The Editor

DONALD GRAY is Professor of English Emeritus at Indiana University, where he has taught since 1956. He is the editor of the Norton Critical Edition of *Alice in Wonderland* and of the anthology *Victorian Poetry*. He has published articles on Victorian poetry, prose, and publishing history.

A NORTON CRITICAL EDITION

Jane Austen

PRIDE AND PREJUDICE

AN AUTHORITATIVE TEXT
BACKGROUNDS AND SOURCES
CRITICISM

THIRD EDITION

Edited by

DONALD GRAY

INDIANA UNIVERSITY

W • W • NORTON & COMPANY • *New York* • *London*

The text of this book is composed in Electra
with the display set in Bernhard Modern.
Composition by Binghamton Valley Composition.
Book design by Antonina Krass.

Library of Congress Cataloging-in-Publication Data

Austen, Jane, 1775–1817.
    Pride and prejudice : an authoritative text, backgrounds and sources,
criticism/Jane Austen ; edited by Donald Gray.—3rd ed.
        p. cm.—(A Norton critical edition)
    Includes bibliographical references.

    ISBN 0-393-97604-1 (pbk.)

    1. England—Fiction. 2. Austen, Jane, 1775–1817. Pride and prejudice.
3. Young women—Fiction. 4. Courtship—fiction. 5. Sisters—Fiction.
I. Gray, Donald J. II. Title.

PR4034.P7   2000
823'.7—dc21

                                                      00-033956

W. W. Norton & Company, Inc., 500 Fifth Avenue, New York, N.Y. 10110
www.wwnorton.com

W. W. Norton & Company Ltd., Castle House, 75/76 Wells Street, London W1T 3QT

Contents

Criticism

Preface

In October 1796, just before she turned twenty-one, Jane Austen began writing a novel she called "First Impressions." She completed the novel the following August, and it immediately became the favorite among the stories and burlesques that for the past ten years she had been writing for her own amusement and for that of her family and friends. Two years later the manuscript was still being reread by members of her family. "I do not wonder at your wanting to read 'First Impressions' again," Austen teased her sister Cassandra in 1799, "so seldom as you have gone through it, and that so long ago." Later the same year she wrote to Cassandra, "I would not let Martha read 'First Impressions' again on any account.... She is very cunning, but I saw through her design; she means to publish it from memory, and one more perusal must enable her to do it."

In 1797 Austen's father offered the novel to a publisher, who refused the chance to become her first publisher without asking to read the manuscript. Austen perhaps continued to work on the novel from time to time during the first decade of the nineteenth century. Certainly she was working hard on its revision in 1812, after a revision of another of her early stories had been published as *Sense and Sensibility* in 1811. By this time the title of the story had been used by another novelist, and when in January of 1813 the novel was finally published, its title was *Pride and Prejudice*.

Many readers who wrote about Austen in the nineteenth and early twentieth centuries have received her fictions as well-composed fantasies (Elizabeth Bennet as Cinderella) that satisfy because they let us forget, or magically resolve, the troubles that ordinarily attend such events as falling in love. Other nineteenth-century readers, such as Richard Whately, Margaret Oliphant, and Richard Simpson, began a still-flourishing tradition in which Austen's novels are understood as stories of ethical and psychological risks, failures, and achievements. In such readings, *Pride and Prejudice*, like her other novels, is about people who learn (though some fail to learn) to recognize good in others, and therefore they themselves become better people. The circumstances of these discoveries would be unremarkable if Austen had not made it clear that a kind of moral salvation depends on what heroines and heroes like Elizabeth and Darcy make of themselves while learning about one another.

Since the middle of the twentieth century literary critics and historians have also become interested in the question of what Austen's novels have to say about the society they represent. Some, such as D. W. Harding, in his influential mid-century essay, read her as a trenchant critic of the pettiness and constraining decorum of the lives she describes. Others, such as Alistair Duckworth and Marilyn Butler, understand her as a thoughtful upholder of the prevailing order of class and gender. Feminist critics and biographers (Nina Auerbach, Claudia L. Johnson, Susan Fraiman, Deborah Kaplan) have engaged the question of how Austen's fiction fits with and acts on the political culture she knew, as have commentators on the tensions and accommodations of class in Austen's fiction (David Spring, Edward Ahearn). The different answers their readings offer to the question illuminate the complexities of Austen's fiction and of the political moment in which it was written and first read.

In the selection of essays and chapters from books included in this edition, I have tried to represent these ethical, psychological, social, and political understandings of Austen in general, and of *Pride and Prejudice* in particular. I have also included some remarks on the recent BBC video version of the novel, which tells us a great deal about what we make of Austen at the end of the twentieth century, and some essays and passages from books by Dorothy Van Ghent, Stuart Tave, Susan Morgan, and Tara Ghoshal Wallace that in their close attention to Austen's craft—another traditional topic in the commentary on her novels—call up social, moral, and epistemological issues. I am grateful to the authors of all these commentaries for their permission to reprint them. When I have deleted passages not immediately relevant to *Pride and Prejudice* or to the topics of the conversation about Austen I wanted to reproduce in this edition, I have tried to preserve the shape and force of their arguments. If I have failed, it is not because the arguments are loose or weak.

The text of *Pride and Prejudice* reprinted in this edition is fundamentally that of the first edition of 1813. The type for the novel was completely reset for its second edition, published in the same year. Austen had no part in the second edition, but I have adopted some of the changes in its text that are obvious corrections of misprintings in the first edition. I have also incorporated some changes entered by her sister Cassandra Austen in her copy of the first edition, and corrected a passage in which, Jane Austen complained in one of her letters, the faulty punctuation of the printers had made two speeches into one. Finally, I have corrected some obvious typographical errors of the 1813 first edition still uncorrected in the second edition, some in spelling ("propect" for "prospect," for example), others in the punctuation of dialogue in which quotation marks were either absent or incorrectly added. In the few instances in which I have changed one word for another ("time" for "mite" in Darcy's speech in Volume I, Chapter III, for example) I have preserved the 1813 text in a footnote. I have not changed Austen's characteristic spellings of such words as "ancle," "stile" (for "style"), and "staid" (for "stayed"). Nor have I modernized the excessive, to our eyes and ears, punctuation of the 1813 text. *Pride and Prejudice* was read aloud, before and after it was put into print, by Austen and members of her family. The punctuation of the 1813 printing gives us an idea of how it sounded, to her and to them.

The Text of
PRIDE AND PREJUDICE

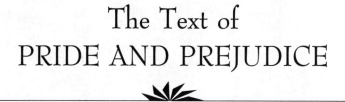

Volume I

Chapter I

It is a truth universally acknowledged, that a single man in possession of a good fortune, must be in want of a wife.

However little known the feelings or views of such a man may be on his first entering a neighborhood, this truth is so well fixed in the minds of the surrounding families, that he is considered as the rightful property of some one or other of their daughters.

"My dear Mr. Bennet," said his lady to him one day, "have you heard that Netherfield Park is let at last?"

Mr. Bennet replied that he had not.

"But it is," returned she; "for Mrs. Long has just been here, and she told me all about it."

Mr. Bennet made no answer.

"Do not you want to know who has taken it?" cried his wife impatiently.

"*You* want to tell me, and I have no objection to hearing it."

This was invitation enough.

"Why, my dear, you must know, Mrs. Long says that Netherfield is taken by a young man of large fortune from the north of England; that he came down on Monday in a chaise and four[1] to see the place, and was so much delighted with it that he agreed with Mr. Morris immediately; that he is to take possession before Michaelmas,[2] and some of his servants are to be in the house by the end of next week."

"What is his name?"

"Bingley."

"Is he married or single?"

"Oh! single, my dear, to be sure! A single man of large fortune; four or five thousand a year.[3] What a fine thing for our girls!"

"How so? how can it affect them?"

"My dear Mr. Bennet," replied his wife, "how can you be so tiresome! You must know that I am thinking of his marrying one of them."

"Is that his design in settling here?"

"Design! nonsense, how can you talk so! But it is very likely that he *may* fall in love with one of them, and therefore you must visit him as soon as he comes."

"I see no occasion for that. You and the girls may go, or you may send them by themselves, which perhaps will be still better, for as you are as handsome as any of them, Mr. Bingley might like you the best of the party."

---

1. A four-wheeled closed carriage, normally used as a family carriage, drawn by four horses.
2. September 29; or, more generally, autumn.
3. See "A Note on Money" (pp. 403–5).

"My dear, you flatter me. I certainly *have* had my share of beauty, but I do not pretend to be any thing extraordinary now. When a woman has five grown up daughters, she ought to give over thinking of her own beauty."

"In such cases, a woman has not often much beauty to think of."

"But, my dear, you must indeed go and see Mr. Bingley when he comes into the neighbourhood."

"It is more than I engage for, I assure you."

"But consider your daughters. Only think what an establishment it would be for one of them. Sir William and Lady Lucas are determined to go, merely on that account, for in general you know they visit no new comers. Indeed you must go, for it will be impossible for *us* to visit him, if you do not."

"You are over scrupulous surely. I dare say Mr. Bingley will be very glad to see you; and I will send a few lines by you to assure him of my hearty consent to his marrying which ever he chuses of the girls; though I must throw in a good word for my little Lizzy."

"I desire you will do no such thing. Lizzy is not a bit better than the others; and I am sure she is not half so handsome as Jane, nor half so good humoured as Lydia. But you are always giving *her* the preference."

"They have none of them much to recommend them," replied he; "they are all silly and ignorant like other girls; but Lizzy has something more of quickness than her sisters."

"Mr. Bennet, how can you abuse your own children in such a way? You take delight in vexing me. You have no compassion on my poor nerves."

"You mistake me, my dear. I have a high respect for your nerves. They are my old friends. I have heard you mention them with consideration these twenty years at least."

"Ah! you do not know what I suffer."

"But I hope you will get over it, and live to see many young men of four thousand a year come into the neighbourhood."

"It will be no use to us, if twenty such should come since you will not visit them."

"Depend upon it, my dear, that when there are twenty, I will visit them all."

Mr. Bennet was so odd a mixture of quick parts, sarcastic humour, reserve, and caprice, that the experience of three and twenty years had been insufficient to make his wife understand his character. *Her* mind was less difficult to develope.[4] She was a woman of mean understanding, little information, and uncertain temper. When she was discontented she fancied herself nervous. The business of her life was to get her daughters married; its solace was visiting and news.

4. Discover, understand.

Chapter II

Mr. Bennet was among the earliest of those who waited on Mr. Bingley. He had always intended to visit him, though to the last always assuring his wife that he should not go; and till the evening after the visit was paid, she had no knowledge of it. It was then disclosed in the following manner. Observing his second daughter employed in trimming a hat, he suddenly addressed her with,

"I hope Mr. Bingley will like it, Lizzy."

"We are not in a way to know *what* Mr. Bingley likes," said her mother resentfully, "since we are not to visit."

"But you forget, mama," said Elizabeth, "that we shall meet him at the assemblies, and that Mrs. Long has promised to introduce him."

"I do not believe Mrs. Long will do any such thing. She has two nieces of her own. She is a selfish, hypocritical woman, and I have no opinion of her."

"No more have I," said Mr. Bennet; "and I am glad to find that you do not depend on her serving you."

Mrs. Bennet deigned not to make any reply; but unable to contain herself, began scolding one of her daughters.

"Don't keep coughing so, Kitty, for heaven's sake! Have a little compassion on my nerves. You tear them to pieces."

"Kitty has no discretion in her coughs," said her father; "she times them ill."

"I do not cough for my own amusement," replied Kitty fretfully.

"When is your next ball to be, Lizzy?"[5]

"To-morrow fortnight."

"Aye, so it is," cried her mother, "and Mrs. Long does not come back till the day before; so, it will be impossible for her to introduce him, for she will not know him herself."

"Then, my dear, you may have the advantage of your friend, and introduce Mr. Bingley to *her*."

"Impossible, Mr. Bennet, impossible, when I am not acquainted with him myself; how can you be so teazing?"

"I honour your circumspection. A fortnight's acquaintance is certainly very little. One cannot know what a man really is by the end of a fortnight. But if *we* do not venture, somebody else will; and after all, Mrs. Long and her nieces must stand their chance; and therefore, as she will think it an act of kindness, if you decline the office, I will take it on myself."

---

5. R. W. Chapman has emended this passage to give this line to Mr. Bennet. " 'When is your next ball to be, Lizzy?' is given to Kitty by all editions. But why should Kitty ask what she must have known? And why should she call it 'your ball'? The speech is of course Mr. Bennet's. In A [the first edition of 1813] it begins a line, and the printer merely failed to indent the first word" (*The Novels of Jane Austen*, 3rd ed. [Oxford, 1932–34] 2:391).

The girls stared at their father. Mrs. Bennet said only, "Nonsense, nonsense!"

"What can be the meaning of that emphatic exclamation?" cried he. "Do you consider the forms of introduction, and the stress that is laid on them, as nonsense? I cannot quite agree with you *there*. What say you, Mary? for you are a young lady of deep reflection I know, and read great books, and make extracts."

Mary wished to say something very sensible, but knew not how.

"While Mary is adjusting her ideas," he continued, "let us return to Mr. Bingley."

"I am sick of Mr. Bingley," cried his wife.

"I am sorry to hear *that*; but why did not you tell me so before? If I had known as much this morning, I certainly would not have called on him. It is very unlucky; but as I have actually paid the visit, we cannot escape the acquaintance now."

The astonishment of the ladies was just what he wished; that of Mrs. Bennet perhaps surpassing the rest; though when the first tumult of joy was over, she began to declare that it was what she had expected all the while.

"How good it was in you, my dear Mr. Bennet! But I knew I should persuade you at last. I was sure you loved your girls too well to neglect such an acquaintance. Well, how pleased I am! and it is such a good joke, too, that you should have gone this morning, and never said a word about it till now."

"Now, Kitty, you may cough as much as you chuse," said Mr. Bennet; and, as he spoke, he left the room, fatigued with the raptures of his wife.

"What an excellent father you have, girls," said she, when the door was shut. "I do not know how you will ever make him amends for his kindness; or me either, for that matter. At our time of life, it is not so pleasant, I can tell you, to be making new acquaintance every day; but for your sakes, we would do any thing. Lydia, my love, though you *are* the youngest, I dare say Mr. Bingley will dance with you at the next ball."

"Oh!" said Lydia stoutly, "I am not afraid; for though I *am* the youngest, I'm the tallest."

The rest of the evening was spent in conjecturing how soon he would return Mr. Bennet's visit, and determining when they should ask him to dinner.

Chapter III

Not all that Mrs. Bennet, however, with the assistance of her five daughters, could ask on the subject was sufficient to draw from her husband any satisfactory description of Mr. Bingley. They attacked him in various ways; with barefaced questions, ingenious supposi- tions, and distant surmises; but he eluded the skill of them all; and they were at last obliged to accept the second-hand intelligence of their neighbour Lady Lucas. Her report was highly favourable. Sir William had been delighted with him. He was quite young, won- derfully handsome, extremely agreeable, and to crown the whole, he meant to be at the next assembly with a large party. Nothing could be more delightful! To be fond of dancing was a certain step towards falling in love; and very lively hopes of Mr. Bingley's heart were entertained.

"If I can but see one of my daughters happily settled at Netherfield," said Mrs. Bennet to her husband, "and all the others equally well mar- ried, I shall have nothing to wish for."

In a few days Mr. Bingley returned Mr. Bennet's visit, and sat about ten minutes with him in his library. He had entertained hopes of being admitted to a sight of the young ladies, of whose beauty he had heard much; but he saw only the father. The ladies were somewhat more fortunate, for they had the advantage of ascertaining from an upper window, that he wore a blue coat and rode a black horse.

An invitation to dinner was soon afterwards dispatched; and already had Mrs. Bennet planned the courses that were to do credit to her housekeeping, when an answer arrived which deferred it all. Mr. Bingley was obliged to be in town the following day, and consequently unable to accept the honour of their invitation, &c. Mrs. Bennet was quite disconcerted. She could not imagine what business he could have in town so soon after his arrival in Hertfordshire; and she began to fear that he might be always flying about from one place to another, and never settled at Netherfield as he ought to be. Lady Lucas quieted her fears a little by starting the idea of his being gone to London only to get a large party for the ball; and a report soon followed that Mr. Bing- ley was to bring twelve ladies and seven gentlemen with him to the assembly. The girls grieved over such a number of ladies; but were comforted the day before the ball by hearing, that instead of twelve, he had brought only six with him from London, his five sisters and a cousin. And when the party entered the assembly room, it consisted of only five altogether; Mr. Bingley, his two sisters, the husband of the eldest, and another young man.

Mr. Bingley was good looking and gentlemanlike; he had a pleasant countenance, and easy, unaffected manners. His sisters were fine women, with an air of decided fashion. His brother-in-law, Mr. Hurst, merely looked the gentleman; but his friend Mr. Darcy soon drew the attention of the room by his fine, tall person, handsome features, noble mien; and the report which was in general circulation within five minutes after his entrance, of his having ten thousand a year. The gentlemen pronounced him to be a fine figure of a man, the ladies declared he was much handsomer than Mr. Bingley, and he was looked at with great admiration for about half the evening, till his manners gave a disgust which turned the tide of his popularity; for he was discovered to be proud, to be above his company, and above being pleased; and not all his large estate in Derbyshire could then save him from having a most forbidding, disagreeable countenance, and being unworthy to be compared with his friend.

Mr. Bingley had soon made himself acquainted with all the principal people in the room; he was lively and unreserved, danced every dance, was angry that the ball closed so early, and talked of giving one himself at Netherfield. Such amiable qualities must speak for themselves. What a contrast between him and his friend! Mr. Darcy danced only once with Mrs. Hurst and once with Miss Bingley, declined being introduced to any other lady, and spent the rest of the evening in walking about the room, speaking occasionally to one of his own party. His character was decided. He was the proudest, most disagreeable man in the world, and every body hoped that he would never come there again. Amongst the most violent against him was Mrs. Bennet, whose dislike of his general behaviour was sharpened into particular resentment, by his having slighted one of her daughters.

Elizabeth Bennet had been obliged, by the scarcity of gentlemen, to sit down for two dances; and during part of that time, Mr. Darcy had been standing near enough for her to overhear a conversation between him and Mr. Bingley, who came from the dance for a few minutes, to press his friend to join it.

"Come, Darcy," said he, "I must have you dance. I hate to see you standing about by yourself in this stupid manner. You had much better dance."

"I certainly shall not. You know how I detest it, unless I am particularly acquainted with my partner. At such an assembly as this, it would be insupportable. Your sisters are engaged, and there is not another woman in the room, whom it would not be a punishment to me to stand up with."

"I would not be so fastidious as you are," cried Bingley, "for a kingdom! Upon my honour, I never met with so many pleasant girls in my life, as I have this evening; and there are several of them you see uncommonly pretty."

"*You* are dancing with the only handsome girl in the room," said Mr. Darcy, looking at the eldest Miss Bennet.

"Oh! she is the most beautiful creature I ever beheld! But there is one of her sisters sitting down just behind you, who is very pretty, and I dare say, very agreeable. Do let me ask my partner to introduce you."

"Which do you mean?" and turning round, he looked for a moment at Elizabeth, till catching her eye, he withdrew his own and coldly said, "She is tolerable; but not handsome enough to tempt *me*; and I am in no humour at present to give consequence to young ladies who are slighted by other men. You had better return to your partner and enjoy her smiles, for you are wasting your time[6] with me."

Mr. Bingley followed his advice. Mr. Darcy walked off; and Elizabeth remained with no very cordial feelings towards him. She told the story however with great spirit among her friends; for she had a lively, playful disposition, which delighted in any thing ridiculous.

The evening altogether passed off pleasantly to the whole family. Mrs. Bennet had seen her eldest daughter much admired by the Netherfield party. Mr. Bingley had danced with her twice, and she had been distinguished by his sisters. Jane was as much gratified by this, as her mother could be, though in a quieter way. Elizabeth felt Jane's pleasure. Mary had heard herself mentioned to Miss Bingley as the most accomplished girl in the neighbourhood; and Catherine and Lydia had been fortunate enough to be never without partners, which was all that they had yet learnt to care for at a ball. They returned therefore in good spirits to Longbourn, the village where they lived, and of which they were the principal inhabitants. They found Mr. Bennet still up. With a book he was regardless of time; and on the present occasion he had a good deal of curiosity as to the event of an evening which had raised such splendid expectations. He had rather hoped that all his wife's views on the stranger would be disappointed; but he soon found that he had a very different story to hear.

"Oh! my dear Mr. Bennet," as she entered the room, "we have had a most delightful evening, a most excellent ball. I wish you had been there. Jane was so admired, nothing could be like it. Every body said how well she looked; and Mr. Bingley thought her quite beautiful, and danced with her twice. Only think of *that* my dear; he actually danced with her twice; and she was the only creature in the room that he asked for a second time. First of all, he asked Miss Lucas. I was so vexed to see him stand up with her; but, however, he did not admire her at all: indeed, nobody can, you know; and he seemed quite struck with Jane as she was going down the dance. So, he enquired who she was, and got introduced, and asked her for the two next. Then, the two third he danced with Miss King, and the two fourth with Maria Lucas, and the two fifth with Jane again, and the two sixth with Lizzy, and the Boulanger."[7]

"If he had had any compassion for *me*," cried her husband impatiently, "he would not have danced half so much! For God's sake, say

6. 1813: mite.
7. A round dance.

no more of his partners. Oh! that he had sprained his ancle in the first dance!"

"Oh! my dear," continued Mrs. Bennet, "I am quite delighted with him. He is so excessively handsome! and his sisters are charming women. I never in my life saw any thing more elegant than their dresses. I dare say the lace upon Mrs. Hurst's gown——"

Here she was interrupted again. Mr. Bennet protested against any description of finery. She was therefore obliged to seek another branch of the subject, and related, with much bitterness of spirit and some exaggeration, the shocking rudeness of Mr. Darcy.

"But I can assure you," she added, "that Lizzy does not lose much by not suiting *his* fancy; for he is a most disagreeable, horrid man, not at all worth pleasing. So high and so conceited that there was no enduring him! He walked here, and he walked there, fancying himself so very great! Not handsome enough to dance with! I wish you had been there, my dear, to have given him one of your set downs. I quite detest the man."

Chapter IV

When Jane and Elizabeth were alone, the former, who had been cautious in her praise of Mr. Bingley before, expressed to her sister how very much she admired him.

"He is just what a young man ought to be," said she, "sensible, good humoured, lively; and I never saw such happy manner!—so much ease, with such perfect good breeding!"

"He is also handsome," replied Elizabeth, "which a young man ought likewise to be, if he possibly can. His character is thereby complete."

"I was very much flattered by his asking me to dance a second time. I did not expect such a compliment."

"Did not you? *I* did for you. But that is one great difference between us. Compliments always take *you* by surprise, and *me* never. What could be more natural than his asking you again? He could not help seeing that you were about five times as pretty as every other woman in the room. No thanks to his gallantry for that. Well, he certainly is very agreeable, and I give you leave to like him. You have liked many a stupider person."

"Dear Lizzy!"

"Oh! you are a great deal too apt you know, to like people in general. You never see a fault in any body. All the world are good and agreeable in your eyes. I never heard you speak ill of a human being in my life."

"I would wish not to be hasty in censuring any one; but I always speak what I think."

"I know you do; and it is *that* which makes the wonder. With *your* good sense, to be so honestly blind to the follies and nonsense of others! Affectation of candour is common enough;—one meets it every where. But to be candid without ostentation or design—to take the good of every body's character and make it still better, and say nothing of the bad—belongs to you alone. And so, you like this man's sisters too, do you? Their manners are not equal to his."

"Certainly not; at first. But they are very pleasing women when you converse with them. Miss Bingley is to live with her brother and keep his house; and I am much mistaken if we shall not find a very charming neighbour in her."

Elizabeth listened in silence, but was not convinced; their behavior at the assembly had not been calculated to please in general; and with more quickness of observation and less pliancy of temper than her sister, and with a judgment too unassailed by any attention to herself, she was very little disposed to approve them. They were in fact very fine ladies; not deficient in good humour when they were pleased, nor in the power of being agreeable where they chose it; but proud and conceited. They were rather handsome, had been educated in one of the first private seminaries in town, had a fortune of twenty thousand pounds, were in the habit of spending more than they ought, and of associating with people of rank; and were therefore in every respect entitled to think well of themselves, and meanly of others. They were of a respectable family in the north of England; a circumstance more deeply impressed on their memories than that their brother's fortune and their own had been acquired by trade.

Mr. Bingley inherited property to the amount of nearly an hundred thousand pounds from his father, who had intended to purchase an estate, but did not live to do it.—Mr. Bingley intended it likewise, and sometimes made choice of his county; but as he was now provided with a good house and the liberty of a manor,[8] it was doubtful to many of those who best knew the easiness of his temper, whether he might not spend the remainder of his days at Netherfield, and leave the next generation to purchase.

His sisters were very anxious for his having an estate of his own; but though he was now established only as a tenant, Miss Bingley was by no means unwilling to preside at his table, nor was Mrs. Hurst, who had married a man of more fashion than fortune, less disposed to consider his house as her home when it suited her. Mr. Bingley had not been of age two years, when he was tempted by an accidental recommendation to look at Netherfield House. He did look at it and into it for half an hour, was pleased with the situation and the principal rooms, satisfied with what the owner said in its praise, and took it immediately.

Between him and Darcy there was a very steady friendship, in spite

---

8. Right to hunt on the fields of an estate.

of a great opposition of character.—Bingley was endeared to Darcy by the easiness, openness, ductility of his temper, though no disposition could offer a greater contrast to his own, and though with his own he never appeared dissatisfied. On the strength of Darcy's regard Bingley had the firmest reliance, and of his judgment the highest opinion. In understanding Darcy was the superior. Bingley was by no means deficient, but Darcy was clever. He was at the same time haughty, reserved, and fastidious, and his manners, though well bred, were not inviting. In that respect his friend had greatly the advantage. Bingley was sure of being liked wherever he appeared, Darcy was continually giving offence.

The manner in which they spoke of the Meryton assembly was sufficiently characteristic. Bingley had never met with pleasanter people or prettier girls in his life; every body had been most kind and attentive to him, there had been no formality, no stiffness, he had soon felt acquainted with all the room; and as to Miss Bennet, he could not conceive an angel more beautiful. Darcy, on the contrary, had seen a collection of people in whom there was little beauty and no fashion, for none of whom he had felt the smallest interest, and from none received either attention or pleasure. Miss Bennet he acknowledged to be pretty, but she smiled too much.

Mrs. Hurst and her sister allowed it to be so—but still they admired her and liked her, and pronounced her to be a sweet girl, and one whom they should not object to know more of. Miss Bennet was therefore established as a sweet girl, and their brother felt authorised by such commendation to think of her as he chose.

Chapter V

Within a short walk of Longbourn lived a family with whom the Bennets were particularly intimate. Sir William Lucas had been formerly in trade in Meryton, where he had made a tolerable fortune and risen to the honour of knighthood by an address to the King, during his mayoralty.[9] The distinction had perhaps been felt too strongly. It had given him a disgust to his business and to his residence in a small market town; and quitting them both, he had removed with his family to a house about a mile from Meryton, denominated from that period Lucas Lodge, where he could think with pleasure of his own importance, and unshackled by business, occupy himself solely in being civil to all the world. For though elated by his rank, it did not render him

9. Knighthoods were sometimes conferred on the occasion of a civic dignitary presenting to the sovereign an address setting out the opinions or good wishes of the citizens of his locality. When he was knighted, Sir William was presented to the king at the palace of St. James, one of the official residences of the sovereigns of England.

supercilious; on the contrary, he was all attention to every body. By nature inoffensive, friendly and obliging, his presentation at St. James's had made him courteous.

Lady Lucas was a very good kind of woman, not too clever to be a valuable neighbour to Mrs. Bennet.—They had several children. The eldest of them, a sensible, intelligent young woman, about twenty-seven, was Elizabeth's intimate friend.

That the Miss Lucases and the Miss Bennets should meet to talk over a ball was absolutely necessary; and the morning after the assembly brought the former to Longbourn to hear and to communicate.

"*You* began the evening well, Charlotte," said Mrs. Bennet with civil self-command to Miss Lucas. "*You* were Mr. Bingley's first choice."

"Yes;—but he seemed to like his second better."

"Oh!—you mean Jane, I suppose—because he danced with her twice. To be sure that *did* seem as if he admired her—indeed I rather believe he *did*—I heard something about it—but I hardly know what—something about Mr. Robinson."

"Perhaps you mean what I overheard between him and Mr. Robinson; did not I mention it to you? Mr. Robinson's asking him how he liked our Meryton assemblies, and whether he did not think there were a great many pretty women in the room, and *which* he thought the prettiest? and his answering immediately to the last question—Oh! the eldest Miss Bennet beyond a doubt, there cannot be two opinions on that point."

"Upon my word!—Well, that was very decided indeed—that does seem as if——but however, it may all come to nothing you know."

"My overhearings were more to the purpose than *yours*, Eliza," said Charlotte. "Mr. Darcy is not so well worth listening to as his friend, is he?—Poor Eliza!—to be only just *tolerable*."

"I beg you would not put it into Lizzy's head to be vexed by his ill-treatment; for he is such a disagreeable man that it would be quite a misfortune to be liked by him. Mrs. Long told me last night that he sat close to her for half an hour without once opening his lips."

"Are you quite sure, Ma'am?—is not there a little mistake?" said Jane.—"I certainly saw Mr. Darcy speaking to her."

"Aye—because she asked him at last how he liked Netherfield, and he could not help answering her;—but she said he seemed very angry at being spoke to."

"Miss Bingley told me," said Jane, "that he never speaks much unless among his intimate acquaintance. With *them* he is remarkably agreeable."

"I do not believe a word of it, my dear. If he had been so very agreeable he would have talked to Mrs. Long. But I can guess how it was;

every body says that he is ate up with pride, and I dare say he had heard somehow that Mrs. Long does not keep a carriage, and had come to the ball in a hack chaise."[1]

"I do not mind his not talking to Mrs. Long," said Miss Lucas, "but I wish he had danced with Eliza."

"Another time, Lizzy," said her mother, "I would not dance with *him*, if I were you."

"I believe, Ma'am, I may safely promise you *never* to dance with him."

"His pride," said Miss Lucas, "does not offend *me* so much as pride often does, because there is an excuse for it. One cannot wonder that so very fine a young man, with family, fortune, every thing in his favour, should think highly of himself. If I may so express it, he has a *right* to be proud."

"That is very true," replied Elizabeth, "and I could easily forgive *his* pride, if he had not mortified *mine*."

"Pride," observed Mary, who piqued herself upon the solidity of her reflections, "is a very common failing I believe. By all that I have ever read, I am convinced that it is very common indeed, that human nature is particularly prone to it, and that there are very few of us who do not cherish a feeling of self-complacency on the score of some quality or other, real or imaginary. Vanity and pride are different things, though the words are often used synonimously. A person may be proud without being vain. Pride relates more to our opinion of ourselves, vanity to what we would have others think of us."

"If I were as rich as Mr. Darcy," cried a young Lucas who came with his sisters, "I should not care how proud I was. I would keep a pack of foxhounds, and drink a bottle of wine every day."

"Then you would drink a great deal more than you ought," said Mrs. Bennet; "and if I were to see you at it I should take away your bottle directly."

The boy protested that she should not; she continued to declare that she would, and the argument ended only with the visit.

Chapter VI

The ladies of Longbourn soon waited on those of Netherfield. The visit was returned in due form. Miss Bennet's pleasing manners grew on the good will of Mrs. Hurst and Miss Bingley; and though the mother was found to be intolerable and the younger sisters not worth speaking to, a wish of being better acquainted with *them*, was expressed towards the two eldest. By Jane this attention was received with the greatest pleasure; but Elizabeth still saw superciliousness in their treat-

---

1. A rented carriage.

ment of every body, hardly excepting even her sister, and could not like them; though their kindness to Jane, such as it was, had a value as arising in all probability from the influence of their brother's admiration. It was generally evident whenever they met, that he *did* admire her; and to *her* it was equally evident that Jane was yielding to the preference which she had begun to entertain for him from the first, and was in a way to be very much in love; but she considered with pleasure that it was not likely to be discovered by the world in general, since Jane united with great strength of feeling, a composure of temper and a uniform cheerfulness of manner, which would guard her from the suspicions of the impertinent. She mentioned this to her friend Miss Lucas.

"It may perhaps be pleasant," replied Charlotte, "to be able to impose on the public in such a case; but it is sometimes a disadvantage to be so very guarded. If a woman conceals her affection with the same skill from the object of it, she may lose the opportunity of fixing him; and it will then be but poor consolation to believe the world equally in the dark. There is so much of gratitude or vanity in almost every attachment, that it is not safe to leave any to itself. We can all *begin* freely—a slight preference is natural enough; but there are very few of us who have heart enough to be really in love without encouragement. In nine cases out of ten, a woman had better shew *more* affection than she feels. Bingley likes your sister undoubtedly; but he may never do more than like her, if she does not help him on."

"But she does help him on, as much as her nature will allow. If *I* can perceive her regard for him, he must be a simpleton indeed not to discover it too."

"Remember, Eliza, that he does not know Jane's disposition as you do."

"But if a woman is partial to a man, and does not endeavour to conceal it, he must find it out."

"Perhaps he must, if he sees enough of her. But though Bingley and Jane meet tolerably often, it is never for many hours together; and as they always see each other in large mixed parties, it is impossible that every moment should be employed in conversing together. Jane should therefore make the most of every half hour in which she can command his attention. When she is secure of him, there will be leisure for falling in love as much as she chuses."

"Your plan is a good one," replied Elizabeth, "where nothing is in question but the desire of being well married; and if I were determined to get a rich husband, or any husband, I dare say I should adopt it. But these are not Jane's feelings; she is not acting by design. As yet, she cannot even be certain of the degree of her own regard, nor of its reasonableness. She has known him only a fortnight. She danced four dances with him at Meryton; she saw him one morning at his own house, and has since dined in company with him four times. This is not quite enough to make her understand his character."

"Not as you present it. Had she merely *dined* with him, she might only have discovered whether he had a good appetite; but you must remember that four evenings have been also spent together—and four evenings may do a great deal."

"Yes; these four evenings have enabled them to ascertain that they both like Vingt-un better than Commerce;[2] but with respect to any other leading characteristic, I do not imagine that much has been unfolded."

"Well," said Charlotte, "I wish Jane success with all my heart; and if she were married to him to-morrow, I should think she had as good a chance of happiness, as if she were to be studying his character for a twelvemonth. Happiness in marriage is entirely a matter of chance. If the dispositions of the parties are ever so well known to each other, or ever so similar before-hand, it does not advance their felicity in the least. They always contrive[3] to grow sufficiently unlike afterwards to have their share of vexation; and it is better to know as little as possible of the defects of the person with whom you are to pass your life."

"You make me laugh, Charlotte; but it is not sound. You know it is not sound, and that you would never act in this way yourself."

Occupied in observing Mr. Bingley's attentions to her sister, Elizabeth was far from suspecting that she was herself becoming an object of some interest in the eyes of his friend. Mr. Darcy had at first scarcely allowed her to be pretty; he had looked at her without admiration at the ball; and when they next met, he had looked at her only to criticise. But no sooner had he made it clear to himself and his friends that she had hardly a good feature in her face, than he began to find it was rendered uncommonly intelligent by the beautiful expression of her dark eyes. To this discovery succeeded some others equally mortifying. Though he had detected with a critical eye more than one failure of perfect symmetry in her form, he was forced to acknowledge her figure to be light and pleasing; and in spite of his asserting that her manners were not those of the fashionable world, he was caught by their easy playfulness. Of this she was perfectly unaware;—to her he was only the man who made himself agreeable no where, and who had not thought her handsome enough to dance with.

He began to wish to know more of her, and as a step towards con-

---

2. Vingt-un is a form of the game commonly called blackjack in America. Commerce is a somewhat more complicated game, a progenitor of poker, in which players buy individual cards from the dealer or barter for them with other players. In some places in England at the end of the eighteenth century, Commerce was a very fashionable game, sometimes played for high stakes.

3. 1813: continue. This change is one of those entered by Cassandra Austen in her copy of the novel. See R. W. Chapman, "Jane Austen's Text," *Times Literary Supplement*, 13 February 1937, 116.

versing with her himself, attended to her conversation with others. His doing so drew her notice. It was at Sir William Lucas's, where a large party were assembled.

"What does Mr. Darcy mean," said she to Charlotte, "by listening to my conversation with Colonel Forster?"

"That is a question which Mr. Darcy only can answer."

"But if he does it any more I shall certainly let him know that I see what he is about. He has a very satirical eye, and if I do not begin by being impertinent myself, I shall soon grow afraid of him."

On his approaching them soon afterwards, though without seeming to have any intention of speaking, Miss Lucas defied her friend to mention such a subject to him, which immediately provoking Elizabeth to do it, she turned to him and said,

"Did not you think, Mr. Darcy, that I expressed myself uncommonly well just now, when I was teazing Colonel Forster to give us a ball at Meryton?"

"With great energy;—but it is a subject which always makes a lady energetic."

"You are severe on us."

"It will be *her* turn soon to be teazed," said Miss Lucas. "I am going to open the instrument, Eliza, and you know what follows."

"You are a very strange creature by way of a friend!—always wanting me to play and sing before any body and every body!—If my vanity had taken a musical turn, you would have been invaluable, but as it is, I would really rather not sit down before those who must be in the habit of hearing the very best performers." On Miss Lucas's persevering, however, she added, "Very well; if it must be so, it must." And gravely glancing at Mr. Darcy, "There is a fine old saying, which every body here is of course familiar with—'Keep your breath to cool your porridge,'—and I shall keep mine to swell my song."

Her performance was pleasing, though by no means capital. After a song or two, and before she could reply to the entreaties of several that she would sing again, she was eagerly succeeded at the instrument by her sister Mary, who having, in consequence of being the only plain one in the family, worked hard for knowledge and accomplishments, was always impatient for display.

Mary had neither genius nor taste; and though vanity had given her application, it had given her likewise a pedantic air and conceited manner, which would have injured a higher degree of excellence than she had reached. Elizabeth, easy and unaffected, had been listened to with much more pleasure, though not playing half so well; and Mary, at the end of a long concerto, was glad to purchase praise and gratitude by Scotch and Irish airs, at the request of her younger sisters, who with some of the Lucases and two or three officers joined eagerly in dancing at one end of the room.

Mr. Darcy stood near them in silent indignation at such a mode of passing the evening, to the exclusion of all conversation, and was too much engrossed by his own thoughts to perceive that Sir William Lucas was his neighbour, till Sir William thus began.

"What a charming amusement for young people this is, Mr. Darcy!—There is nothing like dancing after all.—I consider it as one of the first refinements of polished societies."

"Certainly, Sir;—and it has the advantage also of being in vogue amongst the less polished societies of the world.—Every savage can dance."

Sir William only smiled. "Your friend performs delightfully;" he continued after a pause, on seeing Bingley join the group;—"and I doubt not that you are an adept in the science yourself, Mr. Darcy."

"You saw me dance at Meryton, I believe, Sir."

"Yes, indeed, and received no inconsiderable pleasure from the sight. Do you often dance at St. James's?"

"Never, Sir."

"Do you not think it would be a proper compliment to the place?"

"It is a compliment which I never pay to any place if I can avoid it."

"You have a house in town, I conclude?"

Mr. Darcy bowed.

"I had once some thoughts of fixing in town myself—for I am fond of superior society; but I did not feel quite certain that the air of London would agree with Lady Lucas."

He paused in hopes of an answer; but his companion was not disposed to make any; and Elizabeth at that instant moving towards them, he was struck with the notion of doing a very gallant thing, and called out to her,

"My dear Miss Eliza, why are not you dancing?—Mr. Darcy, you must allow me to present this young lady to you as a very desirable partner.—You cannot refuse to dance, I am sure, when so much beauty is before you." And taking her hand, he would have given it to Mr. Darcy, who, though extremely surprised, was not unwilling to receive it, when she instantly drew back, and said with some discomposure to Sir William,

"Indeed, Sir, I have not the least intention of dancing.—I entreat you not to suppose that I moved this way in order to beg for a partner."

Mr. Darcy with grave propriety requested to be allowed the honour of her hand; but in vain. Elizabeth was determined; nor did Sir William at all shake her purpose by his attempt at persuasion.

"You excel so much in the dance, Miss Eliza, that it is cruel to deny me the happiness of seeing you; and though this gentleman dislikes the amusement in general, he can have no objection, I am sure, to oblige us for one half hour."

"Mr. Darcy is all politeness," said Elizabeth, smiling.

"He is indeed—but considering the inducement, my dear Miss Eliza, we cannot wonder at his complaisance; for who would object to such a partner?"

Elizabeth looked archly, and turned away. Her resistance had not injured her with the gentleman, and he was thinking of her with some complacency, when thus accosted by Miss Bingley,

"I can guess the subject of your reverie."

"I should imagine not."

"You are considering how insupportable it would be to pass many evenings in this manner—in such society; and indeed I am quite of your opinion. I was never more annoyed! The insipidity and yet the noise; the nothingness and yet the self-importance of all these people!—What would I give to hear your strictures on them!"

"Your conjecture is totally wrong, I assure you. My mind was more agreeably engaged. I have been meditating on the very great pleasure which a pair of fine eyes in the face of a pretty woman can bestow."

Miss Bingley immediately fixed her eyes on his face, and desired he would tell her what lady had the credit of inspiring such reflections. Mr. Darcy replied with great intrepidity,

"Miss Elizabeth Bennet."

"Miss Elizabeth Bennet!" repeated Miss Bingley. "I am all astonishment. How long has she been such a favourite?—and pray when am I to wish you joy?"

"That is exactly the question which I expected you to ask. A lady's imagination is very rapid; it jumps from admiration to love, from love to matrimony in a moment. I knew you would be wishing me joy."

"Nay, if you are so serious about it, I shall consider the matter as absolutely settled. You will have a charming mother-in-law, indeed, and of course she will be always at Pemberley with you."

He listened to her with perfect indifference, while she chose to entertain herself in this manner, and as his composure convinced her that all was safe, her wit flowed long.

Chapter VII

Mr. Bennet's property consisted almost entirely in an estate of two thousand a year, which, unfortunately for his daughters, was entailed[4] in default of heirs male, on a distant relation; and their mother's fortune, though ample for her situation in life, could but ill supply the deficiency of his. Her father had been an attorncy in Mcryton, and had left her four thousand pounds.

---

4. That is, the inheritance was restricted. In this case, the entailment stipulated that if Mr. Bennet has no son to continue his line, the property will pass to a male in another branch of the family. On Mr. Bennet's income, and the meaning of money in the novel, see "A Note on Money" (pp. 403–5).

She had a sister married to a Mr. Philips, who had been a clerk to their father, and succeeded him in the business, and a brother settled in London in a respectable line of trade.

The village of Longbourn was only one mile from Meryton; a most convenient distance for the young ladies, who were usually tempted thither three or four times a week, to pay their duty to their aunt and to a milliner's shop just over the way. The two youngest of the family, Catherine and Lydia, were particularly frequent in these attentions; their minds were more vacant than their sisters', and when nothing better offered, a walk to Meryton was necessary to amuse their morning hours and furnish conversation for the evening; and however bare of news the country in general might be, they always contrived to learn some from their aunt. At present, indeed, they were well supplied both with news and happiness by the recent arrival of a militia regiment[5] in the neighbourhood; it was to remain the whole winter, and Meryton was the head quarters.

Their visits to Mrs. Philips were now productive of the most interesting intelligence. Every day added something to their knowledge of the officers' names and connections. Their lodgings were not long a secret, and at length they began to know the officers themselves. Mr. Philips visited them all, and this opened to his nieces a source of felicity unknown before. They could talk of nothing but officers; and Mr. Bingley's large fortune, the mention of which gave animation to their mother, was worthless in their eyes when opposed to the regimentals of an ensign.

After listening one morning to their effusions on this subject, Mr. Bennet coolly observed,

"From all that I can collect by your manner of talking, you must be two of the silliest girls in the country. I have suspected it some time, but I am now convinced."

Catherine was disconcerted, and made no answer; but Lydia, with perfect indifference, continued to express her admiration of Captain Carter, and her hope of seeing him in the course of the day, as he was going the next morning to London.

"I am astonished, my dear," said Mrs. Bennet, "that you should be so ready to think your own children silly. If I wished to think slightingly of any body's children, it should not be of my own however."

"If my children are silly I must hope to be always sensible of it."

---

5. The militia was a military force composed of volunteers who were expected to train only twenty-eight days a year and who were not required to serve abroad. Its principal purpose during the British wars with the French at the end of the eighteenth century and in the first decades of the nineteenth century was to be ready in case of invasion, a periodic anxiety of the time. The exciting presence of soldiers in Austen's story is one of the reminders that it was made from a manuscript novel composed in the late 1790s, when the threat of France was new and strong, and that for most of the rest of her life England was at war.

"Yes—but as it happens, they are all of them very clever."

"This is the only point, I flatter myself, on which we do not agree. I had hoped that our sentiments coincided in every particular, but I must so far differ from you as to think our two youngest daughters uncommonly foolish."

"My dear Mr. Bennet, you must not expect such girls to have the sense of their father and mother.—When they get to our age I dare say they will not think about officers any more than we do. I remember the time when I liked a red coat myself very well—and indeed so I do still at my heart; and if a smart young colonel, with five or six thousand a year, should want one of my girls, I shall not say nay to him; and I thought Colonel Forster looked very becoming the other night at Sir William's in his regimentals."

"Mama," cried Lydia, "my aunt says that Colonel Forster and Captain Carter do not go so often to Miss Watson's as they did when they first came; she sees them now very often standing in Clarke's library."[6]

Mrs. Bennet was prevented replying by the entrance of the footman with a note for Miss Bennet; it came from Netherfield, and the servant waited for an answer. Mrs. Bennet's eyes sparkled with pleasure, and she was eagerly calling out, while her daughter read,

"Well, Jane, who is it from? what is it about? what does he say? well, Jane, make haste and tell us; make haste, my love."

"It is from Miss Bingley," said Jane, and then read it aloud.

"My dear Friend,

"If you are not so compassionate as to dine to-day with Louisa and me, we shall be in danger of hating each other for the rest of our lives, for a whole day's tête-tête between two women can never end without a quarrel. Come as soon as you can on the receipt of this. My brother and the gentlemen are to dine with the officers. Yours ever,
                              "CAROLINE BINGLEY."

"With the officers!" cried Lydia. "I wonder my aunt did not tell us of *that*."

"Dining out," said Mrs. Bennet, "that is very unlucky."

"Can I have the carriage," said Jane.

"No, my dear, you had better go on horseback, because it seems likely to rain; and then you must stay all night."

"That would be a good scheme," said Elizabeth, "if you were sure that they would not offer to send her home."

"Oh! but the gentlemen will have Mr. Bingley's chaise to go to Meryton; and the Hursts have no horses to theirs."

---

6. A circulating library, usually given to popular fiction, like those patronized by Austen and her family. See Mr. Collins's reaction to a book he perceives to be from a circulating library in Volume I, Chapter XV.

"I had much rather go in the coach."

"But, my dear, your father cannot spare the horses, I am sure. They are wanted in the farm, Mr. Bennet, are not they?"

"They are wanted in the farm much oftener than I can get them."

"But if you have got them to day," said Elizabeth, "my mother's purpose will be answered."

She did at last extort from her father an acknowledgment that the horses were engaged, Jane was therefore obliged to go on horseback, and her mother attended her to the door with many cheerful prognostics of a bad day. Her hopes were answered; Jane had not been gone long before it rained hard. Her sisters were uneasy for her, but her mother was delighted. The rain continued the whole evening without intermission; Jane certainly could not come back.

"This was a lucky idea of mine, indeed!" said Mrs. Bennet, more than once, as if the credit of making it rain were all her own. Till the next morning, however, she was not aware of all the felicity of her contrivance. Breakfast was scarcely over when a servant from Netherfield brought the following note for Elizabeth:

> "My dearest Lizzy,
> "I find myself very unwell this morning, which, I suppose, is to be imputed to my getting wet through yesterday. My kind friends will not hear of my returning home till I am better. They insist also on my seeing Mr. Jones—therefore do not be alarmed if you should hear of his having been to me—and excepting a sore-throat and head-ache there is not much the matter with me.
> "Yours, &c."

"Well, my dear," said Mr. Bennet, when Elizabeth had read the note aloud, "if your daughter should have a dangerous fit of illness, if she should die, it would be a comfort to know that it was all in pursuit of Mr. Bingley, and under your orders."

"Oh! I am not at all afraid of her dying. People do not die of little trifling colds. She will be taken good care of. As long as she stays there, it is all very well. I would go and see her, if I could have the carriage."

Elizabeth, feeling really anxious, was determined to go to her, though the carriage was not to be had; and as she was no horsewoman, walking was her only alternative. She declared her resolution.

"How can you be so silly," cried her mother, "as to think of such a thing, in all this dirt! You will not be fit to be seen when you get there."

"I shall be very fit to see Jane—which is all I want."

"Is this a hint to me, Lizzy," said her father, "to send for the horses?"

"No, indeed. I do not wish to avoid the walk. The distance is nothing, when one has a motive; only three miles. I shall be back by dinner."

"I admire the activity of your benevolence," observed Mary, "but every impulse of feeling should be guided by reason; and, in my opinion, exertion should always be in proportion to what is required."

"We will go as far as Meryton with you," said Catherine and Lydia.— Elizabeth accepted their company, and the three young ladies set off together.

"If we make haste," said Lydia, as they walked along, "perhaps we may see something of Captain Carter before he goes."

In Meryton they parted; the two youngest repaired to the lodgings of one of the officers' wives, and Elizabeth continued her walk alone, crossing field after field at a quick pace, jumping over stiles and springing over puddles with impatient activity, and finding herself at last within view of the house, with weary ancles, dirty stockings, and a face glowing with the warmth of exercise.

She was shewn into the breakfast-parlour, where all but Jane were assembled, and where her appearance created a great deal of surprise.— That she should have walked three miles so early in the day, in such dirty weather, and by herself, was almost incredible to Mrs. Hurst and Miss Bingley; and Elizabeth was convinced that they held her in contempt for it. She was received, however, very politely by them; and in their brother's manners there was something better than politeness; there was good humour and kindness.—Mr. Darcy said very little, and Mr. Hurst nothing at all. The former was divided between admiration of the brilliancy which exercise had given to her complexion, and doubt as to the occasion's justifying her coming so far alone. The latter was thinking only of his breakfast.

Her enquiries after her sister were not very favourably answered. Miss Bennet had slept ill, and though up, was very feverish and not well enough to leave her room. Elizabeth was glad to be taken to her immediately; and Jane, who had only been withheld by the fear of giving alarm or inconvenience, from expressing in her note how much she longed for such a visit, was delighted at her entrance. She was not equal, however, to much conversation, and when Miss Bingley left them together, could attempt little beside expressions of gratitude for the extraordinary kindness she was treated with. Elizabeth silently attended her.

When breakfast was over, they were joined by the sisters; and Elizabeth began to like them herself, when she saw how much affection and solicitude they shewed for Jane. The apothecary came, and having examined his patient, said, as might be supposed, that she had caught a violent cold, and that they must endeavour to get the better of it; advised her to return to bed, and promised her some draughts.[7] The advice was followed readily, for the feverish symptoms increased, and

7. Medicine.

her head ached acutely. Elizabeth did not quit her room for a moment, nor were the other ladies often absent; the gentlemen being out, they had in fact nothing to do elsewhere.

When the clock struck three, Elizabeth felt that she must go; and very unwillingly said so. Miss Bingley offered her the carriage, and she only wanted a little pressing to accept it, when Jane testified such concern in parting with her, that Miss Bingley was obliged to convert the offer of the chaise into an invitation to remain at Netherfield for the present. Elizabeth most thankfully consented, and a servant was dispatched to Longbourn to acquaint the family with her stay, and bring back a supply of clothes.

Chapter VIII

At five o'clock the two ladies retired to dress, and at half past six Elizabeth was summoned to dinner. To the civil enquiries which then poured in, and amongst which she had the pleasure of distinguishing the much superior solicitude of Mr. Bingley's, she could not make a very favourable answer. Jane was by no means better. The sisters, on hearing this, repeated three or four times how much they were grieved, how shocking it was to have a bad cold, and how excessively they disliked being ill themselves; and then thought no more of the matter; and their indifference towards Jane when not immediately before them, restored Elizabeth to the enjoyment of all her original dislike.

Their brother, indeed, was the only one of the party whom she could regard with any complacency. His anxiety for Jane was evident, and his attentions to herself most pleasing, and they prevented her feeling herself so much an intruder as she believed she was considered by the others. She had very little notice from any but him. Miss Bingley was engrossed by Mr. Darcy, her sister scarcely less so; and as for Mr. Hurst, by whom Elizabeth sat, he was an indolent man, who lived only to eat, drink, and play at cards, who when he found her prefer a plain dish to a ragout, had nothing to say to her.

When dinner was over, she returned directly to Jane, and Miss Bingley began abusing her as soon as she was out of the room. Her manners were pronounced to be very bad indeed, a mixture of pride and impertinence; she had no conversation, no stile, no taste, no beauty. Mrs. Hurst thought the same, and added,

"She has nothing, in short, to recommend her, but being an excellent walker. I shall never forget her appearance this morning. She really looked almost wild."

"She did indeed, Louisa. I could hardly keep my countenance. Very nonsensical to come at all! Why must *she* be scampering about the country, because her sister had a cold? Her hair so untidy, so blowsy!"

"Yes, and her petticoat; I hope you saw her petticoat, six inches deep in mud, I am absolutely certain; and the gown which had been let down to hide it, not doing its office."

"Your picture may be very exact, Louisa," said Bingley; "but this was all lost upon me. I thought Miss Elizabeth Bennet looked remarkably well, when she came into the room this morning. Her dirty petticoat quite escaped my notice."

"*You* observed it, Mr. Darcy, I am sure," said Miss Bingley; "and I am inclined to think that you would not wish to see *your sister* make such an exhibition."

"Certainly not."

"To walk three miles, or four miles, or five miles, or whatever it is, above her ancles in dirt, and alone, quite alone! what could she mean by it? It seems to me to shew an abominable sort of conceited independence, a most country town indifference to decorum."

"It shews an affection for her sister that is very pleasing," said Bingley.

"I am afraid, Mr. Darcy," observed Miss Bingley, in a half whisper, "that this adventure has rather affected your admiration of her fine eyes."

"Not at all," he replied; "they were brightened by the exercise."—A short pause followed this speech, and Mrs. Hurst began again.

"I have an excessive regard for Jane Bennet, she is really a very sweet girl, and I wish with all my heart she were well settled. But with such a father and mother, and such low connections, I am afraid there is no chance of it."

"I think I have heard you say, that their uncle is an attorney in Meryton."

"Yes; and they have another, who lives somewhere near Cheapside."[8]

"That is capital," added her sister, and they both laughed heartily.

"If they had uncles enough to fill *all* Cheapside," cried Bingley, "it would not make them one jot less agreeable."

"But it must very materially lessen their chance of marrying men of any consideration in the world," replied Darcy.

To this speech Bingley made no answer; but his sisters gave it their hearty assent, and indulged their mirth for some time at the expense of their dear friend's vulgar relations.

With a renewal of tenderness, however, they repaired to her room on leaving the dining-parlour, and sat with her till summoned to coffee. She was still very poorly, and Elizabeth would not quit her at all, till late in the evening, when she had the comfort of seeing her asleep, and when it appeared to her rather right than pleasant that she should

8. A neighborhood in London's commercial district. To be in business rather than to live, as Bingley and Darcy do, from the income of capital or land is to be judged socially inferior by people like Miss Bingley and Mrs. Hurst, even though their own fortune was earned in trade. To live near one's place of business rather than in more fashionable precincts is to confirm their judgment.

go down stairs herself. On entering the drawing-room she found the whole party at loo,[9] and was immediately invited to join them; but suspecting them to be playing high she declined it, and making her sister the excuse, said she would amuse herself for the short time she could stay below with a book. Mr. Hurst looked at her with astonishment.

"Do you prefer reading to cards?" said he; "that is rather singular."

"Miss Eliza Bennet," said Miss Bingley, "despises cards. She is a great reader and has no pleasure in anything else."

"I deserve neither such praise nor such censure," cried Elizabeth; "I am *not* a great reader, and I have pleasure in many things."

"In nursing your sister I am sure you have pleasure," said Bingley; "and I hope it will soon be increased by seeing her quite well."

Elizabeth thanked him from her heart, and then walked towards a table where a few books were lying. He immediately offered to fetch her others; all that his library afforded.

"And I wish my collection were larger for your benefit and my own credit; but I am an idle fellow, and though I have not many, I have more than I ever look into."

Elizabeth assured him that she could suit herself perfectly with those in the room.

"I am astonished," said Miss Bingley, "that my father should have left so small a collection of books.—What a delightful library you have at Pemberley, Mr. Darcy!"

"It ought to be good," he replied, "it has been the work of many generations."

"And then you have added so much to it yourself, you are always buying books."

"I cannot comprehend the neglect of a family library in such days as these."

"Neglect! I am sure you neglect nothing that can add to the beauties of that noble place. Charles, when you build *your* house, I wish it may be half as delightful as Pemberley."

"I wish it may."

"But I would really advise you to make your purchase in that neighbourhood, and take Pemberley for a kind of model. There is not a finer county in England than Derbyshire."

"With all my heart; I will buy Pemberley itself if Darcy will sell it."

"I am talking of possibilities, Charles."

"Upon my word, Caroline, I should think it more possible to get Pemberley by purchase than by imitation."

Elizabeth was so much caught by what passed, as to leave her very little attention for her book; and soon laying it wholly aside, she drew

9. A very popular card game similar to bridge or whist, except that as many as a dozen players could participate.

near the card-table, and stationed herself between Mr. Bingley and his eldest sister, to observe the game.

"Is Miss Darcy much grown since the spring?" said Miss Bingley; "will she be as tall as I am?"

"I think she will. She is now about Miss Elizabeth Bennet's height, or rather taller."

"How I long to see her again! I never met with anybody who delighted me so much. Such a countenance, such manners!——and so extremely accomplished for her age! Her performance on the piano-forte is exquisite."

"It is amazing to me," said Bingley, "how young ladies can have patience to be so very accomplished, as they all are."

"All young ladies accomplished! My dear Charles, what do you mean?"

"Yes, all of them, I think. They all paint tables, cover skreens and net purses. I scarcely know any one who cannot do all this, and I am sure I never heard a young lady spoken of for the first time, without being informed that she was very accomplished."

"Your list of the common extent of accomplishments," said Darcy, "has too much truth. The word is applied to many a woman who deserves it no otherwise than by netting a purse, or covering a skreen. But I am very far from agreeing with you in your estimation of ladies in general. I cannot boast of knowing more than half a dozen, in the whole range of my acquaintance, that are really accomplished."

"Nor I, I am sure," said Miss Bingley.

"Then," observed Elizabeth, "you must comprehend a great deal in your idea of an accomplished woman."

"Yes; I do comprehend a great deal in it."

"Oh! certainly," cried his faithful assistant, "no one can be really esteemed accomplished, who does not greatly surpass what is usually met with. A woman must have a thorough knowledge of music, singing, drawing, dancing, and the modern languages, to deserve the word; and besides all this, she must possess a certain something in her air and manner of walking, the tone of her voice, her address and expressions, or the word will be but half deserved."

"All this she must possess," added Darcy, "and to all this she must yet add something more substantial, in the improvement of her mind by extensive reading."

"I am no longer surprised at your knowing *only* six accomplished women. I rather wonder now at your knowing *any*."

"Are you so severe upon your own sex, as to doubt the possibility of all this?"

"*I* never saw such a woman. *I* never saw such capacity, and taste, and application, and elegance, as you describe, united."

Mrs. Hurst and Miss Bingley both cried out against the injustice of her implied doubt, and were both protesting that they knew many women who answered this description, when Mr. Hurst called them to order, with bitter complaints of their inattention to what was going forward. As all conversation was thereby at an end, Elizabeth soon afterwards left the room.

"Eliza Bennet," said Miss Bingley, when the door was closed on her, "is one of those young ladies who seek to recommend themselves to the other sex, by undervaluing their own; and with many men, I dare say, it succeeds. But, in my opinion, it is a paltry device, a very mean art."

"Undoubtedly," replied Darcy, to whom this remark was chiefly addressed, "there is meanness in *all* the arts which ladies sometimes condescend to employ for captivation. Whatever bears affinity to cunning is despicable."

Miss Bingley was not so entirely satisfied with this reply as to continue the subject.

Elizabeth joined them again only to say that her sister was worse, and that she could not leave her. Bingley urged Mr. Jones's being sent for immediately; while his sisters, convinced that no country advice could be of any service, recommended an express to town for one of the most eminent physicians. This, she would not hear of; but she was not so unwilling to comply with their brother's proposal; and it was settled that Mr. Jones should be sent for early in the morning, if Miss Bennet were not decidedly better. Bingley was quite uncomfortable; his sisters declared that they were miserable. They solaced their wretchedness, however, by duets after supper, while he could find no better relief to his feelings than by giving his housekeeper directions that every possible attention might be paid to the sick lady and her sister.

Chapter IX

Elizabeth passed the chief of the night in her sister's room, and in the morning had the pleasure of being able to send a tolerable answer to the enquiries which she very early received from Mr. Bingley by a housemaid, and some time afterwards from the two elegant ladies who waited on his sisters. In spite of this amendment, however, she requested to have a note sent to Longbourn, desiring her mother to visit Jane, and form her own judgment of her situation. The note was immediately dispatched, and its contents as quickly complied with. Mrs. Bennet, accompanied by her two youngest girls, reached Netherfield soon after the family breakfast.

Had she found Jane in any apparent danger, Mrs. Bennet would have been very miserable; but being satisfied on seeing her that her illness was not alarming, she had no wish of her recovering immediately, as her restoration to health would probably remove her from Netherfield.

She would not listen therefore to her daughter's proposal of being carried home; neither did the apothecary, who arrived about the same time, think it at all advisable. After sitting a little while with Jane, on Miss Bingley's appearance and invitation, the mother and three daughters all attended her into the breakfast parlour. Bingley met them with hopes that Mrs. Bennet had not found Miss Bennet worse than she expected.

"Indeed I have, Sir," was her answer. "She is a great deal too ill to be moved. Mr. Jones says we must not think of moving her. We must trespass a little longer on your kindness."

"Removed!" cried Bingley. "It must not be thought of. My sister, I am sure, will not hear of her removal."

"You can depend upon it, Madam," said Miss Bingley, with cold civility, "that Miss Bennet shall receive every possible attention while she remains with us."

Mrs. Bennet was profuse in her acknowledgments.

"I am sure," she added, "if it was not for such good friends I do not know what would become of her, for she is very ill indeed, and suffers a vast deal, though with the greatest patience in the world, which is always the way with her, for she has, without exception, the sweetest temper I ever met with. I often tell my other girls they are nothing to *her*. You have a sweet room here, Mr. Bingley, and a charming prospect over that gravel walk. I do not know a place in the country that is equal to Netherfield. You will not think of quitting it in a hurry I hope, though you have but a short lease."

"Whatever I do is done in a hurry," replied he; "and therefore if I should resolve to quit Netherfield, I should probably be off in five minutes. At present, however, I consider myself as quite fixed here."

"That is exactly what I should have supposed of you," said Elizabeth.

"You begin to comprehend me, do you?" cried he, turning towards her.

"Oh! yes—I understand you perfectly."

"I wish I might take this for a compliment; but to be so easily seen through I am afraid is pitiful."

"That is as it happens. It does not necessarily follow that a deep, intricate character is more or less estimable than such a one as yours."

"Lizzy," cried her mother, "remember where you are, and do not run on in the wild manner that you are suffered to do at home."

"I did not know before," continued Bingley immediately, "that you were a studier of character. It must be an amusing study."

"Yes; but intricate characters are the *most* amusing. They have at least that advantage."

"The country," said Darcy, "can in general supply but few subjects for such a study. In a country neighbourhood you move in a very confined and unvarying society."

"But people themselves alter so much, that there is something new to be observed in them for ever."

"Yes, indeed," cried Mrs. Bennet, offended by his manner of mentioning a country neighbourhood. "I assure you there is quite as much of *that* going on in the country as in town."

Every body was surprised; and Darcy, after looking at her for a moment, turned silently away. Mrs. Bennet, who fancied she had gained a complete victory over him, continued her triumph.

"I cannot see that London has any great advantage over the country for my part, except the shops and public places. The country is a vast deal pleasanter, is not it, Mr. Bingley?"

"When I am in the country," he replied, "I never wish to leave it; and when I am in town it is pretty much the same. They have each their advantages, and I can be equally happy in either."

"Aye—that is because you have the right disposition. But that gentleman," looking at Darcy, "seemed to think the country was nothing at all."

"Indeed, Mama, you are mistaken," said Elizabeth, blushing for her mother. "You quite mistook Mr. Darcy. He only meant that there were not such a variety of people to be met with in the country as in town, which you must acknowledge to be true."

"Certainly, my dear, nobody said there were; but as to not meeting with many people in this neighbourhood, I believe there are few neighbourhoods larger. I know we dine with four and twenty families."

Nothing but concern for Elizabeth could enable Bingley to keep his countenance. His sister was less delicate, and directed her eye towards Mr. Darcy with a very expressive smile. Elizabeth, for the sake of saying something that might turn her mother's thoughts, now asked her if Charlotte Lucas had been at Longbourn since *her* coming away.

"Yes, she called yesterday with her father. What an agreeable man Sir William is, Mr. Bingley—is not he? so much the man of fashion! so genteel and so easy!—He has always something to say to every body.—*That* is my idea of good breeding; and those persons who fancy themselves very important and never open their mouths, quite mistake the matter."

"Did Charlotte dine with you?"

"No, she would go home. I fancy she was wanted about the mince pies. For my part, Mr. Bingley, I always keep servants that can do their own work; *my* daughters are brought up differently. But every body is to judge for themselves, and the Lucases are very good sort of girls, I assure you. It is a pity they are not handsome! Not that I think Charlotte so *very* plain—but then she is our particular friend."

"She seems a very pleasant young woman," said Bingley.

"Oh! dear, yes;—but you must own she is very plain. Lady Lucas herself has often said so, and envied me Jane's beauty. I do not like to boast of my own child, but to be sure, Jane—one does not often see any body better looking. It is what every body says. I do not trust my own partiality. When she was only fifteen, there was a gentleman at my brother Gardiner's in town, so much in love with her, that my sister-in-law was sure he would make her an offer before we came away. But however he did not. Perhaps he thought her too young. However, he wrote some verses on her, and very pretty they were."

"And so ended his affection," said Elizabeth impatiently. "There has been many a one, I fancy, overcome in the same way. I wonder who first discovered the efficacy of poetry in driving away love!"

"I have been used to consider poetry as the *food* of love," said Darcy.

"Of a fine, stout, healthy love it may. Every thing nourishes what is strong already. But if it be only a slight, thin sort of inclination, I am convinced that one good sonnet will starve it entirely away."

Darcy only smiled; and the general pause which ensued made Elizabeth tremble lest her mother should be exposing herself again. She longed to speak, but could think of nothing to say; and after a short silence Mrs. Bennet began repeating her thanks to Mr. Bingley for his kindness to Jane, with an apology for troubling him also with Lizzy. Mr. Bingley was unaffectedly civil in his answer, and forced his younger sister to be civil also, and say what the occasion required. She performed her part indeed without much graciousness, but Mrs. Bennet was satisfied, and soon afterwards ordered her carriage. Upon this signal, the youngest of her daughters put herself forward. The two girls had been whispering to each other during the whole visit, and the result of it was, that the youngest should tax Mr. Bingley with having promised on his first coming into the country to give a ball at Netherfield.

Lydia was a stout, well-grown girl of fifteen, with a fine complexion and good-humoured countenance; a favorite with her mother, whose affection had brought her into public at an early age. She had high animal spirits, and a sort of natural self-consequence, which the attentions of the officers, to whom her uncle's good dinners and her own easy manners recommended her, had increased into assurance. She was very equal therefore to address Mr. Bingley on the subject of the ball, and abruptly reminded him of his promise; adding, that it would be the most shameful thing in the world if he did not keep it. His answer to this sudden attack was delightful to their mother's ear.

"I am perfectly ready, I assure you, to keep my engagement; and when your sister is recovered, you shall if you please name the very day of the ball. But you would not wish to be dancing while she is ill."

Lydia declared herself satisfied. "Oh! yes—it would be much better to wait till Jane was well, and by that time most likely Captain Carter would be at Meryton again. And when you have given *your* ball," she added, "I shall insist on their giving one also. I shall tell Colonel Forster it will be quite a shame if he does not."

Mrs. Bennet and her daughters then departed, and Elizabeth returned instantly to Jane, leaving her own and her relations' behaviour to the remarks of the two ladies and Mr. Darcy; the latter of whom, however, could not be prevailed on to join in their censure of *her*, in spite of all Miss Bingley's witticisms on *fine eyes*.

Chapter X

The day passed much as the day before had done. Mrs. Hurst and Miss Bingley had spent some hours of the morning with the invalid, who continued, though slowly, to mend; and in the evening Elizabeth joined their party in the drawing-room. The loo table, however, did not appear. Mr. Darcy was writing, and Miss Bingley, seated near him, was watching the progress of his letter, and repeatedly calling off his attention by messages to his sister. Mr. Hurst and Mr. Bingley were at piquet,[1] and Mrs. Hurst was observing their game.

Elizabeth took up some needlework, and was sufficiently amused in attending to what passed between Darcy and his companion. The perpetual commendations of the lady either on his hand-writing, or on the evenness of his lines, or on the length of his letter, with the perfect unconcern with which her praises were received, formed a curious dialogue, and was exactly in unison with her opinion of each.

"How delighted Miss Darcy will be to receive such a letter!"

He made no answer.

"You write uncommonly fast."

"You are mistaken. I write rather slowly."

"How many letters you must have occasion to write in the course of the year! Letters of business too! How odious I should think them!"

"It is fortunate, then, that they fall to my lot instead of to yours."

"Pray tell your sister that I long to see her."

"I have already told her so once, by your desire."

"I am afraid you do not like your pen. Let me mend it for you. I mend pens remarkably well."

"Thank you—but I always mend my own."

"How can you contrive to write so even?"

He was silent.

"Tell your sister I am delighted to hear of her improvement on the harp, and pray let her know that I am quite in raptures with her beautiful little design for a table, and I think it infinitely superior to Miss Grantley's."

"Will you give me leave to defer your raptures till I write again?— At present I have not room to do them justice."

"Oh! it is of no consequence. I shall see her in January. But do you

1. A card game, commonly played by two players; similar to the draw-and-discard games called rummy.

always write such charming long letters to her, Mr. Darcy?"

"They are generally long; but whether always charming, it is not for me to determine."

"It is a rule with me, that a person who can write a long letter, with ease, cannot write ill."

"That will not do for a compliment to Darcy, Caroline," cried her brother—"because he does *not* write with ease. He studies too much for words of four syllables.—Do not you, Darcy?"

"My stile of writing is very different from yours."

"Oh!" cried Miss Bingley, "Charles writes in the most careless way imaginable. He leaves out half his words, and blots the rest."

"My ideas flow so rapidly that I have not time to express them—by which means my letters sometimes convey no ideas at all to my correspondents."

"Your humility, Mr. Bingley," said Elizabeth, "must disarm reproof."

"Nothing is more deceitful," said Darcy, "than the appearance of humility. It is often only carelessness of opinion, and sometimes an indirect boast."

"And which of the two do you call *my* little recent piece of modesty?"

"The indirect boast;—for you are really proud of your defects in writing, because you consider them as proceeding from a rapidity of thought and carelessness of execution, which if not estimable, you think at least highly interesting. The power of doing any thing with quickness is always much prized by the possessor, and often without any attention to the imperfection of the performance. When you told Mrs. Bennet this morning that if you ever resolved on quitting Netherfield you should be gone in five minutes, you meant it to be a sort of panegyric, of compliment to yourself—and yet what is there so very laudable in a precipitance which must leave very necessary business undone, and can be of no real advantage to yourself or any one else?"

"Nay," cried Bingley, "this is too much, to remember at night all the foolish things that were said in the morning. And yet, upon my honour, I believed what I said of myself to be true, and I believe it at this moment. At least, therefore, I did not assume the character of needless precipitance merely to shew off before the ladies."

"I dare say you believed it; but I am by no means convinced that you would be gone with such celerity. Your conduct would be quite as dependant on chance as that of any man I know; and if, as you were mounting your horse, a friend were to say, 'Bingley, you had better stay till next week,' you would probably do it, you would probably not go—and, at another word, might stay a month."

"You have only proved by this," cried Elizabeth, "that Mr. Bingley did not do justice to his own disposition. You have shewn him off now much more than he did himself."

"I am exceedingly gratified," said Bingley, "by your converting what my friend says into a compliment on the sweetness of my temper. But I am afraid you are giving it a turn which that gentleman did by no means intend; for he would certainly think the better of me, if under such a circumstance I were to give a flat denial, and ride off as fast as I could."

"Would Mr. Darcy then consider the rashness of your original intention as atoned for by your obstinacy in adhering to it?"

"Upon my word I cannot exactly explain the matter, Darcy must speak for himself."

"You expect me to account for opinions which you chuse to call mine, but which I have never acknowledged. Allowing the case, however, to stand according to your representation, you must remember, Miss Bennet, that the friend who is supposed to desire his return to the house, and the delay of his plan, has merely desired it, asked it without offering one argument in favour of its propriety."

"To yield readily—easily—to the *persuasion* of a friend is no merit with you."

"To yield without conviction is no compliment to the understanding of either."

"You appear to me, Mr. Darcy, to allow nothing for the influence of friendship and affection. A regard for the requester would often make one readily yield to a request, without waiting for arguments to reason one into it. I am not particularly speaking of such a case as you have supposed about Mr. Bingley. We may as well wait, perhaps, till the circumstance occurs, before we discuss the discretion of his behaviour thereupon. But in general and ordinary cases between friend and friend, where one of them is desired by the other to change a resolution of no very great moment, should you think ill of that person for complying with the desire, without waiting to be argued into it?"

"Will it not be advisable, before we proceed on this subject, to arrange with rather more precision the degree of importance which is to appertain to this request, as well as the degree of intimacy subsisting between the parties?"

"By all means," cried Bingley; "let us hear all the particulars, not forgetting their comparative height and size; for that will have more weight in the argument, Miss Bennet, than you may be aware of. I assure you that if Darcy were not such a great tall fellow, in comparison with myself, I should not pay him half so much deference. I declare I do not know a more aweful object than Darcy, on particular occasions, and in particular places; at his own house especially, and of a Sunday evening when he has nothing to do."

Mr. Darcy smiled; but Elizabeth thought she could perceive that he was rather offended; and therefore checked her laugh. Miss Bingley warmly resented the indignity he had received, in an expostulation with her brother for talking such nonsense.

"I see your design, Bingley," said his friend.—"You dislike an argument, and want to silence this."

"Perhaps I do. Arguments are too much like disputes. If you and Miss Bennet will defer yours till I am out of the room, I shall be very thankful; and then you may say whatever you like of me."

"What you ask," said Elizabeth, "is no sacrifice on my side; and Mr. Darcy had much better finish his letter."

Mr. Darcy took her advice, and did finish his letter.

When that business was over, he applied to Miss Bingley and Elizabeth for the indulgence of some music. Miss Bingley moved with alacrity to the piano-forte, and after a polite request that Elizabeth would lead the way, which the other as politely and more earnestly negatived, she seated herself.

Mrs. Hurst sang with her sister, and while they were thus employed Elizabeth could not help observing as she turned over some music books that lay on the instrument, how frequently Mr. Darcy's eyes were fixed on her. She hardly knew how to suppose that she could be an object of admiration to so great a man; and yet that he should look at her because he disliked her, was still more strange. She could only imagine however at last, that she drew his notice because there was a something about her more wrong and reprehensible, according to his ideas of right, than in any other person present. The supposition did not pain her. She liked him too little to care for his approbation.

After playing some Italian songs, Miss Bingley varied the charm by a lively Scotch air; and soon afterwards Mr. Darcy, drawing near Elizabeth, said to her—

"Do not you feel a great inclination, Miss Bennet, to seize such an opportunity of dancing a reel?"

She smiled, but made no answer. He repeated the question, with some surprise at her silence.

"Oh!" said she, "I heard you before; but I could not immediately determine what to say in reply. You wanted me, I know, to say 'Yes,' that you might have the pleasure of despising my taste; but I always delight in overthrowing those kind of schemes, and cheating a person of their premeditated contempt. I have therefore made up my mind to tell you, that I do not want to dance a reel at all—and now despise me if you dare."

"Indeed I do not dare."

Elizabeth, having rather expected to affront him, was amazed at his gallantry; but there was a mixture of sweetness and archness in her manner which made it difficult for her to affront anybody; and Darcy had never been so bewitched by any woman as he was by her. He really believed, that were it not for the inferiority of her connections, he should be in some danger.

Miss Bingley saw, or suspected enough to be jealous; and her great anxiety for the recovery of her dear friend Jane, received some assistance from her desire of getting rid of Elizabeth.

She often tried to provoke Darcy into disliking her guest, by talking of their supposed marriage, and planning his happiness in such an alliance.

"I hope," said she, as they were walking together in the shrubbery the next day, "you will give your mother-in-law a few hints, when this desirable event takes place, as to the advantage of holding her tongue; and if you can compass it, do cure the younger girls of running after the officers.—And, if I may mention so delicate a subject, endeavour to check that little something, bordering on conceit and impertinence, which your lady possesses."

"Have you any thing else to propose for my domestic felicity?"

"Oh! yes.—Do let the portraits of your uncle and aunt Philips be placed in the gallery at Pemberley. Put them next to your great uncle the judge. They are in the same profession, you know; only in different lines. As for your Elizabeth's picture, you must not attempt to have it taken, for what painter could do justice to those beautiful eyes?"

"It would not be easy, indeed, to catch their expression, but their colour and shape, and the eye-lashes, so remarkably fine, might be copied."

At that moment they were met from another walk, by Mrs. Hurst and Elizabeth herself.

"I did not know that you intended to walk," said Miss Bingley, in some confusion, lest they had been overheard.

"You used us abominably ill," answered Mrs. Hurst, "in running away without telling us that you were coming out."

Then taking the disengaged arm of Mr. Darcy, she left Elizabeth to walk by herself. The path just admitted three. Mr. Darcy felt their rudeness and immediately said,—

"This walk is not wide enough for our party. We had better go into the avenue."

But Elizabeth, who had not the least inclination to remain with them, laughingly answered,

"No, no; stay where you are.—You are charmingly group'd, and appear to uncommon advantage. The picturesque would be spoilt by admitting a fourth.[2] Good bye."

She then ran gaily off, rejoicing as she rambled about, in the hope of being at home again in a day or two. Jane was already so much recovered as to intend leaving her room for a couple of hours that evening.

2. Writers on the picturesque such as William Gilpin (1724–1804), of whose writing the young Jane Austen was very fond, claimed that groups of three (a group of three cows is one of Gilpin's examples) are especially attractive because of their irregularity. Austen's knowledge of the principles and taste of the picturesque is also apparent in her description of Pemberley, Darcy's estate, in Volume III, Chapter XI.

Chapter XI

When the ladies removed after dinner,[3] Elizabeth ran up to her sister, and seeing her well guarded from cold, attended her into the drawing-room; where she was welcomed by her two friends with many professions of pleasure; and Elizabeth had never seen them so agreeable as they were during the hour which passed before the gentlemen appeared. Their powers of conversation were considerable. They could describe an entertainment with accuracy, relate an anecdote with humour, and laugh at their acquaintance with spirit.

But when the gentlemen entered, Jane was no longer the first object. Miss Bingley's eyes were instantly turned towards Darcy, and she had something to say to him before he had advanced many steps. He addressed himself directly to Miss Bennet, with a polite congratulation; Mr. Hurst also made her a slight bow, and said he was "very glad;" but diffuseness and warmth remained for Bingley's salutation. He was full of joy and attention. The first half hour was spent in piling up the fire, lest she should suffer from the change of room; and she removed at his desire to the other side of the fire-place, that she might be farther from the door. He then sat down by her, and talked scarcely to any one else. Elizabeth, at work in the opposite corner, saw it all with great delight.

When tea was over, Mr. Hurst reminded his sister-in-law of the card-table—but in vain. She had obtained private intelligence that Mr. Darcy did not wish for cards; and Mr. Hurst soon found even his open petition rejected. She assured him that no one intended to play, and the silence of the whole party on the subject, seemed to justify her. Mr. Hurst had therefore nothing to do, but to stretch himself on one of the sophas and go to sleep. Darcy took up a book; Miss Bingley did the same; and Mrs. Hurst, principally occupied in playing with her bracelets and rings, joined now and then in her brother's conversation with Miss Bennet.

Miss Bingley's attention was quite as much engaged in watching Mr. Darcy's progress through *his* book, as in reading her own; and she was perpetually either making some inquiry, or looking at his page. She could not win him, however, to any conversation; he merely answered her question, and read on. At length, quite exhausted by the attempt to be amused with her own book, which she had only chosen because it was the second volume of his, she gave a great yawn and said, "How pleasant it is to spend an evening in this way! I declare after all there is no enjoyment like reading! How much sooner one tires of any thing than of a book!—When I have a house of my own, I shall be miserable if I have not an excellent library."

3. It was customary for the women to leave the dinner table before the men, who delayed an interval, usually over wine.

No one made any reply. She then yawned again, threw aside her book, and cast her eyes round the room in quest of some amusement; when hearing her brother mentioning a ball to Miss Bennet, she turned suddenly towards him and said,

"By the bye, Charles, are you really serious in meditating a dance at Netherfield?—I would advise you, before you determine on it, to con- sult the wishes of the present party; I am much mistaken if there are not some among us to whom a ball would be rather a punishment than a pleasure."

"If you mean Darcy," cried her brother, "he may go to bed, if he chuses, before it begins—but as for the ball, it is quite a settled thing; and as soon as Nicholls has made white soup enough I shall send round my cards."[4]

"I should like balls infinitely better," she replied, "if they were carried on in a different manner; but there is something insufferably tedious in the usual process of such a meeting. It would surely be much more rational if conversation instead of dancing made the order of the day."

"Much more rational, my dear Caroline, I dare say, but it would not be near so much like a ball."

Miss Bingley made no answer; and soon afterwards got up and walked about the room. Her figure was elegant, and she walked well;— but Darcy, at whom it was all aimed, was still inflexibly studious. In the desperation of her feelings she resolved on one effort more; and, turning to Elizabeth, said,

"Miss Eliza Bennet, let me persuade you to follow my example, and take a turn about the room.—I assure you it is very refreshing after sitting so long in one attitude."

Elizabeth was surprised, but agreed to it immediately. Miss Bingley succeeded no less in the real object of her civility; Mr. Darcy looked up. He was as much awake to the novelty of attention in that quarter as Elizabeth herself could be, and unconsciously closed his book. He was directly invited to join their party, but he declined it, observing, that he could imagine but two motives for their chusing to walk up and down the room together, with either of which motives his joining them would interfere. "What could he mean? she was dying to know what could be his meaning"—and asked Elizabeth whether she could at all understand him?

"Not at all," was her answer; "but depend upon it, he means to be severe on us, and our surest way of disappointing him, will be to ask nothing about it."

Miss Bingley, however, was incapable of disappointing Mr. Darcy in any thing, and persevered therefore in requiring an explanation of his two motives.

4. Invitations.

"I have not the smallest objection to explaining them," said he, as soon as she allowed him to speak. "You either chuse this method of passing the evening because you are in each other's confidence and have secret affairs to discuss, or because you are conscious that your figures appear to the greatest advantage in walking;—if the first, I should be completely in your way;—and if the second, I can admire you much better as I sit by the fire."

"Oh! shocking!" cried Miss Bingley. "I never heard any thing so abominable. How shall we punish him for such a speech?"

"Nothing so easy, if you have but the inclination," said Elizabeth. "We can all plague and punish one another. Teaze him—laugh at him.—Intimate as you are, you must know how it is to be done."

"But upon my honour I do *not*. I do assure you that my intimacy has not yet taught me *that*. Teaze calmness of temper and presence of mind! No, no—I feel he may defy us there. And as to laughter, we will not expose ourselves, if you please, by attempting to laugh without a subject. Mr. Darcy may hug himself."

"Mr. Darcy is not to be laughed at!" cried Elizabeth. "That is an uncommon advantage, and uncommon I hope it will continue, for it would be a great loss to *me* to have many such acquaintance. I dearly love a laugh."

"Miss Bingley," said he, "has given me credit for more than can be. The wisest and the best of men, nay, the wisest and best of their actions, may be rendered ridiculous by a person whose first object in life is a joke."

"Certainly," replied Elizabeth—"there are such people, but I hope I am not one of *them*. I hope I never ridicule what is wise or good. Follies and nonsense, whims and inconsistencies *do* divert me, I own, and I laugh at them whenever I can.—But these, I suppose, are precisely what you are without."

"Perhaps that is not possible for any one. But it has been the study of my life to avoid those weaknesses which often expose a strong understanding to ridicule."

"Such as vanity and pride."

"Yes, vanity is a weakness indeed. But pride—where there is a real superiority of mind, pride will be always under good regulation."

Elizabeth turned away to hide a smile.

"Your examination of Mr. Darcy is over, I presume," said Miss Bingley;—"and pray what is the result?"

"I am perfectly convinced by it that Mr. Darcy has no defect. He owns it himself without disguise."

"No"—said Darcy, "I have made no such pretension. I have faults enough, but they are not, I hope, of understanding. My temper I dare not vouch for.—It is I believe too little yielding—certainly too little for the convenience of the world. I cannot forget the follies and vices of others so soon as I ought, nor their offences against myself. My feelings are not puffed about with every attempt to move them. My temper would perhaps be called resentful.—My good opinion once lost is lost for ever."

"*That* is a failing indeed!"—cried Elizabeth. "Implacable resentment *is* a shade in a character. But you have chosen your fault well.—I really cannot *laugh* at it. You are safe from me."

"There is, I believe, in every disposition a tendency to some particular evil, a natural defect, which not even the best education can overcome."

"And *your* defect is a propensity to hate every body."

"And yours," he replied with a smile, "is wilfully to misunderstand them."

"Do let us have a little music,"—cried Miss Bingley, tired of a conversation in which she had no share.—"Louisa, you will not mind my waking Mr. Hurst."

Her sister made not the smallest objection, and the piano forte was opened, and Darcy, after a few moments recollection, was not sorry for it. He began to feel the danger of paying Elizabeth too much attention.

Chapter XII

In consequence of an agreement between the sisters, Elizabeth wrote the next morning to her mother, to beg that the carriage might be sent for them in the course of the day. But Mrs. Bennet, who had calculated on her daughters remaining at Netherfield till the following Tuesday, which would exactly finish Jane's week, could not bring herself to receive them with pleasure before. Her answer, therefore, was not propitious, at least not to Elizabeth's wishes, for she was impatient to get home. Mrs. Bennet sent them word that they could not possibly have the carriage before Tuesday; and in her postscript it was added, that if Mr. Bingley and his sister pressed them to stay longer, she could spare them very well.—Against staying longer, however, Elizabeth was positively resolved—nor did she much expect it would be asked; and fearful, on the contrary, as being considered as intruding themselves needlessly long, she urged Jane to borrow Mr. Bingley's carriage immediately, and at length it was settled that their original design of leaving Netherfield that morning should be mentioned, and the request made.

The communication excited many professions of concern; and enough was said of wishing them to stay at least till the following day to work on Jane; and till the morrow, their going was deferred. Miss Bingley was then sorry that she had proposed the delay, for her jealously and dislike of one sister much exceeded her affection for the other.

The master of the house heard with real sorrow that they were to go so soon, and repeatedly tried to persuade Miss Bennet that it would not be safe for her—that she was not enough recovered; but Jane was firm where she felt herself to be right.

To Mr. Darcy it was welcome intelligence—Elizabeth had been at Netherfield long enough. She attracted him more than he liked—and Miss Bingley was uncivil to *her*, and more teazing than usual to himself. He wisely resolved to be particularly careful that no sign of admiration should *now* escape him, nothing that could elevate her with the hope of influencing his felicity; sensible that if such an idea had been suggested, his behaviour during the last day must have material weight in confirming or crushing it. Steady to his purpose, he scarcely spoke ten words to her through the whole of Saturday, and though they were at one time left by themselves for half an hour, he adhered most conscientiously to his book, and would not even look at her.

On Sunday, after morning service, the separation, so agreeable to almost all, took place. Miss Bingley's civility to Elizabeth increased at last very rapidly, as well as her affection for Jane; and when they parted, after assuring the latter of the pleasure it would always give her to see her either at Longbourn or Netherfield, and embracing her most tenderly, she even shook hands with the former.—Elizabeth took leave of the whole party in the liveliest spirits.

They were not welcomed home very cordially by their mother. Mrs. Bennet wondered at their coming, and thought them very wrong to give so much trouble, and was sure Jane would have caught cold again.—But their father, though very laconic in his expressions of pleasure, was really glad to see them; he had felt their importance in the family circle. The evening conversation, when they were all assembled, had lost much of its animation, and almost all its sense, by the absence of Jane and Elizabeth.

They found Mary, as usual, deep in the study of thorough bass and human nature; and had some new extracts to admire, and some new observations of thread-bare morality to listen to. Catherine and Lydia had information for them of a different sort. Much had been done, and much had been said in the regiment since the preceding Wednesday; several of the officers had dined lately with their uncle, a private had been flogged, and it had actually been hinted that Colonel Forster was going to be married.

Chapter XIII

"I hope my dear," said Mr. Bennet to his wife, as they were at breakfast the next morning, "that you have ordered a good dinner to-day, because I have reason to expect an addition to our family party."

"Who do you mean, my dear? I know of nobody that is coming I am sure, unless Charlotte Lucas should happen to call in, and I hope *my* dinners are good enough for her. I do not believe she often sees such at home."

"The person of whom I speak, is a gentleman and a stranger." Mrs. Bennet's eyes sparkled.—"A gentleman and a stranger! It is Mr. Bingley I am sure. Why Jane—you never dropt a word of this; you sly thing! Well, I am sure I shall be extremely glad to see Mr. Bingley.—But— good lord! how unlucky! there is not a bit of fish to be got to-day. Lydia, my love, ring the bell. I must speak to Hill, this moment."

"It is *not* Mr. Bingley," said her husband; "it is a person whom I never saw in the whole course of my life."

This roused a general astonishment; and he had the pleasure of being eagerly questioned by his wife and five daughters at once.

After amusing himself some time with their curiosity, he thus explained. "About a month ago I received this letter, and about a fort-night ago I answered it, for I thought it a case of some delicacy, and requiring early attention. It is from my cousin, Mr. Collins, who, when I am dead, may turn you all out of this house as soon as he pleases."

"Oh! my dear," cried his wife, "I cannot bear to hear that mentioned. Pray do not talk of that odious man. I do think it is the hardest thing in the world, that your estate should be entailed away from your own children; and I am sure if I had been you, I should have tried long ago to do something or other about it."

Jane and Elizabeth attempted to explain to her the nature of an entail. They had often attempted it before, but it was a subject on which Mrs. Bennet was beyond the reach of reason; and she continued to rail bitterly against the cruelty of settling an estate away from a family of five daughters, in favour of a man whom nobody cared any-thing about.

"It certainly is a most iniquitous affair," said Mr. Bennet, "and noth-ing can clear Mr. Collins from the guilt of inheriting Longbourn. But if you will listen to his letter, you may perhaps be a little softened by his manner of expressing himself."

"No, that I am sure I shall not; and I think it was very impertinent of him to write to you at all, and very hypocritical. I hate such false friends. Why could not he keep on quarrelling with you, as his father did before him?"

"Why, indeed, he does seem to have had some filial scruples on that head, as you will hear."

Hunsford, near Westerham, Kent,
15th October.

DEAR SIR,

The disagreement subsisting between yourself and my late honoured father, always gave me much uneasiness, and since I have had the misfortune to lose him, I have frequently wished to heal the breach; but for some time I was kept back by my own doubts, fearing lest it might seem disrespectful to his memory for me to be on good terms with any one, with whom it had always pleased him to be at variance.— "There, Mrs. Bennet."—My mind however is now made up on the subject, for having received ordination at Easter, I have been so fortunate as to be distinguished by the patronage of the Right Honourable Lady Catherine de Bourgh, widow of Sir Lewis de Bourgh, whose bounty and beneficence has preferred me to the valuable rectory of this parish,[5] where it shall be my earnest endeavour to demean myself with grateful respect towards her Ladyship, and be ever ready to perform those rites and ceremonies which are instituted by the Church of England. As a clergyman, moreover, I feel it my duty to promote and establish the blessing of peace in all families within the reach of my influence; and on these grounds I flatter myself that my present overtures of good-will are highly commendable, and that the circumstances of my being next in the entail of Longbourn estate, will be kindly overlooked on your side, and not lead you to reject the offered olive branch. I cannot be otherwise than concerned at being the means of injuring your amiable daughters, and beg leave to apologise for it, as well as to assure you of my readiness to make them every possible amends,—but of this hereafter. If you should have no objection to receive me into your house, I propose myself the satisfaction of waiting on you and your family, Monday, November 18th, by four o'clock, and shall probably trespass on your hospitality till the Saturday se'night[6] following, which I can do without any inconvenience, as Lady Catherine is far from objecting to my occasional absence on a Sunday, provided that some other clergyman is engaged to do the duty of the day. I remain, dear sir, with respectful compliments to your lady and daughters, your well-wisher and friend,

William Collins."

"At four o'clock, therefore, we may expect this peacemaking gentleman," said Mr. Bennet, as he folded up the letter. "He seems to be a most conscientious and polite young man, upon my word; and I doubt not will prove a valuable acquaintance, especially if Lady Catherine should be so indulgent as to let him come to us again."

"There is some sense in what he says about the girls however; and

---

5. Originally, those landowners who built churches or set aside land for the support of the Church were granted advowsons, the right to recommend to bishops candidates for livings or benefices, often the post of rector of a parish. In time the advowsons, which were a useful and often valuable means of patronage, came to be regarded as part of the personal estates of those who held them, and it was literally through the "bounty and beneficence" of people like Lady Catherine that many ambitious clergymen were given their first and subsequent livings. Once preferred to a living, the clergyman held it for life, unless he resigned or was judged grossly incompetent. See Wickham's remarks on the living he was promised (p. 54), and Darcy's (pp. 132–33).

6. A week.

if he is disposed to make them any amends, I shall not be the person to discourage him."

"Though it is difficult," said Jane, "to guess in what way he can mean to make us the atonement he thinks our due, the wish is certainly to his credit."

Elizabeth was chiefly struck with his extraordinary deference for Lady Catherine, and his kind intention of christening, marrying, and burying his parishioners whenever it were required.

"He must be an oddity, I think," said she. "I cannot make him out.—There is something very pompous in his stile.—And what can he mean by apologizing for being next in the entail?—We cannot suppose he would help it, if he could.—Can he be a sensible man, sir?"

"No, my dear; I think not. I have great hopes of finding him quite the reverse. There is a mixture of servility and self-importance in his letter, which promises well. I am impatient to see him."

"In point of composition," said Mary, "his letter does not seem defective. The idea of the olive branch perhaps is not wholly new, yet I think it is well expressed."

To Catherine and Lydia, neither the letter nor its writer were in any degree interesting. It was next to impossible that their cousin should come in a scarlet coat, and it was now some weeks since they had received pleasure from the society of a man in any other colour. As for their mother, Mr. Collin's letter had done away much of her ill-will, and she was preparing to see him with a degree of composure, which astonished her husband and daughters.

Mr. Collins was punctual to his time, and was received with great politeness by the whole family. Mr. Bennet indeed said little; but the ladies were ready enough to talk, and Mr. Collins seemed neither in need of encouragement, nor inclined to be silent himself. He was a tall, heavy looking young man of five and twenty. His air was grave and stately, and his manners were very formal. He had not been long seated before he complimented Mrs. Bennet on having so fine a family of daughters, said he had heard much of their beauty, but that, in this instance, fame had fallen short of the truth; and added, that he did not doubt her seeing them all in due time well disposed of in marriage. This gallantry was not much to the taste of some of his hearers, but Mrs. Bennet, who quarrelled with no compliments, answered most readily,

"You are very kind, sir, I am sure; and I wish with all my heart it may prove so; for else they will be destitute enough. Things are settled so oddly."

"You allude perhaps to the entail of this estate."

"Ah! sir, I do indeed. It is a grievous affair to my poor girls, you must confess. Not that I mean to find fault with *you*, for such things I know are all chance in this world. There is no knowing how estates will go when once they come to be entailed."

"I am very sensible, madam, of the hardship to my fair cousins,—and could say much on the subject, but that I am cautious of appearing forward and precipitate. But I can assure the young ladies that I come prepared to admire them. At present I will not say more, but perhaps when we are better acquainted——"

He was interrupted by a summons to dinner; and the girls smiled on each other. They were not the only objects of Mr. Collins's admiration. The hall, the dining-room, and all its furniture were examined and praised; and his commendation of every thing would have touched Mrs. Bennet's heart, but for the mortifying supposition of his viewing it all as his own future property. The dinner too in its turn was highly admired; and he begged to know to which of his fair cousins, the excellence of its cookery was owing. But here he was set right by Mrs. Bennet, who assured him with asperity that they were very well able to keep a good cook, and that her daughters had nothing to do in the kitchen. He begged pardon for having displeased her. In a softened tone she declared herself not at all offended; but he continued to apologise for about a quarter of an hour.

Chapter XIV

During dinner, Mr. Bennet scarcely spoke at all; but when the servants were withdrawn, he thought it time to have some conversation with his guest, and therefore started a subject in which he expected him to shine, by observing that he seemed very fortunate in his patroness. Lady Catherine de Bourgh's attention to his wishes, and consideration for his comfort, appeared very remarkable. Mr. Bennet could not have chosen better. Mr. Collins was eloquent in her praise. The subject elevated him to more than usual solemnity of manner, and with a most important aspect he protested that he had never in his life witnessed such behaviour in a person of rank—such affability and condescension, as he had himself experienced from Lady Catherine. She had been graciously pleased to approve of both the discourses, which he had already had the honour of preaching before her. She had also asked him twice to dine at Rosings, and had sent for him only the Saturday before, to make up her pool of quadrille[7] in the evening. Lady Catherine was reckoned proud by many people he knew, but *he* had never seen any thing but affability in her. She had always spoken to him as she would to any other gentleman; she made not the smallest objection to his joining in the society of the neighbourhood, nor to his

7. Quadrille is a four-handed card game that by the end of the eighteenth century had become an old-fashioned entertainment, having been displaced by the popularity of whist.

leaving his parish occasionally for a week or two, to visit his relations. She had even condescended to advise him to marry as soon as he could, provided he chose with discretion; and had once paid him a visit in his humble parsonage; where she had perfectly approved all the alterations he had been making, and had even vouchsafed to suggest some her-self,—some shelves in the closets up stairs.[8]

"That is all very proper and civil, I am sure," said Mrs. Bennet, "and I dare say she is a very agreeable woman. It is a pity that great ladies in general are not more like her. Does she live near you, sir?"

"The garden in which stands my humble abode, is separated only by a lane from Rosings Park, her ladyship's residence."

"I think you said she was a widow, sir? has she any family?"

"She has one only daughter, the heiress of Rosings, and of very exten-sive property."

"Ah!" cried Mrs. Bennet, shaking her head, "then she is better off than many girls. And what sort of young lady is she? is she handsome?"

"She is a most charming young lady indeed. Lady Catherine herself says that in point of true beauty, Miss De Bourgh is far superior to the handsomest of her sex; because there is that in her features which marks the young woman of distinguished birth. She is unfortunately of a sickly constitution, which has prevented her making that progress in many accomplishments, which she could not otherwise have failed of; as I am informed by the lady who superintended her education, and who still resides with them. But she is perfectly amiable, and often condescends to drive by my humble abode in her little phaeton[9] and ponies."

"Has she been presented?[1] I do not remember her name among the ladies at court."

"Her indifferent state of health unhappily prevents her being in town; and by that means, as I told Lady Catherine myself one day, has deprived the British court of its brightest ornament. Her ladyship seemed pleased with the idea, and you may imagine that I am happy on every occasion to offer those little delicate compliments which are always acceptable to ladies. I have more than once observed to Lady Catherine, that her charming daughter seemed born to be a duchess, and that the most elevated rank, instead of giving her consequence, would be adorned by her.—These are the kind of little things which please her ladyship, and it is a sort of attention which I conceive myself peculiarly bound to pay."

---

8. In the first edition of 1813 Mr. Collins's praise of Lady Catherine is closed by a quotation mark at this point, although no quotation mark is used to open the speech. Many later editions add a quotation mark after the phrase "he protested that," even though Austen continues to represent Collins speaking in the third person.
9. A four-wheeled light carriage, usually drawn by a pair of horses.
1. Young women of Miss De Bourgh's class marked their entrance into adult society by attending an assembly at one of the residences of the sovereign.

"You judge very properly," said Mr. Bennet, "and it is happy for you that you possess the talent of flattering with delicacy. May I ask whether these pleasing attentions proceed from the impulse of the moment, or are the result of previous study?"

"They arise chiefly from what is passing at the time, and though I sometimes amuse myself with suggesting and arranging such little elegant compliments as may be adapted to ordinary occasions, I always wish to give them as unstudied an air as possible."

Mr. Bennet's expectations were fully answered. His cousin was as absurd as he had hoped, and he listened to him with the keenest enjoyment, maintaining at the same time the most resolute composure of countenance, and except in an occasional glance at Elizabeth, requiring no partner in his pleasure.

By tea-time however the dose had been enough, and Mr. Bennet was glad to take his guest into the drawing-room again, and when tea was over, glad to invite him to read aloud to the ladies. Mr. Collins readily assented, and a book was produced; but on beholding it, (for every thing announced it to be from a circulating library,) he started back, and begging pardon, protested that he never read novels.—Kitty stared at him, and Lydia exclaimed.—Other books were produced, and after some deliberation he chose Fordyce's Sermons.[2] Lydia gaped as he opened the volume, and before he had, with very monotonous solemnity, read three pages, she interrupted him with,

"Do you know, mama, that my uncle Philips talks of turning away Richard, and if he does, Colonel Forster will hire him. My aunt told me so herself on Saturday. I shall walk to Meryton to-morrow to hear more about it, and to ask when Mr. Denny comes back from town."

Lydia was bid by her two eldest sisters to hold her tongue; but Mr. Collins, much offended, laid aside his book, and said,

"I have often observed how little young ladies are interested by books of a serious stamp, though written solely for their benefit. It amazes me, I confess;—for certainly, there can be nothing so advantageous to them as instruction. But I will no longer importune my young cousin."

Then turning to Mr. Bennet, he offered himself as his antagonist at backgammon. Mr. Bennet accepted the challenge, observing that he acted very wisely in leaving the girls to their own trifling amusements. Mrs. Bennet and her daughters apologised most civilly for Lydia's interruption, and promised that it should not occur again, if he would resume his book; but Mr. Collins, after assuring them that he bore his young cousin no ill will, and should never resent her behaviour as any affront, seated himself at another table with Mr. Bennet, and prepared for backgammon.

---

2. James Fordyce's *Sermons to Young Women* (1766) includes deeply conservative warnings to young women about the vanities of fashionable pleasures.

Chapter XV

Mr. Collins was not a sensible man, and the deficiency of nature had been but little assisted by education or society; the greatest part of his life having been spent under the guidance of an illiterate and miserly father; and though he belonged to one of the universities, he had merely kept the necessary terms, without forming at it any useful acquaintance. The subjection in which his father had brought him up, had given him originally great humility of manner, but it was now a good deal counteracted by the self-conceit of a weak head, living in retirement, and the consequential feelings of early and unexpected prosperity. A fortunate chance had recommended him to Lady Catherine de Bourgh when the living of Hunsford was vacant; and the respect which he felt for her high rank, and his veneration for her as his patroness, mingling with a very good opinion of himself, of his authority as a clergyman, and his rights as a rector, made him altogether a mixture of pride and obsequiousness, self-importance and humility.

Having now a good house and very sufficient income, he intended to marry; and in seeking a reconciliation with the Longbourn family he had a wife in view, as he meant to chuse one of the daughters, if he found them as handsome and amiable as they were represented by common report. This was his plan of amends—of atonement—for inheriting their father's estate; and he thought it an excellent one, full of eligibility and suitableness, and excessively generous and disinterested on his own part.

His plan did not vary on seeing them.—Miss Bennet's lovely face confirmed his views, and established all his strictest notions of what was due to seniority; and for the first evening *she* was his settled choice. The next morning, however, made an alteration; for in a quarter of an hour's tête-à tête with Mrs. Bennet before breakfast, a conversation beginning with his parsonage-house, and leading naturally to the avowal of his hopes, that a mistress for it might be found at Longbourn, produced from her, amid very complaisant smiles and general encouragement, a caution against the very Jane he had fixed on.—"As to her *younger* daughters she could not take upon her to say—she could not positively answer—but she did not *know* of any prepossession;—her *eldest* daughter, she must just mention—she felt it incumbent on her to hint, was likely to be very soon engaged."

Mr. Collins had only to change from Jane to Elizabeth—and it was soon done—done while Mrs. Bennet was stirring the fire. Elizabeth, equally next to Jane in birth and beauty, succeeded her of course.

Mrs. Bennet treasured up the hint, and trusted that she might soon have two daughters married; and the man whom she could not bear to speak of the day before, was now high in her good graces.

Lydia's intention of walking to Meryton was not forgotten; every sister except Mary agreed to go with her; and Mr. Collins was to attend them, at the request of Mr. Bennet, who was most anxious to get rid of him, and have his library to himself; for thither Mr. Collins had followed him after breakfast, and there he would continue, nominally engaged with one of the largest folios in the collection, but really talking to Mr. Bennet, with little cessation, of his house and garden at Hunsford. Such doings discomposed Mr. Bennet exceedingly. In his library he had been always sure of leisure and tranquility; and though prepared, as he told Elizabeth, to meet with folly and conceit in every other room in the house, he was used to be free from them there; his civility, therefore, was most prompt in inviting Mr. Collins to join his daughters in their walk; and Mr. Collins, being in fact much better fitted for a walker than a reader, was extremely well pleased to close his large book, and go.

In pompous nothings on his side, and civil assents on that of his cousins, their time passed till they entered Meryton. The attention of the younger ones was then no longer to be gained by *him*. Their eyes were immediately wandering up in the street in quest of the officers, and nothing less than a very smart bonnet indeed, or a really new muslin in a shop window, could recal them.

But the attention of every lady was soon caught by a young man, whom they had never seen before, of most gentlemanlike appearance, walking with an officer on the other side of the way. The officer was the very Mr. Denny, concerning whose return from London Lydia came to inquire, and he bowed as they passed. All were struck with the stranger's air, all wondered who he could be, and Kitty and Lydia, determined if possible to find out, led the way across the street, under pretence of wanting something in an opposite shop, and fortunately had just gained the pavement when the two gentlemen turning back had reached the same spot. Mr. Denny addressed them directly, and entreated permission to introduce his friend, Mr. Wickham, who had returned with him the day before from town, and he was happy to say had accepted a commission in their corps. This was exactly as it should be; for the young man wanted only regimentals to make him completely charming. His appearance was greatly in his favour; he had all the best part of beauty, a fine countenance, a good figure, and very pleasing address. The introduction was followed up on his side by a happy readiness of conversation—a readiness at the same time perfectly correct and unassuming; and the whole party were still standing and talking together very agreeably, when the sound of horses drew their notice, and Darcy and Bingley were seen riding down the street. On distinguishing the ladies of the group, the two gentlemen came directly towards them, and began the usual civilities. Bingley was the principal spokesman, and Miss Bennet the principal object. He was then, he said, on his way to Longbourn on purpose to inquire after her. Mr. Darcy corroborated it with a bow, and was beginning to determine not to fix his eyes on Elizabeth, when they were suddenly arrested by the sight of the stranger, and Elizabeth happening to see the countenance of both as they looked at each other, was all astonishment at the effect of the meeting. Both changed colour, one looked white, the other red. Mr. Wickham, after a few moments, touched his hat—a salutation which Mr. Darcy just deigned to return. What could be the meaning of it?—It was impossible to imagine; it was impossible not to long to know.

In another minute Mr. Bingley, but without seeming to have noticed what passed, took leave and rode on with his friend.

Mr. Denny and Mr. Wickham walked with the young ladies to the door of Mr. Philips's house, and then made their bows, in spite of Miss Lydia's pressing entreaties that they would come in, and even in spite of Mrs. Philips' throwing up the parlour window, and loudly seconding the invitation.

Mrs. Philips was always glad to see her nieces, and the two eldest, from their recent absence, were particularly welcome, and she was eagerly expressing her surprise at their sudden return home, which, as their own carriage had not fetched them, she should have known nothing about, if she had not happened to see Mr. Jones's shop boy in the street, who had told her that they were not to send any more draughts to Netherfield because the Miss Bennets were come away, when her civility was claimed towards Mr. Collins by Jane's introduction of him. She received him with her very best politeness, which he returned with as much more, apologising for his intrusion, without any previous acquaintance with her, which he could not help flattering himself however might be justified by his relationship to the young ladies who introduced him to her notice. Mrs. Philips was quite awed by such an excess of good breeding; but her contemplation of one stranger was soon put an end to by exclamations and inquiries about the other, of whom, however, she could only tell her nieces what they already knew, that Mr. Denny had brought him from London, and that he was to have a lieutenant's commission in the ——shire. She had been watching him the last hour, she said, as he walked up and down the street, and had Mr. Wickham appeared Kitty and Lydia would certainly have continued the occupation, but unluckily no one passed the windows now except a few of the officers, who in comparison with the stranger, were become "stupid, disagreeable fellows." Some of them were to dine with the Philipses the next day, and their aunt promised to make her husband call on Mr. Wickham, and give him an invitation also, if the family from Longbourn would come in the evening. This was agreed to, and Mrs. Philips protested that they would have a nice comfortable noisy game of lottery tickets, and a little bit of hot supper afterwards.[3] The prospect of such delights was very cheering, and they parted in mutual good spirits. Mr. Collins repeated his apologies in quitting the room, and was assured with unwearying civility that they were perfectly needless.

As they walked home, Elizabeth related to Jane what she had seen pass between the two gentlemen; but though Jane would have defended either or both, had they appeared to be wrong, she could no more explain such behaviour than her sister.

Mr. Collins on his return highly gratified Mrs. Bennet by admiring Mrs. Philip's manners and politeness. He protested that except Lady Catherine and her daughter, he had never seen a more elegant woman; for she had not only received him with the utmost civility, but had even pointedly included him in her invitation for the next evening, although utterly unknown to her before. Something he supposed might be attributed to his connection with them, but yet he had never met with so much attention in the whole course of his life.

Chapter XVI

As no objection was made to the young people's engagement with their aunt, and all Mr. Collins's scruples of leaving Mr. and Mrs. Bennet for a single evening during his visit were most steadily resisted, the coach conveyed him and his five cousins at a suitable hour to Meryton; and the girls had the pleasure of hearing, as they entered the drawing-room, that Mr. Wickham had accepted their uncle's invitation, and was then in the house.

When this information was given, and they had all taken their seats, Mr. Collins was at leisure to look around him and admire, and he was so much struck with the size and furniture of the apartment, that he declared he might almost have supposed himself in the small summer breakfast parlour at Rosings; a comparison that did not at first convey much gratification; but when Mrs. Philips understood from him what Rosings was, and who was its proprietor, when she had listened to the description of only one of Lady Catherine's drawing-rooms, and found that the chimney-piece alone had cost eight hundred pounds, she felt all the force of the compliment, and would hardly have resented a comparison with the housekeeper's room.

In describing to her all the grandeur of Lady Catherine and her mansion, with occasional digressions in praise of his own humble

---

3. A very simple card game that can be played with many players, who simply bet that a card dealt face down to one player will be found to match that of another player. The invitation to the Longbourne family is to come to the Philipses after dinner to join the officers, who have been invited to dinner, for cards and a late supper.

abode, and the improvements it was receiving, he was happily employed until the gentlemen joined them; and he found in Mrs. Philips a very attentive listener, whose opinion of his consequence increased with what she heard, and who was resolving to retail it all among her neighbours as soon as she could. To the girls, who could not listen to their cousin, and who had nothing to do but to wish for an instrument, and examine their own indifferent imitations of china[4] on the mantlepiece, the interval of waiting appeared very long. It was over at last however. The gentlemen did approach; and when Mr. Wickham walked into the room, Elizabeth felt that she had neither been seeing him before, nor thinking of him since, with the smallest degree of unreasonable admiration. The officers of the ——shire were in general a very creditable, gentlemanlike set, and the best of them were of the present party; but Mr. Wickham was as far beyond them all in person, countenance, air, and walk, as *they* were superior to the broad-faced stuffy uncle Philips, breathing port wine, who followed them into the room.

Mr. Wickham was the happy man towards whom almost every female eye was turned, and Elizabeth was the happy woman by whom he finally seated himself; and the agreeable manner in which he immediately fell into conversation, though it was only on its being a wet night, and on the probability of a rainy season, made her feel that the commonest, dullest, most threadbare topic might be rendered interesting by the skill of the speaker.

With such rivals for the notice of the fair, as Mr. Wickham and the officers, Mr. Collins seemed likely to sink into insignificance; to the young ladies he certainly was nothing; but he had still at intervals a kind listener in Mrs. Philips, and was, by her watchfulness, most abundantly supplied with coffee and muffin.

When the card tables were placed, he had an opportunity of obliging her in return, by sitting down to whist.

"I know little of the game, at present," said he, "but I shall be glad to improve myself, for in my situation of life—" Mrs. Philips was very thankful for his compliance, but could not wait for his reason.

Mr. Wickham did not play at whist, and with ready delight was he received at the other table between Elizabeth and Lydia. At first there seemed danger of Lydia's engrossing him entirely, for she was a most determined talker; but being likewise extremely fond of lottery tickets, she soon grew too much interested in the game, too eager in making bets and exclaiming after prizes, to have attention for any one in particular. Allowing for the common demands of the game, Mr. Wickham was therefore at leisure to talk to Elizabeth, and she was very willing to hear him, though what she chiefly wished to hear she could not

4. A common diversion of leisured young women was to paint earthenware in imitation of the patterns and scenes on manufactured china.

hope to be told, the history of his acquaintance with Mr. Darcy. She dared not even mention that gentleman. Her curiosity however was unexpectedly relieved. Mr. Wickham began the subject himself. He inquired how far Netherfield was from Meryton; and, after receiving her answer, asked in an hesitating manner how long Mr. Darcy had been staying there.

"About a month," said Elizabeth; and then, unwilling to let the subject drop, added, "He is a man of very large property in Derbyshire, I understand."

"Yes," replied Wickham;—"his estate there is a noble one. A clear ten thousand per annum. You could not have met with a person more capable of giving you certain information on that head than myself— for I have been connected with his family in a particular manner from my infancy."

Elizabeth could not but look surprised.

"You may well be surprised, Miss Bennet, at such an assertion, after seeing, as you probably might, the very cold manner of our meeting yesterday.—Are you much acquainted with Mr. Darcy?"

"As much as I ever wish to be," cried Elizabeth warmly,—"I have spent four days in the same house with him, and I think him very disagreeable."

"I have no right to give *my* opinion," said Wickham, "as to his being agreeable or otherwise. I am not qualified to form one. I have known him too long and too well to be a fair judge. It is impossible for *me* to be impartial. But I believe your opinion of him would in general aston-ish—and perhaps you would not express it quite so strongly anywhere else.—Here you are in your own family."

"Upon my word I say no more *here* than I might say in any house in the neighbourhood, except Netherfield. He is not at all liked in Hert-fordshire. Every body is disgusted with his pride. You will not find him more favourably spoken of by any one."

"I cannot pretend to be sorry," said Wickham, after a short inter-ruption, "that he or that any man should not be estimated beyond their deserts; but with *him* I believe it does not often happen. The world is blinded by his fortune and consequence, or frightened by his high and imposing manners, and sees him only as he chuses to be seen."

"I should take him, even on *my* slight acquaintance, to be an ill-tempered man." Wickham only shook his head.

"I wonder," said he, at the next opportunity of speaking, "whether he is likely to be in this country much longer."

"I do not at all know; but I *heard* nothing of his going away when I was at Netherfield. I hope your plans in favour of the ——shire will not be affected by his being in the neighbourhood."

"Oh! no—it is not for *me* to be driven away by Mr. Darcy. If *he* wishes to avoid seeing *me*, he must go. We are not on friendly terms, and it always gives me pain to meet him, but I have no reason for avoiding *him* but what I might proclaim to all the world; a sense of very great ill usage, and most painful regrets at his being what he is. His father, Miss Bennet, the late Mr. Darcy, was one of the best men that ever breathed, and the truest friend I ever had; and I can never be in company with this Mr. Darcy without being grieved to the soul by a thousand tender recollections. His behaviour to myself has been scandalous; but I verily believe I could forgive him any thing and every thing, rather than his disappointing the hopes and disgracing the memory of his father."

Elizabeth found the interest of the subject increase, and listened with all her heart; but the delicacy of it prevented farther inquiry.

Mr. Wickham began to speak on more general topics, Meryton, the neighbourhood, the society, appearing highly pleased with all that he had yet seen, and speaking of the latter especially, with gentle but very intelligible gallantry.

"It was the prospect of constant society, and good society," he added, "which was my chief inducement to enter the ——shire. I knew it to be a most respectable, agreeable corps, and my friend Denny tempted me farther by his account of their present quarters, and the very great attentions and excellent acquaintance Meryton had procured them. Society, I own, is necessary to me. I have been a disappointed man, and my spirits will not bear solitude. I *must* have employment and society. A military life is not what I was intended for, but circumstances have now made it eligible. The church *ought* to have been my profession—I was brought up for the church, and I should at this time have been in possession of a most valuable living, had it pleased the gentleman we were speaking of just now."

"Indeed!"

"Yes—the late Mr. Darcy bequeathed me the next presentation of the best living in his gift. He was my godfather, and excessively attached to me. I cannot do justice to his kindness. He meant to provide for me amply, and thought he had done it; but when the living fell, it was given elsewhere."

"Good heavens!" cried Elizabeth; "but how could *that* be?—How could his will be disregarded?—Why did not you seek legal redress?"

"There was just such an informality in the terms of the bequest as to give me no hope from law. A man of honour could not have doubted the intention, but Mr. Darcy chose to doubt it—or to treat it as a merely conditional recommendation, and to assert that I had forfeited all claim to it by extravagance, imprudence, in short any thing or nothing. Certain it is, that the living became vacant two years ago, exactly as I was of an age to hold it, and that it was given to another man; and no less certain is it, that I cannot accuse myself of having really done any thing to deserve to lose it. I have a warm, unguarded temper, and I may perhaps have sometimes spoken my opinion *of* him, and *to* him, too freely. I can recal nothing worse. But the fact is, that we are very different sort of men, and that he hates me."

"This is quite shocking!—He deserves to be publicly disgraced."

"Some time or other he *will* be—but it shall not be by *me*. Till I can forget his father, I can never defy or expose *him*."

Elizabeth honoured him for such feelings, and thought him handsomer than ever as he expressed them.

"But what," said she, after a pause, "can have been his motive?—what can have induced him to behave so cruelly?"

"A thorough, determined dislike of me—a dislike which I cannot but attribute in some measure to jealousy. Had the late Mr. Darcy liked me less, his son might have borne with me better; but his father's uncommon attachment to me, irritated him I believe very early in life. He had not a temper to bear the sort of competition in which we stood—the sort of preference which was often given me."

"I had not thought Mr. Darcy so bad as this—though I have never liked him, I had not thought so very ill of him—I had supposed him to be despising his fellow-creatures in general, but did not suspect him of descending to such malicious revenge, such injustice, such inhumanity as this!"

After a few minutes reflection, however, she continued, "I *do* remember his boasting one day, at Netherfield, of the implacability of his resentments, of his having an unforgiving temper. His disposition must be dreadful."

"I will not trust myself on the subject," replied Wickham, "*I* can hardly be just to him."

Elizabeth was again deep in thought, and after a time exclaimed, "To treat in such a manner, the godson, the friend, the favourite of his father!"—She could have added, "A young man too, like *you*, whose very countenance may vouch for your being amiable"—but she contented herself with "And one, too, who had probably been his own companion from childhood, connected together, as I think you said, in the closest manner!"

"We were born in the same parish, within the same park, the greatest part of our youth was passed together; inmates of the same house, sharing the same amusements, objects of the same parental care. *My* father began life in the profession which your uncle, Mr. Philips, appears to do so much credit to—but he gave up everything to be of use to the late Mr. Darcy, and devoted all his time to the care of the Pemberley property. He was most highly esteemed by Mr. Darcy, a most intimate, confidential friend. Mr. Darcy often acknowledged himself to be under the greatest obligations to my father's active superintendance, and when immediately before my father's death, Mr.

Darcy gave him a voluntary promise of providing for me, I am convinced that he felt it to be as much a debt of gratitude to *him*, as of affection to myself."

"How strange!" cried Elizabeth. "How abominable!—I wonder that the very pride of this Mr. Darcy has not made him just to you!—If from no better motive, that he should not have been too proud to be dishonest,—for dishonesty I must call it."

"It *is* wonderful,"—replied Wickham,—"for almost all his actions may be traced to pride;—and pride has often been his best friend. It has connected him nearer with virtue than any other feeling. But we are none of us consistent; and in his behaviour to me, there were stronger impulses even than pride."

"Can such abominable pride as his, have ever done him good?"

"Yes. It has often led him to be liberal and generous,—to give his money freely, to display hospitality, to assist his tenants, and relieve the poor. Family pride, and *filial* pride, for he is very proud of what his father was, have done this. Not to appear to disgrace his family, to degenerate from the popular qualities, or lose the influence of the Pemberley House, is a powerful motive. He has also *brotherly* pride, which with *some* brotherly affection, makes him a very kind and careful guardian of his sister; and you will hear him generally cried up as the most attentive and best of brothers."

"What sort of a girl is Miss Darcy?"

He shook his head.—"I wish I could call her amiable. It gives me pain to speak ill of a Darcy. But she is too much like her brother,—very, very proud.—As a child, she was affectionate and pleasing, and extremely fond of me; and I have devoted hours and hours to her amusement. But she is nothing to me now. She is a handsome girl, about fifteen or sixteen, and I understand highly accomplished. Since her father's death, her home has been London, where a lady lives with her, and superintends her education."

After many pauses and many trials of other subjects, Elizabeth could not help reverting once more to the first, and saying,

"I am astonished at his intimacy with Mr. Bingley! How can Mr. Bingley, who seems good humour itself, and is, I really believe, truly amiable, be in friendship with such a man? How can they suit each other?—Do you know Mr. Bingley?"

"Not at all."

"He is a sweet tempered, amiable, charming man. He cannot know what Mr. Darcy is."

"Probably not;—but Mr. Darcy can please where he chuses. He does not want abilities. He can be a conversible companion if he thinks it worth his while. Among those who are at all his equals in consequence, he is a very different man from what he is to the less prosperous. His pride never deserts him; but with the rich, he is liberal-minded, just, sincere, rational, honourable, and perhaps agreeable,—allowing something for fortune and figure."

The whist party soon afterward breaking up, the players gathered round the other table, and Mr. Collins took his station between his cousin Elizabeth and Mrs. Philips.—The usual inquiries as to his success were made by the latter. It had not been very great; he had lost every point; but when Mrs. Philips began to express her concern thereupon, he assured her with much earnest gravity that it was not of the least importance, that he considered the money as a mere trifle, and begged she would not make herself uneasy.

"I know very well, madam," said he, "that when persons sit down to a card table, they must take their chance of these things,—and happily I am not in such circumstances as to make five shillings any object. There are undoubtedly many who could not say the same, but thanks to Lady Catherine de Bourgh, I am removed far beyond the necessity of regarding little matters."

Mr. Wickham's attention was caught; and after observing Mr. Collins for a few moments, he asked Elizabeth in a low voice whether her relation were very intimately acquainted with the family of de Bourgh.

"Lady Catherine de Bourgh," she replied, "has very lately given him a living. I hardly known how Mr. Collins was first introduced to her notice, but he certainly has not known her long."

"You know of course that Lady Catherine de Bourgh and Lady Anne Darcy were sisters; consequently that she is aunt to the present Mr. Darcy."

"No, indeed, I did not.—I knew nothing at all of Lady Catherine's connections. I never heard of her existence till the day before yesterday."

"Her daughter, Miss de Bourgh, will have a very large fortune, and it is believed that she and her cousin will unite the two estates."

This information made Elizabeth smile, as she thought of poor Miss Bingley. Vain indeed must be all her attentions, vain and useless her affection for his sister and her praise of himself, if he were already self-destined to another.

"Mr. Collins," said she, "speaks highly both of Lady Catherine and her daughter: but from some particulars that he has related of her ladyship, I suspect his gratitude misleads him, and that in spite of her being his patroness, she is an arrogant, conceited woman."

"I believe her to be both in a great degree," replied Wickham; "I have not seen her for many years, but I very well remember that I never liked her, and that her manners were dictatorial and insolent. She has the reputation of being remarkably sensible and clever; but I rather believe she derives part of her abilities from her rank and fortune, part from her authoritative manner, and the rest from the pride of her nephew, who chuses that every one connected with him should have an understanding of the first class."

Elizabeth allowed that he had given a very rational account of it, and they continued talking together with mutual satisfaction till supper put an end to cards; and gave the rest of the ladies their share of Mr. Wickham's attentions. There could be no conversation in the noise of Mrs. Philips's supper party, but his manners recommended him to every body. Whatever he said, was said well; and whatever he did, done gracefully. Elizabeth went away with her head full of him. She could think of nothing but of Mr. Wickham, and of what he had told her, all the way home; but there was not time for her even to mention his name as they went, for neither Lydia nor Mr. Collins were once silent. Lydia talked incessantly of lottery tickets, of the fish[5] she had lost and the fish she had won, and Mr. Collins, in describing the civility of Mr. and Mrs. Philips, protesting that he did not in the least regard his losses at whist, enumerating all the dishes at supper, and repeatedly fearing that he crouded his cousins, had more to say than he could well manage before the carriage stopped at Longbourn House.

Chapter XVII

Elizabeth related to Jane the next day, what had passed between Mr. Wickham and herself. Jane listened with astonishment and concern;—she knew not how to believe that Mr. Darcy could be so unworthy of Mr. Bingley's regard; and yet, it was not in her nature to question the veracity of a young man of such amiable appearance as Wickham.—The possibility of his having really endured such unkindness, was enough to interest all her tender feelings; and nothing therefore remained to be done, but to think well of them both, to defend the conduct of each, and throw into the account of accident or mistake, whatever could not be otherwise explained.

"They have both," said she, "been deceived, I dare say, in some way or other, of which we can form no idea. Interested people have perhaps misrepresented each to the other. It is, in short, impossible for us to conjecture the causes or circumstances which may have alienated them, without actual blame on either side."

"Very true, indeed;—and now, my dear Jane what have you got to say in behalf of the interested people who have probably been concerned in the business?—Do clear *them* too, or we shall be obliged to think ill of somebody."

"Laugh as much as you chuse, but you will not laugh me out of my

---

5. Counters of bone or ivory used as stakes in games.

opinion. My dearest Lizzy, do not consider in what a disgraceful light it places Mr. Darcy, to be treating his father's favourite in such a manner,—one, whom his father had promised to provide for.—It is impossible. No man of common humanity, no man who had any value for his character, could be capable of it. Can his most intimate friends be so excessively deceived in him? oh! no."

"I can much more easily believe Mr. Bingley's being imposed on, than that Mr. Wickham should invent such a history of himself as he gave me last night; names, facts, every thing mentioned without ceremony.—If it be not so, let Mr. Darcy contradict it. Besides, there was truth in his looks."

"It is difficult indeed—it is distressing.—One does not know what to think."

"I beg your pardon;—one knows exactly what to think."

But Jane could think with certainty on only one point,—that Mr. Bingley, if he *had been* imposed on, would have much to suffer when the affair became public.

The two young ladies were summoned from the shrubbery where this conversation passed, by the arrival of some of the very persons of whom they had been speaking; Mr. Bingley and his sisters came to give their personal invitation for the long expected ball at Netherfield, which was fixed for the following Tuesday. The two ladies were delighted to see their dear friend again, called it an age since they had met, and repeatedly asked what she had been doing with herself since their separation. To the rest of the family they paid little attention; avoiding Mrs. Bennet as much as possible, saying not much to Elizabeth, and nothing at all to the others. They were soon gone again, rising from their seats with an activity which took their brother by surprise, and hurrying off as if eager to escape from Mrs. Bennet's civilities.

The prospect of the Netherfield ball was extremely agreeable to every female of the family. Mrs. Bennet chose to consider it as given in compliment to her eldest daughter, and was particularly flattered by receiving the invitation from Mr. Bingley himself, instead of a ceremonious card. Jane pictured to herself a happy evening in the society of her two friends, and the attentions of their brother; and Elizabeth thought with pleasure of dancing a great deal with Mr. Wickham, and of seeing a confirmation of everything in Mr. Darcy's looks and behaviour. The happiness anticipated by Catherine and Lydia, depended less on any single event, or any particular person, for though they each, like Elizabeth, meant to dance half the evening with Mr. Wickham, he was by no means the only partner who could satisfy them, and a ball was at any rate, a ball. And even Mary could assure her family that she had no disinclination for it.

"While I can have my mornings to myself," said she, "it is enough.—
I think it no sacrifice to join occasionally in evening engagements.
Society has claims on us all; and I profess myself one of those who
consider intervals of recreation and amusement as desirable for every
body."

Elizabeth's spirits were so high on the occasion, that though she did
not often speak unnecessarily to Mr. Collins, she could not help asking
him whether he intended to accept Mr. Bingley's invitation, and if he
did, whether he would think it proper to join in the evening's amusement; and she was rather surprised to find that he entertained no scruple whatever on that head, and was very far from dreading a rebuke
either from the Archbishop, or Lady Catherine de Bourgh, by venturing
to dance.

"I am by no means of opinion, I assure you," said he, "that a ball of
this kind, given by a young man of character, to respectable people,
can have any evil tendency; and I am so far from objecting to dancing
myself that I shall hope to be honoured with the hands of all my fair
cousins in the course of the evening, and I take this opportunity of
soliciting yours, Miss Elizabeth, for the two first dances especially,—a
preference which I trust my cousin Jane will attribute to the right
cause, and not to any disrespect for her."

Elizabeth felt herself completely taken in. She had fully proposed
being engaged by Wickham for those very dances:—and to have Mr.
Collins instead!—her liveliness had been never worse timed. There was
no help for it however. Mr. Wickham's happiness and her own was per
force delayed a little longer, and Mr. Collins's proposal accepted with
as good a grace as she could. She was not the better pleased with his
gallantry, from the idea it suggested of something more.—It now first
struck her, that *she* was selected from among her sisters as worthy of
being the mistress of Hunsford Parsonage, and of assisting to form a
quadrille table at Rosings, in the absence of more eligible visitors. The
idea soon reached to conviction, as she observed his increasing civilities
toward herself, and heard his frequent attempt at a compliment on
her wit and vivacity; and though more astonished than gratified herself,
by this effect of her charms, it was not long before her mother gave
her to understand that the probability of their marriage was exceedingly agreeable to *her*. Elizabeth however did not chuse to take the
hint, being well aware that a serious dispute must be the consequence
of any reply. Mr. Collins might never make the offer, and till he did,
it was useless to quarrel about him.

If there had not been a Netherfield ball to prepare for and talk of,
the younger Miss Bennets would have been in a pitiable state at this
time, for from the day of the invitation, to the day of the ball, there
was such a succession of rain as prevented their walking to Meryton
once. No aunt, no officers, no news could be sought after;—the very

shoe-roses[6] for Netherfield were got by proxy. Even Elizabeth might have found some trial of her patience in weather, which totally suspended the improvement of her acquaintance with Mr. Wickham; and nothing less than a dance on Tuesday, could have made such a Friday, Saturday, Sunday and Monday, endurable to Kitty and Lydia.

Chapter XVIII

Till Elizabeth entered the drawing-room at Netherfield and looked in vain for Mr. Wickham among the cluster of red coats there assembled, a doubt of his being present had never occurred to her. The certainty of meeting him had not been checked by any of those recollections that might not unreasonably have alarmed her. She had dressed with more than usual care, and prepared in the highest spirits for the conquest of all that remained unsubdued of his heart, trusting that it was not more than might be won in the course of the evening. But in an instant arose the dreadful suspicion of his being purposely omitted for Mr. Darcy's pleasure in the Bingley's invitation to the officers; and though this was not exactly the case, the absolute fact of his absence was pronounced by his friend Mr. Denny, to whom Lydia eagerly applied, and who told them that Wickham had been obliged to go to town on business the day before, and was not yet returned; adding, with a significant smile,

"I do not imagine his business would have called him away just now, if he had not wished to avoid a certain gentleman here."

This part of his intelligence, though unheard by Lydia, was caught by Elizabeth, and as it assured her that Darcy was not less answerable for Wickham's absence than if her first surmise had been just, every feeling of displeasure against the former was so sharpened by immediate disappointment, that she could hardly reply with tolerable civility to the polite inquiries which he directly afterwards approached to make.—Attention, forbearance, patience with Darcy, was injury to Wickham. She was resolved against any sort of conversation with him, and turned away with a degree of ill humour, which she could not wholly surmount even in speaking to Mr. Bingley, whose blind partiality provoked her.

But Elizabeth was not formed for ill-humour; and though every prospect of her own was destroyed for the evening, it could not dwell long on her spirits; and having told all her griefs to Charlotte Lucas, whom she had not seen for a week, she was soon able to make a voluntary transition to the oddities of her cousin, and to point him out to her particular notice. The two first dances, however, brought a return of distress; they were dances of mortification. Mr. Collins, awkward and

6. Shoe-ties with ribbons bunched in the form of a rose.

solemn, apologising instead of attending, and often moving wrong without being aware of it, gave her all the shame and misery which a disagreeable partner for a couple of dances can give. The moment of her release from him was exstacy.

She danced next with an officer, and had the refreshment of talking of Wickham, and of hearing that he was universally liked. When those dances were over she returned to Charlotte Lucas, and was in conversation with her, when she found herself suddenly addressed by Mr. Darcy, who took her so much by surprise in his application for her hand, that, without knowing what she did, she accepted him. He walked away again immediately, and she was left to fret over her own want of presence of mind; Charlotte tried to console her.

"I dare say you will find him very agreeable."

"Heaven forbid!—*That* would be the greatest misfortune of all!—To find a man agreeable whom one is determined to hate!—Do not wish me such an evil."

When the dancing recommenced, however, and Darcy approached to claim her hand, Charlotte could not help cautioning her in a whisper not to be a simpleton and allow her fancy for Wickham to make her appear unpleasant in the eyes of a man of ten times his consequence. Elizabeth made no answer, and took her place in the set, amazed at the dignity to which she was arrived in being allowed to stand opposite to Mr. Darcy, and reading in her neighbours' looks their equal amazement in beholding it. They stood for some time without speaking a word; and she began to imagine that their silence was to last through the two dances, and at first was resolved not to break it; till suddenly fancying that it would be the greater punishment to her partner to oblige him to talk, she made some slight observation on the dance. He replied, and was silent again. After a pause of some minutes she addressed him a second time with

"It is *your* turn to say something now, Mr. Darcy.—*I* talked about the dance, and *you* ought to make some kind of remark on the size of the room, or the number of couples."

He smiled, and assured her that whatever she wished him to say should be said.

"Very well.—That reply will do for the present.—Perhaps by and bye I may observe that private balls are much pleasanter than public ones.—But *now* we may be silent."

"Do you talk by rule then, while you are dancing?"

"Sometimes. One must speak a little, you know. It would look odd to be entirely silent for half an hour together, and yet for the advantage of *some*, conversation ought to be so arranged as that they may have the trouble of saying as little as possible."

"Are you consulting your own feelings in the present case, or do you imagine that you are gratifying mine?"

"Both," replied Elizabeth archly; "for I have always seen a great similarity in the turn of our minds.—We are each of an unsocial, taciturn disposition, unwilling to speak, unless we expect to say something that will amaze the whole room, and be handed down to posterity with all the eclat of a proverb."

"This is no very striking resemblance of your own character, I am sure," said he. "How near it may be to *mine*, I cannot pretend to say.— *You* think it a faithful portrait undoubtedly."

"I must not decide on my own performance."

He made no answer, and they were again silent till they had gone down the dance, when he asked her if she and her sisters did not very often walk to Meryton. She answered in the affirmative, and, unable to resist the temptation, added, "When you met us there the other day, we had just been forming a new acquaintance."

The effect was immediate. A deeper shade of hauteur overspread his features, but he said not a word, and Elizabeth, though blaming herself for her own weakness, could not go on. At length Darcy spoke, and in a constrained manner said,

"Mr. Wickham is blessed with such happy manners as may ensure his *making* friends—whether he may be equally capable of *retaining* them, is less certain."

"He has been so unlucky as to lose *your* friendship," replied Elizabeth with emphasis, "and in a manner which he is likely to suffer from all his life."

Darcy made no answer, and seemed desirous of changing the subject. At that moment Sir William Lucas appeared close to them, meaning to pass through the set to the other side of the room; but on perceiving Mr. Darcy he stopt with a bow of superior courtesy to compliment him on his dancing and his partner.

"I have been most highly gratified indeed, my dear Sir. Such very superior dancing is not often seen. It is evident that you belong to the first circles. Allow me to say, however, that your fair partner does not disgrace you, and that I must hope to have this pleasure often repeated, especially when a certain desirable event, my dear Miss Eliza, (glancing at her sister and Bingley,) shall take place. What congratulations will then flow in! I appeal to Mr. Darcy:—but let me not interrupt you. Sir.—You will not thank me for detaining you from the bewitching converse of that young lady, whose bright eyes are also upbraiding me."

The latter part of this address was scarcely heard by Darcy; but Sir William's allusion to his friend seemed to strike him forcibly, and his eyes were directed with a very serious expression towards Bingley and Jane, who were dancing together. Recovering himself, however, shortly, he turned to his partner, and said,

"Sir William's interruption has made me forget what we were talking of."

"I do not think we were speaking at all. Sir William could not have interrupted any two people in the room who had less to say for themselves.—We have tried two or three subjects already without success, and what we are to talk of next I cannot imagine."

"What think you of books?" said he, smiling.

"Books—Oh! no.—I am sure we never read the same, or not with the same feelings."

"I am sorry you think so; but if that be the case, there can at least be no want of subject.—We may compare our different opinions."

"No—I cannot talk of books in a ball-room; my head is always full of something else."

"The *present* always occupies you in such scenes—does it?" said he, with a look of doubt.

"Yes, always," she replied, without knowing what she said, for her thoughts had wandered far from the subject, as soon afterwards appeared by her suddenly exclaiming, "I remember hearing you once say, Mr. Darcy, that you hardly ever forgave, that your resentment once created was unappeasable. You are very cautious, I suppose, as to its *being created*."

"I am," said he, with a firm voice.

"And never allow yourself to be blinded by prejudice?"

"I hope not."

"It is particularly incumbent on those who never change their opinion, to be secure of judging properly at first."

"May I ask to what these questions tend?"

"Merely to the illustration of *your* character," said she, endeavouring to shake off her gravity. "I am trying to make it out."

"And what is your success?"

She shook her head. "I do not get on at all. I hear such different accounts of you as puzzle me exceedingly."

"I can readily believe," answered he gravely, "that report may vary greatly with respect to me; and I could wish, Miss Bennet, that you were not to sketch my character at the present moment, as there is reason to fear that the performance would reflect no credit on either."

"But if I do not take your likeness now, I may never have another opportunity."

"I would by no means suspend any pleasure of yours," he coldly replied. She said no more, and they went down the other dance and parted in silence; on each side dissatisfied, though not to an equal degree, for in Darcy's breast there was a tolerable powerful feeling towards her, which soon procured her pardon, and directed all his anger against another.

They had not long separated when Miss Bingley came towards her, and with an expression of civil disdain thus accosted her,

"So, Miss Eliza, I hear you are quite delighted with George Wickham!—Your sister has been talking to me about him, and asking me a thousand questions; and I find that the young man forgot to tell you, among his other communications, that he was the son of old Wickham, the late Mr. Darcy's steward. Let me recommend you, however, as a friend, not to give implicit confidence to all his assertions; for as to Mr. Darcy's using him ill, it is perfectly false; for, on the contrary, he has been always remarkably kind to him, though George Wickham has treated Mr. Darcy in a most infamous manner. I do not know the particulars, but I know very well that Mr. Darcy is not in the least to blame, that he cannot bear to hear George Wickham mentioned, and that though my brother thought he could not well avoid including him in his invitation to the officers, he was excessively glad to find that he had taken himself out of the way. His coming into the country at all, is a most insolent thing indeed, and I wonder how he could presume to do it. I pity you, Miss Eliza, for the discovery of your favourite's guilt; but really considering his descent, one could not expect much better."

"His guilt and his descent appear by your account to be the same," said Elizabeth angrily; "for I have heard you accuse him of nothing worse than of being the son of Mr. Darcy's steward, and of *that*, I can assure you, he informed me himself."

"I beg your pardon," replied Miss Bingley, turning away with a sneer. "Excuse my interference.—It was kindly meant."

"Insolent girl!" said Elizabeth to herself.—"You are much mistaken if you expect to influence me by such a paltry attack as this. I see nothing in it but your own wilful ignorance and the malice of Mr. Darcy." She then sought her eldest sister, who had undertaken to make inquiries on the same subject of Bingley. Jane met her with a smile of such sweet complacency, a glow of such happy expression, as sufficiently marked how well she was satisfied with the occurrences of the evening.—Elizabeth instantly read her feelings, and at that moment solicitude for Wickham, resentment against his enemies, and every thing else gave way before the hope of Jane's being in the fairest way for happiness.

"I want to know," said she, with a countenance no less smiling than her sister's, "what you have learnt about Mr. Wickham. But perhaps you have been too pleasantly engaged to think of any third person; in which case you may be sure of my pardon."

"No," replied Jane, "I have not forgotten him; but I have nothing satisfactory to tell you. Mr. Bingley does not know the whole of his history, and is quite ignorant of the circumstances which have principally offended Mr. Darcy; but he will vouch for the good conduct, the probity and honour of his friend, and is perfectly convinced that Mr. Wickham has deserved much less attention from Mr. Darcy than he has received; and I am sorry to say that by his account as well as his sister's, Mr. Wickham is by no means a respectable young man. I am afraid he has been very imprudent, and has deserved to lose Mr. Darcy's regard."

"Mr. Bingley does not know Mr. Wickham himself?"

"No; he never saw him till the other morning at Meryton."

"This account then is what he has received from Mr. Darcy. I am perfectly satisfied. But what does he say of the living?"

"He does not exactly recollect the circumstances, though he has heard them from Mr. Darcy more than once, but he believes that it was left to him *conditionally* only."

"I have not a doubt of Mr. Bingley's sincerity," said Elizabeth warmly; "but you must excuse my not being convinced by assurances only. Mr. Bingley's defence of his friend was a very able one I dare say, but since he is unacquainted with several parts of the story, and has learnt the rest from that friend himself, I shall venture still to think of both gentlemen as I did before."

She then changed the discourse to one more gratifying to each, and on which there could be no difference of sentiment. Elizabeth listened with delight to the happy, though modest hopes which Jane entertained of Bingley's regard, and said all in her power to heighten her confidence in it. On their being joined by Mr. Bingley himself, Elizabeth withdrew to Miss Lucas; to whose inquiry after the pleasantness of her last partner she had scarcely replied, before Mr. Collins came up to them and told her with great exultation that he had just been so fortunate as to make a most important discovery.

"I have found out," said he, "by a singular accident, that there is now in the room a near relation of my patroness. I happened to overhear the gentleman himself mentioning to the young lady who does the honours of this house the names of his cousin Miss de Bourgh, and of her mother Lady Catherine. How wonderfully these sort of things occur! Who would have thought of my meeting with—perhaps—a nephew of Lady Catherine de Bourgh in this assembly!—I am most thankful that the discovery is made in time for me to pay my respects to him, which I am now going to do, and trust he will excuse my not having done it before. My total ignorance of the connection must plead my apology."

"You are not going to introduce yourself to Mr. Darcy?"

"Indeed I am. I shall intreat his pardon for not having done it earlier. I believe him to be Lady Catherine's *nephew*. It will be in my power to assure him that her ladyship was quite well yesterday se'nnight."

Elizabeth tried hard to dissuade him from such a scheme; assuring him that Mr. Darcy would consider his addressing him without introduction as an impertinent freedom, rather than a compliment to his aunt; that it was not in the least necessary there should be any notice on either side, and that if it were, it must belong to Mr. Darcy, the superior in consequence, to begin the acquaintance.—Mr. Collins listened to her with the determined air of following his own inclination, and when she ceased speaking, replied thus,

"My dear Miss Elizabeth, I have the highest opinion in the world of your excellent judgment in all matters within the scope of your understanding, but permit me to say that there must be a wide difference between the established forms of ceremony amongst the laity, and those which regulate the clergy; for give me leave to observe that I consider the clerical office as equal in point of dignity with the highest rank in the kingdom—provided that a proper humility of behaviour is at the same time maintained. You must therefore allow me to follow the dictates of my conscience on this occasion, which leads me to perform what I look on as a point of duty. Pardon me for neglecting to profit by your advice, which on every other subject shall be my constant guide, though in the case before us I consider myself more fitted by education and habitual study to decide on what is right than a young lady like yourself." And with a low bow he left her to attack Mr. Darcy, whose reception of his advances she eagerly watched, and whose astonishment at being so addressed was very evident. Her cousin prefaced his speech with a solemn bow, and though she could not hear a word of it, she felt as if hearing it all, and saw in the motion of his lips the words "apology," "Hunsford," and "Lady Catherine de Bourgh."—It vexed her to see him expose himself to such a man, Mr. Darcy was eyeing him with unrestrained wonder, and when at last Mr. Collins allowed him time to speak, replied with an air of distant civility. Mr. Collins, however, was not discouraged from speaking again, and Mr. Darcy's contempt seemed abundantly increasing with the length of his second speech, and at the end of it he only made him a slight bow, and moved another way. Mr. Collins then returned to Elizabeth.

"I have no reason, I assure you," said he, "to be dissatisfied with my reception. Mr. Darcy seemed much pleased with the attention. He answered me with the utmost civility, and even paid me the compliment of saying, that he was so well convinced of Lady Catherine's discernment as to be certain she could never bestow a favour unworthily. It was really a very handsome thought. Upon the whole, I am much pleased with him."

As Elizabeth had no longer any interest of her own to pursue, she turned her attention almost entirely on her sister and Mr. Bingley, and the train of agreeable reflections which her observations gave birth to, made her perhaps almost as happy as Jane. She saw her in idea settled in that very house in all the felicity which a marriage of true affection could bestow; and she felt capable under such circumstances, of endeavouring even to like Bingley's two sisters. Her mother's thoughts she plainly saw were bent the same way, and she determined not to venture near her, lest she might hear too much. When they sat down to supper, therefore, she considered it a most unlucky perverseness which placed them within one of each other; and deeply was she vexed to find that her mother was talking to that one person (Lady Lucas) freely, openly, and of nothing else but of her expectation that Jane would be soon married to Mr. Bingley.—It was an animating subject, and Mrs. Bennet seemed incapable of fatigue while enumerating the advantages of the match. His being such a charming young man, and so rich, and living but three miles from them, were the first points of self-gratulation; and then it was such a comfort to think how fond the two sisters were of Jane, and to be certain that they must desire the connection as much as she could do. It was, moreover, such a promising thing for her younger daughters, as Jane's marrying so greatly must throw them in the way of other rich men; and lastly, it was so pleasant at her time of life to be able to consign her single daughters to the care of their sister, that she might not be obliged to go into company more than she liked. It was necessary to make this circumstance a matter of pleasure, because on such occasions it is the etiquette; but no one was less likely than Mrs. Bennet to find comfort in staying at home at any period of her life. She concluded with many good wishes that Lady Lucas might soon be equally fortunate, though evidently and triumphantly believing there was no chance of it.

In vain did Elizabeth endeavour to check the rapidity of her mother's words, or persuade her to describe her felicity in a less audible whisper; for to her inexpressible vexation, she could perceive that the chief of it was overheard by Mr. Darcy, who sat opposite to them. Her mother only scolded her for being nonsensical.

"What is Mr. Darcy to me, pray, that I should be afraid of him? I am sure we owe him no such particular civility as to be obliged to say nothing *he* may not like to hear."

"For heaven's sake, madam, speak lower.—What advantage can it be to you to offend Mr. Darcy?—You will never recommend yourself to his friend by so doing."

Nothing that she could say, however, had any influence. Her mother would talk of her views in the same intelligible tone. Elizabeth blushed and blushed again with shame and vexation. She could not help frequently glancing her eye at Mr. Darcy, though every glance convinced her of what she dreaded; for though he was not always looking at her mother, she was convinced that his attention was invariably fixed by her. The expression of his face changed gradually from indignant contempt to a composed and steady gravity.

At length however Mrs. Bennet had no more to say; and Lady Lucas, who had been long yawning at the repetition of delights which she saw no likelihood of sharing, was left to the comforts of cold ham and chicken. Elizabeth now began to revive. But not long was the interval of tranquility; for when supper was over, singing was talked of, and she had the mortification of seeing Mary, after very little entreaty, preparing to oblige the company. By many significant looks and silent entreaties, did she endeavour to prevent such a proof of complaisance,—but in vain; Mary would not understand them; such an opportunity of exhibiting was delightful to her, and she began her song. Elizabeth's eyes were fixed on her with most painful sensations; and she watched her progress through the several stanzas with an impatience which was very ill rewarded at their close; for Mary, on receiving amongst the thanks of the table, the hint of a hope that she might be prevailed on to favour them again, after the pause of half a minute began another. Mary's powers were by no means fitted for such a display; her voice was weak, and her manner affected.—Elizabeth was in agonies. She looked at Jane, to see how she bore it; but Jane was very composedly talking to Bingley. She looked at his two sisters, and saw them making signs of derision at each other, and at Darcy, who continued however impenetrably grave. She looked at her father to entreat his interference, lest Mary should be singing all night. He took the hint, and when Mary had finished her second song, said aloud,

"That will do extremely well, child. You have delighted us long enough. Let the other young ladies have time to exhibit."

Mary, though pretending not to hear, was somewhat disconcerted; and Elizabeth sorry for her, and sorry for her father's speech, was afraid her anxiety had done no good.—Others of the party were now applied to.

"If I," said Mr. Collins, "were so fortunate as to be able to sing, I should have great pleasure, I am sure, in obliging the company with an air; for I consider music as a very innocent diversion, and perfectly compatible with the profession of a clergyman.—I do not mean however to assert that we can be justified in devoting too much of our time to music, for there are certainly other things to be attended to. The rector of a parish has much to do.—In the first place, he must make such an agreement for tythes as may be beneficial to himself and not offensive to his patron. He must write his own sermons; and the time that remains will not be too much for his parish duties, and the care and improvement of his dwelling, which he cannot be excused from making as comfortable as possible. And I do not think it of light importance that he should have attentive and conciliatory manners towards every body, especially towards those to whom he owes his preferment. I cannot acquit him of that duty; nor could I think well of the man who should omit an occasion of testifying his respect towards any body connected with the family." And with a bow to Mr. Darcy, he concluded his speech, which had been spoken so loud as to be heard by half the room.—Many stared.—Many smiled; but no one looked more amused than Mr. Bennet himself, while his wife seriously commended Mr. Collins for having spoken so sensibly, and observed in a half-whisper to Lady Lucas, that he was a remarkably clever, good kind of young man.

To Elizabeth it appeared, that had her family made an agreement to expose themselves as much as they could during the evening, it would have been impossible for them to play their parts with more spirit, or finer success; and happy did she think it for Bingley and her sister that some of the exhibition had escaped his notice, and that his feelings were not of a sort to be much distressed by the folly which he must have witnessed. That his two sisters and Mr. Darcy, however, should have such an opportunity of ridiculing her relations was bad enough, and she could not determine whether the silent contempt of the gentleman, or the insolent smiles of the ladies, were more intolerable.

The rest of the evening brought her little amusement. She was teazed by Mr. Collins, who continued most perserveringly by her side, and though he could not prevail with her to dance with him again, put it out of her power to dance with others. In vain did she entreat him to stand up with somebody else, and offer to introduce him to any young lady in the room. He assured her that as to dancing, he was perfectly indifferent to it; that his chief object was by delicate attentions to recommend himself to her, and that he should therefore make a point of remaining close to her the whole evening. There was no arguing upon such a project. She owed her greatest relief to her friend Miss Lucas, who often joined them, and good-naturedly engaged Mr. Collins's conversation to herself.

She was at least free from the offence of Mr. Darcy's farther notice; though often standing within a very short distance of her, quite disengaged, he never came near enough to speak. She felt it to be the probable consequence of her allusions to Mr. Wickham, and rejoiced in it.

The Longbourn party were the last of all the company to depart; and by a manœuvre of Mrs. Bennet had to wait for their carriages a quarter of an hour after every body else was gone, which gave them time to see how heartily they were wished away by some of the family. Mrs. Hurst and her sister scarcely opened their mouths except to complain of fatigue, and were evidently impatient to have the house to themselves. They repulsed every attempt of Mrs. Bennet at conversation, and by so doing, threw a languor over the whole party, which was very little relieved by the long speeches of Mr. Collins, who was complimenting Mr. Bingley and his sisters on the elegance of their entertainment, and the hospitality and politeness which had marked their behaviour to their guests. Darcy said nothing at all. Mr. Bennet, in equal silence, was enjoying the scene. Mr. Bingley and Jane were standing together, a little detached from the rest, and talked only to each other. Elizabeth preserved as steady a silence as either Mrs. Hurst or

Miss Bingley; and even Lydia was too much fatigued to utter more than the occasional exclamation of "Lord, how tired I am!" accompanied by a violent yawn.

When at length they arose to take leave, Mrs. Bennet was most pressingly civil in her hope of seeing the whole family soon at Longbourn; and addressed herself particularly to Mr. Bingley, to assure him how happy he would make them, by eating a family dinner with them at any time, without the ceremony of a formal invitation. Bingley was all grateful pleasure, and he readily engaged for taking the earliest opportunity of waiting on her, after his return from London, whither he was obliged to go the next day for a short time.

Mrs. Bennet was perfectly satisfied; and quitted the house under the delightful persuasion that, allowing for the necessary preparations of settlements, new carriages and wedding clothes, she should undoubtedly see her daughter settled at Netherfield, in the course of three or four months. Of having another daughter married to Mr. Collins, she thought with equal certainty, and with considerable, though not equal, pleasure. Elizabeth was the least dear to her of all her children; and though the man and the match were quite good enough for *her*, the worth of each was eclipsed by Mr. Bingley and Netherfield.

Chapter XIX

The next day opened a new scene at Longbourn, Mr. Collins made his declaration in form. Having resolved to do it without loss of time, as his leave of absence extended only to the following Saturday, and having no feelings of diffidence to make it distressing to himself even at the moment, he set about it in a very orderly manner, with all the observances which he supposed a regular part of the business. On finding Mrs. Bennet, Elizabeth, and one of the younger girls together, soon after breakfast, he addressed the mother in these words,

"May I hope, Madam, for your interest with your fair daughter Elizabeth, when I solicit for the honour of a private audience with her in the course of this morning?"

Before Elizabeth had time for any thing but a blush of surprise, Mrs. Bennet instantly answered,

"Oh dear!—Yes—certainly.—I am sure Lizzy will be very happy—I am sure she can have no objection.—Come, Kitty, I want you up stairs." And gathering her work together, she was hastening away, when Elizabeth called out,

"Dear Ma'am, do not go.—I beg you will not go.—Mr. Collins must excuse me.—He can have nothing to say to me that any body need not hear. I am going away myself."

"No, no, nonsense, Lizzy.—I desire you will stay where you are."— And upon Elizabeth's seeming really, with vexed and embarrassed looks, about to escape, she added, "Lizzy, I *insist* upon your staying and hearing Mr. Collins."

Elizabeth would not oppose such an injunction—and a moment's consideration making her also sensible that it would be wisest to get it over as soon and as quietly as possible, she sat down again, and tried to conceal by incessant employment the feelings which were divided between distress and diversion. Mrs. Bennet and Kitty walked off, and as soon as they were gone Mr. Collins began.

"Believe me, my dear Miss Elizabeth, that your modesty, so far from doing you any disservice, rather adds to your other perfections. You would have been less amiable in my eyes had there *not* been this little unwillingness; but allow me to assure you that I have your respected mother's permission for this address. You can hardly doubt the purport of my discourse, however your natural delicacy may lead you to dissemble; my attentions have been too marked to be mistaken. Almost as soon as I entered the house I singled you out as the companion of my future life. But before I am run away with by my feelings on this subject, perhaps it will be advisable for me to state my reasons for marrying—and moreover for coming into Hertfordshire with the design of selecting a wife, as I certainly did."

The idea of Mr. Collins, with all his solemn composure, being run away with by his feelings, made Elizabeth so near laughing that she could not use the short pause he allowed in any attempt to stop him farther, and he continued:

"My reasons for marrying are, first, that I think it a right thing for every clergyman in easy circumstances (like myself) to set the example of matrimony in his parish. Secondly, that I am convinced it will add very greatly in my happiness; and thirdly—which perhaps I ought to have mentioned earlier, that it is the particular advice and recommendation of the very noble lady whom I have the honour of calling patroness. Twice has she condescended to give me her opinion (unasked too!) on this subject; and it was but the very Saturday night before I left Hunsford—between our pools at quadrille, while Mrs. Jenkinson was arranging Miss de Bourgh's foot-stool, that she said, 'Mr. Collins, you must marry. A clergyman like you must marry.—Chuse properly, chuse a gentlewoman for *my* sake; and for your *own*, let her be an active, useful sort of person, not brought up high, but able to make a small income go a good way. This is my advice. Find such a woman as soon as you can, bring her to Hunsford, and I will visit her.' Allow me, by the way, to observe, my fair cousin, that I do not reckon the notice and kindness of Lady Catherine de Bourgh as among the least of the advantages in my power to offer. You will find her manners beyond any thing I can describe; and your wit and vivacity I think must be acceptable to her, especially when tempered with the silence and respect which her rank will inevitably excite. Thus much for my general intention in favour of matrimony; it remains to be told why my views were directed to Longbourn instead of my own neighborhood, where I assure you there are many amiable young women. But the fact is, that being, as I am, to inherit this estate after the death of your honoured father, (who, however, may live many years longer,) I could not satisfy myself without resolving to chuse a wife from among his daughters, that the loss to them might be as little as possible, when the melancholy event takes place—which, however, as I have already said, may not be for several years. This has been my motive, my fair cousin, and I flatter myself it will not sink me in your esteem. And now nothing remains for me but to assure you in the most animated language of the violence of my affection. To fortune I am perfectly indifferent, and shall make no demand of that nature on your father, since I am well aware that it could not be complied with; and that one thousand pounds in the 4 per cents.[7] which will not be yours till after your mother's decease, is all that you may ever be entitled to. On that head, therefore, I shall be uniformly silent; and you may assure yourself that no ungenerous reproach shall ever pass my lips when we are married."

It was absolutely necessary to interrupt him now.

"You are too hasty, Sir," she cried. "You forget that I have made no answer. Let me do it without farther loss of time. Accept my thanks for the compliment you are paying me. I am very sensible of the honour of your proposals, but it is impossible for me to do otherwise than decline them."

"I am not now to learn," replied Mr. Collins, with a formal wave of the hand, "that it is usual with young ladies to reject the addresses of the man whom they secretly mean to accept, when he first applies for their favour; and that sometimes the refusal is repeated a second or even a third time. I am therefore by no means discouraged by what you have just said, and shall hope to lead you to the altar ere long."

"Upon my word, Sir," cried Elizabeth, "your hope is rather an extraordinary one after my declaration. I do assure you that I am not one of those young ladies (if such young ladies there are) who are so daring as to risk their happiness on the chance of being asked a second time. I am perfectly serious in my refusal.—You could not make *me* happy, and I am convinced that I am the last woman in the world who would make *you* so.—Nay, were your friend Lady Catherine to know me, I am persuaded she would find me in every respect ill qualified for the situation."

"Were it certain that Lady Catherine would think so," said Mr. Collins very gravely—"but I cannot imagine that her ladyship would at all

---

7. The "four percents" were government bonds—conservative, safe investments. Elizabeth's inheritance from her mother will provide an annual income of £40, compared to her father's present annual income of £2,000 and, presumably, Mr. Collins's comfortable annual income of several hundred pounds. See "Note on Money," pp. 403–5.

disapprove of you. And you may be certain that when I have the honour of seeing her again I shall speak in the highest terms of your modesty, economy, and other amiable qualifications."

"Indeed, Mr. Collins, all praise of me will be unnecessary. You must give me leave to judge for myself, and pay me the compliment of believing what I say. I wish you very happy and very rich, and by refusing your hand, do all in my power to prevent your being otherwise. In making me the offer, you must have satisfied the delicacy of your feelings with regard to my family, and may take possession of Longbourn estate whenever it falls, without any self-reproach. This matter may be considered, therefore, as finally settled." And rising as she thus spoke, she would have quitted the room, had not Mr. Collins thus addressed her,

"When I do myself the honour of speaking to you next on this subject I shall hope to receive a more favourable answer than you have now given me; though I am far from accusing you of cruelty at present, because I know it to be the established custom of your sex to reject a man on the first application, and perhaps you have even now said as much to encourage my suit as would be consistent with the true delicacy of the female character."

"Really, Mr. Collins," cried Elizabeth with some warmth, "you puzzle me exceedingly. If what I have hitherto said can appear to you in the form of encouragement, I know not how to express my refusal in such a way as may convince you of its being one."

"You must give me leave to flatter myself, my dear cousin, that your refusal of my addresses are merely words of course. My reasons for believing it are briefly these:—It does not appear to me that my hand is unworthy your acceptance, or that the establishment I can offer would be any other than highly desirable. My situation in life, my connections with the family of De Bourgh, and my relationship to your own, are circumstances highly in my favour; and you should take it into farther consideration that in spite of your manifold attractions, it is by no means certain that another offer of marriage may ever be made you. Your portion is unhappily so small that it will in all likelihood undo the effects of your loveliness and amiable qualifications. As I must therefore conclude that you are not serious in your rejection of me, I shall chuse to attribute it to your wish of increasing my love by suspense, according to the usual practice of elegant females."

"I do assure you, Sir, that I have no pretension whatever to that kind of elegance which consists in tormenting a respectable man. I would rather be paid the compliment of being believed sincere. I thank you again and again for the honour you have done me in your proposals, but to accept them is absolutely impossible. My feelings in every respect forbid it. Can I speak plainer? Do not consider me now as an elegant female intending to plague you, but as a rational creature speaking the truth from her heart."

"You are uniformly charming!" cried he, with an air of awkward gallantry; "and I am persuaded that when sanctioned by the express authority of both your excellent parents, my proposals will not fail of being acceptable."

To such perseverance in wilful self-deception Elizabeth would make no reply, and immediately and in silence withdrew; determined, that if he persisted in considering her repeated refusals as flattering encouragement, to apply to her father, whose negative might be uttered in such a manner as must be decisive, and whose behaviour at least could not be mistaken for the affectation and coquetry of an elegant female.

Chapter XX

Mr. Collins was not left long to the silent contemplation of his successful love; for Mrs. Bennet, having dawdled about in the vestibule to watch for the end of the conference, no sooner saw Elizabeth open the door and with quick step pass her towards the staircase, than she entered the breakfast-room, and congratulated both him and herself in warm terms on the happy prospect of their nearer connection. Mr. Collins received and returned these felicitations with equal pleasure, and then proceeded to relate the particulars of their interview, with the result of which he trusted he had every reason to be satisfied, since the refusal which his cousin had steadfastly given him would naturally flow from her bashful modesty and the genuine delicacy of her character.

This information, however, startled Mrs. Bennet;—she would have been glad to be equally satisfied that her daughter had meant to encourage him by protesting against his proposals, but she dared not to believe it, and could not help saying so.

"But depend upon it, Mr. Collins," she added, "that Lizzy shall be brought to reason. I will speak to her about it myself directly. She is a very headstrong foolish girl, and does not know her own interest; but I will *make* her know it."

"Pardon me for interrupting you, Madam," cried Mr. Collins; "but if she is really headstrong and foolish, I know not whether she would altogether be a very desirable wife to a man in my situation, who naturally looks for happiness in the marriage state. If therefore she actually persists in rejecting my suit, perhaps it were better not to force her into accepting me, because if liable to such defects of temper, she could not contribute much to my felicity."

"Sir, you quite misunderstand me," said Mrs. Bennet, alarmed. "Lizzy is only headstrong in such matters as these. In every thing else she is as good natured a girl as ever lived. I will go directly to Mr. Bennet, and we shall very soon settle it with her, I am sure."

She would not give him time to reply, but hurrying instantly to her husband, called out as she entered the library,

"Oh! Mr. Bennet, you are wanted immediately; we are all in an uproar. You must come and make Lizzy marry Mr. Collins, for she vows she will not have him, and if you do not make haste he will change his mind and not have *her*."

Mr. Bennet raised his eyes from his book as she entered, and fixed them on her face with a calm unconcern which was not in the least altered by her communication.

"I have not the pleasure of understanding you," said he, when she had finished her speech. "Of what are you talking?"

"Of Mr. Collins and Lizzy. Lizzy declares she will not have Mr. Collins, and Mr. Collins begins to say that he will not have Lizzy."

"And what am I to do on the occasion?—It seems an hopeless business."

"Speak to Lizzy about it yourself. Tell her that you insist upon her marrying him."

"Let her be called down. She shall hear my opinion."

Mrs. Bennet rang the bell, and Miss Elizabeth was summoned to the library.

"Come here, child," cried her father as she appeared. "I have sent for you on an affair of importance. I understand that Mr. Collins has made you an offer of marriage. Is it true?" Elizabeth replied that it was. "Very well—and this offer of marriage you have refused?"

"I have, Sir."

"Very well. We now come to the point. Your mother insists upon your accepting it. Is not it so, Mrs. Bennet?"

"Yes, or I will never see her again."

"An unhappy alternative is before you, Elizabeth. From this day you must be a stranger to one of your parents.—Your mother will never see you again if you do *not* marry Mr. Collins, and I will never see you again if you *do*."

Elizabeth could not but smile at such a conclusion of such a beginning; but Mrs. Bennet, who had persuaded herself that her husband regarded the affair as she wished, was excessively disappointed.

"What do you mean, Mr. Bennet, by talking in this way? You promised me to *insist* upon her marrying him."

"My dear," replied her husband, "I have two small favours to request. First, that you will allow me the free use of my understanding on the present occasion; and, secondly, of my room. I shall be glad to have the library to myself as soon as may be."

Not yet, however, in spite of her disappointment in her husband, did Mrs. Bennet give up the point. She talked to Elizabeth again and

again; coaxed and threatened her by turns. She endeavoured to secure
Jane in her interest, but Jane with all possible mildness declined inter-
fering;—and Elizabeth sometimes with real earnestness and sometimes
with playful gaiety replied to her attacks. Though her manner varied
however, her determination never did.

Mr. Collins, meanwhile, was meditating in solitude on what had
passed. He thought too well of himself to comprehend on what motive
his cousin could refuse him; and though his pride was hurt, he suffered
in no other way. His regard for her was quite imaginary; and the possibility of her deserving her mother's reproach prevented his feeling
any regret.

While the family were in this confusion, Charlotte Lucas came to
spend the day with them. She was met in the vestibule by Lydia, who,
flying to her, cried in a half whisper, "I am glad you are come, for there
is such fun here!—What do you think has happened this morning?—
Mr. Collins has made an offer to Lizzy, and she will not have him."

Charlotte had hardly time to answer, before they were joined by
Kitty, who came to tell the same news, and no sooner had they entered
the breakfast-room, where Mrs. Bennet was alone, than she likewise
began on the subject, calling on Miss Lucas for her compassion, and
entreating her to persuade her friend Lizzy to comply with the wishes
of all her family. "Pray do, my dear Miss Lucas," she added in a melancholy tone, "for nobody is on my side, nobody takes part with me, I
am cruelly used, nobody feels for my poor nerves."

Charlotte's reply was spared by the entrance of Jane and Elizabeth.

"Aye, there she comes," continued Mrs. Bennet, "looking as unconcerned as may be, and caring no more for us than if we were at York,
provided she can have her own way.—But I tell you what, Miss Lizzy,
if you take it into your head to go on refusing every offer of marriage
in this way, you will never get a husband at all—and I am sure I do
not know who is to maintain you when your father is dead—I shall not
be able to keep you—and so I warn you.—I have done with you from
this very day.—I told you in the library, you know, that I should never
speak to you again, and you will find me as good as my word. I have
no pleasure in talking to undutiful children.—Not that I have much
pleasure indeed in talking to any body. People who suffer as I do from
nervous complaints can have no great inclination for talking. Nobody
can tell what I suffer!—But it is always so. Those who do not complain
are never pitied."

Her daughters listened in silence to this effusion, sensible that any
attempt to reason with or sooth her would only increase the irritation.
She talked on, therefore, without interruption from any of them till
they were joined by Mr. Collins, who entered with an air more stately
than usual, and on perceiving whom, she said to the girls,

"Now, I do insist upon it, that you, all of you, hold your tongues, and let Mr. Collins and me have a little conversation together."

Elizabeth passed quietly out of the room, Jane and Kitty followed, but Lydia stood her ground, determined to hear all she could; and Charlotte, detained first by the civility of Mr. Collins, whose inquiries after herself and all her family were very minute, and then by a little curiosity, satisfied herself with walking to the window and pretending not to hear. In a doleful voice Mrs. Bennet thus began the projected conversation.—"Oh! Mr. Collins!"—

"My dear Madam," replied he, "let us be for ever silent on this point. Far be it from me," he presently continued in a voice that marked his displeasure, "to resent the behaviour of your daughter. Resignation to inevitable evils is the duty of us all; the peculiar duty of a young man who has been so fortunate as I have been in early preferment; and I trust I am resigned. Perhaps not the less so from feeling a doubt of my positive happiness had my fair cousin honoured me with her hand; for I have often observed that resignation is never so perfect as when the blessing denied begins to lose somewhat of its value in our estimation. You will not, I hope, consider me as shewing any disrespect to your family, my dear Madam, by thus withdrawing my pretensions to your daughter's favour, without having paid yourself and Mr. Bennet the compliment of requesting you to interpose your authority in my behalf. My conduct may I fear be objectionable in having accepted my dismission from your daughter's lips instead of your own. But we are all liable to error. I have certainly meant well through the whole affair. My object has been to secure an amiable companion for myself, with due consideration for the advantage of all your family, and if my *manner* has been at all reprehensible, I here beg leave to apologise."

Chapter XXI

The discussion of Mr. Collins's offer was now nearly at an end, and Elizabeth had only to suffer from the uncomfortable feelings necessarily attending it, and occasionally from some peevish allusion of her mother. As for the gentleman himself, *his* feelings were chiefly expressed, not by embarrassment or dejection, or by trying to avoid her, but by stiffness of manner and resentful silence. He scarcely ever spoke to her, and the assiduous attentions which he had been so sensible of himself, were transferred for the rest of the day to Miss Lucas, whose civility in listening to him, was a seasonable relief to them all, and especially to her friend.

The morrow produced no abatement of Mrs. Bennet's ill humour or ill health. Mr. Collins was also in the same state of angry pride. Elizabeth had hoped that his resentment might shorten his visit, but his plan did not appear in the least affected by it. He was always to have gone on Saturday, and to Saturday he still meant to stay.

After breakfast, the girls walked to Meryton to inquire if Mr. Wickham were returned, and to lament over his absence from the Netherfield ball. He joined them on their entering the town and attended them to their aunt's, where his regret and vexation, and the concern of every body was well talked over.—To Elizabeth, however, he voluntarily acknowledged that the necessity of his absence *had* been self imposed.

"I found," said he, "as the time drew near that I had better not meet Mr. Darcy;—that to be in the same room, the same party with him for so many hours together, might be more than I could bear, and that scenes might arise unpleasant to more than myself."

She highly approved his forbearance, and they had leisure for a full discussion of it, and for all the commendation which they civilly bestowed on each other, as Wickham and another officer walked back with them to Longbourn, and during the walk, he particularly attended to her. His accompanying them was a double advantage; she felt all the compliment it offered to herself, and it was most acceptable as an occasion of introducing him to her father and mother.

Soon after their return, a letter was delivered to Miss Bennet; it came from Netherfield, and was opened immediately. The envelope contained a sheet of elegant, little, hot pressed paper,[8] well covered with a lady's fair, flowing hand; and Elizabeth saw her sister's countenance change as she read it, and saw her dwelling intently on some particular passages. Jane recollected herself soon, and putting the letter away, tried to join with her usual cheerfulness in the general conversation; but Elizabeth felt an anxiety on the subject which drew off her attention even from Wickham; and no sooner had he and his companion taken leave, than a glance from Jane invited her to follow her up stairs. When they gained their own room, Jane taking out the letter, said,

"This is from Caroline Bingley; what it contains, has surprised me a good deal. The whole party have left Netherfield by this time, and are on their way to town; and without any intention of coming back again. You shall hear what she says."

She then read the first sentence aloud, which comprised the information of their having just resolved to follow their brother to town directly, and of their meaning to dine that day in Grosvenor street, where Mr. Hurst had a house. The next was in these words. "I do not pretend to regret any thing I shall leave in Hertfordshire, except your society, my dearest friend; but we will hope at some future period, to enjoy many returns of the delightful intercourse we have known, and in the mean while may lessen the pain of separation by a very frequent and most unreserved correspondence. I depend on you for that." To these high flown expressions, Elizabeth listened with all the insensi-

8. Paper with a smooth, glossy surface.

bility of distrust; and though the suddenness of their removal surprised her, she saw nothing in it really to lament; it was not to be supposed that their absence from Netherfield would prevent Mr. Bingley's being there; and as to the loss of their society, she was persuaded that Jane must soon cease to regard it, in the enjoyment of his.

"It is unlucky," said she, after a short pause, "that you should not be able to see your friends before they leave the country. But may we not hope that the period of future happiness to which Miss Bingley looks forward, may arrive earlier than she is aware, and that the delightful intercourse you have known as friends, will be renewed with yet greater satisfaction as sisters?—Mr. Bingley will not be detained in London by them."

"Caroline decidedly says that none of the party will return into Hertfordshire this winter. I will read it to you—

"When my brother left us yesterday, he imagined that the business which took him to London, might be concluded in three or four days, but as we are certain it cannot be so, and at the same time convinced that when Charles gets to town, he will be in no hurry to leave it again, we have determined on following him thither, that he may not be obliged to spend his vacant hours in a comfortless hotel. Many of my acquaintance are already there for the winter; I wish I could hear that you, my dearest friend, had any intention of making one in the croud, but of that I despair. I sincerely hope your Christmas in Hertfordshire may abound in the gaieties which that season generally brings, and that your beaux will be so numerous as to prevent your feeling the loss of the three, of whom we shall deprive you."

"It is evident by this," added Jane, "that he comes back no more this winter."

"It is evident that Miss Bingley does not mean he *should*."

"Why will you think so? It must be his own doing.—He is his own master. But you do not know *all*. I *will* read you the passage which particularly hurts me. I will have no reserves from *you*." "Mr. Darcy is impatient to see his sister, and to confess the truth, *we* are scarcely less eager to meet her again. I really do not think Georgiana Darcy has her equal for beauty, elegance, and accomplishments; and the affection she inspires in Louisa and myself, is heightened into something still more interesting, from the hope we dare to entertain of her being hereafter our sister. I do not know whether I ever before mentioned to you my feelings on this subject, but I will not leave the country without confiding them, and I trust you will not esteem them unreasonable. My brother admires her greatly already, he will have frequent opportunity now of seeing her on the most intimate footing, her relations all wish the connection as much as his own, and a sister's partiality is not misleading me, I think, when I call Charles most capable of engaging any woman's heart. With all these circumstances to favour an attachment and nothing to prevent it, am I wrong, my dearest Jane, in indulging the hope of an event which will secure the happiness of so many?"

"What think you of *this* sentence, my dear Lizzy?"—said Jane as she finished it. "It is not clear enough?—Does it not expressly declare that Caroline neither expects nor wishes me to be her sister; that she is perfectly convinced of her brother's indifference, and that if she suspects the nature of my feelings for him, she means (most kindly!) to put me on my guard? Can there be any other opinion on the subject?"

"Yes, there can; for mine is totally different.—Will you hear it?"

"Most willingly."

"You shall have it in few words. Miss Bingley sees that her brother is in love with you, and wants him to marry Miss Darcy. She follows him to town in the hope of keeping him there, and tries to persuade you that he does not care about you."

Jane shook her head.

"Indeed, Jane, you ought to believe me.—No one who has ever seen you together, can doubt his affection. Miss Bingley I am sure cannot. She is not such a simpleton. Could she have seen half as much love in Mr. Darcy for herself, she would have ordered her wedding clothes. But the case is this. We are not rich enough, or grand enough for them; and she is the more anxious to get Miss Darcy for her brother, from the notion that when there has been *one* intermarriage, she may have less trouble in achieving a second; in which there is certainly some ingenuity, and I dare say it would succeed, if Miss De Bourgh were out of the way. But, my dearest Jane, you cannot seriously imagine that because Miss Bingley tells you her brother greatly admires Miss Darcy, he is in the smallest degree less sensible of *your* merit than when he took leave of you on Tuesday, or that it will be in her power to persuade him that instead of being in love with you, he is very much in love with her friend."

"If we thought alike of Miss Bingley," replied Jane, "your representation of all this, might make me quite easy. But I know the foundation is unjust. Caroline is incapable of wilfully deceiving any one; and all that I can hope in this case is, that she is deceived herself."

"That is right.—You could not have started a more happy idea, since you will not take comfort in mine. Believe her to be deceived by all means. You have now done your duty by her, and must fret no longer."

"But, my dear sister, can I be happy, even supposing the best, in accepting a man whose sisters and friends are all wishing him to marry elsewhere?"

"You must decide for yourself," said Elizabeth, "and if upon mature deliberation, you find that the misery of disobliging his two sisters is more than equivalent to the happiness of being his wife, I advise you by all means to refuse him."

"How can you talk so?"—said Jane faintly smiling,—"you must know that though I should be exceedingly grieved at their disapprobation, I could not hesitate."

"I did not think you would;—and that being the case, I cannot consider your situation with much compassion."

"But if he returns no more this winter, my choice will never be required. A thousand things may arise in six months!"

The idea of his returning no more Elizabeth treated with the utmost contempt. It appeared to her merely the suggestion of Caroline's interested wishes, and she could not for a moment suppose that those wishes, however openly or artfully spoken, could influence a young man so totally independent of every one.

She represented to her sister as forcibly as possible what she felt on the subject, and had soon the pleasure of seeing its happy effect. Jane's temper was not desponding, and she was gradually led to hope, though the diffidence of affection sometimes overcame the hope, that Bingley would return to Netherfield and answer every wish of her heart.

They agreed that Mrs. Bennet should only hear of the departure of the family, without being alarmed on the score of the gentleman's conduct; but even this partial communication gave her a great deal of concern, and she bewailed it as exceedingly unlucky that the ladies should happen to go away, just as they were all getting so intimate together. After lamenting it however at some length, she had the consolation of thinking that Mr. Bingley would be soon down again and soon dining at Longbourn, and the conclusion of all was the comfortable declaration that, though he had been invited only to a family dinner, she would take care to have two full courses.

Chapter XXII

The Bennets were engaged to dine with the Lucases, and again during the chief of the day, was Miss Lucas so kind as to listen to Mr. Collins. Elizabeth took an opportunity of thanking her. "It keeps him in good humour," said she, "and I am more obliged to you than I can express." Charlotte assured her friend of her satisfaction in being useful, and that it amply repaid her for the little sacrifice of her time. This was very amiable, but Charlotte's kindness extended farther than Elizabeth had any conception of;—its object was nothing less, than to secure her from any return of Mr. Collins's addresses, by engaging them towards herself. Such was Miss Lucas's scheme; and appearances were so favourable that when they parted at night, she would have felt almost sure of success if he had not been to leave Hertfordshire so very soon. But here, she did injustice to the fire and independence of his character, for it led him to escape out of Longbourn House the next morning with admirable slyness, and hasten to Lucas Lodge to throw himself at her feet. He was anxious to avoid the notice of his cousins, from a conviction that if they saw him depart, they could not fail to conjecture his design, and he was not willing to have the attempt known till its success could be known likewise; for though feeling almost secure, and with reason, for Charlotte had been tolerably encouraging, he was comparatively diffident since the adventure of Wednesday. His reception however was of the most flattering kind. Miss Lucas perceived him from an upper window as he walked towards the house, and instantly set out to meet him accidentally in the lane. But little had she dared to hope that so much love and eloquence awaited her there.

In as short a time as Mr. Collins's long speeches would allow, every thing was settled between them to the satisfaction of both; and as they entered the house, he earnestly entreated her to name the day that was to make him the happiest of men; and though such a solicitation must be waved for the present, the lady felt no inclination to trifle with his happiness. The stupidity with which he was favoured by nature, must guard his courtship from any charm that could make a woman wish for its continuance; and Miss Lucas, who accepted him solely from the pure and disinterested desire of an establishment, cared not how soon that establishment were gained.

Sir William and Lady Lucas were speedily applied to for their consent; and it was bestowed with a most joyful alacrity. Mr. Collins's present circumstances made it a most eligible match for their daughter, to whom they could give little fortune; and his prospects of future wealth were exceedingly fair. Lady Lucas began directly to calculate with more interest than the matter had ever excited before, how many years longer Mr. Bennet was likely to live; and Sir William gave it as his decided opinion, that whenever Mr. Collins should be in possession of the Longbourn estate, it would be highly expedient that both he and his wife should make their appearance at St. James's. The whole family in short were properly overjoyed on the occasion. The younger girls formed hopes of *coming out*[9] a year or two sooner than they might otherwise have done; and the boys were relieved from their apprehension of Charlotte's dying an old maid. Charlotte herself was tolerably composed. She had gained her point, and had time to consider of it. Her reflections were in general satisfactory. Mr. Collins to be sure was neither sensible nor agreeable; his society was irksome, and his attachment to her must be imaginary. But still he would be her husband.— Without thinking highly either of men or of matrimony, marriage had always been her object; it was the only honourable provision for well-educated young women of small fortune, and however uncertain of giving happiness, must be their pleasantest preservative from want.

9. Formally entering adult society.

This preservative she had now obtained; and at the age of twenty-seven, without having ever been handsome, she felt all the good luck of it. The least agreeable circumstance in the business, was the surprise it must occasion to Elizabeth Bennet, whose friendship she valued beyond that of any other person. Elizabeth would wonder, and probably would blame her; and though her resolution was not to be shaken, her feelings must be hurt by such disapprobation. She resolved to give her the information herself, and therefore charged Mr. Collins when he returned to Longbourn to dinner, to drop no hint of what had passed before any of the family. A promise of secrecy was of course very dutifully given, but it could not be kept without difficulty; for the curiosity excited by his long absence, burst forth in such very direct questions on his return, as required some ingenuity to evade, and he was at the same time exercising great self-denial, for he was longing to publish his prosperous love.

As he was to begin his journey too early on the morrow to see any of the family, the ceremony of leave-taking was performed when the ladies moved for the night; and Mrs. Bennet with great politeness and cordiality said how happy they should be to see him at Longbourn again, whenever his other engagements might allow him to visit them.

"My dear Madam," he replied, "this invitation is particularly gratifying, because it is what I have been hoping to receive; and you may be very certain that I shall avail myself of it as soon as possible."

They were all astonished; and Mr. Bennet, who could by no means wish for so speedy a return, immediately said,

"But is there not danger of Lady Catherine's disapprobation here, my good sir?—You had better neglect your relations, than run the risk of offending your patroness."

"My dear sir," replied Mr. Collins, "I am particularly obliged to you for this friendly caution, and you may depend upon my not taking so material a step without her ladyship's concurrence."

"You cannot be too much on your guard. Risk any thing rather than her displeasure; and if you find it likely to be raised by your coming to us again, which I should think exceedingly probable, stay quietly at home, and be satisfied that we shall take no offence."

"Believe me, my dear sir, my gratitude is warmly excited by such affectionate attention; and depend upon it, you will speedily receive from me a letter of thanks for this, as well as for every other mark of your regard during my stay in Hertfordshire. As for my fair cousins, though my absence may not be long enough to render it necessary, I shall now take the liberty of wishing them health and happiness, not excepting my cousin Elizabeth."

With proper civilities the ladies then withdrew; all of them equally surprised to find that he meditated a quick return. Mrs. Bennet wished to understand by it that he thought of paying his addresses to one of her younger girls, and Mary might have been prevailed on to accept him. She rated his abilities much higher than any of the others; there was a solidity in his reflections which often struck her, and though by no means so clever as herself, she thought that if encouraged to read and improve himself by such an example as her's, he might become a very agreeable companion. But on the following morning, every hope of this kind was done away. Miss Lucas called soon after breakfast, and in a private conference with Elizabeth related the event of the day before.

The possibility of Mr. Collins's fancying himself in love with her friend had once occurred to Elizabeth within the last day or two; but that Charlotte could encourage him, seemed almost as far from possibility as that she could encourage him herself, and her astonishment was consequently so great as to overcome at first the bounds of decorum, and she could not help crying out,

"Engaged to Mr. Collins! my dear Charlotte,—impossible!"

The steady countenance which Miss Lucas had commanded in telling her story, gave way to a momentary confusion here on receiving so direct a reproach; though, as it was no more than she expected, she soon regained her composure, and calmly replied,

"Why should you be surprised, my dear Eliza?—Do you think it incredible that Mr. Collins should be able to procure any woman's good opinion, because he was not so happy as to succeed with you?"

But Elizabeth had now recollected herself, and making a strong effort for it, was able to assure her with tolerable firmness that the prospect of their relationship was highly grateful to her, and that she wished her all imaginable happiness.

"I see what you are feeling," replied Charlotte,—"you must be surprised, very much surprised,—so lately as Mr. Collins was wishing to marry you. But when you have had time to think it all over, I hope you will be satisfied with what I have done. I am not romantic you know. I never was. I ask only a comfortable home; and considering Mr. Collins's character, connections, and situation in life, I am convinced that my chance of happiness with him is as fair, as most people can boast on entering the marriage state."

Elizabeth quietly answered "Undoubtedly;"—and after an awkward pause, they returned to the rest of the family. Charlotte did not stay much longer, and Elizabeth was then left to reflect on what she had heard. It was a long time before she became at all reconciled to the idea of so unsuitable a match. The strangeness of Mr. Collins's making two offers of marriage within three days, was nothing in comparison of his being now accepted. She had always felt that Charlotte's opinion of matrimony was not exactly like her own, but she could not have supposed it possible that when called into action, she would have sacrificed every better feeling to worldly advantage. Charlotte the wife of

Mr. Collins, was a most humiliating picture!—And to the pang of a friend disgracing herself and sunk in her esteem, was added the distressing conviction that it was impossible for that friend to be tolerably happy in the lot she had chosen.

Chapter XXIII

Elizabeth was sitting with her mother and sisters, reflecting on what she had heard, and doubting whether she were authorised to mention it, when Sir William Lucas himself appeared, sent by his daughter to announce her engagement to the family. With many compliments to them, and much self-gratulation on the prospect of a connection between the houses, he unfolded the matter,—to an audience not merely wondering, but incredulous; for Mrs. Bennet, with more perseverance than politeness, protested he must be entirely mistaken, and Lydia, always unguarded and often uncivil, boisterously exclaimed,

"Good Lord! Sir William, how can you tell such a story?—Do not you know that Mr. Collins wants to marry Lizzy?"

Nothing less than the complaisance of a courtier could have borne without anger such treatment, but Sir William's good breeding carried him through it all; and though he begged leave to be positive as to the truth of his information, he listened to all their impertinence with the most forbearing courtesy.

Elizabeth, feeling it incumbent on her to relieve him from so unpleasant a situation, now put herself forward to confirm his account, by mentioning her prior knowledge of it from Charlotte herself; and endeavoured to put a stop to the exclamations of her mother and sisters, by the earnestness of her congratulations to Sir William, in which she was readily joined by Jane, and by making a variety of remarks on the happiness that might be expected from the match, the excellent character of Mr. Collins, and the convenient distance of Hunsford from London.

Mrs. Bennet was in fact too much overpowered to say a great deal while Sir William remained; but no sooner had he left them than her feelings found a rapid vent. In the first place, she persisted in disbelieving the whole of the matter; secondly, she was very sure that Mr. Collins had been taken in; thirdly, she trusted that they would never be happy together; and fourthly, that the match might be broken off. Two inferences, however, were plainly deduced from the whole; one, that Elizabeth was the real cause of all the mischief; and the other, that she herself had been barbarously used by them all; and on these two points she principally dwelt during the rest of the day. Nothing could console and nothing appease her.—Nor did that day wear out her resentment. A week elapsed before she could see Elizabeth without scolding her, a month passed away before she could speak to Sir Wil-

liam or Lady Lucas without being rude, and many months were gone
before she could at all forgive their daughter.

Mr. Bennet's emotions were much more tranquil on the occasion,
and such as he did experience he pronounced to be of a most agreeable
sort; for it gratified him, he said, to discover that Charlotte Lucas,
whom he had been used to think tolerably sensible, was as foolish as
his wife, and more foolish than his daughter!

Jane confessed herself a little surprised at the match; but she said
less of her astonishment than of her earnest desire for their happiness;
nor could Elizabeth persuade her to consider it as improbable. Kitty
and Lydia were far from envying Miss Lucas, for Mr. Collins was only
a clergyman; and it affected them in no other way than as a piece of
news to spread at Meryton.

Lady Lucas could not be insensible of triumph on being able to
retort on Mrs. Bennet the comfort of having a daughter well married;
and she called at Longbourn rather oftener than usual to say how happy
she was, though Mrs. Bennet's sour looks and ill-natured remarks might
have been enough to drive happiness away.

Between Elizabeth and Charlotte there was a restraint which kept
them mutually silent on the subject; and Elizabeth felt persuaded that
no real confidence could ever subsist between them again. Her disappointment in Charlotte made her turn with fonder regard to her sister,
of whose rectitude and delicacy she was sure her opinion could never
be shaken, and for whose happiness she grew daily more anxious, as
Bingley had now been gone a week, and nothing was heard of his
return.

Jane had sent Caroline an early answer to her letter, and was count-
ing the days till she might reasonably hope to hear again. The promised
letter of thanks from Mr. Collins arrived on Tuesday, addressed to their
father, and written with all the solemnity of gratitude which a twelve-
month's abode in the family might have prompted. After discharging
his conscience on that head, he proceeded to inform them, with many
rapturous expressions, of his happiness in having obtained the affection
of their amiable neighbour, Miss Lucas, and then explained that it was
merely with the view of enjoying her society that he had been so ready
to close with their kind wish of seeing him again at Longbourn, whither
he hoped to be able to return on Monday fortnight; for Lady Catherine,
he added, so heartily approved his marriage, that she wished it to take
place as soon as possible, which he trusted would be an unanswerable
argument with his amiable Charlotte to name an early day for making
him the happiest of men.

Mr. Collins's return into Herfordshire was no longer a matter of
pleasure to Mrs. Bennet. On the contrary she was as much disposed to
complain of it as her husband.—It was very strange that he should
come to Longbourn instead of to Lucas Lodge; it was also very incon-

venient and exceedingly troublesome.—She hated having visitors in the house while her health was so indifferent, and lovers were of all people the most disagreeable. Such were the gentle murmurs of Mrs. Bennet, and they gave way only to the greater distress of Mr. Bingley's continued absence.

Neither Jane nor Elizabeth were comfortable on this subject. Day after day passed away without bringing any other tidings of him than the report which shortly prevailed in Meryton of his coming no more to Netherfield the whole winter; a report which highly incensed Mrs. Bennet, and which she never failed to contradict as a most scandalous falsehood.

Even Elizabeth began to fear—not that Bingley was indifferent—but that his sisters would be successful in keeping him away. Unwilling as she was to admit an idea so destructive of Jane's happiness, and so dishonourable to the stability of her lover, she could not prevent its frequently recurring. The united efforts of his two unfeeling sisters and of his overpowering friend, assisted by the attractions of Miss Darcy and the amusements of London, might be too much, she feared, for the strength of his attachment.

As for Jane, *her* anxiety under this suspence was, of course, more painful than Elizabeth's; but whatever she felt she was desirous of concealing, and between herself and Elizabeth, therefore, the subject was never alluded to. But as no such delicacy restrained her mother, an hour seldom passed in which she did not talk of Bingley, express her impatience for his arrival, or even require Jane to confess that if he did not come back, she should think herself very ill used. It needed all Jane's steady mildness to bear these attacks with tolerable tranquility.

Mr. Collins returned most punctually on the Monday fortnight, but his reception at Longbourn was not quite so gracious as it had been on his first introduction. He was too happy, however, to need much attention; and luckily for the others, the business of love-making relieved them from a great deal of his company. The chief of every day was spent by him at Lucas Lodge, and he sometimes returned to Longbourn only in time to make an apology for his absence before the family went to bed.

Mrs. Bennet was really in a most pitiable state. The very mention of any thing concerning the match threw her into an agony of ill humour, and wherever she went she was sure of hearing it talked of. The sight of Miss Lucas was odious to her. As her successor in that house, she regarded her with jealous abhorrence. Whenever Charlotte came to see them she concluded her to be anticipating the hour of possession; and whenever she spoke in a low voice to Mr. Collins, was convinced that they were talking of the Longbourn estate, and resolving to turn herself and her daughters out of the house, as soon as Mr. Bennet were dead. She complained bitterly of all this to her husband.

"Indeed, Mr. Bennet," said she, "it is very hard to think that Charlotte Lucas should ever be mistress of this house, that *I* should be forced to make way for *her*, and live to see her take my place in it!"

"My dear, do not give way to such gloomy thoughts. Let us hope for better things. Let us flatter ourselves that *I* may be the survivor."

This was not very consoling to Mrs. Bennet, and, therefore, instead of making any answer, she went on as before,

"I cannot bear to think that they should have all this estate. If it was not for the entail I should not mind it."

"What should not you mind?"

"I should not mind any thing at all."

"Let us be thankful that you are preserved from a state of such insensibility."

"I never can be thankful, Mr. Bennet, for any thing about the entail. How any one could have the conscience to entail away an estate from one's own daughters I cannot understand; and all for the sake of Mr. Collins too!—Why should *he* have it more than anybody else?"

"I leave it to yourself to determine," said Mr. Bennet.

Volume II

Chapter I

Miss Bingley's letter arrived, and put an end to doubt. The very first sentence conveyed the assurance of their being all settled in London for the winter, and concluded with her brother's regret at not having had time to pay his respects to his friends in Hertfordshire before he left the country.

Hope was over, entirely over; and when Jane could attend to the rest of the letter, she found little, except the professed affection of the writer, that could give her any comfort. Miss Darcy's praise occupied the chief of it. Her many attractions were again dwelt on, and Caroline boasted joyfully of their increasing intimacy, and ventured to predict the accomplishment of the wishes which had been unfolded in her former letter. She wrote also with great pleasure of her brother's being an inmate of Mr. Darcy's house, and mentioned with raptures, some plans of the latter with regard to new furniture.

Elizabeth, to whom Jane very soon communicated the chief of all this, heard it in silent indignation. Her heart was divided between concern for her sister, and resentment against all the others. To Caroline's assertion of her brother's being partial to Miss Darcy she paid no credit. That he was really fond of Jane, she doubted no more than she had ever done; and much as she had always been disposed to like him, she

could not think without anger, hardly without contempt, on that easiness of temper, that want of proper resolution which now made him
the slave of his designing friends, and led him to sacrifice his own
happiness to the caprice of their inclinations. Had his own happiness,
however, been the only sacrifice, he might have been allowed to sport
with it in what ever manner he thought best; but her sister's was
involved in it, as she thought he must be sensible himself. It was a
subject, in short, on which reflection would be long indulged, and must
be unavailing. She could think of nothing else, and yet whether Bingley's regard had really died away, or were suppressed by his friends'
interference; whether he had been aware of Jane's attachment, or
whether it had escaped his observation; whichever were the case,
though her opinion of him must be materially affected by the difference, her sister's situation remained the same, her peace equally
wounded.

A day or two passed before Jane had courage to speak of her feelings
to Elizabeth; but at last on Mrs. Bennet's leaving them together, after
a longer irritation than usual about Netherfield and its master, she
could not help saying,

"Oh! that my dear mother had more command over herself; she can
have no idea of the pain she gives me by her continual reflections on
him. But I will not repine. It cannot last long. He will be forgot, and
we shall all be as we were before."

Elizabeth looked at her sister with incredulous solicitude, but said
nothing.

"You doubt me," cried Jane, slightly colouring; "indeed you have no
reason. He may live in my memory as the most amiable man of my
acquaintance, but that is all. I have nothing either to hope or fear, and
nothing to reproach him with. Thank God! I have not *that* pain. A
little time therefore.—I shall certainly try to get the better."

With a stronger voice she soon added, "I have this comfort immediately, that it has not been more than an error of fancy on my side,
and that it has done no harm to any one but myself."

"My dear Jane!" exclaimed Elizabeth, "you are too good. Your sweetness and disinterestedness are really angelic; I do not know what to say
to you. I feel as if I had never done you justice, or loved you as you
deserve."

Miss Bennet eagerly disclaimed all extraordinary merit, and threw
back the praise on her sister's warm affection.

"Nay," said Elizabeth, "this is not fair. *You* wish to think all the world
respectable, and are hurt if I speak ill of any body. *I* only want to think
you perfect, and you set yourself against it. Do not be afraid of my
running into any excess, of my encroaching on your privilege of universal good will. You need not. There are few people whom I really
love, and still fewer of whom I think well. The more I see of the world,

the more am I dissatisfied with it; and every day confirms my belief of the inconsistency of all human characters, and of the little dependence that can be placed on the appearance of either merit or sense. I have met with two instances lately; one I will not mention; the other is Charlotte's marriage. It is unaccountable! in every view it is unaccountable!"

"My dear Lizzy, do not give way to such feelings as these. They will ruin your happiness. You do not make allowance enough for difference of situation and temper. Consider Mr. Collins's respectability, and Charlotte's prudent, steady character. Remember that she is one of a large family; that as to fortune, it is a most eligible match; and be ready to believe, for every body's sake, that she may feel something like regard and esteem for our cousin."

"To oblige you, I would try to believe almost any thing, but no one else could be benefited by such a belief as this; for were I persuaded that Charlotte had any regard for him, I should only think worse of her understanding, than I now do of her heart. My dear Jane, Mr. Collins is a conceited, pompous, narrow-minded, silly man; you know he is, as well as I do; and you must feel, as well as I do, that the woman who marries him, cannot have a proper way of thinking. You shall not defend her, though it is Charlotte Lucas. You shall not, for the sake of one individual, change the meaning of principle and integrity, nor endeavour to persuade yourself or me, that selfishness is prudence, and insensibility of danger, security for happiness."

"I must think your language too strong in speaking of both," replied Jane, "and I hope you will be convinced of it, by seeing them happy together. But enough of this. You alluded to something else. You mentioned *two* instances. I cannot misunderstand you, but I intreat you, dear Lizzy, not to pain me by thinking *that person* to blame, and saying your opinion of him is sunk. We must not be so ready to fancy ourselves intentionally injured. We must not expect a lively young man to be always so guarded and circumspect. It is very often nothing but our own vanity that deceives us. Women fancy admiration means more than it does."

"And men take care that they should."

"If it is designedly done, they cannot be justified; but I have no idea of there being so much design in the world as some persons imagine."

"I am far from attributing any part of Mr. Bingley's conduct to design," said Elizabeth; "but without scheming to do wrong, or to make others unhappy, there may be error, and there may be misery. Thoughtlessness, want of attention to other people's feelings, and want of resolution, will do the business."

"And do you impute it to either of those?"

"Yes; to the last. But if I go on, I shall displease you by saying what I think of persons you esteem. Stop me whilst you can."

"You persist, then, in supposing his sisters influence him."

"Yes, in conjunction with his friend."

"I cannot believe it. Why should they try to influence him? They can only wish his happiness, and if he is attached to me, no other woman can secure it."

"Your first position is false. They may wish many things besides his happiness; they may wish his increase of wealth and consequence; they may wish him to marry a girl who has all the importance of money, great connections, and pride."

"Beyond a doubt, they *do* wish him to chuse Miss Darcy," replied Jane; "but this may be from better feelings than you are supposing. They have known her much longer than they have known me; no wonder if they love her better. But, whatever may be their own wishes, it is very unlikely they should have opposed their brother's. What sister would think herself at liberty to do it, unless there were something very objectionable? If they believed him attached to me, they would not try to part us; if he were so, they could not succeed. By supposing such an affection, you make every body acting unnaturally and wrong, and me most unhappy. Do not distress me by the idea. I am not ashamed of having been mistaken—or, at least, it is slight, it is nothing in comparison of what I should feel in thinking ill of him or his sisters. Let me take it in the best light, in the light in which it may be understood."

Elizabeth could not oppose such a wish; and from this time Mr. Bingley's name was scarcely ever mentioned between them.

Mrs. Bennet still continued to wonder and repine at his returning no more, and though a day seldom passed in which Elizabeth did not account for it clearly, there seemed little chance of her ever considering it with less perplexity. Her daughter endeavoured to convince her of what she did not believe herself, that his attentions to Jane had been merely the effect of a common and transient liking, which ceased when he saw her no more; but though the probability of the statement was admitted at the time, she had the same story to repeat every day. Mrs. Bennet's best comfort was, that Mr. Bingley must be down again in the summer.

Mr. Bennet treated the matter differently. "So, Lizzy," said he one day, "your sister is crossed in love I find. I congratulate her. Next to being married, a girl likes to be crossed in love a little now and then. It is something to think of, and gives her a sort of distinction among her companions. When is your turn to come? You will hardly bear to be long outdone by Jane. Now is your time. Here are officers enough at Meryton to disappoint all the young ladies in the country. Let Wickham be *your* man. He is a pleasant fellow, and would jilt you creditably."

"Thank you, Sir, but a less agreeable man would satisfy me. We must not all expect Jane's good fortune."

"True," said Mr. Bennet, "but it is a comfort to think that, whatever of that kind may befal you, you have an affectionate mother who will always make the most of it."

Mr. Wickham's society was of material service in dispelling the gloom, which the late perverse occurrences had thrown on many of the Longbourn family. They saw him often, and to his other recommendations was now added that of general unreserve. The whole of what Elizabeth had already heard, his claims on Mr. Darcy, and all that he had suffered from him, was now openly acknowledged and publicly canvassed; and every body was pleased to think how much they had always disliked Mr. Darcy before they had known any thing of the matter.

Miss Bennet was the only creature who could suppose there might be any extenuating circumstances in the case, unknown to the society of Hertfordshire; her mild and steady candour always pleaded for allowances, and urged the possibility of mistakes—but by everybody else Mr. Darcy was condemned as the worst of men.

Chapter II

After a week spent in professions of love and schemes of felicity, Mr. Collins was called from his amiable Charlotte by the arrival of Saturday. The pain of separation, however, might be alleviated on his side, by preparations for the reception of his bride, as he had reason to hope, that shortly after his next return into Hertfordshire, the day would be fixed that was to make him the happiest of men. He took leave of his relations at Longbourn with as much solemnity as before; wished his fair cousins health and happiness again, and promised their father another letter of thanks.

On the following Monday, Mrs. Bennet had the pleasure of receiving her brother and his wife, who came as usual to spend the Christmas at Longbourn. Mr. Gardiner was a sensible, gentlemanlike man, greatly superior to his sister as well by nature as education. The Netherfield ladies would have had difficulty in believing that a man who lived by trade, and within view of his own warehouses, could have been so well bred and agreeable. Mrs. Gardiner, who was several years younger than Mrs. Bennet and Mrs. Philips, was an amiable, intelligent, elegant woman, and a great favourite with all her Longbourn nieces. Between the two eldest and herself especially, there subsisted a very particular regard. They had frequently been staying with her in town.

The first part of Mrs. Gardiner's business on her arrival, was to distribute her presents and describe the newest fashions. When this was done, she had a less active part to play. It became her turn to listen. Mrs. Bennet had many grievances to relate, and much to complain of.

They had all been very ill-used since she last saw her sister.[1] Two of her girls had been on the point of marriage, and after all there was nothing in it.

"I do not blame Jane," she continued, "for Jane would have got Mr. Bingley, if she could. But, Lizzy! Oh, sister! it is very hard to think that she might have been Mr. Collins's wife by this time, had not it been for her own perverseness. He made her an offer in this very room, and she refused him. The consequence of it is, that Lady Lucas will have a daughter married before I have, and that Longbourn estate is just as much entailed as ever. The Lucases are very artful people indeed, sister. They are all for what they can get. I am sorry to say it of them, but so it is. It makes me very nervous and poorly, to be thwarted so in my own family, and to have neighbours who think of themselves before anybody else. However, your coming just at this time is the greatest of comforts, and I am very glad to hear what you tell us, of long sleeves."

Mrs. Gardiner, to whom the chief of this news had been given before, in the course of Jane and Elizabeth's correspondence with her, made her sister a slight answer, and in compassion to her nieces turned the conversation.

When alone with Elizabeth afterwards, she spoke more on the subject. "It seems likely to have been a desirable match for Jane," said she. "I am sorry it went off. But these things happen so often! A young man, such as you describe Mr. Bingley, so easily falls in love with a pretty girl for a few weeks, and when accident separates them, so easily forgets her, that these sort of inconstancies are very frequent."

"An excellent consolation in its way," said Elizabeth, "but it will not do for *us*. We do not suffer by *accident*. It does not often happen that the interference of friends will persuade a young man of independent fortune to think no more of a girl, whom he was violently in love with only a few days before."

"But the expression of 'violently in love' is so hackneyed, so doubtful, so indefinite, that it gives me very little idea. It is as often applied to feelings which arise from an half hour's acquaintance, as to a real, strong attachment. Pray, how *violent was* Mr. Bingley's love?"

"I never saw a more promising inclination. He was growing quite inattentive to other people, and wholly engrossed by her. Every time they met, it was more decided and remarkable. At his own ball he offended two or three young ladies, by not asking them to dance, and I spoke to him twice myself, without receiving an answer. Could there be finer symptoms? Is not general incivility the very essence of love?"

"Oh, yes!—of that kind of love which I suppose him to have felt. Poor Jane! I am sorry for her, because, with her disposition, she may not get over it immediately. It had better have happened to *you*, Lizzy;

---

1. Sister-in-law. See also p. 196, where Mr. Gardiner addresses Mr. Bennet as "My dear Brother."

you would have laughed yourself out of it sooner. But do you think she would be prevailed on to go back with us? Change of scene might be of service—and perhaps a little relief from home, may be as useful as anything."

Elizabeth was exceedingly pleased with this proposal, and felt persuaded of her sister's ready acquiescence.

"I hope," added Mrs. Gardiner, "that no consideration with regard to this young man will influence her. We live in so different a part of town, all our connections are so different, and, as you well know, we go out so little, that it is very improbable they should meet at all, unless he really comes to see her."

"And *that* is quite impossible; for he is now in the custody of his friend, and Mr. Darcy would no more suffer him to call on Jane in such a part of London! My dear aunt, how could you think of it? Mr. Darcy may perhaps have *heard* of such a place as Gracechurch Street,[2] but he would hardly think a month's ablution enough to cleanse him from its impurities, were he once to enter it; and depend upon it, Mr. Bingley never stirs without him."

"So much the better. I hope they will not meet at all. But does not Jane correspond with the sister? *She* will not be able to help calling."

"She will drop the acquaintance entirely."

But in spite of the certainty in which Elizabeth affected to place this point, as well as the still more interesting one of Bingley's being withheld from seeing Jane, she felt a solicitude on the subject which convinced her, on examination, that she did not consider it entirely hopeless. It was possible, and sometimes she thought it probable, that his affection might be re-animated, and the influence of his friends successfully combated by the more natural influence of Jane's attractions.

Miss Bennet accepted her aunt's invitation with pleasure; and the Bingleys were no otherwise in her thoughts at the time, than as she hoped that, by Caroline's not living in the same house with her brother, she might occasionally spend a morning with her, without any danger of seeing him.

The Gardiners staid a week at Longbourn; and what with the Philipses, the Lucases, and the officers, there was not a day without its engagement. Mrs. Bennet had so carefully provided for the entertainment of her brother and sister, that they did not once sit down to a family dinner. When the engagement was for home, some of the officers always made part of it, of which officers Mr. Wickham was sure to be one; and on these occasions, Mrs. Gardiner, rendered suspicious by Elizabeth's warm commendation of him, narrowly observed them both. Without supposing them, from what she saw, to be very seriously

2. Gracechurch Street was in an unfashionable neighborhood near the commercial district of London.

in love, their preference of each other was plain enough to make her a little uneasy; and she resolved to speak to Elizabeth on the subject before she left Hertfordshire, and represent to her the imprudence of encouraging such an attachment.

To Mrs. Gardiner, Wickham had one means of affording pleasure, unconnected with his general powers. About ten or a dozen years ago, before her marriage, she had spent a considerable time in that very part of Derbyshire, to which he belonged. They had, therefore, many acquaintance in common; and, though Wickham had been little there since the death of Darcy's father, five years before, it was yet in his power to give her fresher intelligence of her former friends, than she had been in the way of procuring.

Mrs. Gardiner had seen Pemberley, and known the late Mr. Darcy by character perfectly well. Here consequently was an inexhaustible subject of discourse. In comparing her recollection of Pemberley, with the minute description which Wickham could give, and in bestowing her tribute of praise on the character of its late possessor, she was delighting both him and herself. On being made acquainted with the present Mr. Darcy's treatment of him, she tried to remember something of that gentleman's reputed disposition when quite a lad, which might agree with it, and was confident at last, that she recollected having heard Mr. Fitzwilliam Darcy formerly spoken of as a very proud, ill-natured boy.

Chapter III

Mrs. Gardiner's caution to Elizabeth was punctually and kindly given on the first favourable opportunity of speaking to her alone; after honestly telling her what she thought, she thus went on:

"You are too sensible a girl, Lizzy, to fall in love merely because you are warned against it; and, therefore, I am not afraid of speaking openly. Seriously, I would have you be on your guard. Do not involve yourself, or endeavour to involve him in an affection which the want of fortune would make so very imprudent. I have nothing to say against *him*; he is a most interesting young man; and if he had the fortune he ought to have, I should think you could not do better. But as it is—you must not let your fancy run away with you. You have sense, and we all expect you to use it. Your father would depend on *your* resolution and good conduct, I am sure. You must not disappoint your father."

"My dear aunt, this is being serious indeed."

"Yes, and I hope to engage you to be serious likewise."

"Well, then, you need not be under any alarm. I will take care of myself, and of Mr. Wickham too. He shall not be in love with me, if I can prevent it."

"Elizabeth, you are not serious now."

"I beg your pardon. I will try again. At present I am not in love with Mr. Wickham; no, I certainly am not. But he is, beyond all comparison, the most agreeable man I ever saw—and if he becomes really attached to me—I believe it will be better that he should not. I see the imprudence of it.—Oh! *that* abominable Mr. Darcy!—My father's opinion of me does me the greatest honor; and I should be miserable to forfeit it. My father, however, is partial to Mr. Wickham. In short, my dear aunt, I should be very sorry to be the means of making any of you unhappy; but since we see every day that where there is affection, young people are seldom withheld by immediate want of fortune, from entering into engagements with each other, how can I promise to be wiser than so many of my fellow creatures if I am tempted, or how am I even to know that it would be wisdom to resist? All that I can promise you, therefore, is not to be in a hurry. I will not be in a hurry to believe myself his first object. When I am in company with him, I will not be wishing. In short, I will do my best."

"Perhaps it will be as well, if you discourage his coming here so very often. At least, you should not *remind* your Mother of inviting him."

"As I did the other day," said Elizabeth, with a conscious smile; "very true, it will be wise in me to refrain from *that*. But do not imagine that he is always here so often. It is on your account that he has been so frequently invited this week. You know my mother's ideas as to the necessity of constant company for her friends. But really, and upon my honour, I will try to do what I think to be wisest; and now, I hope you are satisfied."

Her aunt assured her that she was; and Elizabeth having thanked her for the kindness of her hints, they parted; a wonderful instance of advice being given on such a point, without being resented.

Mr. Collins returned into Hertfordshire soon after it had been quitted by the Gardiners and Jane; but as he took up his abode with the Lucases, his arrival was no great inconvenience to Mrs. Bennet. His marriage was now fast approaching, and she was at length so far resigned as to think it inevitable, and even repeatedly to say in an ill-natured tone that she "*wished* they might be happy." Thursday was to be the wedding day, and on Wednesday Miss Lucas[3] paid her farewell visit; and when she rose to take leave, Elizabeth, ashamed of her mother's ungracious and reluctant good wishes, and sincerely affected herself, accompanied her out of the room. As they went down stairs together, Charlotte said,

"I shall depend on hearing from you very often, Eliza."

"*That* you certainly shall."

"And I have another favour to ask. Will you come and see me?"

"We shall often meet, I hope, in Hertfordshire."

3. 1813: Lucy.

"I am not likely to leave Kent for some time. Promise me, therefore, to come to Hunsford."

Elizabeth could not refuse, though she foresaw little pleasure in the visit.

"My father and Maria are to come to me in March," added Charlotte, "and I hope you will consent to be of the party. Indeed, Eliza, you will be as welcome to me as either of them."

The wedding took place; the bride and bridegroom set off for Kent from the church door, and every body had as much to say or to hear on the subject as usual. Elizabeth soon heard from her friend; and their correspondence was as regular and frequent as it had ever been; that it should be equally unreserved was impossible. Elizabeth could never address her without feeling that all the comfort of intimacy was over, and, though determined not to slacken as a correspondent, it was for the sake of what had been, rather than what was. Charlotte's first letters were received with a good deal of eagerness; there could not but be curiosity to know how she would speak of her new home, how she would like Lady Catherine, and how happy she would dare pronounce herself to be; though, when the letters were read, Elizabeth felt that Charlotte expressed herself on every point exactly as she might have foreseen. She wrote cheerfully, seemed surrounded with comforts, and mentioned nothing which she could not praise. The house, furniture, neighbourhood, and roads, were all to her taste, and Lady Catherine's behaviour was most friendly and obliging. It was Mr. Collins's picture of Hunsford and Rosings rationally softened; and Elizabeth perceived that she must wait for her own visit there, to know the rest.

Jane had already written a few lines to her sister to announce their safe arrival in London; and when she wrote again, Elizabeth hoped it would be in her power to say something of the Bingleys.

Her impatience for this second letter was as well rewarded as impatience generally is. Jane had been a week in town, without either seeing or hearing from Caroline. She accounted for it, however, by supposing that her last letter to her friend from Longbourn, had by some accident been lost.

"My aunt," she continued, "is going to-morrow into that part of the town, and I shall take the opportunity of calling in Grosvenor-street."[4]

She wrote again when the visit was paid, and she had seen Miss Bingley. "I did not think Caroline in spirits," were her words, "but she was very glad to see me, and reproached me for giving her no notice of my coming to London. I was right, therefore; my last letter had never reached her. I enquired after their brother, of course. He was well, but so much engaged with Mr. Darcy, that they scarcely ever saw him. I found that Miss Darcy was expected to dinner. I wish I could

4. Grosvenor Street is in a part of London more fashionable than the district in which the Gardiners live.

see her. My visit was not long, as Caroline and Mrs. Hurst were going out. I dare say I shall soon see them here."

Elizabeth shook her head over this letter. It convinced her, that accident only could discover to Mr. Bingley her sister's being in town.

Four weeks passed away, and Jane saw nothing of him. She endeavoured to persuade herself that she did not regret it; but she could no longer be blind to Miss Bingley's inattention. After waiting at home every morning for a fortnight, and inventing every evening a fresh excuse for her, the visitor did at last appear; but the shortness of her stay, and yet more, the alteration of her manner, would allow Jane to deceive herself no longer. The letter which she wrote on this occasion to her sister, will prove what she felt.

"My dearest Lizzy will, I am sure, be incapable of triumphing in her better judgment, at my expence, when I confess myself to have been entirely deceived in Miss Bingley's regard for me. But, my dear sister, though the event has proved you right, do not think me obstinate if I still assert, that, considering what her behaviour was, my confidence was as natural as your suspicion. I do not at all comprehend her reason for wishing to be intimate with me, but if the same circumstances were to happen again, I am sure I should be deceived again. Caroline did not return my visit till yesterday; and not a note, not a line, did I receive in the mean time. When she did come, it was very evident that she had no pleasure in it; she made a slight, formal, apology, for not calling before, said not a word of wishing to see me again, and was in every respect so altered a creature, that when she went away, I was perfectly resolved to continue the acquaintance no longer. I pity, though I cannot help blaming her. She was very wrong in singling me out as she did; I can safely say, that every advance to intimacy began on her side. But I pity her, because she must feel that she has been acting wrong, and because I am very sure that anxiety for her brother is the cause of it. I need not explain myself farther; and though *we* know this anxiety to be quite needless, yet if she feels it, it will easily account for her behaviour to me; and so deservedly dear as he is to his sister, whatever anxiety she may feel on his behalf, is natural and amiable. I cannot but wonder, however, at her having any such fears now, because, if he had at all cared about me, we must have met long, long ago. He knows of my being in town, I am certain, from something she said herself; and yet it should seem by her manner of talking, as if she wanted to persuade herself that he is really partial to Miss Darcy. I cannot understand it. If I were not afraid of judging harshly, I should be almost tempted to say, that there is a strong appearance of duplicity in all this. But I will endeavour to banish every painful thought, and think only of what will make me happy, your affection, and the invariable kindness of my dear uncle and aunt. Let me hear from you very soon.

Miss Bingley said something of his never returning to Netherfield again, of giving up the house, but not with any certainty. We had better not mention it. I am extremely glad that you have such pleasant accounts from our friends at Hunsford. Pray go to see them, with Sir William and Maria. I am sure you will be very comfortable there.

"Yours, &c."

This letter gave Elizabeth some pain; but her spirits returned as she considered that Jane would no longer be duped, by the sister at least. All expectation from the brother was now absolutely over. She would not even wish for any renewal of his attentions. His character sunk on every review of it; and as a punishment for him, as well as a possible advantage to Jane, she seriously hoped he might really soon marry Mr. Darcy's sister, as, by Wickham's account, she would make him abundantly regret what he had thrown away.

Mrs. Gardiner about this time reminded Elizabeth of her promise concerning that gentleman, and required information; and Elizabeth had such to send as might rather give contentment to her aunt than to herself. His apparent partiality had subsided, his attentions were over, he was the admirer of some one else. Elizabeth was watchful enough to see it all, but she could see it and write of it without material pain. Her heart had been but slightly touched, and her vanity was satisfied with believing that *she* would have been his only choice, had fortune permitted it. The sudden acquisition of ten thousand pounds was the most remarkable charm of the young lady, to whom he was now rendering himself agreeable; but Elizabeth, less clear-sighted perhaps in his case than in Charlotte's, did not quarrel with him for his wish of independence. Nothing, on the contrary, could be more natural; and while able to suppose that it cost him a few struggles to relinquish her, she was ready to allow it a wise and desirable measure for both, and could very sincerely wish him happy.

All this was acknowledged to Mrs. Gardiner; and after relating the circumstances, she thus went on:—"I am now convinced, my dear aunt, that I have never been much in love; for had I really experienced that pure and elevating passion, I should at present detest his very name, and wish him all manner of evil. But my feelings are not only cordial towards *him*; they are even impartial towards Miss King. I cannot find out that I hate her at all, or that I am in the least unwilling to think her a very good sort of girl. There can be no love in all this. My watchfulness has been effectual; and though I should certainly be a more interesting object to all my acquaintance, were I distractedly in love with him, I cannot say that I regret my comparative insignificance. Importance may sometimes be purchased too dearly. Kitty and Lydia take his defection much more to heart than I do. They are young in the ways of the world, and not yet open to the mortifying conviction that handsome young men must have something to live on, as well as the plain."

Chapter IV

With no greater events than these in the Longbourn family, and otherwise diversified by little beyond the walks to Meryton, sometimes dirty and sometimes cold, did January and February pass away. March was to take Elizabeth to Hunsford. She had not at first thought very seriously of going thither; but Charlotte, she soon found, was depending on the plan, and she gradually learned to consider it herself with greater pleasure as well as greater certainty. Absence had increased her desire of seeing Charlotte again, and weakened her disgust of Mr. Collins. There was novelty in the scheme, and as, with such a mother and such uncompanionable sisters, home could not be faultless, a little change was not unwelcome for its own sake. The journey would moreover give her a peep at Jane; and, in short, as the time drew near, she would have been very sorry for any delay. Every thing, however, went on smoothly, and was finally settled according to Charlotte's first sketch. She was to accompany Sir William and his second daughter. The improvement of spending a night in London was added in time, and the plan became perfect as plan could be.

The only pain was in leaving her father, who would certainly miss her, and who, when it came to the point, so little liked her going, that he told her to write to him, and almost promised to answer her letter.

The farewell between herself and Mr. Wickham was perfectly friendly; on his side even more. His present pursuit could not make him forget that Elizabeth had been the first to excite and to deserve his attention, the first to listen and to pity, the first to be admired; and in his manner of bidding her adieu, wishing her every enjoyment, reminding her of what she was to expect in Lady Catherine de Bourgh, and trusting their opinion of her—their opinion of every body—would always coincide, there was a solicitude, an interest which she felt must ever attach her to him with a most sincere regard; and she parted from him convinced, that whether married or single, he must always be her model of the amiable and pleasing.

Her fellow-travellers the next day, were not of a kind to make her think him less agreeable. Sir William Lucas, and his daughter Maria, a good humoured girl, but as empty-headed as himself, had nothing to say that could be worth hearing, and were listened to with about as much delight as the rattle of the chaise. Elizabeth loved absurdities, but she had known Sir William's too long. He could tell her nothing new of the wonders of his presentation and knighthood; and his civilities were worn out like his information.

It was a journey of only twenty-four miles, and they began it so early as to be in Gracechurch-street by noon. As they drove to Mr. Gardiner's door, Jane was at a drawing-room window watching their arrival; when they entered the passage she was there to welcome them, and Elizabeth, looking earnestly in her face, was pleased to see it healthful and lovely as ever. On the stairs were a troop of little boys and girls, whose eagerness for their cousin's appearance would not allow them to wait in the drawing-room, and whose shyness, as they had not seen her for a twelve-month, prevented their coming lower. All was joy and kindness. The day passed most pleasantly away; the morning[5] in bustle and shopping, and the evening at one of the theatres.

Elizabeth then contrived to sit by her aunt. Their first subject was her sister; and she was more grieved than astonished to hear, in reply to her minute enquiries, that though Jane always struggled to support her spirits, there were periods of dejection. It was reasonable, however, to hope, that they would not continue long. Mrs. Gardiner gave her the particulars also of Miss Bingley's visit in Gracechurch-street, and repeated conversations occurring at different times between Jane and herself, which proved that the former had, from her heart, given up the acquaintance.

Mrs. Gardiner then rallied her niece on Wickham's desertion, and complimented her on bearing it so well.

"But, my dear Elizabeth," she added, "what sort of girl is Miss King? I should be sorry to think our friend mercenary."

"Pray, my dear aunt, what is the difference in matrimonial affairs, between the mercenary and the prudent motive? Where does discretion end, and avarice begin? Last Christmas you were afraid of his marrying me, because it would be imprudent; and now, because he is trying to get a girl with only ten thousand pounds, you want to find out that he is mercenary."

"If you will only tell me what sort of girl Miss King is, I shall know what to think."

"She is a very good kind of girl, I believe. I know no harm of her."

"But he paid her not the smallest attention, till her grandfather's death made her mistress of this fortune."

"No—why should he? If it was not allowable for him to gain *my* affections, because I had no money, what occasion could there be for making love to a girl whom he did not care about, and who was equally poor?"

"But there seems indelicacy in directing his attentions towards her, so soon after this event."

"A man in distressed circumstances has not time for all those elegant decorums which other people may observe. If *she* does not object to it, why should *we?*"

5. The interval between breakfast (customarily served around 10:00 A.M.) and dinner (served around 4:00 or 5:00 P.M.) was referred to as the morning.

"*Her* not objecting, does not justify *him*. It only shews her being deficient in something herself—sense or feeling."

"Well," cried Elizabeth, "have it as you choose. *He* shall be mercenary, and *she* shall be foolish."

"No, Lizzy, that is what I do *not* choose. I should be sorry, you know, to think ill of a young man who has lived so long in Derbyshire."

"Oh! if that is all, I have a very poor opinion of young men who live in Derbyshire; and their intimate friends who live in Hertfordshire are not much better. I am sick of them all. Thank Heaven! I am going tomorrow where I shall find a man who has not one agreeable quality, who has neither manner nor sense to recommend him. Stupid men are the only ones worth knowing, after all."

"Take care, Lizzy; that speech savours strongly of disappointment."

Before they were separated by the conclusion of the play, she had the unexpected happiness of an invitation to accompany her uncle and aunt in a tour of pleasure which they proposed taking in the summer.

"We have not quite determined how far it shall carry us," said Mrs. Gardiner, "but perhaps to the Lakes."[6]

No scheme could have been more agreeable to Elizabeth, and her acceptance of the invitation was most ready and grateful. "My dear, dear aunt," she rapturously cried, "what delight! what felicity! You give me fresh life and vigour. Adieu to disappointment and spleen. What are men to rocks and mountains? Oh! what hours of transport we shall spend! And when we *do* return, it shall not be like other travellers, without being able to give one accurate idea of any thing. We *will* know where we have gone—we *will* recollect what we have seen. Lakes, mountains, and rivers, shall not be jumbled together in our imaginations; nor, when we attempt to describe any particular scene, will we begin quarrelling about its relative situation. Let *our* first effusions be less insupportable than those of the generality of travellers."

Chapter V

Every object in the next day's journey was new and interesting to Elizabeth; and her spirits were in a state for enjoyment; for she had seen her sister looking so well as to banish all fear for her health, and the prospect of her northern tour was a constant source of delight.

When they left the high road for the lane to Hunsford, every eye was in search of the Parsonage, and every turning expected to bring it in view. The paling[7] of Rosings park was their boundary on one side. Elizabeth smiled at the recollection of all that she had heard of its inhabitants.

At length the Parsonage was discernible. The garden sloping to the

6. The Lake District in the north of England, above Derbyshire.
7. Fence.

road, the house standing in it, the green pales and the laurel hedge, every thing declared they were arriving. Mr. Collins and Charlotte appeared at the door, and the carriage stopped at the small gate, which led by a short gravel walk to the house, amidst the nods and smiles of the whole party. In a moment they were all out of the chaise, rejoicing at the sight of each other. Mrs. Collins welcomed her friend with the liveliest pleasure, and Elizabeth was more and more satisfied with coming, when she found herself so affectionately received. She saw instantly that her cousin's manners were not altered by his marriage; his formal civility was just what it had been, and he detained her some minutes at the gate to hear and satisfy his enquiries after all her family. They were then, with no other delay than his pointing out the neatness of the entrance, taken into the house; and as soon as they were in the parlour, he welcomed them a second time with ostentatious formality to his humble abode, and punctually repeated all his wife's offers of refreshment.

Elizabeth was prepared to see him in his glory; and she could not help fancying that in displaying the good proportion of the room, its aspect and its furniture, he addressed himself particularly to her, as if wishing to make her feel what she had lost in refusing him. But though every thing seemed neat and comfortable, she was not able to gratify him by any sigh of repentance; and rather looked with wonder at her friend that she could have so cheerful an air, with such a companion. When Mr. Collins said any thing of which his wife might reasonably be ashamed, which certainly was not unseldom, she involuntarily turned her eye on Charlotte. Once or twice she could discern a faint blush; but in general Charlotte wisely did not hear. After sitting long enough to admire every article of furniture in the room, from the sideboard to the fender,[8] to give an account of their journey and of all that had happened in London, Mr. Collins invited them to take a stroll in the garden, which was large and well laid out, and to the cultivation of which he attended himself. To work in his garden was one of his most respectable pleasures; and Elizabeth admired the command of countenance with which Charlotte talked of the healthfulness of the exercise, and owned she encouraged it as much as possible. Here, leading the way through every walk and cross walk, and scarcely allowing them an interval to utter the praises he asked for, every view was pointed out with a minuteness which left beauty entirely behind. He could number the fields in every direction, and could tell how many trees there were in the most distant clump. But of all the views which his garden, or which the county, or the kingdom could boast, none were to be compared with the prospect of Rosings, afforded by an opening in the trees that bordered the park nearly opposite the front

---

8. A metal guard before a fireplace.

of his house. It was a handsome modern building, well situated on rising ground.

From his garden, Mr. Collins would have led them round his two meadows, but the ladies not having shoes to encounter the remains of a white frost, turned back; and while Sir William accompanied him, Charlotte took her sister and friend over the house, extremely well pleased, probably, to have the opportunity of shewing it without her husband's help. It was rather small, but well built and convenient; and every thing was fitted up and arranged with a neatness and consistency of which Elizabeth gave Charlotte all the credit. When Mr. Collins could be forgotten, there was really a great air of comfort throughout, and by Charlotte's evident enjoyment of it, Elizabeth supposed he must be often forgotten.

She had already learnt that Lady Catherine was still in the country. It was spoken of again while they were at dinner, when Mr. Collins joining in, observed,

"Yes, Miss Elizabeth, you will have the honour of seeing Lady Catherine de Bourgh on the ensuing Sunday at church, and I need not say you will be delighted with her. She is all affability and condescension, and I doubt not but you will be honoured with some portion of her notice when service is over. I have scarcely any hesitation in saying that she will include you and my sister Maria in every invitation with which she honours us during your stay here. Her behaviour to my dear Charlotte is charming. We dine at Rosings twice every week, and are never allowed to walk home. Her ladyship's carriage is regularly ordered for us. I *should* say, one of her ladyship's carriages, for she has several."

"Lady Catherine is a very respectable, sensible woman indeed," added Charlotte, "and a most attentive neighbour."

"Very true, my dear, that is exactly what I say. She is the sort of woman whom one cannot regard with too much deference."

The evening was spent chiefly in talking over Hertfordshire news, and telling again what had been already written; and when it closed, Elizabeth in the solitude of her chamber had to meditate upon Charlotte's degree of contentment, to understand her address in guiding, and composure in bearing with her husband, and to acknowledge that it was all done very well. She had also to anticipate how her visit would pass, the quiet tenor of their usual employments, the vexatious interruptions of Mr. Collins, and the gaieties of their intercourse with Rosings. A lively imagination soon settled it all.

About the middle of the next day, as she was in her room getting ready for a walk, a sudden noise below seemed to speak the whole house in confusion; and after listening a moment, she heard somebody running up stairs in a violent hurry, and calling loudly after her. She opened the door, and met Maria in the landing place, who, breathless with agitation, cried out,

"Oh, my dear Eliza! pray make haste and come into the dining-room, for there is such a sight to be seen! I will not tell you what it is. Make haste, and come down this moment."

Elizabeth asked questions in vain; Maria would tell her nothing more, and down they ran into the dining-room, which fronted the lane, in quest of this wonder; it was two ladies stopping in a low phaeton at the garden gate.

"And is this all?" cried Elizabeth. "I expected at least that the pigs were got into the garden, and here is nothing but Lady Catherine and her daughter!' "

"La! my dear," said Maria quite shocked at the mistake, "it is not Lady Catherine. The old lady is Mrs. Jenkinson, who lives with them. The other is Miss De Bourgh. Only look at her. She is quite a little creature. Who would have thought she could be so thin and small!"

"She is abominably rude to keep Charlotte out of doors in all this wind. Why does she not come in?"

"Oh! Charlotte says, she hardly ever does. It is the greatest of favours when Miss De Bourgh comes in."

"I like her appearance," said Elizabeth, struck with other ideas. "She looks sickly and cross.—Yes, she will do for him very well. She will make him a very proper wife."

Mr. Collins and Charlotte were both standing at the gate in conversation with the ladies; and Sir William, to Elizabeth's high diversion, was stationed in the door-way, in earnest contemplation of the greatness before him, and constantly bowing whenever Miss De Bourgh looked that way.

At length there was nothing more to be said; the ladies drove on, and the others returned into the house. Mr. Collins no sooner saw the two girls than he began to congratulate them on their good fortune, which Charlotte explained by letting them know that the whole party was asked to dine at Rosings the next day.

Chapter VI

Mr. Collins's triumph in consequence of this invitation was complete. The power of displaying the grandeur of his patroness to his wondering visitors, and of letting them see her civility towards himself and his wife, was exactly what he had wished for; and that an opportunity of doing it should be given so soon, was such an instance of Lady Catherine's condescension as he knew not how to admire enough.

"I confess," said he, "that I should not have been at all surprised by her Ladyship's asking us on Sunday to drink tea and spend the evening at Rosings. I rather expected, from my knowledge of her affability, that it would happen. But who could have foreseen such an attention as this? Who could have imagined that we should receive an invitation to dine there (an invitation moreover including the whole party) so immediately after your arrival!"

"I am the less surprised at what has happened," replied Sir William, "from that knowledge of what the manners of the great really are, which my situation in life has allowed me to acquire. About the Court, such instances of elegant breeding are not uncommon."

Scarcely any thing was talked of the whole day or next morning, but their visit to Rosings. Mr. Collins was carefully instructing them in what they were to expect, that the sight of such rooms, so many servants, and so splendid a dinner might not wholly overpower them.

When the ladies were separating for the toilette, he said to Elizabeth,

"Do not make yourself uneasy, my dear cousin, about your apparel. Lady Catherine is far from requiring that elegance of dress in us, which becomes herself and daughter. I would advise you merely to put on whatever of your clothes is superior to the rest, there is no occasion for any thing more. Lady Catherine will not think the worse of you for being simply dressed. She likes to have the distinction of rank preserved."

While they were dressing, he came two or three times to their different doors, to recommend their being quick, as Lady Catherine very much objected to be kept waiting for her dinner.—Such formidable accounts of her Ladyship, and her manner of living, quite frightened Maria Lucas, who had been little used to company, and she looked forward to her introduction at Rosings, with as much apprehension, as her father had done to his presentation at St. James's.

As the weather was fine, they had a pleasant walk of about half a mile across the park.—Every park has its beauty and its prospects; and Elizabeth saw much to be pleased with, though she could not be in such raptures as Mr. Collins expected the scene to inspire, and was but slightly affected by his enumeration of the windows in front of the house, and his relation of what the glazing altogether had originally cost Sir Lewis De Bourgh.

When they ascended the steps to the hall, Maria's alarm was every moment increasing, and even Sir William did not look perfectly calm.—Elizabeth's courage did not fail her. She had heard nothing of Lady Catherine that spoke her awful from any extraordinary talents or miraculous virtue, and the mere stateliness of money and rank, she thought she could witness without trepidation.

From the entrance hall, of which Mr. Collins pointed out, with a rapturous air, the fine proportion and finished ornaments, they followed the servants through an antichamber, to the room where Lady Catherine, her daughter, and Mrs. Jenkinson were sitting.—Her Ladyship, with great condescension, arose to receive them; and as Mrs. Collins had settled it with her husband that the office of introduction

should be her's, it was performed in a proper manner, without any of
those apologies and thanks which he would have thought necessary.

In spite of having been at St. James's, Sir William was so completely
awed, by the grandeur surrounding him, that he had but just courage
enough to make a very low bow, and take his seat without saying a
word; and his daughter, frightened almost out of her senses, sat on the
edge of her chair, not knowing which way to look. Elizabeth found
herself quite equal to the scene, and could observe the three ladies
before her composedly.—Lady Catherine was a tall, large woman, with
strongly-marked features, which might once have been handsome. Her
air was not conciliating, nor was her manner of receiving them, such
as to make her visitors forget their inferior rank. She was not rendered
formidable by silence; but whatever she said, was spoken in so authoritative a tone, as marked her self-importance, and brought Mr. Wickham immediately to Elizabeth's mind; and from the observation of the
day altogether, she believed Lady Catherine to be exactly what he had
represented.

When, after examining the mother, in whose countenance and
deportment she soon found some resemblance of Mr. Darcy, she
turned her eyes on the daughter, she could almost have joined in
Maria's astonishment, at her being so thin, and so small. There was
neither in figure nor face, any likeness between the ladies. Miss De
Bourgh was pale and sickly; her features, though not plain, were insignificant; and she spoke very little, except in a low voice, to Mrs. Jenkinson, in whose appearance there was nothing remarkable, and who
was entirely engaged in listening to what she said, and placing a screen
in the proper direction before her eyes.

After sitting a few minutes, they were all sent to one of the windows,
to admire the view, Mr. Collins attending them to point out its beauties, and Lady Catherine kindly informing them that it was much better worth looking at in the summer.

The dinner was exceedingly handsome, and there were all the servants, and all the articles of plate which Mr. Collins had promised;
and, as he had likewise foretold, he took his seat at the bottom of the
table, by her ladyship's desire, and looked as if he felt that life could
furnish nothing greater.—He carved, and ate, and praised with
delighted alacrity; and every dish was commended, first by him, and
then by Sir William, who was now enough recovered to echo whatever
his son in law said, in a manner which Elizabeth wondered Lady Catherine could bear. But Lady Catherine seemed gratified by their excessive admiration, and gave most gracious smiles, especially when any
dish on the table proved a novelty to them. The party did not supply
much conversation. Elizabeth was ready to speak whenever there was
an opening, but she was seated between Charlotte and Miss De
Bourgh—the former of whom was engaged in listening to Lady Cath-

erine, and the latter said not a word to her all dinner time. Mrs. Jenkinson was chiefly employed in watching how little Miss De Bourgh ate, pressing her to try some other dish, and fearing she were indisposed. Maria thought speaking out of the question, and the gentlemen did nothing but eat and admire.

When the ladies returned to the drawing room, there was little to be done but to hear Lady Catherine talk, which she did without any intermission till coffee came in, delivering her opinion on every subject in so decisive a manner as proved that she was not used to have her judgment controverted. She enquired into Charlotte's domestic concerns familiarly and minutely, and gave her a great deal of advice, as to the management of them all; told her how every thing ought to be regulated in so small a family as her's, and instructed her as to the care of her cows and her poultry. Elizabeth found that nothing was beneath this great Lady's attention, which could furnish her with an occasion of dictating to others. In the intervals of her discourse with Mrs. Collins, she addressed a variety of questions to Maria and Elizabeth, but especially to the latter, of whose connections she knew the least, and who she observed to Mrs. Collins, was a very genteel, pretty kind of girl. She asked her at different times, how many sisters she had, whether they were older or younger than herself, whether any of them were likely to be married, whether they were handsome, where they had been educated, what carriage her father kept, and what had been her mother's maiden name?—Elizabeth felt all the impertinence of her questions, but answered them very composedly.—Lady Catherine then observed,

"Your father's estate is entailed on Mr. Collins, I think. For your sake," turning to Charlotte, "I am glad of it; but otherwise I see no occasion for entailing estates from the female line.—It was not thought necessary in Sir Lewis de Bourgh's family.—Do you play and sing, Miss Bennet?"

"A little."

"Oh! then—some time or other we shall be happy to hear you. Our instrument is a capital one, probably superior to——You shall try it some day.—Do your sisters play and sing?"

"One of them does."

"Why did not you all learn?—You ought all to have learned. The Miss Webbs all play, and their father has not so good an income as your's.—Do you draw?"

"No, not at all."

"What, none of you?"

"Not one."

"That is very strange. But I suppose you had no opportunity. Your mother should have taken you to town every spring for the benefit of masters."

"My mother would have had no objection, but my father hates London."

"Has your governess left you?"

"We never had any governess."

"No governess! How was that possible? Five daughters brought up at home without a governess!—I never heard of such a thing. Your mother must have been quite a slave to your education."

Elizabeth could hardly help smiling, as she assured her that had not been the case.

"Then, who taught you? who attended to you? Without a governess you must have been neglected."

"Compared with some families, I believe we were; but such of us as wished to learn, never wanted the means. We were always encouraged to read, and had all the masters that were necessary. Those who chose to be idle, certainly might."

"Aye, no doubt; but that is what a governess will prevent, and if I had known your mother, I should have advised her most strenuously to engage one. I always say that nothing is to be done in education without steady and regular instruction, and nobody but a governess can give it. It is wonderful how many families I have been the means of supplying in that way. I am always glad to get a young person well placed out. Four nieces of Mrs. Jenkinson are most delightfully situated through my means; and it was but the other day, that I recommended another young person, who was merely accidentally mentioned to me, and the family are quite delighted with her. Mrs. Collins, did I tell you of Lady Metcalfe's calling yesterday to thank me? She finds Miss Pope a treasure. 'Lady Catherine,' said she, 'you have given me a treasure.' Are any of your younger sisters out, Miss Bennet?"

"Yes, Ma'am, all."

"All!—What, all five out at once? Very odd!—And you only the second.—The younger ones out before the elder are married!—Your younger sisters must be very young?"

"Yes, my youngest is not sixteen. Perhaps *she* is full young to be much in company. But really, Ma'am, I think it would be very hard upon younger sisters, that they should not have their share of society and amusement because the elder may not have the means or inclination to marry early.—The last born has as good a right to the pleasures of youth, as the first. And to be kept back on *such* a motive!—I think it would not be very likely to promote sisterly affection or delicacy of mind."

"Upon my word," said her Ladyship, "you give your opinion very decidedly for so young a person.—Pray, what is your age?"

"With three younger sisters grown up," replied Elizabeth smiling, "your Ladyship can hardly expect me to own it."

Lady Catherine seemed quite astonished at not receiving a direct answer; and Elizabeth suspected herself to be the first creature who had ever dared to trifle with so much dignified impertinence.

"You cannot be more than twenty, I am sure,—therefore you need not conceal your age."

"I am not one and twenty."

When the gentlemen had joined them, and tea was over, the card tables were placed. Lady Catherine, Sir William, and Mr. and Mrs. Collins sat down to quadrille; and as Miss De Bourgh chose to play at cassino,[9] the two girls had the honour of assisting Mrs. Jenkinson to make up her party. Their table was superlatively stupid. Scarcely a syllable was uttered that did not relate to the game, except when Mrs. Jenkinson expressed her fears Miss De Bourgh's being too hot or too cold, or having too much or too little light. A great deal more passed at the other table. Lady Catherine was generally speaking—stating the mistakes of the three others, or relating some anecdote of herself. Mr. Collins was employed in agreeing to everything her Ladyship said, thanking her for every fish he won, and apologising if he thought he won too many. Sir William did not say much. He was storing his memory with anecdotes and noble names.

When Lady Catherine and her daughter had played as long as they chose, the tables were broke up, the carriage was offered to Mrs. Collins, gratefully accepted, and immediately ordered. The party then gathered round the fire to hear Lady Catherine determine what weather they were to have on the morrow. From these instructions they were summoned by the arrival of the coach, and with many speeches of thankfulness on Mr. Collins's side, and as many bows on Sir William's, they departed. As soon as they had driven from the door, Elizabeth was called on by her cousin, to give her opinion of all that she had seen at Rosings, which, for Charlotte's sake, she made more favourable than it really was. But her commendation, though costing her some trouble, could by no means satisfy Mr. Collins, and he was very soon obliged to take her Ladyship's praise into his own hands.

Chapter VII

Sir William staid only a week at Hunsford; but his visit was long enough to convince him of his daughter's being most comfortably settled, and of her possessing such a husband and such a neighbour as were not often met with. While Sir William was with them, Mr. Collins devoted his mornings to driving him out in his gig, and shewing him the country; but when he went away, the whole family returned to their usual employments, and Elizabeth was thankful to find that they did not see more of her cousin by the alteration, for the chief of the

---

9. A card game that can be played by two, three, or four people. Quadrille: a card game similar to bridge and whist and more complicated than cassino.

time between breakfast and dinner was now passed by him either at
work in the garden, or in reading and writing, and looking out of window in his own book room, which fronted the road. The room in which
the ladies sat was backwards.[1] Elizabeth at first had rather wondered
that Charlotte should not prefer the dining parlour for common use;
it was a better sized room, and had a pleasanter aspect; but she soon
saw that her friend had an excellent reason for what she did, for Mr.
Collins would undoubtedly have been much less in his own apartment,
had they sat in one equally lively; and she gave Charlotte credit for the
arrangement.

From the drawing room they could distinguish nothing in the lane,
and were indebted to Mr. Collins for the knowledge of what carriages
went along, and how often especially Miss De Bourgh drove by in her
phaeton, which he never failed coming to inform them of, though it
happened almost every day. She not unfrequently stopped at the Parsonage, and had a few minutes' conversation with Charlotte, but was
scarcely ever prevailed on to get out.

Very few days passed in which Mr. Collins did not walk to Rosings,
and not many in which his wife did not think it necessary to go likewise;
and till Elizabeth recollected that there might be other family livings
to be disposed of, she could not understand the sacrifice of so many
hours. Now and then, they were honoured with a call from her Ladyship, and nothing escaped her observation that was passing in the room
during these visits. She examined into their employments, looked at
their work, and advised them to do it differently; found fault with the
arrangement of the furniture, or detected the housemaid in negligence;
and if she accepted any refreshment, seemed to do it only for the sake
of finding out that Mrs. Collins's joints of meat were too large for her
family.

Elizabeth soon perceived that though this great lady was not in the
commission of the peace[2] for the county, she was a most active mag-
istrate in her own parish, the minutest concerns of which were carried
to her by Mr. Collins; and whenever any of the cottagers were disposed
to be quarrelsome, discontented or too poor, she sallied forth into the
village to settle their differences, silence their complaints, and scold
them into harmony and plenty.

The entertainment of dining at Rosings was repeated about twice a
week; and, allowing for the loss of Sir William, and there being only
one card table in the evening, every such entertainment was the counterpart of the first. Their other engagements were few; as the style of
living of the neighbourhood in general, was beyond the Collinses'
reach. This however was no evil to Elizabeth, and upon the whole she

---

1. I.e., at the back rather than at the front of the house, looking out on the lane.
2. Commissioned as justice of the peace, with the authority to judge and punish minor offend-
   ers.

spent her time comfortably enough; there were half hours of pleasant conversation with Charlotte, and the weather was so fine for the time of year, that she had often great enjoyment out of doors. Her favourite walk, and where she frequently went while the others were calling on Lady Catherine, was along the open grove which edged that side of the park, where there was a nice sheltered path, which no one seemed to value but herself, and where she felt beyond the reach of Lady Catherine's curiosity.

In this quiet way, the first fortnight of her visit soon passed away. Easter was approaching, and the week preceding it, was to bring an addition to the family at Rosings, which in so small a circle must be important. Elizabeth had heard soon after her arrival, that Mr. Darcy was expected there in the course of a few weeks, and though there were not many of her acquaintance whom she did not prefer, his coming would furnish one comparatively new to look at in their Rosings parties, and she might be amused in seeing how hopeless Miss Bingley's designs on him were, by his behaviour to his cousin, for whom he was evidently destined by Lady Catherine; who talked of his coming with the greatest satisfaction, spoke of him in terms of the highest admiration, and seemed almost angry to find that he had already been frequently seen by Miss Lucas and herself.

His arrival was soon known at the Parsonage, for Mr. Collins was walking the whole morning within view of the lodges opening into Hunsford Lane, in order to have the earliest assurance of it; and after making his bow as the carriage turned into the Park, hurried home with the great intelligence. On the following morning he hastened to Rosings to pay his respects. There were two nephews of Lady Catherine to require them, for Mr. Darcy had brought with him a Colonel Fitzwilliam, the younger son of his uncle, Lord —— and to the great surprise of all the party, when Mr. Collins returned the gentlemen accompanied him. Charlotte had seen them from her husband's room, crossing the road, and immediately running into the other, told the girls what an honour they might expect, adding.

"I may thank you, Eliza, for this piece of civility. Mr. Darcy would never have come so soon to wait upon me."

Elizabeth had scarcely time to disclaim all right to the compliment, before their approach was announced by the door-bell, and shortly afterwards the three gentlemen entered the room. Colonel Fitzwilliam, who led the way, was about thirty, not handsome, but in person and address most truly the gentleman. Mr. Darcy looked just as he had been used to look in Hertfordshire, paid his compliments, with his usual reserve, to Mrs. Collins; and whatever might be his feelings towards her friend, met her with every appearance of composure. Elizabeth merely curtseyed to him, without saying a word.

Colonel Fitzwilliam entered into conversation directly with the readiness and ease of a well-bred man, and talked very pleasantly; but his cousin, after having addressed a slight observation on the house and garden to Mrs. Collins, sat for some time without speaking to any body. At length, however, his civility was so far awakened as to enquire of Elizabeth after the health of her family. She answered him in the usual way, and after a moment's pause, added,

"My eldest sister has been in town these three months. Have you never happened to see her there?"

She was perfectly sensible that he never had; but she wished to see whether he would betray any consciousness of what had passed between the Bingleys and Jane; and she thought he looked a little confused as he answered that he had never been so fortunate as to meet Miss Bennet. The subject was pursued no farther, and the gentlemen soon afterwards went away.

Chapter VIII

Colonel Fitzwilliam's manners were very much admired at the parsonage, and the ladies all felt that he must add considerably to the pleasure of their engagements at Rosings. It was some days, however, before they received any invitation thither, for while there were visitors in the house, they could not be necessary; and it was not till Easter-day, almost a week after the gentlemen's arrival, that they were honoured by such an attention, and then they were merely asked on leaving church to come there in the evening. For the last week they had seen very little of either Lady Catherine or her daughter. Colonel Fitzwilliam had called at the parsonage more than once during the time, but Mr. Darcy they had only seen at church.

The invitation was accepted of course, and at a proper hour they joined the party in Lady Catherine's drawing room. Her ladyship received them civilly, but it was plain that their company was by no means so acceptable as when she could get nobody else; and she was, in fact, almost engrossed by her nephews, speaking to them, especially to Darcy, much more than to any other person in the room.

Colonel Fitzwilliam seemed really glad to see them; any thing was a welcome relief to him at Rosings; and Mrs. Collins's pretty friend had moreover caught his fancy very much. He now seated himself by her, and talked so agreeably of Kent and Hertfordshire, of travelling and staying at home, of new books and music, that Elizabeth had never been half so well entertained in that room before; and they conversed with so much spirit and flow, as to draw the attention of Lady Catherine herself, as well as of Mr. Darcy. *His* eyes had been soon and repeatedly turned towards them with a look of curiosity; and that her

ladyship after a while shared the feeling, was more openly acknowledged, for she did not scruple to call out,

"What is that you are saying, Fitzwilliam? What is it you are talking
of? What are you telling Miss Bennet? Let me hear what it is."

"We are speaking of music, Madam," said he, when no longer able
to avoid a reply.

"Of music! Then pray speak aloud. It is of all subjects my delight. I
must have my share in the conversation, if you are speaking of music.
There are few people in England, I suppose, who have more true enjoyment of music than myself, or a better natural taste. If I had ever learnt,
I should have been a great proficient. And so would Anne, if her health
had allowed her to apply. I am confident that she would have performed delightfully. How does Georgiana get on, Darcy?"

Mr. Darcy spoke with affectionate praise of his sister's proficiency.

"I am very glad to hear such a good account of her," said Lady
Catherine; "and pray tell her from me, that she cannot expect to excel,
if she does not practise a great deal."

"I assure you, Madam," he replied, "that she does not need such
advice. She practises very constantly."

"So much the better. It cannot be done too much; and when I next
write to her, I shall charge her not to neglect it on any account. I often
tell young ladies, that no excellence in music is to be acquired, without
constant practice. I have told Miss Bennet several times, that she will
never play really well, unless she practises more; and though Mrs. Collins has no instrument, she is very welcome, as I have often told her,
to come to Rosings every day, and play on the piano forte in Mrs.
Jenkinson's room. She would be in nobody's way, you know, in that
part of the house."

Mr. Darcy looked a little ashamed of his aunt's ill breeding, and
made no answer.

When coffee was over, Colonel Fitzwilliam reminded Elizabeth of
having promised to play to him; and she sat down directly to the instrument. He drew a chair near her. Lady Catherine listened to half a song,
and then talked, as before, to her other nephew; till the latter walked
away from her, and moving with his usual deliberation towards the
piano forte, stationed himself so as to command a full view of the fair
performer's countenance. Elizabeth saw what he was doing, and at the
first convenient pause, turned to him with an arch smile, and said,

"You mean to frighten me, Mr. Darcy, by coming in all this state to
hear me? But I will not be alarmed though your sister *does* play so well.
There is a stubbornness about me that never can bear to be frightened
at the will of others. My courage always rises with every attempt to
intimidate me."

"I shall not say that you are mistaken," he replied, "because you could not really believe me to entertain any design of alarming you; and I have had the pleasure of your acquaintance long enough to know, that you find great enjoyment in occasionally professing opinions which in fact are not your own."

Elizabeth laughed heartily at this picture of herself, and said to Colonel Fitzwilliam, "Your cousin will give you a very pretty notion of me, and teach you not to believe a word I say. I am particularly unlucky in meeting with a person so well able to expose my real character, in a part of the world, where I had hoped to pass myself off with some degree of credit. Indeed, Mr. Darcy, it is very ungenerous in you to mention all that you knew to my disadvantage in Hertfordshire—and, give me leave to say, very impolitic too—for it is provoking me to retaliate, and such things may come out, as will shock your relations to hear."

"I am not afraid of you," said he, smilingly.

"Pray let me hear what you have to accuse him of," cried Colonel Fitzwilliam. "I should like to know how he behaves among strangers."

"You shall hear then—but prepare yourself for something very dreadful. The first time of my ever seeing him in Hertfordshire, you must know, was at a ball—and at this ball, what do you think he did? He danced only four dances! I am sorry to pain you—but so it was. He danced only four dances, though gentlemen were scarce; and, to my certain knowledge, more than one young lady was sitting down in want of a partner. Mr. Darcy, you cannot deny the fact."

"I had not at that time the honour of knowing any lady in the assembly beyond my own party."

"True; and nobody can ever be introduced in a ball room. Well, Colonel Fitzwilliam, what do I play next? My fingers wait your orders."

"Perhaps," said Darcy, "I should have judged better, had I sought an introduction, but I am ill qualified to recommend myself to strangers."

"Shall we ask your cousin the reason of this?" said Elizabeth, still addressing Colonel Fitzwilliam. "Shall we ask him why a man of sense and education, and who has lived in the world, is ill qualified to recommend himself to strangers?"

"I can answer your question," said Fitzwilliam, "without applying to him. It is because he will not give himself the trouble."

"I certainly have not the talent which some people possess," said Darcy, "of conversing easily with those I have never seen before. I cannot catch their tone of conversation, or appear interested in their concerns, as I often see done."

"My fingers," said Elizabeth, "do not move over this instrument in the masterly manner which I see so many women's do. They have not the same force or rapidity, and do not produce the same expression. But then I have always supposed it to be my own fault—because I would not take the trouble of practising. It is not that I do not believe *my* fingers as capable as any other woman's of superior execution."

Darcy smiled and said, "You are perfectly right. You have employed your time much better. No one admitted to the privilege of hearing you, can think any thing wanting. We neither of us perform to strangers."

Here they were interrupted by Lady Catherine, who called out to know what they were talking of. Elizabeth immediately began playing again. Lady Catherine approached, and, after listening for a few minutes, said to Darcy,

"Miss Bennet would not play at all amiss, if she practised more, and could have the advantage of a London master. She has a very good notion of fingering, though her taste is not equal to Anne's. Anne would have been a delightful performer, had her health allowed her to learn."

Elizabeth looked at Darcy to see how cordially he assented to his cousin's praise; but neither at the moment nor at any other could she discern any symptom of love; and from the whole of his behaviour to Miss De Bourgh she derived this comfort for Miss Bingley, that he might have been just as likely to marry *her*, had she been his relation.

Lady Catherine continued her remarks on Elizabeth's performance, mixing with them many instructions on execution and taste. Elizabeth received them with all the forbearance of civility; and at the request of the gentlemen remained at the instrument till her Ladyship's carriage was ready to take them all home.

Chapter IX

Elizabeth was sitting by herself the next morning, and writing to Jane, while Mrs. Collins and Maria were gone on business into the village, when she was startled by a ring at the door, the certain signal of a visitor. As she had heard no carriage, she thought it not unlikely to be Lady Catherine, and under that apprehension was putting away her half-finished letter that she might escape all impertinent questions, when the door opened, and to her very great surprise, Mr. Darcy, and Mr. Darcy only, entered the room.

He seemed astonished too on finding her alone, and apologised for his intrusion, by letting her know that he had understood all the ladies to be within.

They then sat down, and when her enquiries after Rosings were made, seemed in danger of sinking into total silence. It was absolutely necessary, therefore, to think of something, and in this emergency recollecting *when* she had seen him last in Hertfordshire, and feeling curious to know what he would say on the subject of their hasty departure, she observed,

"How very suddenly you all quitted Netherfield last November, Mr. Darcy! It must have been a most agreeable surprise to Mr. Bingley to see you all after him so soon; for, if I recollect right, he went but the day before. He and his sisters were well, I hope, when you left London."

"Perfectly so—I thank you."

She found that she was to receive no other answer—and, after a short pause, added,

"I think I have understood that Mr. Bingley has not much idea of ever returning to Netherfield again?"

"I have never heard him say so; but it is probable that he may spend very little of his time there in future. He has many friends, and he is at a time of life when friends and engagements are continually increasing."

"If he means to be but little at Netherfield, it would be better for the neighbourhood that he should give up the place entirely, for then we might possibly get a settled family there. But perhaps Mr. Bingley did not take the house so much for the convenience of the neighbourhood as for his own, and we must expect him to keep or quit it on the same principle."

"I should not be surprised," said Darcy, "if he were to give it up, as soon as any eligible purchase offers."

Elizabeth made no answer. She was afraid of talking longer of his friend; and, having nothing else to say, was now determined to leave the trouble of finding a subject to him.

He took the hint, and soon began with, "This seems a very comfortable house. Lady Catherine, I believe, did a great deal to it when Mr. Collins first came to Hunsford."

"I believe she did—and I am sure she could not have bestowed her kindness on a more grateful object."

"Mr. Collins appears very fortunate in his choice of a wife."

"Yes, indeed; his friends may well rejoice in his having met with one of the very few sensible women who would have accepted him, or have made him happy if they had. My friend has an excellent understanding—though I am not certain that I consider her marrying Mr. Collins as the wisest thing she ever did. She seems perfectly happy, however, and in a prudential light, it is certainly a very good match for her."

"It must be very agreeable to her to be settled within so easy a distance of her own family and friends."

"An easy distance do you call it? It is nearly fifty miles."

"And what is fifty miles of good road? Little more than half a day's journey. Yes, I call it a *very* easy distance."

"I should never have considered the distance as one of the *advantages* of the match," cried Elizabeth. "I should never have said Mrs. Collins was settled *near* her family."

"It is a proof of your own attachment to Hertfordshire. Any thing beyond the very neighbourhood of Longbourn, I suppose, would appear far."

As he spoke there was a sort of smile, which Elizabeth fancied she understood; he must be supposing her to be thinking of Jane and Netherfield, and she blushed as she answered,

"I do not mean to say that a woman may not be settled too near her family. The far and the near must be relative, and depend on many varying circumstances. Where there is fortune to make the expence of travelling unimportant, distance becomes no evil. But that is not the case *here*. Mr. and Mrs. Collins have a comfortable income, but not such a one as will allow of frequent journeys—and I am persuaded my friend would not call herself *near* her family under less than *half* the present distance."

Mr. Darcy drew his chair a little towards her, and said, "*You* cannot have a right to such very strong local attachment. *You* cannot have been always at Longbourn."

Elizabeth looked surprised. The gentleman experienced some change of feeling; he drew back his chair, took a newspaper from the table, and, glancing over it, said, in a colder voice,

"Are you pleased with Kent?"

A short dialogue on the subject of the country ensued, on either side calm and concise—and soon put an end to by the entrance of Charlotte and her sister, just returned from their walk. The tête à tête surprised them. Mr. Darcy related the mistake which had occasioned his intruding on Miss Bennet, and after sitting a few minutes longer without saying much to any body, went away.

"What can be the meaning of this!" said Charlotte, as soon as he was gone. "My dear Eliza he must be in love with you, or he would never have called on us in this familiar way."

But when Elizabeth told of his silence, it did not seem very likely, even to Charlotte's wishes, to be the case; and after various conjectures, they could at last only suppose his visit to proceed from the difficulty of finding any thing to do, which was the more probable from the time of year. All field sports were over. Within doors there was Lady Catherine, books, and a billiard table, but gentlemen cannot be always within doors; and in the nearness of the Parsonage, or the pleasantness of the walk to it, or of the people who lived in it, the two cousins found a temptation from this period of walking thither almost every day. They called at various times of the morning, sometimes separately, sometimes together, and now and then accompanied by their aunt. It was plain to them all that Colonel Fitzwilliam came because he had pleasure in their society, a persuasion which of course recommended him still more; and Elizabeth was reminded by her own satisfaction in being with him, as well as by his evident admiration of her, of her former favourite George Wickham; and though, in comparing them, she saw there was less captivating softness in Colonel Fitzwilliam's manners, she believed he might have the best informed mind.

But why Mr. Darcy came so often to the Parsonage, it was more difficult to understand. It could not be for society, as he frequently sat there ten minutes together without opening his lips; and when he did speak, it seemed the effect of necessity rather than of choice—a sacrifice to propriety, not a pleasure to himself. He seldom appeared really animated. Mrs. Collins knew not what to make of him. Colonel Fitzwilliam's occasionally laughing at his stupidity, proved that he was generally different, which her own knowledge of him could not have told her; and as she would have liked to believe this change the effect of love, and the object of that love, her friend Eliza, she sat herself seriously to work to find it out.—She watched him whenever they were at Rosings, and whenever he came to Hunsford; but without much success. He certainly looked at her friend a great deal, but the expression of that look was disputable. It was an earnest, stedfast gaze, but she often doubted whether there were much admiration in it, and sometimes it seemed nothing but absence of mind.

She had once or twice suggested to Elizabeth the possibility of his being partial to her, but Elizabeth always laughed at the idea; and Mrs. Collins did not think it right to press the subject, from the danger of raising expectations which might only end in disappointment; for in her opinion it admitted not of a doubt, that all her friend's dislike would vanish, if she could suppose him to be in her power.

In her kind schemes for Elizabeth, she sometimes planned her marrying Colonel Fitzwilliam. He was beyond comparison the pleasantest man; he certainly admired her, and his situation in life was most eligible; but, to counterbalance these advantages, Mr. Darcy had considerable patronage in the church, and his cousin could have none at all.

Chapter X

More than once did Elizabeth in her ramble within the Park, unexpectedly meet Mr. Darcy.—She felt all the perverseness of the mischance that should bring him where no one else was brought; and to prevent its ever happening again, took care to inform him at first, that it was a favourite haunt of hers.—How it could occur a second time therefore was very odd!—Yet it did, and even a third. It seemed like wilful ill-nature, or a voluntary penance, for on these occasions it was not merely a few formal enquiries and an awkward pause and then away, but he actually thought it necessary to turn back and walk with her. He never said a great deal, nor did she give herself the trouble of talking or of listening much; but it struck her in the course of their third rencontre that he was asking some odd unconnected questions—about her pleasure in being at Hunsford, her love of solitary walks, and her opinion of Mr. and Mrs. Collins's happiness; and that in speaking of Rosings and her not perfectly understanding the house, he seemed to expect that whenever she came into Kent again she would be staying *there* too. His words seemed to imply it. Could he have Colonel Fitzwilliam in his thoughts? She supposed, if he meant any thing, he must mean an allusion to what might arise in that quarter. It distressed her a little, and she was quite glad to find herself at the gate in the pales opposite the Parsonage.

She was engaged one day as she walked, in re-perusing Jane's last letter, and dwelling on some passages which proved that Jane had not written in spirits, when, instead of being again surprised by Mr. Darcy, she saw on looking up that Colonel Fitzwilliam was meeting her. Putting away the letter immediately and forcing a smile, she said,

"I did not know before that you ever walked this way."

"I have been making the tour of the Park," he replied, "as I generally do every year, and intend to close it with a call at the Parsonage. Are you going much farther?"

"No, I should have turned in a moment."

And accordingly she did turn, and they walked towards the Parsonage together.

"Do you certainly leave Kent on Saturday?" said she.

"Yes—if Darcy does not put it off again. But I am at his disposal. He arranges the business just as he pleases."

"And if not able to please himself in the arrangement, he has at least great pleasure in the power of choice. I do not know any body who seems more to enjoy the power of doing what he likes than Mr. Darcy."

"He likes to have his own way very well," replied Colonel Fitzwilliam. "But so we all do. It is only that he has better means of having it than many others, because he is rich, and many others are poor. I speak feelingly. A younger son, you know, must be inured to self-denial and dependence."

"In my opinion, the younger son of an Earl can know very little of either. Now, seriously, what have you ever known of self-denial and dependence? When have you been prevented by want of money from going wherever you choose, or procuring any thing you had a fancy for?"

"These are home questions—and perhaps I cannot say that I have experienced many hardships of that nature. But in matters of greater weight, I may suffer from the want of money. Younger sons cannot marry where they like."

"Unless where they like women of fortune, which I think they very often do."

"Our habits of expence make us too dependant, and there are not many in my rank of life who can afford to marry without some attention to money."

"Is this," thought Elizabeth, "meant for me?" and she coloured at
the idea; but, recovering herself, said in a lively tone, "and pray, what
is the usual price of an Earl's younger son? Unless the elder brother is
very sickly, I suppose you would not ask above fifty thousand pounds."

He answered her in the same style, and the subject dropped. To
interrupt a silence which might make him fancy her affected with what
had passed, she soon afterwards said,

"I imagine your cousin brought you down with him chiefly for the
sake of having somebody at his disposal. I wonder he does not marry,
to secure a lasting convenience of that kind. But, perhaps his sister
does as well for the present, and, as she is under his sole care, he may
do what he likes with her."

"No," said Colonel Fitzwilliam, "that is an advantage which he must
divide with me. I am joined with him in the guardianship of Miss
Darcy."

"Are you, indeed? And pray what sort of guardians do you make?
Does your charge give you much trouble? Young ladies of her age, are
sometimes a little difficult to manage, and if she has the true Darcy
spirit, she may like to have her own way."

As she spoke, she observed him looking at her earnestly, and the
manner in which he immediately asked her why she supposed Miss
Darcy likely to give them any uneasiness, convinced her that she had
somehow or other got pretty near the truth. She directly replied,

"You need not be frightened. I never heard any harm of her; and I
dare say she is one of the most tractable creatures in the world. She is
a very great favourite with some ladies of my acquaintance, Mrs. Hurst
and Miss Bingley. I think I have heard you say that you know them."

"I know them a little. Their brother is a pleasant gentleman-like
man—he is a great friend of Darcy's."

"Oh! yes," said Elizabeth drily—"Mr. Darcy is uncommonly kind to
Mr. Bingley, and takes a prodigious deal of care of him."

"Care of him!—Yes, I really believe Darcy does take care of him in
those points where he most wants care. From something that he told
me in our journey hither, I have reason to think Bingley very much
indebted to him. But I ought to beg his pardon, for I have no right to
suppose that Bingley was the person meant. It was all conjecture."

"What is it you mean?"

"It is a circumstance which Darcy of course would not wish to be
generally known, because if it were to get round to the lady's family,
it would be an unpleasant thing."

"You may depend upon my not mentioning it."

"And remember that I have not much reason for supposing it to be
Bingley. What he told me was merely this; that he congratulated himself on having lately saved a friend from the inconveniences of a most
imprudent marriage, but without mentioning names or any other par-

ticulars, and I only suspected it to be Bingley from believing him the kind of young man to get into a scrape of that sort, and from knowing them to have been together the whole of last summer."

"Did Mr. Darcy give you his reasons for this interference?"

"I understood that there were some very strong objections against the lady."

"And what arts did he use to separate them?"

"He did not talk to me of his own arts," said Fitzwilliam smiling. "He only told me, what I have now told you."

Elizabeth made no answer, and walked on, her heart swelling with indignation. After watching her a little, Fitzwilliam asked her why she was so thoughtful.

"I am thinking of what you have been telling me," said she. "Your cousin's conduct does not suit my feelings. Why was he to be the judge?"

"You are rather disposed to call his interference officious?"

"I do not see what right Mr. Darcy had to decide on the propriety of his friend's inclination, or why, upon his own judgment alone, he was to determine and direct in what manner that friend was to be happy." "But," she continued, recollecting herself, "as we know none of the particulars, it is not fair to condemn him. It is not to be supposed that there was much affection in the case."

"That is not an unnatural surmise," said Fitzwilliam, "but it is lessening the honour of my cousin's triumph very sadly."

This was spoken jestingly, but it appeared to her so just a picture of Mr. Darcy, that she would not trust herself with an answer; and, therefore, abruptly changing the conversation, talked on indifferent matters till they reached the parsonage. There, shut into her own room, as soon as their visitor left them, she could think without interruption of all that she had heard. It was not to be supposed that any other people could be meant than those with whom she was connected. There could not exist in the world *two* men, over whom Mr. Darcy could have such boundless influence. That he had been concerned in the measures taken to separate Mr. Bingley and Jane, she had never doubted; but she had always attributed to Miss Bingley the principal design and arrangement of them. If his own vanity, however, did not mislead him, *he* was the cause, his pride and caprice were the cause of all that Jane had suffered, and still continued to suffer. He had ruined for a while every hope of happiness for the most affectionate, generous heart in the world; and no one could say how lasting an evil he might have inflicted.

"There were some very strong objections against the lady," were Colonel Fitzwilliam's words, and these strong objections probably were, her having one uncle who was a country attorney, and another who was in business in London.

"To Jane herself," she exclaimed, "there could be no possibility of objection. All loveliness and goodness as she is! Her understanding excellent, her mind improved, and her manners captivating. Neither could any thing be urged against my father, who, though with some peculiarities, has abilities which Mr. Darcy himself need not disdain, and respectability which he will probably never reach." When she thought of her mother indeed, her confidence gave way a little, but she would not allow that any objections *there* had material weight with Mr. Darcy, whose pride, she was convinced, would receive a deeper wound from the want of importance in his friend's connections, than from their want of sense; and she was quite decided at last, that he had been partly governed by this worst kind of pride, and partly by the wish of retaining Mr. Bingley for his sister.

The agitation and tears which the subject occasioned, brought on a head-ache; and it grew so much worse towards the evening that, added to her unwillingness to see Mr. Darcy, it determined her not to attend her cousins to Rosings, where they were engaged to drink tea. Mrs. Collins, seeing that she was really unwell, did not press her to go, and as much as possible prevented her husband from pressing her, but Mr. Collins could not conceal his apprehension of Lady Catherine's being rather displeased by her staying at home.

Chapter XI

When they were gone, Elizabeth, as if intending to exasperate herself as much as possible against Mr. Darcy, chose for her employment the examination of all the letters which Jane had written to her since her being in Kent. They contained no actual complaint, nor was there any revival of past occurrences, or any communication of present suffering. But in all, and in almost every line of each, there was a want of that cheerfulness which had been used to characterize her style, and which, proceding from the serenity of a mind at ease with itself, and kindly disposed towards every one, had been scarcely ever clouded. Elizabeth noticed every sentence conveying the idea of uneasiness, with an attention which it had hardly received on the first perusal. Mr. Darcy's shameful boast of what misery he had been able to inflict, gave her a keener sense of her sister's sufferings. It was some consolation to think that his visit to Rosings was to end on the day after the next, and a still greater, that in less than a fortnight she should herself be with Jane again, and enabled to contribute to the recovery of her spirits, by all that affection could do.

She could not think of Darcy's leaving Kent, without remembering that his cousin was to go with him; but Colonel Fitzwilliam had made it clear that he had no intentions at all, and agreeable as he was, she did not mean to be unhappy about him.

While settling this point, she was suddenly roused by the sound of the door bell, and her spirits were a little fluttered by the idea of its being Colonel Fitzwilliam himself, who had once before called late in the evening, and might now come to enquire particularly after her. But this idea was soon banished, and her spirits were very differently affected, when, to her utter amazement, she saw Mr. Darcy walk into the room. In an hurried manner he immediately began an enquiry after her health, imputing his visit to a wish of hearing that she were better. She answered him with cold civility. He sat down for a few moments, and then getting up walked about the room. Elizabeth was surprised, but said not a word. After a silence of several minutes he came towards her in an agitated manner, and thus began,

"In vain have I struggled. It will not do. My feelings will not be repressed. You must allow me to tell you how ardently I admire and love you."

Elizabeth's astonishment was beyond expression. She stared, coloured, doubted, and was silent. This he considered sufficient encouragement, and the avowal of all that he felt and had long felt for her, immediately followed. He spoke well, but there were feelings besides those of the heart to be detailed, and he was not more eloquent on the subject of tenderness than of pride. His sense of her inferiority— of its being a degradation—of the family obstacles which judgment had always opposed to inclination, were dwelt on with a warmth which seemed due to the consequence he was wounding, but was very unlikely to recommend his suit.

In spite of her deeply-rooted dislike, she could not be insensible to the compliment of such a man's affection, and though her intentions did not vary for an instant, she was at first sorry for the pain he was to receive; till, roused to resentment by his subsequent language, she lost all compassion in anger. She tried, however, to compose herself to answer him with patience, when he should have done. He concluded with representing to her the strength of that attachment which, in spite of all his endeavours, he had found impossible to conquer; and with expressing his hope that it would now be rewarded by her acceptance of his hand. As he said this, she could easily see that he had no doubt of a favourable answer. He *spoke* of apprehension and anxiety, but his countenance expressed real security. Such a circumstance could only exasperate farther, and when he ceased, the colour rose into her cheeks, and she said,

"In such cases as this, it is, I believe, the established mode to express a sense of obligation for the sentiments avowed, however unequally they may be returned. It is natural that obligation should be felt, and if I could *feel* gratitude, I would now thank you. But I cannot—I have never desired your good opinion, and you have certainly bestowed it most unwillingly. I am sorry to have occasioned pain to any one. It has been most unconsciously done, however, and I hope will be of short duration. The feelings which, you tell me, have long prevented the acknowledgment of your regard, can have little difficulty in overcoming it after this explanation."

Mr. Darcy, who was leaning against the mantle-piece with his eyes fixed on her face, seemed to catch her words with no less resentment than surprise. His complexion became pale with anger, and the disturbance of his mind was visible in every feature. He was struggling for the appearance of composure, and would not open his lips, till he believed himself to have attained it. The pause was to Elizabeth's feelings dreadful. At length, in a voice of forced calmness, he said,

"And this is all the reply which I am to have the honour of expecting! I might, perhaps, wish to be informed why, with so little *endeavour* at civility, I am thus rejected. But it is of small importance."

"I might as well enquire," replied she, "why with so evident a design of offending and insulting me, you chose to tell me that you liked me against your will, against your reason, and even against your character? Was not this some excuse for incivility, if I *was* uncivil? But I have other provocations. You know I have. Had not my own feelings decided against you, had they been indifferent, or had they even been favourable, do you think that any consideration would tempt me to accept the man, who has been the means of ruining, perhaps for ever, the happiness of a most beloved sister?"

As she pronounced these words, Mr. Darcy changed colour; but the emotion was short, and he listened without attempting to interrupt her while she continued.

"I have every reason in the world to think ill of you. No motive can excuse the unjust and ungenerous part you acted *there*. You dare not, you cannot deny that you have been the principal, if not the only means of dividing them from each other, of exposing one to the censure of the world for caprice and instability, the other to its derision for disappointed hopes, and involving them both in misery of the acutest kind."

She paused, and saw with no slight indignation that he was listening with an air which proved him wholly unmoved by any feeling of remorse. He even looked at her with a smile of affected incredulity.

"Can you deny that you have done it?" she repeated.

With assumed tranquillity he then replied, "I have no wish of denying that I did every thing in my power to separate my friend from your sister, or that I rejoice in my success. Towards *him* I have been kinder than towards myself."

Elizabeth disdained the appearance of noticing this civil reflection, but its meaning did not escape, nor was it likely to conciliate her.

"But it is not merely this affair," she continued, "on which my dislike is founded. Long before it had taken place, my opinion of you was decided. Your character was unfolded in the recital which I received many months ago from Mr. Wickham. On this subject, what can you have to say? In what imaginary act of friendship can you here defend yourself? or under what misrepresentation, can you here impose upon others?"

"You take an eager interest in that gentleman's concerns," said Darcy in a less tranquil tone, and with a heightened colour.

"Who that knows what his misfortunes have been, can help feeling an interest in him?"

"His misfortunes!" repeated Darcy contemptuously; "yes, his misfortunes have been great indeed."

"And of your infliction," cried Elizabeth with energy. "You have reduced him to his present state of poverty, comparative poverty. You have withheld the advantages, which you must know to have been designed for him. You have deprived the best years of his life, of that independence which was no less his due than his desert. You have done all this! and yet you can treat the mention of his misfortunes with contempt and ridicule."

"And this," cried Darcy, as he walked with quick steps across the room, "is your opinion of me! This is the estimation in which you hold me! I thank you for explaining it so fully. My faults, according to this calculation, are heavy indeed! But perhaps," added he, stopping in his walk, and turning towards her, "these offences might have been overlooked, had not your pride been hurt by my honest confession of the scruples that had long prevented my forming any serious design. These bitter accusations might have been suppressed, had I with greater policy concealed my struggles, and flattered you into the belief of my being impelled by unqualified, unalloyed inclination; by reason, by reflection, by every thing. But disguise of every sort is my abhorrence. Nor am I ashamed of the feelings I related. They were natural and just. Could you expect me to rejoice in the inferiority of your connections? To congratulate myself on the hope of relations, whose condition in life is so decidedly beneath my own?"

Elizabeth felt herself growing more angry every moment; yet she tried to the utmost to speak with composure when she said,

"You are mistaken, Mr. Darcy, if you suppose that the mode of your declaration affected me in any other way, than as it spared me the concern which I might have felt in refusing you, had you behaved in a more gentleman-like manner."

She saw him start at this, but he said nothing, and she continued,

"You could not have made me the offer of your hand in any possible way that would have tempted me to accept it."

Again his astonishment was obvious; and he looked at her with an expression of mingled incredulity and mortification. She went on.

"From the very beginning, from the first moment I may almost say, of my acquaintance with you, your manners impressing me with the fullest belief of your arrogance, your conceit, and your selfish disdain of the feelings of others, were such as to form that ground-work of disapprobation, on which succeeding events have built so immoveable a dislike; and I had not known you a month before I felt that you were the last man in the world whom I could ever be prevailed on to marry."

"You have said quite enough, madam. I perfectly comprehend your feelings, and have now only to be ashamed of what my own have been. Forgive me for having taken up so much of your time, and accept my best wishes for your health and happiness."

And with these words he hastily left the room, and Elizabeth heard him the next moment open the front door and quit the house.

The tumult of her mind was now painfully great. She knew not how to support herself, and from actual weakness sat down and cried for half an hour. Her astonishment, as she reflected on what had passed, was increased by every review of it. That she should receive an offer of marriage from Mr. Darcy! that he should have been in love with her for so many months! so much in love as to wish to marry her in spite of all the objections which had made him prevent his friend's marrying her sister, and which must appear at least with equal force in his own case, was almost incredible! it was gratifying to have inspired unconsciously so strong an affection. But his pride, his abominable pride, his shameless avowal of what he had done with respect to Jane, his unpardonable assurance in acknowledging, though he could not justify it, and the unfeeling manner in which he had mentioned Mr. Wickham, his cruelty towards whom he had not attempted to deny, soon overcame the pity which the consideration of his attachment had for a moment excited.

She continued in very agitating reflections till the sound of Lady Catherine's carriage made her feel how unequal she was to encounter Charlotte's observation, and hurried her away to her room.

Chapter XII

Elizabeth awoke the next morning to the same thoughts and meditations which had at length closed her eyes. She could not yet recover from the surprise of what had happened; it was impossible to think of any thing else, and totally indisposed for employment, she resolved soon after breakfast to indulge herself in air and exercise. She was proceeding directly to her favourite walk, when the recollection of Mr. Darcy's sometimes coming there stopped her, and instead of entering the park, she turned up the lane, which led her farther from the turnpike road. The park paling was still the boundary on one side, and she soon passed one of the gates into the ground.

After walking two or three times along that part of the lane, she was tempted, by the pleasantness of the morning, to stop at the gates and look into the park. The five weeks which she had now passed in Kent, had made a great difference in the country, and every day was adding to the verdure of the early trees. She was on the point of continuing her walk, when she caught a glimpse of a gentleman within the sort of grove which edged the park; he was moving that way; and fearful of its being Mr. Darcy, she was directly retreating. But the person who advanced, was now near enough to see her, and stepping forward with eagerness, pronounced her name. She had turned away, but on hearing herself called, though in a voice which proved it to be Mr. Darcy, she moved again towards the gate. He had by that time reached it also, and holding out a letter, which she instinctively took, said with a look of haughty composure, "I have been walking in the grove some time in the hope of meeting you. Will you do me the honour of reading that letter?"—And then, with a slight bow, turned again into the plan-tation,[3] and was soon out of sight.

With no expectation of pleasure, but with the strongest curiosity, Elizabeth opened the letter, and to her still increasing wonder, per-ceived an envelope containing two sheets of letter paper, written quite through, in a very close hand.—The envelope[4] itself was likewise full.—Pursuing her way along the lane, she then began it. It was dated from Rosings, at eight o'clock in the morning, and was as follows:—

"Be not alarmed, Madam, on receiving this letter, by the apprehen-sion of its containing any repetition of those sentiments, or renewal of those offers, which were last night so disgusting to you. I write without any intention of paining you, or humbling myself, by dwelling on wishes, which, for the happiness of both, cannot be too soon forgotten; and the effort which the formation, and the perusal of this letter must occasion, should have been spared, had not my character required it to be written and read. You must, therefore, pardon the freedom with which I demand your attention; your feelings, I know, will bestow it unwillingly, but I demand it of your justice.

"Two offences of a very different nature, and by no means of equal magnitude, you last night laid to my charge. The first mentioned was, that, regardless of the sentiments of either, I had detached Mr. Bingley from your sister,—and the other, that I had, in defiance of various claims, in defiance of honour and humanity, ruined the immediate prosperity, and blasted the prospects of Mr. Wickham.—Wilfully and wantonly to have thrown off the companion of my youth, the acknowl-edged favourite of my father, a young man who had scarcely any other dependence than on our patronage, and who had been brought up to expect its exertion, would be a depravity, to which the separation of

3. Wood of planted trees.
4. Darcy has enclosed the two pages of letter paper within another sheet of paper and written on this third sheet too.

two young persons, whose affection could be the growth of only a few weeks, could bear no comparison.—But from the severity of that blame which was last night so liberally bestowed, respecting each circumstance, I shall hope to be in future secured, when the following account of my actions and their motives has been read.—If, in the explanation of them which is due to myself, I am under the necessity of relating feelings which may be offensive to your's, I can only say that I am sorry.—The necessity must be obeyed—and farther apology would be absurd. I had not been long in Hertfordshire, before I saw, in common with others, that Bingley preferred your eldest sister, to any other young woman in the country.—But it was not till the evening of the dance at Netherfield that I had any apprehension of his feeling a serious attachment.—I had often seen him in love before.—At that ball, while I had the honour of dancing with you, I was first made acquainted, by Sir William Lucas's accidental information, that Bingley's attentions to your sister had given rise to a general expectation of their marriage. He spoke of it as a certain event, of which the time alone could be undecided. From that moment I observed my friend's behaviour attentively; and I could then perceive that his partiality for Miss Bennet was beyond what I had ever witnessed in him. Your sister I also watched.— Her look and manners were open, cheerful and engaging as ever, but without any symptom of peculiar regard, and I remained convinced from the evening's scrutiny, that though she received his attentions with pleasure, she did not invite them by any participation of sentiment.—If *you* have not been mistaken here, *I* must have been in an error. Your superior knowledge of your sister must make the latter probable.—If it be so, if I have been misled by such error, to inflict pain on her, your resentment has not been unreasonable. But I shall not scruple to assert, that the serenity of your sister's countenance and air was such, as might have given the most acute observer, a conviction that, however amiable her temper, her heart was not likely to be easily touched.—That I was desirous of believing her indifferent is certain,— but I will venture to say that my investigations and decisions are not usually influenced by my hopes or fears.—I did not believe her to be indifferent because I wished it;—I believed it on impartial conviction, as truly as I wished it in reason.—My objections to the marriage were not merely those, which I last night acknowledged to have required the utmost force of passion to put aside, in my own case; the want of connection could not be so great an evil to my friend as to me.—But there were other causes of repugnance;—causes which, though still existing, and existing to an equal degree in both instances, I had myself endeavoured to forget, because they were not immediately before me.—These causes must be stated, though briefly.—The situation of your mother's family, though objectionable, was nothing in comparison of that total want of propriety so frequently, so almost uniformly betrayed by herself, by your three younger sisters, and occasionally even by your father.—Pardon me.—It pains me to offend you. But amidst your concern for the defects of your nearest relations, and your displeasure at this representation of them, let it give you consolation to consider that, to have conducted yourselves so as to avoid any share of the like censure, is praise no less generally bestowed on you and your eldest sister, than it is honourable to the sense and disposition of both.—I will only say farther, that from what passed that evening, my opinion of all parties was confirmed, and every inducement heightened, which could have led me before, to preserve my friend from what I esteemed a most unhappy connection.—He left Netherfield for London, on the day following, as you, I am certain, remember, with the design of soon returning.—The part which I acted, is now to be explained.—His sisters' uneasiness had been equally excited with my own; our coincidence of feeling was soon discovered; and, alike sensible that no time was to be lost in detaching their brother, we shortly resolved on joining him directly in London.—We accordingly went— and there I readily engaged in the office of pointing out to my friend, the certain evils of such a choice.—I described, and enforced them earnestly.—But, however this remonstrance might have staggered or delayed his determination, I do not suppose that it would ultimately have prevented the marriage, had it not been seconded by the assurance which I hesitated not in giving, of your sister's indifference. He had before believed her to return his affection with sincere, if not with equal regard.—But Bingley has great natural modesty, with a stronger dependence on my judgment than on his own.—To convince him, therefore, that he had deceived himself, was no very difficult point. To persuade him against returning into Hertfordshire, when that conviction had been given, was scarcely the work of a moment.—I cannot blame myself for having done thus much. There is but one part of my conduct in the whole affair, on which I do not reflect with satisfaction; it is that I condescended to adopt the measures of art so far as to conceal from him your sister's being in town. I knew it myself, as it was known to Miss Bingley, but her brother is even yet ignorant of it.— That they might have met without ill consequence, is perhaps probable;—but his regard did not appear to me enough extinguished for him to see her without some danger.—Perhaps this concealment, this disguise, was beneath me.—It is done, however, and it was done for the best.—On this subject I have nothing more to say, no other apology to offer. If I have wounded your sister's feelings, it was unknowingly done; and though the motives which governed me may to you very naturally appear insufficient, I have not yet learnt to condemn them.— With respect to that other, more weighty accusation, of having injured Mr. Wickham, I can only refute it by laying before you the whole of his connection with my family. Of what he has *particularly* accused me

I am ignorant; but of the truth of what I shall relate, I can summon more than one witness of undoubted veracity. Mr. Wickham is the son of a very respectable man, who had for many years the management of all the Pemberley estates; and whose good conduct in the discharge of his trust, naturally inclined my father to be of service to him, and on George Wickham, who was his god-son, his kindness was therefore liberally bestowed. My father supported him at school, and afterwards at Cambridge;—most important assistance, as his own father, always poor from the extravagance of his wife, would have been unable to give him a gentleman's education. My father was not only fond of this young man's society, whose manners were always engaging; he had also the highest opinion of him, and hoping the church would be his profession, intended to provide for him in it. As for myself, it is many, many years since I first began to think of him in a very different manner. The vicious propensities—the want of principle which he was careful to guard from the knowledge of his best friend, could not escape the observation of a young man of nearly the same age with himself, and who had opportunities of seeing him in unguarded moments, which Mr. Darcy could not have. Here again I shall give you pain—to what degree you only can tell. But whatever may be the sentiments which Mr. Wickham has created, a suspicion of their nature shall not prevent me from unfolding his real character. It adds even another motive. My excellent father died about five years ago; and his attachment to Mr. Wickham was to the last so steady, that in his will he particularly recommended it to me, to promote his advancement in the best manner that his profession might allow, and if he took orders, desired that a valuable family living might be his as soon as it became vacant. There was also a legacy of one thousand pounds. His own father did not long survive mine, and within half a year from these events, Mr. Wickham wrote to inform me that, having finally resolved against taking orders, he hoped I should not think it unreasonable for him to expect some more immediate pecuniary advantage, in lieu of the preferment, by which he could not be benefited. He had some intention, he added, of studying the law, and I must be aware that the interest of one thousand pounds would be a very insufficient support therein. I rather wished, than believed him to be sincere; but at any rate, was perfectly ready to accede to his proposal. I knew that Mr. Wickham ought not to be a clergyman. The business was therefore soon settled. He resigned all claim to assistance in the church, were it possible that he could ever be in a situation to receive it, and accepted in return three thousand pounds. All connection between us seemed now dissolved. I thought too ill of him, to invite him to Pemberley, or admit his society in town. In town I believe he chiefly lived, but his studying the law was a mere pretence, and being now free from all restraint, his life was a life of idleness and dissipation. For about three years I heard little of him; but on the decease of the incumbent of the living which had been designed for him, he applied to me again by letter for the presentation. His circumstances, he assured me, and I had no difficulty in believing it, were exceedingly bad. He had found the law a most unprofitable study, and was now absolutely resolved on being ordained, if I would present him to the living in question—of which he trusted there could be little doubt, as he was well assured that I had no other person to provide for, and I could not have forgotten my revered father's intentions. You will hardly blame me for refusing to comply with this entreaty, or for resisting every repetition of it. His resentment was in proportion to the distress of his circumstances—and he was doubtless as violent in his abuse of me to others, as in his reproaches to myself. After this period, every appearance of acquaintance was dropt. How he lived I know not. But last summer he was again most painfully obtruded on my notice. I must now mention a circumstance which I would wish to forget myself, and which no obligation less than the present should induce me to unfold to any human being. Having said thus much, I feel no doubt of your secrecy. My sister, who is more than ten years my junior, was left to the guardianship of my mother's nephew, Colonel Fitzwilliam, and myself. About a year ago, she was taken from school, and an establishment formed for her in London; and last summer she went with the lady who presided over it, to Ramsgate; and thither also went Mr. Wickham, undoubtedly by design; for there proved to have been a prior acquaintance between him and Mrs. Younge, in whose character we were most unhappily deceived; and by her connivance and aid, he so far recommended himself to Georgiana, whose affectionate heart retained a strong impression of his kindness to her as a child, that she was persuaded to believe herself in love, and to consent to an elopement. She was then but fifteen, which must be her excuse; and after stating her imprudence, I am happy to add, that I owed the knowledge of it to herself. I joined them unexpectedly a day or two before the intended elopement, and then Georgiana, unable to support the idea of grieving and offending a brother whom she almost looked up to as a father, acknowledged the whole to me. You may imagine what I felt and how I acted. Regard for my sister's credit and feelings prevented any public exposure, but I wrote to Mr. Wickham, who left the place immediately, and Mrs. Younge was of course removed from her charge. Mr. Wickham's chief object was unquestionably my sister's fortune, which is thirty thousand pounds; but I cannot help supposing that the hope of revenging himself on me, was a strong inducement. His revenge would have been complete indeed. This, madam, is a faithful narrative of every event in which we have been concerned together; and if you do not absolutely reject it as false, you will, I hope, acquit me henceforth of cruelty towards Mr. Wickham. I know not in what manner, under what form of falsehood he has imposed on you; but his success is not perhaps to be wondered at, ignorant as you previously were of every thing concerning either. Detection could not be in your power, and suspicion certainly not in your inclination.[5] You may possibly wonder why all this was not told you last night. But I was not then master enough of myself to know what could or ought to be revealed. For the truth of every thing here related, I can appeal more particularly to the testimony of Colonel Fitzwilliam, who from our near relationship and constant intimacy, and still more as one of the executors of my father's will, has been unavoidably acquainted with every particular of these transactions. If your abhorrence of *me* should make *my* assertions valueless, you cannot be prevented by the same cause from confiding in my cousin; and that there may be the possibility of consulting him, I shall endeavour to find some opportunity of putting this letter in your hands in the course of the morning. I will only add, God bless you.

"FITZWILLIAM DARCY"

Chapter XIII

If Elizabeth, when Mr. Darcy gave her the letter, did not expect it to contain a renewal of his offers, she had formed no expectation at all of its contents. But such as they were, it may well be supposed how eagerly she went through them, and what a contrariety of emotion they excited. Her feelings as she read were scarcely to be defined. With amazement did she first understand that he believed any apology to be in his power; and stedfastly was she persuaded that he could have no explanation to give, which a just sense of shame would not conceal. With a strong prejudice against every thing he might say, she began his account of what had happened at Netherfield. She read, with an eagerness which hardly left her power of comprehension, and from impatience of knowing what the next sentence might bring, was incapable of attending to the sense of the one before her eyes. His belief of her sister's insensibility, she instantly resolved to be false, and his account of the real, the worst objections to the match, made her too angry to have any wish of doing him justice. He expressed no regret for what he had done which satisfied her; his style was not penitent, but haughty. It was all pride and insolence.

But when this subject was succeeded by his account of Mr. Wickham, when she read with somewhat clearer attention, a relation of events, which, if true, must overthrow every cherished opinion of his worth, and which bore so alarming an affinity to his own history of

---

5. In his edition of the novel R. W. Chapman emends this passage to read: "but his success is not to be wondered at. Ignorant as you previously were of everything concerning either, detection could not be in your power . . ." (*The Novels of Jane Austen*, 3rd ed. [Oxford, 1932–34] 2:293.

himself, her feelings were yet more acutely painful and more difficult of definition. Astonishment, apprehension, and even horror, oppressed her. She wished to discredit it entirely, repeatedly exclaiming, "This must be false! This cannot be! This must be the grossest falsehood!"— and when she had gone through the whole letter, though scarcely knowing any thing of the last page or two, put it hastily away, protesting that she would not regard it, that she would never look in it again.

In this perturbed state of mind, with thoughts that could rest on nothing, she walked on; but it would not do; in half a minute the letter was unfolded again, and collecting herself as well as she could, she again began the mortifying perusal of all that related to Wickham, and commanded herself so far as to examine the meaning of every sentence. The account of his connection with the Pemberley family, was exactly what he had related himself; and the kindness of the late Mr. Darcy, though she had not before known its extent, agreed equally well with his own words. So far each recital confirmed the other: but when she came to the will, the difference was great. What Wickham had said of the living was fresh in her memory, and as she recalled his very words, it was impossible not to feel that there was gross duplicity on one side or the other; and, for a few moments, she flattered herself that her wishes did not err. But when she read, and re-read with the closest attention, the particulars immediately following of Wickham's resigning all pretensions to the living, of his receiving in lieu, so considerable a sum as three thousand pounds, again was she forced to hesitate. She put down the letter, weighed every circumstance with what she meant to be impartiality—deliberated on the probability of each statement— but with little success. On both sides it was only assertion. Again she read on. But every line proved more clearly that the affair, which she had believed it impossible that any contrivance could so represent, as to render Mr. Darcy's conduct in it less than infamous, was capable of a turn which must make him entirely blameless throughout the whole.

The extravagance and general profligacy which he scrupled not to lay to Mr. Wickham's charge, exceedingly shocked her; the more so, as she could bring no proof of its injustice. She had never heard of him before his entrance into the ——shire Militia, in which he had engaged at the persuasion of the young man, who, on meeting him accidentally in town, had there renewed a slight acquaintance. Of his former way of life, nothing had been known in Hertfordshire but what he told himself. As to his real character, had information been in her power, she had never felt a wish of enquiring. His countenance, voice, and manner, had established him at once in the possession of every virtue. She tried to recollect some instance of goodness, some distinguished trait of integrity or benevolence, that might rescue him from the attacks of Mr. Darcy; or at least, by the predominance of virtue, atone for those casual errors, under which she would endeavour to class, what

Mr. Darcy had described as the idleness and vice of many years continuance. But no such recollection befriended her. She could see him instantly before her, in every charm of air and address; but she could remember no more substantial good than the general approbation of the neighbourhood, and the regard which his social powers had gained him in the mess. After pausing on this point a considerable while, she once more continued to read. But, alas! the story which followed of his designs on Miss Darcy, received some confirmation from what had passed between Colonel Fitzwilliam and herself only the morning before; and at last she was referred for the truth of every particular to Colonel Fitzwilliam himself—from whom she had previously received the information of his near concern in all his cousin's affairs, and whose character she had no reason to question. At one time she had almost resolved on applying to him, but the idea was checked by the awkwardness of the application, and at length wholly banished by the conviction that Mr. Darcy would never have hazarded such a proposal, if he had not been well assured of his cousin's corroboration.

She perfectly remembered every thing that had passed in conversation between Wickham and herself, in their first evening at Mr. Philips's. Many of his expressions were still fresh in her memory. She was *now* struck with the impropriety of such communications to a stranger, and wondered it had escaped her before. She saw the indelicacy of putting himself forward as he had done, and the inconsistency of his professions with his conduct. She remembered that he had boasted of having no fear of seeing Mr. Darcy—that Mr. Darcy might leave the country, but that *he* should stand his ground; yet he had avoided the Netherfield ball the very next week. She remembered also, that till the Netherfield family had quitted the country, he had told his story to no one but herself; but that after their removal, it had been every where discussed; that he had then no reserves, no scruples in sinking Mr. Darcy's character, though he had assured her that respect for the father, would always prevent his exposing the son.

How differently did every thing now appear in which he was concerned! His attentions to Miss King were now the consequence of views solely and hatefully mercenary; and the mediocrity of her fortune proved no longer the moderation of his wishes, but his eagerness to grasp at any thing. His behaviour to herself could now have had no tolerable motive; he had either been deceived with regard to her fortune, or had been gratifying his vanity by encouraging the preference which she believed she had most incautiously shewn. Every lingering struggle in his favour grew fainter and fainter; and in farther justification of Mr. Darcy, she could not but allow that Mr. Bingley, when questioned by Jane, had long ago asserted his blamelessness in the affair; that proud and repulsive as were his manners, she had never, in the whole course of their acquaintance, an acquaintance which had latterly brought them much together, and given her a sort of intimacy with his ways, seen any thing that betrayed him to be unprincipled or unjust—any thing that spoke him of irreligious or immoral habits. That among his own connections he was esteemed and valued—that even Wickham had allowed him merit as a brother, and that she had often heard him speak so affectionately of his sister as to prove him capable of *some* amiable feeling. That had his actions been what Wickham represented them, so gross a violation of every thing right could hardly have been concealed from the world; and that friendship between a person capable of it, and such an amiable man as Mr. Bingley, was incomprehensible.

She grew absolutely ashamed of herself.—Of neither Darcy nor Wickham could she think, without feeling that she had been blind, partial, prejudiced, absurd.

"How despicably have I acted!" she cried.—"I, who have prided myself on my discernment!—I, who have valued myself on my abilities! who have often disdained the generous candour of my sister, and gratified my vanity, in useless or blameable distrust.—How humiliating is this discovery!—Yet, how just a humiliation!—Had I been in love, I could not have been more wretchedly blind. But vanity, not love, has been my folly.—Pleased with the preference of one, and offended by the neglect of the other, on the very beginning of our acquaintance, I have courted prepossession and ignorance, and driven reason away, where either were concerned. Till this moment, I never knew myself."

From herself to Jane—from Jane to Bingley, her thoughts were in a line which soon brought to her recollection that Mr. Darcy's explanation *there*, had appeared very insufficient; and she read it again. Widely different was the effect of a second perusal.—How could she deny that credit to his assertions, in one instance, which she had been obliged to give in the other?—He declared himself to have been totally unsuspicious of her sister's attachment;—and she could not help remembering what Charlotte's opinion had always been.—Neither could she deny the justice of his description of Jane.—She felt that Jane's feelings, though fervent, were little displayed, and that there was a constant complacency in her air and manner, not often united with great sensibility.

When she came to that part of the letter, in which her family were mentioned, in terms of such mortifying, yet merited reproach, her sense of shame was severe. The justice of the charge struck her too forcibly for denial, and the circumstances to which he particularly alluded, as having passed at the Netherfield ball, and as confirming all his first disapprobation, could not have made a stronger impression on his mind than on hers.

The compliment to herself and her sister, was not unfelt. It soothed, but it could not console her for the contempt which had been thus self-attracted by the rest of her family;—and as she considered that Jane's disappointment had in fact been the work of her nearest relations, and reflected how materially the credit of both must be hurt by such impropriety of conduct, she felt depressed beyond any thing she had ever known before.

After wandering along the lane for two hours, giving way to every variety of thought; re-considering events, determining probabilities, and reconciling herself as well as she could, to a change so sudden and so important, fatigue, and a recollection of her long absence, made her at length return home; and she entered the house with the wish of appearing cheerful as usual, and the resolution of repressing such reflections as must make her unfit for conversation.

She was immediately told, that the two gentlemen from Rosings had each called during her absence; Mr. Darcy, only for a few minutes to take leave, but that Colonel Fitzwilliam had been sitting with them at least an hour, hoping for her return, and almost resolving to walk after her till she could be found.—Elizabeth could but just *affect* concern in missing him; she really rejoiced at it. Colonel Fitzwilliam was no longer an object. She could think only of her letter.

Chapter XIV

The two gentlemen left Rosings the next morning; and Mr. Collins having been in waiting near the lodges, to make them his parting obeisance, was able to bring home the pleasing intelligence, of their appearing in very good health, and in as tolerable spirits as could be expected, after the melancholy scene so lately gone through at Rosings. To Rosings he then hastened to console Lady Catherine, and her daughter; and on his return, brought back, with great satisfaction, a message from her Ladyship, importing that she felt herself so dull as to make her very desirous of having them all to dine with her.

Elizabeth could not see Lady Catherine without recollecting, that had she chosen it, she might by this time have been presented to her, as her future niece; nor could she think, without a smile, of what her ladyship's indignation would have been. "What would she have said?— how would she have behaved?" were questions with which she amused herself.

Their first subject was the diminution of the Rosings party.—"I assure you, I feel it exceedingly," said Lady Catherine; "I believe nobody feels the loss of friends so much as I do. But I am particularly attached to these young men; and know them to be so much attached to me!—They were excessively sorry to go! But so they always are. The dear colonel rallied his spirits tolerably till just at last; but Darcy seemed to feel it most acutely, more I think than last year. His attachment to Rosings, certainly increases."

Mr. Collins had a compliment, and an allusion to throw in here, which were kindly smiled on by the mother and daughter.

Lady Catherine observed, after dinner, that Miss Bennet seemed out of spirits, and immediately accounting for it herself, by supposing that she did not like to go home again so soon, she added,

"But if that is the case, you must write to your mother to beg that you may stay a little longer. Mrs. Collins will be very glad of your company, I am sure."

"I am much obliged to your ladyship for your kind invitation," replied Elizabeth, "but it is not in my power to accept it.—I must be in town next Saturday."

"Why, at that rate, you will have been here only six weeks. I expected you to stay two months. I told Mrs. Collins so before you came. There can be no occasion for your going so soon. Mrs. Bennet could certainly spare you for another fortnight."

"But my father cannot.—He wrote last week to hurry my return."

"Oh! your father of course may spare you, if your mother can.— Daughters are never of so much consequence to a father. And if you will stay another *month* complete, it will be in my power to take one of you as far as London, for I am going there early in June, for a week; and as Dawson does not object to the Barouche box,[6] there will be very good room for one of you—and indeed, if the weather should happen to be cool, I should not object to taking you both, as you are neither of you large."

"You are all kindness, Madam; but I believe we must abide by our original plan."

Lady Catherine seemed resigned.—

"Mrs. Collins, you must send a servant with them. You know I always speak my mind, and I cannot bear the idea of two young women travelling post[7] by themselves. It is highly improper. You must contrive to send somebody. I have the greatest dislike in the world to that sort of thing.—Young women should always be properly guarded and attended, according to their situation in life. When my niece Georgiana went to Ramsgate last summer, I made a point of her having two men servants go with her.—Miss Darcy, the daughter of Mr. Darcy, of Pemberley, and Lady Anne, could not have appeared with propriety in a different manner.—I am excessively attentive to all those things. You must send John with the young ladies, Mrs. Collins. I am glad it occurred to me to mention it; for it would really be discreditable to *you* to let them go alone."

"My uncle is to send a servant for us."

"Oh!—Your uncle!—He keeps a man-servant, does he?—I am very

6. That is, the servant Dawson does not object to riding on the outside of the barouche, a large carriage with a convertible top.
7. Traveling by carriage and hiring horses at stages of the journey.

glad you have somebody who thinks of those things. Where shall you change horses?—Oh! Bromley, of course.—If you mention my name at the Bell, you will be attended to."

Lady Catherine had many other questions to ask respecting their journey, and as she did not answer them all herself, attention was necessary, which Elizabeth believed to be lucky for her; or, with a mind so occupied, she might have forgotten where she was. Reflection must be reserved for solitary hours; whenever she was alone, she gave way to it as the greatest relief; and not a day went by without a solitary walk, in which she might indulge in all the delight of unpleasant recollections.

Mr. Darcy's letter, she was in a fair way of soon knowing by heart. She studied every sentence: and her feelings towards its writer were at times widely different. When she remembered the style of his address, she was still full of indignation; but when she considered how unjustly she had condemned and upbraided him, her anger was turned against herself; and his disappointed feelings became the object of compassion. His attachment excited gratitude, his general character respect; but she could not approve him; nor could she for a moment repent her refusal, or feel the slightest inclination ever to see him again. In her own past behaviour, there was a constant source of vexation and regret; and in the unhappy defects of her family a subject of yet heavier chagrin. They were hopeless of remedy. Her father, contented with laughing at them, would never exert himself to restrain the wild giddiness of his youngest daughters; and her mother, with manner so far from right herself, was entirely insensible of the evil. Elizabeth had frequently united with Jane in an endeavour to check the imprudence of Catherine and Lydia; but while they were supported by their mother's indulgence, what chance could there be of improvement? Catherine, weak-spirited, irritable, and completely under Lydia's guidance, had been always affronted by their advice; and Lydia, self-willed and careless, would scarcely give them a hearing. They were ignorant, idle, and vain. While there was an officer in Meryton, they would flirt with him; and while Meryton was within a walk of Longbourn, they would be going there for ever.

Anxiety on Jane's behalf, was another prevailing concern, and Mr. Darcy's explanation, by restoring Bingley to all her former good opinion, heightened the sense of what Jane had lost. His affection was proved to have been sincere, and his conduct cleared of all blame, unless any could attach to the implicitness of his confidence in his friend. How grievous then was the thought that, of a situation so desirable in every respect, so replete with advantage, so promising for happiness, Jane had been deprived, by the folly and indecorum of her own family!

When to these recollections was added the developement of Wickham's character, it may be easily believed that the happy spirits which had seldom been depressed before, were now so much affected as to make it almost impossible for her to appear tolerably cheerful.

Their engagements at Rosings were as frequent during the last week of her stay, as they had been at first. The very last evening was spent there; and her Ladyship again enquired minutely into the particulars of their journey, gave them directions as to the best method of packing, and was so urgent on the necessity of placing gowns in the only right way, that Maria thought herself obliged, on her return, to undo all the work of the morning, and pack her trunk afresh.

When they parted, Lady Catherine, with great condescension, wished them a good journey, and invited them to come to Hunsford again next year; and Miss De Bourgh exerted herself so far as to curtsey and hold our her hand to both.

Chapter XV

On Saturday morning Elizabeth and Mr. Collins met for breakfast a few minutes before the others appeared; and he took the opportunity of paying the parting civilities which he deemed indispensably necessary.

"I know not, Miss Elizabeth," said he, "whether Mrs. Collins has yet expressed her sense of your kindness in coming to us, but I am very certain you will not leave the house without receiving her thanks for it. The favour of your company has been much felt, I assure you. We know how little there is to tempt any one to our humble abode. Our plain manner of living, our small rooms, and few domestics, and the little we see of the world, must make Hunsford extremely dull to a young lady like yourself; but I hope you will believe us grateful for the condescension, and that we have done everything in our power to prevent your spending your time unpleasantly."

Elizabeth was eager with her thanks and assurances of happiness. She had spent six weeks with great enjoyment; and the pleasure of being with Charlotte, and the kind attentions she had received, must make *her* feel the obliged. Mr. Collins was gratified; and with a more smiling solemnity replied,

"It gives me the greatest pleasure to hear that you have passed your time not disagreeably. We have certainly done our best; and most fortunately having it in our power to introduce you to very superior society, and from our connections with Rosings, the frequent means of varying the humble home scene, I think we may flatter ourselves that your Hunsford visit cannot have been entirely irksome. Our situation with regard to Lady Catherine's family is indeed the sort of extraordinary advantage and blessing which few can boast. You see on what a footing we are. You see how continually we are engaged there.

In truth I must acknowledge that, with all the disadvantages of this humble parsonage, I should not think any one abiding in it an object of compassion, while they are sharers of our intimacy at Rosings."

Words were insufficient for the elevation of his feelings; and he was obliged to walk about the room, while Elizabeth tried to unite civility and truth in a few short sentences.

"You may, in fact, carry a very favourable report of us into Hertfordshire, my dear cousin. I flatter myself at least that you will be able to do so. Lady Catherine's great attentions to Mrs. Collins you have been a daily witness of; and altogether I trust it does not appear that your friend has drawn an unfortunate—but on this point it will be as well to be silent. Only let me assure you, my dear Miss Elizabeth, that I can from my heart most cordially wish you equal felicity in marriage. My dear Charlotte and I have but one mind and one way of thinking. There is in every thing a most remarkable resemblance of character and ideas between us. We seem to have been designed for each other."

Elizabeth could safely say that it was a great happiness where that was the case, and with equal sincerity could add that she firmly believed and rejoiced in his domestic comforts. She was not sorry, however, to have the recital of them interrupted by the entrance of the lady from whom they sprung. Poor Charlotte!—it was melancholy to leave her to such society!—But she had chosen it with her eyes open; and though evidently regretting that her visitors were to go, she did not seem to ask for compassion. Her home and her housekeeping, her parish and her poultry, and all their dependent concerns, had not yet lost their charms.

At length the chaise arrived, the trunks were fastened on, the parcels placed within, and it was pronounced to be ready. After an affectionate parting between the friends, Elizabeth was attended to the carriage by Mr. Collins, and as they walked down the garden, he was commissioning her with his best respects to all her family, not forgetting his thanks for the kindness he had received at Longbourn in the winter, and his compliments to Mr. and Mrs. Gardiner, though unknown. He then handed her in, Maria followed, and the door was on the point of being closed, when he suddenly reminded them, with some consternation, that they had hitherto forgotten to leave any message for the ladies of Rosings.

"But," he added, "you will of course wish to have your humble respects delivered to them, with your grateful thanks for their kindness to you while you have been here."

Elizabeth made no objection;—the door was then allowed to be shut, and the carriage drove off.

"Good gracious!" cried Maria, after a few minutes silence, "it seems but a day or two since we first came!—and yet how many things have happened!"

"A great many indeed," said her companion with a sigh.

"We have dined nine times at Rosings, besides drinking tea there twice!—How much I shall have to tell!"[8]

Elizabeth privately added, "and how much I shall have to conceal."

Their journey was performed without much conversation, or any alarm; and within four hours of their leaving Hunsford, they reached Mr. Gardiner's house, where they were to remain a few days.

Jane looked well, and Elizabeth had little opportunity of studying her spirits, amidst the various engagements which the kindness of her aunt had reserved for them. But Jane was to go home with her, and at Longbourn there would be leisure enough for observation.

It was not without an effort meanwhile that she could wait even for Longbourn, before she told her sister of Mr. Darcy's proposals. To know that she had the power of revealing what would so exceedingly astonish Jane, and must, at the same time, so highly gratify whatever of her own vanity she had not yet been able to reason away, was such a temptation to openness as nothing could have conquered, but the state of indecision in which she remained, as to the extent of what she should communicate; and her fear, if she once entered on the subject, of being hurried into repeating something of Bingley, which might only grieve her sister farther.

Chapter XVI

It was the second week in May, in which the three young ladies set out together from Gracechurch-street, for the town of —— in Hertfordshire; and, as they drew near the appointed inn where Mr. Bennet's carriage was to meet them, they quickly perceived, in token of the coachman's punctuality, both Kitty and Lydia looking out of a dining room up stairs. These two girls had been above an hour in the place, happily employed in visiting an opposite milliner, watching the sentinel on guard, and dressing a sallad and cucumber.

After welcoming their sisters, they triumphantly displayed a table set out with such cold meat as an inn larder usually affords, exclaiming, "Is not this nice? is not this an agreeable surprise?"

"And we mean to treat you all," added Lydia; "but you must lend us the money, for we have just spent ours at the shop out there." Then shewing her purchases: "Look here, I have bought this bonnet. I do not think it is very pretty; but I thought I might as well buy it as not. I shall put it to pieces as soon as I get home, and see if I can make it up any better."

And when her sisters abused it as ugly, she added, with perfect unconcern, "Oh! but there were two or three much uglier in the shop;

8. In the 1813 edition this passage is mistakenly set without a paragraph break after "with a sigh," so that the speech appears to be Elizabeth's rather than Maria's.

and when I have bought some prettier-coloured satin to trim it with fresh, I think it will be very tolerable. Besides, it will not much signify what one wears this summer, after the —— shire have left Meryton, and they are going in a fortnight."

"Are they indeed?" cried Elizabeth, with the greatest satisfaction.

"They are going to be encamped near Brighton; and I do so want papa to take us all there for the summer! It would be such a delicious scheme, and I dare say would hardly cost any thing at all. Mamma would like to go too of all things! Only think what a miserable summer else we shall have!"

"Yes," thought Elizabeth, "*that* would be a delightful scheme, indeed, and completely do for us at once. Good Heaven! Brighton, and a whole campful of soldiers, to us, who have been overset already by one poor regiment of militia, and the monthly balls of Meryton."

"Now I have got some news for you," said Lydia, as they sat down to table. "What do you think? It is excellent news, capital news, and about a certain person that we all like."

Jane and Elizabeth looked at each other, and the waiter was told that he need not stay. Lydia laughed, and said,

"Aye, that is just like your formality and discretion. You thought the waiter must not hear, as if he cared! I dare say he often hears worse things said than I am going to say. But he is an ugly fellow! I am glad he is gone. I never saw such a long chin in my life. Well, but now for my news: it is about dear Wickham; too good for the waiter, is it not? There is no danger of Wickham's marrying Mary King. There's for you! She is gone down to her uncle at Liverpool; gone to stay. Wickham is safe."

"And Mary King is safe!" added Elizabeth; "safe from a connection imprudent as to fortune."

"She is a great fool for going away, if she liked him."

"But I hope there is no strong attachment on either side," said Jane.

"I am sure there is not on *his*. I will answer for it he never cared three straws about her. Who *could* about such a nasty little freckled thing?"

Elizabeth was shocked to think that, however incapable of such coarseness of *expression* herself, the coarseness of the *sentiment* was little other than her own breast had formerly harboured and fancied liberal!

As soon as all had ate, and the elder ones paid, the carriage was ordered; and after some contrivance, the whole party, with all their boxes, work-bags, and parcels, and the unwelcome addition of Kitty's and Lydia's purchases, were seated in it.

"How nicely we are crammed in!" cried Lydia. "I am glad I bought my bonnet, if it is only for the fun of having another bandbox! Well, now let us be quite comfortable and snug, and talk and laugh all the way home. And in the first place, let us hear what has happened to you all, since you went away. Have you seen any pleasant men? Have you had any flirting? I was in great hopes that one of you would have got a husband before you came back. Jane will be quite an old maid soon, I declare. She is almost three and twenty! Lord, how ashamed I should be of not being married before three and twenty! My aunt Philips wants you so to get husbands, you can't think. She says Lizzy had better have taken Mr. Collins; but *I* do not think there would have been any fun in it. Lord! how I should like to be married before any of you; and then I would chaperon you about to all the balls. Dear me! we had such a good piece of fun the other day at Colonel Forster's. Kitty and me were to spend the day there, and Mrs. Forster promised to have a little dance in the evening; (by the bye, Mrs. Forster and me are *such* friends!) and so she asked the two Harringtons to come, but Harriet was ill, and so Pen was forced to come by herself; and then, what do you think we did? We dressed up Chamberlayne in woman's clothes, on purpose to pass for a lady,—only think what fun! Not a soul knew of it, but Col. and Mrs. Forster, and Kitty and me, except my aunt, for we were forced to borrow one of her gowns; and you cannot imagine how well he looked! When Denny, and Wickham, and Pratt, and two or three more of the men came in, they did not know him in the least. Lord! how I laughed! and so did Mrs. Forster. I thought I should have died. And *that* made the men suspect something, and then they soon found out what was the matter."

With such kind of histories of their parties and good jokes, did Lydia, assisted by Kitty's hints and additions, endeavour to amuse her companions all the way to Longbourn. Elizabeth listened as little as she could, but there was no escaping the frequent mention of Wickham's name.

Their reception at home was most kind. Mrs. Bennet rejoiced to see Jane in undiminished beauty; and more than once during dinner did Mr. Bennet say voluntarily to Elizabeth,

"I am glad you are come back, Lizzy."

Their party in the dining-room was large, for almost all the Lucases came to meet Maria and hear the news: and various were the subjects which occupied them; lady Lucas was enquiring of Maria across the table, after the welfare and poultry of her eldest daughter; Mrs. Bennet was doubly engaged, on one hand collecting an account of the present fashions from Jane, who sat some way below her, and on the other, retailing them all to the younger Miss Lucases; and Lydia, in a voice rather louder than any other person's, was enumerating the various pleasures of the morning to any body who would hear her.

"Oh! Mary," said she, "I wish you had gone with us, for we had such fun! as we went along, Kitty and me drew up all the blinds, and pretended there was nobody in the coach; and I should have gone so all the way, if Kitty had not been sick; and when we got to the George, I do think we behaved very handsomely, for we treated the other three with the nicest cold luncheon in the world, and if you would have gone, we would have treated you too. And then when we came away it was such fun! I thought we never should have got into the coach. I was ready to die of laughter. And then we were so merry all the way home! we talked and laughed so loud, that any body might have heard us ten miles off!"

To this, Mary very gravely replied, "Far be it from me, my dear sister, to deprecate such pleasures. They would doubtless be congenial with the generality of female minds. But I confess they would have no charms for *me*. I should infinitely prefer a book."

But of this answer Lydia heard not a word. She seldom listened to any body for more than half a minute, and never attended to Mary at all.

In the afternoon Lydia was urgent with the rest of the girls to walk to Meryton and see how every body went on; but Elizabeth steadily opposed the scheme. It should not be said, that the Miss Bennets could not be at home half a day before they were in pursuit of the officers. There was another reason too for her opposition. She dreaded seeing Wickham again, and was resolved to avoid it as long as possible. The comfort to *her*, of the regiment's approaching removal, was indeed beyond expression. In a fortnight they were to go, and once gone, she hoped there could be nothing more to plague her on his account.

She had not been many hours at home, before she found that the Brighton scheme, of which Lydia had given them a hint at the inn, was under frequent discussion between her parents. Elizabeth saw directly that her father had not the smallest intention of yielding; but his answers were at the same time so vague and equivocal, that her mother, though often disheartened, had never yet despaired of succeeding at last.

Chapter XVII

Elizabeth's impatience to acquaint Jane with what had happened could no longer be overcome; and at length resolving to suppress every particular in which her sister was concerned, and preparing her to be surprised, she related to her the next morning the chief of the scene between Mr. Darcy and herself.

Miss Bennet's astonishment was soon lessened by the strong sisterly partiality which made any admiration of Elizabeth appear perfectly natural; and all surprise was shortly lost in other feelings. She was sorry that Mr. Darcy should have delivered his sentiments in a manner so little suited to recommend them; but still more was she grieved for the unhappiness which her sister's refusal must have given him.

"His being so sure of succeeding, was wrong," said she; "and certainly ought not to have appeared; but consider how much it must increase his disappointment."

"Indeed," replied Elizabeth, "I am heartily sorry for him; but he has other feelings which will probably soon drive away his regard for me. You do not blame me, however, for refusing him?"

"Blame you! Oh, no."

"But you blame me for having spoken so warmly of Wickham."

"No—I do not know that you were wrong in saying what you did."

"But you *will* know it, when I have told you what happened the very next day."

She then spoke of the letter, repeating the whole of its contents as far as they concerned George Wickham. What a stroke was this for poor Jane! who would willingly have gone through the world without believing that so much wickedness existed in the whole race of mankind, as was here collected in one individual. Nor was Darcy's vindication, though grateful to her feelings, capable of consoling her for such discovery. Most earnestly did she labour to prove the probability of error, and seek to clear one, without involving the other.

"This will not do," said Elizabeth. "You never will be able to make both of them good for any thing. Take your choice, but you must be satisfied with only one. There is but such a quantity of merit between them; just enough to make one good sort of man; and of late it has been shifting about pretty much. For my part, I am inclined to believe it all Mr. Darcy's, but you shall do as you chuse."

It was some time, however, before a smile could be extorted from Jane.

"I do not know when I have been more shocked," said she. "Wickham so very bad! It is almost past belief. And poor Mr. Darcy! dear Lizzy, only consider what he must have suffered. Such a disappointment! and with the knowledge of your ill opinion too! and having to relate such a thing of his sister! It is really too distressing. I am sure you must feel it so."

"Oh! no, my regret and compassion are all done away by seeing you so full of both. I know you will do him such ample justice, that I am growing every moment more unconcerned and indifferent. Your profusion makes me saving; and if you lament over him much longer, my heart will be as light as a feather."

"Poor Wickham; there is such an expression of goodness in his countenance! such an openness and gentleness in his manner."

"There certainly was some great mismanagement in the education of those two young men. One has got all the goodness, and the other all the appearance of it."

"I never thought Mr. Darcy so deficient in the *appearance* of it as you used to do."

"And yet I meant to be uncommonly clever in taking so decided a dislike to him, without any reason. It is such a spur to one's genius, such an opening for wit to have a dislike of that kind. One may be continually abusive without saying any thing just; but one cannot be always laughing at a man without now and then stumbling on something witty."

"Lizzy, when you first read that letter, I am sure you could not treat the matter as you do now."

"Indeed I could not. I was uncomfortable enough. I was very uncomfortable, I may say unhappy. And with no one to speak to, of what I felt, no Jane to comfort me and say that I had not been so very weak and vain and nonsensical as I knew I had! Oh! how I wanted you!"

"How unfortunate that you should have used such very strong expressions in speaking of Wickham to Mr. Darcy, for now they *do* appear wholly undeserved."

"Certainly. But the misfortune of speaking with bitterness, is a most natural consequence of the prejudices I had been encouraging. There is one point, on which I want your advice. I want to be told whether I ought, or ought not to make our acquaintance in general understand Wickham's character."

Miss Bennett paused a little and then replied, "Surely there can be no occasion for exposing him so dreadfully. What is your own opinion?"

"That it ought not to be attempted. Mr. Darcy has not authorised me to make his communication public. On the contrary every particular relative to his sister, was meant to be kept as much as possible to myself; and if I endeavour to undeceive people as to the rest of his conduct, who will believe me? The general prejudice against Mr. Darcy is so violent, that it would be the death of half the good people in Meryton, to attempt to place him in an amiable light. I am not equal to it. Wickham will soon be gone; and therefore it will not signify to anybody here, what he really is. Sometime hence it will be all found out, and then we may laugh at their stupidity in not knowing it before. At present I will say nothing about it."

"You are quite right. To have his errors made public might ruin him for ever. He is now perhaps sorry for what he has done, and anxious to re-establish a character. We must not make him desperate."

The tumult of Elizabeth's mind was allayed by this conversation. She had got rid of two of the secrets which had weighed on her for a fortnight, and was certain of a willing listener in Jane, whenever she might wish to talk again of either. But there was still something lurking behind, of which prudence forbad the disclosure. She dared not relate the other half of Mr. Darcy's letter, nor explain to her sister how sincerely she had been valued by his friend. Here was knowledge in which no one could partake; and she was sensible that nothing less than a perfect understanding between the parties could justify her in throwing off this last incumbrance of mystery. "And then," said she, "if that very improbable event should ever take place, I shall merely be able to tell what Bingley may tell in a much more agreeable manner himself. The liberty of communication cannot be mine till it has lost all its value!"

She was now, on being settled at home, at leisure to observe the real state of her sister's spirits. Jane was not happy. She still cherished a very tender affection for Bingley. Having never even fancied herself in love before, her regard had all the warmth of first attachment, and from her age and disposition, greater steadiness than first attachments often boast; and so fervently did she value his remembrance, and prefer him to every other man, that all her good sense, and all her attention to the feelings of her friends, were requisite to check the indulgence of those regrets, which must have been injurious to her own health and their tranquillity.

"Well, Lizzy," said Mrs. Bennet one day, "what is your opinion *now* of this sad business of Jane's? For my part, I am determined never to speak of it again to anybody. I told my sister Philips so the other day. But I cannot find out that Jane saw any thing of him in London. Well, he is a very undeserving young man—and I do not suppose there is the least chance in the world of her ever getting him now. There is no talk of his coming to Netherfield again in the summer; and I have enquired of every body too, who is likely to know."

"I do not believe that he will ever live at Netherfield any more."

"Oh, well! it is just as he chooses. Nobody wants him to come. Though I shall always say that he used my daughter extremely ill; and if I was her, I would not have put up with it. Well, my comfort is, I am sure Jane will die of a broken heart, and then he will be sorry for what he has done."

But as Elizabeth could not receive comfort from any such expectation, she made no answer.

"Well, Lizzy," continued her mother soon afterwards, "and so the Collinses live very comfortable, do they? Well, well, I only hope it will last. And what sort of table do they keep? Charlotte is an excellent manager, I dare say. If she is half as sharp as her mother, she is saving enough. There is nothing extravagant in *their* housekeeping, I dare say."

"No, nothing at all."

"A great deal of good management, depend upon it. Yes, yes. *They* will take care not to outrun their income. *They* will never be distressed for money. Well, much good may it do them! And so, I suppose, they often talk of having Longbourn when your father is dead. They look upon it quite as their own, I dare say, whenever that happens."

"It was a subject which they could not mention before me."

"No. It would have been strange if they had. But I make no doubt, they often talk of it between themselves. Well, if they can be easy with an estate that is not lawfully their own, so much the better. *I* should be ashamed of having one that was only entailed on me."

Chapter XVIII

The first week of their return was soon gone. The second began. It was the last of the regiment's stay in Meryton, and all the young ladies in the neighbourhood were drooping apace. The dejection was almost universal. The elder Miss Bennets alone were still able to eat, drink, and sleep, and pursue the usual course of their employments. Very frequently were they reproached for this insensibility by Kitty and Lydia, whose own misery was extreme, and who could not comprehend such hard-heartedness in any of the family.

"Good Heaven! What is to become of us! What are we to do!" would they often exclaim in the bitterness of woe. "How can you be smiling so, Lizzy?"

Their affectionate mother shared all their grief; she remembered what she had herself endured on a similar occasion, five and twenty years ago.

"I am sure," she said, "I cried for two days together when Colonel Millar's regiment went away. I thought I should have broke my heart."

"I am sure I shall break *mine*," said Lydia.

"If one could but go to Brighton!" observed Mrs. Bennet.

"Oh, yes!—if one could but go to Brighton! But papa is so disagreeable."

"A little sea-bathing would set me up for ever."

"And my aunt Philips is sure it would do *me* a great deal of good," added Kitty.

Such were the kind of lamentations resounding perpetually through Longbourn-house. Elizabeth tried to be diverted by them; but all sense of pleasure was lost in shame. She felt anew the justice of Mr. Darcy's objections; and never had she before been so much disposed to pardon his interference in the views of his friend.

But the gloom of Lydia's prospect was shortly cleared away; for she received an invitation from Mrs. Forster, the wife of the Colonel of the regiment, to accompany her to Brighton. This invaluable friend was a very young woman, and very lately married. A resemblance in good humour and good spirits had recommended her and Lydia to each other, and out of their *three* months' acquaintance they had been intimate *two*.

The rapture of Lydia on this occasion, her adoration of Mrs. Forster, the delight of Mrs. Bennet, and the mortification of Kitty, are scarcely to be described. Wholly inattentive to her sister's feelings, Lydia flew about the house in restless ecstacy, calling for every one's congratulations, and laughing and talking with more violence than ever; whilst the luckless Kitty continued in the parlour repining at her fate in terms as unreasonable as her accent was peevish.

"I cannot see why Mrs. Forster should not ask *me* as well as Lydia," said she, "though I am *not* her particular friend. I have just as much right to be asked as she has, and more too, for I am two years older."

In vain did Elizabeth attempt to make her reasonable, and Jane to make her resigned. As for Elizabeth herself, this invitation was so far from exciting in her the same feelings as in her mother and Lydia, that she considered it as the death-warrant of all possibility of common sense for the latter; and detestable as such a step must make her were it known, she could not help secretly advising her father not to let her go. She represented to him all the improprieties of Lydia's general behaviour, the little advantage she could derive from the friendship of such a woman as Mrs. Forster, and the probability of her being yet more imprudent with such a companion at Brighton, where the temptations must be greater than at home. He heard her attentively, and then said,

"Lydia will never be easy till she has exposed herself in some public place or other, and we can never expect her to do it with so little expense or inconvenience to her family as under the present circumstances."

"If you were aware," said Elizabeth, "of the very great disadvantage to us all, which must arise from the public notice of Lydia's unguarded and imprudent manner; nay, which has already arisen from it, I am sure you would judge differently in the affair."

"Already arisen!" repeated Mr. Bennet. "What, has she frightened away some of your lovers? Poor little Lizzy! But do not be cast down. Such squeamish youths as cannot bear to be connected with a little absurdity, are not worth a regret. Come, let me see the list of the pitiful fellows who have been kept aloof by Lydia's folly."

"Indeed you are mistaken. I have no such injuries to resent. It is not of peculiar, but of general evils, which I am now complaining. Our importance, our respectability in the world, must be affected by the wild volatility, the assurance and disdain of all restraint which mark Lydia's character. Excuse me—for I must speak plainly. If you, my dear father, will not take the trouble of checking her exuberant spirits, and of teaching her that her present pursuits are not to be the business of her life, she will soon be beyond the reach of amendment. Her character will be fixed, and she will, at sixteen, be the most determined flirt that ever made herself and her family ridiculous. A flirt too, in the worst and meanest degree of flirtation; without any attraction beyond youth and a tolerable person; and from the ignorance and emptiness of her mind, wholly unable to ward off any portion of that universal contempt which her rage for admiration will excite. In this danger Kitty

is also comprehended. She will follow wherever Lydia leads. Vain, ignorant, idle, and absolutely uncontrouled! Oh! my dear father, can you
suppose it possible that they will not be censured and despised
wherever they are known, and that their sisters will not be often
involved in the disgrace?"

Mr. Bennet saw that her whole heart was in the subject; and affectionately taking her hand, said in reply,

"Do not make yourself uneasy, my love. Wherever[9] you and Jane are
known, you must be respected and valued; and you will not appear to
less advantage for having a couple of—or I may say, three very silly
sisters. We shall have no peace at Longbourn if Lydia does not go to
Brighton. Let her go then. Colonel Forster is a sensible man, and will
keep her out of any real mischief; and she is luckily too poor to be an
object of prey to any body. At Brighton she will be of less importance
even as a common flirt than she has been here. The officers will find
women better worth their notice. Let us hope, therefore, that her being
there may teach her her own insignificance. At any rate, she cannot
grow many degrees worse, without authorizing us to lock her up for
the rest of her life."

With this answer Elizabeth was forced to be content; but her own
opinion continued the same, and she left him disappointed and sorry.
It was not in her nature, however, to increase her vexations, by dwelling
on them. She was confident of having performed her duty, and to fret
over unavoidable evils, or augment them by anxiety, was no part of her
disposition.

Had Lydia and her mother known of the substance of her conference
with her father, their indignation would hardly have found expression
in their united volubility. In Lydia's imagination, a visit to Brighton
comprised every possibility of earthly happiness. She saw with the creative eye of fancy, the streets of that gay bathing place covered with
officers. She saw herself the object of attention, to tens and to scores
of them at present unknown. She saw all the glories of the camp; its
tents stretched forth in beauteous uniformity of lines, crowded with
the young and the gay, and dazzling with scarlet; and to complete the
view, she saw herself seated beneath a tent, tenderly flirting with at
least six officers at once.

Had she known that her sister sought to tear her from such prospects
and such realities as these, what would have been her sensations? They
could have been understood only by her mother, who might have felt
nearly the same. Lydia's going to Brighton was all that consoled her
for the melancholy conviction of her husband's never intending to go
there himself.

9. 1813: Whenever.

But they were entirely ignorant of what had passed; and their raptures continued with little intermission to the very day of Lydia's leaving home.

Elizabeth was now to see Mr. Wickham for the last time. Having been frequently in company with him since her return, agitation was pretty well over; the agitations of former partiality entirely so. She had even learnt to detect, in the very gentleness which had first delighted her, an affectation and a sameness to disgust and weary. In his present behaviour to herself, moreover, she had a fresh source of displeasure, for the inclination he soon testified of renewing those attentions which had marked the early part of their acquaintance, could only serve, after what had since passed, to provoke her. She lost all concern for him in finding herself thus selected as the object of such idle and frivolous gallantry; and while she steadily repressed it, could not but feel the reproof contained in his believing, that however long, and for whatever cause, his attentions had been withdrawn, her vanity would be gratified and her preference secured at any time by their renewal.

On the very last day of the regiment's remaining in Meryton, he dined with others of the officers at Longbourn; and so little was Elizabeth disposed to part from him in good humour, that on his making some enquiry as to the manner in which her time had passed at Hunsford, she mentioned Colonel Fitzwilliam's and Mr. Darcy's having both spent three weeks at Rosings, and asked him if he were acquainted with the former.

He looked surprised, displeased, alarmed; but with a moment's recollection and a returning smile, replied, that he had formerly seen him often; and after observing that he was a very gentlemanlike man, asked her how she had liked him. Her answer was warmly in his favour. With an air of indifference he soon afterwards added, "How long did you say that he was at Rosings?"

"Nearly three weeks."

"And you saw him frequently?"

"Yes, almost every day."

"His manners are very different from his cousin's."

"Yes, very different. But I think Mr. Darcy improves on acquaintance."

"Indeed!" cried Wickham with a look which did not escape her. "And pray may I ask?" but checking himself, he added in a gayer tone, "Is it in address that he improves? Has he deigned to add ought of civility to his ordinary style? for I dare not hope," he continued in a lower and more serious tone, "that he is improved in essentials."

"Oh, no!" said Elizabeth. "In essentials, I believe, he is very much what he ever was."

While she spoke, Wickham looked as if scarcely knowing whether to rejoice over her words, or to distrust their meaning. There was a something in her countenance which made him listen with an apprehensive and anxious attention, while she added,

"When I said that he improved on acquaintance, I did not mean that either his mind or manners were in a state of improvement, but that from knowing him better, his disposition was better understood."

Wickham's alarm now appeared in a heightened complexion and agitated look; for a few minutes he was silent; till, shaking off his embarrassment, he turned to her again, and said in the gentlest of accents,

"You, who so well know my feelings towards Mr. Darcy, will readily comprehend how sincerely I must rejoice that he is wise enough to assume even the *appearance* of what is right. His pride, in that direction, may be of service, if not to himself, to many others, for it must deter him from such foul misconduct as I have suffered by. I only fear that the sort of cautiousness, to which you, I imagine, have been alluding, is merely adopted on his visits to his aunt, of whose good opinion and judgment he stands much in awe. His fear of her, has always operated, I know, when they were together; and a good deal is to be imputed to his wish of forwarding the match with Miss De Bourgh, which I am certain he has very much at heart."

Elizabeth could not repress a smile at this, but she answered only by a slight inclination of the head. She saw that he wanted to engage her on the old subject of his grievances, and she was in no humour to indulge him. The rest of the evening passed with the *appearance*, on his[1] side, of usual cheerfulness, but with no farther attempt to distinguish Elizabeth; and they parted at last with mutual civility, and possibly a mutual desire of never meeting again.

When the party broke up, Lydia returned with Mrs. Forster to Meryton, from whence they were to set out early the next morning. The separation between her and her family was rather noisy than pathetic. Kitty was the only one who shed tears; but she did weep from vexation and envy. Mrs. Bennet was diffuse in her good wishes for the felicity of her daughter, and impressive in her injunctions that she would not miss the opportunity of enjoying herself as much as possible; advice, which there was every reason to believe would be attended to; and in the clamorous happiness of Lydia herself in bidding farewell, the more gentle adieus of her sisters were uttered without being heard.

Chapter XIX

Had Elizabeth's opinion been all drawn from her own family, she could not have formed a very pleasing picture of conjugal felicity or

---

1. 1813 first edition: her. Corrected to "his" in the second edition.

domestic comfort. Her father, captivated by youth and beauty, and that appearance of good humour, which youth and beauty generally give, had married a woman whose weak understanding and illiberal mind, had very early in their marriage put an end to all real affection for her. Respect, esteem, and confidence, had vanished for ever; and all his views of domestic happiness were overthrown. But Mr. Bennet was not of a disposition to seek comfort for the disappointment which his own imprudence had brought on, in any of those pleasures which too often console the unfortunate for their folly or their vice. He was fond of the country and of books; and from these tastes had arisen his principal enjoyments. To his wife he was very little otherwise indebted, than as her ignorance and folly had contributed to his amusement. This is not the sort of happiness which a man would in general wish to owe to his wife; but where other powers of entertainment are wanting, the true philosopher will derive benefit from such as are given.

Elizabeth, however, had never been blind to the impropriety of her father's behaviour as a husband. She had always seen it with pain; but respecting his abilities, and grateful for his affectionate treatment of herself, she endeavoured to forget what she could not overlook, and to banish from her thoughts that continual breach of conjugal obligation and decorum which, in exposing his wife to the contempt of her own children, was so highly reprehensible. But she had never felt so strongly as now, the disadvantages which must attend the children of so unsuitable a marriage, nor ever been so fully aware of the evils arising from so ill-judged a direction of talents; talents which rightly used, might at least have preserved the respectability of his daughters, even if incapable of enlarging the mind of his wife.

When Elizabeth had rejoiced over Wickham's departure, she found little other cause for satisfaction in the loss of the regiment. Their parties abroad were less varied than before; and at home she had a mother and sister whose constant repinings at the dulness of every thing around them, threw a real gloom over their domestic circle; and, though Kitty might in time regain her natural degree of sense, since the disturbers of her brain were removed, her other sister, from whose disposition greater evil might be apprehended, was likely to be hardened in all her folly and assurance, by a situation of such double danger as a watering place and a camp. Upon the whole, therefore, she found, what has been sometimes found before, that an event to which she had looked forward with impatient desire, did not in taking place, bring all the satisfaction she had promised herself. It was consequently necessary to name some other period for the commencement of actual felicity; to have some other point on which her wishes and hopes might be fixed, and by again enjoying the pleasure of anticipation, console herself for the present, and prepare for another disappointment. Her tour to the Lakes was now the object of her happiest thoughts; it was her best consolation for all the uncomfortable hours, which the dis-contentedness of her mother and Kitty made inevitable; and could she have included Jane in the scheme, every part of it would have been perfect.

"But it is fortunate," thought she "that I have something to wish for. Were the whole arrangement complete, my disappointment would be certain. But here, by[2] carrying with me one ceaseless source of regret in my sister's absence, I may reasonably hope to have all my expecta-tions of pleasure realized. A scheme of which every part promises delight, can never be successful; and general disappointment is only warded off by the defence of some little peculiar vexation."

When Lydia went away, she promised to write very often and very minutely to her mother and Kitty; but her letters were always long expected, and always very short. Those to her mother, contained little else, than that they were just returned from the library, where such and such officers had attended them, and where she had seen such beautiful ornaments as made her quite wild; that she had a new gown, or a new parasol, which she would have described more fully, but was obliged to leave off in a violent hurry, as Mrs. Forster called her, and they were going to the camp;—and from her correspondence with her sister, there was still less to be learnt—for her letters to Kitty, though rather longer, were much too full of lines under the words to be made public.

After the first fortnight or three weeks of her absence, health, good humour and cheerfulness began to re-appear at Longbourn. Everything wore a happier aspect. The families who had been in town for the winter came back again, and summer finery and summer engagements arose. Mrs. Bennet was restored to her usual querulous serenity, and by the middle of June Kitty was so much recovered as to be able to enter Meryton without tears; an event of such happy promise as to make Elizabeth hope, that by the following Christmas, she might be so tolerably reasonable as not to mention an officer above once a day, unless by some cruel and malicious arrangement at the war-office, another regiment should be quartered in Meryton.

The time fixed for the beginning of their Northern tour was now fast approaching; and a fortnight only was wanting of it, when a letter arrived from Mrs. Gardiner, which at once delayed its commencement and curtailed its extent. Mr. Gardiner would be prevented by business from setting out till a fortnight later in July, and must be in London again within a month; and as that left too short a period for them to go so far, and see so much as they had proposed, or at least to see it with the leisure and comfort they had built on, they were obliged to

2. 1813: my.

give up the Lakes, and substitute a more contracted tour; and, according to the present plan, were to go no farther northward than Derbyshire. In that county, there was enough to be seen, to occupy the chief of their three weeks; and to Mrs. Gardiner it had a peculiarly strong attraction. The town where she had formerly passed some years of her life, and where they were now to spend a few days, was probably as great an object of her curiosity, as all the celebrated beauties of Matlock, Chatsworth, Dovedale, or the Peak.

Elizabeth was excessively disappointed; she had set her heart on seeing the Lakes; and still thought there might have been time enough. But it was her business to be satisfied—and certainly her temper to be happy; and all was soon right again.

With the mention of Derbyshire, there were many ideas connected. It was impossible for her to see the word without thinking of Pemberley and its owner. "But surely," said she, "I may enter his county with impunity, and rob it of a few petrified spars[3] without his perceiving me."

The period of expectation was now doubled. Four weeks were to pass away before her uncle and aunt's arrival. But they did pass away, and Mr. and Mrs. Gardiner, with their four children, did at length appear at Longbourn. The children, two girls of six and eight years old, and two younger boys, were to be left under the particular care of their cousin Jane, who was the general favourite, and whose steady sense and sweetness of temper exactly adapted her for attending to them in every way—teaching them, playing with them, and loving them.

The Gardiners staid only one night at Longbourn, and set off the next morning with Elizabeth in pursuit of novelty and amusement. One enjoyment was certain—that of suitableness as companions; a suitableness which comprehended health and temper to bear inconveniences—cheerfulness to enhance every pleasure—and affection and intelligence, which might supply it among themselves if there were disappointments abroad.

It is not the object of this work to give a description of Derbyshire, nor of any of the remarkable places through which their route thither lay; Oxford, Blenheim, Warwick, Kenelworth, Birmingham, &c. are sufficiently known. A small part of Derbyshire is all the present concern. To the little town of Lambton, the scene of Mrs. Gardiner's former residence, and where she had lately learned that some acquaintance still remained, they bent their steps, after having seen all the principal wonders of the country; and within five miles of Lambton, Elizabeth found from her aunt, that Pemberley was situated. It was not in their direct road, nor more than a mile or two out of it. In talking

3. Crystallized minerals.

over their route the evening before, Mrs. Gardiner expressed an inclination to see the place again. Mr. Gardiner declared his willingness, and Elizabeth was applied to for her approbation.

"My love, should not you like to see a place of which you have heard so much?" said her aunt. "A place too, with which so many of your acquaintance are connected. Wickham passed all his youth there, you know."

Elizabeth was distressed. She felt that she had no business at Pemberley, and was obliged to assume a disinclination for seeing it. She must own that she was tired of great houses; after going over so many, she really had no pleasure in fine carpets or satin curtains.

Mrs. Gardiner abused her stupidity. "If it were merely a fine house richly furnished," said she, "I should not care about it myself; but the grounds are delightful. They have some of the finest woods in the country."

Elizabeth said no more—but her mind could not acquiesce. The possibility of meeting Mr. Darcy, while viewing the place, instantly occurred. It would be dreadful! She blushed at the very idea; and thought it would be better to speak openly to her aunt, than to run such a risk. But against this, there were objections; and she finally resolved that it could be the last resource, if her private enquiries as to the absence of the family, were unfavourably answered.

Accordingly, when she retired at night, she asked the chambermaid whether Pemberley were not a very fine place, what was the name of its proprietor, and with no little alarm, whether the family were down for the summer. A most welcome negative followed the last question— and her alarms being now removed, she was at leisure to feel a great deal of curiosity to see the house herself; and when the subject was revived the next morning, and she was again applied to, could readily answer, and with a proper air of indifference, that she had not really any dislike to the scheme.

To Pemberley, therefore, they were to go.

Volume III

Chapter I

Elizabeth, as they drove along, watched for the first appearance of Pemberley Woods with some perturbation; and when at length they turned in at the lodge, her spirits were in a high flutter.

The park was very large, and contained great variety of ground. They entered it in one of its lowest points, and drove for some time through a beautiful wood, stretching over a wide extent.

Elizabeth's mind was too full for conversation, but she saw and admired every remarkable spot and point of view. They gradually ascended for half a mile, and then found themselves at the top of a considerable eminence, where the wood ceased, and the eye was instantly caught by Pemberley House, situated on the opposite side of a valley, into which the road with some abruptness wound. It was a large, handsome, stone building, standing well on rising ground, and backed by a ridge of high woody hills;—and in front, a stream of some natural importance was swelled into greater, but without any artificial appearance. Its banks were neither formal, nor falsely adorned. Elizabeth was delighted. She had never seen a place for which nature had done more, or where natural beauty had been so little counteracted by an awkward taste. They were all of them warm in their admiration; and at that moment she felt, that to be mistress of Pemberley might be something!

They descended the hill, crossed the bridge, and drove to the door; and, while examining the nearer aspect of the house, all her apprehensions of meeting its owner returned. She dreaded lest the chambermaid had been mistaken. On applying to see the place, they were admitted into the hall; and Elizabeth, as they waited for the housekeeper, had leisure to wonder at her being where she was.

The housekeeper came; a respectable-looking, elderly woman, much less fine, and more civil, than she had any notion of finding her. They followed her into the dining-parlour. It was a large, well-proportioned room, handsomely fitted up. Elizabeth, after slightly surveying it, went to a window to enjoy its prospect. The hill, crowned with wood, from which they had descended, receiving increased abruptness from the distance, was a beautiful object. Every disposition of the ground was good; and she looked on the whole scene, the river, the trees scattered on its banks, and the winding of the valley, as far as she could trace it, with delight. As they passed into other rooms, these objects were taking different positions; but from every window there were beauties to be seen. The rooms were lofty and handsome, and their furniture suitable to the fortune of their proprietor; but Elizabeth saw, with admiration of his taste, that it was neither gaudy nor uselessly fine; with less of splendor, and more real elegance, than the furniture of Rosings.

"And of this place," thought she, "I might have been mistress! With these rooms I might now have been familiarly acquainted! Instead of viewing them as a stranger, I might have rejoiced in them as my own, and welcomed to them as visitors my uncle and aunt.—But no."— recollecting herself,—"that could never be: my uncle and aunt would have been lost to me: I should not have been allowed to invite them."

This was a lucky recollection—it saved her from something like regret.

She longed to enquire of the housekeeper, whether her master were really absent, but had not courage for it. At length, however, the question was asked by her uncle; and she turned away with alarm, while Mrs. Reynolds replied, that he was, adding, "but we expect him tomorrow, with a large party of friends." How rejoiced was Elizabeth that their own journey had not by any circumstances been delayed a day!

Her aunt now called her to look at a picture. She approached, and saw the likeness of Mr. Wickham suspended, amongst several other miniatures, over the mantlepiece. Her aunt asked her, smilingly, how she liked it. The housekeeper came forward, and told them it was the picture of a young gentleman, the son of her late master's steward, who had been brought up by him at his own expense.—"He is now gone into the army," she added, "but I am afraid he has turned out very wild."

Mrs. Gardiner looked at her niece with a smile, but Elizabeth could not return it.

"And that," said Mrs. Reynolds, pointing to another of the miniatures, "is my master—and very like him. It was drawn at the same time as the other—about eight years ago."

"I have heard much of your master's fine person," said Mrs. Gardiner, looking at the picture; "it is a handsome face. But, Lizzy, you can tell us whether it is like or not."

Mrs. Reynold's respect for Elizabeth seemed to increase on this intimation of her knowing her master.

"Does that young lady know Mr. Darcy?"

Elizabeth coloured, and said—"A little."

"And do not you think him a very handsome gentleman, Ma'am?"

"Yes, very handsome."

"I am sure I know none so handsome; but in the gallery up stairs you will see a finer, larger picture of him than this. This room was my late master's favourite room, and these miniatures are just as they used to be then. He was very fond of them."

This accounted to Elizabeth for Mr. Wickham's being among them.

Mrs. Reynolds then directed their attention to one of Miss Darcy, drawn when she was only eight years old.

"And is Miss Darcy as handsome as her brother?" said Mr. Gardiner.

"Oh! yes—the handsomest young lady that ever was seen; and so accomplished!—She plays and sings all day long. In the next room is a new instrument just come down for her—a present from my master; she comes here to-morrow with him."

Mr. Gardiner, whose manners were easy and pleasant, encouraged her communicativeness by his questions and remarks; Mrs. Reynolds, either from pride or attachment, had evidently great pleasure in talking of her master and his sister.

"Is your master much at Pemberley in the course of the year?"

"Not so much as I could wish, Sir; but I dare say he may spend half his time here; and Miss Darcy is always down for the summer months."

"Except," thought Elizabeth, "when she goes to Ramsgate."

"If your master would marry, you might see more of him."

"Yes, Sir; but I do not know when *that* will be. I do not know who is good enough for him."

Mr. and Mrs. Gardiner smiled. Elizabeth could not help but saying, "It is very much to his credit, I am sure, that you should think so."

"I say no more than the truth, and what every body will say that knows him," replied the other. Elizabeth thought this was going pretty far; and she listened with increasing astonishment as the housekeeper added, "I have never had a cross word from him in my life, and I have known him ever since he was four years old."

This was praise, of all others most extraordinary, most opposite to her ideas. That he was not a good-tempered man, had been her firmest opinion. Her keenest attention was awakened; she longed to hear more, and was grateful to her uncle for saying,

"There are very few people of whom so much can be said. You are lucky in having such a master."

"Yes, Sir, I know I am. If I was to go through the world, I could not meet with a better. But I have always observed, that they who are good-natured when children, are good-natured when they grow up; and he was always the sweetest-tempered, most generous-hearted, boy in the world."

Elizabeth almost stared at her.—"Can this be Mr. Darcy!" thought she.

"His father was an excellent man," said Mrs. Gardiner.

"Yes, Ma'am, that he was indeed; and his son will be just like him—just as affable to the poor."

Elizabeth listened, wondered, doubted, and was impatient for more. Mrs. Reynolds could interest her on no other point. She related the subject of the pictures, the dimensions of the rooms, and the price of the furniture, in vain. Mr. Gardiner, highly amused by the kind of family prejudice, to which he attributed her excessive commendation of her master, soon led again to the subject; and she dwelt with energy on his many merits, as they proceeded together up the great staircase.

"He is the best landlord, and the best master," said she, "that ever lived. Not like the wild young men now-a-days, who think of nothing but themselves. There is not one of his tenants or servants but what will give him a good name. Some people call him proud; but I am sure I never saw any thing of it. To my fancy, it is only because he does not rattle away like other young men."

"In what an amiable light does this place him!" thought Elizabeth.

"This fine account of him," whispered her aunt, as they walked, "is not quite consistent with his behaviour to our poor friend."

"Perhaps we might be deceived."

"That is not very likely; our authority was too good."

On reaching the spacious lobby above, they were shewn into a very pretty sitting-room, lately fitted up with greater elegance and lightness than the apartments below; and were informed that it was but just done, to give pleasure to Miss Darcy, who had taken a liking to the room, when last at Pemberley.

"He is certainly a good brother," said Elizabeth, as she walked towards one of the windows.

Mrs. Reynolds anticipated Miss Darcy's delight, when she should enter the room. "And this is always the way with him," she added.— "Whatever can give his sister any pleasure, is sure to be done in a moment. There is nothing he would not do for her."

The picture gallery, and two or three of the principal bed-rooms, were all that remained to be shewn. In the former were many good paintings; but Elizabeth knew nothing of the art; and from such as had been already visible below, she had willingly turned to look at some drawings of Miss Darcy's, in crayons, whose subjects were usually more interesting, and also more intelligible.

In the gallery there were many family portraits, but they could have little to fix the attention of a stranger. Elizabeth walked on in quest of the only face whose features would be known to her. At last it arrested her—and she beheld a striking resemblance of Mr. Darcy, with such a smile over the face, as she remembered to have sometimes seen, when he looked at her. She stood several minutes before the picture in earnest contemplation, and returned to it again before they quitted the gallery. Mrs. Reynolds informed them, that it had been taken in his father's life time.

There was certainly at this moment, in Elizabeth's mind, a more gentle sensation towards the original, than she had ever felt in the height of their acquaintance. The commendation bestowed on him by Mrs. Reynolds was of no trifling nature. What praise is more valuable than the praise of an intelligent servant? As a brother, a landlord, a master, she considered how many people's happiness were in his guardianship!—How much of pleasure or pain it was in his power to bestow!—How much of good or evil must be done by him! Every idea that had been brought forward by the housekeeper was favourable to his character, and as she stood before the canvas, on which he was represented, and fixed his eyes upon herself, she thought of his regard with a deeper sentiment of gratitude than it had ever raised before; she remembered its warmth, and softened its impropriety of expression.

When all of the house that was open to general inspection had been seen, they returned down stairs, and taking leave of the housekeeper, were consigned over to the gardener, who met them at the hall door.

As they walked across the lawn towards the river, Elizabeth turned back to look again; her uncle and aunt stopped also, and while the former was conjecturing as to the date of the building, the owner of it himself suddenly came forward from the road, which led behind it to the stables.

They were within twenty yards of each other, and so abrupt was his appearance, that it was impossible to avoid his sight. Their eyes instantly met, and the cheeks of each were overspread with the deepest blush. He absolutely started, and for a moment seemed immoveable from surprise; but shortly recovering himself, advanced towards the party, and spoke to Elizabeth, if not in terms of perfect composure, at least of perfect civility.

She had instinctively turned away; but, stopping on his approach, received his compliments with an embarrassment impossible to be overcome. Had his first appearance, or his resemblance to the picture they had just been examining, been insufficient to assure the other two that they now saw Mr. Darcy, the gardener's expression of surprise, on beholding his master, must immediately have told it. They stood a little aloof while he was talking to their niece, who, astonished and confused, scarcely dared lift her eyes to his face, and knew not what answer she returned to his civil enquiries after her family. Amazed at the alteration in his manner since they last parted, every sentence that he uttered was increasing her embarrassment; and every idea of the impropriety of her being found there, recurring to her mind, the few minutes in which they continued together, were some of the most uncomfortable of her life. Nor did he seem much more at ease; when he spoke, his accent had none of its usual sedateness; and he repeated his enquiries as to the time of her having left Longbourn, and of her stay in Derbyshire, so often, and in so hurried a way, as plainly spoke the distraction of his thoughts.

At length, every idea seemed to fail him; and, after standing a few moments without saying a word, he suddenly recollected himself, and took leave.

The others then joined her, and expressed their admiration of his figure; but Elizabeth heard not a word, and, wholly engrossed by her own feelings, followed them in silence. She was overpowered by shame and vexation. Her coming there was the most unfortunate, the most ill-judged thing in the world! How strange must it appear to him! In what a disgraceful light might it not strike so vain a man! It might seem as if she had purposely thrown herself in his way again! Oh! why did she come? or, why did he thus come a day before he was expected? Had they been only ten minutes sooner, they should have been beyond the reach of his discrimination, for it was plain that he was that moment arrived, that moment alighted from his horse or his carriage. She blushed again and again over the perverseness of the meeting. And his behaviour, so strikingly altered,—what could it mean? That he should even speak to her was amazing!—but to speak with such civility, to enquire after her family! Never in her life had she seen his manners so little dignified, never had he spoken with such gentleness as on this unexpected meeting. What a contrast did it offer to his last address in Rosing's Park, when he put his letter into her hand! She knew not what to think, nor how to account for it.

They had now entered a beautiful walk by the side of the water, and every step was bringing forward a nobler fall of ground, or a finer reach of the woods to which they were approaching; but it was some time before Elizabeth was sensible of any of it; and, though she answered mechanically to the repeated appeals of her uncle and aunt, and seemed to direct her eyes to such objects as they pointed out, she distinguished no part of the scene. Her thoughts were all fixed on that one spot of Pemberley House, whichever it might be, where Mr. Darcy then was. She longed to know what at that moment was passing in his mind; in what manner he thought of her, and whether, in defiance of every thing, she was still dear to him. Perhaps he had been civil, only because he felt himself at ease; yet there had been *that* in his voice, which was not like ease. Whether he had felt more of pain or of pleasure in seeing her, she could not tell, but he certainly had not seen her with composure.

At length, however, the remarks of her companions on her absence of mind roused her, and she felt the necessity of appearing more like herself.

They entered the woods, and bidding adieu to the river for a while, ascended some of the higher grounds; whence, in spots where the opening of the trees gave the eye power to wander, were many charming views of the valley, the opposite hills, with the long range of woods overspreading many, and occasionally part of the stream. Mr. Gardiner expressed a wish of going round the whole Park, but feared it might be beyond a walk. With a triumphant smile, they were told, that it was ten miles round. It settled the matter; and they pursued the accustomed circuit; which brought them again, after some time, in a descent among hanging woods,[4] to the edge of the water, in one of its narrowest parts. They crossed it by a simple bridge, in character with the general air of the scene; it was a spot less adorned than any they had yet visited; and the valley, here contracted into a glen, allowed room only for the stream, and a narrow walk amidst the rough coppice-wood which bordered it. Elizabeth longed to explore its windings; but when they had crossed the bridge, and perceived their distance from the house, Mrs. Gardiner, who was not a great walker, could go no farther, and thought only of returning to the carriage as quickly as possible. Her niece was, therefore, obliged to submit, and they took their way towards the house on the opposite side of the river, in the nearest direction; but their

4. Woods on a steep slope.

progress was slow, for Mr. Gardiner, though seldom able to indulge the taste, was very fond of fishing, and was so much engaged in watching the occasional appearance of some trout in the water, and talking to the man about them, that he advanced but little. Whilst wandering on in this slow manner, they were again surprised, and Elizabeth's astonishment was quite equal to what it had been at first, by the sight of Mr. Darcy approaching them, and at no great distance. The walk being here less sheltered than on the other side, allowed them to see him before they met. Elizabeth, however astonished, was at least more prepared for an interview than before, and resolved to appear and to speak with calmness, if he really intended to meet them. For a few moments, indeed, she felt that he would probably strike into some other path. This idea lasted while a turning in the walk concealed him from their view; then turning past, he was immediately before them. With a glance she saw, that he had lost none of his recent civility; and, to imitate his politeness, she began, as they met, to admire the beauty of the place; but she had not got beyond the words "delightful," and "charming," when some unlucky recollections obtruded, and she fancied that praise of Pemberley from her, might be mischievously construed. Her colour changed, and she said no more.

Mrs. Gardiner was standing a little behind; and on her pausing, he asked her, if she would do him the honour of introducing him to her friends. This was a stroke of civility for which she was quite unprepared; and she could hardly suppress a smile, at his being now seeking the acquaintance of some of those very people, against whom his pride had revolted, in his offer to herself. "What will be his surprise," thought she, "when he knows who they are! He takes them now for people of fashion."

The introduction, however, was immediately made; and as she named their relationship to herself, she stole a sly look at him, to see how he bore it; and was not without the expectation of his decamping as fast as he could from such disgraceful companions. That he was *surprised* by the connexion was evident; he sustained it however with fortitude, and so far from going away, turned back with them, and entered into conversation with Mr. Gardiner. Elizabeth could not but be pleased, could not but triumph. It was consoling, that he should know she had some relations for whom there was no need to blush. She listened most attentively to all that passed between them, and gloried in every expression, every sentence of her uncle, which marked his intelligence, his taste, or his good manners.

The conversation soon turned upon fishing, and she heard Mr. Darcy invite him, with the greatest civility, to fish there as often as he chose, while he continued in the neighbourhood, offering at the same time to supply him with fishing tackle, and pointing out those parts of the stream where there was usually most sport. Mrs. Gardiner, who was walking arm in arm with Elizabeth, gave her a look expressive of her wonder. Elizabeth said nothing, but it gratified her exceedingly; the compliment must be all for herself. Her astonishment, however, was extreme; and continually was she repeating, "Why is he so altered? From what can it proceed? It cannot be for *me*, it cannot be for *my* sake that his manners are thus softened. My reproofs at Hunsford could not work such a change as this. It is impossible that he should still love me."

After walking some time in this way, the two ladies in front, the two gentlemen behind, on resuming their places, after descending to the brink of the river for the better inspection of some curious water-plant, there chanced to be a little alteration. It originated in Mrs. Gardiner, who, fatigued by the exercise of the morning, found Elizabeth's arm inadequate to her support, and consequently preferred her husband's. Mr. Darcy took her place by her niece, and they walked on together. After a short silence, the lady first spoke. She wished him to know that she had been assured of his absence before she came to the place, and accordingly began by observing, that his arrival had been very unexpected—"for your housekeeper," she added, "informed us that you would certainly not be here till to-morrow; and indeed, before we left Bakewell, we understood that you were not immediately expected in the country." He acknowledged the truth of it all; and said that business with his steward had occasioned his coming forward a few hours before the rest of the party with whom he had been travelling. "They will join me early to-morrow," he continued, "and among them are some who will claim an acquaintance with you,—Mr. Bingley and his sisters."

Elizabeth answered only by a slight bow. Her thoughts were instantly driven back to the time when Mr. Bingley's name had been last mentioned between them; and if she might judge from his complexion, *his* mind was not very differently engaged.

"There is also one other person in the party," he continued after a pause, "who more particularly wishes to be known to you,—Will you allow me, or do I ask too much, to introduce my sister to your acquaintance during your stay at Lambton?"

The surprise of such an application was great indeed; it was too great for her to know in what manner she acceded to it. She immediately felt that whatever desire Miss Darcy might have of being acquainted with her, must be the work of her brother, and without looking farther, it was satisfactory; it was gratifying to know that his resentment had not made him think really ill of her.

They now walked on in silence; each of them deep in thought. Elizabeth was not comfortable; that was impossible; but she was flattered and pleased. His wish of introducing his sister to her, was a compliment of the highest kind. They soon outstripped the others, and when they had reached the carriage, Mr. and Mrs. Gardiner were half a quarter of a mile behind.

He then asked her to walk into the house—but she declared herself not tired, and they stood together on the lawn. At such a time, much might have been said, and silence was very awkward. She wanted to talk, but there seemed an embargo on every subject. At last she recollected that she had been travelling, and they talked of Matlock and Dovedale with great perseverance. Yet time and her aunt moved slowly—and her patience and her ideas were nearly worn out before the tête-à-tête was over. On Mr. and Mrs. Gardiner's coming up, they were all pressed to go into the house and take some refreshment; but this was declined, and they parted on each side with the utmost politeness. Mr. Darcy handed the ladies into the carriage, and when it drove off, Elizabeth saw him walking slowly towards the house.

The observations of her uncle and aunt now began; and each of them pronounced him to be infinitely superior to any thing they had expected. "He is perfectly well behaved, polite, and unassuming," said her uncle.

"There *is* something a little stately in him to be sure," replied her aunt, "but it is confined to his air, and is not unbecoming. I can now say with the housekeeper, that though some people may call him proud, *I* have seen nothing of it."

"I was never more surprised than by his behaviour to us. It was more than civil; it was really attentive; and there was no necessity for such attention. His acquaintance with Elizabeth was very trifling."

"To be sure, Lizzy," said her aunt, "he is not so handsome as Wickham; or rather he has not Wickham's countenance, for his features are perfectly good. But how came you to tell us that he was so disagreeable?"

Elizabeth excused herself as well as she could; said that she had liked him better when they met in Kent than before, and that she had never seen him so pleasant as this morning.

"But perhaps he may be a little whimsical in his civilities," replied her uncle. "Your great men often are; and therefore I shall not take him at his word about fishing, as he might change his mind another day, and warn me off his grounds."

Elizabeth felt that they had entirely mistaken his character, but said nothing.

"From what we have seen of him," continued Mrs. Gardiner, "I really should not have thought that he could have behaved in so cruel a way by any body, as he has done by poor Wickham. He has not an ill-natured look. On the contrary, there is something pleasing about his mouth when he speaks. And there is something of dignity in his countenance, that would not give one an unfavourable idea of his heart. But to be sure, the good lady who shewed us the house, did give him a most flaming character! I could hardly help laughing aloud some-times. But he is a liberal master, I suppose, and *that* in the eye of a servant comprehends every virtue."

Elizabeth here felt herself called on to say something in vindication of his behaviour to Wickham; and therefore gave them to understand, in as guarded a manner as she could, that by what she had heard from his relations in Kent, his actions were capable of a very different con-struction; and that his character was by no means so faulty, nor Wick-ham's so amiable, as they had been considered in Hertfordshire. In confirmation of this, she related the particulars of all the pecuniary transactions in which they had been connected, without actually nam-ing her authority, but stating it to be such as might be relied on.

Mrs. Gardiner was surprised and concerned; but as they were now approaching the scene of her former pleasures, every idea gave way to the charm of recollection; and she was too much engaged in pointing out to her husband all the interesting spots in its environs, to think of any thing else. Fatigued as she had been by the morning's walk, they had no sooner dined than she set off again in quest of her former acquaintance, and the evening was spent in the satisfaction of an inter-course renewed after many years discontinuance.

The occurrences of the day were too full of interest to leave Eliza-beth much attention for any of these new friends; and she could do nothing but think, and think with wonder, of Mr. Darcy's civility, and above all, of his wishing her to be acquainted with his sister.

Chapter II

Elizabeth had settled it that Mr. Darcy would bring his sister to visit her, the very day after her reaching Pemberley; and was consequently resolved not to be out of sight of the inn the whole of that morning. But her conclusion was false; for on the very morning after their own arrival at Lambton, these visitors came. They had been walking about the place with some of their new friends, and were just returned to the inn to dress themselves for dining with the same family, when the sound of a carriage drew them to a window, and they saw a gentleman and lady in a curricle,[5] driving up the street. Elizabeth immediately recognising the livery,[6] guessed what it meant, and imparted no small degree of surprise to her relations, by acquainting them with the hon-our which she expected. Her uncle and aunt were all amazement; and the embarrassment of her manner as she spoke, joined to the circum-stance itself, and many of the circumstances of the preceding day, opened to them a new idea on the business. Nothing had ever sug-gested it before, but they now felt that there was no other way of

5. A small two-wheeled carriage.
6. Distinctive garments worn by servants of a large house.

accounting for such attentions from such a quarter, than by supposing a partiality for their niece. While these newly-born notions were passing in their heads, the perturbation of Elizabeth's feelings was every moment increasing. She was quite amazed at her own discomposure; but amongst other causes of disquiet, she dreaded lest the partiality of the brother should have said too much in her favour; and more than commonly anxious to please, she naturally suspected that every power of pleasing would fail her.

She retreated from the window, fearful of being seen; and as she walked up and down the room, endeavouring to compose herself, saw such looks of enquiring surprise in her uncle and aunt, as made every thing worse.

Miss Darcy and her brother appeared, and this formidable introduction took place. With astonishment did Elizabeth see, that her new acquaintance was at least as much embarrassed as herself. Since her being at Lambton, she had heard that Miss Darcy was exceedingly proud; but the observation of a very few minutes convinced her, that she was only exceedingly shy. She found it difficult to obtain even a word from her beyond a monosyllable.

Miss Darcy was tall, and on a larger scale than Elizabeth; and, though little more than sixteen, her figure was formed, and her appearance womanly and graceful. She was less handsome than her brother, but there was sense and good humour in her face, and her manners were perfectly unassuming and gentle. Elizabeth, who had expected to find in her as acute and unembarrassed an observer as ever Mr. Darcy had been, was much relieved by discerning such different feelings.

They had not been long together, before Darcy told her that Bingley was also coming to wait on her; and she had barely time to express her satisfaction, and prepare for such a visitor, when Bingley's quick step was heard on the stairs, and in a moment he entered the room. All Elizabeth's anger against him had been long done away; but, had she still felt any, it could hardly have stood its ground against the unaffected cordiality with which he expressed himself, on seeing her again. He enquired in a friendly, though general way, after her family, and looked and spoke with the same good-humoured ease that he had ever done.

To Mr. and Mrs. Gardiner he was scarcely a less interesting personage than to herself. They had long wished to see him. The whole party before them, indeed, excited a lively attention. The suspicions which had just arisen of Mr. Darcy and their niece, directed their observation towards each with an earnest, though guarded, enquiry; and they soon drew from those enquiries the full conviction that one of them at least knew what it was to love. Of the lady's sensations they remained a little in doubt; but that the gentleman was overflowing with admiration was evident enough.

Elizabeth, on her side, had much to do. She wanted to ascertain the feelings of each of her visitors, she wanted to compose her own, and to make herself agreeable to all; and in the latter object, where she feared most to fail, she was most sure of success, for those to whom she endeavoured to give pleasure were prepossessed in her favour. Bingley was ready, Georgiana was eager, and Darcy determined, to be pleased.

In seeing Bingley, her thoughts naturally flew to her sister; and oh! how ardently did she long to know, whether any of his were directed in a like manner. Sometimes she could fancy, that he talked less than on former occasions, and once or twice pleased herself with the notion that as he looked at her, he was trying to trace a resemblance. But, though this might be imaginary, she could not be deceived as to his behaviour to Miss Darcy, who had been set up as a rival of Jane. No look appeared on either side that spoke particular regard. Nothing occurred between them that could justify the hopes of his sister. On this point she was soon satisfied; and two or three little circumstances occurred ere they parted, which, in her anxious interpretation, denoted a recollection of Jane, not untinctured by tenderness, and a wish of saying more that might lead to the mention of her, had he dared. He observed to her, at a moment when the others were talking together, and in a tone which had something of real regret, that it "was a very long time since he had had the pleasure of seeing her;" and, before she could reply, he added, "It is above eight months. We have not met since the 26th of November, when we were all dancing together at Netherfield."

Elizabeth was pleased to find his memory so exact; and he afterwards took occasion to ask her, when unattended to by any of the rest, whether *all* her sisters were at Longbourn. There was not much in the question, nor in the preceding remark, but there was a look and a manner which gave them meaning.

It was not often that she could turn her eyes on Mr. Darcy himself; but, whenever she did catch a glimpse, she saw an expression of general complaisance, and in all that he said, she heard an accent so far removed from hauteur or disdain of his companions, as convinced her that the improvement of manners which she had yesterday witnessed, however temporary its existence might prove, had at least outlived one day. When she saw him thus seeking the acquaintance, and courting the good opinion of people, with whom any intercourse a few months ago would have been a disgrace; when she saw him thus civil, not only to herself, but to the very relations whom he had openly disdained, and recollected their last lively scene in Hunsford Parsonage, the difference, the change was so great, and struck so forcibly on her mind, that she could hardly restrain her astonishment from being visible. Never, even in the company of his dear friends at Netherfield, or his dignified relations st Rosings, had she seen him so desirous to please, so free from self-consequence, or unbending reserve as now, when no importance could result from the success of his endeavours, and when even the acquaintance of those to whom his attentions were addressed, would draw down the ridicule and censure of the ladies both of Netherfield and Rosings.

Their visitors staid with them above half an hour, and when they arose to depart, Mr. Darcy called on his sister to join him in expressing their wish of seeing Mr. and Mrs. Gardiner, and Miss Bennet, to dinner at Pemberley, before they left the country. Miss Darcy, though with a diffidence which marked her little in the habit of giving invitations, readily obeyed. Mrs. Gardiner looked at her niece, desirous of knowing how *she*, whom the invitation most concerned, felt disposed as to its acceptance, but Elizabeth had turned away her head. Presuming, however, that this studied avoidance spoke rather a momentary embarrassment, than any dislike of the proposal, and seeing in her husband, who was fond of society, a perfect willingness to accept it, she ventured to engage for her attendance, and the day after the next was fixed on.

Bingley expressed great pleasure in the certainty of seeing Elizabeth again, having still a great deal to say to her, and many enquiries to make after all their Hertfordshire friends. Elizabeth, construing all this into a wish of hearing her speak of her sister, was pleased; and on this account, as well as some others, found herself, when their visitors left them, capable of considering the last half hour with some satisfaction, though while it was passing, the enjoyment of it had been little. Eager to be alone, and fearful of enquiries or hints from her uncle and aunt, she staid with them only long enough to hear their favourable opinion of Bingley, and then hurried away to dress.

But she had no reason to fear Mr. and Mrs. Gardiner's curiosity; it was not their wish to force her communication. It was evident that she was much better acquainted with Mr. Darcy than they had before any idea of; it was evident that he was very much in love with her. They saw much to interest, but nothing to justify enquiry.

Of Mr. Darcy it was now a matter of anxiety to think well; and, as far as their acquaintance reached, there was no fault to find. They could not be untouched by his politeness, and had they drawn his character from their own feelings, and his servant's report, without any reference to any other account, the circle in Hertfordshire to which he was known, would not have recognised it for Mr. Darcy. There was now an interest, however, in believing the housekeeper; and they soon became sensible, that the authority of a servant who had known him since he was four years old, and whose own manners indicated respectability, was not to be hastily rejected. Neither had any thing occurred in the intelligence of their Lambton friends, that could materially lessen its weight. They had nothing to accuse him of but pride; pride he probably had, and if not, it would certainly be imputed by the inhabitants of a small market-town, where the family did not visit.[7] It was acknowledged, however, that he was a liberal man, and did much good among the poor.

With respect to Wickham, the travellers soon found that he was not held there in much estimation; for though the chief of his concerns, with the son of his patron, were imperfectly understood, it was yet a well known fact that, on his quitting Derbyshire, he had left many debts behind him, which Mr. Darcy afterwards discharged.

As for Elizabeth, her thoughts were at Pemberley this evening more than the last; and the evening, though as it passed it seemed long, was not long enough to determine her feelings towards *one* in that mansion; and she lay awake two whole hours, endeavouring to make them out. She certainly did not hate him. No; hatred had vanished long ago, and she had almost as long been ashamed of ever feeling a dislike against him, that could be so called. The respect created by the conviction of his valuable qualities, though at first unwillingly admitted, had for some time ceased to be repugnant to her feelings; and it was now heightened into somewhat of a friendlier nature, by the testimony so highly in his favour, and bringing forward his disposition in so amiable a light, which yesterday had produced. But above all, above respect and esteem, there was a motive within her of good will which could not be overlooked. It was gratitude.—Gratitude, not merely for having once loved her, but for loving her still well enough, to forgive all the petulance and acrimony of her manner in rejecting him, and all the unjust accusations accompanying her rejection. He who, she had been persuaded, would avoid her as his greatest enemy, seemed, on this accidental meeting, most eager to preserve the acquaintance, and without any indelicate display of regard, or any peculiarity of manner, where their two selves only were concerned, was soliciting the good opinion of her friends, and bent on making her known to his sister. Such a change in a man of so much pride, excited not only astonishment but gratitude—for to love, ardent love, it must be attributed; and as such its impression on her was of a sort to be encouraged, as by no means unpleasing, though it could not be exactly defined. She respected, she esteemed, she was grateful to him, she felt a real interest in his welfare; and she only wanted to know how far she wished that welfare to depend upon herself, and how far it would be for the happiness of both that she should employ the power, which her fancy told her she still possessed, of bringing on the renewal of his addresses.

It had been settled in the evening, between the aunt and niece, that such a striking civility as Miss Darcy's, in coming to them on the very day of her arrival at Pemberley, for she had reached it only to a late

7. I.e., on whose principal families the residents of Pemberley did not call socially.

breakfast, ought to be imitated, though it could not be equalled, by some exertion of politeness on their side; and, consequently, that it would be highly expedient to wait on her at Pemberley the following morning. They were, therefore, to go.—Elizabeth was pleased, though, when she asked herself the reason, she had very little to say in reply.

Mr. Gardiner left them soon after breakfast. The fishing scheme had been renewed the day before, and a positive engagement made of his meeting some of the gentlemen at Pemberley by noon.

Chapter III

Convinced as Elizabeth now was that Miss Bingley's dislike of her had originated in jealousy, she could not help feeling how very unwelcome her appearance at Pemberley must be to her, and was curious to know with how much civility on that lady's side, the acquaintance would now be renewed.

On reaching the house, they were shewn through the hall into the saloon, whose northern aspect rendered it delightful for summer. Its windows opening to the ground, admitted a most refreshing view of the high woody hills behind the house, and of the beautiful oaks and Spanish chestnuts which were scattered over the intermediate lawn.

In this room they were received by Miss Darcy, who was sitting there with Mrs. Hurst and Miss Bingley, and the lady with whom she lived in London. Georgiana's reception of them was very civil; but attended with all that embarrassment which, though proceeding from shyness and the fear of doing wrong, would easily give to those who felt themselves inferior, the belief of her being proud and reserved. Mrs. Gardiner and her niece, however, did her justice, and pitied her.

By Mrs. Hurst and Miss Bingley, they were noticed only by a curtsey; and on their being seated, a pause, awkward as such pauses must always be, succeeded for a few moments. It was first broken by Mrs. Annesley, a genteel, agreeable-looking woman, whose endeavour to introduce some kind of discourse, proved her to be more truly well bred than either of the others; and between her and Mrs. Gardiner, with occasional help from Elizabeth, the conversation was carried on. Miss Darcy looked as if she wished for courage enough to join in it; and sometimes did venture a short sentence, when there was least danger of its being heard.

Elizabeth soon saw that she was herself closely watched by Miss Bingley, and that she could not speak a word, especially to Miss Darcy, without calling her attention. This observation would not have prevented her from trying to talk to the latter, had they not been seated at an inconvenient distance; but she was not sorry to be spared the necessity of saying much. Her own thoughts were employing her. She expected every moment that some of the gentlemen would enter the room. She wished, she feared that the master of the house might be amongst them; and whether she wished or feared it most, she could scarcely determine. After sitting in this manner a quarter of an hour, without hearing Miss Bingley's voice, Elizabeth was roused by receiving from her a cold enquiry after the health of her family. She answered with equal indifference and brevity, and the other said no more.

The next variation which their visit afforded was produced by the entrance of servants with cold meat, cake, and a variety of all the finest fruits in season; but this did not take place till after many a significant look and smile from Mrs. Annesley to Miss Darcy had been given, to remind her of her post. There was now employment for the whole party; for though they could not all talk, they could all eat; and the beautiful pyramids of grapes, nectarines, and peaches, soon collected them round the table.

While thus engaged, Elizabeth had a fair opportunity of deciding whether she most feared or wished for the appearance of Mr. Darcy, by the feelings which prevailed on his entering the room; and then, though but a moment before she had believed her wishes to predominate, she began to regret that he came.

He had been some time with Mr. Gardiner, who, with two or three other gentlemen from the house, was engaged by the river, and had left him only on learning that the ladies of the family intended a visit to Georgiana that morning. No sooner did he appear, than Elizabeth wisely resolved to be perfectly easy and unembarrassed;—a resolution the more necessary to be made, but perhaps not the more easily kept, because she saw that the suspicions of the whole party were awakened against them, and that there was scarcely an eye which did not watch his behaviour when he first came into the room. In no countenance was attentive curiosity so strongly marked as in Miss Bingley's, in spite of the smiles which overspread her face whenever she spoke to one of its objects; for jealousy had not yet made her desperate, and her attentions to Mr. Darcy were by no means over. Miss Darcy, on her brother's entrance, exerted herself much more to talk; and Elizabeth saw that he was anxious for his sister and herself to get acquainted, and forwarded, as much as possible, every attempt at conversation on either side. Miss Bingley saw all this likewise; and, in the imprudence of anger, took the first opportunity of saying, with sneering civility,

"Pray, Miss Eliza, are not the ——shire militia removed from Meryton? They must be a great loss to *your* family."

In Darcy's presence she dared not mention Wickham's name; but Elizabeth instantly comprehended that he was uppermost in her thoughts; and the various recollections connected with him gave her a moment's distress; but, exerting herself vigorously to repel the ill-natured attack, she presently answered the question in a tolerably disengaged tone. While she spoke, an involuntary glance shewed her

Darcy with an heightened complexion, earnestly looking at her, and his sister overcome with confusion, and unable to lift up her eyes. Had Miss Bingley known what pain she was then giving her beloved friend, she undoubtedly would have refrained from the hint; but she had merely intended to discompose Elizabeth, by bringing forward the idea of a man to whom she believed her partial, to make her betray a sensibility which might injure her in Darcy's opinion, and perhaps to remind the latter of all the follies and absurdities, by which some part of her family were connected with that corps. Not a syllable had ever reached her of Miss Darcy's meditated elopement. To no creature had it been revealed, where secresy was possible, except to Elizabeth; and from all Bingley's connections her brother was particularly anxious to conceal it, from that very wish which Elizabeth had long ago attributed to him, of their becoming hereafter her own. He had certainly formed such a plan, and without meaning that it should affect his endeavour to separate him from Miss Bennet, it is probable that it might add something to his lively concern for the welfare of his friend.

Elizabeth's collected behaviour, however, soon quieted his emotion; and as Miss Bingley, vexed and disappointed, dared not approach nearer to Wickham, Georgiana also recovered in time, though not enough to be able to speak any more. Her brother, whose eye she feared to meet, scarcely recollected her interest in the affair, and the very circumstance which had been designed to turn his thoughts from Elizabeth, seemed to have fixed them on her more, and more cheerfully.

Their visit did not continue long after the question and answer above-mentioned; and while Mr. Darcy was attending them to their carriage, Miss Bingley was venting her feelings in criticisms on Elizabeth's person, behaviour, and dress. But Georgiana would not join her. Her brother's recommendation was enough to ensure her favour: his judgment could not err, and he had spoken in such terms of Elizabeth, as to leave Georgiana without the power of finding her otherwise than lovely and amiable. When Darcy returned to the saloon, Miss Bingley could not help repeating to him some part of what she had been saying to his sister.

"How very ill Eliza Bennet looks this morning, Mr. Darcy," she cried; "I never in my life saw any one so much altered as she is since the winter. She is grown so brown and coarse! Louisa and I were agreeing that we should not have known her again."

However little Mr. Darcy might have liked such an address, he contented himself with coolly replying, that he perceived no other alteration than her being rather tanned,—no miraculous consequence of travelling in the summer.

"For my own part," she rejoined, "I must confess that I never could see any beauty in her. Her face is too thin; her complexion has no brilliancy; and her features are not at all handsome. Her nose wants character; there is nothing marked in its lines. Her teeth are tolerable, but not out of the common way; and as for her eyes, which have sometimes been called so fine, I never could perceive any thing extraordinary in them. They have a sharp, shrewish look, which I do not like at all; and in her air altogether, there is a self-sufficiency without fashion, which is intolerable."

Persuaded as Miss Bingley was that Darcy admired Elizabeth, this was not the best method of recommending herself; but angry people are not always wise; and in seeing him at last look somewhat nettled, she had all the success she expected. He was resolutely silent however; and, from a determination of making him speak, she continued,

"I remember, when we first knew her in Hertfordshire, how amazed we all were to find that she was a reputed beauty; and I particularly recollect your saying one night, after they had been dining at Netherfield, 'She a beauty!—I should as soon call her mother a wit.' But afterwards she seemed to improve on you, and I believe you thought her rather pretty at one time."

"Yes," replied Darcy, who could contain himself no longer, "but *that* was only when I first knew her, for it is many months since I have considered her as one of the handsomest women of my acquaintance."

He then went away, and Miss Bingley was left to all the satisfaction of having forced him to say what gave no one any pain but herself.

Mrs. Gardiner and Elizabeth talked of all that had occurred, during their visit, as they returned, except what had particularly interested them both. The looks and behaviour of every body they had seen were discussed, except of the person who had mostly engaged their attention. They talked of his sister, his friends, his house, his fruit, of every thing but himself; yet Elizabeth was longing to know what Mrs. Gardiner thought of him, and Mrs. Gardiner would have been highly gratified by her niece's beginning the subject.

Chapter IV

Elizabeth had been a good deal disappointed in not finding a letter from Jane, on their first arrival at Lambton; and this disappointment had been renewed on each of the mornings that had now been spent there; but on the third, her repining was over, and her sister justified by the receipt of two letters from her at once, on one of which was marked that it had been missent elsewhere. Elizabeth was not surprised at it, as Jane had written the direction[8] remarkably ill.

They had just been preparing to walk as the letters came in; and her uncle and aunt, leaving her to enjoy them in quiet, set off by themselves. The one missent must be first attended to; it had been written

8. Address.

five days ago. The beginning contained an account of all their little parties and engagements, with such news as the country afforded; but the latter half, which was dated a day later, and written in evident agitation, gave more important intelligence. It was to this effect:

"Since writing the above, dearest Lizzy, something has occurred of a most unexpected and serious nature; but I am afraid of alarming you—be assured that we are all well. What I have to say relates to poor Lydia. An express came at twelve last night, just as we were all gone to bed, from Colonel Forster, to inform us that she was gone off to Scotland with one of his officers; to own the truth, with Wickham!— Imagine our surprise. To Kitty, however, it does not seem so wholly unexpected. I am very, very sorry. So imprudent a match on both sides!—But I am willing to hope the best, and that his character has been misunderstood. Thoughtless and indiscreet I can easily believe him, but this step (and let us rejoice over it) marks nothing bad at heart. His choice is disinterested at least, for he must know my father can give her nothing. Our poor mother is sadly grieved. My father bears it better. How thankful am I, that we never let them know what has been said against him; we must forget it ourselves. They were off Saturday night about twelve, as is conjectured, but were not missed till yesterday morning at eight. The express was sent off directly. My dear Lizzy, they must have passed within ten miles of us. Colonel Forster gives us reason to expect him here soon. Lydia left a few lines for his wife, informing her of their intention. I must conclude, for I cannot be long from my poor mother. I am afraid you will not be able to make it out, but I hardly know what I have written."

Without allowing herself time for consideration, and scarcely knowing what she felt, Elizabeth on finishing this letter, instantly seized the other, and opening it with the utmost impatience, read as follows: it had been written a day later than the conclusion of the first.

"By this time, my dearest sister, you have received my hurried letter; I wish this may be more intelligible, but though not confined for time, my head is so bewildered that I cannot answer for being coherent. Dearest Lizzy, I hardly know what I would write, but I have bad news for you, and it cannot be delayed. Imprudent as a marriage between Mr. Wickham and our poor Lydia would be, we are now anxious to be assured it has taken place, for there is but too much reason to fear they are not gone to Scotland. Colonel Forster came yesterday, having left Brighton the day before, not many hours after the express. Though Lydia's short letter to Mrs. F. gave them to understand that they were going to Gretna Green,[9] something was dropped by Denny expressing his belief that W. never intended to go there, or to marry Lydia at all,

9. Scottish law did not require the consent of parents to the marriage of a minor. As the most accessible village on the Scottish side of the border with England, Gretna Green was the customary destination of eloping couples in which one partner was not yet of age.

which was repeated to Colonel F. who instantly taking the alarm, set off from B. intending to trace their route. He did trace them easily to Clapham, but no farther; for on entering that place they removed into a hackney-coach[1] and dismissed the chaise that brought them from Epsom. All that is known after this is, that they were seen to continue the London road. I know not what to think. After making every possible enquiry on that side London, Colonel F. came on into Hertfordshire, anxiously renewing them at all the turnpikes, and at the inns in Barnet and Hatfield, but without any success, no such people had been seen to pass through. With the kindest concern he came on to Longbourn, and broke his apprehensions to us in a manner most creditable to his heart. I am sincerely grieved for him and Mrs. F. but no one can throw any blame on them. Our distress, my dear Lizzy, is very great. My father and mother believe the worst, but I cannot think so ill of him. Many circumstances might make it more eligible for them to be married privately in town than to pursue their first plan; and even if *he* could form such a design against a young woman of Lydia's connections, which is not likely, can I suppose her so lost to every thing?—Impossible. I grieve to find, however, that Colonel F. is not disposed to depend upon their marriage; he shook his head when I expressed my hopes, and said he feared W. was not a man to be trusted. My poor mother is really ill and keeps her room. Could she exert herself it would be better, but this is not to be expected; and as to my father, I never in my life saw him so affected. Poor Kitty has anger for having concealed their attachment; but as it was a matter of confidence one cannot wonder. I am truly glad, dearest Lizzy, that you have been spared something of these distressing scenes; but now as the first shock is over, shall I own that I long for your return? I am not so selfish, however, as to press for it, if inconvenient. Adieu. I take up my pen again to do, what I have just told you I would not, but circumstances are such, that I cannot help earnestly begging you all to come here, as soon as possible. I know my dear uncle and aunt so well, that I am not afraid of requesting it, though I have still something more to ask of the former. My father is going to London with Colonel Forster instantly, to try to discover her. What he means to do, I am sure I know not; but his excessive distress will not allow him to pursue any measure in the best and safest way, and Colonel Forster is obliged to be at Brighton again to-morrow evening. In such an exigence my uncle's advice and assistance would be every thing in the world; he will immediately comprehend what I must feel, and I rely upon his goodness."

"Oh! where, where is my uncle?" cried Elizabeth, darting from her seat as she finished the letter, in eagerness to follow him, without losing a moment of the time so precious; but as she reached the door, it was

1. Hired coach.

opened by a servant, and Mr. Darcy appeared. Her pale face and impetuous manner made him start, and before he could recover himself enough to speak, she, in whose mind every idea was superseded by Lydia's situation, hastily exclaimed, "I beg your pardon, but I must leave you. I must find Mr. Gardiner this moment, on business that cannot be delayed; I have not an instant to lose."

"Good God! what is the matter?" cried he, with more feeling than politeness; then recollecting himself, "I will not detain you a minute, but let me, or let the servant, go after Mr. and Mrs. Gardiner. You are not well enough;—you cannot go yourself."

Elizabeth hesitated, but her knees trembled under her, and she felt how little would be gained by her attempting to pursue them. Calling back the servant, therefore, she commissioned him, though in so breathless an accent as made her almost unintelligible, to fetch his master and mistress home, instantly.

On his quitting the room, she sat down, unable to support herself, and looking so miserably ill, that it was impossible for Darcy to leave her, or to refrain from saying, in a tone of gentleness and commiseration, "Let me call your maid. Is there nothing you could take, to give you present relief?—A glass of wine;—shall I get you one?—You are very ill."

"No, I thank you;" she replied, endeavouring to recover herself. "There is nothing the matter with me. I am quite well. I am only distressed by some dreadful news which I have just received from Longbourn."

She burst into tears as she alluded to it, and for a few minutes could not speak another word. Darcy, in wretched suspense, could only say something indistinctly of his concern, and observe her in compassionate silence. At length, she spoke again. "I have just had a letter from Jane, with such dreadful news. It cannot be concealed from any one. My youngest sister has left all her friends—has eloped;—has thrown herself into the power of—of Mr. Wickham. They are gone off together from Brighton. *You* know him too well to doubt the rest. She has no money, no connections, nothing that can tempt him to—she is lost for ever."

Darcy was fixed in astonishment. "When I consider," she added, in a yet more agitated voice, "that *I* might have prevented it!—*I* who knew what he was. Had I but explained some part of it only—some part of what I learnt, to my own family! Had his character been known, this could not have happened. But it is all, all too late now."

"I am grieved, indeed," cried Darcy; "grieved—shocked. But is it certain, absolutely certain?"

"Oh yes!—They left Brighton together on Sunday night, and were traced almost to London, but not beyond; they are certainly not gone to Scotland."

"And what has been done, what has been attempted, to recover her?"

"My father is gone to London, and Jane has written to beg my uncle's immediate assistance, and we shall be off, I hope, in half an hour. But nothing can be done; I know very well that nothing can be done. How is such a man to be worked on? How are they even to be discovered? I have not the smallest hope. It is every way horrible!"

Darcy shook his head in silent acquiescence.

"When *my* eyes were opened to his real character.—Oh! had I known what I ought, what I dared, to do! But I knew not—I was afraid of doing too much. Wretched, wretched, mistake!"

Darcy made no answer. He seemed scarcely to hear her, and was walking up and down the room in earnest meditation; his brow contracted, his air gloomy. Elizabeth soon observed, and instantly understood it. Her power was sinking; every thing *must* sink under such a proof of family weakness, such an assurance of the deepest disgrace. She could neither wonder nor condemn, but the belief of his self-conquest brought nothing consolatory to her bosom, afforded no palliation of her distress. It was, on the contrary, exactly calculated to make her understand her own wishes; and never had she so honestly felt that she could have loved him, as now, when all love must be vain.

But self, though it would intrude, could not engross her. Lydia—the humiliation, the misery, she was bringing on them all, soon swallowed up every private care; and covering her face with her handkerchief, Elizabeth was soon lost to every thing else; and, after a pause of several minutes, was only recalled to a sense of her situation by the voice of her companion, who, in a manner, which though it spoke compassion, spoke likewise restraint, said, "I am afraid you have been long desiring my absence, nor have I any thing to plead in excuse of my stay, but real, though unavailing, concern. Would to heaven that any thing could be either said or done on my part, that might offer consolation to such distress.—But I will not torment you with vain wishes, which may seem purposely to ask for your thanks. This unfortunate affair will, I fear, prevent my sister's having the pleasure of seeing you at Pemberley to day."

"Oh, yes. Be so kind as to apologize for us to Miss Darcy. Say that urgent business calls us home immediately. Conceal the unhappy truth as long as it is possible.—I know it cannot be long."

He readily assured her of his secrecy—again expressed his sorrow for her distress, wished it a happier conclusion than there was at present reason to hope, and leaving his compliments for her relations, with only one serious, parting, look, went away.

As he quitted the room, Elizabeth felt how improbable it was that they should ever see each other again on such terms of cordiality as had marked their several meetings in Derbyshire; and as she threw a retrospective glance over the whole of their acquaintance, so full of contradictions and varieties, sighed at the perverseness of those feelings which would now have promoted its continuance, and would formerly have rejoiced in its termination.

If gratitude and esteem are good foundations of affection, Elizabeth's change of sentiment will be neither improbable nor faulty. But if otherwise, if the regard springing from such sources is unreasonable or unnatural, in comparison of what is so often described as arising on a first interview with its object, and even before two words have been exchanged, nothing can be said in her defence, except that she had given somewhat of a trial to the latter method, in her partiality for Wickham, and that its ill-success might perhaps authorise her to seek the other less interesting mode of attachment. Be that as it may, she saw him go with regret; and in this early example of what Lydia's infamy must produce, found additional anguish as she reflected on that wretched business. Never, since reading Jane's second letter, had she entertained a hope of Wickham's meaning to marry her. No one but Jane, she thought, could flatter herself with such an expectation. Surprise was the least of her feelings on this developement. While the contents of the first letter remained on her mind, she was all surprise— all astonishment that Wickham should marry a girl, whom it was impossible he could marry for money; and how Lydia could ever have attached him, had appeared incomprehensible. But now it was all too natural. For such an attachment as this, she might have sufficient charms; and though she did not suppose Lydia to be deliberately engaging in an elopement, without the intention of marriage, she had no difficulty in believing that neither her virtue nor her understanding would preserve her from falling an easy prey.

She had never perceived, while the regiment was in Hertfordshire, that Lydia had any partiality for him, but she was convinced that Lydia had wanted only encouragement to attach herself to any body. Sometimes one officer, sometimes another had been her favourite, as their attentions raised them in her opinion. Her affections had been continually fluctuating, but never without an object. The mischief of neglect and mistaken indulgence towards such a girl.—Oh! how acutely did she now feel it.

She was wild to be at home—to hear, to see, to be upon the spot, to share with Jane in the cares that must now fall wholly upon her, in a family so deranged; a father absent, a mother incapable of exertion, and requiring constant attendance; and though almost persuaded that nothing could be done for Lydia, her uncle's interference seemed of the utmost importance, and till he entered the room, the misery of her impatience was severe. Mr. and Mrs. Gardiner had hurried back in alarm, supposing, by the servant's account, that their niece was taken suddenly ill;—but satisfying them instantly on that head, she eagerly communicated the cause of their summons, reading the two letters aloud, and dwelling on the postscript of the last, with trembling energy.—Though Lydia had never been a favourite with them, Mr. and Mrs. Gardiner could not but be deeply affected. Not Lydia only, but all were concerned in it; and after the first exclamations of surprise and horror, Mr. Gardiner readily promised every assistance in his power.—Elizabeth, though expecting no less, thanked him with tears of gratitude; and all three being actuated by one spirit, every thing relating to their journey was speedily settled. They were to be off as soon as possible. "But what is to be done about Pemberley?" cried Mrs. Gardiner. "John told us Mr. Darcy was here when you sent for us;—was it so?"

"Yes; and I told him we should not be able to keep our engagement. *That* is all settled."

"That is all settled;" repeated the other, as she ran into her room to prepare. "And are they upon such terms as for her to disclose the real truth! Oh, that I knew how it was!"

But wishes were vain; or at best could serve only to amuse her in the hurry and confusion of the following hour. Had Elizabeth been at leisure to be idle, she would have remained certain that all employment was impossible to one so wretched as herself; but she had her share of business as well as her aunt, and amongst the rest there were notes to be written to all their friends in Lambton, with false excuses for their sudden departure. An hour, however, saw the whole completed; and Mr. Gardiner meanwhile having settled his account at the inn, nothing remained to be done but to go; and Elizabeth, after all the misery of the morning, found herself, in a shorter space of time than she could have supposed, seated in the carriage, and on the road to Longbourn.

Chapter V

"I have been thinking it over again, Elizabeth," said her uncle, as they drove from the town; "and really, upon serious consideration, I am much more inclined than I was to judge as your eldest sister does of the matter. It appears to me so very unlikely, that any young man should form such a design against a girl who is by no means unprotected or friendless, and who was actually staying in his colonel's family, that I am strongly inclined to hope the best. Could he expect that her friends would not step forward? Could he expect to be noticed again by the regiment, after such an affront to Colonel Forster? His temptation is not adequate to the risk."

"Do you really think so?" cried Elizabeth, brightening up for a moment.

"Upon my word," said Mrs. Gardiner, "I begin to be of your uncle's opinion. It is really too great a violation of decency, honour, and interest, for him to be guilty of it. I cannot think so very ill of Wickham.

Can you, yourself, Lizzy, so wholly give him up, as to believe him capable of it?"

"Not perhaps of neglecting his own interest. But of every other neglect I can believe him capable. If, indeed, it should be so! But I dare not hope it. Why should they not go on to Scotland, if that had been the case?"

"In the first place," replied Mr. Gardiner, "there is no absolute proof that they are not gone to Scotland."

"Oh! but their removing from the chaise into an hackney coach is such a presumption! And, besides, no traces of them were to be found on the Barnet road."

"Well, then—supposing them to be in London. They may be there, though for the purpose of concealment, for no more exceptionable purpose. It is not likely that money should be very abundant on either side; and it might strike them that they could be more economically, though less expeditiously, married in London, than in Scotland."

"But why all this secrecy? Why any fear of detection? Why must their marriage be private? Oh! no, no, this is not likely. His most particular friend, you see by Jane's account, was persuaded of his never intending to marry her. Wickham will never marry a woman without some money. He cannot afford it. And what claims has Lydia, what attractions has she beyond youth, health, and good humour, that could make him for her sake, forego every chance of benefiting himself by marrying well. As to what restraint the apprehension of disgrace in the corps might throw on a dishonourable elopement with her, I am not able to judge; for I know nothing of the effects that such a step might produce. But as to your other objection, I am afraid it will hardly hold good. Lydia has no brothers to step forward; and he might imagine, from my father's behaviour, from his indolence and the little attention he has ever seemed to give to what was going forward in his family, that *he* would do as little, and think as little about it, as any father could do, in such a matter."

"But can you think that Lydia is so lost to every thing but love of him, as to consent to live with him on any other terms than marriage?"

"It does seem, and it is most shocking indeed," replied Elizabeth, with tears in her eyes, "that a sister's sense of decency and virtue in such a point should admit of doubt. But, really, I know not what to say. Perhaps I am not doing her justice. But she is very young; she has never been taught to think on serious subjects; and for the last half year, nay, for a twelvemonth, she has been given up to nothing but amusement and vanity. She has been allowed to dispose of her time in the most idle and frivolous manner, and to adopt any opinions that came in her way. Since the ——shire were first quartered in Meryton, nothing but love, flirtation, and officers, have been in her head. She has been doing every thing in her power by thinking and talking on the subject, to give greater—what shall I call it? susceptibility to her feelings; which are naturally lively enough. And we all know that Wickham has every charm of person and address that can captivate a woman."

"But you see that Jane," said her aunt, "does not think so ill of Wickham, as to believe him capable of the attempt."

"Of whom does Jane ever think ill? And who is there, whatever might be their former conduct, that she would believe capable of such an attempt, till it were proved against them? But Jane knows, as well as I do, what Wickham really is. We both know that he has been profligate in every sense of the word. That he has neither integrity nor honour. That he is as false and deceitful, as he is insinuating."

"And do you really know all this?" cried Mrs. Gardiner, whose curiosity as to the mode of her intelligence was all alive.

"I do, indeed," replied Elizabeth, colouring. "I told you the other day, of his infamous behaviour to Mr. Darcy; and you, yourself, when last at Longbourn, heard in what manner he spoke of the man, who had behaved with such forbearance and liberality towards him. And there are other circumstances which I am not at liberty—which it is not worth while to relate; but his lies about the whole Pemberley family are endless. From what he said of Miss Darcy, I was thoroughly prepared to see a proud, reserved, disagreeable girl. Yet he knew to the contrary himself. He must know that she was as amiable and unpretending as we have found her."

"But does Lydia know nothing of this? Can she be ignorant of what you and Jane seem so well to understand?"

"Oh, yes!—that, that is the worst of all. Till I was in Kent, and saw so much both of Mr. Darcy and his relation, Colonel Fitzwilliam, I was ignorant of the truth myself. And when I returned home, the ——shire was to leave Meryton in a week or fortnight's time. As that was the case, neither Jane, to whom I related the whole, nor I, thought it necessary to make our knowledge public; for what use could it apparently be to any one, that the good opinion which all the neighbourhood had of him, should then be overthrown? And even when it was settled that Lydia should go with Mrs. Forster, the necessity of opening her eyes to his character never occurred to me. That *she* could be in any danger from the deception never entered my head. That such a consequence as *this* should ensue, you may easily believe was far enough from my thoughts."

"When they all removed to Brighton, therefore, you had no reason, I suppose, to believe them fond of each other."

"Not the slightest. I can remember no symptom of affection on either side; and had any thing of the kind been perceptible, you must be aware that ours is not a family, on which it could be thrown away.

When first he entered the corps, she was ready enough to admire him; but so we all were. Every girl in, or near Meryton, was out of her senses about him for the first two months; but he never distinguished *her* by any particular attention, and, consequently, after a moderate period of extravagant and wild admiration, her fancy for him gave way, and others of the regiment, who treated her with more distinction, again became her favourites."

———

It may be easily believed, that however little of novelty could be added to their fears, hopes, and conjectures, on this interesting subject, by its repeated discussion, no other could detain them from it long, during the whole of the journey. From Elizabeth's thoughts it was never absent. Fixed there by the keenest of all anguish, self reproach, she could find no interval of ease or forgetfulness.

They travelled as expeditiously as possible; and sleeping one night on the road, reached Longbourn by dinner-time the next day. It was a comfort to Elizabeth to consider that Jane could not have been wearied by long expectations.

The little Gardiners, attracted by the sight of a chaise, were standing on the steps of the house, as they entered the paddock;[2] and when the carriage drove up to the door, the joyful surprise that lighted up their faces, and displayed itself over their whole bodies, in a variety of capers and frisks, was the first pleasing earnest of their welcome.

Elizabeth jumped out; and, after giving each of them an hasty kiss, hurried into the vestibule, where Jane, who came running down stairs from her mother's apartment, immediately met her.

Elizabeth, as she affectionately embraced her, whilst tears filled the eyes of both, lost not a moment in asking whether any thing had been heard of the fugitives.

"Not yet," replied Jane. "But now that my dear uncle is come, I hope every thing will be well."

"Is my father in town?"

"Yes, he went on Tuesday as I wrote you word."

"And have you heard from him often?"

"We have heard only once. He wrote me a few lines on Wednesday, to say that he had arrived in safety, and to give me his directions, which I particularly begged him to do. He merely added, that he should not write again, till he had something of importance to mention."

"And my mother—How is she? How are you all?"

"My mother is tolerably well, I trust; though her spirits are greatly shaken. She is up stairs, and will have great satisfaction in seeing you all. She does not yet leave her dressing-room. Mary and Kitty, thank Heaven! are quite well."

---

2. A small enclosed field, usually a pasture, near a house or stable.

"But you—How are you?" cried Elizabeth. "You look pale. How much you must have gone through!"

Her sister, however, assured her, of her being perfectly well; and their conversation, which had been passing while Mr. and Mrs. Gardiner were engaged with their children, was now put an end to, by the approach of the whole party. Jane ran to her uncle and aunt, and welcomed and thanked them both, with alternate smiles and tears.

When they were all in the drawing room, the questions which Elizabeth had already asked, were of course repeated by the others, and they soon found that Jane had no intelligence to give. The sanguine hope of good, however, which the benevolence of her heart suggested, had not yet deserted her; she still expected that it would all end well, and that every morning would bring some letter, either from Lydia or her father, to explain their proceedings, and perhaps announce the marriage.

Mrs. Bennet, to whose apartment they all repaired, after a few minutes conversation together, received them exactly as might be expected; with tears and lamentations of regret, invectives against the villanous conduct of Wickham, and complaints of her own sufferings and ill usage, blaming every body but the person to whose ill judging indulgence the errors of her daughter must be principally owing.[3]

"If I had been able," said she, "to carry my point of going to Brighton, with all my family, *this* would not have happened; but poor dear Lydia had nobody to take care of her. Why did the Forsters ever let her go out of their sight? I am sure there was some great neglect or other on their side, for she is not the kind of girl to do such a thing, if she had been well looked after. I always thought they were very unfit to have the charge of her; but I was over-ruled, as I always am. Poor dear child! And now here's Mr. Bennet gone away, and I know he will fight Wickham, wherever he meets him, and then he will be killed, and what is to become of us all? The Collinses will turn us out, before he is cold in his grave; and if you are not kind to us, brother, I do not know what we shall do."

They all exclaimed against such terrific ideas; and Mr. Gardiner, after general assurances of his affection for her and all her family, told her that he meant to be in London the very next day, and would assist Mr. Bennet in every endeavour for recovering Lydia.

"Do not give way to useless alarm," added he, "though it is right to be prepared for the worst, there is no occasion to look on it as certain. It is not quite a week since they left Brighton. In a few days more, we may gain some news of them, and till we know that they are not married, and have no design of marrying, do not let us give the matter over as lost. As soon as I get to town, I shall go to my brother, and make

3. The 1813 edition puts a period after "ill-usage" in this sentence and capitalizes the first letter of "blaming."

him come home with me to Gracechurch Street, and then we may consult together as to what is to be done."

"Oh! my dear brother," replied Mrs. Bennet, "that is exactly what I could most wish for. And now do, when you get to town, find them out, wherever they may be; and if they are not married already, *make* them marry. And as for wedding clothes, do not let them wait for that, but tell Lydia she shall have as much money as she chuses, to buy them, after they are married. And, above all things, keep Mr. Bennet from fighting. Tell him what a dreadful state I am in,—that I am frightened out of my wits; and have such tremblings, such flutterings, all over me, such spasms in my side, and pains in my head, and such beatings at heart, that I can get no rest by night nor by day. And tell my dear Lydia, not to give any directions about her clothes, till she has seen me, for she does not know which are the best warehouses.[4] Oh, brother, how kind you are! I know you will contrive it all."

But Mr. Gardiner, though he assured her again of his earnest endeavours in the cause, could not avoid recommending moderation to her, as well in her hopes as her fears; and, after talking with her in this manner till dinner was on table, they left her to vent all her feelings on the housekeeper, who attended, in the absence of her daughters.

Though her brother and sister were persuaded that there was no real occasion for such a seclusion from the family, they did not attempt to oppose it, for they knew that she had not prudence enough to hold her tongue before the servants, while they waited at table, and judged it better that *one* only of the household, and the one whom they could most trust, should comprehend all her fears and solicitude on the subject.

In the dining-room they were soon joined by Mary and Kitty, who had been too busily engaged in their separate apartments, to make their appearance before. One came from her books, and the other from her toilette. The faces of both, however, were tolerably calm; and no change was visible in either, except that the loss of her favourite sister, or the anger which she had herself incurred in the business, had given something more of fretfulness than usual, to the accents of Kitty. As for Mary, she was mistress enough of herself to whisper to Elizabeth with a countenance of grave reflection, soon after they were seated at table,

"This is a most unfortunate affair; and will probably be much talked of. But we must stem the tide of malice, and pour into the wounded bosoms of each other, the balm of sisterly consolation."

Then, perceiving in Elizabeth no inclination of replying, she added, "Unhappy as the event must be for Lydia, we may draw from it this useful lesson; that loss of virtue in a female is irretrievable—that one

4. Shops.

false step involves her in endless ruin—that her reputation is no less brittle than it is beautiful,—and that she cannot be too much guarded in her behaviour towards the undeserving of the other sex."

Elizabeth lifted up her eyes in amazement, but was too much oppressed to make any reply. Mary, however, continued to console herself with such kind of moral extractions from the evil before them.

In the afternoon, the two elder Miss Bennets were able to be for half an hour by themselves; and Elizabeth instantly availed herself of the opportunity of making many enquiries, which Jane was equally eager to satisfy. After joining in general lamentations over the dreadful sequel of this event, which Elizabeth considered as all but certain, and Miss Bennet could not assert to be wholly impossible; the former continued the subject, by saying, "But tell me all and every thing about it, which I have not already heard. Give me farther particulars. What did Colonel Forster say? Had they no apprehension of any thing before the elopement took place? They must have seen them together for ever."

"Colonel Forster did own that he had often suspected some partiality, especially on Lydia's side, but nothing to give him any alarm. I am so grieved for him. His behaviour was attentive and kind to the utmost. He *was* coming to us, in order to assure us of his concern, before he had any idea of their not being gone to Scotland: when that apprehension first got abroad, it hastened his journey."

"And was Denny convinced that Wickham would not marry? Did he know of their intending to go off? Had Colonel Forster seen Denny himself?"

"Yes; but when questioned by *him* Denny denied knowing any thing of their plan, and would not give his real opinion about it. He did not repeat his persuasion of their not marrying—and from *that*, I am inclined to hope, he might have been misunderstood before."

"And till Colonel Forster came himself, not one of you entertained a doubt, I suppose, of their being really married?"

"How was it possible that such an idea should enter our brains! I felt a little uneasy—a little fearful of my sister's happiness with him in marriage, because I knew that his conduct had not been always quite right. My father and mother knew nothing of that, they only felt how imprudent a match it must be. Kitty then owned, with a very natural triumph on knowing more than the rest of us, that in Lydia's last letter, she had prepared her for such a step. She had known, it seems, of their being in love with each other, many weeks."

"But not before they went to Brighton?"

"No, I believe not."

"And did Colonel Forster appear to think ill of Wickham himself? Does he know his real character?"

"I must confess that he did not speak so well of Wickham as he formerly did. He believed him to be imprudent and extravagant. And since this sad affair has taken place, it is said, that he left Meryton greatly in debt; but I hope this may be false."

"Oh, Jane, had we been less secret, had we told what we knew of him, this could not have happened!"

"Perhaps it would have been better;" replied her sister. "But to expose the former faults of any person, without knowing what their present feelings were, seemed unjustifiable. We acted with the best intentions."

"Could Colonel Forster repeat the particulars of Lydia's note to his wife?"

"He brought it with him for us to see."

Jane then took it from her pocket-book, and gave it to Elizabeth. These were the contents:

MY DEAR HARRIET,

"You will laugh when you know where I am gone, and I cannot help laughing myself at your surprise to-morrow morning, as soon as I am missed. I am going to Gretna Green, and if you cannot guess with who, I shall think you a simpleton, for there is but one man in the world I love, and he is an angel. I should never be happy without him, so think it no harm to be off. You need not send them word at Longbourn of my going, if you do not like it, for it will make the surprise the greater, when I write to them, and sign my name Lydia Wickham. What a good joke it will be! I can hardly write for laughing. Pray make my excuses to Pratt, for not keeping my engagement, and dancing with him to night. Tell him I hope he will excuse me when he knows all, and tell him I will dance with him at the next ball we meet, with great pleasure. I shall send for my clothes when I get to Longbourn; but I wish you would tell Sally to mend a great slit in my worked muslin gown, before they are packed up. Good bye. Give my love to Colonel Forster, I hope you will drink to our good journey.

"Your affectionate friend,
"LYDIA BENNET."

"Oh! thoughtless, thoughtless Lydia!" cried Elizabeth when she had finished it. "What a letter is this, to be written at such a moment. But at least it shews, that *she* was serious in the object of her journey. Whatever he might afterwards persuade her to, it was not on her side a *scheme* of infamy. My poor father! how he must have felt it!"

"I never saw any one so shocked. He could not speak a word for full ten minutes. My mother was taken ill immediately, and the whole house in such confusion!"

"Oh! Jane," cried Elizabeth, "was there a servant belonging to it, who did not know the whole story before the end of the day?"

"I do not know.—I hope there was.—But to be guarded at such a time, is very difficult. My mother was in hysterics, and though I endeavoured to give her every assistance in my power, I am afraid I did not do so much as I might have done! But the horror of what might possibly happen, almost took from me my faculties."

"Your attendance upon her, has been too much for you. You do not look well. Oh! that I had been with you, you have had every care and anxiety upon yourself alone."

"Mary and Kitty have been very kind, and would have shared in every fatigue, I am sure, but I did not think it right for either of them. Kitty is slight and delicate, and Mary studies so much, that her hours of repose should not be broken in on. My aunt Philips came to Longbourn on Tuesday, after my father went away; and was so good as to stay till Thursday with me. She was of great use and comfort to us all, and lady Lucas has been very kind; she walked here on Wednesday morning to condole with us, and offered her services, or any of her daughters, if they could be of use to us."

"She had better have stayed at home," cried Elizabeth; "perhaps she *meant* well, but, under such a misfortune as this, one cannot see too little of one's neighbours. Assistance is impossible; condolence, insufferable. Let them triumph over us at a distance, and be satisfied."

She then proceeded to enquire into the measures which her father had intended to pursue, while in town, for the recovery of his daughter.

"He meant, I believe," replied Jane, "to go to Epsom, the place where they last changed horses, see the postilions, and try if any thing could be made out from them. His principal object must be, to discover the number of the hackney coach which took them from Clapham. It had come with a fare from London; and as he thought the circumstance of a gentleman and lady's removing from one carriage into another, might be remarked, he meant to make enquiries at Clapham. If he could any how discover at what house the coachman had before set down his fare, he determined to make enquiries there, and hoped it might not be impossible to find out the stand and number of the coach. I do not know of any other designs that he had formed: but he was in such a hurry to be gone, and his spirits so greatly discomposed, that I had difficulty in finding out even so much as this."

Chapter VI

The whole party were in hopes of a letter from Mr. Bennet the next morning, but the post came in without bringing a single line from him. His family knew him to be on all common occasions, a most negligent and dilatory correspondent, but at such a time, they had hoped for exertion. They were forced to conclude, that he had no pleasing intelligence to send, but even of *that* they would have been glad to be certain. Mr. Gardiner had waited only for the letters before he set off.

When he was gone, they were certain at least of receiving constant information of what was going on, and their uncle promised, at parting, to prevail on Mr. Bennet to return to Longbourn, as soon as he could, to the great consolation of his sister, who considered it as the only security for her husband's not being killed in a duel.

Mrs. Gardiner and the children were to remain in Hertfordshire a few days longer, as the former thought her presence might be service- able to her nieces. She shared in their attendance on Mrs. Bennet, and was a great comfort to them, in their hours of freedom. Their other aunt also visited them frequently, and always, as she said, with the design of cheering and heartening them up, though as she never came without reporting some fresh instance of Wickham's extravagance or irregularity, she seldom went away without leaving them more dispir- ited than she found them.

All Meryton seemed striving to blacken the man, who, but three months before, had been almost an angel of light. He was declared to be in debt to every tradesman in the place, and his intrigues, all hon- oured with the title of seduction, had been extended into every trades- man's family. Every body declared that he was the wickedest young man in the world; and every body began to find out, that they had always distrusted the appearance of his goodness. Elizabeth, though she did not credit above half of what was said, believed enough to make her former assurance of her sister's ruin still more certain; and even Jane, who believed still less of it, became almost hopeless, more especially as the time was now come, when if they had gone to Scot- land, which she had never before entirely despaired of, they must in all probability have gained some news of them.

Mr. Gardiner left Longbourn on Sunday; on Tuesday, his wife received a letter from him; it told them, that on his arrival, he had immediately found out his brother, and persuaded him to come to Gracechurch street. That Mr. Bennet had been to Epsom and Cla- pham, before his arrival, but without gaining any satisfactory infor- mation; and that he was now determined to enquire at all the principal hotels in town, as Mr. Bennet thought it possible they might have gone to one of them, on their first coming to London, before they procured lodgings. Mr. Gardiner himself did not expect any success from this measure, but as his brother was eager in it, he meant to assist him in pursuing it. He added, that Mr. Bennet seemed wholly disinclined at present, to leave London, and promised to write again very soon. There was also a postscript to this effect.

"I have written to Colonel Forster to desire him to find out, if pos- sible, from some of the young man's intimates in the regiment, whether Wickham has any relations or connections, who would be likely to know in what part of the town he has now concealed himself. If there were any one, that one could apply to, with a probability of gaining such a clue as that, it might be of essential consequence. At present we have nothing to guide us. Colonel Forster will, I dare say, do every thing in his power to satisfy us on this head. But, on second thoughts, perhaps Lizzy could tell us, what relations he has now living, better than any other person."

Elizabeth was at no loss to understand from whence this deference for her authority proceeded; but it was not in her power to give any information of so satisfactory a nature, as the compliment deserved.

She had never heard of his having had any relations, except a father and mother, both of whom had been dead many years. It was possible, however, that some of his companions in the ——shire, might be able to give more information; and, though she was not very sanguine in expecting it, the application was something to look forward to.

Every day at Longbourn was now a day of anxiety; but the most anxious part of each was when the post was expected. The arrival of letters was the first grand object of every morning's impatience. Through letters, whatever of good or bad was to be told, would be communicated, and every succeeding day was expected to bring some news of importance.

But before they heard again from Mr. Gardiner, a letter arrived for their father, from a different quarter, from Mr. Collins; which, as Jane had received directions to open all that came for him in his absence, she accordingly read; and Elizabeth, who knew what curiosities his letters always were, looked over her, and read it likewise. It was as follows:

"MY DEAR SIR,

"I feel myself called upon, by our relationship, and my situation in life, to condole with you on the grievous affliction you are now suffering under, of which we were yesterday informed by a letter from Hertford-shire. Be assured, my dear Sir, that Mrs. Collins and myself sincerely sympathise with you, and all your respectable family, in your present distress, which must be of the bitterest kind, because proceeding from a cause which no time can remove. No arguments shall be wanting on my part, that can alleviate so severe a misfortune; or that may comfort you, under a circumstance that must be of all others most afflicting to a parent's mind. The death of your daughter would have been a bless-ing in comparison of this. And it is the more to be lamented, because there is reason to suppose, as my dear Charlotte informs me, that this licentiousness of behaviour in your daughter, has proceeded from a faulty degree of indulgence, though, at the same time, for the conso-lation of yourself and Mrs. Bennet, I am inclined to think that her own disposition must be naturally bad, or she could not be guilty of such an enormity, at so early an age. Howsoever that may be, you are griev-ously to be pitied, in which opinion I am not only joined by Mrs. Collins, but likewise by lady Catherine and her daughter, to whom I have related the affair. They agree with me in apprehending that this false step in one daughter, will be injurious to the fortunes of all the others, for who, as lady Catherine herself condescendingly says, will connect themselves with such a family. And this consideration leads me moreover to reflect with augmented satisfaction on a certain event of last November, for had it been otherwise, I must have been involved in all your sorrow and disgrace. Let me advise you then, my dear Sir, to console yourself as much as possible, to throw off your unworthy child from your affection for ever, and leave her to reap the fruits of her own heinous offence.

I am, dear Sir, &c. &c."

Mr. Gardiner did not write again, till he had received an answer from Colonel Forster; and then he had nothing of a pleasant nature to send. It was not known that Wickham had a single relation, with whom he kept up any connection, and it was certain that he had no near one living. His former acquaintance had been numerous; but since he had been in the militia, it did not appear that he was on terms of particular friendship with any of them. There was no one therefore who could be pointed out, as likely to give any news of him. And in the wretched state of his own finances, there was a very powerful motive for secrecy, in addition to his fear of discovery by Lydia's relations, for it had just transpired that he had left gaming debts behind him, to a very consid- erable amount. Colonel Forster believed that more than a thousand pounds would be necessary to clear his expences at Brighton. He owed a good deal in the town, but his debts of honour[5] were still more for- midable. Mr. Gardiner did not attempt to conceal these particulars from the Longbourn family, Jane heard them with horror. "A game- ster!" she cried. "This is wholly unexpected. I had not an idea of it."

Mr. Gardiner added in his letter, that they might expect to see their father at home on the following day, which was Saturday. Rendered spiritless by the ill-success of all their endeavours, he had yielded to his brother-in-law's intreaty that he would return to his family, and leave it to him to do, whatever occasion might suggest to be advisable for continuing their pursuit. When Mrs. Bennet was told of this, she did not express so much satisfaction as her children expected, consid- ering what her anxiety for his life had been before.

"What, is he coming home, and without poor Lydia!" she cried. "Sure he will not leave London before he has found them. Who is to fight Wickham, and make him marry her, if he comes away?"

As Mrs. Gardiner began to wish to be at home, it was settled that she and her children should go to London, at the same time that Mr.

---

5. "Debts of honour" are gambling or other debts owed to fellow officers and other gentlemen. The honor of a gentleman requires that these debts be paid, unlike those owed to trades- people and other less socially elevated citizens of the town.

Bennet came from it. The coach, therefore, took them the first stage of their journey, and brought its master back to Longbourn.

Mrs. Gardiner went away in all the perplexity about Elizabeth and her Derbyshire friend, that had attended her from that part of the world. His name had never been voluntarily mentioned before them by her niece; and the kind of half-expectation which Mrs. Gardiner had formed, of their being followed by a letter from him, had ended in nothing. Elizabeth had received none since her return, that could come from Pemberley.

The present unhappy state of the family, rendered any other excuse for the lowness of her spirits unnecessary; nothing, therefore, could be fairly conjectured from *that*, though Elizabeth, who was by this time tolerably well acquainted with her own feelings, was perfectly aware, that, had she known nothing of Darcy, she could have borne the dread of Lydia's infamy somewhat better. It would have spared her, she thought, one sleepless night out of two.

When Mr. Bennet arrived, he had all the appearance of his usual philosophic composure. He said as little as he had ever been in the habit of saying; made no mention of the business that had taken him away, and it was some time before his daughters had courage to speak of it.

It was not till the afternoon, when he joined them at tea, that Elizabeth ventured to introduce the subject; and then, on her briefly expressing her sorrow for what he must have endured, he replied, "Say nothing of that. Who should suffer but myself? It has been my own doing, and I ought to feel it."

"You must not be too severe upon yourself," replied Elizabeth.

"You may well warn me against such an evil. Human nature is so prone to fall into it! No, Lizzy, let me once in my life feel how much I have been to blame. I am not afraid of being overpowered by the impression. It will pass away soon enough."

"Do you suppose them to be in London?"

"Yes; where else can they be so well concealed?"

"And Lydia used to want to go to London," added Kitty.

"She is happy, then," said her father, drily; "and her residence there will probably be of some duration."

Then, after a short silence, he continued, "Lizzy, I bear you no ill-will for being justified in your advice to me last May, which, considering the event, shews some greatness of mind."

They were interrupted by Miss Bennet, who came to fetch her mother's tea.

"This is a parade," cried he, "which does one good; it gives such an elegance to misfortune! Another day I will do the same; I will sit in my library, in my night cap and powdering gown, and give as much trouble as I can,—or, perhaps, I may defer it, till Kitty runs away."

"I am not going to run away, Papa," said Kitty, fretfully; "if I should ever go to Brighton, I would behave better than Lydia."

"You go to Brighton!—I would not trust you so near it as East Bourne, for fifty pounds! No, Kitty, I have at last learnt to be cautious, and you will feel the effects of it. No officer is ever to enter my house again, nor even to pass through the village. Balls will be absolutely prohibited, unless you stand up with one of your sisters. And you are never to stir out of doors, till you can prove, that you have spent ten minutes of every day in a rational manner."

Kitty, who took all these threats in a serious light, began to cry.

"Well, well," said he, "do not make yourself unhappy. If you are a good girl for the next ten years, I will take you to a review[6] at the end of them."

Chapter VII

Two days after Mr. Bennet's return, as Jane and Elizabeth were walking together in the shrubbery behind the house, they saw the housekeeper coming towards them, and, concluding that she came to call them to their mother, went forward to meet her; but, instead of the expected summons, when they approached her, she said to Miss Bennet, "I beg your pardon, madam, for interrupting you, but I was in hopes you might have got some good news from town, so I took the liberty of coming to ask."

"What do you mean, Hill? We have heard nothing from town."

"Dear madam," cried Mrs. Hill, in great astonishment, "don't you know there is an express come for master from Mr. Gardiner? He has been here this half hour, and master has had a letter."

Away ran the girls, too eager to get in to have time for speech. They ran through the vestibule into the breakfast room; from thence to the library;—their father was in neither; and they were on the point of seeking him up stairs with their mother, when they were met by the butler, who said,

"If you are looking for my master, ma'am, he is walking toward the little copse."

Upon this information, they instantly passed through the hall once more, and ran across the lawn after their father, who was deliberately pursuing his way towards a small wood on one side of the paddock.

Jane, who was not so light, nor so much in the habit of running as Elizabeth, soon lagged behind, while her sister, panting for breath, came up with him, and eagerly cried out, "Oh, Papa, what news? what news? have you heard from my uncle?"

"Yes, I have had a letter from him by express."

6. Perhaps, take you to attend a military review. Or perhaps, reconsider the prohibition.

"Well, and what news does it bring? good or bad?"

"What is there of good to be expected?" said he, taking the letter from his pocket; "but perhaps you would like to read it."

Elizabeth impatiently caught it from his hand. Jane now came up.

"Read it aloud," said their father, "for I hardly know myself what it is about."

"Gracechurch-street, Monday,

August 2.

"MY DEAR BROTHER,

"At last I am able to send you some tidings of my niece, and such as, upon the whole, I hope will give you satisfaction. Soon after you left me on Saturday, I was fortunate enough to find out in what part of London they were. The particulars, I reserve till we meet. It is enough to know they are discovered, I have seen them both—"

"Then it is, as I always hoped," cried Jane; "they are married!"

Elizabeth read on; "I have seen them both. They are not married, nor can I find there was any intention of being so; but if you are willing to perform the engagements which I have ventured to make on your side, I hope it will not be long before they are. All that is required of you is, to assure to your daughter, by settlement, her equal share of the five thousand pounds, secured among your children after the decease of yourself and my sister; and, moreover, to enter into an engagement of allowing her, during your life, one hundred pounds per annum. These are conditions, which, considering every thing, I had no hesitation in complying with, as far as I thought myself privileged, for you. I shall send this by express, that no time may be lost in bringing me your answer. You will easily comprehend, from these particulars, that Mr. Wickham's circumstances are not so hopeless as they are generally believed to be. The world has been deceived in that respect; and I am happy to say, there will be some little money, even when all his debts are discharged, to settle on my niece, in addition to her own fortune. If, as I conclude will be the case, you send me full powers to act in your name, throughout the whole of this business, I will immediately give directions to Haggerston for preparing a proper settlement. There will not be the smallest occasion for your coming to town again; therefore, stay quietly at Longbourn, and depend on my diligence and care. Send back your answer as soon as you can, and be careful to write explicitly. We have judged it best, that my niece should be married from this house, of which I hope you will approve. She comes to us to-day. I shall write again as soon as any thing more is determined on. Your's, &c.

"EDW. GARDINER."

"Is it possible!" cried Elizabeth, when she had finished. "Can it be possible that he will marry her?"

"Wickham is not so undeserving, then, as we have thought him;" said her sister. "My dear father, I congratulate you."

"And have you answered the letter?" said Elizabeth.

"No; but it must be done soon."

Most earnestly did she then intreat him to lose no more time before he wrote.

"Oh! my dear father," she cried, "come back, and write immediately. Consider how important every moment is, in such a case."

"Let me write for you," said Jane, "if you dislike the trouble yourself."

"I dislike it very much," he replied; "but it must be done."

And so saying, he turned back with them, and walked towards the house.

"And may I ask?" said Elizabeth, "but the terms, I suppose, must be complied with."

"Complied with! I am only ashamed of his asking so little."

"And they *must* marry! Yet he is *such* a man!"

"Yes, yes, they must marry. There is nothing else to be done. But there are two things that I want very much to know:—one is, how much money your uncle has laid down, to bring it about; and the other, how I am ever to pay him."

"Money! my uncle!" cried Jane, "what do you mean, Sir?"

"I mean, that no man in his senses, would marry Lydia on so slight a temptation as one hundred a-year during my life, and fifty after I am gone."

"That is very true," said Elizabeth; "though it had not occurred to me before. His debts to be discharged, and something still to remain! Oh! it must be my uncle's doings! Generous, good man, I am afraid he has distressed himself. A small sum could not do all this."

"No," said her father, "Wickham's a fool, if he takes her with a farthing less than ten thousand pounds. I should be sorry to think so ill of him, in the very beginning of our relationship."

"Ten thousand pounds! Heaven forbid! How is half such a sum to be repaid?"

Mr. Bennet made no answer, and each of them, deep in thought, continued silent till they reached the house, Their father then went to the library to write, and the girls walked into the breakfast-room.

"And they are really to be married!" cried Elizabeth, as soon as they were by themselves. "How strange this is! And for *this* we are to be thankful. That they should marry, small as is their chance of happiness, and wretched as is his character, we are forced to rejoice! Oh, Lydia!"

"I comfort myself with thinking," replied Jane, "that he certainly would not marry Lydia, if he had not a real regard for her. Though our kind uncle has done something towards clearing him, I cannot believe that ten thousand pounds, or any thing like it, has been advanced. He has children of his own, and may have more. How could he spare half ten thousand pounds?"

"If we are ever able to learn what Wickham's debts have been," said Elizabeth, "and how much is settled on his side on our sister, we shall exactly know what Mr. Gardiner has done for them, because Wickham has not sixpence of his own. The kindness of my uncle and aunt can never be requited. Their taking her home, and affording her their personal protection and countenance, is such a sacrifice to her advantage, as years of gratitude cannot enough acknowledge. By this time she is actually with them! If such goodness does not make her miserable now, she will never deserve to be happy! What a meeting for her, when she first sees my aunt!"

"We must endeavour to forget all that has passed on either side," said Jane: "I hope and trust they will yet be happy. His consenting to marry her is a proof, I will believe, that he is come to a right way of thinking. Their mutual affection will steady them; and I flatter myself they will settle so quietly, and live in so rational a manner, as may in time make their past imprudence forgotten."

"Their conduct has been such," replied Elizabeth, "as neither you, nor I, nor any body, can ever forget. It is useless to talk of it."

It now occurred to the girls that their mother was in all likelihood perfectly ignorant of what had happened. They went to the library, therefore, and asked their father, whether he would not wish them to make it known to her. He was writing, and, without raising his head, coolly replied, "Just as you please."

"May we take my uncle's letter to read to her?"

"Take whatever you like, and get away."

Elizabeth took the letter from his writing table, and they went up stairs together. Mary and Kitty were both with Mrs. Bennet: one communication would, therefore, do for all. After a slight preparation for good news, the letter was read aloud. Mrs. Bennet could hardly contain herself. As soon as Jane had read Mr. Gardiner's hope of Lydia's being soon married, her joy burst forth, and every following sentence added to its exuberance. She was now in an irritation as violent from delight, as she had ever been fidgetty from alarm and vexation. To know that her daughter would be married was enough. She was disturbed by no fear for her felicity, nor humbled by any remembrance of her misconduct.

"My dear, dear Lydia!" she cried: "This is delightful indeed!—She will be married!—I shall see her again!—She will be married at sixteen!—My good, kind brother!—I knew how it would be—I knew he would manage every thing. How I long to see her! and to see dear Wickham too! But the clothes, the wedding clothes! I will write to my sister Gardiner about them directly. Lizzy, my dear, run down to your father, and ask him how much he will give her. Stay, stay, I will go myself. Ring the bell, Kitty, for Hill. I will put on my things in a moment. My dear, dear Lydia!—How merry we shall be together when we meet!"

Her eldest daughter endeavoured to give some relief to the violence of these transports, by leading her thoughts to the obligations which Mr. Gardiner's behaviour laid them all under.

"For we must attribute this happy conclusion," she added, "in a great measure, to his kindness. We are persuaded that he had pledged himself to assist Mr. Wickham with money."

"Well," cried her mother, "it is all very right; who should do it but her own uncle? If he had not had a family of his own, I and my children must have had all his money you know, and it is the first time we have ever had any thing from him, except a few presents. Well! I am so happy. In a short time, I shall have a daughter married. Mrs. Wickham! How well it sounds. And she was only sixteen last June. My dear Jane, I am in such a flutter, that I am sure I can't write; so I will dictate, and you write for me. We will settle with your father about the money afterwards; but the things should be ordered immediately."

She was then proceeding to all the particulars of calico, muslin, and cambric, and would shortly have dictated some very plentiful orders, had not Jane, though with some difficulty, persuaded her to wait, till her father was at leisure to be consulted. One day's delay she observed, would be of small importance; and her mother was too happy, to be quite so obstinate as usual. Other schemes too came into her head.

"I will go to Meryton," said she, "as soon as I am dressed, and tell the good, good news to my sister Philips. And as I come back, I can call on Lady Lucas and Mrs. Long. Kitty, run down and order the carriage. An airing would do me a great deal of good, I am sure. Girls, can I do any thing for you in Meryton? Oh! here comes Hill. My dear Hill, have you heard the good news? Miss Lydia is going to be married; and you shall all have a bowl of punch, to make merry at her wedding."

Mrs. Hill began instantly to express her joy. Elizabeth received her congratulations amongst the rest, and then, sick of this folly, took refuge in her own room, that she might think with freedom.

Poor Lydia's situation must, at best, be bad enough; but that it was no worse, she had need to be thankful. She felt it so; and though, in looking forward, neither rational happiness nor worldly prosperity, could be justly expected for her sister; in looking back to what they had feared, only two hours ago, she felt all the advantages of what they had gained.

Chapter VIII

Mr. Bennet had very often wished, before this period of his life, that, instead of spending his whole income, he had laid by an annual sum, for the better provision of his children, and of his wife, if she survived him. He now wished it more than ever. Had he done his duty in that respect, Lydia need not have been indebted to her uncle, for whatever of honour or credit could now be purchased for her. The satisfaction of prevailing on one of the most worthless young men in Great Britain to be her husband, might then have rested in its proper place.

He was seriously concerned, that a cause of so little advantage to any one, should be forwarded at the sole expence of his brother-in-law, and he was determined, if possible, to find out the extent of his assistance, and to discharge the obligation as soon as he could.

When first Mr. Bennet had married, economy was held to be perfectly useless; for, of course, they were to have a son. This son was to join in cutting off the entail, as soon as he should be of age, and the widow and younger children would by that means be provided for. Five daughters successively entered the world, but yet the son was to come; and Mrs. Bennet, for many years after Lydia's birth, had been certain that he would. This event had at last been despaired of, but it was then too late to be saving. Mrs. Bennet had no turn for economy, and her husband's love of independence had alone prevented their exceeding their income.

Five thousand pounds was settled by marriage articles on Mrs. Bennet and the children. But in what proportions it should be divided amongst the latter, depended on the will of the parents. This was one point, with regard to Lydia at least, which was now to be settled, and Mr. Bennet could have no hesitation in acceding to the proposal before him. In terms of grateful acknowledgment for the kindness of his brother, though expressed most concisely, he then delivered on paper his perfect approbation of all that was done, and his willingness to fulfil the engagements that had been made for him. He had never before supposed that, could Wickham be prevailed on to marry his daughter, it would be done with so little inconvenience to himself, as by the present arrangement. He would scarcely be ten pounds a-year the loser, by the hundred that was to be paid them; for, what with her board and pocket allowance, and the continual presents in money, which passed to her, through her mother's hands, Lydia's expences had been very little within that sum.

That it would be done with such trifling exertion on his side, too, was another very welcome surprise; for his chief wish at present, was to have as little trouble in the business as possible. When the first transports of rage which had produced his activity in seeking her were over, he naturally returned to all his former indolence. His letter was soon dispatched; for though dilatory in undertaking business, he was quick in its execution. He begged to know farther particulars of what he was indebted to his brother; but was too angry with Lydia, to send any message to her.

The good news quickly spread through the house; and with proportionate speed through the neighbourhood. It was borne in the latter with decent philosophy. To be sure it would have been more for the advantage of conversation, had Miss Lydia Bennet come upon the town; or, as the happiest alternative, been secluded from the world, in some distant farm house.[7] But there was much to be talked of, in marrying her; and the good-natured wishes for her well-doing, which had proceeded before, from all the spiteful old ladies in Meryton, lost but little of their spirit in this change of circumstances, because with such an husband, her misery was considered certain.

It was a fortnight since Mrs. Bennet had been down stairs, but on this happy day, she again took her seat at the head of her table, and in spirits oppressively high. No sentiment of shame gave a damp to her triumph. The marriage of a daughter, which had been the first object of her wishes, since Jane was sixteen, was now on the point of accomplishment, and her thoughts and her words ran wholly on those attendants of elegant nuptials, fine muslins, new carriages, and servants. She was busily searching through the neighbourhood for a proper situation[8] for her daughter, and, without knowing or considering what their income might be, rejected many as deficient in size and importance.

"Haye-Park might do," said she, "if the Gouldings would quit it, or the great house of Stoke, if the drawing-room were larger; but Ashworth is too far off! I could not bear to have her ten miles from me; and as for Purvis Lodge, the attics are dreadful."

Her husband allowed her to talk on without interruption, while the servants remained. But when they had withdrawn, he said to her, "Mrs. Bennet, before you take any, or all of these houses, for your son and daughter, let us come to a right understanding. Into *one* house in this neighbourhood, they shall never have admittance. I will not encourage the impudence of either, by receiving them at Longbourn."

A long dispute followed this declaration; but Mr. Bennet was firm: it soon led to another; and Mrs. Bennet found, with amazement and horror, that her husband would not advance a guinea to buy clothes for his daughter. He protested that she should receive from him no mark of affection whatever, on the occasion. Mrs. Bennet could hardly comprehend it. That his anger could be carried to such a point of inconceivable resentment, as to refuse his daughter a privilege, without which her marriage would scarcely seem valid, exceeded all that she could believe possible. She was more alive to the disgrace, which the want of new clothes must reflect on her daughter's nuptials, than to

---

7. According to Francis Grose's A *Classical Dictionary of the Vulgar Tongue*, 3rd ed. (1796), to be "upon the town" is to engage in prostitution or thievery. The "happiest alternative" would be seclusion during the term of pregnancy.
8. House.

any sense of shame at her eloping and living with Wickham, a fortnight before they took place.

Elizabeth was now most heartily sorry that she had, from the distress of the moment, been led to make Mr. Darcy acquainted with their fears for her sister; for since her marriage would so shortly give the proper termination to the elopement, they might hope to conceal its unfavourable beginning, from all those who were not immediately on the spot.

She had no fear of its spreading farther, through his means. There were few people on whose secrecy she would have more confidently depended; but at the same time, there was no one, whose knowledge of a sister's frailty would have mortified her so much. Not, however, from any fear of disadvantage from it, individually to herself; for at any rate, there seemed a gulf impassable[9] between them. Had Lydia's marriage been concluded on the most honourable terms, it was not to be supposed that Mr. Darcy would connect himself with a family, where to every other objection would now be added, an alliance and relationship of the nearest kind with the man whom he so justly scorned.

From such a connection she could not wonder that he should shrink. The wish of procuring her regard, which she had assured herself of his feeling in Derbyshire, could not in rational expectation survive such a blow as this. She was humbled, she was grieved; she repented, though she hardly knew of what. She became jealous of his esteem, when she could no longer hope to be benefited by it. She wanted to hear of him, when there seemed the least chance of gaining intelligence. She was convinced that she could have been happy with him; when it was no longer likely they should meet.

What a triumph for him, as she often thought, could he know that the proposals which she had proudly spurned only four months ago, would now have been gladly and gratefully received! He was as generous, she doubted not, as the most generous of his sex. But while he was mortal, there must be a triumph.

She began now to comprehend that he was exactly the man, who, in disposition and talents, would most suit her. His understanding and temper, though unlike her own, would have answered all her wishes. It was an union that must have been to the advantage of both; by her ease and liveliness, his mind might have been softened, his manners improved, and from his judgment, information, and knowledge of the world, she must have received benefit of greater importance.

But no such happy marriage could now teach the admiring multitude what connubial felicity really was. An union of a different tendency, and precluding the possibility of the other, was soon to be formed in their family.

9. 1813 first edition: impossible. Changed in second edition.

How Wickham and Lydia were to be supported in tolerable independence, she could not imagine. But how little of permanent happiness could belong to a couple who were only brought together because their passions were stronger than their virtue, she could easily conjecture.

Mr. Gardiner soon wrote again to his brother. To Mr. Bennet's acknowledgments he briefly replied, with assurances of his eagerness to promote the welfare of any of his family; and concluded with intreaties that the subject might never be mentioned to him again. The principal purport of his letter was to inform them, that Mr. Wickham had resolved on quitting the Militia.

"It was greatly my wish that he should do so," he added, "as soon as his marriage was fixed on. And I think you will agree with me, in considering a removal from that corps as highly advisable, both on his account and my niece's. It is Mr. Wickham's intention to go into the regulars; and, among his former friends, there are still some who are able and willing to assist him in the army. He has the promise of an ensigncy in General ———'s regiment, now quartered in the North. It is an advantage to have it so far from this part of the kingdom. He promises fairly, and I hope among different people, where they may each have a character to preserve, they will both be more prudent. I have written to Colonel Forster, to inform him of our present arrangements, and to request that he will satisfy the various creditors of Mr. Wickham in and near Brighton, with assurances of speedy payment, for which I have pledged myself. And will you give yourself the trouble of carrying similar assurances to his creditors in Meryton, of whom I shall subjoin a list, according to his information. He has given in all his debts; I hope at least he has not deceived us. Haggerston has our directions, and all will be completed in a week. They will then join his regiment, unless they are first invited to Longbourn; and I understand from Mrs. Gardiner, that my niece is very desirous of seeing you all, before she leaves the South. She is well, and begs to be dutifully remembered to you and her mother—Your's, &c.

                                                         "E. GARDINER."

Mr. Bennet and his daughters saw all the advantages of Wickham's removal from the ——shire, as clearly as Mr. Gardiner could do. But Mrs. Bennet, was not so well pleased with it. Lydia's being settled in the North, just when she had expected most pleasure and pride in her company, for she had by no means given up her plan of their residing in Hertfordshire, was a severe disappointment; and besides, it was such a pity that Lydia should be taken from a regiment where she was acquainted with every body, and had so many favourites.

"She is so fond of Mrs. Forster," said she, "it will be quite shocking to send her away! And there are several of the young men, too, that she likes very much. The officers may not be so pleasant in General ———'s regiment."

His daughter's request, for such it might be considered, of being admitted into her family again, before she set off for the North, received at first an absolute negative. But Jane and Elizabeth, who agreed in wishing, for the sake of their sister's feelings and consequence, that she should be noticed on her marriage by her parents, urged him so earnestly, yet so rationally and so mildly, to receive her and her husband at Longbourn, as soon as they were married, that he was prevailed on to think as they thought, and act as they wished. And their mother had the satisfaction of knowing, that she should be able to shew her married daughter in the neighbourhood, before she was banished to the North. When Mr. Bennet wrote again to his brother, therefore, he sent his permission for them to come; and it was settled, that as soon as the ceremony was over, they should proceed to Longbourn. Elizabeth was surprised, however, that Wickham should consent to such a scheme, and, had she consulted only her own inclination, any meeting with him would have been the last object of her wishes.

Chapter IX

Their sister's wedding day arrived; and Jane and Elizabeth felt for her probably more than she felt for herself. The carriage was sent to meet them at ———, and they were to return in it, by dinner-time. Their arrival was dreaded by the elder Miss Bennets; and Jane more especially, who gave Lydia the feelings which would have attended herself, had *she* been the culprit, was wretched in the thought of what her sister must endure.

They came. The family were assembled in the breakfast room, to receive them. Smiles decked the face of Mrs. Bennet, as the carriage drove up to the door; her husband looked impenetrably grave; her daughters, alarmed, anxious, uneasy.

Lydia's voice was heard in the vestibule; the door was thrown open, and she ran into the room. Her mother stepped forwards, embraced her, and welcomed her with rapture; gave her hand with an affectionate smile to Wickham, who followed his lady, and wished them both joy, with an alacrity which shewed no doubt of their happiness.

Their reception from Mr. Bennet, to whom they then turned, was not quite so cordial. His countenance rather gained in austerity; and he scarcely opened his lips. The easy assurance of the young couple, indeed, was enough to provoke him. Elizabeth was disgusted, and even Miss Bennet was shocked. Lydia was Lydia still; untamed, unabashed, wild, noisy, and fearless. She turned from sister to sister, demanding their congratulations, and when at length they all sat down, looked eagerly round the room, took notice of some little alteration in it, and observed, with a laugh, that it was a great while since she had been there.

Wickham was not at all more distressed than herself, but his manners were always so pleasing, that had his character and his marriage been exactly what they ought, his smiles and his easy address, while he claimed their relationship, would have delighted them all. Elizabeth had not before believed him quite equal to such assurance; but she sat down, resolving within herself, to draw no limits in future to the impudence of an impudent man. *She* blushed, and Jane blushed; but the cheeks of the two who caused their confusion, suffered no variation of colour.

There was no want of discourse. The bride and her mother could neither of them talk fast enough; and Wickham, who happened to sit near Elizabeth, began enquiring after his acquaintance in that neighbourhood, with a good humoured ease, which she felt very unable to equal in her replies. They seemed each of them to have the happiest memories in the world. Nothing of the past was recollected with pain; and Lydia led voluntarily to subjects, which her sisters would not have alluded to for the world.

"Only think of its being three months," she cried, "since I went away; it seems but a fortnight I declare; and yet there have been things enough happened in the time. Good gracious! when I went away, I am sure I had no more idea of being married till I came back again! though I thought it would be very good fun if I was."

Her father lifted up his eyes. Jane was distressed. Elizabeth looked expressively at Lydia; but she, who never heard nor saw any thing of which she chose to be insensible, gaily continued, "Oh! mamma, do the people here abouts know I am married to day? I was afraid they might not; and we overtook William Goulding in his curricle, so I was determined he should know it, and so I let down the side glass next to him, and took off my glove, and let my hand just rest upon the window frame, so that he might see the ring, and then I bowed and smiled like any thing."

Elizabeth could bear it no longer. She got up, and ran out of the room; and returned no more, till she heard them passing through the hall to the dining parlour. She then joined them soon enough to see Lydia, with anxious parade, walk up to her mother's right hand, and hear her say to her eldest sister, "Ah! Jane, I take your place now, and you must go lower, because I am a married woman."

It was not to be supposed that time would give Lydia that embarrassment, from which she had been so wholly free at first. Her ease and good spirits increased. She longed to see Mrs. Philips, the Lucasses, and all their other neighbours, and to hear herself called "Mrs. Wickham," by each of them; and in the mean time, she went after dinner to shew her ring and boast of being married, to Mrs. Hill and the two housemaids.

"Well, mamma," said she, when they were all returned to the breakfast room, "and what do you think of my husband? Is not he a charming man? I am sure my sisters must all envy me. I only hope they may have half my good luck. They must all go to Brighton. That is the place to get husbands. What a pity it is, mamma, we did not all go."

"Very true; and if I had my will, we should. But my dear Lydia, I don't at all like your going such a way off. Must it be so?"

"Oh, lord! yes;—there is nothing in that. I shall like it of all things. You and papa, and my sisters, must come down and see us. We shall be at Newcastle all the winter, and I dare say there will be some balls, and I will take care to get good partners for them all."

"I should like it beyond any thing!" said her mother.

"And then when you go away! you may leave one or two of my sisters behind you; and I dare say I shall get husbands for them before the winter is over."

"I thank you for my share of the favour," said Elizabeth; "but I do not particularly like your way of getting husbands."

Their visitors were not to remain above ten days with them. Mr. Wickham had received his commission before he left London, and he was to join his regiment at the end of a fortnight.

No one but Mrs. Bennet, regretted that their stay would be so short; and she made the most of the time, by visiting about with her daughter, and having very frequent parties at home. These parties were acceptable to all; to avoid a family circle was even more desirable to such as did think, than such as did not.

Wickham's affection for Lydia, was just what Elizabeth had expected to find it; not equal to Lydia's for him. She had scarcely needed her present observation to be satisfied, from the reason of things, that their elopement had been brought on by the strength of her love, rather than by his; and she would have wondered why, without violently caring for her, he chose to elope with her at all had she not felt certain that his flight was rendered necessary by distress of circumstances; and if that were the case, he was not the young man to resist an opportunity of having a companion.

Lydia was exceedingly fond of him. He was her dear Wickham on every occasion; no one was to be put in competition with him. He did every thing best in the world; and she was sure he would kill more birds on the first of September,[1] than any body else in the country.

One morning, soon after their arrival, as she was sitting with her two elder sisters, she said to Elizabeth,

"Lizzy, I never gave *you* an account of my wedding, I believe. You

---

1. The beginning of the bird-hunting season.

were not by, when I told mamma, and the others, all about it. Are not you curious to hear how it was managed?"

"No really," replied Elizabeth; "I think there cannot be too little said on the subject."

"La! You are so strange! But I must tell you how it went off. We were married, you know, at St. Clements, because Wickham's lodgings were in that parish. And it was settled that we should all be there by eleven o'clock. My uncle and aunt and I were to go together; and the others were to meet us at the church. Well, Monday morning came, and I was in such a fuss! I was so afraid you know that something would happen to put it off, and then I should have gone quite distracted.[2] And there was my aunt, all the time I was dressing, preaching and talking away just as if she was reading a sermon. However, I did not hear above one word in ten, for I was thinking, you may suppose, of my dear Wickham. I longed to know whether he would be married in his blue coat.

"Well, and so we breakfasted at ten as usual; I thought it would never be over; for, by the bye, you are to understand, that my uncle and aunt were horrid unpleasant all the time I was with them. If you'll believe me, I did not once put my foot out of doors, though I was there a fortnight. Not one party, or scheme, or any thing. To be sure London was rather thin, but however the little Theatre was open. Well, and so just as the carriage came to the door, my uncle was called away upon business to that horrid man Mr. Stone.[3] And then, you know, when once they get together, there is no end of it. Well, I was so frightened I did not know what to do, for my uncle was to give me away; and if we were beyond the hour, we could not be married all day. But, luckily, he came back again in ten minutes time, and then we all set out. However, I recollected afterwards, that if he *had* been prevented going, the wedding need not be put off, for Mr. Darcy might have done as well."

"Mr. Darcy!" repeated Elizabeth, in utter amazement.

"Oh, yes!—he was to come there with Wickham, you know. But gracious me! I quite forgot! I ought not have said a word about it. I promised them so faithfully! What will Wickham say? It was to be such a secret!"

"If it was to be secret," said Jane, "say not another word on the subject. You may depend upon my seeking no further."

"Oh! certainly," said Elizabeth, though burning with curiosity; "we will ask you no questions."

"Thank you," said Lydia, "for if you did, I should certainly tell you all, and then Wickham would be angry."

2. Deranged.
3. Lydia misremembers the name of Haggerston, Mr. Gardiner's attorney (see above, p. 196).

On such encouragement to ask, Elizabeth was forced to put it out of her power, by running away.

But to live in ignorance on such a point was impossible; or at least it was impossible not to try for information. Mr. Darcy had been at her sister's wedding. It was exactly a scene, and exactly among people, where he had apparently least to do, and least temptation to go. Conjectures as to the meaning of it, rapid and wild, hurried into her brain; but she was satisfied with none. Those that best pleased her, as placing his conduct in the noblest light, seemed most improbable. She could not bear such suspense; and hastily seizing a sheet of paper, wrote a short letter to her aunt, to request an explanation of what Lydia had dropt, if it were compatible with the secrecy which had been intended.

"You may readily comprehend," she added, "what my curiosity must be to know how a person unconnected with any of us, and (comparatively speaking) a stranger to our family, should have been amongst you at such a time. Pray write instantly, and let me understand it— unless it is, for very cogent reasons, to remain in the secrecy which Lydia seems to think necessary; and then I must endeavour to be satisfied with ignorance."

"Not that I *shall* though," she added to herself, as she finished the letter; "and my dear aunt, if you do not tell me in an honourable manner, I shall certainly be reduced to tricks and stratagems to find it out."

Jane's delicate sense of honour would not allow her to speak to Elizabeth privately of what Lydia had let fall; Elizabeth was glad of it;— till it appeared whether her inquiries would receive any satisfaction, she had rather be without a confidante.

Chapter X

Elizabeth had the satisfaction of receiving an answer to her letter, as soon as she possibly could. She was no sooner in possession of it, than hurrying into the little copse, where she was least likely to be interrupted, she sat down on one of the benches, and prepared to be happy; for the length of the letter convinced her, that it did not contain a denial.

"Gracechurch-street, Sept. 6

"My dear Niece,

"I have just received your letter, and shall devote this whole morning to answering it, as I forsee that a *little* writing will not comprise what I have to tell you. I must confess myself surprised by your application; I did not expect it from *you*. Don't think me angry, however, for I only mean to let you know, that I had not imagined such enquiries to be necessary on *your* side. If you do not choose to understand me, forgive my impertinence. Your uncle is as much surprised as I am—and nothing but the belief of your being a party concerned, would have allowed him to act as he has done. But if you are really innocent and ignorant, I must be more explicit. On the very day of my coming home from Longbourn, your uncle had a most unexpected visitor. Mr. Darcy called, and was shut up with him several hours. It was all over before I arrived; so my curiosity was not so dreadfully racked as *your's* seems to have been. He came to tell Mr. Gardiner that he had found out where your sister and Mr. Wickham were, and that he had seen and talked with them both, Wickham repeatedly, Lydia once. From what I can collect, he left Derbyshire only one day after ourselves, and came to town with the resolution of hunting for them. The motive professed, was his conviction of its being owing to himself that Wickham's worthlessness had not been so well known, as to make it impossible for any young woman of character, to love or confide in him. He generously imputed the whole to his mistaken pride, and confessed that he had before thought it beneath him, to lay his private actions open to the world. His character was to speak for itself. He called it, therefore, his duty to step forward, and endeavour to remedy an evil, which had been brought on by himself. If he *had another* motive, I am sure it would never disgrace him. He had been some days in town, before he was able to discover them; but he had something to direct his search, which was more than *we* had; and the consciousness of this, was another reason for his resolving to follow us. There is a lady, it seems, a Mrs. Younge, who was some time ago governess to Miss Darcy, and was dismissed from her charge on some cause of disapprobation, though he did not say what. She then took a large house in Edward-street, and has since maintained herself by letting lodgings. This Mrs. Younge was, he knew, intimately acquainted with Wickham; and he went to her for intelligence of him, as soon as he got to town. But it was two or three days before he could get from her what he wanted. She would not betray her trust, I suppose, without bribery and corruption, for she really did know where her friend was to be found. Wickham indeed had gone to her, on their first arrival in London, and had she been able to receive them into her house, they would have taken up their abode with her. At length, however, our kind friend procured the wished-for direction. They were in ——street. He saw Wickham, and afterwards insisted on seeing Lydia. His first object with her, he acknowledged, had been to persuade her to quit her present disgraceful situation, and return to her friends as soon as they could be prevailed on to receive her, offering his assistance, as far as it would go. But he found Lydia absolutely resolved on remaining where she was. She cared for none of her friends, she wanted no help of his, she would not hear of leaving Wickham. She was sure they should be married some time or other, and it did not much signify when. Since such were her feelings, it only remained, he thought, to secure and expedite a marriage, which, in his very first conversation with Wickham, he easily learnt, had never been *his* design. He confessed himself obliged to leave the regiment, on account of some debts of honour, which were very pressing; and scrupled not to lay all the ill-consequences of Lydia's flight, on her own folly alone. He meant to resign his commission immediately; and as to his future situation, he could conjecture very little about it. He must go somewhere, but he did not know where, and he knew he should have nothing to live on. Mr. Darcy asked him why he had not married your sister at once. Though Mr. Bennet was not imagined to be very rich, he would have been able to do something for him, and his situation must have been benefited by marriage. But he found, in reply to this question, that Wickham still cherished the hope of more effectually making his fortune by marriage, in some other country. Under such circumstances, however, he was not likely to be proof against the temptation of immediate relief. They met several times, for there was much to be discussed. Wickham of course wanted more than he could get; but at length was reduced to be reasonable. Every thing being settled between *them*, Mr. Darcy's next step was to make your uncle acquainted with it, and he first called in Gracechurch-street the evening before I came home. But Mr. Gardiner could not be seen, and Mr. Darcy found, on further enquiry, that your father was still with him, but would quit town the next morning. He did not judge your father to be a person whom he could so properly consult as your uncle, and therefore readily postponed seeing him, till after the departure of the former. He did not leave his name, and till the next day, it was only known that a gentleman had called on business. On Saturday he came again. Your father was gone, your uncle at home, and, as I said before, they had a great deal of talk together. They met again on Sunday, and then *I* saw him too. It was not all settled before Monday: as soon as it was, the express was sent off to Longbourn. But our visitor was very obstinate. I fancy, Lizzy, that obstinacy is the real defect of his character after all. He has been accused of many faults at different times; but *this* is the true one. Nothing was to be done that he did not do himself; though I am sure (and I do not speak it to be thanked, therefore say nothing about it,) your uncle would most readily have settled the whole. They battled it together for a long time, which was more than either the gentleman or lady concerned in it deserved. But at last your uncle was forced to yield, and instead of being allowed to be of use to his niece, was forced to put up with only having the probable credit of it, which went sorely against the grain; and I really believe your letter this morning gave him great pleasure, because it required an explanation that would rob him of his borrowed feathers, and give the praise where it was due. But, Lizzy, this must go no farther than yourself, or Jane at most. You know pretty well, I suppose, what has been done for the young people. His debts are to be paid, amounting, I believe, to considerably more than a thousand pounds, another thousand in addition to her own settled upon *her*, and his commission purchased. The reason why all this was to be done by him alone, was such as I have given above. It was owing to him, to his reserve, and want of proper consideration, that Wickham's character had been so misunderstood, and consequently that he had been received and noticed as he was. Perhaps there was some truth in *this*; though I doubt whether *his* reserve, or *anybody's* reserve, can be answerable for the event. But in spite of all this fine talking, my dear Lizzy, you may rest perfectly assured, that your uncle would never have yielded, if we had not given him credit for *another interest* in the affair. When all this was resolved on, he returned again to his friends, who were still staying at Pemberley; but it was agreed that he should be in London once more when the wedding took place, and all money matters were then to receive the last finish. I believe I have now told you every thing. It is a relation which you tell me is to give you great surprise; I hope at least it will not afford you any displeasure. Lydia came to us; and Wickham had constant admission to the house. *He* was exactly what he had been, when I knew him in Hertfordshire; but I would not tell you how little I was satisfied with *her* behaviour while she staid with us, if I had not perceived, by Jane's letter last Wednesday, that her conduct on coming home was exactly of a piece with it, and therefore what I now tell you, can give you no fresh pain. I talked to her repeatedly in the most serious manner, representing to her all the wickedness of what she had done, and all the unhappiness she had brought on her family. If she heard me, it was by good luck, for I am sure she did not listen. I was sometimes quite provoked, but then I recollected my dear Elizabeth and Jane, and for their sakes had patience with her. Mr. Darcy was punctual in his return, and as Lydia informed you, attended the wedding. He dined with us the next day, and was to leave town again on Wednesday or Thursday. Will you be very angry with me, my dear Lizzy, if I take this opportunity of saying (what I was never bold enough to say before) how much I like him. His behaviour to us has, in every respect, been as pleasing as when we were in Derbyshire. His understanding and opinions all please me; he wants nothing but a little more liveliness, and *that*, if he marry *prudently*, his wife may teach him. I thought him very sly;—he hardly ever mentioned your name. But slyness seems the fashion. Pray forgive me, if I have been very presuming, or at least do not punish me so far, as to exclude me from P. I shall never be quite happy till I have been all round the park. A low phaeton, with a nice little pair of ponies, would be the very thing. But I must write no more. The children have been wanting me this half hour. Your's, very sincerely,

"M. Gardiner."

The contents of this letter threw Elizabeth into a flutter of spirits, in which it was difficult to determine whether pleasure or pain bore the greatest share. The vague and unsettled suspicions which uncertainty had produced of what Mr. Darcy might have been doing to forward her sister's match, which she had feared to encourage, as an exertion of goodness too great to be probable, and at the same time dreaded to be just, from the pain of obligation, were proved beyond their greatest extent to be true! He had followed them purposely to town, he had taken on himself all the trouble and mortification attendant on such a research; in which supplication had been necessary to a woman whom he must abominate and despise, and where he was reduced to meet, frequently meet, reason with, persuade, and finally bribe, the man whom he always most wished to avoid, and whose very name was punishment to him to pronounce. He had done all this for a girl whom he could neither regard nor esteem. Her heart did whisper, that he had done it for her. But it was a hope shortly checked by other considerations, and she soon felt that even her vanity was insufficient, when required to depend on his affection for her, for a woman who had already refused him, as able to overcome a sentiment so natural as abhorrence against relationship with Wickham. Brother-in-law of Wickham! Every kind of pride must revolt from the connection. He had to be sure done much. She was ashamed to think how much. But he had given a reason for his interference, which asked no extraordinary stretch of belief. It was reasonable that he should feel he had been wrong; he had liberality, and he had the means of exercising it; and though she would not place herself as his principal inducement, she could, perhaps, believe, that remaining partiality for her, might assist his endeavours in a cause where her peace of mind must be materially concerned. It was painful, exceedingly painful, to know that they were under obligations to a person who could never receive a return. They owed the restoration of Lydia, her character, every thing to him. Oh! how heartily did she grieve over every ungracious sensation she had ever encouraged, every saucy speech she had ever directed towards him. For herself she was humbled; but she was proud of him. Proud that in a cause of compassion and honour, he had been able to get the better of himself. She read over her aunt's commendation of him again and again. It was hardly enough; but it pleased her. She was even sensible of some pleasure, though mixed with regret, on finding how steadfastly both she and her uncle had been persuaded that affection and confidence subsisted between Mr. Darcy and herself.

She was roused from her seat, and her reflections, by some one's approach; and before she could strike into another path, she was overtaken by Wickham.

"I am afraid I interrupt your solitary ramble, my dear sister?" said he, as he joined her.

"You certainly do," she replied with a smile; "but it does not follow that the interruption must be unwelcome."

"I should be sorry indeed, if it were. We were always good friends; and now we are better."

"True. Are the others coming out?"

"I do not know. Mrs. Bennet and Lydia are going in the carriage to Meryton. And so, my dear sister, I find from our uncle and aunt, that you have actually seen Pemberley."

She replied in the affirmative.

"I almost envy you the pleasure, and yet I believe it would be too much for me, or else I could take it in my way to Newcastle. And you saw the old housekeeper, I suppose? Poor Reynolds, she was always very fond of me. But of course she did not mention my name to you."

"Yes, she did."

"And what did she say?"

"That you were gone into the army, and she was afraid had—not turned out well. At such a distance as *that*, you know, things are strangely misrepresented."

"Certainly," he replied, biting his lips. Elizabeth hoped she had silenced him; but he soon afterwards said,

"I was surprised to see Darcy in town last month. We passed each other several times. I wonder what he can be doing there."

"Perhaps preparing for his marriage with Miss de Bourgh," said Elizabeth. "It must be something particular, to take him there at this time of year."

"Undoubtedly. Did you see him while you were at Lambton? I thought I understood from the Gardiners that you had."

"Yes; he introduced us to his sister."

"And do you like her?"

"Very much."

"I have heard, indeed, that she is uncommonly improved within this year or two. When I last saw her, she was not very promising. I am very glad you liked her. I hope she will turn out well."

"I dare say she will; she has got over the most trying age."

"Did you go by the village of Kympton?"

"I do not recollect that we did."

"I mention it, because it is the living which I ought to have had. A most delightful place! Excellent Parsonage House! It would have suited me in every respect."

"How should you have liked making sermons?"

"Exceedingly well. I should have considered it as part of my duty, and the exertion would soon have been nothing. One ought not to repine;—but, to be sure, it would have been such a thing for me! The quiet, the retirement of such a life, would have answered all my ideas of happiness! But it was not to be. Did you ever hear Darcy mention the circumstance, when you were in Kent?"

"I *have* heard from authority, which I thought *as good*, that it was left you conditionally only, and at the will of the present patron."

"You have. Yes, there was something in *that*; I told you so from the first, you may remember."

"I *did* hear, too, that there was a time, when sermon-making was not so palatable to you, as it seems to be at present; that you actually declared your resolution of never taking orders, and that the business had been compromised accordingly."

"You did! and it was not wholly without foundation. You may remember what I told you on that point, when first we talked of it."

They were now almost at the door of the house, for she had walked fast to get rid of him; and unwilling, for her sister's sake, to provoke him, she only said in reply, with a good-humoured smile,

"Come, Mr. Wickham, we are brother and sister, you know. Do not let us quarrel about the past. In future, I hope we shall be always of one mind."

She held out her hand; he kissed it with affectionate gallantry, though he hardly knew how to look, and they entered the house.

Chapter XI

Mr. Wickham was so perfectly satisfied with this conversation, that he never again distressed himself, or provoked his dear sister Elizabeth, by introducing the subject of it; and she was pleased to find that she had said enough to keep him quiet.

The day of his and Lydia's departure soon came, and Mrs. Bennet was forced to submit to a separation, which, as her husband by no means entered into her scheme of their all going to Newcastle, was likely to continue at least a twelvemonth.

"Oh! my dear Lydia," she cried, "when shall we meet again?"

"Oh, lord! I don't know. Not these two or three years perhaps."

"Write to me very often, my dear."

"As often as I can. But you know married women have never much time for writing. My sisters may write to *me*. They will have nothing else to do."

Mr. Wickham's adieus were much more affectionate than his wife's. He smiled, looked handsome, and said many pretty things.

"He is as fine a fellow," said Mr. Bennet, as soon as they were out of the house, "as ever I saw. He simpers, and smirks, and makes love to us all. I am prodigiously proud of him. I defy even Sr. William Lucas himself, to produce a more valuable son-in-law."

The loss of her daughter made Mrs. Bennet very dull for several days.

"I often think," said she, "that there is nothing so bad as parting with one's friends. One seems so forlorn without them."

"This is the consequence you see, Madam, of marrying a daughter," said Elizabeth. "It must make you better satisfied that your other four are single."

"It is no such thing. Lydia does not leave me because she is married; but only because her husband's regiment happens to be so far off. If that had been nearer, she would not have gone so soon."

But the spiritless condition which this event threw her into, was shortly relieved, and her mind opened again to the agitation of hope, by an article of news, which then began to be in circulation. The house-keeper at Netherfield had received orders to prepare for the arrival of her master, who was coming down in a day or two, to shoot there for several weeks. Mrs. Bennet was quite in the fidgets. She looked at Jane, and smiled, and shook her head by turns.

"Well, well, and so Mr. Bingley is coming down, sister," (for Mrs. Philips first brought her the news.) "Well, so much the better. Not that I care about it, though. He is nothing to us, you know, and I am sure *I* never want to see him again. But, however, he is very welcome to come to Netherfield, if he likes it. And who knows what *may* happen? But that is nothing to us. You know, sister, we agreed long ago never to mention a word about it. And so, is it quite certain he is coming?"

"You may depend on it," replied the other, "for Mrs. Nicholls was in Meryton last night; I saw her passing by, and went out myself on purpose to know the truth of it; and she told me that it was certain true. He comes down on Thursday at the latest, very likely on Wednesday. She was going to the butcher's, she told me, on purpose to order in some meat on Wednesday, and she has got three couple of ducks, just fit to be killed."

Miss Bennet had not been able to hear of his coming, without changing colour. It was many months since she had mentioned his name to Elizabeth; but now, as soon as they were alone together, she said,

"I saw you look at me to day, Lizzy, when my aunt told us of the present report; and I know I appeared distressed. But don't imagine it was from any silly cause. I was only confused for the moment, because I felt that I *should* be looked at. I do assure you, that the news does not affect me either with pleasure or pain. I am glad of one thing, that he comes alone; because we shall see the less of him. Not that I am afraid of *myself*, but I dread other people's remarks."

Elizabeth did not know what to make of it. Had she not seen him in Derbyshire, she might have supposed him capable of coming there, with no other view than what was acknowledged; but she still thought him partial to Jane, and she wavered as to the greater probability of his coming there *with* his friend's permission, or being bold enough to come without it.

"Yet it is hard," she sometimes thought, "that this poor man cannot come to a house, which he has legally hired, without raising all this speculation! I *will* leave him to himself."

In spite of what her sister declared, and really believed to be her feelings, in the expectation of his arrival, Elizabeth could easily perceive that her spirits were affected by it. They were more disturbed, more unequal, than she had often seen them.

The subject which had been so warmly canvassed between their parents, about a twelvemonth ago, was now brought forward again.

"As soon as ever Mr. Bingley comes, my dear," said Mrs. Bennet, "you will wait on him of course."

"No, no. You forced me into visiting him last year, and promised if I went to see him, he should marry one of my daughters. But it ended in nothing, and I will not be sent on a fool's errand again."

His wife represented to him how absolutely necessary such an attention would be from all the neighbouring gentlemen, on his returning to Netherfield.

" 'Tis an etiquette I despise," said he. "If he wants our society, let him seek it. He knows where we live. I will not spend *my* hours in running after my neighbours every time they go away, and come back again."

"Well, all I know is, that it will be abominably rude if you do not wait on him. But, however, that shan't prevent my asking him to dine here, I am determined. We must have Mrs. Long and the Gouldings soon. That will make thirteen with ourselves, so there will be just room at table for him."

Consoled by this resolution, she was the better able to bear her husband's incivility; though it was very mortifying to know that her neighbours might all see Mr. Bingley in consequence of it, before *they* did. As the day of his arrival drew near,

"I begin to be sorry that he comes at all," said Jane to her sister. "It would be nothing; I could see him with perfect indifference, but I can hardly bear to hear it thus perpetually talked of. My mother means well; but she does not know, no one can know how much I suffer from what she says. Happy shall I be, when his stay at Netherfield is over!"

"I wish I could say any thing to comfort you," replied Elizabeth; "but it is wholly out of my power. You must feel it; and the usual satisfaction of preaching patience to a sufferer is denied me, because you have always so much."

Mr. Bingley arrived. Mrs. Bennet, through the assistance of servants, contrived to have the earliest tidings of it, that the period of anxiety and fretfulness on her side, might be as long as it could. She counted the days that must intervene before their invitation could be sent; hopeless of seeing him before. But on the third morning after his arrival in Hertfordshire, she saw him from her dressing-room window, enter the paddock, and ride towards the house.

Her daughters were eagerly called to partake of her joy. Jane resolutely kept her place at the table; but Elizabeth, to satisfy her mother, went to the window—she looked—she saw Mr. Darcy with him, and sat down again by her sister.

"There is a gentleman with him, mamma," said Kitty; "who can it be?"

"Some acquaintance or other, my dear, I suppose; I am sure I do not know."

"La!" replied Kitty, "it looks just like that man that used to be with him before. Mr. what's his name. That tall, proud man."

"Good gracious! Mr. Darcy!—and so it does I vow. Well, any friend of Mr. Bingley's will always be welcome here to be sure; but else I must say that I hate the very sight of him."

Jane looked at Elizabeth with surprise and concern. She knew but little of their meeting in Derbyshire, and therefore felt for the awkwardness which must attend her sister, in seeing him almost for the first time after receiving his explanatory letter. Both sisters were uncomfortable enough. Each felt for the other, and of course for themselves; and their mother talked on, of her dislike of Mr. Darcy, and her resolution to be civil to him only as Mr. Bingley's friend, without being heard by either of them. But Elizabeth had sources of uneasiness which could not be suspected by Jane, to whom she had never yet had courage to shew Mrs. Gardiner's letter, or to relate her own change of sentiment towards him. To Jane, he could be only a man whose proposals she had refused, and whose merit she had undervalued; but to her own more extensive information, he was the person, to whom the whole family were indebted for the first of benefits, and whom she regarded herself with an interest, if not quite so tender, at least as reasonable and just, as what Jane felt for Bingley. Her astonishment at his coming—at his coming to Netherfield, to Longbourn, and voluntarily seeking her again, was almost equal to what she had known on first witnessing his altered behaviour in Derbyshire.

The color which had been driven from her face, returned for half a minute with an additional glow, and a smile of delight added lustre to her eyes, as she thought for that space of time, that his affection and wishes must still be unshaken. But she would not be secure.

"Let me first see how he behaves," said she; "it will then be early enough for expectation."

She sat intently at work, striving to be composed, and without daring to lift up her eyes, till anxious curiosity carried them to the face of her sister, as the servant was approaching the door. Jane looked a little paler than usual, but more sedate than Elizabeth had expected. On the gentlemen's appearing, her colour increased; yet she received them with tolerable ease, and with a propriety of behaviour equally free from any symptom of resentment, or any unnecessary complaisance.

Elizabeth said as little to either as civility would allow, and sat down again to her work, with an eagerness which it did not often command. She had ventured only one glance at Darcy. He looked serious as usual; and she thought, more as he had been used to look in Hertfordshire, than as she had seen him at Pemberley. But, perhaps he could not in her mother's presence be what he was before her uncle and aunt. It was a painful, but not an improbable, conjecture.

Bingley, she had likewise seen for an instant, and in that short period saw him looking both pleased and embarrassed. He was received by Mrs. Bennet with a degree of civility, which made her two daughters ashamed, especially when contrasted with the cold and ceremonious politeness of her curtsey and address to his friend.

Elizabeth particularly, who knew that her mother owed to the latter the preservation of her favourite daughter from irremediable infamy, was hurt and distressed to a most painful degree by a distinction so ill applied.

Darcy, after enquiring of her how Mr. and Mrs. Gardiner did, a question which she could not answer without confusion, said scarcely any thing. He was not seated by her; perhaps that was the reason of his silence; but it had not been so in Derbyshire. There he had talked to her friends, when he could not to herself. But now several minutes elapsed, without bringing the sound of his voice; and when occasionally, unable to resist the impulse of curiosity, she raised her eyes to his face, she as often found him looking at Jane, as at herself, and frequently on no object but the ground. More thoughtfulness, and less anxiety to please than when they last met, were plainly expressed. She was disappointed, and angry with herself for being so.

"Could I expect it to be otherwise!" said she. "Yet why did he come?"

She was in no humour for conversation with any one but himself; and to him she had hardly courage to speak.

She enquired after his sister, but could do no more.

"It is a long time, Mr. Bingley, since you went away," said Mrs. Bennet.

He readily agreed to it.

"I began to be afraid you would never come back again. People *did* say, you meant to quit the place entirely at Michaelmas; but, however, I hope it is not true. A great many changes have happened in the neighbourhood, since you went away. Miss Lucas is married and settled. And one of my own daughters. I suppose you have heard of it; indeed, you must have seen it in the papers. It was in the Times and the Courier, I know; though it was not put in as it ought to be. It was only said, 'Lately, George Wickham, Esq. to Miss Lydia Bennet,' without there being a syllable said of her father, or the place where she lived, or any thing. It was my brother Gardiner's drawing up too, and

I wonder how he came to make such an awkward business of it. Did you see it?"

Bingley replied that he did, and made his congratulations. Elizabeth dared not lift up her eyes. How Mr. Darcy looked, therefore, she could not tell.

"It is a delightful thing, to be sure, to have a daughter well married," continued her mother; "but at the same time, Mr. Bingley, it is very hard to have her taken such a way from me. They are gone down to Newcastle, a place quite northward, it seems, and there they are to stay, I do not know how long. His regiment is there; for I suppose you have heard of his leaving the ——shire, and of his being gone into the regulars. Thank Heaven! he has *some* friends, though perhaps not so many as he deserves."

Elizabeth, who knew this to be levelled at Mr. Darcy, was in such misery of shame, that she could hardly keep her seat. It drew from her, however, the exertion of speaking, which nothing else had so effectually done before; and she asked Bingley, whether he meant to make any stay in the country at present. A few weeks, he believed.

"When you have killed all your own birds, Mr. Bingley," said her mother, "I beg you will come here, and shoot as many as you please, on Mr. Bennet's manor. I am sure he will be vastly happy to oblige you, and will save all the best of the covies for you."

Elizabeth's misery increased, at such unnecessary, such officious attention! Were the same fair prospect to arise at present, as had flattered them a year ago, every thing, she was persuaded, would be hastening to the same vexatious conclusion. At that instant she felt, that years of happiness could not make Jane or herself amends, for moments of such painful confusion.

"The first wish of my heart," said she to herself, "is never more to be in company with either of them. Their society can afford no pleasure, that will atone for such wretchedness as this! Let me never see either one or the other again!"

Yet the misery, for which years of happiness were to offer no compensation, received soon afterwards material relief, from observing how much the beauty of her sister re-kindled the admiration of her former lover. When first he came in, he had spoken to her but little; but every five minutes seemed to be giving her more of his attention. He found her as handsome as she had been last year; as good natured, and as unaffected, though not quite so chatty. Jane was anxious that no difference should be perceived in her at all, and was really persuaded that she talked as much as ever. But her mind was so busily engaged, that she did not always know when she was silent.

When the gentlemen rose to go away, Mrs. Bennet was mindful of her intended civility, and they were invited and engaged to dine at Longbourn in a few days time.

"You are quite a visit in my debt, Mr. Bingley," she added, "for when you went to town last winter, you promised to take a family dinner with us, as soon as you returned. I have not forgot, you see; and I assure you, I was very much disappointed that you did not come back and keep your engagement."

Bingley looked a little silly at this reflection, and said something of his concern, at having been prevented by business. They then went away.

Mrs. Bennet had been strongly inclined to ask them to stay and dine there, that day; but, though she always kept a very good table, she did not think any thing less than two courses, could be good enough for a man, on whom she had such anxious designs, or satisfy the appetite and pride of one who had ten thousand a-year.

Chapter XII

As soon as they were gone, Elizabeth walked out to recover her spirits; or in other words, to dwell without interruption on those subjects that must deaden them more. Mr. Darcy's behaviour astonished and vexed her.

"Why, if he came only to be silent, grave, and indifferent," said she, "did he come at all?"

She could settle it in no way that gave her pleasure.

"He could be still amiable, still pleasing, to my uncle and aunt, when he was in town; and why not to me? If he fears me, why come hither? If he no longer cares for me, why silent? Teazing, teazing, man! I will think no more about him."

Her resolution was for a short time involuntarily kept by the approach of her sister, who joined her with a cheerful look, which shewed her better satisfied with their visitors, than Elizabeth.

"Now," said she, "that this first meeting is over, I feel perfectly easy. I know my own strength, and I shall never be embarrassed again by his coming. I am glad he dines here on Tuesday. It will then be publicly seen, that on both sides, we meet only as common and indifferent acquaintance."

"Yes, very indifferent indeed," said Elizabeth, laughingly. "Oh, Jane, take care."

"My dear Lizzy, you cannot think me so weak, as to be in danger now."

"I think you are in very great danger of making him as much in love with you as ever."

They did not see the gentlemen again till Tuesday; and Mrs. Bennet, in the meanwhile, was giving way to all the happy schemes, which the good humour, and common politeness of Bingley, in half an hour's visit, had revived.

On Tuesday there was a large party assembled at Longbourn; and the two, who were most anxiously expected, to the credit of their punctuality as sportsmen, were in very good time. When they repaired to the dining-room, Elizabeth eagerly watched to see whether Bingley would take the place, which, in all their former parties, had belonged to him, by her sister. Her prudent mother, occupied by the same ideas, forbore to invite him to sit by herself. On entering the room, he seemed to hesitate; but Jane happened to look round, and happened to smile: it was decided. He placed himself by her.

Elizabeth, with a triumphant sensation, looked towards his friend. He bore it with noble indifference, and she would have imagined that Bingley had received his sanction to be happy, had she not seen his eyes likewise turned towards Mr. Darcy, with an expression of half-laughing alarm.

His behaviour to her sister was such, during dinner time, as shewed an admiration of her, which, though more guarded than formerly, persuaded Elizabeth, that if left wholly to himself, Jane's happiness, and his own, would be speedily secured. Though she dared not depend upon the consequence, she yet received pleasure from observing his behaviour. It gave her all the animation that her spirits could boast; for she was in no cheerful humour. Mr. Darcy was almost as far from her, as the table could divide them. He was on one side of her mother. She knew how little such a situation would give pleasure to either, or make either appear to advantage. She was not near enough to hear any of their discourse, but she could see how seldom they spoke to each other, and how formal and cold was their manner, whenever they did. Her mother's ungraciousness, made the sense of what they owed him more painful to Elizabeth's mind; and she would, at times, have given any thing to be privileged to tell him, that his kindness was neither unknown nor unfelt by the whole of the family.

She was in hopes that the evening would afford some opportunity of bringing them together; that the whole of the visit would not pass away without enabling them to enter into something more of conversation, than the mere ceremonious salutation attending his entrance. Anxious and uneasy, the period which passed in the drawing-room, before the gentlemen came, was wearisome and dull to a degree, that almost made her uncivil. She looked forward to their entrance, as the point on which all her chance of pleasure for the evening must depend.

"If he does not come to me, *then*," said she, "I shall give him up for ever."

The gentlemen came; and she thought he looked as if he would have answered her hopes; but, alas! the ladies had crowded round the table, where Miss Bennet was making tea, and Elizabeth pouring out the coffee, in so close a confederacy, that there was not a single vacancy near her, which would admit of a chair. And on the gentlemen's approaching, one of the girls moved closer to her than ever, and said, in a whisper,

"The men shan't come and part us, I am determined. We want none of them; do we?"

Darcy had walked away to another part of the room. She followed him with her eyes, envied every one to whom he spoke, had scarcely patience enough to help anybody to coffee; and then was enraged against herself for being so silly!

"A man who has once been refused! How could I ever be foolish enough to expect a renewal of his love? Is there one among the sex, who would not protest against such a weakness as a second proposal to the same woman? There is no indignity so abhorrent to their feelings!"

She was a little revived, however, by his bringing back his coffee cup himself; and she seized the opportunity of saying,

"Is your sister at Pemberley still?"

"Yes, she will remain there till Christmas."

"And quite alone? Have all her friends left her?"

"Mrs. Annesley is with her. The others have been gone on to Scarborough, these three weeks."

She could think of nothing more to say; but if he wished to converse with her, he might have better success. He stood by her, however, for some minutes, in silence; and, at last, on the young lady's whispering to Elizabeth again, he walked away.

When the tea-things were removed, and the card tables placed, the ladies all rose, and Elizabeth was then hoping to be soon joined by him, when all her views were overthrown, by seeing him fall a victim to her mother's rapacity for whist players, and in a few moments after seated with the rest of the party. She now lost every expectation of pleasure. They were confined for the evening at different tables, and she had nothing to hope, but that his eyes were so often turned towards her side of the room, as to make him play as unsuccessfully as herself.

Mrs. Bennet had designed to keep the two Netherfield gentlemen to supper; but their carriage was unluckily ordered before any of the others, and she had no opportunity of detaining them.

"Well girls," said she, as soon as they were left to themselves, "What say you to the day? I think every thing has passed off uncommonly well, I assure you. The dinner was as well dressed as any I ever saw. The venison was roasted to a turn—and everybody said, they never saw so fat a haunch. The soup was fifty times better than what we had at the Lucas's last week; and even Mr. Darcy acknowledged, that the partridges were remarkably well done; and I suppose he has two or three

French cooks at least. And, my dear Jane, I never saw you look in greater beauty. Mrs. Long said so too, for I asked her whether you did not. And what do you think she said besides? 'Ah! Mrs. Bennet, we shall have her at Netherfield at last.' She did indeed. I do think Mrs. Long is as good a creature as ever lived—and her nieces are very pretty behaved girls, and not at all handsome: I like them prodigiously."

Mrs. Bennet, in short, was in very great spirits; she had seen enough of Bingley's behaviour to Jane, to be convinced that she would get him at last; and her expectations of advantage to her family, when in a happy humour, were so far beyond reason, that she was quite disappointed at not seeing him there again the next day, to make his proposals.

"It has been a very agreeable day," said Miss Bennet to Elizabeth. "The party seemed so well selected, so suitable one with the other. I hope we may often meet again."

Elizabeth smiled.

"Lizzy, you must not do so. You must not suspect me. It mortifies me. I assure you that I have now learnt to enjoy his conversation as an agreeable and sensible young man, without having a wish beyond it. I am perfectly satisfied from what his manners now are, that he never had any design of engaging my affection. It is only that he is blessed with greater sweetness of address, and a stronger desire of generally pleasing than any other man."

"You are very cruel," said her sister, "you will not let me smile, and are provoking me to it every moment."

"How hard it is in some cases to be believed!"

"And how impossible in others!"[4]

"But why should you wish to persuade me that I feel more than I acknowledge?"

"That is a question which I hardly know how to answer. We all love to instruct, though we can teach only what is not worth knowing. Forgive me; and if you persist in indifference, do not make *me* your confidante."

Chapter XIII

A few days after this visit, Mr. Bingley called again, and alone. His friend had left him that morning for London, but was to return home in ten days time. He sat with them above an hour, and was in remarkably good spirits. Mrs. Bennet invited him to dine with them; but, with many expressions of concern, he confessed himself engaged elsewhere.

"Next time you call," said she, "I hope we shall be more lucky."

4. Jane Austen notes in one of her letters to her sister Cassandra (4 February 1813) that the printers of the first edition had punctuated these two lines as a single speech. The error was not corrected in the second edition. Cassandra corrected the error in her copy of the novel.

He should be particularly happy at any time, &c. &c.; and if she would give him leave, would take an early opportunity of waiting on them.

"Can you come to-morrow?"

Yes, he had no engagement at all for to-morrow; and her invitation was accepted with alacrity.

He came, and in such very good time, that the ladies were none of them dressed. In ran Mrs. Bennet to her daughter's room, in her dressing gown, and with her hair half finished, crying out,

"My dear Jane, make haste and hurry down. He is come—Mr. Bingley is come.—He is, indeed. Make haste, make haste. Here, Sarah, come to Miss Bennet this moment, and help her on with her gown. Never mind Miss Lizzy's hair."

"We will be down as soon as we can," said Jane; "but I dare say Kitty is forwarder than either of us, for she went up stairs half an hour ago."

"Oh! hang Kitty! what has she to do with it? Come be quick, be quick! where is your sash my dear?"

But when her mother was gone, Jane would not be prevailed on to go down without one of her sisters.

The same anxiety to get them by themselves, was visible again in the evening. After tea, Mr. Bennet retired to the library, as was his custom, and Mary went up stairs to her instrument. Two obstacles of the five being thus removed, Mrs. Bennet sat looking and winking at Elizabeth and Catherine for a considerable time, without making any impression on them. Elizabeth would not observe her; and when at last Kitty did, she very innocently said, "What is the matter mamma? What do you keep winking at me for? What am I to do?"

"Nothing child, nothing. I did not wink at you." She then sat still five minutes longer; but unable to waste such a precious occasion, she suddenly got up, and saying to Kitty,

"Come here, my love, I want to speak to you," took her out of the room. Jane instantly gave a look at Elizabeth, which spoke her distress at such premeditation, and her intreaty that *she* would not give into it. In a few minutes, Mrs. Bennet half opened the door and called out,

"Lizzy, my dear, I want to speak with you."

Elizabeth was forced to go.

"We may as well leave them by themselves you know;" said her mother as soon as she was in the hall. "Kitty and I are going up stairs to sit in my dressing room."

Elizabeth made no attempt to reason with her mother, but remained quietly in the hall, till she and Kitty were out of sight, then returned into the drawing room.

Mrs. Bennet's schemes for this day were ineffectual. Bingley was every thing that was charming, except the professed lover of her daughter. His ease and cheerfulness rendered him a most agreeable addition to their evening party; and he bore with the ill-judged officiousness of the mother, and heard all her silly remarks with a forbearance and command of countenance, particularly grateful to the daughter.

He scarcely needed an invitation to stay supper; and before he went away, an engagement was formed, chiefly through his own and Mrs. Bennet's means, for his coming next morning to shoot with her husband.

After this day, Jane said no more of her indifference. Not a word passed between the sisters concerning Bingley; but Elizabeth went to bed in the happy belief that all must speedily be concluded, unless Mr. Darcy returned within the stated time. Seriously, however, she felt tolerably persuaded that all this must have taken place with that gentleman's concurrence.

Bingley was punctual to his appointment; and he and Mr. Bennet spent the morning together, as had been agreed on. The latter was much more agreeable than his companion expected. There was nothing of presumption or folly in Bingley, that could provoke his ridicule, or disgust him into silence; and he was more communicative, and less eccentric than the other had ever seen him. Bingley of course returned with him to dinner; and in the evening Mrs. Bennet's invention was again at work to get every body away from him and her daughter. Elizabeth, who had a letter to write, went into the breakfast room for that purpose soon after tea; for as the others were all going to sit down to cards, she could not be wanted to counteract her mother's schemes.

But on returning to the drawing room, when her letter was finished, she saw, to her infinite surprise, there was reason to fear that her mother had been too ingenious for her. On opening the door, she perceived her sister and Bingley standing together over the hearth, as if engaged in earnest conversation; and had this led to no suspicion, the faces of both as they hastily turned round, and moved away from each other, would have told it all. *Their* situation was awkward enough; but *her's* she thought was still worse. Not a syllable was uttered by either; and Elizabeth was on the point of going away again, when Bingley, who as well as the other had sat down, suddenly rose, and whispering a few words to her sister, ran out of the room.

Jane could have no reserves from Elizabeth, where confidence would give pleasure; and instantly embracing her, acknowledged, with the liveliest emotion, that she was the happiest creature in the world.

" 'Tis too much!" she added, "by far too much. I do not deserve it. Oh! why is not every body as happy?"

Elizabeth's congratulations were given with a sincerity, a warmth, a delight, which words could but poorly express. Every sentence of kindness was a fresh source of happiness to Jane. But she would not allow herself to stay with her sister, or say half that remained to be said, for the present.

"I must go instantly to my mother;" she cried. "I would not on any account trifle with her affectionate solicitude; or allow her to hear it from any one but myself. He is gone to my father already. Oh! Lizzy, to know that what I have to relate will give such pleasure to all my dear family! how shall I bear so much happiness!"

She then hastened away to her mother, who had purposely broken up the card party, and was sitting up stairs with Kitty.

Elizabeth, who was left by herself, now smiled at the rapidity and ease with which an affair was finally settled, that had given them so many previous months of suspense and vexation.

"And this," said she, "is the end of his friend's anxious circumspection! of all his sister's falsehood and contrivance! the happiest, wisest, most reasonable end!"

In a few minutes she was joined by Bingley, whose conference with her father had been short and to the purpose.

"Where is your sister?" said he hastily, as he opened the door.

"With my mother up stairs. She will be down in a moment I dare say."

He then shut the door, and coming up to her, claimed the good wishes and affection of a sister. Elizabeth honestly and heartily expressed her delight in the prospect of their relationship. They shook hands with great cordiality; and then till her sister came down, she had to listen to all he had to say, of his own happiness, and of Jane's perfections; and in spite of his being a lover, Elizabeth really believed all his expectations of felicity, to be rationally founded, because they had for basis the excellent understanding, and super-excellent disposition of Jane, and a general similarity of feeling and taste between her and himself.

It was an evening of no common delight to them all; the satisfaction of Miss Bennet's mind gave a glow of such sweet animation to her face, as made her look handsomer than ever. Kitty simpered and smiled, and hoped her turn was coming soon. Mrs. Bennet could not give her consent, or speak her approbation in terms warm enough to satisfy her feelings, though she talked to Bingley of nothing else, for half an hour; and when Mr. Bennet joined them at supper, his voice and manner plainly shewed how really happy he was.

Not a word, however, passed his lips in allusion to it, till their visitor took his leave for the night; but as soon as he was gone, he turned to his daughter and said,

"Jane, I congratulate you. You will be a very happy woman."

Jane went to him instantly, kissed him, and thanked him for his goodness.

"You are a good girl;" he replied, "and I have great pleasure in think-ing you will be so happily settled. I have not a doubt of your doing very well together. Your tempers are by no means unlike. You are each of you so complying, that nothing will ever be resolved on; so easy, that every servant will cheat you; and so generous, that you will always exceed your income."

"I hope not so. Imprudence or thoughtlessness in money matters, would be unpardonable in *me*."

"Exceed their income! My dear Mr. Bennet," cried his wife, "what are you talking of? Why, he has four or five thousand a-year, and very likely more." Then addressing her daughter, "Oh! my dear, dear Jane, I am so happy! I am sure I sha'nt get a wink of sleep all night. I knew how it would be. I always said it must be so, at last. I was sure you could not be so beautiful for nothing! I remember, as soon as ever I saw him, when he first came into Hertfordshire last year, I thought how likely it was that you should come together. Oh! he is the hand-somest young man that ever was seen!"

Wickham, Lydia, were all forgotten. Jane was beyond competition her favorite child. At that moment, she cared for no other. Her youn-gest sisters soon began to make interest with her for objects of hap-piness which she might in future be able to dispense.

Mary petitioned for the use of the library at Netherfield; and Kitty begged very hard for a few balls there every winter.

Bingley, from this time, was of course a daily visitor at Longbourn; coming frequently before breakfast, and always remaining till after sup-per; unless when some barbarous neighbour, who could not be enough detested, had given him an invitation to dinner, which he thought himself obliged to accept.

Elizabeth had now but little time for conversation with her sister; for while he was present, Jane had no attention to bestow on any one else; but she found herself considerably useful to both of them, in those hours of separation that must sometimes occur. In the absence of Jane, he always attached himself to Elizabeth, for the pleasure of talking of her; and when Bingley was gone, Jane constantly sought the same means of relief.

"He has made me so happy," said she, one evening, "by telling me, that he was totally ignorant of my being in town last spring! I had not believed it possible."

"I suspected as much," replied Elizabeth. "But how did he account for it?"

"It must have been his sister's doing. They were certainly no friends to his acquaintance with me, which I cannot wonder at, since he might have chosen so much more advantageously in many respects. But when they see, as I trust they will, that their brother is happy with me, they will learn to be contented, and we shall be on good terms again; though we can never be what we once were to each other."

"That is the most unforgiving speech," said Elizabeth, "that I ever heard you utter. Good girl! It would vex me, indeed, to see you again the dupe of Miss Bingley's pretended regard."

"Would you believe it, Lizzy, that when he went to town last November, he really loved me, and nothing but a persuasion of *my* being indifferent, would have prevented his coming down again!"

"He made a little mistake to be sure; but it is to the credit of his modesty."

This naturally introduced a panegyric from Jane on his diffidence, and the little value he put on his own good qualities.

Elizabeth was pleased to find, that he had not betrayed the interference of his friend,[5] for, though Jane had the most generous and forgiving heart in the world, she knew it was a circumstance which must prejudice her against him.

"I am certainly the most fortunate creature that ever existed!" cried Jane. "Oh! Lizzy, why am I thus singled from my family, and blessed above them all! If I could but see *you* as happy! If there *were* but such another man for you!"

"If you were to give me forty such men, I never could be so happy as you. Till I have your disposition, your goodness, I never can have your happiness. No, no, let me shift for myself; and, perhaps, if I have very good luck, I may meet with another Mr. Collins in time."

The situation of affairs in the Longbourn family could not be long a secret. Mrs. Bennet was privileged to whisper it to Mrs. Philips, and *she* ventured, without any permission, to do the same by all her neighbours in Meryton.

The Bennets were speedily pronounced to be the luckiest family in the world, though only a few weeks before, when Lydia had first run away, they had been generally proved to be marked out for misfortune.

Chapter XIV

One morning, about a week after Bingley's engagement with Jane had been formed, as he and the females of the family were sitting together in the dressing-room[6] their attention was suddenly drawn to the window, by the sound of a carriage; and they perceived a chaise and four driving up the lawn. It was too early in the morning for visitors, and besides, the equipage did not answer to that of any of their neighbours. The horses were post; and neither the carriage, nor the livery of the servant who preceded it, were familiar to them. As it was certain, however, that somebody was coming, Bingley instantly prevailed on

5. 1813: friends.
6. 1813: dining room. Cassandra Austen's correction.

Miss Bennet to avoid the confinement of such an intrusion, and walk away with him into the shrubbery. They both set off, and the conjectures of the remaining three continued, though with little satisfaction, till the door was thrown open, and their visitor entered. It was Lady Catherine De Bourgh.

They were of course all intending to be surprised; but their astonishment was beyond their expectation; and on the part of Mrs. Bennet and Kitty, though she was perfectly unknown to them, even inferior to what Elizabeth felt.

She entered the room with an air more than usually ungracious, made no other reply to Elizabeth's salutation, than a slight inclination of the head, and sat down without saying a word. Elizabeth had mentioned her name to her mother, on her ladyship's entrance, though no request of introduction had been made.

Mrs. Bennet all amazement, though flattered by having a guest of such high importance, received her with the utmost politeness. After sitting for a moment in silence, she said very stiffly to Elizabeth,

"I hope you are well, Miss Bennet. That lady I suppose is your mother."

Elizabeth replied very concisely that she was.

"And *that* I suppose is one of your sisters."

"Yes, madam," said Mrs. Bennet, delighted to speak to a lady Catherine. "She is my youngest girl but one. My youngest of all, is lately married, and my eldest is some-where about the grounds, walking with a young man, who I believe will soon become a part of the family."

"You have a very small park here," returned lady Catherine after a short silence.

"It is nothing in comparison of Rosings, my lady, I dare say; but I assure you it is much larger than Sir William Lucas's."

"This must be a most inconvenient sitting room for the evening, in summer; the windows are full west."

Mrs. Bennet assured her that they never sat there after dinner; and then added,

"May I take the liberty of asking your ladyship whether you left Mr. and Mrs. Collins well."

"Yes, very well. I saw them the night before last."

Elizabeth now expected that she would produce a letter for her from Charlotte, as it seemed the only probable motive for her calling. But no letter appeared, and she was completely puzzled.

Mrs. Bennet, with great civility, begged her ladyship to take some refreshment; but Lady Catherine very resolutely, and not very politely, declined eating any thing; and then rising up, said to Elizabeth,

"Miss Bennet, there seemed to be a prettyish kind of a little wilderness on one side of your lawn. I should be glad to take a turn in it, if you will favour me with your company."

"Go, my dear," cried her mother, "and shew her ladyship about the different walks. I think she will be pleased with the hermitage."[7]

Elizabeth obeyed, and running into her own room for her parasol, attended her noble guest down stairs. As they passed through the hall, Lady Catherine opened the doors into the dining-parlour and drawing-room, and pronouncing them, after a short survey, to be decent looking rooms, walked on.

Her carriage remained at the door, and Elizabeth saw that her waiting-woman was in it. They proceeded in silence along the gravel walk that led to the copse; Elizabeth was determined to make no effort for conversation with a woman, who was now more than usually insolent and disagreeable.

"How could I ever think her like her nephew?" said she, as she looked in her face.

As soon as they entered the copse, Lady Catherine began in the following manner—

"You can be at no loss, Miss Bennet, to understand the reason of my journey hither. Your own heart, your own conscience, must tell you why I come."

Elizabeth looked with unaffected astonishment.

"Indeed, you are mistaken, Madam. I have not been at all able to account for the honour of seeing you here."

"Miss Bennet," replied her ladyship, in an angry tone, "you ought to know, that I am not to be trifled with. But however insincere *you* may choose to be, you shall not find *me* so. My character has ever been celebrated for its sincerity and frankness, and in a cause of such moment as this, I shall certainly not depart from it. A report of a most alarming nature, reached me two days ago. I was told, that not only your sister was on the point of being most advantageously married, but that *you*, that Miss Elizabeth Bennet, would, in all likelihood, be soon afterwards united to my nephew, my own nephew, Mr. Darcy. Though I *know* it must be a scandalous falsehood; though I would not injure him so much as to suppose the truth of it possible, I instantly resolved on setting off for this place, that I might make my sentiments known to you."

"If you believed it impossible to be true," said Elizabeth, colouring with astonishment and disdain, "I wonder you took the trouble of coming so far. What could your ladyship propose by it?"

"At once to insist upon having such a report universally contradicted."

"Your coming to Longbourn, to see me and my family," said Elizabeth, coolly, "will be rather a confirmation of it; if, indeed, such a report is in existence."

7. A secluded place; here the copse, or bower of small trees, on the grounds.

"If! do you then pretend to be ignorant of it? Has it not been indus-triously circulated by yourselves? Do you not know that such a report is spread abroad?"

"I never heard that it was."

"And can you likewise declare, that there is no *foundation* for it?"

"I do not pretend to possess equal frankness with your ladyship. *You* may ask questions, which *I* shall not choose to answer."

"This is not to be borne. Miss Bennet, I insist on being satisfied. Has he, has my nephew, made you an offer of marriage?"

"Your ladyship has declared it to be impossible."

"It ought to be so; it must be so, while he retains the use of his reason. But *your* arts and allurements may, in a moment of infatuation, have made him forget what he owes to himself and to all his family. You may have drawn him in."

"If I have, I shall be the last person to confess it."

"Miss Bennet, do you know who I am? I have not been accustomed to such language as this. I am almost the nearest relation he has in the world, and am entitled to know all his dearest concerns."

"But you are not entitled to know *mine*; nor will such behaviour as this, ever induce me to be explicit."

"Let me be rightly understood. This match, to which you have the presumption to aspire, can never take place. No, never. Mr. Darcy is engaged to *my daughter*. Now what have you to say?"

"Only this; that if he is so, you can have no reason to suppose he will make an offer to me."

Lady Catherine hesitated for a moment, and then replied,

"The engagement between them is of a peculiar kind. From their infancy, they have been intended for each other. It was the favourite wish of *his* mother, as well as of her's. While in their cradles, we planned the union: and now, at the moment when the wishes of both sisters would be accomplished, is[8] their marriage, to be prevented by a young woman of inferior birth, of no importance in the world, and wholly unallied to the family? Do you pay no regard to the wishes of his friends? To his tacit engagement with Miss De Bourgh? Are you lost to every feeling of propriety and delicacy? Have you not heard me say, that from his earliest hours he was destined for his cousin?"[9]

"Yes, and I had heard it before. But what is that to me? If there is no other objection to my marrying your nephew, I shall certainly not be kept from it, by knowing that his mother and aunt wished him to marry Miss De Bourgh. You both did as much as you could, in planning the marriage. Its completion depended on others. If Mr. Darcy is nei-

8. 1813: in.
9. The marriage of cousins was not unusual in English landed families. The practice combined estates and prevented their passing outside the family, as Miss De Bourgh's inheritance would if she married someone to whom she was not related.

ther by honour nor inclination confined to his cousin, why is not he to make another choice? And if I am that choice, why may not I accept him?"

"Because honour, decorum, prudence, nay, interest, forbid it. Yes, Miss Bennet, interest; for do not expect to be noticed by his family or friends, if you wilfully act against the inclinations of all. You will be censured, slighted, and despised, by every one connected with him. Your alliance will be a disgrace; your name will never even be mentioned by any of us."

"These are heavy misfortunes," replied Elizabeth. "But the wife of Mr. Darcy must have such extraordinary sources of happiness necessarily attached to her situation, that she could, upon the whole, have no cause to repine."

"Obstinate, headstrong girl! I am ashamed of you! Is this your gratitude for my attentions to you last spring? Is nothing due to me on that score?

"Let us sit down. You are to understand, Miss Bennet, that I came here with the determined resolution of carrying my purpose; nor will I be dissuaded from it. I have not been used to submit to any person's whims. I have not been in the habit of brooking disappointment."

"*That* will make your ladyship's situation at present more pitiable; but it will have no effect on *me*."

"I will not be interrupted. Hear me in silence. My daughter and my nephew are formed for each other. They are descended on the maternal side, from the same noble line; and, on the father's, from respectable, honourable, and ancient, though untitled families. Their fortune on both sides is splendid. They are destined for each other by the voice of every member of their respective houses; and what is to divide them? The upstart pretensions of a young woman without family, connections, or fortune. Is this to be endured! But it must not, shall not be. If you were sensible of your own good, you would not wish to quit the sphere, in which you have been brought up."

"In marrying your nephew, I should not consider myself as quitting that sphere. He is a gentleman; I am a gentleman's daughter; so far we are equal."

"True. You *are* a gentleman's daughter. But who was your mother? Who are your uncles and aunts? Do not imagine me ignorant of their condition."

"Whatever my connections may be," said Elizabeth, "if your nephew does not object to them, they can be nothing to *you*."

"Tell me once for all, are you engaged to him?"

Though Elizabeth would not, for the mere purpose of obliging Lady Catherine, have answered this question; she could not but say, after a moment's deliberation,

"I am not."

Lady Catherine seemed pleased.

"And will you promise me, never to enter into such an engagement?"

"I will make no promise of the kind."

"Miss Bennet, I am shocked and astonished. I expected to find a more reasonable young woman. But do not deceive yourself into a belief that I will ever recede. I shall not go away, till you have given me the assurance I require."

"And I certainly *never* shall give it. I am not to be intimidated into anything so wholly unreasonable. Your ladyship wants Mr. Darcy to marry your daughter; but would my giving you the wished-for promise, make *their* marriage at all more probable? Supposing him to be attached to me, would *my* refusing to accept his hand, make him wish to bestow it on his cousin? Allow me to say, Lady Catherine, that the arguments with which you have supported this extraordinary application, have been as frivolous as the application was ill-judged. You have widely mistaken my character, if you think I can be worked on by such persuasions as these. How far your nephew might approve of your interference in *his* affairs, I cannot tell; but you have certainly no right to concern yourself in mine. I must beg, therefore, to be importuned no farther on the subject."

"Not so hasty, if you please. I have by no means done. To all the objections I have already urged, I have still another to add. I am no stranger to the particulars of your youngest sister's infamous elopement. I know it all; that the young man's marrying her, was a patched-up business, at the expence of your father and uncle.[1] And is *such* a girl to be my nephew's sister? Is *her* husband, is the son of his late father's steward, to be his brother? Heaven and earth!—of what are you thinking? Are the shades of Pemberley to be thus polluted?"

"You can *now* have nothing farther to say," she resentfully answered. "You have insulted me, in every possible method. I must beg to return to the house."

And she rose as she spoke. Lady Catherine rose also, and they turned back. Her ladyship was highly incensed.

"You have no regard, then, for the honour and credit of my nephew! Unfeeling, selfish girl! Do you not consider that a connection with you, must disgrace him in the eyes of everybody."

"Lady Catherine, I have nothing farther to say. You know my sentiments."

"You are then resolved to have him?"

"I have said no such thing. I am only resolved to act in that manner, which will, in my own opinion, constitute my happiness, without reference to *you*, or to any person so wholly unconnected with me."

"It is well. You refuse, then, to oblige me. You refuse to obey the

1. 1813: uncles.

claims of duty, honour, and gratitude. You are determined to ruin him in the opinion of all his friends, and make him the contempt of the world."

"Neither duty, nor honour, nor gratitude," replied Elizabeth, "have any possible claim on me, in the present instance. No principle of either, would be violated by my marriage with Mr. Darcy. And with regard to the resentment of his family, or the indignation of the world, if the former *were* excited by his marrying me, it would not give me one moment's concern—and the world in general would have too much sense to join in the scorn."

"And this is your real opinion! This is your final resolve! Very well. I shall now know how to act. Do not imagine, Miss Bennet, that your ambition will ever be gratified. I came to try you. I hoped to find you reasonable; but depend upon it I will carry my point."

In this manner Lady Catherine talked on, till they were at the door of the carriage, when turning hastily round, she added,

"I take no leave of you, Miss Bennet. I send no compliments to your mother. You deserve no such attention. I am most seriously displeased."

Elizabeth made no answer; and without attempting to persuade her ladyship to return into the house, walked quietly into it herself. She heard the carriage drive away as she proceeded up stairs. Her mother impatiently met her at the door of the dressing-room, to ask why Lady Catherine would not come in again and rest herself.

"She did not choose it," said her daughter, "she would go."

"She is a very fine-looking woman! and her calling here was prodigiously civil! for she only came, I suppose, to tell us the Collinses were well. She is on her road somewhere, I dare say, and so passing through Meryton, thought she might as well call on you. I suppose she had nothing particular to say to you, Lizzy?"

Elizabeth was forced to give into a little falsehood here; for to acknowledge the substance of their conversation was impossible.

Chapter XV

The discomposure of spirits, which this extraordinary visit threw Elizabeth into, could not be easily overcome; nor could she for many hours, learn to think of it less than incessantly. Lady Catherine it appeared, had actually taken the trouble of this journey from Rosings, for the sole purpose of breaking off her supposed engagement with Mr. Darcy. It was a rational scheme to be sure! but from what the report of their engagement could originate, Elizabeth was at a loss to imagine; till she recollected that *his* being the intimate friend of Bingley, and *her* being the sister of Jane, was enough, at a time when the expectation of one wedding, made every body eager for another, to supply the idea.

She had not herself forgotten to feel that the marriage of her sister must bring them more frequently together. And her neighbours at Lucas lodge, therefore, (for through their communication with the Collinses, the report she concluded had reached lady Catherine) had only set *that* down, as almost certain and immediate, which *she* had looked forward to as possible, at some future time.

In revolving lady Catherine's expressions, however, she could not help feeling some uneasiness as to the possible consequence of her persisting in this interference. From what she had said of her resolution to prevent their marriage, it occurred to Elizabeth that she must meditate an application to her nephew, and how *he* might take a similar representation of the evils attached to a connection with her, she dared not pronounce. She knew not the exact degree of his affection for his aunt, or his dependence on her judgment, but it was natural to suppose that he thought much higher of her ladyship than *she* could do; and it was certain, that in enumerating the miseries of a marriage with *one*, whose immediate connections were so unequal to his own, his aunt would address him on his weakest side. With his notions of dignity, he would probably feel that the arguments, which to Elizabeth had appeared weak and ridiculous, contained much good sense and solid reasoning.

If he had been wavering before, as to what he should do, which had often seemed likely, the advice and intreaty of so near a relation might settle every doubt, and determine him at once to be as happy, as dignity unblemished could make him. In that case he would return no more. Lady Catherine might see him in her way through town; and his engagement to Bingley of coming again to Netherfield must give way.

"If, therefore, an excuse for not keeping his promise, should come to his friend within a few days," she added, "I shall know how to understand it. I shall then give over every expectation, every wish of his constancy. If he is satisfied with only regretting me, when he might have obtained my affections and hand, I shall soon cease to regret him at all."

The surprise of the rest of the family, on hearing who their visitor had been, was very great; but they obligingly satisfied it, with the same kind of supposition, which had appeased Mrs. Bennet's curiosity; and Elizabeth was spared from much teazing on the subject.

The next morning, as she was going down stairs, she was met by her father, who came out of his library with a letter in his hand.

"Lizzy," said he, "I was going to look for you; come into my room."

She followed him thither; and her curiosity to know what he had to tell her, was heightened by the supposition of its being in some manner connected with the letter he held. It suddenly struck her that it might be from lady Catherine; and she anticipated with dismay all the consequent explanations.

She followed her father to the fire-place, and they both sat down. He then said,

"I have received a letter this morning that has astonished me exceedingly. As it principally concerns yourself, you ought to know its contents. I did not know before, that I had *two* daughters on the brink of matrimony. Let me congratulate you, on a very important conquest."

The colour now rushed into Elizabeth's cheeks in the instantaneous conviction of its being a letter from the nephew, instead of the aunt; and she was undetermined whether most to be pleased that he explained himself at all, or offended that his letter was not rather addressed to herself; when her father continued,

"You look conscious. Young ladies have great penetration in such matters as these; but I think I may defy even *your* sagacity, to discover the name of your admirer. This letter is from Mr. Collins."

"From Mr. Collins! and what can *he* have to say?"

"Something very much to the purpose of course. He begins with congratulations to the approaching nuptials of my eldest daughter, of which it seems he has been told, by some of the good-natured, gossiping Lucases. I shall not sport with your impatience, by reading what he says on that point. What relates to yourself, is as follows. 'Having thus offered you the sincere congratulations of Mrs. Collins and myself on this happy event, let me now add a short hint on the subject of another; of which we have been advertised by the same authority. Your daughter Elizabeth, it is presumed, will not long bear the name of Bennet, after her elder sister has resigned it, and the chosen partner of her fate, may be reasonably looked up to, as one of the most illustrious personages in this land.'

"Can you possibly guess, Lizzy, who is meant by this? 'This young gentleman is blessed in a peculiar way, with every thing the heart of mortal can most desire,—splendid property, noble kindred, and extensive patronage. Yet in spite of all these temptations, let me warn my cousin Elizabeth, and yourself, of what evils you may incur, by a precipitate closure with this gentleman's proposals, which, of course, you will be inclined to take immediate advantage of.'

"Have you any idea, Lizzy, who this gentleman is? But now it comes out.

" 'My motive for cautioning you, is as follows. We have reason to imagine that his aunt, lady Catherine de Bourgh, does not look on the match with a friendly eye.'

"*Mr. Darcy*, you see, is the man! Now, Lizzy, I think I *have* surprised you. Could he, or the Lucases, have pitched on any man, within the circle of our acquaintance, whose name would have given the lie more effectually to what they related? Mr. Darcy, who never looks at any woman but to see a blemish, and who probably never looked at *you* in his life! It is admirable!"

Elizabeth tried to join in her father's pleasantry, but could only force one most reluctant smile. Never had his wit been directed in a manner so little agreeable to her.

"Are you not diverted?"

"Oh! yes. Pray read on."

" 'After mentioning the likelihood of this marriage to her ladyship last night, she immediately, with her usual condescension, expressed what she felt on the occasion; when it became apparent, that on the score of some family objections on the part of my cousin, she would never give her consent to what she termed so disgraceful a match. I thought it my duty to give the speediest intelligence of this to my cousin, that she and her noble admirer may be aware of what they are about, and not run hastily into a marriage which has not been properly sanctioned.' Mr. Collins moreover adds, 'I am truly rejoiced that my cousin Lydia's sad business has been so well hushed up, and am only concerned that their living together before the marriage took place, should be so generally known. I must not, however, neglect the duties of my station, or refrain from declaring my amazement, at hearing that you received the young couple into your house as soon as they were married. It was an encouragement of vice; and had I been the rector of Longbourn, I should very strenuously have opposed it. You ought certainly to forgive them as a christian, but never to admit them in your sight, or allow their names to be mentioned in your hearing.' *That* is his notion of christian forgiveness! The rest of his letter is only about his dear Charlotte's situation, and his expectation of a young olive-branch. But, Lizzy, you look as if you did not enjoy it. You are not going to be *Missish*,[2] I hope, and pretend to be affronted at an idle report. For what do we live, but to make sport for our neighbours, and laugh at them in our turn?"

"Oh!" cried Elizabeth, "I am excessively diverted. But it is so strange!"

"Yes—*that* is what makes it amusing. Had they fixed on any other man it would have been nothing; but *his* perfect indifference, and your pointed dislike, make it so delightfully absurd! Much as I abominate writing, I would not give up Mr. Collins's correspondence for any consideration. Nay, when I read a letter of his, I cannot help giving him the preference even over Wickham, much as I value the impudence and hypocrisy of my son-in-law. And pray, Lizzy, what said Lady Catherine about this report? Did she call to refuse her consent?"

To this question his daughter replied only with a laugh; and as it had been asked without the least suspicion, she was not distressed by his repeating it. Elizabeth had never been more at a loss to make her feelings appear what they were not. It was necessary to laugh, when

2. Behave like an affectedly prim and decorous young girl.

she would rather have cried. Her father had most cruelly mortified her, by what he said of Mr. Darcy's indifference, and she could do nothing but wonder at such a want of penetration, or fear that perhaps, instead of his seeing too *little*, she might have fancied too *much*.

Chapter XVI

Instead of receiving any such letter of excuse from his friend, as Elizabeth half expected Mr. Bingley to do, he was able to bring Darcy with him to Longbourn before many days had passed after Lady Catherine's visit. The gentlemen arrived early; and, before Mrs. Bennet had time to tell him of their having seen his aunt, of which her daughter sat in momentary dread, Bingley, who wanted to be alone with Jane, proposed their all walking out. It was agreed to. Mrs. Bennet was not in the habit of walking, Mary could never spare time, but the remaining five set off together. Bingley and Jane, however, soon allowed the others to outstrip them. They lagged behind, while Elizabeth, Kitty, and Darcy, were to entertain each other. Very little was said by either; Kitty was too much afraid of him to talk; Elizabeth was secretly forming a desperate resolution; and perhaps he might be doing the same.

They walked towards the Lucases, because Kitty wished to call upon Maria; and as Elizabeth saw no occasion for making it a general concern, when Kitty left them, she went boldly on with him alone. Now was the moment for her resolution to be executed, and, while her courage was high, she immediately said,

"Mr. Darcy, I am a very selfish creature; and, for the sake of giving relief to my own feelings, care not how much I may be wounding your's. I can no longer help thanking you for you unexampled kindness to my poor sister. Ever since I have known it, I have been most anxious to acknowledge to you how gratefully I feel it. Were it known to the rest of my family, I should not have merely my own gratitude to express."

"I am sorry, exceedingly sorry," replied Darcy, in a tone of surprise and emotion, "that you have ever been informed of what may, in a mistaken light, have given you uneasiness. I did not think Mrs. Gardiner was so little to be trusted."

"You must not blame my aunt. Lydia's thoughtlessness first betrayed to me that you had been concerned in the matter; and, of course, I could not rest till I knew the particulars. Let me thank you again and again, in the name of all my family, for that generous compassion which induced you to take so much trouble, and bear so many mortifications, for the sake of discovering them."

"If you *will* thank me," he replied, "let it be for yourself alone. That the wish of giving happiness to you, might add force to the other inducements which led me on, I shall not attempt to deny. But your *family* owe me nothing. Much as I respect them, I believe, I thought only of *you*."

Elizabeth was too much embarrassed to say a word. After a short pause, her companion added, "You are too generous to trifle with me. If your feelings are still what they were last April, tell me so at once. *My* affections and wishes are unchanged, but one word from you will silence me on this subject for ever."

Elizabeth feeling all the more than common awkwardness and anxiety of his situation, now forced herself to speak; and immediately, though not very fluently, gave him to understand, that her sentiments had undergone so material a change, since the period to which he alluded, as to make her receive with gratitude and pleasure, his present assurances. The happiness which this reply produced, was such as he had probably never felt before; and he expressed himself on the occasion as sensibly and as warmly as a man violently in love can be supposed to do. Had Elizabeth been able to encounter his eye, she might have seen how well the expression of heart-felt delight, diffused over his face, became him; but, though she could not look, she could listen, and he told her of feelings, which, in proving of what importance she was to him, made his affection every moment more valuable.

They walked on, without knowing in what direction. There was too much to be thought, and felt, and said, for attention to any other objects. She soon learnt that they were indebted for their present good understanding to the efforts of his aunt, who *did* call on him in her return through London, and there relate her journey to Longbourn, its motive, and the substance of her conversation with Elizabeth; dwelling emphatically on every expression of the latter, which, in her ladyship's apprehension, peculiarly denoted her perverseness and assurance, in the belief that such a relation must assist her endeavours to obtain that promise from her nephew, which *she* had refused to give. But, unluckily for her ladyship, its effect had been exactly contrariwise.

"It taught me to hope," said he, "as I had scarcely ever allowed myself to hope before. I knew enough of your disposition to be certain, that, had you been absolutely, irrevocably decided against me, you would have acknowledged it to Lady Catherine, frankly and openly."

Elizabeth coloured and laughed as she replied, "Yes, you know enough of my *frankness* to believe me capable of *that*. After abusing you so abominably to your face, I could have no scruple in abusing you to all your relations."

"What did you say of me, that I did not deserve? For, though your accusations were ill-founded, formed on mistaken premises, my behaviour to you at the time, had merited the severest reproof. It was unpardonable. I cannot think of it without abhorrence."

"We will not quarrel for the greater share of blame annexed to that evening," said Elizabeth. "The conduct of neither, if strictly examined, will be irreproachable; but since then, we have both, I hope, improved in civility."

"I cannot be so easily reconciled to myself. The recollection of what I then said, of my conduct, my manners, my expressions during the whole of it, is now, and has been many months, inexpressibly painful to me. Your reproof, so well applied, I shall never forget: 'had you behaved in a more gentleman-like manner.' Those were your words. You know not, you can scarcely conceive, how they have tortured me; —though it was some time, I confess, before I was reasonable enough to allow their justice."

"I was certainly very far from expecting them to make so strong an impression. I had not the smallest idea of their being ever felt in such a way."

"I can easily believe it. You thought me then devoid of every proper feeling, I am sure you did. The turn of your countenance I shall never forget, as you said that I could not have addressed you in any possible way, that would induce you to accept me."

"Oh! do not repeat what I then said. These recollections will not do at all. I assure you, that I have long been most heartily ashamed of it."

Darcy mentioned his letter. "Did it," said he, "did it *soon* make you think better of me? Did you, on reading it, give any credit to its contents?"

She explained what its effect on her had been, and how gradually all her former prejudices had been removed.

"I knew," said he, "that what I wrote must give you pain, but it was necessary. I hope you have destroyed the letter. There was one part especially, the opening of it, which I should dread your having the power of reading again. I can remember some expressions which might justly make you hate me."

"The letter shall certainly be burnt, if you believe it essential to the preservation of my regard; but, though we have both reason to think my opinions not entirely unalterable, they are not, I hope, quite so easily changed as that implies."

"When I wrote that letter," replied Darcy, "I believed myself perfectly calm and cool, but I am since convinced that it was written in a dreadful bitterness of spirit."

"The letter, perhaps, began in bitterness, but it did not end so. The adieu is charity itself. But think no more of the letter. The feelings of the person who wrote, and the person who received it, are now so widely different from what they were then, that every unpleasant circumstance attending it, ought to be forgotten. You must learn some of my philosophy. Think only of the past as its remembrance gives you pleasure."

"I cannot give you credit for any philosophy of the kind. *Your* retrospections must be so totally void of reproach, that the contentment arising from them, is not of philosophy, but what is much better, of innocence.[3] But with *me*, it is not so. Painful recollections will intrude, which cannot, which ought not to be repelled. I have been a selfish being all my life, in practice, though not in principle. As a child I was taught what was *right*, but not taught to correct my temper. I was given good principles, but left to follow them in pride and conceit. Unfortunately an only son, (for many years an only *child*) I was spoilt by my parents, who though good themselves, (my father particularly, all that was benevolent and amiable,) allowed, encouraged, almost taught me to be selfish and overbearing, to care for none beyond my own family circle, to think meanly of all the rest of the world, to *wish* at least to think meanly of their sense and worth compared with my own. Such I was, from eight to eight and twenty; and such I might still have been but for you, dearest, loveliest Elizabeth! What do I not owe you! You taught me a lesson, hard indeed at first, but most advantageous. By you, I was properly humbled. I came to you without a doubt of my reception. You shewed me how insufficient were all my pretensions to please a woman worthy of being pleased."

"Had you then persuaded yourself that I should?"

"Indeed I had. What will you think of my vanity? I believed you to be wishing, expecting my addresses."

"My manners must have been in fault, but not intentionally I assure you. I never meant to deceive you, but my spirits might often lead me wrong. How you must have hated me after *that* evening?"

"Hate you! I was angry perhaps at first, but my anger soon began to take a proper direction."

"I am almost afraid of asking what you thought of me, when we met at Pemberley. You blamed me for coming?"

"No indeed; I felt nothing but surprise."

"Your surprise could not be greater than *mine* in being noticed by you. My conscience told me that I deserved no extraordinary politeness, and I confess that I did not expect to receive *more* than my due."

"My object *then*," replied Darcy, "was to shew you, by every civility in my power, that I was not so mean as to resent the past; and I hoped to obtain your forgiveness, to lessen your ill opinion, by letting you see that your reproofs had been attended to. How soon any other wishes introduced themselves I can hardly tell, but I believe in about half an hour after I had seen you."

He then told her of Georgiana's delight in her acquaintance, and of her disappointment at its sudden interruption; which naturally leading to the cause of that interruption, she soon learnt that his resolution of following her from Derbyshire in quest of her sister, had been formed

3. 1813: ignorance. Cassandra Austen's correction.

before he quitted the inn, and that his gravity and thoughtfulness there, had arisen from no other struggles than what such a purpose must comprehend.

She expressed her gratitude again, but it was too painful a subject to each, to be dwelt on farther.

After walking several miles in a leisurely manner, and too busy to know any thing about it, they found at last, on examining their watches, that it was time to be at home.

"What could become of Mr. Bingley and Jane!" was a wonder which introduced the discussion of *their* affairs. Darcy was delighted with their engagement; his friend had given him the earliest information of it.

"I must ask whether you were surprised?" said Elizabeth.

"Not at all. When I went away, I felt that it would soon happen."

"That is to say, you had given your permission. I guessed as much." And though he exclaimed at the term, she found that it had been pretty much the case.

"On the evening before my going to London," said he "I made a confession to him, which I believe I ought to have made long ago. I told him of all that had occurred to make my former interference in his affairs, absurd and impertinent. His surprise was great. He had never had the slightest suspicion. I told him, moreover, that I believed myself mistaken in supposing, as I had done, that your sister was indifferent to him; and as I could easily perceive that his attachment to her was unabated, I felt no doubt of their happiness together."

Elizabeth could not help smiling at his easy manner of directing his friend.

"Did you speak from your own observation," said she, "when you told him that my sister loved him, or merely from my information last spring?"

"From the former. I had narrowly observed her during the two visits which I had lately made here;[4] and I was convinced of her affection."

"And your assurance of it, I suppose, carried immediate conviction to him."

"It did. Bingley is most unaffectedly modest. His diffidence had prevented his depending on his own judgment in so anxious a case, but his reliance on mine made every thing easy. I was obliged to confess one thing, which for a time, and not unjustly, offended him. I could not allow myself to conceal that your sister had been in town three months last winter, that I had known it, and purposely kept it from him. He was angry. But his anger, I am persuaded, lasted no longer than he remained in any doubt of your sister's sentiments. He has heartily forgiven me now."

4. 1813: her here. Cassandra Austen's correction.

Elizabeth longed to observe that Mr. Bingley had been a most delightful friend; so easily guided that his worth was invaluable; but she checked herself. She remembered that he had yet to learn to be laught at, and it was rather too early to begin. In anticipating the happiness of Bingley, which of course was to be inferior only to his own, he continued the conversation till they reached the house. In the hall they parted.

Chapter XVII

"My dear Lizzy, where can you have been walking to?" was a question which Elizabeth received from Jane as soon as she entered their[5] room, and from all the others when they sat down to table. She had only to say in reply, that they had wandered about, till she was beyond her own knowledge. She coloured as she spoke; but neither that, nor any thing else, awakened a suspicion of the truth.

The evening passed quietly, unmarked by any thing extraordinary. The acknowledged lovers talked and laughed, the unacknowledged were silent. Darcy was not of a disposition in which happiness overflows in mirth; and Elizabeth, agitated and confused, rather *knew* that she was happy, than *felt* herself to be so; for, besides the immediate embarrassment, there were other evils before her. She anticipated what would be felt in the family when her situation became known; she was aware that no one liked him but Jane; and even feared that with the others it was a *dislike* which not all his fortune and consequence might do away.

At night she opened her heart to Jane. Though suspicion was very far from Miss Bennet's general habits, she was absolutely incredulous here.

"You are joking, Lizzy. This cannot be!—engaged to Mr. Darcy! No, no, you shall not deceive me. I know it to be impossible."

"This is a wretched beginning indeed! My sole dependence was on you; and I am sure nobody else will believe me, if you do not. Yet, indeed, I am in earnest. I speak nothing but the truth. He still loves me, and we are engaged."

Jane looked at her doubtingly. "Oh, Lizzy! it cannot be. I know how much you dislike him."

"You know nothing of the matter. *That* is all to be forgot. Perhaps I did not always love him as well as I do now. But in such cases as these, a good memory is unpardonable. This is the last time I shall ever remember it myself."

Miss Bennet still looked all amazement. Elizabeth again, and more seriously assured her of its truth.

5. 1813: the. Cassandra Austen's correction.

"Good Heaven! can it be really so! Yet now I must believe you," cried Jane. "My dear, dear Lizzy, I would—I do congratulate you—but are you certain? forgive the question—are you quite certain that you can be happy with him?"

"There can be no doubt of that. It is settled between us already, that we are to be the happiest couple in the world. But are you pleased, Jane? Shall you like to have such a brother?"

"Very, very much. Nothing could give either Bingley or myself more delight. But we considered it, we talked of it as impossible. And do you really love him quite well enough? Oh, Lizzy! do any thing rather than marry without affection. Are you quite sure that you feel what you ought to do?"

"Oh, yes! You will only think I feel *more* than I ought to do, when I tell you all."

"What do you mean?"

"Why, I must confess, that I love him better than I do Bingley. I am afraid you will be angry."

"My dearest sister, now be[6] serious. I want to talk very seriously. Let me know every thing that I am to know, without delay. Will you tell me how long you have loved him?"

"It has been coming on so gradually, that I hardly know when it began. But I believe I must date it from my first seeing his beautiful grounds at Pemberley."

Another intreaty that she would be serious, however, produced the desired effect; and she soon satisfied Jane by her solemn assurances of attachment. When convinced on that article, Miss Bennet had nothing farther to wish.

"Now I am quite happy," said she, "for you will be as happy as myself. I always had a value for him. Were it for nothing but his love of you, I must always have esteemed him; but now, as Bingley's friend and your husband, there can be only Bingley and yourself more dear to me. But Lizzy, you have been very sly, very reserved with me. How little did you tell me of what passed at Pemberley and Lambton! I owe all that I know of it, to another, not to you."

Elizabeth told her the motives of her secrecy. She had been unwilling to mention Bingley; and the unsettled state of her own feelings had made her equally avoid the name of his friend. But now she would no longer conceal from her, his share in Lydia's marriage. All was acknowledged, and half the night spent in conversation.

———

"Good gracious!" cried Mrs. Bennet, as she stood at a window the next morning, "if that disagreeable Mr. Darcy is not coming here again with our dear Bingley! What can he mean by being so tiresome as to

6. 1813: *be* be serious. Cassandra Austen's correction.

be always coming here? I had no notion but he would go a shooting, or something or other, and not disturb us with his company. What shall we do with him? Lizzy, you must walk out with him again, that he may not be in Bingley's way."

Elizabeth could hardly help laughing at so convenient a proposal; yet was really vexed that her mother should be always giving him such an epithet.

As soon as they entered, Bingley looked at her so expressively, and shook hands with such warmth, as left no doubt of his good information; and he soon afterwards said aloud, "Mrs. Bennet,[7] have you no more lanes hereabouts in which Lizzy may lose her way again to-day?"

"I advise Mr. Darcy, and Lizzy, and Kitty," said Mrs. Bennet, "to walk to Oakham Mount this morning. It is a nice long walk, and Mr. Darcy has never seen the view."

"It may do very well for the others," replied Mr. Bingley; "but I am sure it will be too much for Kitty. Won't it, Kitty?"

Kitty owned that she had rather stay at home. Darcy professed a great curiosity to see the view from the Mount, and Elizabeth silently consented. As she went up stairs to get ready, Mrs. Bennet followed her, saying,

"I am quite sorry, Lizzy, that you should be forced to have that disagreeable man all to yourself. But I hope you will not mind it: it is all for Jane's sake, you know; and there is no occasion for talking to him, except just now and then. So, do not put yourself to inconvenience."

During their walk, it was resolved that Mr. Bennet's consent should be asked in the course of the evening. Elizabeth reserved to herself the application for her mother's. She could not determine how her mother would take it; sometimes doubting whether all his wealth and grandeur would be enough to overcome her abhorrence of the man. But whether she were violently set against the match, or violently delighted with it, it was certain that her manner would be equally ill adapted to do credit to her sense; and she could no more bear that Mr. Darcy should hear the first raptures of her joy, than the first vehemence of her disapprobation.

––––––

In the evening, soon after Mr. Bennet withdrew to the library, she saw Mr. Darcy rise also and follow him, and her agitation on seeing it was extreme. She did not fear her father's opposition, but he was going to be made unhappy, and that it should be through her means, that *she*, his favourite child, should be distressing him by her choice, should be filling him with fears and regrets in disposing of her, was a wretched reflection, and she sat in misery till Mr. Darcy appeared again, when, looking at him, she was a little relieved by his smile. In a few minutes he approached the table where she was sitting with Kitty; and, while pretending to admire her work, said in a whisper, "Go to your father, he wants you in the library." She was gone directly.

Her father was walking about the room, looking grave and anxious. "Lizzy," said he, "what are you doing? Are you out of your senses, to be accepting this man? Have not you always hated him?"

How earnestly did she then wish that her former opinions had been more reasonable, her expressions more moderate! It would have spared her from explanations and professions which it was exceedingly awkward to give; but they were now necessary, and she assured him with some confusion, of her attachment to Mr. Darcy.

"Or in other words, you are determined to have him. He is rich, to be sure, and you may have more fine clothes and fine carriages than Jane. But will they make you happy?"

"Have you any other objection," said Elizabeth, "than your belief of my indifference?"

"None at all. We all know him to be a proud, unpleasant sort of man; but this would be nothing if you really liked him."

"I do, I do like him," she replied, with tears in her eyes, "I love him. Indeed he has no improper pride. He is perfectly amiable. You do not know what he really is; then pray do not pain me by speaking of him in such terms."

"Lizzy," said her father, "I have given him my consent. He is the kind of man, indeed, to whom I should never dare refuse any thing, which he condescended to ask. I now give it to *you*, if you are resolved on having him. But let me advise you to think better of it. I know your disposition, Lizzy. I know that you could be neither happy nor respectable, unless you truly esteemed your husband; unless you looked up to him as a superior. Your lively talents would place you in the greatest danger in an unequal marriage. You could scarcely escape discredit and misery. My child, let me not have the grief of seeing *you* unable to respect your partner in life. You know not what you are about."

Elizabeth, still more affected, was earnest and solemn in her reply; and at length, by repeated assurances that Mr. Darcy was really the object of her choice, by explaining the gradual change which her estimation of him had undergone, relating her absolute certainty that his affection was not the work of a day, but had stood the test of many months suspense, and enumerating with energy all his good qualities, she did conquer her father's incredulity, and reconcile him to the match.

"Well, my dear," said he, when she ceased speaking, "I have no more to say. If this be the case, he deserves you. I could not have parted with you, my Lizzy, to any one less worthy."

To complete the favourable impression, she then told him what Mr. Darcy had voluntarily done for Lydia. He heard her with astonishment.

"This is an evening of wonders, indeed! And so, Darcy did every thing; made up the match, gave the money, paid the fellow's debts, and got him his commission! So much the better. It will save me a world of trouble and economy. Had it been your uncle's doing, I must and *would* have paid him; but these violent young lovers carry every thing their own way. I shall offer to pay him to-morrow; he will rant and storm about his love for you, and there will be an end of the matter."

He then recollected her embarrassment a few days before, on his reading Mr. Collins's letter; and after laughing at her some time, allowed her at last to go—saying, as she quitted the room, "If any young men come for Mary or Kitty, send them in, for I am quite at leisure."

Elizabeth's mind was now relieved from a very heavy weight; and, after half an hour's quiet reflection in her own room, she was able to join the others with tolerable composure. Every thing was too recent for gaiety, but the evening passed tranquilly away; there was no longer any thing material to be dreaded, and the comfort of ease and familiarity would come in time.

When her mother went up to her dressing-room at night, she followed her, and made the important communication. Its effect was most extraordinary; for on first hearing it, Mrs. Bennet sat quite still, and unable to utter a syllable. Nor was it under many, many minutes, that she could comprehend what she heard; though not in general backward to credit what was for the advantage of her family, or that came in the shape of a lover to any of them. She began at length to recover, to fidget about in her chair, get up, sit down again, wonder, and bless herself.

"Good gracious! Lord bless me! only think! dear me! Mr. Darcy! Who would have thought it! And is it really true? Oh! my sweetest Lizzy! how rich and how great you will be! What pin-money, what jewels, what carriages you will have! Jane's is nothing to it—nothing at all. I am so pleased—so happy. Such a charming man!—so handsome! so tall!—Oh, my dear Lizzy! pray apologise for my having disliked him so much before. I hope he will overlook it. Dear, dear Lizzy. A house in town! Every thing that is charming! Three daughters married! Ten thousand a year! Oh, Lord! What will become of me? I shall go distracted."

This was enough to prove that her approbation need not be doubted: and Elizabeth, rejoicing that such an effusion was heard only by herself, soon went away, But before she had been three minutes in her own room, her mother followed her.

"My dearest child," she cried, "I can think of nothing else! Ten thousand a year, and very likely more! 'Tis as good as a Lord! And a special license.[8] You must and shall be married by a special license. But my dearest love, tell me what dish Mr. Darcy is particularly fond of, that I may have it to-morrow."

This was a sad omen of what her mother's behaviour to the gentleman himself might be; and Elizabeth found, that though in the certain possession of his warmest affection, and secure of her relations' consent, there was still something to be wished for. But the morrow passed off much better than she expected; for Mrs. Bennet luckily stood in such awe of her intended son-in-law, that she ventured not to speak to him, unless it was in her power to offer him any attention, or mark her deference for his opinion.

Elizabeth had the satisfaction of seeing her father taking pains to get acquainted with him; and Mr. Bennet soon assured her that he was rising every hour in his esteem.

"I admire all my three sons-in-law highly," said he. "Wickham, perhaps, is my favourite; but I think I shall like *your* husband quite as well as Jane's."

Chapter XVIII

Elizabeth's spirits soon rising to playfulness again, she wanted Mr. Darcy to account for his having ever fallen in love with her. "How could you begin?" said she. "I can comprehend your going on charmingly, when you had once made a beginning; but what could set you off in the first place?"

"I cannot fix on the hour, or the spot, or the look, or the words, which laid the foundation. It is too long ago. I was in the middle before I knew that I *had* begun."

"My beauty you had early withstood, and as for my manners—my behavior to *you* was at least always bordering on the uncivil, and I never spoke to you without rather wishing to give you pain than not. Now be sincere; did you admire me for my impertinence?'

"For the liveliness of your mind, I did."

"You may as well call it impertinence at once. It was very little less. The fact is, that you were sick of civility, of deference, of officious attention. You were disgusted with the women who were always speaking and looking, and thinking for *your* approbation alone. I roused, and interested you, because I was so unlike *them*. Had you not been really amiable you would have hated me for it; but in spite of the pains you took to disguise yourself, your feelings were always noble and just; and in your heart, you thoroughly despised the persons who so assiduously courted you. There—I have saved you the trouble of accounting for it;

8. Permission to marry procured from a bishop or archbishop and used in lieu of the publishing of banns. Because a special license was usually only available to members of the aristocracy, its use carried a social cachet.

and really, all things considered, I begin to think it perfectly reasonable. To be sure, you know no actual good of me—but nobody thinks of *that* when they fall in love."

"Was there no good in your affectionate behaviour to Jane, while she was ill at Netherfield?"

"Dearest Jane! who could have done less for her? But make a virtue of it by all means. My good qualities are under your protection, and you are to exaggerate them as much as possible; and, in return, it belongs to me to find occasions for teazing and quarrelling with you as often as may be; and I shall begin directly by asking you what made you so unwilling to come to the point at last. What made you so shy of me, when you first called, and afterwards dined here? Why, especially, when you called, did you look as if you did not care about me?"

"Because you were grave and silent, and gave me no encouragement."

"But I was embarrassed."

"And so was I."

"You might have talked to me more when you came to dinner."

"A man who had felt less, might."

"How unlucky that you should have a reasonable answer to give, and that I should be so reasonable as to admit it! But I wonder how long you *would* have gone on, if you had been left to yourself. I wonder when you *would* have spoken, if I had not asked you! My resolution of thanking you for your kindness to Lydia had certainly great effect. *Too much*, I am afraid; for what becomes of the moral, if our comfort springs from a breach of promise, for I ought not to have mentioned the subject? This will never do."

"You need not distress yourself. The moral will be perfectly fair. Lady Catherine's unjustifiable endeavours to separate us, were the means of removing all my doubts. I am not indebted for my present happiness to your eager desire of expressing your gratitude. I was not in a humour to wait for any opening of your's. My aunt's intelligence had given me hope, and I was determined at once to know every thing."

"Lady Catherine has been of infinite use, which ought to make her happy, for she loves to be of use. But tell me, what did you come down to Netherfield for? Was it merely to ride to Longbourn and be embarrassed? or had you intended any more serious consequence?"

"My real purpose was to see *you*, and to judge, if I could, whether I might ever hope to make you love me. My avowed one, or what I avowed to myself, was to see whether your sister were still partial to Bingley, and if she were, to make the confession to him which I have since made."

"Shall you ever have courage to announce to Lady Catherine, what is to befall her?"

"I am more likely to want time than courage, Elizabeth. But it ought to be done, and if you will give me a sheet of paper, it shall be done directly."

"And if I had not a letter to write myself, I might sit by you, and admire the evenness of your writing, as another young lady once did. But I have an aunt, too, who must not be longer neglected."

From an unwillingness to confess how much her intimacy with Mr. Darcy had been over-rated, Elizabeth had never yet answered Mrs. Gardiner's long letter, but now, having *that* to communicate which she knew would be most welcome, she was almost ashamed to find, that her uncle and aunt had already lost three days of happiness, and immediately wrote as follows:

"I would have thanked you before, my dear aunt, as I ought to have done, for your long, kind, satisfactory, detail of particulars; but to say the truth, I was too cross to write. You supposed more than really existed. But *now* suppose as much as you chuse; give a loose to your fancy, indulge your imagination in every possible flight which the subject will afford, and unless you believe me actually married, you cannot greatly err. You must write again very soon, and praise him a great deal more than you did in your last. I thank you, again and again, for not going to the Lakes. How could I be so silly as to wish it! Your idea of the ponies is delightful. We will go round the Park every day. I am the happiest creature in the world. Perhaps other people have said so before, but not one with such justice. I am happier even than Jane; she only smiles, I laugh. Mr. Darcy sends you all the love in the world, that he can spare from me. You are all to come to Pemberley at Christmas. Your's, &c."

Mr. Darcy's letter to Lady Catherine, was in a different style; and still different from either, was what Mr. Bennet sent to Mr. Collins, in reply to his last.

"DEAR SIR,

"I must trouble you once more for congratulations. Elizabeth will soon be the wife of Mr. Darcy. Console Lady Catherine as well as you can. But, if I were you, I would stand by the nephew. He has more to give.

"Your's sincerely, &c."

Miss Bingley's congratulations to her brother, on his approaching marriage, were all that was affectionate and insincere. She wrote even to Jane on the occasion, to express her delight, and repeat all her former professions of regard. Jane was not deceived, but she was affected; and though feeling no reliance on her, could not help writing her a much kinder answer than she knew was deserved.

The joy which Miss Darcy expressed on receiving similar information, was as sincere as her brother's in sending it. Four sides of paper were insufficient to contain all her delight, and all her earnest desire of being loved by her sister.

Before any answer could arrive from Mr. Collins, or any congratulations to Elizabeth, from his wife, the Longbourn family heard that the Collinses were come themselves to Lucas lodge. The reason of this sudden removal was soon evident. Lady Catherine had been rendered so exceedingly angry by the contents of her nephew's letter, that Charlotte, really rejoicing in the match, was anxious to get away till the storm was blown over. At such a moment, the arrival of her friend was a sincere pleasure to Elizabeth, though in the course of their meetings she must sometimes think the pleasure dearly bought, when she saw Mr. Darcy exposed to all the parading and obsequious civility of her husband. He bore it however with admirable calmness. He could even listen to Sir William Lucas, when he complimented him on carrying away the brightest jewel of the country, and expressed his hopes of their all meeting frequently at St. James's, with very decent composure. If he did shrug his shoulders, it was not till Sir William was out of sight.

Mrs. Philip's vulgarity was another, and perhaps a greater tax on his forbearance; and though Mrs. Philips, as well as her sister, stood in too much awe of him to speak with the familiarity which Bingley's good humour encouraged, yet, whenever she *did* speak, she must be vulgar. Nor was her respect for him, though it made her more quiet, at all likely to make her more elegant. Elizabeth did all she could, to shield him from the frequent notice of either, and was ever anxious to keep him to herself, and to those of her family with whom he might converse without mortification; and though the uncomfortable feelings arising from all this took from the season of courtship much of its pleasure, it added to the hope of the future; and she looked forward with delight to the time when they should be removed from society so little pleasing to either, to all the comfort and elegance of their family party at Pemberley.

Chapter XIX

Happy for all her maternal feelings was the day on which Mrs. Bennet got rid of her two most deserving daughters. With what delighted pride she afterwards visited Mrs. Bingley and talked of Mrs. Darcy may be guessed. I wish I could say, for the sake of her family, that the accomplishment of her earnest desire in the establishment of so many of her children, produced so happy an effect as to make her a sensible, amiable, well-informed woman for the rest of her life; though perhaps it was lucky for her husband, who might not have relished domestic felicity in so unusual a form, that she still was occasionally nervous and invariably silly.

Mr. Bennet missed his second daughter exceedingly; his affection for her drew him oftener from home than any thing else could do. He delighted in going to Pemberley, especially when he was least expected.

Mr. Bingley and Jane remained at Netherfield only a twelvemonth. So near a vicinity to her mother and Meryton relations was not desirable even to *his* easy temper, or *her* affectionate heart. The darling wish of his sisters was then gratified; he bought an estate in a neighbouring county to Derbyshire, and Jane and Elizabeth, in addition to every other source of happiness, were within thirty miles of each other.

Kitty, to her very material advantage, spent the chief of her time with her two elder sisters. In society so superior to what she had generally known, her improvement was great. She was not of so ungovernable a temper as Lydia, and, removed from the influence of Lydia's example, she became, by proper attention and management, less irritable, less ignorant, and less insipid. From the farther disadvantage of Lydia's society she was of course carefully kept, and though Mrs. Wickham frequently invited her to come and stay with her, with the promise of balls and young men, her father would never consent to her going.

Mary was the only daughter who remained at home; and she was necessarily drawn from the pursuit of accomplishments by Mrs. Bennet's being quite unable to sit alone. Mary was obliged to mix more with the world, but she could still moralize over every morning visit; and as she was no longer mortified by comparisons between her sisters' beauty and her own, it was suspected by her father that she submitted to the change without much reluctance.

As for Wickham and Lydia, their characters suffered no revolution from the marriage of her sisters. He bore with philosophy the conviction that Elizabeth must now become acquainted with whatever of his ingratitude and falsehood had before been unknown to her; and in spite of every thing, was not wholly without hope that Darcy might yet be prevailed on to make his fortune. The congratulatory letter which Elizabeth received from Lydia on her marriage, explained to her that, by his wife at least, if not by himself, such a hope was cherished. The letter was to this effect:

"MY DEAR LIZZY,

"I wish you joy. If you love Mr. Darcy half as well as I do my dear Wickham, you must be very happy. It is a great comfort to have you so rich, and when you have nothing else to do, I hope you will think of us. I am sure Wickham would like a place at court very much, and I do not think we shall have quite money enough to live upon without some help. Any place would do, of about three or four hundred a year; but, however, do not speak to Mr. Darcy about it, if you had rather not.

"Your's &c."

As it happened that Elizabeth had *much* rather not; she endeavoured in her answer to put an end to every intreaty and expectation of the kind. Such relief, however, as it was in her power to afford, by the practice of what might be called economy in her own private expences, she frequently sent them. It had always been evident to her that such an income as theirs, under the direction of two persons so extravagant in their wants, and heedless of the future, must be very insufficient to their support; and whenever they changed their quarters, either Jane or herself were sure of being applied to, for some little assistance towards discharging their bills. Their manner of living, even when the restoration of peace[9] dismissed them to a home, was unsettled in the extreme. They were always moving from place to place in quest of a cheap situation, and always spending more than they ought. His affection for her soon sunk into indifference; hers lasted a little longer; and in spite of her youth and her manners, she retained all the claims to reputation which her marriage had given her.

Though Darcy could never receive *him* at Pemberley, yet, for Elizabeth's sake, he assisted him farther in his profession. Lydia was occasionally a visitor there, when her husband was gone to enjoy himself in London or Bath; and with the Bingleys they both of them frequently staid so long, that even Bingley's good humour was overcome, and he proceeded so far as to *talk* of giving them a hint to be gone.

Miss Bingley was very deeply mortified by Darcy's marriage; but as she thought it advisable to retain the right of visiting at Pemberley, she dropt all her resentment; was fonder than ever of Georgiana, almost as attentive to Darcy as heretofore, and paid off every arrear of civility to Elizabeth.

Pemberley was now Georgiana's home; and the attachment of the sisters was exactly what Darcy had hoped to see. They were able to love each other, even as well as they intended. Georgiana had the highest opinion in the world of Elizabeth; though at first she often listened with an astonishment bordering on alarm, at her lively, sportive, manner of talking to her brother. He, who had always inspired in herself a respect which almost overcame her affection, she now saw the object of open pleasantry. Her mind received knowledge which had never before fallen in her way. By Elizabeth's instructions she began to comprehend that a woman may take liberties with her husband, which a brother will not always allow in a sister more than ten years younger than himself.

Lady Catherine was extremely indignant on the marriage of her

---

9. In many particulars, the chronology of the novel is based on almanacs for 1811 and 1812. This reference to peace, however, may be to the temporary interruption of the war against Napoleon by the Peace of Amiens of 1802. It is plausible that when in 1811 Austen began seriously to convert "First Impressions," the manuscript novel she wrote in 1796–97, into *Pride and Prejudice*, she still imagined its principal events as occurring in the 1790s. See R. W. Chapman's note on chronology (Oxford edition 2: 400–407).

nephew; and as she gave way to all the genuine frankness of her character, in her reply to the letter which announced its arrangement, she sent him language so very abusive, especially of Elizabeth, that for some time all intercourse was at an end. But at length, by Elizabeth's persuasion, he was prevailed on to overlook the offence, and seek a reconciliation; and, after a little farther resistance on the part of his aunt, her resentment gave way, either to her affection for him, or her curiosity to see how his wife conducted herself; and she condescended to wait on them at Pemberley, in spite of that pollution which its woods had received, not merely from the presence of such a mistress, but the visits of her uncle and aunt from the city.

With the Gardiners, they were always on the most intimate terms. Darcy, as well as Elizabeth, really loved them; and they were both ever sensible of the warmest gratitude towards the persons who, by bringing her into Derbyshire, had been the means of uniting them.

FINIS.

BACKGROUNDS
AND SOURCES

Biography

HENRY AUSTEN

Biographical Notice of the Author†

* * * Short and easy will be the task of the mere biographer. A life of usefulness, literature, and religion, was not by any means a life of event. To those who lament their irreparable loss, it is consolatory to think that, as she never deserved disapprobation, so, in the circle of her family and friends, she never met reproof; that her wishes were not only reasonable, but gratified; and that to the little disappointments incidental to human life was never added, even for a moment, an abatement of good-will from any who knew her.

Jane Austen was born on the 16th of December, 1775, at Steventon, in the county of Hants [Hampshire]. Her father was Rector of that parish upwards of forty years. There he resided, in the conscientious and unassisted discharge of his ministerial duties, until he was turned of seventy years. Then he retired with his wife, our authoress, and her sister [Cassandra], to Bath, for the remainder of his life, a period of about four years. Being not only a profound scholar, but possessing a most exquisite taste in every species of literature, it is not wonderful that his daughter Jane should, at a very early age, have become sensible to the charms of style, and enthusiastic in the cultivation of her own language. On the death of her father she removed, with her mother and sister, for a short time, to Southampton, and finally, in 1809, to the pleasant village of Chawton, in the same county. From this place she sent into the world those novels, which by many have been placed on the same shelf as the works of a D'Arblay and an Edgeworth.[1] Some of these novels had been the gradual performances of her previous life. For though in compositions she was equally rapid and correct, yet an

---

† Henry Austen's biographical sketch of his sister was first published as a preface to the post-humous volume containing *Persuasion* and *Northanger Abbey* (London: John Murray, 1818) 1:v–ix, xi–iv, xvi. All notes are by the editor of this Norton Critical Edition. It was reprinted in 1833 in the first of the collected editions of Jane Austen's novels.
1. Maria Edgeworth (1767–1849) was a popular, somewhat didactic novelist. D'Arblay was the married name of Fanny Burney (1752–1840), whose novels *Evelina* (1778) and *Cecilia* (1782) went through several editions by the end of the eighteenth century.

invincible distrust of her own judgement induced her to withhold her works from the public, till time and many perusals had satisfied her that the charm of recent composition was dissolved. The natural constitution, the regular habits, the quiet and happy occupations of our authoress, seemed to promise a long succession of amusement to the public, and a gradual increase of reputation to herself. But the symptoms of a decay, deep and incurable, began to shew themselves in the commencement of 1816. Her decline was at first deceitfully slow; and until the spring of this present year [1817], those who knew their happiness to be involved in her existence could not endure to despair. But in the month of May, 1817, it was found advisable that she should be removed to Winchester for the benefit of constant medical aid, which none even then dared to hope would be permanently beneficial. She supported, during two months, all the varying pain, irksomeness, and tedium, attendant on decaying nature, with more than resignation, with a truly elastic cheerfulness. She retained her faculties, her memory, her fancy, her temper, and her affections, warm, clear, and unimpaired, to the last. Neither her love of God, nor of her fellow creatures flagged for a moment. She made a point of receiving the sacrament before excessive bodily weakness might have rendered her perception unequal to her wishes. She wrote whilst she could hold a pen, and with a pencil when a pen was become too laborious. The day preceding her death she composed some stanzas replete with fancy and vigour. Her last voluntary speech conveyed thanks to her medical attendant; and to the final question asked of her, purporting to know her wants, she replied, "I want nothing but death."

She expired shortly after, on Friday the 18th of July, 1817, in the arms of her sister, who, as well as the relator of these events, feels too surely that they shall never look upon her like again.

* * *

If there be an opinion current in the world, that perfect placidity of temper is not reconcileable to the most lively imagination, and the keenest relish for wit, such an opinion will be rejected for ever by those who have had the happiness of knowing the authoress of the following works. Though the frailties, foibles, and follies of others could not escape her immediate detection, yet even on their vices did she never trust herself to comment with unkindness. The affectation of candour is not uncommon; but she had no affectation. Faultless herself, as nearly as human nature can be, she always sought, in the faults of others, something to excuse, to forgive or forget. Where extenuation was impossible, she had a sure refuge in silence. She never uttered either a hasty, a silly, or a severe expression. In short, her temper was as polished as her wit. Nor were her manners inferior to her temper. They were of the happiest kind. No one could be often in her company without feeling a strong desire of obtaining her friendship, and cherishing a hope of having obtained it. She was tranquil without reserve or stiffness; and communicative without intrusion or self-sufficiency. She became an authoress entirely from taste and inclination. Neither the hope of fame nor profit mixed with her early motives. Most of her works, as before observed, were composed many years previous to their publication. It was with extreme difficulty that her friends, whose partiality she suspected whilst she honoured their judgement, could prevail on her to publish her first work. Nay, so persuaded was she that its sale would not repay the expense of publication, that she actually made a reserve from her very moderate income to meet the expected loss. * * * She read aloud with very great taste and effect. Her own works, probably, were never heard to so much advantage as from her own mouth; for she partook largely in all the best gifts of the comic muse. She was a warm and judicious admirer of landscape, both in nature and on canvass. At a very early age she was enamoured of Gilpin[2] on the Picturesque; and she seldom changed her opinions either on books or men.

* * *

One trait only remains to be touched on. It makes all others unimportant. She was thoroughly religious and devout; fearful of giving offence to God, and incapable of feeling it towards any fellow creature. On serious subjects she was well-instructed, both by reading and meditation, and her opinions accorded strictly with those of our Established Church.

J. E. AUSTEN-LEIGH

[Beginning to Write]†

* * *

It is impossible to say at how early an age she began [to write]. There are copy-books extant containing tales, some of which must have been composed while she was a young girl, as they had amounted to a considerable number by the time she was sixteen. Her earliest stories are of a slight and flimsy texture, and are generally intended to be nonsensical, but the nonsense has much spirit in it. They are usually preceded by a dedication of mock solemnity to some one of her family. It

---

2. William Gilpin (1724–1804) was the author of books on the picturesque in landscape. See above, p. 36, n. 2.
† From J. E. Austen-Leigh, A Memoir of Jane Austen, 2nd ed. (London: Bentley, 1871) 42–47. J. E. Austen-Leigh was Austen's nephew; he was nineteen years old when she died.

would seem that the grandiloquent dedications prevalent in those days had not escaped her youthful penetration. Perhaps the most characteristic feature in those early productions is that, however puerile the matter, they are always composed in pure simple English, quite free from the over-ornamented style which might be expected from so young a writer. * * *

Her own mature opinion of the desirableness of such an early habit of composition is given in the following words of a niece:—[1]

"As I grew older, my aunt would talk to me more seriously of my reading and my amusements. I had taken early to writing verses and stories, and I am sorry to think how I troubled her with reading them. She was very kind about it, and always had some praise to bestow, but at last she warned me against spending too much time upon them. She said—how well I recollect it!—that she knew writing stories was a great amusement, and *she* thought a harmless one, though many people, she was aware, thought otherwise; but that at my age it would be bad for me to be much taken up with my own compositions. Later still—it was after she had gone to Winchester—she sent me a message to this effect, that if I would take her advice I should cease writing till I was sixteen; that she had herself often wished she had read more, and written less in the corresponding years of her own life." As this niece was only twelve years old at the time of her aunt's death, these words seem to imply that the juvenile tales to which I have referred had, some of them at least, been written in her childhood.

But between these childish effusions, and the composition of her living works, there intervened another stage of her progress, during which she produced some stories, not without merit, but which she never considered worthy of publication. During this preparatory period her mind seems to have been working in a very different direction from that into which it ultimately settled. Instead of presenting faithful copies of nature, these tales were generally burlesques, ridiculing the improbable events and exaggerated sentiments which she had met with in sundry silly romances. Something of this fancy is to be found in "Northanger Abbey," but she soon left it far behind in her subsequent course. It would seem as if she were first taking note of all the faults to be avoided, and curiously considering how she ought *not* to write before she attempted to put forth her strength in the right direction. The family have, rightly, I think, declined to let these early works be published. * * *

1. Louisa Knight (1804–1889) [*Editor*].

CLAIRE TOMALIN

[Jane Austen's Childhood]†

* * *

Growing up in a school[1] meant that Jane knew exactly what to expect of boys, and was always at ease with them; boys were her natural environment, and boys' jokes and boys' interests were the first she learnt about. This is obvious in what has survived of her earliest writing; although there is none from before the age of twelve, the influence is clear. It is full of boys' humour, starting with the talk of horses and vehicles, journeys and accidents, all topics young men were as much obsessed with then as modern boys are with motor bikes and cars. There is a lot about drunkenness too, always good for a laugh among boys. There are drunken quarrels, and characters are found "dead drunk," or actually die of drink.

Food is another source of jokes, "stinking" fish and game, underdone veal and curry with no seasoning, and other dishes likely to have been unpopular with schoolboys, fried cow-heel and onion, tripe, red herrings, liver and "crow" (i.e., giblets). A man at an inn orders "a whole egg" to be boiled for his and his servants' dinner. Food is funny in itself, and by association. A girl's face turns "as White as a Whipt syllabub"[2] when her future husband is killed; another—called Cassandra—devours six ices at a pastry-cook's shop, refuses to pay for them and knocks down the pastry-cook; a third remains, under provocation, "as cool as a cream cheese." Of two sisters, one loves drawing pictures, the other drawing pullets[3]: schoolchildren's word play. And there is a fine boys' joke about a man jilting his bride because the marriage date coincides with the first day of shooting.

Ugly and deformed girls provide another source of humour: one is "short, fat and disagreeable," another has a "forbidding Squint," "greazy tresses" and a "swelling Back." Female efforts to improve appearances with red and white cosmetic paint are good for a laugh too. There is a great deal of cheerful violence, including several incidents which might be called fun murders. There is a hanging. There is a steel mantrap that catches a girl by the leg. There are characters driven by hunger to bite off their own fingers.

Jane Austen was a tough and unsentimental child, drawn to rude

---

† From *Jane Austen: A Life* (New York: Alfred A. Knopf; London: Peters Fraser and Dunlop, 1997) 30–31. Reprinted by permission of Alfred A. Knopf, a Division of Random House, Inc., and the Peters Fraser and Dunlop Group Ltd. All notes are by the editor of this Norton Critical Edition.
1. During her childhood Jane Austen's father taught and boarded pupils in the rectory.
2. Sweetened or flavored curdled milk.
3. Eviscerating chickens.

anarchic imaginings and black jokes. She found a good source for this ferocious style of humour in the talk she heard, and doubtless some times joined in, among her parents' pupils, bursting out of childhood into young manhood. If she was sometimes shocked as she listened, she herself was learning how to shock by writing things down.

* * *

WILLIAM AUSTEN-LEIGH, RICHARD ARTHUR AUSTEN-LEIGH, AND DEIRDRE LE FAYE

[Prospects of Marriage]†

* * *

Charles brought his sisters back to Steventon [from Bath, to which the family had moved in 1801] on 28 October [1802], and on 25 November Jane and Cassandra moved on to visit their old friends Catherine and Alethea Bigg at Manydown, intending to stay with them two or three weeks.

However, only one week later, on Friday 3 December, Mary Lloyd[1] was surprised to see a carriage draw up unexpectedly outside Steventon Rectory, containing her sisters-in-law and their two friends. To her further surprise, a scene of tearful and affectionate farewells took place in the hall, and as soon as the carriage had gone Cassandra and Jane declared it was absolutely necessary for them to return to Bath the next day, and that James must conduct them there. Saturday was of course a most inconvenient day for a single-handed parson to leave his parish and arrange for the Sunday duty to be taken at such short notice; but the sisters refused to remain until Monday, nor would they give any reason for this refusal, so that James was therefore obliged to yield and to go with them to Bath. Eventually the explanation was given—on the evening of 2 December Harris Bigg-Wither had asked Jane to marry him and she had accepted, but then on the following morning had changed her mind and withdrawn her consent. In later years Mary Lloyd passed on this tale to her daughter Caroline, who pondered about the matter: "Mr. Wither was very plain in person—awkward, &

---

† Reprinted by permission of the publisher, from William Austen-Leigh and Richard Arthur Austen-Leigh, *Jane Austen: A Family Record*, revised and enlarged by Deirdre Le Faye (London: The British Library, and Boston: G. K. Hall, 1989) 121–22, 126–27. William and Richard Austen-Leigh prepared the first *Life and Letters of Jane Austen* in 1913; Le Faye's enlargement of this biography greatly amplifies it by adding information from published and unpublished documents. All notes are by the editor of this Norton Critical Edition.

1. The second wife of Austen's oldest brother, James, who took over his father's duties as rector at Steventon when the family moved to Bath in 1801.

even uncouth in manner—nothing but his size to recommend him—he was a fine big man—but one need not look about for secret reason to account for a young lady's *not* loving him—a great many would have taken him *without* love—& I believe the wife he did get was very fond of him, & that they were a happy couple—He had sense in plenty & went through life very respectably, as a country gentleman—I *conjecture* that the advantages he could offer, & her gratitude for his love, & her long friendship with his family, induced my Aunt to decide that she would marry him *when* he should ask her—but that having accepted him she found she was miserable & that the place & fortune which would certainly be *his*, could not alter the *man*—She was staying in his *Father's* house—old Mr. Wither was then alive—To be sure she should not have said yes—over night—but I have always respected her for the courage in cancelling that yes—the next morning—All worldly advantages would have been to her—& she was of an age to know *this* quite well—My Aunts had very small fortunes & on their Father's death they & their Mother would be, they were aware, but poorly off—I beleive most young women so circumstanced would have taken Mr. W. & trusted to love after marriage . . ."[2] * * *

* * *

There is a tradition that during one of these seaside holidays between 1801–04 Jane met the only man whom she could seriously have wished to marry, had fortune been kinder to her. Cassandra knew the details of this brief episode, but in her later life passed on to Caroline Austen[3] merely the barest outline of what had happened years before. In 1870 Caroline wrote out the account, for her brother's use in preparing the second edition of his *Memoir*: "All that I know is this. At Newtown, Aunt Cassandra was staying with us [i.e., with Caroline and her mother, Mary Lloyd—they lived at Newtown, near Newbury, from 1825–36] when we made acquaintance [during 1828] with a certain Mr. Henry Eldridge, of the Engineers. He was very pleasing and very good-looking. My aunt was very much struck with him, and *I* was struck by her commendation; she so rarely admired strangers. Afterwards, at another time—I do not remember exactly when [probably early 1829]—she spoke of him as of one so unusually gifted with all that was agreeable, and said that he reminded her strongly of a gentleman whom they had met one summer when they were by the sea—I think she said in Devonshire; I don't think she named the place, and I am sure she did not say Lyme,[4] for that I should have remembered—that he seemed greatly attracted by my Aunt Jane—I suppose it was

2. Caroline Mary Craven Austen to Amy Austen-Leigh, 17 June 1870; see also Joan Austen-Leigh, "New Light Thrown on Jane Austen's Refusal of Harris Bigg-Wither," *Persuasions* 8 (1986): 34–36.
3. Daughter of James Austen and Mary Lloyd.
4. Lyme is the setting of part of *Persuasion* (1818).

an intercourse of some weeks—and that when they had to part (I imagine he was a visitor also, but his family might have lived near) he was urgent to know where they would be the next summer, implying or perhaps saying that he should be there also, wherever it might be. I can only say that the impression left on Aunt Cassandra was that he had fallen in love with her sister, and was quite in earnest. Soon afterwards they heard of his death. Mr. Henry Eldridge also died of a sudden illness [on 6 November 1828] soon after we had seen him at Newtown, and I suppose it was that coincidence of early death that led my aunt to speak of him—the unknown—at all. I am sure she thought he was worthy of her sister, from the way in which she recalled his memory, and also that she did not doubt, either, that he would have been a successful suitor." Caroline's statement, imprecise though it is, is the fullest and earliest account available and, bearing in mind her reputation in the family for having a wonderfully accurate and retentive memory, must be considered reliable, stemming as it does from the unimpeachable authority of Cassandra herself. * * *

DAVID NOKES

[Bath and Southampton]†

* * *

Biographers and critics have been greatly puzzled by the strange silence which fell upon Jane Austen during her Bath and Southampton years [1801–09]. During her last three years at Steventon rectory she produced three full-length novels, 'First Impressions', 'Elinor and Marianne' and 'Susan'.[1] Yet it was as if, on leaving Steventon, her imagination had run dry. No new novels were undertaken, and no serious revisions planned to those already in existence. 'First Impressions' was seldom brought out to be read aloud for the amusement of family parties. No publisher's interest was sought for 'Elinor and Marianne', even under its grand new title of *Sense and Sensibility*. To many of Jane Austen's biographers, this apparent evidence of a desiccation of her imaginative powers during the Bath and Southampton years merely confirms their sense of the feelings of unhappiness and displacement which she must have experienced in these busy cities. The true sources of her inspiration, it might appear, lay deep in the rural countryside of her native Hampshire. And it comes as little surprise to these biogra-

---

† From *Jane Austen: A Life* (London: Fourth Estate; New York: Farrar, Straus and Giroux, 1997) 350–53. Reprinted by permission of the publishers. All notes are by the editor of this Norton Critical Edition.
1. Revised and published as, respectively, *Pride and Prejudice* (1813), *Sense and Sensibility* (1812), and *Northanger Abbey* (1818).

phers that Jane Austen's genius seemed to flourish again, as if by magic, as soon as she was established in the homely village retreat of Chawton.

While this interpretation has much to recommend it, it seems to presuppose our own conviction that novel-writing was Jane Austen's peculiar province, and the activity to which she ought most usefully to devote her life. She herself acknowledged no such settled sense of public literary ambitions or literary destiny. Her juvenile writings make great play of claims to literary fame, but, like the spoofs and parodies which they introduce, these hyperbolic claims form part of an elaborate rhetoric of self-mockery. Yet, when Thomas Cadell declined to take an interest in reading 'First Impressions' with a view to publication,[2] she had made no attempt to have it considered by other publishers. For her, the first design of all her writings at Steventon was as a form of private amusement, shared between Cassandra and herself, or as a literary diversion for the entertainment of the wider circle of family and friends. At Steventon, all their entertainments had been of this home-made kind; Bath and Southampton, by contrast, afforded such abundance of public diversions and amusements; and presented such plentiful opportunities for new and varied acquaintances, that there was neither the time nor the inclination for private literary diversions. Nor is there any evidence that Jane Austen considered the curtailment of her former literary pastimes, in favour of visits to the Pump Room, the Assembly Rooms, Sydney Gardens or the theatre, as any form of sacrifice. Her biographers have chosen to imagine that unhappiness at her unsettled, hectic city life cast a pall over her imagination in the years between 1800 and 1809. Yet happiness may be just as destructive of literary dedication as unhappiness. And it is equally possible to suggest that it was an abundance of amusements, rather than the absence of inspiration, that prevented her from writing. Her silence might then be interpreted not as evidence of mental dejection, but as a natural consequence of alternative distractions. 'I assure you, I am as tired of writing long letters as you can be,' she wrote to Cassandra from God-mersham[3] in the summer of 1808, at a time when her mind was filled with dreams of eating ice, drinking French wine, and indulging all the other delights of a life of 'Elegance & Ease & Luxury'.[4] If her life seemed frequently too full of other distractions for writing long letters to Cassandra, there should be less surprise that there was little time for writing novels.

2. Thomas Cadell was the publisher to whom Jane Austen's father offered the early version of *Pride and Prejudice* in 1797.
3. Godmersham was the estate of Edward, Jane Austen's elder brother. Edward had been adopted by the Knights, a wealthy family related by marriage to the Austens, took the name of Knight, and inherited their property at the end of the eighteenth century. See the essay by David Spring reprinted on pp. 392–99 of this volume.
4. *Jane Austen's Letters*, 3rd ed., ed. Deirdre Le Faye (Oxford and New York: Oxford University Press, 1995), 30 June–1 July 1808, 137–38.

At Chawton, things would be very different. There, once again, they would be compelled to furnish their own amusements. There could be nothing more suitable for filling the long afternoons and evenings, when they were neither visiting nor visited, or when the weather was not suitable for walking, or when her mood did not incline to playing her pianoforte, than reading and writing. In recent months, Jane's pleasure in her own compositions had been rekindled by the lively interest that young Fanny[5] seemed to show in them. 'I am gratified by her having pleasure in what I write,' she told Cassandra, then added: 'but I wish the knowledge of my being exposed to her discerning criticism may not hurt my stile, by inducing too great a solicitude. I begin already to weigh my words & sentences more than I did, & am looking about for a sentiment, an illustration or a metaphor in every corner of the room. One corner of the room seemed to provide a particularly apt comparison for her leaky imagination. 'Could my ideas flow as fast as the rain in the store-closet, it would be charming,' she wrote.[6] Yet Fanny's admiration, however gratifying, was not sufficient on its own to induce her to write to Richard Crosby.[7] That decision proceeded from more rational considerations.

It was now beyond a doubt, whatever kindly hopes old Mrs Birch or Mrs Knight might yet entertain of the matter, that there was to be no legacy, no 'handsome present' to rescue her from vulgar economies.[8] At thirty-three she was also well beyond any expectation of 'eligible offers' of another kind. Yet, without vanity, she knew she might fairly boast a certain skill in the way of novel writing. And whilst her family might well be guilty of some partiality in their generous opinions of her work, it had long been universally acknowledged amongst them that her writings far exceeded the productions of several other literary ladies. If Mrs Grant's *American Lady* ('still the same faults'), Mrs Sykes's *Marigana* ('a very fine villain') and Miss Owenson's *Ida of Athens* ('it might be worth reading in this weather'),[9] could all find pub-

5. Knight, Edward's daughter.
6. *Letters*, 24 Jan. 1809, 169.
7. The publisher Richard Crosby had purchased the manuscript of the novel eventually published as *Northanger Abbey* in 1803, but he never brought out the book. In 1809 Jane Austen wrote to him (under the name Mrs. Ashton Dennis; she signed the letter with the initials M.A.D.) to inquire whether he intended to publish. He did not, and he offered to sell the manuscript back to her for the Ł10 he had paid for it. She eventually did buy the manuscript in 1816.
8. Shortly before she and her daughters moved to Chawton, Mrs. Austen's brother and her cousin were involved in negotiations concerning the inheritance of a large estate. She was disappointed in her hopes that she and her daughters would in some way benefit from the agreement that settled the inheritance. Mrs. Knight was the wife of Thomas, who adopted Edward Austen; Mrs. Birch was a friend of the family who, with her "usual distinguished kindness," had written to Jane Austen that she "shall not be at all satisfied unless a very *handsome* present is made immediately" by Jane and Cassandra's uncle (*Letters*, 10–11 Jan. 1809, 163).
9. The novels by Anne Grant and Mrs. S. Sykes were published in 1808, that by Sydney Owenson (later Lady Morgan) in 1809. The parenthetical judgments of the novels are in Austen's *Letters*, 10–11 Jan. 1809, 164; 17–18 Jan. 1809, 166.

lishers for their works, it was surely not beyond the bounds of reason to suppose that she might do likewise.* * *

PARK HONAN

[Last Years at Chawton]†

* * *

It is very important that we should have an accurate picture of her at just this time and luckily we do, since Cassandra sketched her and Charlotte-Maria wrote two descriptions of her that help to confirm the accuracy of Cassandra's sketch. The descriptions came to light as recently as 1985. Charlotte-Maria Middleton,[1] who later married her cousin Charles Beckford, was in old age not at all pleased by the round-faced, sweet-looking picture of Jane that illustrates the 1870 *Memoir* about the novelist. "Jane's likeness is hardly what I remember," Charlotte-Maria writes of that Victorian picture (it is the one engraved by Lizars from an idealized drawing worked up by a Mr. Andrews of Maidenhead). No, Jane Austen was rather different: "There *is* a look, & that is all—I remember her as a tall thin *spare* person, with very high cheek bones, great colour—sparkling Eyes not large but joyous & intelligent, the face by *no means so broad* & plump as represented; perhaps it was taken when very young, but the *Cap looks womanly*— her keen sense of humour I quite remember, it oozed out very much in Mr. Bennett's Style—Altogether I remember we liked her greatly as children from her entering into all Games &c." And again "We saw her often," Charlotte-Maria remembered. "She was a most kind & enjoyable person *to Children* but somewhat stiff & cold to strangers. She used to sit at Table at Dinner parties without uttering much, probably collecting matter for her charming novels which in those days we knew nothing about—her Sister Cassandra was very lady-like but *very prim*, but my remembrance of Jane is that of her entering into all Children's Games & liking her extremely.—We were often asked to meet her young nephews & nieces [who] were *at Chawton with them*."

In recalling her childhood, Caroline wrote of her two aunts in a similar vein: "Of the two," Caroline says, "Aunt Jane was by far my favorite—I did not *dislike* Aunt Cassandra—but if my visit had at any time chanced to fall out during *her* absence, I don't think I should have

† From *Jane Austen: Her Life* (New York: St. Martin's Press; London: Weidenfeld and Nicholson, 1987) 270, 351–53. Copyright © 1988 by Park Honan. Reprinted with permission of St. Martin's Press, Inc., New York, N.Y.
1. Charlotte-Maria Middleton was a neighbor whose family leased the estate of Austen's brother Edward. Her reminiscences were published in a letter from Deirdre Le Faye, *Times Literary Supplement* 3 May 1985: 495 [*Editor*].

missed her—whereas, *not* to have found Aunt Jane at Chawton, *would* have been a blank indeed."[2]

* * *

Mrs Austen and the three younger women were busy in a disciplined, efficient ménage in which idleness in daylight hours was unusual. When Mrs Austen could not work in the garden she sat with her patch-works or prided herself on sewing them when bedridden. Jane, with her light household duties, was not only shielded and favoured by Cas-sandra and Martha[3] but actively helped by their critical opinions and at least by Cassandra's willingness to argue over details in a story. The fact that Jane's novels had begun to win public admiration could only have confirmed in the eyes of her companions the rightness and worth of her labours; and if the cottage attracted too many family visitors, it was otherwise a good place for uninterrupted work. In an atmosphere in which others kept at their duties one did not have to apologize for being busy with a manuscript, and with indulgent companions one had a sense of being valued with a respectful tolerance. Here Jane Austen's mild peculiarities—her private laughter, absence of mind, obsessive enquiries into factual details, or her wish to conceal her novel-writing as much as she could from all outsiders—were well understood. A vis-itor would be kept away from the drawing room where she wrote, or, upon entering, would find her in a cap and work-smock as if jotting a shopping list. She could write "when sitting with her family," and when alone she had a special protection. She "wrote upon small sheets of paper, which could easily be put away, or covered with a piece of blot-ting paper. There was, between the front door and the offices, a swing door which creaked when it was opened," her nephew recorded later, "but she objected to having this little inconvenience remedied, because it gave her notice when anyone was coming."[4] If the door was vital, it was the vigilance of older women that left her secure so that her imag-ination and recollections were free to interact. For composing she pre-pared with elaborate care, folding ordinary sheets of writing paper in half until she had a number of them to make fascicles of perhaps thirty-two, forty-eight, or eighty pages, to judge from her *Sanditon* MS. These were, at some point, stitched to form small booklets, so that she had a sense of her novel coming physically into being; and the tidy home-stitching of folded pages seems to have been her very early practice. She thus had a neat arena for her pen—before or after the stitching. Her corrections altered her rhythms or attended to fine details of dic-

---

2. Caroline Austen, *My Aunt Jane Austen* (London: Jane Austen Society, 1952) 5–6.
3. Martha Lloyd was the sister of the wife of one of Jane Austen's brothers, and she later (1828) married another of her brothers. She lived with the Austens at both Southampton and Chaw-ton [*Editor*].
4. J. E. Austen Leigh, A *Memoir of Jane Austen* (London: Bentley, 1871) 96.

tion and phrasing, and though the space she allowed herself was narrow or cramped it helped her to focus upon phrasing and cadence. With a mature sense of the challenge and craftsmanship entailed she relished her art—and valued her companions who ensured that she had "much time" for it. The practical world was always at hand, but its demands were largely met by her housemates.

The price of her success, as she well knew, was her anonymity. To have become known as "Jane Austen, novelist" would be to be left open to those who would accuse her of autobiography, of writing from experience, or of having lived through the ordeals of her characters. That would have inhibited her freedom as an artist. Further, her notoriety could damage the Austen family; it might be assumed that their circumstances had obliged her to try to support herself by earning money. By temperament too she needed her concealment to help her in the modest roles she had as a daughter, sister and aunt.

*   *   *

Letters[†]

To Cassandra Austen

Saturday 9–Sunday 10 January 1796
Steventon

* * * You scold me so much in the nice long letter which I have this moment received from you, that I am almost afraid to tell you how my Irish friend[1] and I behaved. Imagine to yourself everything most profligate and shocking in the way of dancing and sitting down together. I *can* expose myself, however, only *once more*, because he leaves the country soon after next Friday, on which day we *are* to have a dance at Ashe after all. He is a very gentlemanlike, good-looking, pleasant young man, I assure you. But as to our having ever met, except at the three last balls, I cannot say much; for he is so excessively laughed at about me at Ashe, that he is ashamed of coming to Steventon, and ran away when we called on Mrs Lefroy a few days ago.

*   *   *

* * * After I had written the above, we received a visit from Mr Tom Lefroy and his cousin George. The latter is really very well-behaved now; and as for the other, he has but *one* fault, which time will, I trust, entirely remove—it is that his morning coat is a great deal too light. He is a very great admirer of Tom Jones,[2] and therefore wears the same coloured clothes, I imagine, which *he* did when he was wounded. * * *

[†] From *Jane Austen's Letters*, 3rd ed., ed. Deirdre Le Faye (Oxford and New York: Oxford University Press, 1995) 1–2, 4, 26, 68–69, 84–85, 197, 201–2, 203, 216–17, 251, 268–69, 275, 279–81, 285–86, 306, 323, 328–29. Reproduced by permission of Oxford University Press. All notes are by the editor of this Norton Critical Edition.

1. Thomas Lefroy (1776–1869) was staying with his uncle and aunt at Ashe, a neighboring rectory, in 1796. He later became Lord Chief Justice of Ireland and in his old age affected to remember a "boyish love" for Jane Austen (*Jane Austen: A Family Record* 87).
2. The eponymous hero of the novel by Henry Fielding (1707–1754).

To Cassandra Austen

Thursday 14–Friday 15 January 1796
Steventon

* * *

Friday.—At length the Day is come on which I am to flirt my last with Tom Lefroy, & when you receive this it will be over——My tears flow as I write, at the melancholy idea. Wm. Chute called here yesterday. I wonder what he means by being so civil. There is a report that Tom[3] is going to be married to a Lichfield lass. John Lyford and his sister bring Edward home to-day, dine with us, and we shall all go together to Ashe. I understand that we are to draw for partners. I shall be extremely impatient to hear from you again, that I may know how Eliza is, and when you are to return.

With best love, &c., I am affec:^tely yours,

J. Austen

To Cassandra Austen

Tuesday 18–Wednesday 19 December 1798
Steventon

* * * I have received a very civil note from Mrs Martin requesting my name as a Subscriber to her Library which opens the 14th of January, & my name, or rather Yours is accordingly given. My Mother finds the Money. * * *—As an inducement to subscribe Mrs Martin tells us that her Collection is not to consist only of Novels, but of every kind of Literature &c &c—She might have spared this pretension to *our* family, who are great Novel-readers & not ashamed of being so;—but it was necessary I suppose to the self-consequence of half her Subscribers. * * *

To Cassandra Austen

Saturday 3–Monday 5 January 1801
Steventon

* * * I get more & more reconciled to the idea of our removal.[4] We have lived long enough in this Neighbourhood, the Basingstoke[5] Balls are certainly on the decline, there is something interesting in the bustle

---

3. Tom Chute, younger brother of William.
4. At the end of 1801 Austen's father retired and decided to move from the rectory at Steventon to Bath with his wife and two daughters. The family remained in Bath until, after her father's death in 1805 Jane Austen moved with Cassandra and their mother first to Southampton and finally to Chawton in 1809, in the same county as Steventon.
5. A town near Steventon.

of going away, & the prospect of spending future summers by the Sea or in Wales is very delightful.—For a time we shall now possess many of the advantages which I have often thought of with Envy in the wives of Sailors or Soldiers.—It must not be generally known however that I am not sacrificing a great deal in quitting the Country—or I can expect to inspire no tenderness, no interest in those we leave behind. * * *

To Cassandra Austen

Tuesday 12–Wednesday 13 May 1801
Paragon [Bath]

* * * In the evening I hope you honoured my Toilette & Ball with a thought; I dressed myself as well as I could, & had all my finery much admired at home. By nine o'clock my Uncle, Aunt & I entered the rooms & linked Miss Winstone on to us.—Before tea, it was rather a dull affair; but then the beforetea did not last long, for there was only one dance, danced by four couple.—Think of four couple, surrounded by about an hundred people, dancing in the upper rooms at Bath!— After tea we *cheered up*; the breaking up of private parties sent some scores more to the Ball, & tho' it was shockingly & inhumanly thin for this place, there were people enough I suppose to have made five or six very pretty Basingstoke assemblies.—I then got Mr Evelyn to talk to, & Miss Twisleton to look at; and I am proud to say that I have a very good eye at an Adultress, for tho' repeatedly assured that another in the same party was the *She*, I fixed upon the right one from the first.—A resemblance to Mrs Leigh was my guide. She is not so pretty as I expected; her face has the same defect of baldness as her sister's, & her features not so handsome;—she was highly rouged, & looked rather quietly & contentedly silly than anything else.—Mrs Badcock & two young Women were of the same party, except when Mrs Badcock thought herself obliged to leave them, to run round the room after her drunken Husband.—His avoidance, & her pursuit, with the probable intoxication of both, was an amusing scene. * * *

To Martha Lloyd[6]

Sunday 29–Monday 30 November 1812
Chawton

* * * P. & P. is sold.—Egerton gives £110 for it.—I would rather have had £150, but we could not both be pleased, & I am not at all surprised that he should not chuse to hazard so much.—Its' being sold will I hope be a great saving of Trouble to Henry, & therefore must be

6. See note on p. 268.

welcome to me.—The Money is to be paid at the end of the twelve-month. * * *

To Cassandra Austen

Friday 29 January 1813
Chawton

* * * I want to tell you that I have got my own darling Child[7] from London; * * * Miss Benn dined with us on the very day of the Books coming, & in the even^g we set fairly at it & read half the I^st vol. to her—prefacing that having intelligence from Henry that such a work w^d soon appear we had desired him to send it whenever it came out—& I beleive it passed with her unsuspected.—She was amused, poor soul! *that* she c^d not help you know, with two such people to lead the way; but she really does seem to admire Elizabeth. I must confess that *I* think her as delightful a creature as ever appeared in print, & how I shall be able to tolerate those who do not like *her* at least, I do not know.—There are a few Typical errors—& a "said he" or a "said she" would sometimes make the Dialogue more immediately clear—but "I do not write for such dull Elves"

"As have not a great deal of Ingenuity themselves."[8]—The 2^d vol. is shorter than I c^d wish—but the difference is not so much in reality as in look, there being a larger proportion of Narrative in that part. I have lopt & cropt so successfully however that I imagine it must be rather shorter than S. & S. [*Sense and Sensibility*] altogether. * * *

To Cassandra Austen

Thursday 4 February 1813
Chawton

My dear Cassandra

Your letter was truely welcome & I am much obliged to you all for your praise; it came at a right time, for I had had some fits of disgust;—our 2^d evening's reading to Miss Benn had not pleased me so well, but I beleive something must be attributed to my Mother's too rapid way of getting on—& tho' she perfectly understands the Characters herself, she cannot speak as they ought.—Upon the whole however I am quite vain enough & well satisfied enough.—The work is rather too light & bright & sparkling;—it wants shade;—it wants to be stretched out here & there with a long Chapter—of sense if it could be had, if not of solemn specious nonsense—about something unconnected with the story; an Essay on Writing, a critique on Walter Scott, or the history

---

7. The volumes of *Pride and Prejudice*. In the first edition, the author is identified only as "a lady," which allowed Austen to practice the innocent deception she describes in this letter.
8. A quotation from Sir Walter Scott's narrative poem *Marmion* (1808).

of Buonaparte—or anything that would form a contrast & bring the reader with increased delight to the playfulness & Epigrammatism of the general stile.—I doubt your quite agreeing with me here—I know your starched Notions. * * *

To Francis Austen[9]

Saturday 3–Tuesday 6 July 1813
Chawton

* * * I wonder whether you happened to see Mr Blackall's marriage[1] in the Papers last Jan^{ry}. We did. He was married at Clifton to a Miss Lewis, whose Father had been late of Antigua. I should very much like to know what sort of a Woman she is. He was a piece of Perfection, noisy Perfection himself which I always recollect with regard.—We had noticed a few months before his succeeding to a College Living, the very Living which we remembered his talking of & wishing for; an exceeding good one, Great Cadbury in Somersetshire.—I would wish Miss Lewis to be of a silent turn & rather ignorant, but naturally intelligent & wishing to learn;—fond of cold veal pies, green tea in the afternoon, & a green window blind at night.

*   *   *

[Postscript upside down at top of p. 1]
You will be glad to hear that every Copy of S.&S. is sold & that it has brought me £140—besides the Copyright, if that sh^d ever be of any value.—I have now therefore written myself into £250.—which only makes me long for more.—I have something in hand—which I hope on the credit of P.&P. will sell well, tho' not half so entertaining. * * *

To Cassandra Austen

Saturday 6–Sunday 7 November 1813
Godmersham Park

* * * Miss Lee I found very conversible; she admires Crabbe[2] as she ought.—She is at an age of reason, ten years older than myself at least. She was at the famous Ball at Chilham Castle, so of course you remember her.—By the bye, as I must leave off being young, I find many

9. Jane Austen's brother, then at sea.
1. The Rev. Samuel Blackall visited the Austens in 1798 and was regarded by some friends of the family as a potential suitor of Jane Austen. She seems not to have been much interested and to be unperturbed by his failure really to initiate his suit; her wishes for his wife express, among other sentiments, her memory of his cautious and solemn character.
2. English poet George Crabbe (1754–1832).

Douceurs in being a sort of Chaperon for I am put on the Sofa near the Fire & can drink as much wine as I like. We had Music in the Even^g, Fanny & Miss Wildman played, & Mr James Wildman sat close by & listened, or pretended to listen. * * *

To Anna Austen[3]

Wednesday 10–Thursday 18 August 1814
Chawton

Wednesday 17.—We have just finished the 1st of the 3 Books I had the pleasure of receiving yesterday; *I* read it aloud—& we are all very much amused, & like the work quite as well as ever. * * * My Corrections have not been more important than before;—here & there, we have thought the sense might be expressed in fewer words—and I have scratched out Sir Tho: from walking with the other Men to the Stables &c the very day after his breaking his arm—for though I find your Papa *did* walk out immediately after *his* arm was set, I think it can be so little usual as to *appear* unnatural in a book—& it does not seem to be material that Sir Tho: should go with them.—Lyme will not do. Lyme is towards 40 miles distance from Dawlish & would not be talked of there.—I have put Starcross indeed.—If you prefer *Exeter*, that must be always safe.—I have also scratched out the Introduction between Lord P. & his Brother, & Mr Griffin. A Country Surgeon (dont tell Mr C. Lyford) would not be introduced to Men of their rank.—And when Mr Portman is first brought in, he w^d not be introduced as *the Honble— That* distinction is never mentioned at such times;—at least I beleive not.—Now, we have finished the 2^d book—or rather the 5th—I *do* think you had better omit Lady Helena's postscript;—to those who are acquainted with P. & P it will seem an Imitation. * * *

Thursday. We finished it last night, after our return from drinking tea at the G^t House.—The last Chapter does not please us quite so well, we do not thoroughly like the *Play*; perhaps from having had too much of Plays in that way lately. * * * —Your Aunt C. does not like desultory novels, & is rather fearful yours will be too much so, that there will be too frequent a change from one set of people to another, & that circumstances will be sometimes introduced of apparent consequence, which will lead to nothing.—It will not be so great an objection to *me*, if it does. I allow much more Latitude than She does—& think Nature & Spirit cover many sins of a wandering story—and People in general do not care so much about it—for your comfort. * * *

---

3. Anna Austen was the daughter of Jane Austen's brother James. Anna was about twenty-one when she sought advice from her aunt about the novel she was writing. Anna's novel was never published.

To Anna Austen

Friday 9–Sunday 18 September 1814
Chawton

* * * You are now collecting your People delightfully, getting them exactly into such a spot as is the delight of my life;—3 or 4 Families in a Country Village is the very thing to work on—& I hope you will write a great deal more, & make full use of them while they are so very favourably arranged. You are but *now* coming to the heart & beauty of your book; till the heroine grows up, the fun must be imperfect—but I expect a great deal of entertainment from the next 3 or 4 books, & I hope you will not resent these remarks by sending me no more. * * *

To Fanny Knight[4]

Friday 18–Sunday 20 November 1814
Chawton

* * * Poor dear Mr J. P!—Oh! dear Fanny, Your mistake has been one that thousands of women fall into. He was the *first* young Man who attached himself to you. That was the charm, & most powerful it is.—Among the multitudes however that make the same mistake with Yourself, there can be few indeed who have so little reason to regret it;—*his* Character & *his* attachment leave you nothing to be ashamed of.—Upon the whole, what is to be done? You certainly *have* encouraged him to such a point as to make him feel almost secure of you—you have no inclination for any other person—His situation in life, family, friends, & above all his Character—his uncommonly amiable mind, strict principles, just notions, good habits—*all* that *you* know so well how to value, *All* that really is of the first importance—everything of this nature pleads his cause most strongly.—You have no doubt of his having superior Abilities—he has proved it at the University—he is I dare say such a Scholar as your agreable, idle Brothers would ill bear a comparison with.—Oh! my dear Fanny, the more I write about him, the warmer my feelings become, the more strongly I feel the sterling worth of such a young Man & the desirableness of your growing in love with him again. I recommend this most thoroughly.—There *are* such beings in the World perhaps, one in a Thousand, as the Creature You & I should think perfection, where Grace & Spirit are united to Worth, where the Manners are equal to the Heart & Understanding, but such a person may not come in your way, or if he does, he may

---

4. Fanny Knight was the eldest daughter of Jane Austen's brother Edward, who took the name Knight when he was adopted by relatives who made him their heir. Fanny was about twenty-one when she sought advice from her aunt about the young men with whom she was, or was not, falling in love.

not be the eldest son of a Man of Fortune, the Brother of your particular friend, & belonging to your own County.—Think of all this Fanny.
M[r] J. P.-has advantages which do not often meet in one person. His
only fault indeed seems Modesty. If he were less modest, he would be
more agreable, speak louder & look Impudenter;—and is not it a fine
Character, of which Modesty is the only defect?—I have no doubt that
he will get more lively & more like yourselves as he is more with you;—
he will catch your ways if he belongs to you. And as to there being any
objection from his *Goodness*, from the danger of his becoming even
Evangelical, I cannot admit *that*. I am by no means convinced that we
ought not all to be Evangelicals, & am at least persuaded that they
who are so from Reason & Feeling, must be happiest & safest.—Do
not be frightened from the connection by your Brothers having most
wit. Wisdom is better than Wit, & in the long run will certainly have
the laugh on her side; & don't be frightened by the idea of his acting
more strictly up to the precepts of the New Testament than others.—
And now, my dear Fanny, having written so much on one side of the
question, I shall turn round & entreat you not to commit yourself
farther, & not to think of accepting him unless you really do like him.
Anything is to be preferred or endured rather than marrying without
Affection; and if his deficiencies of Manner &c &c strike you more
than all his good qualities, if you continue to think strongly of them,
give him up at once.—Things are now in such a state, that you must
resolve upon one or the other, either to allow him to go on as he has
done, or whenever you are together behave with a coldness which may
convince him that he has been deceiving himself.—I have no doubt
of his suffering a good deal for a time, a great deal, when he feels that
he must give you up;—but it is no creed of mine, as you must be well
aware, that such sort of Disappointments kill anybody. * * * You will
be glad to hear that the first Edit: of M. P. [*Mansfield Park*] is all
sold.—Your Uncle Henry is rather wanting me to come to Town, to
settle about a 2[d] Edit:—but as I could not very conveniently leave
home now, I have written him my Will & pleasure, & unless he still
urges it, shall not go.—I am very greedy & want to make the most of
it;—but as you are much above caring about money, I shall not plague
you with any particulars.—The pleasures of Vanity are more within
your comprehension, & you will enter into mine, at receiving the *praise*
which every now & then comes to me, through some channel or
other. * * *

To Fanny Knight

Wednesday 30 November 1814
23 Hans Place[5]

* * * Now my dearest Fanny, I will begin a subject which comes in very naturally.—You frighten me out of my Wits by your reference. Your affection gives me the highest pleasure, but indeed you must not let anything depend on my opinion. Your own feelings & none but your own, should determine such an important point.—So far however as answering your question, I have no scruple.—I am perfectly convinced that your present feelings, supposing you were to marry *now*, would be sufficient for his happiness;—but when I think how very, very far it is from a *Now*, & take everything that *may be*, into consideration, I dare not say, "determine to accept him." The risk is too great for *you*, unless your own Sentiments prompt it.—You will think me perverse perhaps; in my last letter I was urging everything in his favour, & now I am inclining the other way; but I cannot help it; I am at present more impressed with the possible Evil that may arise to *You* from engaging yourself to him—in word or mind—than with anything else.—When I consider how few young Men you have yet seen much of—how capable you are (yes, I do still think you *very* capable) of being really in love—and how full of temptation the next 6 or 7 years of your Life will probably be—(it is the very period of Life for the *strongest* attachments to be formed)—I cannot wish you with your present very cool feelings to devote yourself in honour to him. It is very true that you never may attach another Man, his equal altogether, but if that other Man has the power of attaching you *more*, he will be in your eyes the most perfect.—I shall be glad if you *can* revive past feelings, & from your unbiassed self resolve to go on as you have done, but this I do not expect, and without it I cannot wish you to be fettered. I should not be afraid of your *marrying* him;—with all his Worth, you would soon love him enough for the happiness of both; but I should dread the continuance of this sort of tacit engagement, with such an uncertainty as there is, of *when* it may be completed.—Years may pass, before he is Independant.—You like him well enough to marry, but not well enough to wait.—The unpleasantness of appearing fickle is certainly great—but if you think you want Punishment for past Illusions, there it is—and nothing can be compared to the misery of being bound *without* Love, bound to one, & preferring another. *That* is a Punishment which you do *not* deserve. * * *

---

5. Hans Place was the address of the London house of Jane Austen's brother Henry, then a banker.

To James Stanier Clarke[6]

Monday 11 December 1815

* * * I am quite honoured by your thinking me capable of drawing such a Clergyman as you gave the sketch of in your note of Nov: 16. But I assure you I am *not*. The comic part of the Character I might be equal to, but not the Good, the Enthusiastic, the Literary. Such a Man's Conversation must at times be on subjects of Science & Philosophy of which I know nothing—or at least be occasionally abundant in quotations & allusions which a Woman, who like me, knows only her own Mother-tongue & has read very little in that, would be totally without the power of giving.—A Classical Education, or at any rate, a very extensive acquaintance with English Literature, Ancient & Modern, appears to me quite Indispensable for the person who w^d do any justice to your Clergyman—And I think I may boast myself to be, with all possible Vanity, the most unlearned, & uninformed Female who ever dared to be an Authoress.

Believe me, dear Sir,
Your obligd & faith Hum. Servt.
J. A.

To James Edward Austen[7]

Monday 16—Tuesday 17 December 1816
Chawton

* * * Uncle Henry writes very superior Sermons.—You & I must try to get hold of one or two, & put them into our Novels;—it would be a fine help to a volume; & we could make our Heroine read it aloud of a Sunday Evening, just as well as Isabella Wardour in the Antiquary,[8] is made to read the History of the Hartz Demon in the ruins of St Ruth—tho' I believe, upon recollection, Lovell is the Reader.—By the bye, my dear Edward, I am quite concerned for the loss your Mother mentions in her Letter; two Chapters & a half to be missing is monstrous! It is well that *I* have not been at Steventon lately, & therefore cannot be suspected of purloining them;—two strong twigs & a half towards a Nest of my own, would have been something.—I do not think however that any theft of that sort would be really very useful to

---

6. Clarke was the domestic chaplain and librarian to the Prince of Wales, later George IV. When the prince, who admired Austen's novels, heard that she was in London he sent Mr. Clarke to offer to show her the library. Clarke then wrote suggesting that she write about the life of a clergyman or (later) a romance founded on the history of the prince's family. At his suggestion *Emma* was dedicated to the prince.
7. James Edward Austen was the author of a memoir (1871) of his aunt Jane Austen (see p. 259). He too seems to have been writing a novel.
8. A novel by Sir Walter Scott (1771–1832), published in the year in which this letter was written.

me. What should I do with your strong, manly, spirited Sketches, full of Variety & Glow?—How could I possibly join them on to the little bit (two Inches wide) of Ivory on which I work with so fine a Brush, as produces little effect after much labour? * * *

To Fanny Knight

Thursday 20—Friday 21 February 1817
Chawton

My dearest Fanny,

You are inimitable, irresistable. You are the delight of my Life. Such Letters, such entertaining Letters as you have lately sent!—Such a description of your queer little heart!—Such a lovely display of what Imagination does. * * * You are the Paragon of all that is Silly & Sensible, common-place & eccentric, Sad & Lively, Provoking & Interesting.—Who can keep pace with the fluctuations of your Fancy, the Capprizios of your Taste, the Contradictions of your Feelings?—You are so odd!   & all the time, so perfectly natural—so peculiar in yourself, & yet so like everybody else!—It is very, very gratifying to me to know you so intimately. You can hardly think what a pleasure it is to me, to have such thorough pictures of your Heart.—Oh! what a loss it will be, when you are married. You are too agreable in your single state, too agreable as a Neice. I shall hate you when your delicious play of Mind is all settled down into conjugal & maternal affections. Mʳ J. W. frightens me.—He will have you.—I see you at the Altar. * * *

Early Writing

From Love and Freindship†

Letter 5th   Laura to Marianne

One Evening in December as my Father, my Mother and myself, were arranged in social converse round our Fireside, we were on a sudden, greatly astonished, by hearing a violent knocking on the outward Door of our rustic Cot.

My Father started—"What noise is that," (said he.) "It sounds like a loud rapping at the Door"—(replied my Mother.) "[i]t does indeed." (cried I.) "I am of your opinion; (said my Father) it certainly does appear to proceed from some uncommon violence exerted against our unoffending Door." "Yes (exclaimed I) I cannot help thinking it must be somebody who knocks for Admittance."

"That is another point (replied he;) We must not pretend to determine on what motive the person may knock—tho' that someone *does* rap at the Door, I am partly convinced."

Here, a 2d tremendous rap interrupted my Father in his speech and somewhat alarmed my Mother and me.

"Had we not better go and see who it is,? (said she) the Servants are out." "I think we had." (replied I.) "Certainly, (added my Father) by all means." "Shall we go now?" (said my Mother.) "The sooner the better." (answered he). "Oh! let no time be lost." (cried I.)

A third more violent Rap than ever again assaulted our ears. "I am certain there is somebody knocking at the Door." (said my Mother.) "I think there must," (replied my Father) "I fancy the Servants are returned; (said I) I think I hear Mary going to the Door." "I'm glad of it (cried my Father) for I long to know who it is."

I was right in my Conjecture; for Mary instantly entering the Room, informed us that a young Gentleman & his Servant were at the Door, who had lossed their way, were very cold and begged leave to warm themselves by our fire.

---

† From *Volume the Second*, ed. B. C. Southam (Oxford: Clarendon Press, 1963) 6–13. Reprinted by permission of Athlone Press. *Love and Freindship* was composed in 1790. A short novel told in fifteen letters, it burlesques the conventions of sentimental fiction. All notes are by the editor of this Norton Critical Edition.

"Wont you admit them?" (said I) "You have no objection, my Dear?" (said my Father.) "None in the World." (replied my Mother.)

Mary, without waiting for any further commands immediately left the room and quickly returned introducing the most beauteous and amiable Youth, I had ever beheld. The servant, She kept to herself.

My natural Sensibility had already been greatly affected by the sufferings of the unfortunate Stranger and no sooner did I first behold him, than I felt that on him the happiness or Misery of my future Life must depend.

adeiu.

Laura

Letter 6th   Laura to Marianne

The noble Youth informed us that his name was Lindsay—for particular reasons however I shall conceal it under that of Talbot. He told us that he was the son of an English Baronet, that his Mother had been many years no more and that he had a Sister of the middle size. "My Father (he continued) is a mean and mercenary wretch—it is only to such particular friends as this Dear Party that I would thus betray his failings. Your Virtues my amiable Polydore (addressing himself to my father) yours Dear Claudia and yours my Charming Laura call on me to repose in you, my Confidence." We bowed. "My Father, seduced by the false glare of Fortune and the Deluding Pomp of Title, insisted on my giving my hand to Lady Dorothea. No never exclaimed I. Lady Dorothea is lovely and Engaging; I prefer no woman to her; but know Sir, that I scorn to marry her in compliance with your wishes. No! Never shall it be said that I obliged my Father,"

We all admired the noble Manliness of his reply. He continued.

"Sir Edward was surprized; he had perhaps little expected to meet with so spirited an opposition to his will. 'Where Edward in the name of wonder (said he) did you pick up this unmeaning Gibberish? You have been studying Novels I suspect.' I scorned to answer: it would have been beneath my Dignity. I mounted my Horse and followed by my faithful William set forwards for my Aunts."

"My Father's house is situated in Bedfordshire, my Aunt's in Middlesex, and tho' I flatter myself with being a tolerable proficienz in Geography, I know not how it happened, but I found myself entering this beautifull Vale which I find is in South Wales, when I had expected to have reached my Aunts."

"After having wandered some time on the Banks of the Uske without knowing which way to go, I began to lament my cruel Destiny in the bitterest and most pathetic Manner. It was now perfectly dark, not a single Star was there to direct my steps, and I know not what might have befallen me had I not at length discerned thro' the solemn Gloom that surrounded me a distant Light, which as I approached it, I discovered to be the chearfull Blaze of your fire. Impelled by the combination of Misfortunes under which I laboured, namely Fear, Cold and Hunger I hesitated not to ask admittance which at length I have gained; and now my Adorable Laura (continued he taking my Hand) when may I hope to receive that reward of all the painfull sufferings I have undergone during the course of my Attachment to you, to which I have ever aspired? Oh! when will you reward me with Yourself?"

"This instant, Dear and Amiable Edward." (replied I.). We were immediately united by my Father, who tho' he had never taken orders[1] had been bred to the Church.

adeium.

Laura

From A Collection of Letters†

Letter the Third

FROM A YOUNG LADY IN DISTRESS'D CIRCUMSTANCES TO HER FRIEND.

A few days ago I was at a private Ball given by Mr. Ashburnham. As my Mother never goes out she entrusted me to the care of Lady Greville who did me the honour of calling for me in her way & of allowing me to sit forwards, which is a favour about which I am very indifferent especially as I know it is considered as confering a great obligation on me. "So Miss Maria (said her Ladyship as she saw me advancing to the door of the Carriage) you seem very smart tonight—*My* poor Girls will appear quite to disadvantage by *you*. I only hope your Mother may not have distressed herself to set *you* off. Have you got a new Gown on?"

"Yes Ma'am," replied I with as much indifference as I could assume.

"Aye, and a fine one too I think—(feeling it, as by her permission I seated myself by her) I dare say it is all very smart—But I must own, for you know I always speak my mind, that I think it was quite a needless peice of expence—Why could not you have worn your old striped one? It is not my way to find fault with people because they are poor, for I always think that they are more to be despised & pitied than blamed for it, especially if they cannot help it, but at the same time I must say that in my opinion your old striped Gown would have been

---

1. Been ordained as a clergyman.
† From *Volume the Second*, ed B. C. Southam (Oxford: Clarendon Press, 1963) 164–72. Reprinted by permission of Athlone Press. *A Collection of Letters* was probably written before the end of 1792. It is a very short burlesque of five letters whose subtitles ("From a Young Lady crossed in Love to her Freind"; "From a Young Lady very much in love to her Freind") suggest its tone and targets. All notes are by the editor of this Norton Critical Edition.

quite fine enough for its wearer—for to tell you the truth (I always speak my mind) I am very much afraid that one half of the people in the room will not know whether you have a Gown on or not—But I suppose you intend to make your fortune tonight—Well, the sooner the better; & I wish you success."

"Indeed Ma'am I have no such intention.—"

"Who ever heard a Young Lady own that she was a Fortune-hunter?" Miss Greville laughed, but I am sure Ellen felt for me.

"Was your Mother gone to bed before you left her?" said her Ladyship.

"Dear Ma'am" said Ellen, "it is but nine o'clock."

"True Ellen, but Candles cost money, and Mrs Williams is too wise to be extravagant."

"She was just sitting down to supper Ma'am."

"And what had she got for Supper?" "I did not observe". "Bread & Cheese I suppose." "I should never wish for a better supper". said Ellen. "You have never any reason" replied her Mother, "as a better is always provided for you." Miss Greville laughed excessively, as she constantly does at her Mother's wit.

Such is the humiliating Situation in which I am forced to appear while riding in her Ladyship's Coach—I dare not be impertinent, as my Mother is always admonishing me to be humble & patient if I wish to make my way in the world. She insists on my accepting every invitation of Lady Greville, or you may be certain that I would never enter either her House, or her Coach, with the disagreeable certainty I always have of being abused for my Poverty while I am in them.— When we arrived at Ashburnham, it was nearly ten o'clock, which was an hour and a half later than we were desired to be there; but Lady Greville is too fashionable (or fancies herself to be so) to be punctual. The Dancing however was not begun as they waited for Miss Greville. I had not been long in the room before I was engaged to dance by Mr. Bernard but just as we were going to stand up, he recollected that his Servant had got his white Gloves, & immediately ran out to fetch them. In the mean time the Dancing began & Lady Greville in passing to another room went exactly before me.— She saw me & instantly stopping, said to me though there were several people close to us;

"Hey day, Miss Maria! What cannot you get a partner? Poor Young Lady! I am afraid your new Gown was put on for nothing. But do not despair; perhaps you may get a hop before the Evening is over." So saying, she passed on without hearing my repeated assurance of being engaged, & leaving me very provoked at being so exposed before every one—Mr Bernard however soon returned & by coming to me the moment he entered the room, and leading me to the Dancers, my Character I hope was cleared from the imputation Lady Greville had thrown on it, in the eyes of all the old Ladies who had heard her speech.

I soon forgot all my vexations in the pleasure of dancing and of having the most agreable partner in the room. As he is moreover heir to a very large Estate I could see that Lady Greville did not look very well pleased when she found who had been his Choice.— She was determined to mortify me, and accordingly when we were sitting down between the dances, she came to me with *more* than her usual insulting importance attended by Miss Mason and said loud enough to be heard by half the people in the room, "Pray Miss Maria in what way of business was your Grandfather? for Miss Mason & I cannot agree whether he was a Grocer or a Bookbinder." I saw that she wanted to mortify me and was resolved if I possibly could to prevent her seeing that her scheme succeeded. "Neither Madam; he was a Wine Merchant." "Aye, I knew he was in some such low way—He broke[1] did not he?" "I beleive not Ma'am." "Did not he abscond?" "I never heard that he did" "At least he died insolvent?" "I was never told so before." "Why was not your Father as poor as a Rat?" "I fancy not;" "Was not he in the Kings Bench once?" "I never saw him there." *She* gave me *such* a look, & turned away in a great passion; while I was half delighted with myself for my impertinence, & half afraid of being thought too saucy. As Lady Greville was extremely angry with me, she took no further notice of me all the evening, and indeed had I been in favour I should have been equally neglected, as she was got into a party of great folks & she never speaks to me when she can to any one else. Miss Greville was with her Mother's party at Supper, but Ellen preferred staying with the Bernards & me. We had a very pleasant Dance & as Lady G— slept all the way home, I had a very comfortable ride.

The next day while we were at Dinner Lady Greville's Coach stopped at the door, for that is the time of day she generally contrives it should. She sent in a message by the Servant to say that "she should not get out but that Miss Maria must come to the Coach-door, as she wanted to speak to her, and that she must make haste & come immediately—" "What an impertinent Message Mama!" said I—"Go Maria—" replied She—Accordingly I went & was obliged to stand there at her Ladyships pleasure though the Wind was extremely high and very cold.

"Why I think Miss Maria you are not quite so smart as you were last night—But I did not come to examine your dress, but to tell you that you may dine with us the day after tomorrow—Not tomorrow, remember, do not come tomorrow, for we expect Lord and Lady Clermont & Sir Thomas Stanley's family—There will be no occasion for your being very fine for I shant send the Carriage—If it rains you may take an umbrella—" I could hardly help laughing at hearing her give me leave to keep myself dry—"and pray remember to be in time, for I shant wait—I hate my Victuals over-done—But you need not come *before*

1. Went bankrupt. The King's Bench to which Lady Greville later refers is a court that hears criminal cases, including bankruptcy cases.

the time—How does your Mother do—? She is at dinner is not she?" "Yes Ma'am we were in the middle of dinner when your Ladyship came." "I am afraid you find it very cold Maria." said Ellen. "Yes, it is an horrible East wind"—said her Mother—"I assure you I can hardly bear the window down—But you are used to be blown about the wind Miss Maria & that is what has made your Complexion so ruddy & coarse. You young Ladies who cannot often ride in a Carriage never mind what weather you trudge in, or how the wind shrews your legs. I would not have *my* Girls stand out of doors as you do in such a day as this. But some sort of people have no feelings either of cold or Delicacy—Well, remember that we shall expect you on Thursday at 5 o'clock—You must tell your Maid to come for you at night—There will be no Moon—and you will have an horrid walk home—My Compts[2] to your Mother—I am afraid your dinner will be cold—Drive on—" And away she went, leaving me in a great passion with her as she always does.

Maria Williams

---

2. Compliments.

CRITICISM

RICHARD WHATELY

[Technique and Moral Effect
in Jane Austen's Fiction]†

*   *   *

* * * We remarked, in a former Number, in reviewing a work of the author now before us, that "a new style of novel has arisen, within the last fifteen or twenty years, differing from the former in the points upon which the interest hinges; neither alarming our credulity nor amusing our imagination by wild variety of incident, or by those pictures of romantic affection and sensibility, which were formerly as certain attributes of fictitious characters as they are of rare occurrence among those who actually live and die. The substitute for these excitements, which had lost much of their poignancy by the repeated and injudicious use of them, was the art of copying from nature as she really exists in the common walks of life, and presenting to the reader, instead of the splendid scenes of an imaginary world, a correct and striking representation of that which is daily taking place around him."[1]

Now, though the origin of this new school of fiction may probably be traced, as we there suggested, to the exclusion of the mines from which materials for entertainment had been hitherto extracted, and the necessity of gratifying the natural craving of the reader for variety, by striking into an untrodden path; the consequences resulting from this change have been far greater than the mere supply of this demand. When this Flemish painting, as it were, is introduced—this accurate and unexaggerated delineation of events and characters—it necessarily follows, that a novel, which makes good its pretensions of giving a perfectly correct picture of common life, becomes a far more *instructive* work than one of equal or superior merit of the other class; it guides the judgment, and supplies a kind of artificial experience.

*   *   *

For most of that instruction which used to be presented to the world in the shape of formal dissertations, or shorter and more desultory moral essays, such as those of the Spectator and Rambler,[2] we may now resort to the pages of the acute and judicious, but not less amusing,

---

† From "Modern Novels," *Quarterly Review* 24 (1821): 352–53, 357, 359–60. All notes are by the editor of this Norton Critical Edition. In 1821 Whately was a Church of England clergyman and a fellow of an Oxford college who wrote on religious as well as literary topics. In 1831 he was appointed archbishop of Dublin.
1. Whately is quoting (using an editorial "We") from Walter Scott's review of Austen's *Emma* (*Quarterly Review* 14 [1815]: 188–201).
2. Weekly series of essays, those in the *Spectator* written by Joseph Addison and Richard Steele in 1711–12 and again in 1714, those in the *Rambler* written by Samuel Johnson in 1750–52.

novelists who have lately appeared. If their views of men and manners are no less just than those of the essayists who preceded them, are they to be rated lower because they present to us these views, not in the language of general description, but in the form of well-constructed fictitious narrative? If the practical lessons they inculcate are no less sound and useful, it is surely no diminution of their merit that they are conveyed by example instead of precept: nor, if their remarks are neither less wise nor less important, are they the less valuable for being represented as thrown out in the course of conversations suggested by the circumstances of the speakers, and perfectly in character. The praise and blame of the moralist are surely not the less effectual for being bestowed, not in general declamation, on classes of men, but on individuals representing those classes, who are so clearly delineated and brought into action before us, that we seem to be acquainted with them, and feel an interest in their fate.

*   *   *

Miss Austin [*sic*] has the merit (in our judgment most essential) of being evidently a Christian writer: a merit which is much enhanced, both on the score of good taste, and of practical utility, by her religion being not at all obtrusive. She might defy the most fastidious critic to call any of her novels, (as Cœlebs[3] was designated, we will not say altogether without reason,) a "dramatic sermon." The subject is rather alluded to, and that incidentally, than studiously brought forward and dwelt upon. In fact she is more sparing of it than would be thought desirable by some persons; perhaps even by herself, had she consulted merely her own sentiments; but she probably introduced it as far as she thought would be generally acceptable and profitable: for when the purpose of inculcating a religious principle is made too palpably prominent, many readers, if they do not throw aside the book with disgust, are apt to fortify themselves with that respectful kind of apathy with which they undergo a regular sermon, and prepare themselves as they do to swallow a dose of medicine, endeavouring to *get it down* in large gulps, without tasting it more than is necessary.

The moral lessons also of this lady's novels, though clearly and impressively conveyed, are not offensively put forward, but spring incidentally from the circumstances of the story; they are not forced upon the reader, but he is left to collect them (though without any difficulty) for himself: her's is that unpretending kind of instruction which is furnished by real life; and certainly no author has ever conformed more closely to real life, as well in the incidents, as in the characters and descriptions. Her fables appear to us to be in their own way, nearly

3. *Coelebs in Search of a Wife* (1809) is a didactic novel written by Hannah More (1745–1833)

faultless; they do not consist (like those of some of the writers who
have attempted this kind of common-life novel writing) of a string of
unconnected events which have little or no bearing on one main plot,
and are introduced evidently for the sole purpose of bringing in characters and conversations; but have all that compactness of plan and
unity of action which is generally produced by a sacrifice of probability:
yet they have little or nothing that is not probable; the story proceeds
without the aid of extraordinary accidents; the events which take place
are the necessary or natural consequences of what has preceded; and
yet (which is a very rare merit indeed) the final catastrophe is scarcely
ever clearly foreseen from the beginning, and very often comes, upon
the generality of readers at least, quite unexpected. We know not
whether Miss Austin ever had access to the precepts of Aristotle; but
there are few, if any, writers of fiction who have illustrated them more
successfully.

*   *   *

MARGARET OLIPHANT

[Miss Austen]†

* * * To be sure, Miss Austen's ladies and gentlemen are seldom
fine; but they are all to be found in the same kind of house with the
same kind of surroundings. Their poverties, when they have any, are
caused in a genteel way by the entail of an estate, or by the premature
death of the father without leaving an adequate provision of his lovely
and accomplished girls. The neglect which leaves the delicate heroine
without a horse to ride, or the injury conveyed in the fact that she has
to travel post without a servant, is the worst that happens. If it were
not that the class to which she thus confines herself was the one most
intimately and thoroughly known to her, we should be disposed to
consider it, as we have said, a piece of self-denial on Miss Austen's part
to relinquish all stronger lights and shadows; but perhaps it is better
to say that she was conscientious in her determination to describe only
what she knew, and that nature aided principle in this singular limitation. Of itself, however, it throws a certain light upon her character,
which is not the simple character it appears at the first glance, but one
full of subtle power, keenness, finesse, and self-restraint—a type not

† From "Miss Austen and Miss Mitford," *Blackwood's* 107 (1870): 294–96. Oliphant (1822–
1897) was a prolific novelist and a frequent contributor of literary commentary to *Blackwood's*.
Her essay is a review of the first edition of Henry Austen-Leigh's memoir.

at all unusual among women of high cultivation, especially in the retirement of the country, where such qualities are likely enough to be unappreciated or misunderstood.

Mr. Austen Leigh, without meaning it, throws out of his dim little lantern a passing gleam of light upon the fine vein of feminine cynicism which pervades his aunt's mind. It is something altogether different from the rude and brutal male quality that bears the same name. It is the soft and silent disbelief of a spectator who has to look at a great many things without showing any outward discomposure, and who has learned to give up any moral classification of social sins, and to place them instead on the level of absurdities. She is not surprised or offended, much less horror-stricken or indignant, when her people show vulgar or mean traits of character, when they make it evident how selfish and self-absorbed they are, or even when they fall into those social cruelties which selfish and stupid people are so often guilty of, not without intention, but yet without the power of realising half the pain they inflict. She stands by and looks on, and gives a soft half-smile, and tells the story with an exquisite sense of its ridiculous side, and fine stinging yet soft-voiced contempt for the actors in it. She sympathises with the sufferers, yet she can scarcely be said to be sorry for them; giving them unconsciously a share in her own sense of the covert fun of the scene, and gentle disdain of the possibility that meanness and folly and stupidity could ever really wound any rational creature. The position of mind is essentially feminine, and one which may be readily identified in the personal knowledge of most people. It is the natural result of the constant, though probably quite unconscious, observation in which a young woman, with no active pursuit to occupy her, spends, without knowing it, so much of her time and youth. Courses of lectures, no doubt, or balls, or any decided out-of-door interest, interferes with this involuntary training; but such disturbances were rare in Miss Austen's day. A certain soft despair of any one human creature ever doing any good to another—of any influence overcoming those habits and moods and peculiarities of mind which the observer sees to be more obstinate than life itself—a sense that nothing is to be done but to look on, to say perhaps now and then a softening word, to make the best of it practically and theoretically, to smile and hold up one's hands and wonder why human creatures should be such fools,—such are the foundations upon which the feminine cynicism which we attribute to Miss Austen is built. It includes a great deal that is amiable, and is full of toleration and patience, and that habit of making allowance for others which lies at the bottom of all human charity. But yet it is not charity, and its toleration has none of the sweetness which proceeds from that highest of Christian graces. It is not absolute contempt either, but only a softened tone of general disbelief—amusement, nay enjoyment, of all those humours of humanity

which are so quaint to look at as soon as you dissociate them from any
rigid standard of right or wrong.

*   *   *

RICHARD SIMPSON

[The Critical Faculty of Jane Austen]†

*   *   *

Her plots always presuppose an organized society of families, of
fathers and mothers long married, whose existence has been fulfilled
in having given birth to the heroes and heroines of the stories. Now,
these people are almost always represented as living together in fair
comfort; and yet there is scarcely a single pair of them who have not,
on the usual novelist's scale of propriety, been wofully mismatched.
Sense and stupidity, solidity and frivolity, are represented as in everyday life cosily uniting, and making up the elements of a home with the
usual average of happiness and comfort. Miss Austen does not absolutely tell us that the special ends which she takes so much trouble to
bring about are anything short of the highest happiness, or that such
happiness could possibly be obtained by any other means. On the contrary, she appears as earnest as other novelists for the success of her
favourites. But there is enough in her evident opinions, in her bywords,
in her arguments, to prove to any sufficiently clear sight that it would
be, after all, much the same whether the proper people intermarried,
or whether they were mismatched by some malevolent Puck. Dr. Johnson thought it nonsense to say that marriages were made in heaven,
and held that any woman and any man might, if they determined upon
it, live well enough together, and settle down into the prosaic happiness
of a comfortable couple. In similar manner Miss Austen believed in
the ultimate possible happiness of every marriage. * * * Thus the great
coil Miss Austen makes to bring the right people together is really
much ado about nothing. * * * Now, what is this other than taking a
humourist's view of that which as a novelist she was treating as the
summum bonum of existence? That predestination of love, that pre-
ordained fitness, which decreed that one and one only should be the
complement and fulfilment of another's being—that except in union
with each other each must live miserably, and that no other solace
could be found for either than the other's society—she treated as mere

† From "Jane Austen," *North British Review* 52 (1870): 135–40. Simpson (1820–1876) was a
  liberal Roman Catholic writer and editor. All notes are by the editor of this Norton Critical
  Edition.

moonshine, while she at the same time founded her novels on the assumption of it as a hypothesis. * * * Friendship, to judge from her novels, was enough for her; she did not want to exaggerate it into passionate love. In it she in fact seems to have found sufficient tenderness and support to satisfy her cravings; she was contented with her home, with her brothers and sister, and did not want a husband. This gave her a great advantage for describing the perturbations of love. She sat apart on her rocky tower, and watched the poor souls struggling in the waves beneath. And her sympathies were not too painfully engaged; for she knew that it was only an Ariel's magic tempest,[1] and that no loss of life was to follow. Hence she could consider the struggles of the mariners with an amused and ironical complacency, and observe minutely all the hairbreadth escapes of their harmless peril. Accordingly her view of the life she described was that of a humourist, but of a very kindly one. She did not precisely think that all she described was vanity and vexation of spirit. But she thought that, in ordinary language, and especially in that of romance-writers, it was screwed up to a higher tension than the facts warranted. * * * She is so true because she is consciously exceeding the truth. Others may believe in the stability of raptures, and in the eternity of a momentary fancy; she knows exactly what they are worth; and, though she puts into the mouths of her puppets the language of faith, she knows how to convey to her readers a feeling of her own skepticism.

* * * She exhibits no ideal characters, no perfect virtue, no perfect vice. She shows strength dashed with feebleness, feebleness braced with some fibres of strength. * * * It is her philosophy to see not only the soul of goodness in things evil, but also to see on the face of goodness the impress of weakness and caducity. This is one reason which obliges her to compound her characters. Another is even stronger. It is her thorough consciousness that man is a social being, and that apart from society there is not even the individual. She was too great a realist to abstract and isolate the individual, and to give a portrait of him in the manner of Theophrastus or La Bruyère.[2] Even as a unit, man is only known to her in the process of his formation by social influences. She broods over his history, not over his individual soul and its secret workings, nor over the analysis of its faculties and organs. She sees him, not as a solitary being complete in himself, but only as completed in society. Again, she contemplates virtues, not as fixed quantities, or as definable qualities, but as continual struggles and conquests, as progressive states of mind, advancing by repulsing their contraries, or los-

---

1. Ariel is the sprite who creates the storm in Shakespeare's *The Tempest*.
2. Theophrastus was a classical Greek philosopher who wrote character sketches as a way of classifying human types; the characters of La Bruyère, a seventeenth-century French writer, satirized types of people.

ing ground by being overcome. Hence again the individual mind can only be represented by her as a battle-field, where contending hosts are marshalled, and where victory inclines now to one side, now to another. A character therefore unfolded itself to her, not in statuesque repose, not as a model without motion, but as a dramatic sketch, a living history, a composite force, which could only exhibit what it was by exhibiting what it did. * * *

* * * She defined her own sphere when she said that three or four families in a country village were the thing for a novelist to work upon. Each of these "little social common wealths" became a distinct personal entity to her imagination, with its own range of ideas, its own subjects of discourse, its own public opinion on all social matters. Indeed there is nothing in her novels to prove that she had any conception of society itself, but only of the coterie of three or four families mixing together, with differences of intellect, wealth, or character, but without any grave social inequalities. Of organized society she manifests no idea. She had no interest for the great political and social problems which were being debated with so much blood in her day. * * * There is not the least attempt to bring public opinion to bear on any one. Some of the characters are said to show too much or too little deference to public opinion; but it is only spoken of, not represented. It is an abstract notion, a word not a thing, an idea not a force. Yet if it had been within the sphere of her power she might have made excellent opportunities for using it. She delights in introducing her heroines in their girlhood, shapeless but of good material, like malleable and ductile masses of gold. We have the flower in the germ, the woman's thought dark in the child's brain; the dream of the artist still involved in the marble block which some external force is to chip and carve and mould. She must have known the force of public opinion in doing work of this kind, and she would no doubt have dramatized public opinion, and exhibited its workings, if she had possessed any such knowledge of it as is displayed by George Eliot or by Mrs. Browning. She was perfect in dramatizing the combination of a few simple forces; but it never struck her to try to dramatize the action and reaction of all.

Platonist as she was in her feelings, she could rise to contemplate the soul as a family, but not as a republic. The disturbances in it were not insurrections or revolutions, but only family quarrels; and the scapegrace passion did not necessarily lose the affections of the family ruler. There is no capital punishment, not even transportation[3] or imprisonment for life, in her ethical statue-book.

* * *

3. In the eighteenth and nineteenth centuries in Britain certain crimes were punished by transporting the criminal, for a fixed period or for life, to Australia or another British colony.

D. W. HARDING

"Regulated Hatred": An Aspect in the Work of Jane Austen †

The impression of Jane Austen which has filtered through to the reading public down from the first-hand critics, through histories of literature, university courses, literary journalism and polite allusion, deters many who might be her best readers from bothering with her at all. How can this popular impression be described? In my experience the first idea to be absorbed from the atmosphere surrounding her work was that she offered exceptionally favourable openings to the exponents of urbanity. Gentlemen of an older generation than mine spoke of their intention of re-reading her on their deathbeds; Eric Linklater's cultured Prime Minister in *The Impregnable Women* [1938] passes from surreptitious to abandoned reading of her novels as a national crisis deepens. With this there also came the impression that she provided a refuge for the sensitive when the contemporary world grew too much for them. So Beatrice Kean Seymour writes (*Jane Austen*: 1937): "In a society which has enthroned the machine-gun and carried it aloft even into the quiet heavens, there will always be men and women—Escapist or not, as you please—who will turn to her novels with an unending sense of relief and thankfulness."

I was given to understand that her scope was of course extremely restricted, but that within her limits she succeeded admirably in expressing the gentler virtues of a civilised social order. She could do this because she lived at a time when, as a sensitive person of culture, she could still feel that she had a place in society and could address the reading public as sympathetic equals; she might introduce unpleasant people into her stories but she could confidently expose them to a public opinion that condemned them. Chiefly, so I gathered, she was a delicate satirist, revealing with inimitable lightness of touch the comic foibles and amiable weaknesses of the people whom she lived amongst and liked.

All this was enough to make me quite certain I didn't want to read her. And it is, I believe, a seriously misleading impression. Fragments of the truth have been incorporated in it but they are fitted into a pattern whose total effect is false. And yet the wide currency of this false impression is an indication of Jane Austen's success in an essential part of her complex intention as a writer: her books are, as she meant

† From *Scrutiny* 8 (1940): 346–47, 351–54, 362. Reprinted with the permission of Athlone Press. Professor Harding's essay has also been reprinted in a collection of essays, *"Regulated Hatred" and Other Essays on Jane Austen*, edited by Monica Lawlor (London and Atlantic Heights, NJ: Athlone Press, 1998).

them to be, read and enjoyed by precisely the sort of people whom she disliked; she is a literary classic of the society which attitudes like hers, held widely enough, would undermine.

* * *

To speak of this aspect of her work as "satire" is perhaps misleading. She has none of the underlying didactic intention ordinarily attributed to the satirist. Her object is not missionary; it is the more desperate one of merely finding some mode of existence for her critical attitudes. To her the first necessity was to keep on reasonably good terms with the associates of her everyday life; she had a deep need of their affection and a genuine respect for the ordered, decent civilisation that they upheld. And yet she was sensitive to their crudenesses and complacencies and knew that her real existence depended on resisting many of the values they implied. The novels gave her a way out of this dilemma. This, rather than the ambition of entertaining a posterity of urbane gentlemen, was her motive force in writing.

As a novelist, therefore, part of her aim was to find the means for unobtrusive spiritual survival, without open conflict with the friendly people around her whose standards in simpler things she could accept and whose affection she greatly needed. She found, of course, that one of the most useful peculiarities of her society was its willingness to remain blind to the implications of a caricature. She found people eager to laugh at faults they tolerated in themselves and their friends, so long as the faults were exaggerated and the laughter "good-natured"—so long, that is, as the assault on society could be regarded as a mock assault and not genuinely disruptive. Satire such as this is obviously a means not of admonition but of self-preservation.

Hence one of Jane Austen's most successful methods is to offer her readers every excuse for regarding as rather exaggerated figures of fun people whom she herself detests and fears. Mrs. Bennet, according to the Austen tradition, is one of "our" richly comic characters about whom we can feel superior, condescending, perhaps a trifle sympathetic, and above all heartily amused and free from care. Everything conspires to make this the natural interpretation once you are willing to overlook Jane Austen's bald and brief statement of her own attitude to her: "She was a woman of mean understanding, little information, and uncertain temper." How many women amongst Jane Austen's acquaintance and amongst her most complacent readers to the present day that phrase must describe! How gladly they enjoy the funny side of the situations Mrs. Bennet's unpleasant nature creates, and how easy it is made for them to forget or never observe that Jane Austen, none the less for seeing how funny she is, goes on detesting her. The thesis that the ruling standards of our social group leave a perfectly comfortable niche for detestable people and give them sufficient sanction to persist, would, if it were argued seriously, arouse the most violent opposition, the most determined apologetics for things as they are, and the most reproachful pleas for a sense of proportion.

Caricature served Jane Austen's purpose perfectly. Under her treatment one can never say where caricature leaves off and the claim to serious portraiture begins. Mr. Collins is only given a trifle more comic exaggeration than Lady Catherine de Bourgh, and by her standards is a possible human being. Lady Catherine in turn seems acceptable as a portrait if the criterion of verisimilitude is her nephew Mr. Darcy. And he, finally, although to some extent a caricature, is near enough natural portraiture to stand beside Elizabeth Bennet, who, like all the heroines, is presented as an undistorted portrait. The simplest comic effects are gained by bringing the caricatures into direct contact with the real people, as in Mr. Collins' visit to the Bennets and his proposal to Elizabeth. But at the same time one knows that, though from some points of view [he is a] caricature, in other directions he does, by easy stages, fit into the real world. He is real enough to Mrs. Bennet; and she is real enough to Elizabeth to create a situation of real misery for her when she refuses. Consequently the proposal scene is not only comic fantasy, but it is also, for Elizabeth, a taste of the fantastic nightmare in which economic and social institutions have such power over the values of personal relationships that the comic monster is nearly able to get her.

The implications of her caricatures as criticism of real people in real society is brought out in the way they dovetail into their social setting. The decent, stodgy Charlotte puts up cheerfully with Mr. Collins as a husband; and Elizabeth can never quite become reconciled to the idea that her friend is the wife of her comic monster. And that, of course, is precisely the sort of idea that Jane Austen herself could never grow reconciled to. The people she hated were tolerated, accepted, comfortably ensconced in the only human society she knew; they were, for her, society's embarrassing unconscious comment on itself. A recent writer on Jane Austen, Elizabeth Jenkins [*Jane Austen*: 1938], puts forward the polite and more comfortable interpretation in supposing Charlotte's marriage to be explained solely by the impossibility of young women's earning their own living at that period. But Charlotte's complaisance goes deeper than that: it is shown as a considered indifference to personal relationships when they conflict with cruder advantages in the wider social world:

> She had always felt that Charlotte's opinion of matrimony was not exactly like her own, but she could not have supposed it possible that, when called into action, she would have sacrificed every better feeling to worldly advantage.

We know too, at the biographical level, that Jane Austen herself, in a precisely similar situation to Charlotte's, spent a night of psychological crisis in deciding to revoke her acceptance of an "advantageous" proposal made the previous evening. And her letters to Fanny Knight show how deep her convictions went at this point.

It is important to notice that Elizabeth makes no break with her friend on account of the marriage. This was the sort of friend—"a friend disgracing herself and sunk in her esteem"—that went to make up the available social world which one could neither escape materially nor be independent of psychologically.

* * *

This attempt to suggest a slightly different emphasis in the reading of Jane Austen is not offered as a balanced appraisal of her work. It is deliberately lop-sided, neglecting the many points at which the established view seems adequate. I have tried to underline one or two features of her work that claim the sort of readers who sometimes miss her—those who would turn to her not for relief and escape but as a formidable ally against things and people which were to her, and still are, hateful.

DOROTHY VAN GHENT

On *Pride and Prejudice*†

It is the frequent response of readers who are making their first acquaintance with Jane Austen that her subject matter is itself so limited—limited to the manners of a small section of English country gentry who apparently never have been worried about death or sex, hunger or war, guilt or God—that it can offer no contiguity with modern interests. This is a very real difficulty in an approach to an Austen novel, and we should not obscure it; for by taking it initially into consideration, we can begin to come closer to the actual toughness and subtlety of the Austen quality. The greatest novels have been great in range as well as in technical invention; they have explored human experience a good deal more widely and deeply than Jane Austen was able to explore it. It is wronging an Austen novel to expect of it what it makes no pretense to rival—the spiritual profundity of the very greatest novels. But if we expect artistic mastery of limited materials, we shall not be disappointed.

The exclusions and limitations are deliberate; they do not necessarily

† From *The English Novel, Form and Function* (New York: Holt, Rinehart and Winston, 1953) 105–23. Copyright © 1953. Reprinted by permission of Henry Holt and Company.

represent limitations of Jane Austen's personal experience. Though she
led the life of a maiden gentlewoman, it was not actually a sheltered
life—not sheltered, that is, from the apparition of a number of the
harsher human difficulties. She was a member of a large family whose
activities ramified in many directions, in a period when a cousin could
be guillotined, when an aunt and uncle could be jailed for a year on a
shopkeeper's petty falsification,[1] and when the pregnancies and child-
bed mortalities of relatives and friends were kept up at a barnyard rate.
Her letters show in her the ironical mentality and the eighteenth-
century gusto that are the reverse of the puritanism and naïveté that
might be associated with the maidenly life. What she excludes from
her fictional material does not, then, reflect a personal obliviousness,
but, rather, a critically developed knowledge of the character of her
gift and a restriction of its exercise to the kind of subject matter which
she could shape into most significance. When we begin to look upon
these limitations, not as having the negative function of showing how
much of human life Jane Austen left out, but as having, rather, the
positive function of defining the form and meaning of the book, we
begin also to understand that kind of value that can lie in artistic
mastery over a restricted range. This "two inches of ivory" (the metaphor which she herself used to describe her work), though it may
resemble the handle of a lady's fan when looked on scantly, is in substance an elephant's tusk; it is a savagely probing instrument as well
as a masterpiece of refinement.

Time and space are small in *Pride and Prejudice*. Time is a few
months completely on the surface of the present, with no abysses of
past or future, no room for mystery; there is time only for a sufficiently
complicated business of getting wived and husbanded and of adapting
oneself to civilization and civilization to oneself. Space can be covered
in a few hours of coach ride between London and a country village or
estate; but this space is a *physical* setting only in the most generalized
sense; it is space as defined by a modern positivistic philosopher—"a
place for an argument." The concern is rational and social. What is
relevant is the way minds operate in certain social circumstances, and
the physical particular has only a derived and subordinate relevance,
as it serves to stimulate attitudes between persons. Even the social
circumstances are severely restricted: they are the circumstances of
marriageable young women coming five to a leisure-class family with
reduced funds and prospects. What can be done with this time and
space and these circumstances? What Jane Austen does is to dissect—

1. The first husband of Austen's cousin Eliza de Feuillide was executed in Paris in 1794. Eliza
later married Austen's brother Henry. Austen's aunt, Mrs. Leigh-Perrot, was accused of shop-
lifting by a shopkeeper in Bath in 1799 and remained in jail over seven months until she was
found innocent at her trial [*Editor*].

with what one critic has called "regulated hatred"[2]—the monster in the skin of the civilized animal, the irrational acting in the costumes and on the stage of the rational; and to illuminate the difficult and delicate reconciliation of the sensitively developed individual with the terms of his social existence.

"It is a truth universally acknowledged, that a single man in possession of a good fortune must be in want of a wife." This is the first sentence of the book. What we read in it is its opposite—a single woman must be in want of a man with a good fortune—and at once we are inducted into the Austen language, the ironical Austen attack, and the energy, peculiar to an Austen novel, that arises from the compression between a barbaric subsurface marital warfare and a surface of polite manners and civilized conventions. Marriage—that adult initiatory rite that is centrally important in most societies whether barbarous or advanced—is the upper-most concern. As motivated for the story, it is as primitively powerful an urgency as is sex in a novel by D. H. Lawrence. The tale is that of a man hunt, with the female the pursuer and the male a shy and elusive prey. The desperation of the hunt is the desperation of economic survival: girls in a family like that of the Bennets must succeed in running down solvent young men in order to survive. But the marriage motivation is complicated by other needs of a civilized community: the man hunters must observe the most refined behavior and sentiments. The female is a "lady" and the male is a "gentleman"; they must "fall in love." Not only must civilized appearances be preserved before the eyes of the community, but it is even necessary to preserve dignity and fineness of feeling in one's own eyes.

The second sentence outlines the area in which the aforementioned "truth universally acknowledged" is to be investigated—a small settled community, febrile with social and economic rivalry.

> However little known the feelings or views of such a man may be on his first entering a neighborhood, this truth is so well fixed in the minds of the surrounding families, that he is considered as the rightful property of some one or other of their daughters.

Here a high valuation of property is so dominant a culture trait that the word "property" becomes a metaphor for the young man himself; and the phrasing of the sentence, with typical Austen obliquity, adds a further sly emphasis to this trait when it uses an idiom associated with the possession of wealth—"well fixed"—as a qualifier of the standing of "truth." We are told that the young man may have "feelings or views" of his own (it becomes evident, later, that even daughters

2. D. W. Harding, "Regulated Hatred: An Aspect of the Work of Jane Austen," *Security* 8 (1940): 346–620. [See pp. 296–99 of this volume—*Editor*.]

are capable of a similar willful subjectivity); and we are warned of the
embarrassment such "feelings or views" will cause, whether to the individual or to the community, when we read of those "surrounding families" in whom "truth" is "so well fixed"—portentous pressure! And
now we are given a light preliminary draft of the esteemed state of
marriage, in the little drama of conflicting perceptions and wills that
the first chapter presents between the imbecilic Mrs. Bennet and her
indifferent, sarcastic husband. "The experience of three and twenty
years had been insufficient to make his wife understand his character."
The marriage problem is set broadly before us in this uneasy parental
background, where an ill-mated couple must come to terms on the
finding of mates for their five daughters. A social call must be made,
in any case, on the single gentleman of good fortune who has settled
in the neighborhood. With the return of the call, and with the daughters set up for view—some of whom are "handsome," some "good-
natured"—no doubt he will buy, that is to say, "fall in love" (with such
love, perhaps, as we have seen between Mr. and Mrs. Bennet themselves).

In this first chapter, the fundamental literary unit of the single
word—"fortune," "property," "possession," "establishment," "business"—has consistently been setting up the impulsion of economic
interest against those nonutilitarian interests implied by the words
"feelings" and "love."[3] The implications of the word "marriage" itself
are ambivalent; for as these implications are controlled in the book,
"marriage" does not mean an act of ungoverned passion (not even in
Lydia's and Wickham's rash elopement does it mean this: for Wickham has his eye on a settlement by blackmail, and Lydia's infatuation
is rather more with a uniform than with a man); marriage means a
complex engagement between the marrying couple and society—that
is, it means not only "feelings" but "property" as well. In marrying, the
individual marries society as well as his mate, and "property" provides
the necessary articles of this other marriage. With marriage so defined,
as the given locus of action, the clash and reconciliation of utility interests with interests that are nonutilitarian will provide a subtle drama
of manners; for whatever spiritual creativity may lie in the individual
personality, that creativity will be able to operate only within publicly
acceptable modes of deportment. These modes of deportment, however public and traditional, must be made to convey the secret life of
the individual spirit, much as a lens conveys a vision of otherwise invisible constellations. Language itself is the lens in this case—the linguistic habits of social man.

3. This point of view is developed by Mark Schorer in the essay "Fiction and the 'Analogical
   Matrix,'" in *Critiques and Essays on Modern Fiction*, edited by John W. Aldridge (New York:
   Ronald, 1952); 83–98. [Schorer's essay was first printed in *Kenyon Review* 11 (1949): 539–60,
   and reprinted in his collection of essays, *The World We Imagine* (New York: Farrar, Straus,
   Giroux, 1968) 24–45—*Editor*.]

* * *

Among the "daughters" and the "young men of fortune" there are a few sensitive individuals, civilized in spirit as well as in manner. For these few, "feeling" must either succumb to the paralysis of utility or else must develop special delicacy and strength. The final adjustment with society, with "property" and "establishment," must be made in any case, for in this book the individual is unthinkable without the social environment, and in the Austen world that environment has been given once and forever—it is unchangeable and it contains the only possibilities for individual development. For the protagonists, the marriage rite will signify an "ordeal" in that traditional sense of a moral testing which is the serious meaning of initiation in any of the important ceremonies of life. What will be tested will be their integrity of "feeling" under the crudely threatening social pressures. The moral life, then, will be equated with delicacy and integrity of feeling, and its capacity for growth under adverse conditions. In the person of the chief protagonist, Elizabeth, it really will be equated with intelligence. In this conception of the moral life, Jane Austen shows herself the closest kin to Henry James in the tradition of the English novel; for by James, also, the moral life was located in emotional intelligence, and he too limited himself to observation of its workings in the narrow area of a sophisticated civilization.

The final note of the civilized in *Pride and Prejudice* is, as we have said, reconciliation. The protagonists do not "find themselves" by leaving society, divorcing themselves from its predilections and obsessions. In the union of Darcy and Elizabeth, Jane and Bingley, the obsessive social formula of marriage-to-property is found again, but now as the happy reward of initiates who have travailed and passed their "ordeal." The incongruities between savage impulsions and the civilized conventions in which they are buried, between utility and morality, are reconciled in the symbolic act of a marriage which society itself—bent on useful marriages—has paradoxically done everything to prevent. Rightly, the next to the last word in the book is the word "uniting."

* * *

* * * An Austen novel offers a particularly luminous illustration of the function of style in determining the major form. It is here, in style, in the language base itself, that we are able to observe Jane Austen's most deft and subtle exploitation of her material.

The first sentence of the book—"It is a truth universally acknowledged, that a single man in possession of a good fortune must be in want of a wife"—again affords an instance in point. As we have said, the sentence ironically turns itself inside out, thus: a single woman must be in want of a man with a good fortune. In this doubling of the

inverse meaning over the surface meaning, a very modest-looking statement sums up the chief conflicting forces in the book: a decorous
convention of love (which holds the man to be the pursuer) embraces
a savage economic compulsion (the compulsion of the insolvent female
to run down male "property"), and in the verbal embrace they appear
as a unit. The ironic mode here is a mode of simultaneous opposition
and union: civilized convention and economic primitivism unite in the
sentence as they do in the action, where "feelings" and "fortune," initially in conflict, are reconciled in the socially creative union of marriage.

This is but one type of verbal manipulation with which the book
luxuriates. Another we shall illustrate with a sentence from Mr. Collins'
proposal to Elizabeth, where "significant form" lies in elaborate rather
than in modest phrasing. Mr. Collins manages to wind himself up
almost inextricably in syntax.

> "But the fact is, that being as I am, to inherit this estate after the
> death of your honored father, (who, however, may live many years
> longer,) I could not satisfy myself without resolving to chuse a
> wife from among his daughters, that the loss to them might be as
> little as possible, when the melancholy event takes place—which,
> however, as I have already said, may not be for several years."

Fancy syntax acts here, not as an expression of moral and intellectual
refinement (as Mr. Collins intends it to act), but as an expression of
stupidity, the antithesis of that refinement. The elaborate language in
which Mr. Collins gets himself fairly *stuck* is a mimesis of an action of
the soul, the soul that becomes self dishonest through failure to know
itself, and that overrates itself at the expense of social context, just as
it overrates verbalism at the expense of meaning. We have suggested
that moral life, in an Austen novel, is identified with emotional intelligence; and it is precisely through failure of intelligence—the wit to
know his own limitations—that Mr. Collins appears as a moral mon-
strosity. Language is the mirror of his degeneracy. Against Mr. Collins'
elaborate style of speech we may place the neat and direct phrasing of
a sentence such as "It is a truth universally acknowledged . . ." where
the balance of overt thesis and buried antithesis acts as a kind of signature of the intelligential life—its syntactical modesty conveying a
very deft and energetic mental dance.

* * *

Finally we should remark upon what is perhaps the most formative
and conclusive activity of style in the book: the effect of a narrowly
mercantile and materialistic vocabulary in setting up meanings. Let us
go down a few lists of typical words, categorizing them rather crudely
and arbitrarily, but in such a manner as to show their direction of

reference.[4] The reader will perhaps be interested in adding to these merely suggestive lists, for in watching the Austen language lies the real excitement of the Austen novel. We shall set up such categories as "trade," "arithmetic," "money," "material possessions," simply in order to indicate the kind of language Jane Austen inherited from her culture and to which she was confined—and in order to suggest what she was able to do with her language, how much of the human drama she was able to get into such confines. We could add such verbal categories as those referring to "patronage," "law," "skill" (a particularly interesting one, covering such words as "design," "cunning," "arts," "schemes," and so on; a category obviously converging with the "trade" category, but whose vocabulary, as it appears in this book, is used derogatorily—the stupid people, like Mrs. Bennet, Lady Catherine de Bourgh, Wickham, and Mr. Collins, are the ones who "scheme" and have "designs").

TRADE	ARITHMETIC	MONEY	MATERIAL POSSESSIONS	SOCIAL INTEGRATION
employed	equally	pounds	estate	town
due form	added	credit	property	society
collect	proportion	capital	owner	civil
receipt	addition	pay	house	neighborhood
buy	enumerate	fortune	manor	county
sell	figure	valuable	tenant	fashion
business	calculated	principal	substantial	breeding
supply	amount	interest	establishment	genteel
terms	amounting	afford	provided	marriage
means	inconsiderable	indebted	foundation	husband
venture	consideration	undervalue	belongs to	connection

* * * The general directions of reference taken by Jane Austen's language, as indicated by such lists as those given above (and the lists, with others like them, could be extended for pages), are clearly materialistic. They reflect a culture whose institutions are solidly defined by materialistic interests—property and banking and trade and the law that keeps order in these matters—institutions which determine, in turn, the character of family relations, the amenities of community life, and the whole complex economy of the emotions. By acknowledgment of the fact that the materialistic assumptions of our own culture are even more persuasive than those reflected in this book, and that their governance over our emotions and our speech habits is even more grim, more sterilizing, and more restrictive, we should be somewhat aided in appreciation of the "contemporaneity" of Jane Austen herself.

But where then, we must ask, does originality lie, if an author's very language is dictated in so large a part by something, as it were, "out-

---

4. Mr. Schorer's essay "Fiction and the 'Analogical Matrix,'" cited above, closely examines this aspect of Jane Austen's style.

side" himself—by the culture into which he is accidentally born? How can there be any free play of individual genius, the free and original play with the language by which we recognize the insight and innovations of genius? The question has to be answered separately for the work of each artist, but as for Jane Austen's work we have been finding answers all along—in her exploitation of antithetical structures to convey ambivalent attitudes, in her ironic use of syntactical elaborations that go against the grain of the language and that convey moral aberrations, and finally in her direct and oblique play with an inherited vocabulary that is materialistic in reference and that she forces—or blandishes or intrigues—into spiritual duties.

The language base of the Austen novel gives us the limiting conditions of the culture. Somehow, using this language of acquisitiveness and calculation and materialism, a language common to the most admirable characters as well as to the basest characters in the book, the spiritually creative persons will have to form their destinies. The project would be so much easier if the intelligent people and the stupid people, the people who are morally alive and the people who are morally dead, had each their different language to distinguish and publicize their differences! But unfortunately for that ease, they have only one language. Fortunately for the drama of the Austen novel, there is this difficulty of the single materialistic language; for drama subsists on difficulty. Within the sterile confines of public assumptions, the Austen protagonists find with difficulty the fertility of honest and intelligent individual feeling. On a basis of communication that is drawn always from the public and savage theology of "property," the delicate lines of spiritual adjustment are explored. The final fought-for recognitions of value are recognitions of the unity of experience—a unity between the common culture and the individual development. No one more knowledgeably than this perceptive and witty woman, ambushed by imbecility, could have conducted such an exploration.

ALISTAIR DUCKWORTH

Pride and Prejudice: The Reconstitution of Society†

More successfully than *Sense and Sensibility*, *Pride and Prejudice* moves from an initial condition of potential social fragmentation to a resolution in which the grounds of society are reconstituted as the principal characters come together in marriage. As in the former novel, there is

---

† From *The Improvement of the Estate: A Study of Jane Austen's Novels* (Baltimore and London: The Johns Hopkins University Press, 1971) 116–28, 140–43. Reprinted by permission of the publisher.

a recognition of widespread economic motivation in human conduct, but a more important bar, initially, to the continuity of a traditionally grounded society is the existence everywhere of separations—between classes in the context of society as a whole, between minds in the smaller context of the home.

The fragmentary nature of the novel's world is humorously evident from the beginning in the constitution of the Bennet family itself, as any number of scenes could illustrate. Consider, for example, the various reactions to Mr. Collins's letter announcing his intention to visit Longbourn:

> "There is some sense in what he says about the girls however;" [said Mrs. Bennet] "and if he is disposed to make them any amends, I shall not be the person to discourage him."
>
> "Though it is difficult," said Jane, "to guess in what way he can mean to make us the atonement he thinks our due, the wish is certainly to his credit."
>
> Elizabeth was chiefly struck with his extraordinary deference for Lady Catherine, and his kind intention of christening, marrying, and burying his parishioners whenever it were required.
>
> "He must be an oddity, I think," said she. "I cannot make him out.—There is something very pompous in his stile.—And what can he mean by apologizing for being next in the entail?—We cannot suppose he would help it, if he could.—Can he be a sensible man, sir?"
>
> "No, my dear; I think not. I have great hopes of finding him quite the reverse. There is a mixture of servility and self-importance in his letter, which promises well. I am impatient to see him."
>
> "In point of composition," said Mary, "his letter does not seem defective. The idea of the olive branch perhaps is not wholly new, yet I think it is well expressed."
>
> To Catherine and Lydia, neither the letter nor its writer were in any degree interesting. It was next to impossible that their cousin should come in a scarlet coat. . . .

Mr. Bennet's somewhat cynical irony, his wife's fixed concern to marry off her daughters, Jane's indiscriminate benevolence, Mary's pedantry, the youngest sisters' love of the military, are all evident, as, too, are Elizabeth's perceptiveness and special position (hers are the only thoughts reported). But beyond the humorous revelation of character the scene discloses an important concern of the novel. The meaning of any statement or action, such a method suggests, is not single, but multiple in ratio to the number of minds perceiving it. In such an individualistic—almost Shandean—world,[1] meaning is in danger of

---

1. The idiosyncratic world of Laurence Sterne's (1713–1768) *The Life and Options of Tristam Shandy, Gentleman* (1760–64) [*Editor*].

becoming a function of private desire, and all that does not accord with the individual vision is in danger of being discredited. Only when self-interest encounters self-interest, seemingly, is communication, indeed conversation, possible. Mr. Collins and Mrs. Bennet understand each other perfectly in their "tête-à-tête" before breakfast at Longbourn. When coincidence of interest is absent, mind is closed to mind and conversation is in vain, as Mrs. Bennet interminably complains about the injustice of the entail, Sir William Lucas recalls his presentation at St. James's, Mr. Collins descants on the beauty of Rosings.

The distances of the drawing room, moreover, are the mirror of social distances outside. As a "gulf impassable" seems to loom between Darcy and Elizabeth, so there are seemingly uncrossable distances between the aristocracy (Darcy and Lady Catherine), the gentry (the Bennets), and "trade" (the Philipses and the Gardiners). Those who were "formerly in trade"—the Lucases and the Bingleys—add mobility, but hardly continuity, to the social moment, as they seek landed security at their different levels.

How in this world of distances are people, and classes, to come together? This, the crucial question underlying *Pride and Prejudice*, is answered primarily through the education of the hero and heroine, whose union is not only to their mutual advantage, but brings together widely separate outlooks and social positions. As many critics have argued, it is in the mutuality of the concessions made by Elizabeth and Darcy that the novel's attraction lies. If Elizabeth's private vision is shown to be insufficient, then so, too, is Darcy's arrogant assumption that status is value-laden. Only when Elizabeth recognizes that individualism must find its social limits, and Darcy concedes that tradition without individual energy is empty form, can the novel reach its eminently satisfactory conclusion.[2]

That Darcy's pride is convincingly humiliated needs little documentation, but it is more important, I think, to consider Elizabeth's education in the novel. Hers is the only mind to which we are granted continual access, and through her internal development from a private to a social outlook we discover again that for Jane Austen an individ-

2. That *Pride and Prejudice* achieves an ideal relation between the individual and society seems now to be generally agreed. Cf. Lionel Trilling's succinct summary of the novel's thesis: "a formal rhetoric, traditional and rigorous, must find a way to accommodate a female vivacity, which in turn must recognize the principled demands of the strict male syntax" (*The Opposing Self* [1955] 222). Samuel Klinger's brilliant article, "Jane Austen's *Pride and Prejudice* in the Eighteenth-Century Mode," *University of Toronto Quarterly*, 16 (1947): 357–70, sets the novel in the context of the history of ideas, by showing how the various relationships of the novel depend upon commonplace antitheses of ethical and aesthetic debate—art and nature, the rules and originality—the impulse of the whole being toward a reconciliation of extremes and the establishment of a normative mean. Noting the "Whig" resonance of the hero's name, Donald J. Greene, in "Jane Austen and the Peerage," *PMLA*, 68 (1953): 1017–31, argues for a historical rapprochement, suggesting as a "unifying thesis" of the novel (and of Jane Austen's fiction) "the rise of the middle class, a process of which the middle class itself became acutely conscious when Pitt, in effect, overthrew the entrenched political power of the Whig aristocracy in 1784."

ual's moral duty is necessarily to society, properly understood, and that any retreat into a subjective morality is misguided. While *Pride and Prejudice* quite clearly looks with a critical eye upon automatic social responses, it also validates inherited social principles as they are made relevant to the conditions of the moment and properly informed by individual commitment. To support this argument, it will be necessary, first, to demonstrate how carefully Jane Austen has qualified Elizabeth's largely admirable individualism.[3]

For a long time the inadequacy of the heroine's outlook is concealed, as the narrative strategy emphasizes its undoubted virtues. Elizabeth's morality, when seen in action, is praiseworthy. * * * What is important to her are friendship and love, the mutual reciprocation of kindness and concern by two people—sisters, lovers, or friends. This present, all is excusable; this absent, nothing is. But the very reduction of the area of her moral concern renders her outlook susceptible, for, if the other in a close relationship fails to reciprocate affection or trust, disappointment must ensue. * * *

Elizabeth's experience with Wickham, of course, reveals this inadequacy * * *. Wickham is at first view "most gentlemanlike"; "he had all the best part of beauty, a fine countenance, a good figure, and very pleasing address." But these are external qualities only, and it is significant that we hear nothing of his "character," "understanding," "mind" —the inner qualities which Jane Austen invariably requires to inform the outward show. As Elizabeth herself will later realize, the "impropriety" of Wickham's communications at the first meeting is blatant; but, already prejudiced against Darcy, she accepts Wickham's slanderous perspective, and in later refusing Darcy's proposal of marriage will adduce as a major reason his treatment of Wickham: "In what imaginary act of *friendship* can you here defend yourself?" (my italics).

Wickham, it seems to Elizabeth initially, like herself and Jane, holds brief for the holiness of the heart's affections. He discovers value, so it appears, in friendship or in the spontaneous action of the self, and not in a conformity to sterile social principles. In this way, he is the opposite of Darcy, who, in Elizabeth's eyes, allows "nothing for the influence of friendship and affection." Thus, when Jane wishes to see both Wickham and Darcy as in some way right—"do but consider in what a disgraceful light it places Mr. Darcy"—Elizabeth refuses to be persuaded that Wickham's view is just another perspective on Darcy's character. "There was truth in his looks," she says of Wickham, "one

---

3. Not everyone would agree that *Pride and Prejudice* is a novel of the heroine's education. Marvin Mudrick, for example, finds Elizabeth's attitudes admirable and normative: "Like Mary Crawford later, Elizabeth is a recognizable and striking aspect of her author" (*Jane Austen: Irony as Defense and Discovery* [1952] 120). There is, Mudrick argues, "no compulsion—personal, thematic, or moral—toward denying the heroine her own powers of judgment" (197). But such a reading ignores the heroine's own gradual awareness of the excesses of her individualism.

knows exactly what to think." And at the Netherfield ball which follows, although it is Wickham and not Darcy who is absent—in spite of the former's assertion that he has "no reason for avoiding" Darcy—it is against Darcy that Elizabeth's "feeling of displeasure" is directed.

*   *   *

The relativistic (or better, perspectivistic) aspects involved in knowing another person are touched upon at the Netherfield Ball, where a conversation between Elizabeth and Darcy reveals the extent to which initial interpretations of character are constructions, or sketches, based on available (and often inadequate) information. When Elizabeth accuses Darcy of "an unsocial, taciturn disposition," he concedes that this may be a "faithful portrait" in her eyes; and when Elizabeth later questions him about his "temper," she admits that her questions are intended to provide an "illustration" of his character. Darcy has earlier been made aware of her meeting with Wickham, a fact that has bearing on the following exchange:

> She shook her head. "I do not get on at all. I hear such different accounts of you as puzzle me exceedingly."
>
> "I can readily believe," answered he gravely, "that report may vary greatly with respect to me; and I could wish, Miss Bennet, that you were not to sketch my character at the present moment, as there is reason to fear that the performance would reflect no credit on either."
>
> "But if I do not take your likeness now, I may never have another opportunity."

Darcy is here suggesting that Elizabeth should avoid basing her judgment of him on "report," whether the general report of Meryton or the particular report of Wickham. In either case the sketch she will draw will be partial, for its perspective will be limited. Darcy's true character is not to be immediately derived, as Wickham's character has been by Elizabeth, from external appearances. Unwilling to accede to Darcy's implied request that she postpone her judgment, however, Elizabeth takes his likeness now. Her decision angers Darcy, and they part, not to meet again until they come together at Hunsford.

There, in his letter to her following her rejection of his proposal, Elizabeth begins to see Darcy's character in a different "light" and to recognize how badly she has misjudged him from a too easy acceptance of Wickham's partial view and a too hasty response to externals—"every charm of air and address." The perspectivist theme is more importantly continued in the second great recognition scene, Elizabeth's visit to Pemberley. At Darcy's estate Elizabeth comes to an awareness of Darcy's intrinsically worthy character and of the deficiencies of her own outlook. Taken with her response to his letter, her visit to Derbyshire marks a crucial change in the direction of her critical views, which now turn inward on herself and her family, at the same time as her ethical outlook broadens to take in other than personal and interpersonal factors. At first, Pemberley seems only to add contradictory perspectives on the man; but on larger view the visit refutes perspectivism as a bar to true moral discrimination as it recognizes its inevitable existence in human relations.

*   *   *

At Pemberley, Darcy is "so desirous to please, so free from self-consequence" that had she and the Gardiners "drawn his character from their own feelings, and his servant's report, without any reference to any other account, the circle in Hertfordshire to which he was known, would not have recognized it for Mr. Darcy."[4] In his home Darcy is exemplary, and the description of his estate, though general, is a natural analogue of his social and moral character.

Pemberley is a model estate, possessing those indications of value that Jane Austen everywhere provides in her descriptions of properly run estates—beautiful trees, well-disposed landscapes, a handsome house, and finely proportioned rooms. Its grounds, while aesthetically pleasing, are quite without pretension or evidence of extravagance. There is a kind of scenic *mediocritas* about the estate, a mean between the extremes of the improver's art and uncultivated nature:

> It was a large, handsome, stone building, standing well on rising ground, and backed by a ridge of high woody hills;—and in front, a stream of some natural importance was swelled into greater, but without any artificial appearance. Its banks were neither formal, nor falsely adorned. Elizabeth was delighted. She had never seen a place for which nature had done more, or where natural beauty had been so little counteracted by an awkward taste.

Darcy had evidently given his estate the kind of "modern dress" Edmund Bertram calls for at Sotherton [in *Mansfield Park*]. There is perhaps something here, too, of a Shaftesburian recognition that excellent aesthetic taste denotes an excellence of moral character.[5] Thus, when Elizabeth comes to exclaim to herself that "to be mistress of Pemberley might be something," she has, we might conjecture, come to recognize not merely the money and the status of Pemberley, but its value as the setting of a traditional social and ethical orientation,

---

4. Mrs. Reynolds is not, however, without "family prejudice," and Jane Austen is careful to provide more than one view of Darcy even at Pemberley. The Lambton community view has "nothing to accuse him of but pride" but they also acknowledge his liberality and charity.

5. A point made by Walton Litz in *Jane Austen: A Study of Her Artistic Development* (1965) 103–4. Cf. also Martin Price's remarks in "The Picturesque Moment," in *From Sensibility to Romanticism*, ed. Frederick W. Hilles and Harold Bloom (1965) 268.

its possibilities—seemingly now only hypothetical—as a context for her responsible social activity.

Following Elizabeth's journey through the park the perspectivist theme is interestingly continued as she accompanies the housekeeper into the dining parlor:

> It was a large, well-proportioned room, handsomely fitted up. Elizabeth, after slightly surveying it, went to a window to enjoy its prospect. The hill, crowned with wood, from which they had descended, receiving increased abruptness from the distance, was a beautiful object. Every disposition of the ground was good; and she looked on the whole scene, the river, the trees scattered on its banks, and the winding of the valley, as far as she could trace it, with delight. As they passed into other rooms, these objects were taking different positions; but from every window there were beauties to be seen.

By looking through the dining parlor window, Elizabeth sees the "whole scene" from one point of view and "as far as she could trace it." She recognizes the harmony of the scene with delight. As she moves from room to room, however, the "objects were taking different positions." Nevertheless, it is still the same landscape that she views. Her position, not the disposition of the ground, is what has altered. By traveling first through the park, then by looking back over it, Elizabeth is made aware of the permanence of the estate and yet of the necessarily partial and angled view of the individual. She sees that no overall view is possible to the single vision, but that an approximation to such a view is possible provided the individual is both retrospective and circumspect. More than this, it is not only the angle of the view but the distance from the object which renders the individual sight fallible. An abrupt hill may have its steepness emphasized, just as Darcy's personal abruptness may be exaggerated, by the distance from which it is viewed.

Elizabeth's journey through the park, from its boundary to the house, is a spatial recapitulation of her association with Darcy from her first prejudiced impressions of his external appearance, through a recognition of other (and seemingly contradictory) views, to a final arrival at the central core of his character. As the reader follows Elizabeth's journey, he learns that although relativism and perspectivism are facts of existence—different people will see life from different windows, and movement through time and space inevitably provides different angles of view—variability is a function of human perception and not a characteristic of truth itself. That which is good and true in life resists the perversions of the individual viewpoint, as Pemberley is a beautiful scene from wherever it is viewed by Elizabeth.

*   *   *

As we see Elizabeth's prejudice modified, so we see Darcy's pride humbled.[6] But we have also learned, with Elizabeth, that Darcy possesses a "proper pride"—whose definition Mary Bennet, characteristically, has already supplied—and that much (if not all) of what had seemed "so high and so conceited" in his early behavior is open, retrospectively, to a more favorable interpretation.[7] Darcy's "proper pride" is not merely a stereotyped literary attitude but a well-established commitment to propriety in a time of collapsing standards—the pride of a responsible landlord who recognizes with some apprehension "in such days as these" that the norms by which men have lived for generations are in danger of neglect or destruction. * * * Darcy sees his role in life as a permanent one which will fix the nature of the self. "Disguise of every sort" is his abhorrence. His role-behavior is not to be considered an act of *mauvaise foi*, though the Sartrean accusation permits an instructive comparison. Like the "Presiding Judge" and "Chief Treasurer" for whom Sarte has so much distaste, Darcy—as Jane Austen describes him—identifies himself with his role.[8] There is nothing pejorative for Jane Austen in the belief that pride in function is a safeguard against contingency. Whereas for Sartre the acceptance of a role is the evasion of personal freedom, the refusal to see that we can act roles other than the one we now act, for Jane Austen freedom is only authentic when given a proper social context. This is not to say that social position for Jane Austen inevitably confers personal worth—the absurd pretensions of Lady Catherine and Mr. Collins, based as they are solely on position, are satirically exposed. It is to argue that Jane Austen affirms a positive interpretation of social role. Charlotte's marriage to Collins is not the total loss of integrity that Elizabeth considers it, for it shows her willingness to become part of society, to play a social part. Mr. Bennet, on the other hand, so much more witty and attractive than Charlotte, is a less than responsible character in his refusal to play a part. Always the spectator who watches others play their roles, quick to observe discrepancies or ridiculous mannerisms in a performance, Mr. Bennet himself refuses to adopt the role of father and landowner. His chosen freedom from social commitment and his withdrawal from the proper stage of his behavior are serious faults in his character.

* * * Though certain critics have seen the novel as the celebration

6. For an interesting reading of Darcy as a deflated version of the "patrician hero" figure in eighteenth century fiction, and of Elizabeth as an "anti-Evelina," refusing to take the sycophantic role of the typical Richardson-Burney heroine, see Kenneth L. Moler's chapter in *Jane Austen's Art of Allusion* (1968). Though Moler goes on to show that Jane Austen "does not allow her anti-Evelina to rout her patrician hero completely" [102], he is clearly not concerned to stress—as I am—the education of the heroine in the novel.
7. Reuben Brower points out how "the simultaneity of tonal layers" in the early conversations of the novel permits a favorable interpretation of many of Darcy's apparently rude utterances. (" 'Light and Bright and Sparkling': Irony and Fiction in *Pride and Prejudice*," in *The Fields of Light* [1951]).
8. Jean Paul Sartre, *Being and Nothingness*, trans. Hazel Barnes (1956) 485.

of the individual spirit, this is at best only half the story. The individual vision is inevitably partial, prone to relativistic impressionism, and in need of a social context. The special attraction of the novel is that it allows a vital personality herself to learn through retrospection the limitations of a private view. Elizabeth's final location within the park of Pemberley is also the self's limitation of its power to define its own essence, the heroine's recognition of moral and social limits within which she must live.

As Elizabeth enters the park, so what had been an enclosure opens to receive an infusion of individual energy. Though an admirable model of society, Pemberley, unlike Mansfield Park, is not a central focus, but a peripheral ideal to which Elizabeth moves. When Darcy leaves his ideal center and moves into the center of less perfect worlds—the assemblies of Meryton or the drawing rooms of Longbourn—his deficiencies become apparent. If Elizabeth's movement is from personality to character, Darcy's movement is from *persona* to person. His strict attention to his station and its duties, admirable as it is, must yet allow access to the claims of spontaneity and relaxation, whilst remaining vigilantly opposed to the social and ethical subversion of both unbridled freedom and passive indolence. If Elizabeth—to put it in the scenic terms of the novel—is out of place with muddy petticoats in the Netherfield drawing room, Darcy is equally "out of his element in a Ball-room."[9] When he wishes to introduce responsibility and tradition there by asking Elizabeth what she thinks of books, he is to be told, "I cannot talk of books in a ballroom." There are still spaces for spontaneity in the world of *Pride and Prejudice.* * * *

The novel is structurally balanced between the basic orientations of the two principals. The central chapters of Darcy's proposal and letter reveal that Elizabeth's objections to him are dual: he has ruined the happiness of her sister by his influence over Bingley, and he has been unjust to Wickham. If, as we have seen, Elizabeth's acceptance of Wickham's charges seriously called into question her personalist ethic, her first accusation is more valid. Darcy's prudent and social point of departure has led him to be blind to the real love that exists between Bingley and Jane. The best solution, clearly, is neither society alone, nor self alone, but self-in-society, the vitalized reconstitution of a social totality, the dynamic compromise between past and present, the simultaneous reception of what is valuable in an inheritance and the liberation of the originality, energy and spontaneity in the living moment. * * *

Recognizing (in "A Letter to William Elliot, Esq." [1795]) that authority needs "other support than the poise of its own gravity," [Edmund] Burke might be describing the characteristic limitation of

9. This quotation actually describes Lord Osborne in *The Watsons*, a character in some respects like Darcy.

Fitzwilliam Darcy. In calling "the impulses of individuals at once to the aid and control of authority," he might be describing Elizabeth's movement in the novel.[1] And in a passage from the *Reflections*, we may discover the thesis and antithesis of *Pride and Prejudice*. Burke requires as qualities of his ideal statesman a "disposition to preserve and an ability to improve" (193–94), and it is exactly these requirements which are united in the marriage of Darcy and Elizabeth. Darcy's is the disposition to preserve, Elizabeth's the ability to improve, and taken together they achieve a synthesis which is not only (as Elizabeth recognizes) a "union . . . to the advantage of both" but a guarantee of a broader union in the fictional world of the novel. By crossing the "gulf impassable," Elizabeth and Darcy provide a fixed moral and social center around which the other marriages group themselves. The Collinses—all prudence—and the Bingleys—all benevolence—will remain; ruling passions will continue to prevail in the Longbourn drawing room and at Lucas Lodge; the Wickhams will continue to move from place to place; relativism and perspectivism will not miraculously vanish from the Meryton community. All these faults, however, are but the surface discontinuities of a ground that is, by the marriage of Elizabeth and Darcy, substantial and well disposed.

STUART TAVE

Limitations and Definitions†

Jane Austen was fond of dancing and excelled in it. She often writes about it in her letters. It is the sort of thing one might expect, that enjoyment and ability in moving with significant grace in good time in a restricted space. In the earliest letter of hers that survives, written when she was twenty, she says, "I danced twice with Warren last night, and once with Mr. Charles Watkins, and, to my inexpressible astonishment, I entirely escaped John Lyford. I was forced to fight hard for it, however."[1] There is a lot of action going on in that small space. Even more important, three years later we find that she did dance with John Lyford, on an evening when she had what she calls an odd set of partners. "I had a very pleasant evening, however," she tells her sister, "though you will probably find out that there was no particular reason for it; but I do not think it worth while to wait for enjoyment until

---

1. *The Works of Edmund Burke* (1906) 5.77, 79–80.
† From *Some Words of Jane Austen* (Chicago: University of Chicago Press, 1973) 1–2, 12–15, 33–35. Reprinted by permission of The University of Chicago Press. The author's notes have been edited to provide references to the recent edition of Austen's letters.
1. *Jane Austen's Letters*, 3rd ed., ed. Deirdre Le Faye (Oxford and New York: Oxford University Press, 1995), 9–10 Jan. 1796, 2.

there is some real opportunity for it."[2] She does not fight for escape but makes the best use of the conditions, and if that's not the whole of art at least that is where it begins and that is where it ends. We need not fret or labor to refute them who think her novels limited because their dimensions are limited. It was never a problem that bothered her. She knew better. Those lines, forever quoted—about the little bit of ivory two inches wide and the work with so fine a brush as produces little effect after much labor—are not a serious account of her own art; they are quite other, an ironic contrast of her chapters with those of her schoolboy nephew who, in her affectionate fun, writes "strong, manly, spirited Sketches, full of Variety and Glow."[3] She knew that she had made the choice not of weakness and the merely female, but the choice of difficulty, originality, and meaning. She had always known the absurdity of an art that thinks it is strong and full and large because it tries to run in a large world.

* * *

The chronology of Jane Austen's novels is usually worked out with a quiet but unfailing care. She doesn't force the dates and their movement on the reader's attention, but they are there and they can be and have been worked out; they are evidently part of the basic structure which simply must be there for her to tell a story as they are primary conditions of life. In *Pride and Prejudice*, for example, the date of the ball at Netherfield is not given to us, but it can be determined from other information to be Tuesday, November 26. Much later in the novel this is confirmed when Bingley meets Elizabeth and says, "It is above eight months. We have not met since the 26th of November, when we were all dancing together at Netherfield." That exactness is important—"Elizabeth was pleased to find his memory so exact"— because it means that he remembers with feeling the last time he saw Jane. Whatever can happen happens in time, day by day, week by week, month by month. It is only in the romantic fancy of Catherine Morland [in *Northanger Abbey*] that nine years is "a trifle of time." In Jane Austen's reality things happen in a shorter compass and with measured urgency. What we are given of Elizabeth Bennet's life is about a year, from about October to October, the year in which she becomes twenty-one, and we can follow her in the parts of that time. If nothing much seems to be happening at any time we must be concerned for her. "With no greater events than these in the Longbourn family, and otherwise diversified by little beyond walks to Meryton, sometimes dirty and sometimes cold, did January and February pass away. March was to take Elizabeth to Hunsford." In the confines of little beyond the walks to Meryton Elizabeth has got to be doing better than letting the

2. *Letters*, 21–23 Jan. 1799, 38.
3. *Letters*, 16–17 Dec. 1816, 323.

time pass away. To go to Hunsford, for a welcome change, is not what she needs most. What has happened at this point is that the young woman who began this year with all her attractions and excellence of mind has, by a series of unfortunate events and chiefly her own mis-judgments, of which she is not yet aware, found herself disappointed. The danger for her is that what has happened will not lead her to rethink what she has been doing, to understand better those people who have not acted as she expected they would, to understand better why she was mistaken, to know herself better and gain in experience and strength. There was a time when she would not, for the sake of one individual, "change the meaning" of principle and integrity or blur the line between selfishness and prudence in matrimonial affairs. Now she is asking cynically what the difference is between the mercenary and the prudent motive, and where does discretion end and avarice begin. Now she is thankful to be visiting Hunsford, home of Mr. Collins and Charlotte, because stupid men are the only ones worth knowing after all. Now she is finding what she thinks is fresh life and vigor in the prospect of a tour to the Lake country. "What are men to rocks and mountains?" But those journeys become valuable only because they bring into her life not open spaces without responsibility but the surprising impetus of pressing new times.

In Jane Austen time moves softly but certainly, as a natural and inevitable line of life. It is measured by the watch and by the calendar, which mark its divisions, and in those divisions the characters must act appropriately if they are to live with a real fresh life and vigor. In those lives that seem to continue in much the same way from day to day, with little variety of incident, little touched by the world of large action, fixed in one place, there come, again and again, times to make a judg-ment, times to make a moral choice, and there is a certain amount of time in which to make it, an amount appropriate to know what should be known, feel what should be felt, think what should be thought, do what should be done, neither too quickly nor too slowly for the occa-sion. There is no choice of standing still. One cannot "dwell." If the Elizabeth Bennet who begins her twenty-first year does not respond properly, as she is faced by the successive events, of the shock of Char-lotte's marriage, of the seeming attractiveness and then the defection of Wickham, and so on through the many successive tests that face her, month by month, in this critical year of her life, if she does not learn from their experience more of the world and of herself, and whom she should love, if she succumbs to disappointment, she will not be the same girl in the same place one year older. She will be worse. There are examples of those to whom being in the same place year after year means becoming a vegetable, dozing on a sofa like Lady Bertram [in *Mansfield Park*]; she is innocuous, Lady Bertram, but she does harm by not acting, by not even knowing that she should be acting. Elizabeth is in greater danger and has her example of that close at home, because she has a lively mind; if it cannot grow under the pressures of time it will deteriorate and corrupt. She has seen in her father how a disappointment brought on by his own mistake, in choosing badly when he married, has made him reprehensible. He has abilities Elizabeth respects, she is grateful for his affectionate treatment of herself, but his behavior as a husband, his exposure of his wife to the contempt of her own children, is highly reprehensible. The talents he has, which might have done much for his daughters, in their ill-judged direction are productive of evils. The reader, who can afford to enjoy these talents, and who can see where Elizabeth derives hers, can see the ill-judged direction in which she may move.

*　*　*

The real freedom is in the life triumphing over the illusion that it escapes those limits which hold smaller spirits; it is in the life that transforms every impediment into an acquisition and fills its rooms and its moment.

That tight and demarcated little world, which may seem to us so restricted in its scope and in its assumptions about reality, becomes enormously exhilarating and liberating; it offers to those who are capable of exerting themselves to discover its meaning the control of the essential qualities of their lives; it challenges our own narrowness, our assumption of powerlessness or rebellion. The restrictions in the world of Jane Austen's heroines do not make their choices less significant. As boundaries become clear and close and alternatives are few and final, choice becomes more heroic. The more valuable way to approach her novels is not through the list of all the mighty matters and all the odd corners that she omits, as though her primary concern were to reject or withdraw from what she could not or did not want to touch in art. It is not helpful to say, with one critic of many, that she "feels compelled to tidy up life's customary messiness," because to say that is to make an assumption about life that is not hers. She knows, and she shows us in her novels, messy lives, and most people are leading them, even when the surface of life seems proper; but custom is not the first fact of life. Life is not a disorder to be ordered, a given mess on which those of tidy compulsions impose a tidiness. It is not a meaningless heap from which meaning is extracted by reduction and exclusion. Meaning is the first fact. It is obscured by inexperience, by miseducation, by deception, above all by internal blindness, but it is there and it is clear to the opened eye. She does not omit any more than a dancer omits clumsiness, but begins directly with what is essential, as the dancer begins with grace. The form of the dance does not suppress significant motion; by its order it sets free the dancer. Jane Austen's world is full, it has all the parts it needs and all of them are fully given to us as far as they are needed. All parts become luminous in a defining vision. Each part is located, each part can be explained, as far as it must be for purposeful word and action. Strong feelings rise in her characters, rightly and necessarily at moments of crisis, with pleasures and pains beyond what they have ever felt: the characteristic accompaniment of this increase of feeling is an increase in articulateness; they must often struggle for it but their stature is in proportion to their willingness to try for it and their eventual success in achieving the brightness of command.

That definition, clarity of atmosphere, fullness of articulation, with which she gives us the actions of men and women in common life, give her stories such original simplicity that it is understandable why even sophisticated critics have thought of her as a primitive. Her stories have a freshness and firstness, even while what we see seems to have happened many times before, and will happen again, because it is in the inevitable order of things; it is an old story, always beginning, the same story, always different. In that sense hers is a timeless world, where life repeats and renews itself in each well-lived individual life. And in that sense it is a spacious world, in which the measured movement of the dance can be found in every place. "There is nothing like dancing after all," Sir William Lucas says to Mr. Darcy. "I consider it as one of the first refinements of polished societies." "Certainly, Sir," Darcy replies, "and it has the advantage also of being in vogue amongst the less polished societies of the world.—Every savage can dance." Each man is right, of course, but of course each is being foolish in his exclusive statement. There is good dancing everywhere that men and women have mastered the arts of time and space, to move with meaning.

MARILYN BUTLER

Jane Austen and the War of Ideas:
Pride and Prejudice†

Of all the Austen novels, *Pride and Prejudice* seems at first glance the least likely to yield a conservative theme. Jane Austen herself playfully confessed that the impression it made was not serious:

> The work is rather too light, and bright, and sparkling; it wants shade; it wants to be stretched out here and there with a long chapter of sense, if it could be had; if not, of solemn specious

---

† From *Jane Austen and the War of Ideas* (Oxford: Clarendon Press, 1975) 197–98, 203–7, 210–13. Reprinted by permission of Oxford University Press. The author's notes have been edited to provide references to the recent edition of Austen's letters.

nonsense, about something unconnected with the story; an essay on writing, a critique on Walter Scott, or the history of Buonaparté, or anything that would form a contrast, and bring the reader with increased delight to the playfulness and epigrammatism of the general style.[1]

Although the remedies Jane Austen suggests are intentionally absurd, the critical observation itself reads like a genuine one. At any rate, generations of Jane Austen readers have agreed in finding *Pride and Prejudice* the lightest, most consistently entertaining, and least didactic of the novels.

It would not be in keeping with the serious-mindedness of modern scholarship to rest content with the popular view of *Pride and Prejudice* as having no meaning at all. But the commonest interpretations, however they differ from each other, agree in placing it well outside the sphere of the antijacobin novel.[2] Many modern critics have suggested that it appears deliberately to run counter to the conservative tendency which can hardly be gainsaid in *Sense and Sensibility* and *Mansfield Park*. In appearing before her readers in the guise of Elizabeth Bennet, Jane Austen—or so the argument runs—reveals herself the critic of various forms of orthodoxy.

A powerful and systematic interpreter of *Pride and Prejudice* as a progressive novel is Mr. Samuel Kliger, author of the essay "Jane Austen's *Pride and Prejudice* in the Eighteenth Century Mode."[3] Mr. Kliger develops the argument that *Pride and Prejudice* uses the familiar eighteenth-century antithesis between art and nature "as the ground of the book's action and its mode of organization" (362). He marshals a considerable number of instances in which the antithesis appears in relation to Elizabeth. Her "natural" piano-playing is compared, for example, with Mary's artificial performance; her impulsive walk through the mud to Netherfield contrasts with the cold, formal reservations expressed first by Mary, later by Miss Bingley. A series of episodes, in short, presents Elizabeth on the side of nature, feeling, impulse, originality, spontaneity. Mr. Kliger takes care, as he begins, to introduce a caveat. "Although Jane Austen's partiality for Elizabeth's vivid style is obvious, it would be a serious mistake to conclude that it was possible for either Jane Austen or her period to deprecate art altogether" (358). Nevertheless he does not doubt that on the whole Jane Austen sympathizes with a "natural" Elizabeth, a view which has star-

1. *Jane Austen's Letters*, 3rd ed., ed. Deirdre Le Faye (Oxford and New York: Oxford University Press, 1995) 4 Feb. 1813, 203.
2. By the anti-jacobin novel, Butler means late-eighteenth-century British fiction that in its plots and characterization participated in the reaction to ideas and threats enacted in the French Revolution. Anti-jacobin fiction, in Butler's argument, was especially concerned to offer a counterforce to sentimental writing that assumed human instincts were essentially good and that honored individual desire over the constraints and requirements of established institutions and practices [*Editor*].
3. *University of Toronto Quarterly*, 16 (1946–7): 357–71.

tling implications when he transfers his attention from style to the sphere of morals, and, especially, of class relationships. He sees the movement of the book as one of compromise and mutual instruction, as Elizabeth learns to take class into account, and Darcy comes to share "Elizabeth's genius for treating all people with respect for their natural dignity."[4] Nevertheless, the tendency of Mr. Kliger's closing paragraphs, in which he compares Elizabeth with the seventeenth-century Levellers, is clear-cut enough. According to this reading, Elizabeth, even if not wholly victorious, is Jane Austen's revolutionary heroine.

*   *   *

The more one examines the novel the more difficult it becomes to read into it authorial approval of the element in Elizabeth which is rebellious. It is true that, like all Jane Austen's fiction, *Pride and Prejudice* has an element of antithetical patterning. It is not true that the pattern is adequately summarized in the terms "nature" versus "art." To begin with, Mr. Kliger's simple transition from the aesthetic sphere to the socio-political sphere is a long step, far too long one suspects for Jane Austen. He remarks of the aesthetic discussion that the taste and temper of the times "required that excellence be found in a mean between two extremes" (358). It may be true of art, but it is not true of politics, especially in the aftermath of the French Revolution. There the debate is about the nature and hence the rights of man, and it scarcely admits of trimming. As it happens, all novels built on the consciously antithetical pattern, from Sterne's comparison in *Tristram Shandy* of the feeling with the intellectualizing, to Maria Edgeworth's many comparisons of the rational with the unthinking, are about the human question, not the aesthetic question, and are—as one would expect—perfectly clear about which side they favour.

In fact the antitheses in the novel by no means match Mr. Kliger's equation. They are far more complex and bewildering, since in many respects they cut across one another. To be sure Elizabeth, independent and informal, can be contrasted with Darcy, who is socially established and formal; Elizabeth's "low" mother, sisters and aunt offer themselves for comparison with Darcy's haughty aunt and cousin. But, equally, Elizabeth and Darcy together, each of them complex and censorious, are balanced against the simpler Jane and Bingley, and this may prove in the long run to be the more significant comparison. The obvious social contrasts between the two extended families and their connections have encouraged, latterly, some unduly sociological interpretations, in which the characters come to stand for certain classes and class attitudes. Elizabeth and Darcy, for example, believe respec-

---

4. 367. For a sophisticated variant of this reading—that Jane Austen shows herself, through Elizabeth, a "Tory radical," with a strong anti-aristocratic bias—see D. J. Greene. "Jane Austen and the Peerage," *PMLA* 68 (1953): 1017–31.

tively in "a personalist ethic" and "a prudent and social point of departure," and the parties behind them follow suit: "the novel is structurally balanced between the basic orientation of the two principals."[5] Yet of all the points made by the complex action, the most decisive are surely those which affect Darcy and Elizabeth in their private capacity, as individuals. And if this is true, the notion of a structure which opposes the two is at best a half-truth, at worst misleading.

When Darcy and Elizabeth are first introduced, we are aware of great differences of personality between them: enough, one might think, to justify the idea that they are indeed presented as polar opposites. At the first assembly Darcy is "discovered to be proud, to be above his company, and above being pleased; and not all his large estate in Derbyshire could then save him from having a most forbidding, disagreeable countenance." His hauteur seems as different as possible from Elizabeth's informality. "She had a lively, playful disposition, which delighted in anything ridiculous." Elizabeth certainly continues in the notion that she and Darcy are so different as to be totally incompatible. Her teasing of him while they dance reveals the extent of the contrast as she sees it:

> ". . . for the advantage of *some*, conversation ought to be so arranged as that they may have the trouble of saying as little as possible."
>
> "Are you consulting your own feelings in the present case, or do you imagine that you are gratifying mine?"
>
> "Both," replied Elizabeth archly; "for I have always seen a great similarity in the turn of our minds.—We are each of an unsocial, taciturn disposition, unwilling to speak, unless we expect to say something that will amaze the whole room, and be handed down to posterity with all the éclat of a proverb."
>
> "This is no very striking resemblance of your own character, I am sure," said he. "How near it may be to *mine*, I cannot pretend to say."

This, then, ironically conveys Elizabeth's view that there is no similarity in the turn of their minds: a hasty conclusion based on her hostile first impression of Darcy. And Darcy's view of Elizabeth is also coloured by his sense of a gulf between them; although for him it is not a difference of personality but of social status, an objective fact related to the dignity of his own family, and to the vulgarity of some of Elizabeth's connections.

Apparently many readers are persuaded by the opinions of the two protagonists that they should see in the love-story of *Pride and Prejudice* a meeting of opposites. Yet from the beginning the evidence sup-

5. Alistair Duckworth, *"Pride and Prejudice:* The Reconstitution of Society," *The Improvement of the Estate* (1971) 142. [See pp. 306–15 in this volume—*Editor.*]

plied by independent witnesses and, surely, by the author herself shows that the two protagonists are mistaken. Whenever Elizabeth discusses Darcy's faults, she touches, though often unconsciously, upon her own. She notices at once, for example, that he is, like her, a critic of others. "He has a very satirical eye, and if I do not begin by being impertinent myself, I shall soon grow afraid of him." In discussing his faults with Darcy, she gets him to admit to what he calls resentfulness, which is an unwillingness to change his mind once he has decided to censure someone. "My good opinion once lost is lost for ever." Elizabeth calls this "a failing indeed"; but Darcy's disapproval of Wickham is not more obstinate (and of course it turns out to be more reasonably founded) than Elizabeth's own wilful dislike of Darcy. Although for different reasons, both are equally likely to be severe on others:

> "There is, I believe, in every disposition a tendency to some particular evil, a natural defect, which not even the best education can overcome."
> "And *your* defect is a propensity to hate everybody."
> "And yours," he replied with a smile, "is wilfully to misunderstand them."[6]

Darcy's theory of human nature implies a curiously blended attitude towards his own: in theory he admits he is fallible, but the real impression left is one of pride. For Elizabeth, too, the quality that goes with severity about others is complacency towards the self. As Jane Austen's prayers show, this disposition to think well of the self and ill of others is the opposite of what she conceives to be the Christian's duty:

> Incline us oh God! to think humbly of ourselves, to be severe only in the examination of our own conduct, to consider our fellow-creatures with kindness, and to judge of all they say and do with that charity which we would desire from them ourselves.[7]

In *Pride and Prejudice* Jane Austen presents Miss Bingley and her sister Mrs. Hurst, who are "proud and conceited," and, because fashionable, conceive themselves "entitled to think well of themselves, and meanly of others." These have also been Darcy's faults, as eventually he humbly confesses;

> "I have been a selfish being all my life, in practice, though not in principle. As a child . . . I was given good principles, but left to follow them in pride and conceit . . . I was spoilt by my parents, who . . . allowed, encouraged, almost taught me to be selfish and overbearing, to care for none beyond my own family circle, to think meanly of all the rest of the world, to *wish* at least to think

---

6. In this case, as in many others, Elizabeth's phrasing is far more exaggerated, and in fact untrue, in relation to Darcy, than his perfectly accurate observation about her.
7. *Minor Works*, ed. R. W. Chapman, rev. ed. (1963) 189.

meanly of their sense and worth compared with my own. . . . You
taught me a lesson, hard indeed at first, but most advantageous.
By you, I was properly humbled."

The subject of *Pride and Prejudice* is what the title indicates: the sin
of pride, obnoxious to the Christian, which takes the form of a complacency about the self and a correspondingly lower opinion, or prejudice, about others. Darcy's pride is humbled mid-way through the
novel, when he proposes to Elizabeth and to his astonishment is
rejected. The lesson he has to learn is not quite that it is hard for a
rich man to enter the kingdom of heaven; it is more that we have no
innate worth, either of social status or abilities. We have to earn our
right to consideration by respect for others, and continuous watchfulness of ourselves.

Elizabeth's corresponding sin is more subtle and her enlightenment
requires the space of the whole book. To begin with she seems unconscious that she suffers from pride at all. Quick of observation, encouraged by her father's example to take delight in the follies and vanities
of others, she sees everyone's mistakes but her own. The false proffers
of friendship from Miss Bingley and Mrs. Hurst do not deceive her:
she already has too low an opinion of them. She is quick to see and
enjoy the foibles of Mr. Collins, as she has always taken pleasure from
those of Sir William Lucas. But she also quite unreasonably persists in
thinking ill of Darcy, and, just as perversely, in thinking well of Wickham, even when the evidence that he is a fortune-hunter is placed
before her. Elizabeth's pride in her own fallible perceptions is her governing characteristic.

*   *   *

The most central of the antitheses in the novel is the one which
contrasts the attitudes of the two pairs of central characters to the
people around them. Darcy and Elizabeth are similar in being "satirical": they tend consistently to adopt a low opinion of others. In this
they are continuously compared with the other couple, Bingley and
Jane, who are modest about themselves and charitable about others.
"Your humility, Mr. Bingley, must disarm reproof," says Elizabeth, in
pointed reference to the arrogance of Darcy. Bingley thinks well of the
people of Meryton, Darcy ill. The arrogant Darcy is convinced, wrongly,
that Elizabeth loves him; Bingley is too diffident about himself to
believe that Jane returns his feeling. The same contrast is more thoroughly worked out in the conversations between Elizabeth and Jane,
where it is of more moment because Elizabeth's moral errors matter
more to the reader than Darcy's. Elizabeth has always admired Jane
for her "candour," her generous capacity to think well of others, and
at several points in the novel she pays general tribute to the quality

while in the individual case persisting in her own characteristically astringent view. Jane is surely too kind in thinking Charlotte's motives in marrying Mr Collins may not be narrowly prudential; she has to admit that she was overcharitable about Miss Bingley; she did not see through Wickham; but she was right in two important instances, in detecting goodness where it really was—in Bingley and in Darcy. After Wickham has spread his slanders about Darcy at Meryton, Jane alone resists taking a prejudiced, hasty, or ill-natured view:

> . . . everybody was pleased to think how much they had always disliked Mr. Darcy before they had known anything of the matter.
>   Miss Bennet was the only creature who could suppose there might be any extenuating circumstances in the case, unknown to the society of Hertfordshire; her mild and steady candour always pleaded for allowances, and urged the possibility of mistakes— but by everybody else Mr. Darcy was condemned as the worst of men.

Elizabeth's conversations with Jane, in which she is gently urged to take a more candid view, counterpoint her conversations with Darcy, in which we see her ill-founded prejudices in action.

Now this clearly *is* the kind of antithesis in which a balance is meant to be struck. Many critics have echoed Elizabeth's remark, "intricate characters are the *most* amusing." We would not exchange Elizabeth's intelligence for Jane's innocence, nor Darcy's consistency for Bingley's pliancy, even though the faults of the central couple lead them into worse moral error. But in fact the author does not want us to—it is clear that her view of the truly Christian character blends the best qualities of all four. Elizabeth and Darcy take a properly pessimistic view of human liability to err, and, rightly applied, their perceptiveness will be a great moral quality: for Jane Austen insists that the scrupulous self-knowledge which she prizes is the product of their kind of sceptical intelligence. The example of the other couple helps them to harness their talents to more Christian ends, by showing charity towards others and humility towards themselves. To this extent Mr. Kliger's general- ization applies: in the comparison between the two central couples, faults are identified with excesses in either extreme, and excellence lies in the mean. But the different beliefs that divide Elizabeth and Jane are not fundamental, for they concern the proper application of prin- ciples which they both share. Elizabeth's satire versus Jane's candour is a very different polarization from nature versus art, and it can never suggest to us that over the novel as a whole Jane Austen compromises between two views of human nature. Her moral ideal is clear: it is mostly nearly approached by Darcy and Elizabeth at the point when they have acknowledged the necessity of Jane and Bingley's humility and candour. In their ultimate state of enlightenment, Jane Austen's hero and heroine illustrate a view of human nature that derives from orthodox Christian pessimism, not from progressive optimism. The theme of the moral education of Elizabeth, which is paralleled by that of Darcy, does not sanction but rebukes the contemporary doctrine of faith in the individual.

If in nothing else, a clue to the conservatism of the novel lies in the original title, "First Impressions." Mr. B. C. Southam has suggested that *Pride and Prejudice* may have begun as a burlesque on that popular theme.[8] Jane Austen had already employed it satirically more than once, for both *Love and Friendship* and *Sense and Sensibility* mock the convention of love at first sight; and, in doing so, express conservative scepticism about the "truth" of man's spontaneous feelings. It is possible that Jane Austen meant to ridicule the hackneyed theme by standing it on its head: what *she* offers is hate at first sight. In any case, as she develops her plot in the final version, it is clear that to her love at first sight and hate at first sight are essentially the same. Both are emotional responses, built on insufficient or wrong evidence, and fostered by pride and complacency towards the unreliable subjective consciousness. It may well have been that with such a title the early version was more dogmatic; it belongs, after all, to 1796–7, years of great partisan activity in the novel, and approximately the era of the early work on *Sense and Sensibility*. Yet, for all its polish and technical maturity, the finished *Pride and Prejudice* has not, evidently, modified its ideological stance. As a novel it is far better than *Sense and Sensibility*, but no less conservative.

* * *

NINA AUERBACH

Waiting Together: *Pride and Prejudice*†

Anxious and uneasy, the period which passed in the drawing-room, before the gentlemen came, was wearisome and dull to a degree, that almost made her uncivil. She looked forward to their entrance, as the point on which all her chance of pleasure for the evening must depend.

---

8. *Jane Austen's Literary Manuscripts* (1964) 59–62.
† Reprinted by permission of the publisher from *Communities of Women: An Idea in Fiction* by Nina Auerbach (Cambridge: Harvard University Press, 1978) 38–46, 48–55. Copyright © 1978 by The President and Fellows of Harvard College. The notes have been edited to provide references to the recent edition of Austen's letters.

Since Elizabeth Bennet has passed her life in a world of waiting women, and we have passed it with her for much of the previous two volumes of the novel, this passage need describe such a world only as a temptation to lose one's temper. The story, the glow, will begin with the opening of the door.

In an earlier description of a similar situation we are given a chance, not so much to hear what women say to each other during this excruciating period, as to have our attention called to the distrust and emotional pressure that forbid their saying anything:

> Elizabeth soon saw that she was herself closely watched by Miss Bingley, and that she could not speak a word, especially to Miss Darcy, without calling her attention. This observation would not have prevented her from trying to talk to the latter, had they not been seated at an inconvenient distance; but she was not sorry to be spared the necessity of saying much. Her own thoughts were employing her. She expected every moment that some of the gentlemen would enter the room. She wished, she feared that the master of the house might be amongst them; and whether she wished or feared it most, she could scarcely determine.

Darcy has gently commanded that Elizabeth and his sister like each other, but his absent presence is the only emotional point of reference for all three women. Waiting for the entrance of the gentlemen, their shared world is a limbo of suspension and suspense, which cannot take shape until it is given one by the opening of the door.

The unexpressed intensity of this collective waiting for the door to open and a Pygmalion to bring life into limbo defines the female world of *Pride and Prejudice*; its agonized restraint is reflected microcosmically in the smaller community of the Bennet family, and macrocosmically in the larger community of England itself. With a nod to Pritchett, Jane Austen's most recent biographer allows her to touch British history in a manner that most admirers of her self-enclosed miniatures have forbidden: "In his *George Meredith and English Comedy*, V. S. Pritchett has a challenging aside in which he describes Jane Austen as a war novelist, pointing out that the facts of the long war are basic to all her books. She knew all about the shortage of men, the high cost of living, and . . . about the vital part played by the Navy."[1] In presenting these drawing rooms full of women watching the door and watching each other, Jane Austen tells us what an observant, genteel woman has to tell about the Napoleonic Wars: she writes novels about waiting.

As her England is in large part a country of women whose business it is to wait for the return of the men who have married them or may

1. Jane Aiken Hodge, *Only A Novel: The Double Life of Jane Austen* (1973) 238–39.

do so, so her heroine's family has occupied much of its history in waiting, with increasing hopelessness, for a male to enter it:

> When first Mr. Bennet had married, economy was held to be perfectly useless; for, of course, they were to have a son. This son was to join in cutting off the entail, as soon as he should be of age, and the widow and younger children would by that means be provided for. Five daughters successively entered the world, but yet the son was to come; and Mrs. Bennet, for many years after Lydia's birth, had been certain that he would. This event had at last been despaired of, but it was then too late to be saving. Mrs. Bennet had no turn for economy, and her husband's love of independence had alone prevented their exceeding their income.

In the family microcosm, the male whom all await can alone bring substance: by inheriting the estate, he will ensure the family the solidity and continuity of income and land. Without him, their emotional and financial resources, and ultimately the family itself, can only evaporate. The quality of the Bennet household is determined by the Beckett-like realization that the period of protracted waiting is not a probationary interim before life begins: waiting for a male is life itself.

The Bennet home, as its name indicates, is not an autonomous, self-sustaining entity: unlike Lucas Lodge, the home of their neighbors, Longbourn House bears the name of the village in which it is set, although a son might have changed its name to his own. This interchangeability of name between village and home suggests the primacy of "the neighborhood" in *Pride and Prejudice*, a primacy which nobody questions. The walls of the family are made of brittle glass: when Longbourn House receives a piece of news, its inhabitants do not gather together to savor it; * * * they disperse it instantly to the neighborhood, which makes of it what malicious use it may. Elizabeth Bennet accepts this primacy, though like her father, she makes conversational capital out of its absurdity: "If he means to be but little at Netherfield, it would be better for the neighborhood that he should give up the place entirely, for then we might possibly get a settled family there. But perhaps Mr. Bingley did not take the house so much for the convenience of the neighborhood as for his own, and we must expect him to keep or quit it on the same principle." The family exists to feed the neighborhood, and not the other way round. The reductio ad absurdum of this priority is Mr. Bennet's mordant: "For what do we live, but to make sport for our neighbors, and laugh at them in our turn?" Although the habitual Bennet note of self-mockery makes these speeches slippery as statements of belief, "we" clearly cannot live for families who are so nearly interchangeable with neighbors; and in fact, when Elizabeth and Jane marry Darcy and Bingley, we learn of their activities in their new neighborhood of Derbyshire rather than of the new families they start. This is a world far from Jo March's euphoric cry at the conclusion of [Louisa May Alcott's] *Little Women*: "I do think that families are the most beautiful things in all the world!" In *Pride and Prejudice* they are the most beautiful things in all the world to leave: "There was novelty in the scheme [of Elizabeth's journey to Hunsford], and as, with such a mother and such uncompanionable sisters, home could not be faultless, a little change was not unwelcome for its own sake."

The two evasive double negatives that suggest Elizabeth's nonfeeling for her nonfamily suggest also the most striking characteristic of the Bennet ménage: its nonexistence. Austen boasted to her sister of the success with which she had "lop't and crop't"[2] the manuscript of *Pride and Prejudice*, and I suspect that it was the scenes among the Bennets that were lop't and crop't, for the version we have contains scarcely any fully developed sequence in which the family are alone together. It is true that in the second chapter, "the girls" all flock around Mr. Bennet in rapture at his having paid a call on Bingley, but this is the last time they act in concert. After their first shared joy at this possible escape from home * * * the unity between the sisters fractures, the two younger raucously pursuing officers in Meryton and the two elder more decorously pursuing gentility at Netherfield, while plain Mary disappears at home into being a mouthpiece of platitudes. The groupings between the sisters are rigidly separate and hierarchical. During her brief infatuation with Wickham, Elizabeth steps across a wide gulf as she moves from Jane's camp into Lydia's and, when her vision clears, shifts with mortification back into Jane's. There is none of the emotional fluidity that exists among the March sisters, with each older girl mothering a younger one, the one most different from herself: the passionate tomboy Jo appropriates saintly Beth, while gentle, domestic Meg nurtures vain, ambitious Amy. In *Pride and Prejudice* this cross-fertilization and balance of opposing temperaments would threaten to complete a circle that by definition can never be complete, as long as a "single man in possession of a good fortune" exists who is "in want of a wife"—or is wanted by one. For, according to the mother-evolved dictum of the famous first sentence, such a quintessence of eligibility *must* be both wanting and wanted. These two words take us out of the novelistic sphere of contingent, palpable reality into a world of wish and vision, somewhere between injunction and hope, command and prayer. Its replacement of "is" by "must be" lifts us from the empirical to the absolute, in a false, feminine similitude of logical necessity whose note of wishful command gives the texture of a world ruled by women but possessed by men.

We are not allowed to see Longbourn House until a man does; for

---

2. *Jane Austen's Letters*, 3rd ed., ed. Deirdre Le Faye (Oxford and New York: Oxford University, Press, 1995), 29 Jan. 1813, 202 [*Editor*].

the reader as for its inhabitants, it is an insubstantial place that exists to be left. Though Jane Austen's descriptions never number the streaks of the tulip, she is almost always precise; but Longbourn is so impalpable that even such a precisionist as R. W. Chapman must search for a misprint to explain its shifting design.[3] When the unregenerate Lydia returns to make everybody miserable as the family's first bride, and looks "eagerly round the room, [takes] notice of some little alteration in it, and observe[s], with a laugh, that it [is] a great while since she [has] been there," it matters to nobody what the little alteration might be. Details of Longbourn are not "known, and *loved* because they are known," as George Eliot will put it in *The Mill on the Floss*: here and elsewhere, notice of the house evokes the joy of absence from it, not presence in it. Lydia's wedding parties crystallize the role of the household in the novel as a whole: "these parties were acceptable to all; to avoid a family circle was even more desirable to such as did think, than such as did not." Meg, the eldest and so the natural first bride of the March household, will turn longingly back to the circle immediately after her wedding ceremony, crying, "The first kiss for Marmee!" But Lydia, the youngest and her mother's favorite, leaves with never a backward glance a family we have never seen together, a house with wavering contours and rooms we cannot visualize. The near-invisibility of Longbourn and the collective life of the Bennets within it is at one with its economic invisibility under an entail which denies a family of women legal existence. Mrs. Bennet is a constant shrill reminder of the entail's overweening power over the family unit, and Jane Austen presents Longbourn House in part as Mrs. Bennet perceives it—as an inherently lost and already half-vanished mirage.

Further erosion of Longbourn's solidity comes from its lack of a past. The inhabitant with whom we are most intimate is Elizabeth, and for her the house has none of the density and texture which a childhood in it would bring. Though she scrupulously watches and analyzes and talks, Elizabeth is beyond a certain point devoid of memory. "The *present* always occupies you in such scenes—does it?" says Darcy to her "with a look of doubt," and she answers half-consciously, "yes, always." Later he tries to lead her back into her past by saying, "*You* cannot have a right to such very strong local attachment. *You* cannot have been always at Longbourn." We never know the answer. Elizabeth merely "look[s] surprised" and is silent. Elizabeth Bennet is the only one of Austen's heroines who is deprived of a childhood and a setting for her childhood. Marianne Dashwood's rhapsody [in *Sense and Sensibility*] to the "dear, dear Norland" she is forced out of would have

3. In his edition of the novel R. W. Chapman preserves a sentence that, he later discovered, had been corrected by Cassandra Austen in her copy of the novel: an upstairs dressing room had mistakenly been described as a downstairs drawing room (Oxford edition 2:395–96) [*Editor*].

some resonance for all the rest. Only Elizabeth shares none of Maggie Tulliver's later panic at childhood dislodged [in George Eliot's *The Mill on the Floss*]: "The end of our life will have nothing in it like the beginning." With her home a vacuum and her memory a blank, such an end can only be Elizabeth's dearest wish.

After the engagement, when she is coming sufficiently close to Darcy to begin to educate him, one of her first pedagogical gifts is her cool repudiation of memory: "You must learn some of my philosophy. Think only of the past as its remembrance gives you pleasure." Darcy chivalrously denies such a philosophy in his "dearest, loveliest Elizabeth"; but shortly thereafter, in speaking of him to Jane, she uses this philosophy to obliterate a great part of Darcy: "You know nothing of [my dislike of him]. *That* is all to be forgot. Perhaps I did not always love him so well as I do now. But in such cases as these, a good memory is unpardonable. This is the last time I shall ever remember it myself." The novel's mode of perception suggests the seriousness of Elizabeth's jokes. If she shares nothing else with her mother, her faculty of non-remembrance confirms Mrs. Bennet's perception of the nonlife they have had together.

Oddly, it is men who bring domestic substance into the representation of this world. Dorothy Van Ghent writes beautifully about the physicality that somehow emerges from Jane Austen's spare language: "Curiously and quite wonderfully, out of her restricted concern for the rational and social definition of the human performance there does arise a strong implication of the physical."[4] But men alone endow female existence with this physicality. Mrs. Bennet is perpetually begging any and all eligible males to come to a dinner we have never seen the family at Longbourn eat, as if only in their presence can nourishment present itself. The first male to grace their table is Mr. Collins, and in token of the reality of male appetite, Mrs. Bennet gives us the first domestic detail of Longbourn we have seen—a fish they do not have: "But—good lord! how unlucky! there is not a bit of fish to be got to-day. Lydia, my love, ring the bell. I must speak to Hill, this moment." Mr. Collins brings a sense of domestic reality to Longbourn by his interminable descriptions of the arrangements and situation of Hunsford; he even permits us to hear about "some shelves in the closets up stairs," which stand out vividly in a house that as far as we know has neither closets nor shelves. While the sonorous presentation of these details reminds us primarily of the weighty tedium of Mr. Collins' self-absorption, like Miss Bates's outpourings in *Emma* they also unob-

---

4. Dorothy Van Ghent, *The English Novel: Form and Function* (1953) 103. [See pp. 299–306— *Editor*.] Ellen Moers's discussion of "female realism" in *Literary Women* (1976) 67–89, uses *Pride and Prejudice* and *Little Women* to construct a female tradition honoring the "Monday voices" of concrete and pragmatic workaday reality. But in the Bennet family at least, money and the job are most strongly felt by virtue of their thwarting absence.

trusively fill the world in a manner that looks forward to the opulently detailed presentation of Darcy's Pemberley.

Pemberley is Elizabeth's initiation into physicality, providing her with all the architectural solidity and domestic substance Longbourn lacks. It has real grounds, woods, paths, streams, rooms, furniture; real food is eaten there: "The next variation which their visit afforded was produced by the entrance of servants with cold meat, cake, and a variety of all the finest fruits in season; . . . though they could not all talk, they could all eat, and the beautiful pyramids of grapes, nectarines, and peaches, soon collected them round the table." The "pyramids" of fruit suggest both architectural and natural power, neither of which is available in the blank space of her mother's house. Surely, to be mistress of Pemberley is "something," in view of the imprisoning nothing of being mistress at Longbourn. But when Bingley and Darcy appear there for dinner at last, in all the glory of prospective husbandness, food seems to spring into abundance for the first time: "The dinner was as well dressed as any I ever saw. The venison was roasted to a turn—and everybody said, they never saw so fat a haunch. The soup was fifty times better than we had at the Lucas's last week; and even Mr. Darcy acknowledged, that the partridges were remarkably well done; and I suppose he has two or three French cooks at least." For the first time, Mrs. Bennet applies the numbers with which she is obsessed, not to abstract and invisible sums of money, but to the immediately edible and nourishing. Contrary to sentimental myth, it is not women but available men whose presence makes a house a home.

If men can bring what seems a cornucopian abundance to the scanty Bennet dinner table, men also create whatever strength of sisterhood we see in the novel. If at times the fight for male approval prevents cooperation among women,[5] the mysterious power of a man can also draw women together under its aegis. During the many confidences we see between Elizabeth and Jane, they talk of nothing but Bingley and Darcy, speculating over their motives and characters with the relish of two collaborators working on a novel. Moreover, Lydia is never so much their sister as when she disgraces herself with Wickham and seems to spoil their chances of marriage as well: unwanted family solidarity is created by sexual disgrace as it is celebrated in sexual triumph. *The Watsons*, Austen's fragmentary beginning of a novel, defines more baldly the law that a family of women is never so much a family as when one member finds a man to remove her from it: "We must not all expect to be individually lucky replied Emma. The Luck of one member of a Family is Luck to all.—"[6] Not merely is the descriptive

---

5. As it almost invariably does in Patricia Beer's witty book, *Reader, I Married Him: A Study of the Women Characters of Jane Austen, Charlotte Brontë, Elizabeth Gaskell and George Eliot* (1974) 76.

6. *Minor Works*, ed. R. W. Chapman (1969) 321.

energy of the novel reserved for the homes the girls marry into: only the presence of suitors brings substance to the families they leave. The law governing the technique of *Pride and Prejudice* is at one with Mrs. Bennet's economic obsession: marriage and marriage alone gives the world contour.

The vaporousness of Longbourn, as a narrative center and as an empty reflection in memory, is surprising in view of the primacy of the family in Austen's other novels. Darcy will emphasize its role as moral shaper, second in significance only to his loving adult encounters with his "dearest, loveliest Elizabeth." In the other novels, no matter how distant family relationships might be, expulsion thence is in some sense a loss of Eden; the family is enriched by its traditional incarnation as a microcosm of society, endowing the life within it with weight and purpose, if not the intimacy later writers learned to want.[7]

*   *   *

The lack of texture in Austen's delineation of a family of women is the more surprising in that during her major creative period she lived in one. The household at Chawton in which she lived between 1809 and her death in 1817 consisted of herself, her sister Cassandra, their widowed mother, their unmarried friend Martha Lloyd, and sometimes brother James' daughter Cassy, lacking even the token nonauthoritative male the novels provide to give the little community official identity. * * *

Except in the independent and possibly defensive orbit between Jane and Cassandra, this community of four manless women is never depicted as intimate, but always as encroaching and intruding. Yet the Jane Austen we still want to know about was born there; it was at Chawton that she finally outgrew the role of family court jester and came to see herself as a serious writer, her books as alive. It is significant that her first serious projects there were almost certainly the recasting of *Sense and Sensibility* and *Pride and Prejudice*, both of which deal extensively with the vacuum that is the lives of "superfluous" women. If these novels were originally epistolary, as some critics suggest, her recasting from letters into dramatized narrative would throw the sisters into a proximity impossible in the old form, which may reflect the intimacy of the new female world in which she lived.[8] Though she may have been inspired by a sense of her new life's vacuity, inspired she was, and the Chawton community, almost always deplored as an impediment, must be given credit for some of the same generative power that living with George Henry Lewes possessed for George Eliot.

---

7. For Austen's relation to the tradition of the familial Eden, see R. F. Brissenden, "Mansfield Park: Freedom and the Family," in *Jane Austen: Bicentenary Essays*, ed. John Halperin (1975) 156–71.
8. See B. C. Southam, *Jane Austen's Literary Manuscripts* (1964) 55–60.

Some of the strength of Chawton's productive impetus may have come from the fact that, as with Longbourn House, its existence as a family was indistinguishable from its life as a neighborhood. Not only did it function as a clearinghouse for the next generation of Austens and their social lives, but the house itself was caught between its private and public characters: according to the *Memoir* written by Jane Austen's nephew [*A Memoir of Jane Austen* (2nd ed., 1871)], it was originally built as an inn and after 1845 was divided into "tenements for labourers," retaining some of its original collective function (85–86). "Very snug" they might have been at Chawton, but the outside world poured through it, and the pressure of people fed into the pressure of art, endowing a real female community with a power for which we must be grateful.

But it is on this very issue of direct female power that Jane Austen's novels are most equivocal. Beginning with such trivial incidents as the married Lydia's displacement of her older and more level-headed sister Jane at the head of the table, or the married Mrs. Elton taking precedence over the elegant Emma at a ball, there is an unnervingly arbitrary and grotesque quality to the assumption of power by women. If flabby fathers are to be deplored in the novels, strong mothers or mother-substitutes like Lady Susan [in *Catharine*], Mrs. Norris [*Mansfield Park*], and Lady Russell [*Persuasion*] are almost always pernicious in their authority: female power is effectively synonymous with power abused. Mrs. Bennet's desire to establish Jane at Netherfield is depicted only as a series of murderous attacks upon the pliant girl, despite the fact that in the end, Jane's illness at Netherfield does further her marriage as Mrs. Bennet had planned, leading Elizabeth toward glory as well. Like Chawton, Mrs. Bennet is given credit only for obstructing; as one critic says well, "Mrs. Bennet moves in an atmosphere of repugnance that is scarcely explained."[9]

It was Mrs. Bennet's grotesque specter that led the Victorian feminist Harriet Martineau to back into an oblique apology for the little authority Englishwomen were allowed: "I was asked whether it was possible that the Bennet family would act as they are represented in 'Pride and Prejudice': whether a foolish mother, with grown up daughters, would be allowed to spoil the two youngest, instead of the sensible daughters taking the case into their own hands. It is certainly true that in America the superior minds of the family would take the lead; while in England, however the domestic affairs might gradually arrange themselves, no person would be found breathing the suggestion of superseding the mother's authority."[1] Given such meager-minded despotism, Martineau might have better understood why men looked with repudiation on the idea of female participation in the government of

9. Julia Prewit Brown, *Jane Austen's Novels*, (1971) 71.
1. Harriet Martineau, *Society in America*, 2 vols. 2: 276.

their countries; but despite Mrs. Bennet's aura of awfulness, she is in league with her creator as she drives her daughters out of a nonhome into the establishments they deserve. "The business of her life [is] to get her daughters married," in fact as well as obsessed fantasy; though in the case of the three most nubile, the end crowns the whole, her government is shown to be at one with the usurpation that is the paramount characteristic of Mrs. Bennet's counterpart in the larger social world—the overpowering Lady Catherine de Bourgh.[2]

* * *This monster of misgovernment is the only character other than Mrs. Bennet to deplore the exclusively male right of inheritance, which the sprightly, iconoclastic Elizabeth seems to accept as a matter of course: "I am glad of it; but otherwise I see no occasion for entailing estates from the female line.—It was not thought necessary in Sir Lewis de Bourgh's family." This interesting fact makes clear one role that Lady Catherine plays in the novel: she functions as an image of the overweening matriarchate that would result could widow and daughters inherit the estate Mrs. Bennet craves. In her futile confrontation with Elizabeth, Lady Catherine makes clear that her private great society runs on matriarchal principles:

> "I will not be interrupted. Hear me in silence. My daughter and my nephew are formed for each other. They are descended on the maternal side, from the same noble line; and, on the father's, from respectable, honourable, and ancient, though untitled families." [After this condescending inclusion of the lesser paternal line, Lady Catherine goes on to warn Elizabeth not to "quit the sphere" in which she was brought up.]
>
> "In marrying your nephew, I should not consider myself as quitting that sphere. He is a gentleman; I am a gentleman's daughter; so far we are equal."
>
> "True. You *are* a gentleman's daughter. But who was your mother?"

This bit of dialogue, particularly Lady Catherine's final challenge, throws Elizabeth back on the female, matriarchal dream world she is trying to escape. In asserting the primary reality of men and patrilineal inheritance, she comes close to denying that she is her mother's daughter. In the context of the novel's artistic methods and its social scheme, the male principle Elizabeth invokes is the invincible "reality" that counters Lady Catherine's fantasy of matriarchal omnipotence, whose visionary impossibility is reflected even in its syntax: "While in their

2. See Marvin Mudrick, *Jane Austen: Irony as Defense and Discovery* (1952) 103: "By her insulting condescension toward Elizabeth, [Lady Catherine] helps Darcy to balance off his distaste of Mrs. Bennet's not dissimilar shortcomings"; and Joseph Wiesenfarth, *The Errand of Form: An Assay of Jane Austen's Art* (1967) 63: "The wonderful interference of the egregious Lady Catherine de Bourgh in his affairs has yet to make Darcy realize that his aunt's title is nothing more than a cover that keeps the skeleton in the family closet from rattling as loudly as the bumbling Mrs. Bennet."

cradles, we planned the union." Given the real, masculine center of power in the novel, Lady Catherine's trumpeting of her divine omnipresence is as hollow a delusion as she is herself: "Do not deceive yourself into a belief that I will ever recede," she says, receding. Lady Catherine's withdrawal, and the reassuringly ardent Darcy's quick appearance in her place, suggests the salutary recession of the usurped power of all mothers before the meaning and form only men can bestow.

The acknowledged center of power in the novel is the shadowy Darcy. "As a brother, a landlord, a master, she considered how many people's happiness were in his guardianship!—How much of pleasure or pain it was in his power to bestow!—How much of good or evil must be done by him!" Looking at Darcy as his portrait immortalizes him, Elizabeth is overcome by a kind of social vitalism: she is drawn not to the benignity and wisdom of Darcy's power, but to its sheer extent as such, for evil as well as good. What compels her in the portrait is the awesomely institutionalized power of a man, a power that her own father has let fall and her mother, grotesquely usurped. Loathing the idea of any kinship to her mother, Elizabeth will doubtless be content not to have her own portrait displayed after her marriage, as Austen speculates: "I can only imagine that Mr. D. prizes any Picture of her too much to like it should be exposed to the public eye.—I can imagine he wd. have that sort [of] feeling—that mixture of Love, Pride & Delicacy" (*Letters* 24 May 1813, 213). After the clamorous anonymity of Longbourn, marriage waits for her as a hard-won release into a privacy only Darcy can bestow.

Underneath this pervasive largesse, Darcy has as shadowy a selfhood as his aunt, Lady Catherine. If Elizabeth's childhood is obliterated in memory, Darcy's is a muddled contradiction. The man who caught Elizabeth's eye before audibly insulting her was, according to his "intelligent" housekeeper, a fount of virtue from the beginning of his life. He was merely too modest to declare his goodness, and Elizabeth too prejudiced to see it: "I have never had a cross word from him in my life, and I have known him ever since he was four years old. . . . I have always observed, that they who are good-natured when children, are good-natured when they grow up; and he was always the sweetest-tempered, most generous-hearted, boy in the world. . . . Some people call him proud; but I am sure I never saw any thing of it. To my fancy, it is only because he does not rattle away like other young men." A good deal of weight is put on this testimony, though it is oddly redolent of Mr. Collins extolling the condescension of Lady Catherine; also, it meshes neither with the reliable Mrs. Gardiner's "having heard Mr. Fitzwilliam Darcy formerly spoken of as a very proud, ill-natured boy," nor with Darcy's own meticulous diagnosis of his boyhood:

"As a child I was taught what was *right*, but I was not taught to correct my temper. I was given good principles, but left to follow them in pride and conceit. Unfortunately an only son, (for many years an only *child*) I was spoilt by my parents, who though good themselves . . . allowed, encouraged, almost taught me to be self-ish and overbearing, to care for none beyond my own family circle, to think meanly of all the rest of the world, to *wish* at least to think meanly of their sense and worth compared with my own. Such I was, from eight to eight and twenty; and such I might still have been but for you, dearest, loveliest Elizabeth! What do I not owe you! You taught me a lesson, hard indeed at first, but most advantageous. By you, I was properly humbled."

Darcy the man is as muddled a figure as Darcy the boy. Is he indeed converted into humanity by Elizabeth's spontaneity and spirit, or was he always the perfection that maturity allows her to see? Oddly, Elizabeth herself prefers the latter interpretation, which replaces her power over him with a reassuring silliness: "And yet I meant to be uncommonly clever in taking so decided a dislike to him, without any reason. It is such a spur to one's genius, such an opening for wit to have a dislike of that kind. One may be continually abusive without saying any thing just; but one cannot be always laughing at a man without now and then stumbling on something witty." Elizabeth's selective memory serves her well here by erasing the fact that she had, and has, several good reasons for disliking Darcy; but she seems to need a sense of her own wrongness to justify the play of her mind. In choosing to emphasize her own prejudice over Darcy's most palpable pride, she can wonder freely at the power in his portrait while her own (if there is one) will be closeted away, invisible to all eyes but her husband's. * * *

The sanctioned power of management with which [Austen] endows Darcy allows him to prove his heroism in the third volume by taking over the mother's role: like the shadowy "Duke of dark corners" in *Measure for Measure*, he moves behind the scenes and secretly arranges the marriages of the three Bennet girls. The end of the novel finds the neighborhood of families that centers around Pemberley busily improving Kitty for a good match, leaving only the lumpish Mary still at home to be displayed by her mother, their alliance a fitting penance for the pedantry of the one and the presumption of the other. The last page tells us incidentally that the war has ended, and, with Darcy's will to harmony, perhaps the waiting will as well. In becoming the novel's providential matchmaker, Darcy brings about the comic conclusion by an administrative activity for which Mrs. Bennet and Lady Catherine were, and Emma Woodhouse will be, severely condemned. In the end, the malevolent power of the mother is ennobled by being transferred to the hero,[3] and the female community of Longbourn, an oppressive blank in a dense society, is dispersed with relief in the solidity of marriage.

SUSAN MORGAN

[Perception and *Pride and Prejudice*]†

*   *   *

What I claim for Austen is an intellectual position which, rejecting the inheritance of Locke, explores ideas of perception as temporal and creative by means of inventing and arranging her fictions. This is not to say that Austen is a systematic thinker or that the novels, when pressed, release a theory of knowledge full formed enough to be a systematic epistemology. It is to say that Austen's work, as properly as Wordsworth's or many other writers', yields "the philosophic mind." Because Austen is a woman, a novelist in an era of sublime poetry, a spinster whose subject is how young ladies marry, readers have been unwilling to notice the philosophic basis of her work—as they do so easily for male writers who compose poetry advertising its philosophic dimension. We have granted her morality and manners, technical genius and an observant eye. We have not granted her an original mind. It has been easier with George Eliot: not only was she explicitly philosophic but she could also read German. I offer a reading of Austen's novels as speculative resolutions to questions about the sources of truth and value. The novels do not reflect a society or defend one side or another of a historical debate. To assume they do is to limit her achievement to mimesis and polemic. Austen is no portrait artist, but a luminous maker of the world she sings.

The subject of Austen's fiction, like that of the major poets of her time, is the relation between the mind and its objects. Perception becomes a problem and a fit subject for fiction for two reasons: the nature of character and the nature of reality. These two tend to merge, since the reality we struggle to comprehend consists primarily of other people. As Austen tells us in *Northanger Abbey*, character is mixed.

---

3. See Kenneth L. Moler, *Jane Austen's Art of Allusion* (1968) 75–108, for a discussion of the managing, marrying Darcy in relation to his Godlike prototype, Sir Charles Grandison. It is part of Austen's feminization of Richardson's material that in *Pride and Prejudice* it is initially the mother's "business" to get her daughters married, and Darcy merely replaces her in the job.

† From *In the Meantime: Character and Perception in Jane Austen's Fiction* (Chicago: University of Chicago Press, 1980) 4–5, 10–12, 78–81, 90–92, 98, 101–104. Reprinted by permission of The University of Chicago Press.

Truth, or the reality we wish to understand, is uncertain. Truth changes because people change. And our relation to it, unlike that of the narrator in *Joseph Andrews*,[1] can never be the neutral distance of an objective observer toward a completed world. Our perceptions must be active and changing, and continuously so. Austen acknowledges that there are completions, when the secrets are revealed and the truth is sure and clear. But those completions are the end of fiction as well. Her novels take place during the time of our lives: that meantime, that "in between time," as an old song has it, before everything is known. The temporal quality of truth and of character means that judgment must also be a matter of time. Without a fixed truth, without characters like Fielding's lawyer whom we have known these four thousand years, what are the grounds of knowledge? What does it mean to be good? How do we go about acting in the world? Simple problems, familiar and even mundane. They are, as Austen presented them, the common problems of common life.

*   *   *

To recognize that Austen's subject is perception allows us to see how thoroughly the question of the mind's approaches to its objects pervades her fiction. Given a fluid reality, the move to truth requires being able to live in uncertainties, the ability to sustain judgments which are temporary and incomplete. Austen's commitment to an optimistic skepticism which allows her characters a continuing process of perceiving has similarities not only to Keats's definition of negative capability in 1817[2] but also to the kind of skepticism Shelley can depict even in such a transcendent poem as "Mont Blanc" in 1816. The basis of these similarities may be that, like most of her poetic contemporaries, Austen's commitment is to particulars. The forms of thought which often blind us begin as generalities. The famous opening of *Pride and Prejudice*, "it is a truth universally acknowledged, that a single man in possession of a good fortune, must be in want of a wife," locates the subject of the book in our tendency to generalize. To invoke universals is to live in a world of forms, to think with all the spaciousness and all the hollowness of preconceptions and thus withdraw from life in its demanding and inconclusive particularity. Such objectifying keeps us from the risks and thereby the hopes of an involved intelligence.

*   *   *

But if idealism codifies mystery, realism denies it entirely. In Austen's fiction realism looms as the greatest evil, a state of mind far more

---

1. A novel by Henry Fielding (1707–1754) [Editor].
2. Keats defined negative capability as that state in which "man is capable of being in uncertainties, Mysteries, doubts, without any irritable reaching after fact & reason," capable "of remaining content with half knowledge" (To George and Tom Keats, 21–27 December 1817, *The Letters of John Keats*, ed. Hyder Edward Rollins [1958] 1: 193–94 [*Editor*].

destructive, far more the focus of her attention, than such material events as unmarried women running off with men. Realism is the attitude which, under the guise of seeing things as they really are, portrays the world in shabby, ugly, greedy ways. It generalizes the worst rather than the purest, and claims for itself an objectivity of perception untainted by any rose. And the motive is always the same: a selfishness which disclaims involvement or responsibility. Again and again the realists are condemned. Mrs. Bennet is a vulgar fool. But Mr. Bennet, gifted by nature with a better understanding, is a portrait of waste. * * * And there is no forgetting Charlotte Lucas as she tells Elizabeth Bennet that "I am not romantic, you know. I never was." But Austen is. She always was. And in her work sentimentalists and realists, superficially so different, share that corruption of mind which prefers certainty to possibility. Substituting preconceptions for active judgment, both attitudes reduce life. Structures are necessary. But so is the recognition that they are no more than that, only fictions when is all done.

Against such regulated views Austen offers the landscape her characters actually see. The potential of everyday life, the romance to be found in familiar circumstances, is the premise of Austen's fiction. And how that potential is to be realized, that romance to be discovered, is always a matter of particulars. When we look for continuity in the novels we see immediately that Austen has no pure truths to tell. This is merely to say what many readers have seen, that Austen's are partial truths, both in not being absolute and in being truths of the heart.

* * *

Pride and Prejudice has a charmed place as the most popular of Austen's novels. Elizabeth, witty, self-confident, with those dancing eyes, and not quite beautiful face, depicts for all of us what is flawed and irresistible about real people. Trilling has observed about *Emma* that we like Mr. Knightley "because we perceive that he cherishes Emma not merely in spite of her subversive self-assertion but because of it."[3] This applies to Mr. Darcy as well, and Elizabeth, perfectly aware that it does, cannot resist inquiring when she demands an account of his having fallen in love with her: "Did you admire me for my impertinence?" Her impertinence, of course, is why generations of readers have admired her and why we recognize that the major concern of the book is with the possibilities and responsibility of free and lively thought. *Pride and Prejudice* explores the special question of the meaning of freedom, given the premise which Austen assumes throughout her fiction, that the relation between character and public reality is at once difficult and necessary.

Elizabeth's freedom is basically the freedom to think for herself.

---

3. Lionel Trilling, *Sincerity and Authenticity* (1972) 77.

Unlike Catherine Morland [in *Northanger Abbey*] and Emma Wood-house [in *Emma*], one of whom follows external structures and the other of whom is preoccupied with creating her own, Elizabeth sees herself as already beyond those forms which direct or control our perceptions. She begins her story believing that she does judge from her own observations rather than from preconceptions. But like Catherine and Emma, Elizabeth is self-deceived. We watch her move from a belief in her own logic to a more fluid interpretation of knowing and of intelligence in terms of the backgrounds, contexts, and particulars which inform truth. And we learn to acknowledge that the pressing importance of such a movement rests not on our hopes for being right but on our hopes for being free.

Miss Bingley describes Elizabeth's free spirit as "an abominable sort of conceited independence, a most country town indifference to decorum." Certainly, Elizabeth hurrying through the muddy countryside to visit Jane, springing over puddles and jumping over stiles, is not a decorous sight. And just as certainly, those muddy petticoats and glowing cheeks contribute a great deal to Mr. Darcy's falling in love. The importance of Elizabeth's sense of freedom and the necessity of relating that idea to her growth in the novel may account for the fact that so many critics have sought to discuss *Pride and Prejudice* in terms of a dualism (suggested by the title) in which Elizabeth's freedom constitutes one pole and some sort of social sense the other. Her progress can then be understood as a movement from polarity to a merging or harmony, represented by her marriage to Mr. Darcy. Thus Alistair Duckworth finds it generally agreed that *Pride and Prejudice* "achieves an ideal relation between the individual and society."[4] Dorothy Van Ghent sees the book as illuminating "the difficult and delicate reconciliation of the sensitively developed individual with the terms of his social existence."[5] Marvin Mudrick, then, would account for Elizabeth's wrong-headedness as a failure to acknowledge the social context, and Samuel Kliger, in variant terms, places the dichotomy as that between nature and art.[6] All would locate the embodiment of that final harmony among the stately and tasteful grounds of Pemberley.

Although most of these individual discussions, and others like them, are both valuable and persuasive, they share that familiar assumption which in Austen criticism has sunk to a truism, that her perspective is one of social and rational good. The general objection to this prevailing view is its orderliness when applied to *Pride and Prejudice*. It is hard to

---

4. Alistair Duckworth, *The Improvement of the Estate* (1971) 118n. [See pp. 306–15 in this volume—*Editor*.]
5. Dorothy Van Ghent, *The English Novel: Form and Function* (1953) 100. [See pp. 299–306 in this volume—*Editor*.]
6. Marvin Mudrick, *Jane Austen: Irony as Defense and Discovery* (1952); Samuel Kliger, "Jane Austen's *Pride and Prejudice* in the Eighteenth-Century Mode," *University of Toronto Quarterly* 16 (1947): 357–70.

see where in that vision of social and emotional harmony with which so many would have the novel end there could be room for the doubts, the blindness, and the mistakes which Elizabeth still exhibits and which are a continuing part of every major character Austen creates. I do not at all mean to imply that beyond the lightness there is some dark side to the novelist, some sort of regulated hatred or repression. I do mean to ask where there would be room for the life which, as Austen was perfectly aware, goes on beyond all our formulations of it. Tave reminds us that "She knows, and she shows in her novels, messy lives, and most people are leading them, even when the surface of life seems proper."[7] We have been too eager to assume that Austen's was a conclusive vision, a sort of apotheosis of the optimism of premodern fiction. To understand *Pride and Prejudice* in terms of some ideal blend of the individual and the social is to speak of finalities about a writer who herself chooses to speak of the possible, the continuous, the incomplete. Austen's "social" concerns are with human relations, not society. Her own reference to "the little bit (two inches wide) of Ivory" can only be called unfortunate in the light of the critical weight given that suspiciously humble remark. Austen offers neither Chinese miniatures nor Dutch interiors nor any surface so finished that meanings are conclusive as well. It is hardly possible to speak of her themes as social (or as rational) without involving, by implication alone, that too familiar image of her as outside her own time and belonging to an earlier and more ordered age.

A more particular objection to the prevailing view of *Pride and Prejudice* is that it violates the evidence of the text. If Mr. Darcy is to represent society and Elizabeth a rebellious individualism, how can we account for the fact that the first major breach of society's rules is made by Mr. Darcy, when he insults Elizabeth within her hearing at the Meryton ball? It seems evasive to conclude, with Mary Lascelles, that at the moment Mr. Darcy is out of character and the remark is a technical flaw.[8] Unquestionably, Mr. Darcy is an outstanding member of society, a landowner with both power and responsibility. His position and an accompanying sense of duties and obligations justify a proper kind of pride. Yet this should not obscure the fact that Mr. Darcy's nature, far from being social, is reserved, independent, isolated, private, and vain. And it is Elizabeth who points to this discrepancy when she remarks to Colonel Fitzwilliam on Mr. Darcy's rude conduct at the Meryton dance: "Shall we ask him why a man of sense and education, and who has lived in the world, is ill qualified to recommend himself to strangers?"

Elizabeth's failures in judgment, with Charlotte Lucas but primarily with Mr. Wickham and Mr. Darcy, cannot be adequately explained as

---

7. *Some Words of Jane Austen* (1973) 33. [See pp. 315–19 in this volume—*Editor.*]
8. Mary Lascelles, *Jane Austen and Her Art* (1939) 160.

a headstrong insistence on private judgment in the face of social values. It is inaccurate to claim that Elizabeth should have been swayed by the fact that Mr. Wickham "is a dispossessed man in an acquisitive society" (Mudrick 110). He has a military commission, and military service, like naval service, is an honorable, gentlemanly occupation composing a respected part of Austen's social scheme. It would be just as distorting for Elizabeth to find Mr. Darcy socially acceptable simply because he owns Pemberley, whatever Charlotte Lucas may think. It is Charlotte, after all, who advises Elizabeth "not to be a simpleton and allow her fancy for Wickham to make her appear unpleasant in the eyes of a man of ten times his consequence." Charlotte chooses "not to be a simpleton" and will spend the rest of her life with Mr. Collins. To judge others in economic or social terms is the very sort of thinking Austen would expose. Mr. Wickham is socially unacceptable for moral rather than economic reasons—not because he has no possessions but because he has no principles. Judging him is no more a question of manners than it is of position or money. Mr. Wickham can be as pleasantly talkative and polite as Mr. Darcy can be unpleasantly reserved and rude. Elizabeth misjudges them both, but not through an individualism that fails to appreciate class or social values. If that were true, *Pride and Prejudice* would be a lesser novel. Elizabeth's failure is one of intelligence.

*   *   *

Austen has deliberately and obviously made Mr. Wickham a stock character in order to point to Elizabeth's central moral weakness, that she does not take life seriously. Raised by a foolish mother and a cynical father who has abdicated all responsibility, encouraged to distinguish herself from her sisters, Elizabeth sees the world as some sort of entertaining game. She is not silly in the way that Lydia and Kitty are (though she is sometimes surprisingly similar to them), but she cannot imagine that anything could be expected of her. Elizabeth is morally disengaged. What she wants is to understand what she sees and she also hopes that what she sees will be exciting, will be worth understanding. And excitement, of course, is just what she thinks Mr. Wickham offers. His stereotyped charm confers no individual feelings and invokes no personal obligations. His tale is bizarre, out of the ordinary, and shocking, with the initial flattering appeal of being a privileged confidence. It is told to Elizabeth and the reader literally as the recounting of a sentimental story. On Elizabeth's part the hearing is complete with the proper forms of response, with expectations ("what she chiefly wished to hear she could not hope to be told, the history of his acquaintance with Mr. Darcy") and the appropriate stated exclamations (such as "Indeed!", "Good heavens!", "This is quite shocking!", "How strange!", and "How abominable!").

Elizabeth chooses to believe Mr. Wickham's story, and the reason she gives Jane is that "there was truth in his looks." We might accept this as having the familiar meaning that Mr. Wickham has an honest face if it were not that throughout Mr. Wickham's account Austen has Elizabeth think about his good looks. She responds to his declarations of honoring Mr. Darcy's father (declarations made suspect as much by the triteness of their phrasing as by the fact that Mr. Wickham is even now dishonoring the father by exposing Mr. Darcy to Elizabeth) by the remarkable thought that Mr. Wickham was "handsomer than ever as he expressed them." And she silently remarks that Mr. Wickham is a young man "whose very countenance may vouch for [his] being amiable." We cannot simply explain these responses by understanding Elizabeth, as we do Lydia, as a silly and ignorant flirt without any sense. Yet for her the credibility of Mr. Wickham's story is inseparable from his handsome face. Both Mr. Wickham's story and his looks have a glamour which is exceptional and dramatic without being either unpredictable or unique.

Because Austen depicts both Elizabeth's credence and her feelings in the familiar and suspect language of sentimental fiction we must conclude that Elizabeth no more seriously believes Mr. Wickham's tale than she seriously believes she is in love with him. We need only think of how Austen depicts the classic situation of a woman looking forward to seeing a man at a dance. Elizabeth, hoping to see Mr. Wickham at the Netherfield ball, "had dressed with more than usual care, and prepared in the highest spirits for the conquest of all that remained unsubdued of his heart, trusting that it was not more than might be won in the course of the evening." Her own high spirits are the most dramatic note here, and when Mr. Wickham does not come, the extent of Elizabeth's real regret may be gauged by Austen's comment that "Elizabeth was not formed for ill-humour; and though every prospect of her own was destroyed for the evening, it could not dwell long on her spirits; and having told all her griefs to Charlotte Lucas, whom she had not seen in a week, she was soon able to make a voluntary transition to the oddities of her cousin." We doubt whether Elizabeth would have found more pleasure in dancing with Mr. Wickham than she does in laughing at Mr. Collins, or whether, indeed, there is finally much difference between the two activities. Both are the expressions of a mind and heart essentially uninvolved. Elizabeth has allowed herself to be taken in by a style which she can later recognize as stale affectation because she views the very artificiality of her connection to Mr. Wickham as an assurance of freedom. * * *

Perhaps the worst moment of Elizabeth's objectivity is her letter to Mrs. Gardiner telling of Mr. Wickham's defection to Miss King. Her sisters, she says, are more hurt than she for they "are young in the ways of the world, and not yet open to the mortifying conviction that hand-

some young men must have something to live on, as well as the plain."
It is a terrible sentence, terrible in its distance from her feelings, its
self-satisfied realism, its "way of the world." And what is most painful
is to see Elizabeth choosing to make sense of her experience in such
cold and easy terms.

The sense of blasted hopes which passes as a realistic intelligence
with Charlotte Lucas and Mr. Bennet is not allowed to influence Elizabeth unchallenged. The cynicism of these two is opposed by a warmer
vision, that of Jane Bennet. Elizabeth's "disappointment in Charlotte
made her turn with fonder regard to her sister, of whose rectitude and
delicacy she was sure her opinion could never be shaken." It is Jane
who replies to Elizabeth's despair at human nature and at Charlotte's
marriage with the comment, "Do not give way to such feelings as these.
They will ruin your happiness." For it is Jane who understands that to
view the world coldly is to be neither perceptive nor superior nor safe
from wrong. It is to be irresponsible and to abandon the difficulties of
trust for the finalities of easy generalization. Jane's prepossession to
think well of people does not lead her to be perceptive, and she is
obviously wrong about the Bingley sisters. Yet Jane's kind of misunderstanding, unlike the generalizing which presumes certainty, is
acceptable to her author in a way that the disposition to think ill of
people is not. And her role as the opponent of negativity is central to
understanding Elizabeth's mistakes, her choices, and her intellectual
growth.

*   *   *

The willingness to commit oneself to experience, in its unknown
dangers as well as its possibilities, comes naturally to Jane, and perhaps
that is why she is not the central character of *Pride and Prejudice*. She
has never deliberately chosen involvement over clarity. Austen's major
interest is always with those whose connections to reality, in terms of
knowledge and goodness, are at once more questionable and more difficult. Jane is an innocent. Yet she teaches us that involvement can
lead to a kind of perceptiveness inaccessible to those who understand
clarity as something gained through avoiding involvement. Elizabeth's
freedom, insofar as it leads to judgments she likes to think are untouched by commitment or concern, does not bring understanding. In
accounting to Jane for her unfairness to Mr. Darcy, Elizabeth admits
that "I meant to be uncommonly clever in taking so decided a dislike
to him, without any reason. It is such a spur to one's genius, such an
opening for wit to have a dislike of that kind. One may be continually
abusive without saying anything just; but one cannot be always laughing at a man without now and then stumbling on something witty."
* * * But to look only for flaws is not objective but selfish and distorting, and cuts oneself off from one's kind. Between candor and cynicism

there can be a way of understanding which presupposes neither human evil nor human good, yet allows for both by the very suspension of any fixed view.

During that long walk in the lane at Hunsford Elizabeth offers, for the first time in her story, a picture of her mind at work. The neutral observer, the instant clarity, the conclusive wit, are gone. They must vanish before a dilemma requiring discrimination between versions of a truth she had previously found so clear. Elizabeth moves from feelings "scarcely to be defined" to "feelings yet more acutely painful and more difficult of definition" to a "perturbed state of mind, with thoughts that could rest on nothing" to careful recollections and "pausing on a point a considerable while" to, at last, the realization that "I, who have prided myself on my discernment, . . . have courted prepossession and ignorance, and driven reason away." This scene, comprising a whole chapter, looks forward to Isabel Archer's meditative vigil,[9] the "representation simply of her motionlessly *seeing*," of which James was so proud. In her responses to Darcy's letter Elizabeth does not at all demonstrate that "quickness" her father had praised her for. And that is her victory. Understanding comes slowly, with a depth of feeling Mr. Bennet will never reach in his appreciation of being quick.

One of the most powerful facts in *Pride and Prejudice* is that after Elizabeth's critical moments of shame and revelation at Hunsford so many of her perceptions continue to be quite wrong. She does see through Wickham, but she can learn to detect his artificiality only because she knows the truth. Her judgment not to expose him turns out to be almost disastrous to her own family. And she is still nearly always wrong about Mr. Darcy. She interprets his silence at Lambton on learning of Lydia's elopement with complete assurance: "her power was sinking; every thing *must* sink under such proof of family weakness, such an assurance of the deepest disgrace. She could neither wonder nor condemn." After Lady Catherine's visit, Elizabeth speculates that if his aunt appeals to Mr. Darcy to give her up, "With his notions of dignity, he would probably feel that the arguments, which to Elizabeth had appeared weak and ridiculous, contained much good sense and solid reasoning." Even when all these confusions are resolved by Darcy's second proposal, the two must still spend much of their courtship in the charming yet quite necessary explanations of all those motives and actions so misunderstood. Austen, who did not compose love scenes for their emotional appeal, reminds the reader that in human relations, even of the kind reputed to provide immediate understanding, there is a great deal that intuition and surmise do not reveal.

We must ask what, after all, Elizabeth has learned and what her

---

9. In *Portrait of a Lady*, by Henry James (1843–1916) [*Editor*].

story is about if after the acknowledgment of prejudice and vanity in the lane at Hunsford her judgment seems hardly more accurate than before. Austen has so arranged the plot that her heroine's moment of revelation and chagrin comes nearly in the middle of the story. After Hunsford there are few scenes of Elizabeth's quickness and wit, and much of the action seems not to depend on her at all. The Gardiners' delayed vacation and wish to visit Pemberley, the combination of Mrs. Forster's invitation, Wickham's mounting debts and Lydia's reckless-ness which precipitate the elopement, and Mr. Darcy's arrival at the Lambton inn at the moment of Elizabeth's receiving the news, all remind us that Elizabeth can have little control over people or events, while both may be crucial to her. The second half of *Pride and Prejudice* may be less sparkling than the first, but the quieter pleasure it offers is an extended view of Elizabeth's fate entwined with the lives of those around her.

What Elizabeth is doing in these later scenes, with a directness and care which were absent from her earlier casual wit, is seriously trying to understand the particular situations she finds herself in and the people she cares about. This effort is given more space in *Pride and Prejudice* than it was in *Northanger Abbey* or will be in *Emma*. By plac-ing Elizabeth's moment of crisis in the middle of the novel rather than at the end, Austen can present Elizabeth as a heroine who needs to be educated and also as a heroine who is properly involved in her world. Whether she is trying to compose her feelings enough at the Lambton inn to receive Georgiana Darcy and her brother, or paying a morning visit to the ladies at Pemberley, or accepting what she believes to be Darcy's giving her up after the elopement, or speculating (with the Gardiners and Jane) on Mr. Wickham's intentions, or surmising Mr. Darcy's reaction to his aunt's interference, Elizabeth is constantly engaged in trying to see and respond to other points of view. She is often wrong—and for quite the same reasons that she was wrong in the beginning, that her partialities and ignorance must limit her. The difference is that Elizabeth no longer sees her world as a place of easily discovered folly from which, in self-defense as much as in amusement, she must stand apart if she is to see the truth. She has come to value the connections and partialities which inform truth and to understand the lesson of Hunsford, that a lively intelligence is personal and engaged. She can now use that quick mind to reach for hopes and suggestive meanings rather than killing finalities.

* * *

CLAUDIA L. JOHNSON

Pride and Prejudice and the Pursuit of Happiness†

* * *

In its readiness to ratify and to grant our happiness, *Pride and Prejudice* is almost shamelessly wish fulfilling. The fantasies it satisfies, however, are not merely private—a poor but deserving girl catches a rich husband. They are pervasively political as well. If *Pride and Prejudice* legitimizes a progressive yearning for pleasure, it also gratifies a conservative yearning for a strong, attentive, loving, and paradoxically perhaps, at times even submissive authority. At no other time in Austen's career would she indulge a fantasy of this magnitude to this degree, for it is Darcy himself who secures the happiness the novel celebrates. As an authority figure, "a brother, a landlord, a master" who holds, as Elizabeth remarks, "many people's happiness . . . in his guardianship," Darcy is singularly free from the faults that underline comparable figures elsewhere—General Tilney's repressiveness [in *Northanger Abbey*], for example, or Sir Walter's foolishness [in *Persuasion*]. *Pride and Prejudice* is thus a profoundly conciliatory work, and of all Austen's novels it most affirms established social arrangements without damaging their prestige or fundamentally challenging their wisdom or equity. Whereas *Sense and Sensibility* excoriates the traditional family and *Mansfield Park* subjects characters of Darcy's stature to disabling satire, on the surface at least, *Pride and Prejudice* corroborates conservative myths which had argued that established forms cherished rather than prohibited true liberty, sustained rather than disrupted real happiness, and safeguarded rather than repressed individual merit. Its hero accordingly is a sober-minded exemplar of the great gentry, a dutiful son and affectionate brother. Its villain is an ungrateful upstart who, by attempting to elope with a female of good family, seeks not simply to enrich himself but also to sully the scutcheons of legitimate male power—as Darcy puts it, "Mr. Wickham's chief object, was unquestionably my sister's fortune, which is thirty thousand pounds; but I cannot help supposing that the hope of revenging himself on me, was a strong inducement." And its turning point is the heroine's contemplation of the household of a private gentleman. Prepared to find Pemberley a grandiose estate designed expressly to overbear subordinates with awe, Elizabeth finds instead an unpretentiously elegant manor, and rather than testimonials to the insolence of power, she hears tributes to a kind master, a beloved landlord, tributes which

---

† From *Jane Austen: Women, Politics, and the Novel* (Chicago: University of Chicago Press, 1988) 73–75, 80–84, 87–89. Reprinted by permission of The University of Chicago Press.

moreover are not tainted by "prejudice," that ultimate progressive pejorative.

To some, Pride and Prejudice has a markedly fairy-tale-like quality which, while accounting for much of the novel's enduring popular success, is politically suspect. One of Austen's recent critics observes that the novel's wishful, though aesthetically satisfying, "romantic conclusion" fudges the ideological contraditions uncovered earlier between the "individualistic perspective inherent in the bourgeois value system *and* the authoritarian hierarchy retained from traditional, paternalistic society."[1] By this account, the happy ending of Pride and Prejudice is an "aesthetic solution" that cannot really address the "social problems" the novel itself uncovers, and indeed that actually conceals their depth. But while these objections are partly true, we should not let our own rather modern preference for ideological conflict predispose us to undervalue Austen's achievement in Pride and Prejudice. To imagine versions of authority responsive to criticism and capable of transformation is not necessarily to "escape" from urgent problems into "romance" and to settle for politically irresponsible "consolations of form" which offer us a never-never land and leave the structures of the "real world" unchanged (Poovey 207). When we recall that Austen's preceding novel could locate her protagonists' contentment only in a retreat from and renunciation of power, Austen's decision here to engage her exceptionally argumentative antagonists in direct, extensive, and mutually improving debates can just as well be viewed as a step towards, rather than an "escape" from, constructive political commentary.

*   *   *

In all Austen's novels, but especially in Pride and Prejudice, pursuing happiness is the business of life. Austen trots character after character before our attention so that we may consider what pleases or, conversely, what vexes and mortifies them, thus inviting us to assess the quality and durability of their happiness. At the outset, at least, Darcy's sense of self-consequence is characterized by a haughty determination to be mortified by everyone outside his small circle. Unlike the easy-going Bingley, who has an agreeable disposition to be pleased anywhere, Darcy is much as the neighborhood around Meryton first perceives him: "proud . . . above his company . . . above being pleased." But if this refusal to be pleased is a serious moral failing, as Darcy himself later admits, a determination to be imperturbably agreeable is little better. Knighthood has given Sir William Lucas license to spend

1. Mary Poovey, The Proper Lady and the Woman Writer: Ideology as Style in the Works of Mary Wollstonecraft, Mary Shelley, and Jane Austen (1984) 205.

all his time thinking "with pleasure of his own importance," and he feels this pleasure most acutely by being pleased—quite indiscriminately—with everything, smiling graciously even as Darcy snubs him with quips about the savagery of dancing, or even as Mrs. Bennet insults the claims of his daughter to marry Mr. Collins. With her "high animal spirits" Lydia Bennet, by contrast, finds her boisterous pleasures in redcoats and balls. Because she has never been taught that "her present pursuits are not to be the business of her life," a visit to the encampment at Brighton "comprised every possibility of earthly happiness." Mrs. Bennet's grip on happiness is considerably weaker, and she is hardly able to take any pleasure at all. Though marrying off her daughters is the chief "business" of her life, so firmly is she convinced that the world conspires to irritate her "poor nerves" and thwart her wishes that she passes most of her time in vexation.

Austen's care to establish the standards of her characters' happiness provides us with an index to their moral imaginations, tempers, and resources that enables us to engage in judicious moral evaluation without resorting to the conclusive moralizing characteristic of some of her contemporaries. By leaving censorious reflections on Lydia's elopement to the "spiteful old ladies in Meryton" and to the pompous Mary, for example, Austen distances herself from prescriptive pronouncements on this subject, and no specifically authorial moral opprobrium is ever attached to Charlotte's frankly mercenary marriage to Collins. It is enough instead that Lydia's abrupt lapse into conjugal indifference and pecuniary want shows just how little her previous ideas of "earthly happiness" comprehended after all, and that Charlotte's choice of and apparently successful adjustment to Mr. Collins as a husband indicates where she rates the exigencies of physical maintenance relative to the pleasures of rational society. Thus, although Austen's refusal to settle the differences in what her characters seek as desirable—in *Persuasion* Admiral Croft likes and Anne Elliot dreads the prospect of "future war"—implies a toleration of some ethical relativity which some of her contemporaries could have found disturbing, she nevertheless does not leave us bereft of rational means for ethical discrimination.

The attention devoted to happiness in *Pride and Prejudice* does not stop with characterization. Happiness itself has distinctive social and political ramifications which the novel carefully develops. First of all, in keeping with the liberal tradition of moral philosophy to which *Pride and Prejudice* is affiliated, happiness is something many of the characters feel they have a basic right to. Darcy's central fault, after all, is to have been careless about pleasing other people, to have had what Elizabeth stingingly terms "a selfish disdain of the feelings of others," and Lady Catherine and he both are judged wanting precisely because their own pride renders them incapable of regarding the happiness of their inferiors. * * *

Lady Catherine, as Collins assures Elizabeth, "likes to have the distinction of rank preserved." Rather than make others feel at ease, she patronizes Elizabeth so superciliously that even Darcy looks "a little ashamed of his aunt's ill breeding." But Elizabeth also takes him to task for a carelessness of pleasing, and when he lamely pleads shyness with strangers, she taxes him with [an] ugly failure of civility: * * * "Shall we ask him [Darcy] why a man of sense and education, and who has lived in the world, is ill qualified to recommend himself to strangers?" Fitzwilliam, who happily does possess "the readiness and ease of a well-bred man," answers in Darcy's stead: "It is because he will not give himself the trouble." Just as Lady Catherine takes every "occasion of dictating to others," Darcy too, as Elizabeth puts it, enjoys "the power of doing what he likes," without troubling himself with the consideration that others have what [Samuel] Johnson calls "the same claim to deference."[2]

Nowhere is Darcy's failure of deference to others clearer than in his proposal, bearing as it does an appalling resemblance to that of Collins. To Collins only one person is worthy of deference. Accordingly, he expects Elizabeth to be gratified to learn that he is proposing to her on Lady Catherine's advice that he choose "an active, useful sort of person, not brought up high, but able to make a small income go a good way." But as deferent as Collins is to Lady Catherine, his principal concern is with himself, and consequently he expresses no wish to contribute to Elizabeth's happiness but rather only a conviction that matrimony will add to his own. Even after he must accept the reality of Elizabeth's negative, Collins believes that a refusal of himself can derive only from a "defect of temper" on Elizabeth's part, rather than a failure to please on his own. Like Collins, Darcy also parades hollow gallantries that do not veil his assurance of immediate success and that tax Elizabeth with her unfavourable fortune and connections. So little is Darcy concerned for Elizabeth's happiness that he does not hesitate to inform her of the damage he is doing to his own self-consequence by proposing marriage to her in the first place, expressing his "sense of her inferiority—of its being a degradation—of the family obstacles which judgment had always opposed to inclination."

Considered with respect to the liberal ideas about personal happiness, Darcy's failures of politeness are quite momentous, and Johnson once again elucidates them with a morally fervent solicitude for the unempowered that shows us why progressive social critics liked him, his approval of subordination notwithstanding:

> Though all are not equally culpable with Trypherus, it is scarcely
> possible to find any man who does not frequently, like him,

2. The Rambler, no. 56 (29 September 1750), in The Yale Edition of the Works of Samuel Johnson, ed. W. J. Bate and Albrecht B. Strauss, vol. 3 (1969) 302.

indulge his own pride by forcing others into a comparison with himself, when he knows the advantage is on his side, without considering that unnecessarily to obtrude unpleasing ideas is a species of oppression; and that it is little more criminal to deprive another of some real advantage, than to interrupt that forgetfulness of its absence which is the next happiness to actual possession.(*Rambler* 98)

Although Johnson does not go so far as Hume in vindicating vanity, he employs politically charged language which describes the offensiveness of hauteur as just short of criminal, a theft of that self-approbation to which, he implies, we all have a right. Johnson's remarks can suggest how Elizabeth's initial pique with Darcy ought to be considered as more than "merely" injured vanity, an implicitly rearguard construction which places the problems squarely in Elizabeth's court. Elizabeth effortlessly concurs with Charlotte's opinion that Darcy "has a *right* to be proud," but she believes that she has a right to pride as well: "I could easily forgive *his* pride, if he had not mortified *mine*." Readers who contend that *Pride and Prejudice* is a didactic novel consistent with the orthodox morality expounded in sermons and conduct books typically observe here that Elizabeth is guilty of the "sin" of pride, either in her all-too-fallible private judgments or in her personal attractions, for both of these wounds to her self-esteem render her susceptible to Wickham's flattery.[3] Yet *Pride and Prejudice* invites us not to chide Elizabeth with threadbare morality about original sin, but on the contrary, if not actually to flatter people's pride as Wickham and Collins do, then at least to honor it. In Johnson's words, "unnecessarily to obtrude unpleasing ideas" onto people about themselves is almost criminally to take their happiness away. Defending the honesty of his proposal, Darcy insists that "reason" vindicates him in confronting Elizabeth with painful truths about her circumstances, but to Johnson it is no excuse that "reason" may be on the side of the offender: "a thousand incivilities may be committed, and a thousand offices neglected, without any remorse of conscience, or reproach from reason" (*Rambler* 98).

Unless we acknowledge that Darcy's pride is a "criminal" assault on Elizabeth's happiness, we will not appreciate the profundity of his eventual transformation. Darcy himself later explains that Elizabeth taught him "how insufficient were all my pretensions to please a woman worthy of being pleased." The "most certain way of giving any man pleasure," as Johnson explains the economy of social pleasures, "is to persuade him that you receive pleasure from him" (*Rambler* 72), and this is precisely what Darcy cannot do when he still thinks "meanly of all the rest of the world" outside his family circle. Elizabeth can

3. See, for example, Marilyn Butler, *Jane Austen and the War of Ideas* (1975) 206. [See pp. 319–26 in this volume—*Editor*.]

easily account for Colonel Fitzwilliam's visits at Hunsford: he "came because he had pleasure in their society, a persuasion which of course recommended him still more." But Darcy's visits remain a puzzle: they seem "the effect of necessity rather than of choice—a sacrifice to propriety, not a pleasure to himself." When Darcy improves his manners, however, he becomes "desirous to please" Elizabeth, and "determined, to be pleased" by her, and it is this finally which impresses her with grateful desire that their happiness depend upon each other. Austen's concern with good manners, then, has decidedly political underpinnings: to be guilty of hauteur is to deprive people of a pleasing sense of self-esteem that it is legitimate for them to have.

* * *

Austen's simultaneously bold and delicate handling of the confrontation between Elizabeth and Lady Catherine typifies her entire relationship to the novelistic tradition of social criticism under discussion here. The treatment is decisively progressive because Elizabeth does not consider the interests of the ruling class to be morally binding upon her: "Neither duty, nor honour, nor gratitude," Elizabeth holds, "have any possible claim on me, in the present instance. No principle of either, would be violated by my marriage with Mr. Darcy." Defending her love of laughter from charges of cynicism, Elizabeth proclaims, "I hope I never ridicule what is wise or good," and this promise of principled restraint differentiates Elizabeth's laughter from Lydia's animal glee. But at a time when Hannah More, among others, was writing conduct books for the middle classes and tracts for the lower, enjoining both not to question the wisdom of Providence in placing them in humbler spheres, Elizabeth's disclaimer is not quite as innocuous as it may appear, for the point of contention is exactly what or who is "wise or good," and Elizabeth appears not to doubt her own qualifications to decide for herself, and has no trouble censuring a Lady's officious airs or ridiculing a pompous patrician with his failure to behave like a gentleman. As far as Elizabeth is concerned, "extraordinary talents or miraculous virtue" will always command her respect, but the "mere stateliness of money and rank" will not awe her. Convinced that they occupied high ground, progressive novelists seize on the same kinds of distinctions and exploit them for all they are worth, contending, more systematically and more conspicuously of course, that the defenders of money and rank marshal speciously ethical artillery—such as Lady Catherine's "duty," "honour," and "gratitude"—in order to sustain their hegemony, and that it is only by force of "prejudice" that we are either bullied or duped into equating our moral imperatives with their interests.

Although this much is clearly true, the conflict between Elizabeth and Lady Catherine nevertheless remains exceedingly discreet in that even as it demarcates this politically volatile issue, it circumnavigates it at the same time. Austen dramatizes social prejudice, and her revised title highlights that buzzword. But people lower on the social scale can be prejudiced too, and the disputants themselves stand well back from polemical jargon. *Pride and Prejudice* thus alternatively verges on and recoils from radical criticism: Lady Catherine is not quite so extreme as to claim outright that the well-being of the kingdom depends on the purity of her family line. And for her part, Elizabeth claims not that she has the right to quit the "sphere" of her birth, but rather that in marrying Darcy, she would be staying within that sphere: "He is a gentleman; I am a gentleman's daughter; so far we are equal." To the extent that this assertion of equality demystifies the great gentry, it serves reformist ends, for it deprives men like Darcy of any rationale for their pride. But in the meantime, it leaves the social structure radicals had assailed substantially intact. Elizabeth, after all, changes her mind about Darcy when she realizes how conscientiously he tends to the happiness of those in his charge as a good master, landlord, and brother: "How many people's happiness were in his guardianship!— How much of pleasure or pain it was in his power to bestow."

The challenge Elizabeth poses to the power of rank and wealth is further diminished when we consider Lady Catherine's sex as well as her utter ridiculousness. Unlike Mrs. Smith in *Sense and Sensibility* and Lady Russell in *Persuasion*, who both figure as alternatives to male authority, women such as Lady Catherine and Mrs. Ferrars [in *Sense and Sensibility*] are parodies of male authority. As such, although they defend and collude in the interests of the patriarchal family, they themselves obviously are not the most formidable embodiments of it. Because these surrogates are easier to assail than, say, fathers and uncles, they make it possible to show what is oppressive about the power of rank and wealth, and what is overbearing about their assumptions of superiority. Further, they also make it possible to represent rebellion against the claims of familial authority, because in Austen's novels, at least, female authority figures are invariably defied by their young male relations. Though they may hold some purse strings, they hold virtually no moral sway. Because they cannot enforce obedience, their imperiousness is risible. This need not have been so. Austen could have endowed Lady Catherine with some of the daunting majesty [Fanny] Burney extends to Mrs. Delvile in *Cecilia* [1782], for example, a figure who for similar reasons makes similar appeals to the heroine's honor and gratitude, but who does command the respect and voluntary obedience of both her son and Cecilia. But far from being dignified, Lady Catherine is in her own way every bit as ludicrous as Mrs. Bennet. If Austen's use of a weak and ridiculous female authority figure makes it possible to dramatize effectual resistance, it is at the cost of minimizing the extent and perhaps even obscuring the object of that resistance. Quite simply, it is left unclear whether all attempts on the part of the high and mighty to meddle in the autonomous choices of others are to be deemed insufferable, or whether it is merely that Lady Catherine's attempts to wield power are incompetent, inappropriate and eccentric.

Elizabeth's and Darcy's defiance of Lady Catherine exemplifies the balancing act everywhere in evidence in *Pride and Prejudice* and indicates the advantages as well as the limitations of complying, even critically, with conservative myths about the gentry as Austen does in this novel. The figure of Lady Catherine invites as well as dispels a critique of authority, for she receives all of the opprobrium we are never permitted to aim directly at Darcy or his parents, or at great gentry families in general. Though Darcy assures Elizabeth that his parents were "good themselves (my father particularly . . .)," they evidently share the same sentiments which prompt Lady Catherine to assert her authority on their behalf: solicitude for the "shades of Pemberley" demands it. Conflict with the aunt thus averts a more politically potent and sentimentally complicated conflict with parents. Here, the family is spared a frontal attack. We have to read closely in order to discover that Darcy's own parents taught him to "care for none beyond my own family circle, to think meanly of all the rest of the world," and by the time we learn this, it does not matter any more, for they are deceased, and Darcy is too touched by filial piety to dishonor their memories. But even though the "shades of Pemberley" are finally "polluted" by Elizabeth, her middle-class relations, a steward's rascally son, and the barely respectable Lydia, the majesty of Pemberley itself is still affirmed, and any suspicion on our part that it may have been tarnished is soon set to rest by our confidence that the now properly proud Darcy would never permit any real compromise of its integrity. Austen thus disclaims and exploits mythology about the gentry that counterrevolutionary writers employ. The insolence of rank and power has been chastized, but never radically enough to make us doubt their prestige or wonder whether it really would be "something" after all, as Elizabeth says, "to be mistress of Pemberley." The same worldly advantages that have not been allowed to bully Elizabeth into respect have still been allowed to exalt her in the end.

* * *

356

SUSAN FRAIMAN

The Humiliation of Elizabeth Bennet†

* * *

* * * Mr. Bennet is not actually a bad father—just a modern one. Smooth-browed advocate of instruction over discipline, user of reason instead of force, he typifies the benevolent father proposed by John Locke in his often reprinted tract, *Some Thoughts Concerning Education* (1693). * * * Apparently benign to the point of irresponsibility, Mr. Bennet may seem to wield nothing sharper than his sarcasm, but what he actually wields is the covert power of the Lockean patriarch, which is all the more effective for its subtlety. This aloof, unseen power of Mr. Bennet's suggests to me, for several reasons, the peculiar power of an author. As evidence of his literary disposition, Mr. Bennet takes refuge from the world in his library, prefers the inner to the outer life, chooses books over people. He asks two things only: the free use of his understanding and his room, precisely those things Virginia Woolf [in "A Room of One's Own"] associates with the privilege of the male writer and privation of the female. Above all, among women whose solace is news, Mr. Bennet keeps the upper hand by withholding information—that is, by creating suspense.

In the opening scene, for example, Mr. Bennet refuses to visit the new bachelor in town, deliberately frustrating Mrs. Bennet's expectation and desire. In fact, "he had always intended to visit him, though to the last always assuring his wife that he should not go; and till the evening after the visit was paid, she had no knowledge of it." Like any writer, Mr. Bennet relishes the power to contain his reader's pleasure and then, with his dénouement, to relieve and enrapture her. But the suspense is not over, for Elizabeth's father continues to be as stingy with physical description as some fathers are with pocket money. He controls his family by being not tightfisted but tight-lipped, and in this he resembles Austen herself. George Lewes[1] first noted the remarkable paucity of concrete details in Austen, her reluctance to tell us what people, their clothes, houses, or gardens look like. If female readers flocked to Richardson for Pamela's meticulous descriptions of what she packed in her trunk,[2] we may imagine their frustration at Austen's

---

† From *Unbecoming Women: British Women Writers and the Novel of Development* (New York: Columbia University Press, 1993) 69–87. Copyright © 1993 Columbia University Press. Reprinted with the permission of the publisher. Some references have been revised to a form consistent with bibliographic citations in this volume.
1. George Henry Lewes, "The Novels of Jane Austen," *Blackwood's* 86 (1859): 99–113.
2. See Ian Watt's comments on the "wealth of minutely described domestic detail" in Samuel Richardson's *Pamela* (1740): *The Rise of the Novel* (Berkeley: University of California Press, 1957) 153.

reticence about such matters. So Mr. Bennet only follows Austen when, secretive about Bingley's person and estate, he keeps the ladies in the dark. Their curiosity is finally gratified by another, less plain-styled father, Sir William Lucas, whose report they receive "second-hand" from Lady Lucas. For much as women talk in this novel, the flow of important words, of what counts as "intelligence," is regulated largely by men; in this verbal economy, women get the trickle-down of news.

The scene following Mr. Collins's proposal to Elizabeth offers another instance of this, as Mr. Bennet again contrives to keep his female audience hanging. In a stern prologue he pretends to support his wife—insisting that Lizzie marry her clerical cousin—only to undermine Mrs. Bennet in a surprise conclusion: "An unhappy alternative is before you, Elizabeth. From this day you must be a stranger to one of your parents.—Your mother will never see you again if you do *not* marry Mr. Collins, and I will never see you again if you *do*." Not only this particular coup but the entire episode demonstrates the efficacy of paternal words. Throughout his proposal, much to Elizabeth's distress and the reader's amusement, Mr. Collins completely ignores her many impassioned refusals. He discounts what she says as "merely words of course," for even his dim, self-mired mind correctly perceives that a lady's word carries no definitive weight. Mr. Collins accuses Elizabeth of wishing to increase his love "by suspense, according to the usual practice of elegant females," yet creating suspense is exactly what Elizabeth, rhetorically disadvantaged, cannot do. She has no choice but "to apply to her father, whose negative might be uttered in such a manner as must be decision." Mr. Bennet's power resides, as I say, in his authorial prerogative, his right to have the last word.

Though Mr. Bennet uses this right to ridicule and disappoint his wife, he uses it in an opposite fashion to praise, protect, and apparently enable his daughter. Like so many heroines in women's fiction, Elizabeth has a special relationship to her father. She is immediately distinguished, both as a family member and as a character, by his preference for her and hers for him. Entail aside, she is in many respects his heir, for Mr. Bennet bequeaths to Elizabeth his ironic distance from the world, his habit of studying and appraising those around him, his role of social critic. Colleagues in this role, father and daughter scan Mr. Collins's letter together, dismissing man and letter with a few, skeptical words. Mr. Bennet enables Elizabeth, in short, by sharing with her an authorial mandate that is Austen's own: the need and ability to frame a moral discourse and to judge characters accordingly. Through her father, Elizabeth gains provisional access to certain authorial powers. But Mr. Bennet also shares with her, illogically enough, his disdain for women. He respects Elizabeth only insofar as she is unlike other girls, so that bonding with him means breaking with her mother or even reneging on femaleness altogether. In this sense Elizabeth is less a daughter than a surrogate son: like a son, by giving up the mother and giving in to the father, she reaps the spoils of maleness. Freud's charting of female development supplies an alternative view. In this scheme, girls turn, disillusioned, from the mother to the father out of penis envy. To complete their oedipal task, however, they must cease to identify with the powerful father, come to accept their own "castration," and learn to desire a baby as a substitute for the phallus.[3] In these terms the cocky Elizabeth of the book's first half is charmingly arrested in the early phase of male-identification, victim of what Freud would call a "masculinity complex." And in either case—whether one sees her as an honorary boy who has completed his oedipal task or as a backward, wayward girl who refuses to complete hers—Elizabeth's discursive power arises from an alliance and identification with her father. As the scene with Mr. Collins shows, the force of her words is highly contingent, any authority she has merely borrowed. Like a woman writing under a male pseudonym, Elizabeth's credibility depends on the father's signature.

* * * For in Austen the male bonding between father and daughter is set up to collapse. Sooner or later, what Adrienne Rich calls "compulsory heterosexuality"[4]—a conspiracy of economic need and the ideology of romance—forces Elizabeth out of the library, into the ballroom, and up to the altar. The father's business in this ritual is, in every sense, to give the daughter away. If Mr. Bennet is supportive up to a point, her marriage obliges him to objectify Elizabeth and hand her over. At this juncture, he not only withdraws his protection and empowerment but also gives away her true "castrated" gender, revealing her incapacity for action in a phallocentric society.[5] This ceremony—posing father as giver, daughter as gift—could be said to underlie and ultimately to belie the relation of fathers to daughters in *Pride and Prejudice*.

*   *   *

3. The relevant essays are "The Dissolution of the Oedipus Complex" (1924), "Some Psychical Consequences of the Anatomical Distinction between the Sexes" (1925), "Female Sexuality" (1931), and "Femininity" (1932). Nancy Chodorow [in *The Reproduction of Mothering* (Berkeley: University of California Press, 1978)] offers a helpful recapitulation of Freud on fathers and daughters (94–99); see also Sarah Kofman [*The Enigma of Woman: Women in Freud's Writings*, trans. Catherine Porter (Ithaca: Cornell University Press, 1985)] for a further glossing of the Oedipus and masculinity complexes (199–206).
4. Adrienne Rich, "Compulsory Heterosexuality and Lesbian Existence," *Signs* 5 (1980): 631–60.
5. In a letter to a favorite niece, Austen more explicitly and bitterly represents marriage as a loss, for women, ushering in a period of inactivity: "Oh! what a loss it will be, when you are married. You are too agreable in your single state, too agreable as a Neice. I shall hate you when your delicious play of Mind is settled down into conjugal & maternal affections" (*Jane Austen's Letters*, 3rd ed., ed. Deirdre Le Faye [Oxford and New York: Oxford University Press, 1995], 20–21 Feb 1817, 329.

In his discussion of marriage and the incest taboo, Lévi-Strauss[6] famously proposed that the exchange of women among kin groups serves, like the exchange of money or words, to negotiate relationships among men. He explained that women function as a kind of currency, their circulation binding and organizing male society (61), and I am suggesting that *Pride and Prejudice* may offer a similar anthropology. Here, too, marriage betrays the tie between father and daughter in favor of ties among men with agendas of their own, involving both male sexuality and male class ambitions. To begin with the first, I appeal to Georges Bataille[7] regarding the (bestowing) father's libidinal investment in the marriage ceremony:

> Marriage is a matter less for the partners than for the man who gives the woman away, the man whether father or brother who might have freely enjoyed the woman, daughter or sister, yet who bestows her on someone else. This gift is perhaps a substitute for the sexual act. (218)

According to Bataille, marriage substitutes for the incestuous hetero-sexual act a homoerotic exchange in which the father gives his own flesh, as it were, to another man. Dropping the daughter from the sexual equation except as a mediating term, this substitution italicizes male sexuality at the expense of female sexuality. Revising Bataille, one might say that marriage is at once an expression/renunciation of the father's desire for the daughter and the renunciation of the daughter's right to a sexual agenda of her own. As anthropologist Gayle Rubin observes in "The Traffic in Women,"[8] the systematic exchange of women imprisons female desire in a "debt nexus":

> If a girl is promised in infancy, her refusal to participate as an adult would disrupt the flow of debts and promises. It would be in the interests of such a system if the woman in question did not have too many ideas of her own about whom she might want to sleep with. (182)

* * *

The fathers' other interest in the daughter's circulation concerns, as I say, class ambitions. Mr. Bennet's obvious interest in the Elizabeth-Darcy match is similar to Elizabeth's own. He may laugh at Mrs. Bennet's schemes, but the fact remains that he, too, will benefit from a noble connection. And despite his philosophic detachment, Mr. Ben-

---

6. Claude Lévi-Strauss, *The Elementary Structures of Kinship*, revised edition, translated by James Harle Bell, John Richard von Sturner, and Rodney Needham (Boston: Beacon Press, 1969).
7. *Death and Sensuality: A Study of Eroticism and the Taboo* (New York: Arno, 1977).
8. In *Toward an Anthropology of Women*, ed. Royna R. Deiter (New York: Monthly Review Press, 1975).

net is not without a streak of pragmatism—after all, he has always intended to visit Mr. Bingley. Capable of being impressed by wealth and rank, he is frankly delighted that Darcy has used his money and influence to straighten out the Lydia-Wickham affair. "So much the better," he exults. "It will save me a world of trouble and economy." Sounding even, for a moment, strangely like Mr. Collins, Elizabeth's father consents to her marriage with little of his habitual irony. "I have given him my consent," he tells her. "He is the kind of man, indeed, to whom I should never dare refuse any thing, which he condescended to ask." Though Mr. Darcy's class interests may seem to rule against a tie to the Bennets, they too are subtly at work here. Eighteenth-century Cinderella matches not only brought titles to the middle class but also, by distributing merchant profits, put oft-needed cash into the coffers of the well-born. Only with *Persuasion*'s Sir Walter Elliot does Austen fully represent the material as well as moral impoverishment of her landed contemporaries; yet by *Sense and Sensibility* she has already given us one Willoughby who, unsure of his aristocratic heritage, leaves Marianne for a certain Miss Grey with fifty thousand pounds. Of course, in *Pride and Prejudice* capital flows the other way, but even here a decline in aristocratic welfare is nevertheless suggested by the sickly Miss De Bourgh. It may well be the enfeeblement of his own class that encourages Darcy to look below him for a wife with greater stamina. As a figure for the ambitious bourgeoisie, Elizabeth pumps richer, more robust blood into the collapsing veins of the nobility, even as she boosts the social standing of her relatives in trade. Most important, however— to the patriarchs of both classes—she eases tensions between them. By neutralizing class antagonisms, she promotes the political stability essential to industrial prosperity and the fortunes of middle-class and noble men alike. What does it mean, *Pride and Prejudice* encourages one to ask, for female development and destiny to be thoroughly entangled in patriarchal enmities and interests so far beyond the purview of any one girl?

* * *

This brings me to Mr. Darcy—a father by virtue of his age, class, and a paternalism extending to friends and dependents alike. A man given to long letters and polysyllables, a man with an excellent library and even hand, Darcy may also be seen as an aspiring authorial figure. If Mr. Bennet sets out to create suspense, Mr. Darcy hankers to resolve it. They are literary as well as sexual rivals, and Elizabeth is the prize— or would be, were this surrogate son, father's heir, not herself a contender for authorial status. In these terms, Elizabeth's and Darcy's matching of wits, more than flirtation, is a struggle for control of the text. There are two heated and defining moments in this struggle: Elizabeth's refusal of Darcy's first proposal and the morning after when he delivers his letter. The first begins with Elizabeth alone at the Collins's house in Kent, studying Jane's letters. Suddenly Darcy bursts in and blurts out a proposal; the chapter closes by resuming Elizabeth's internal dialogue, "the tumult of her mind" after Darcy's departure. But where has the reader been throughout this chapter if not in the heroine's formidable mind? By all rights this should be Darcy's scene, his say, while in fact Austen transcribes relatively few of his actual words. His amatory discourse is quickly taken over by a narrator who represents the scene and renders even Darcy's language wholly from Elizabeth's point of view: "His sense of her inferiority . . . [was] dwelt on with a warmth which . . . was very unlikely to recommend his suit." The text of Darcy's proposal is completely glossed and glossed over by Elizabeth's response to it. Of her refusal, on the other hand, Austen includes every unmediated word, a direct quotation four times as long as that permitted Darcy, and this sets the pattern for what follows. Each time Darcy opens his mouth, he is superseded by a speech of greater length and vehemence. She answers his question—why is he so rudely rejected?—with a tougher question of her own.

> I might as well enquire . . . why with so evident a design of offending and insulting me, you chose to tell me that you liked me against your will, against your reason, and even against your character? Was not this some excuse for incivility, if I *was* uncivil?

Conceding nothing, she accuses him at some length of everything: of breaking Jane's heart and unmaking Wickham's fortune, of earning and continually confirming her own dislike. She betters his scorn for her family by scorning him. "I have every reason in the world to think ill of you," she declares. Her language, her feelings, and her judgments overwhelm his and put them to shame. Driving poor Darcy to platitude, apology, and hasty retreat, they leave Elizabeth the easy winner of this first rhetorical round.

The following day, however, Elizabeth is obsessed by Darcy: "It was the impossible to think of anything else." As the man crowds out all other thoughts, so the letter he delivers soon crowds out all other words, monopolizing the narrative for the next seven pages. Longer than the entire preceding chapter, it completely dispels Elizabeth's inspired performance of the day before. If Darcy was not "master enough" of himself then, he regains his mastery now. In a play for literary hegemony (to be author and critic both), he recovers his story and manages its interpretation. The letter establishes, for example, that Darcy's judgment of Jane was entirely impartial:

> That I was desirous of believing her indifferent is certain,—but I will venture to say that my investigations and decisions are not

usually influenced by my hopes and fears.—I did not believe her to be indifferent because I wished it;—I believed it on impartial conviction.

As for Wickham, the letter documents Darcy's early suspicions and the events that follow, proving him right. It demonstrates, too, Darcy's fatherly influence upon others, the moral sway he holds over Bingley and Georgiana: his friend has "a stronger dependence on [Darcy's] judgment than on his own"; his sister, fearing big brother's disapproval, decides not to elope after all. Only after Darcy's unabridged text does the narrator describes Elizabeth's reaction to it. She reads "with an eagerness which hardly left her power of comprehension, and from impatience of knowing what the next sentence might bring, was incapable of attending to the sense of the one before her eyes." Darcy's letter saps her power to comprehend, disables her attention. She is addressed as reader—recall with what certainty she dispatched a letter from her previous suitor—only to be indisposed in this role. At first Elizabeth protests: "This must be false! This cannot be! This must be the grossest falsehood!" She rushes through the letter and resolves to put it away forever, but the text, unrelenting, demands to be taken out, to be read and read again. Against the broad chest of Darcy's logic, Elizabeth pounds the ineffectual fists of her own. She puts the paper firmly down, then "weighed every circumstance with what she meant to be impartiality—deliberated on the probability of each statement—but with little success." Resolutions, procrastinations, do nothing to stop the inexorable drive of Darcy's narrative to its foregone conclusion. * * *

* * *

Soon after receiving Darcy's letter, Elizabeth meets up with Kitty and Lydia. Officer-crazy as ever, Lydia gushes on about Brighton and her plans to join the regiment there for its summer encampment. This first reference to Brighton unfolds into an unexpectedly earnest seduction plot—latent perhaps in Lydia's very character, throwback to earlier, too sentimental heroines—that might be more at home in a novel by Richardson or Burney. That such a seemingly anomalous plot should surface now and dominate for more than seven chapters is not accidental. For one thing, the Lydia-Wickham fiasco serves to reveal both Bennet's inadequacy and Darcy's capacity. Elizabeth first doubts her father regarding his decision to let Lydia go to Brighton, and she blames him bitterly for the subsequent scandal. For Darcy, by contrast, the calamity is a chance to display his nobility of heart and purse, his wish to rectify and his power to do so. The Lydia plot thus accomplishes Elizabeth's separation from her father as well as her reattachment to another: a changing of the paternal guard. By showcasing

Darcy, the upstart story that appears to delay and even to replace Elizabeth's and Darcy's courtship actually works to advance it.

But there is another reason that Lydia's seduction moves into the foreground at this moment. It happens to occupy the curious gap between Elizabeth's first, private softening and her final, public surrender to Darcy. This leads me to suspect that Elizabeth's narrative is displaced for the length of these chapters onto her sister's, that Lydia's seduction codes an emotional drama—of coercion, capitulation, and lamentation—missing from but underlying Elizabeth's story proper. Far from being an unrelated plot, Lydia's may be its ruder, telltale twin. Of course Lydia is a foil for Elizabeth, one sister's folly held up to the other's wisdom, yet there remains a sense in which they, or their fates, are similar. When Lydia calls Mary King "a nasty little freckled thing," Elizabeth admits that "however incapable of such coarseness of *expression* herself, the coarseness of the *sentiment* was little other than her own breast had formerly harbored." Taking seriously this point that Lydia and Elizabeth may differ more in style than substance, I find that Lydia's interpolated tale does not so much distract from the central courtship as distill its darkest meaning. While the overread version of Elizabeth's *Bildung* marks her gaining of self-knowledge and security, the eruption into Elizabeth's midst of Lydia's more sordid history points to a counternarrative of seduction and surrender.

* * *

According to one critical truism, *Pride and Prejudice* manages a kind of bilateral disarmament: Elizabeth gives up her prejudice, while Darcy relinquishes his pride.[9] I am arguing, however, that Darcy woos away not Elizabeth's "prejudice," but her judgment entire. For while Darcy defends the impartiality of his views, Elizabeth confesses to the partiality of hers; while his representation of the world is taken to be objective, raised to the level of universality, hers (like that of women generally) is condemned for being subjective and dismissed as mere "prejudice." But what does Austen's record actually show? Elizabeth was certainly wrong about Wickham, but was she really that wrong about Darcy? He may warm up a bit, and his integrity is rightly affirmed, but he is hardly less arrogant than Elizabeth at first supposed.

9. John Halperin (*The Life of Jane Austen* [Baltimore and London: Johns Hopkins University Press, 1984]) is particularly complacent before this formulation: "It is unnecessary to rehearse again the process by which Darcy's pride is humbled and Elizabeth's prejudices exposed—'your defect is a propensity to hate every body,' she tells him early in the novel; 'And yours . . . is wilfully to misunderstand them,' he replies" (70). Alison Sulloway (*Jane Austen and the Province of Womanhood* [Philadelphia: University of Pennsylvania Press, 1989]), by contrast, revises the cliché by historicizing the terms *pride* and *prejudice*, demonstrating their embeddedness in eighteenth-century feminist texts (66–69); in the polemical writings of Mary Astell, Catherine Macaulay, Mary Wollstonecraft, and Mary Hays, as in novels by Burney, Edgeworth, and Austen, these frequently used terms come to operate as "code words to describe men's pride in their dominion and their prejudice against the sex they dominated" (66).

Her comment to Fitzwilliam is ever exact: "I do not know any body who seems more to enjoy the power of doing what he likes than Mr. Darcy." And what about Darcy's own accuracy? His judgment of Jane is just as mistaken—and, though he denies it, as partial—as Elizabeth's view of Wickham. Yet Darcy's credibility remains intact. Finally admitting to having misinterpreted Jane, Darcy explains that he was corrected not by Elizabeth but by his own subsequent observations, and on this basis he readvises the ever-pliant Bingley. Whereas Lizzie's mistake discredits her judgment for good, Mr. Darcy's, far from disqualifying him, gives him an opportunity to judge again. What happens in *Pride and Prejudice*, then, is not simply that an a priori prejudiced character at last sees the error of her ways. Rather, a character introduced as reliable, whose clarity of vision is evidently the author's own, is re-presented—in the context of her marriageability—as prejudiced. In my reading, the psychological drama of a heroine "awakening" to her true identity is brought into conflict with the social drama of an outspoken girl entering a world whose voices drown out her own.

If Elizabeth does not overcome her "prejudice," neither does Darcy abandon his pride. Early in the book Elizabeth declares, "I could easily forgive *his* pride, if he had not mortified *mine.*" But by the last volume she suggests just the opposite:

> They owed the restoration of Lydia, her character, every thing to him. Oh! how heartily did she grieve over every ungracious sensation she had ever encouraged, every saucy speech she had ever directed towards him. For herself she was humbled; but she was proud of him.

There is a rueful women's joke about how "it was one of those love-hate relationships: by the end of it we both loved him and both hated me." At the outset, Elizabeth and Darcy are each proud, each skeptical of the other, yet finally they reach what is in some sense the conjugal consensus of this joke: in the end both are skeptical of her, both proud of him. But wait. Doesn't Darcy make a pretty speech to his bride confessing, "By you, I was properly humbled"? Here it is useful to see how the novel itself defines "pride" and how this definition relates to Mr. Darcy. The bookish Mary (another figure for Austen, if a self-mocking one) distinguishes "pride" from "vanity": "Pride relates more to our opinion of ourselves, vanity to what we would have others think of us." As for Darcy, Charlotte Lucas contends that his pride is excusable: "One cannot wonder that so very fine a young man, with family, fortune, every thing in his favor, should think highly of himself. If I may so express it, he has a *right* to be proud." A younger Lucas puts it more bluntly: "If I were as rich as Mr. Darcy, I should not care how proud I was. I would keep a pack of foxhounds and drink a bottle of wine every day." The practical Lucases have a point. Darcy's richness gives him if not the "right" then the ability, in Mary's formulation, to be proud. A man in Darcy's social position need not consider any opinion but his own; he is proud because he does not have to be vain. In this sense, pride is less a psychological attribute than a social one—it comes with the territory and is therefore, if anything, heightened by Darcy's enhanced status in *Pride and Prejudice*'s last act.

Vanity, by contrast, is the adaptive strategy of those who depend on the kindness of strangers. In these terms, pride and vanity are arguably gender as well as class specific. * * * Dependent on what the neighbors say for their status as proper ladies, reliant on male admiration and marriage for their economic survival, middle-class women are vain because they cannot afford to be proud. The story I am tracing of Elizabeth's decline involves not only the interrogation of her judgment but her fall from a "male" impersonation of pride into the vanity of other girls. John Berger[1] might put it that the heroine shifts from proudly "acting" on her own behalf to merely "appearing" in the eyes of others; from seeing the world herself to seeing only herself *being seen* by the world.

To begin with, Elizabeth resists maternal efforts to school her in self-display. Warned by Mrs. Bennet that if she walks to Netherfield she "will not be fit *to be seen*," Elizabeth firmly activates her mother's passive voice. "I shall be very fit *to see* Jane—which is all I want," she replies (my emphases). Three chapters later, Miss Bingley and Mr. Darcy stroll along discussing Elizabeth's portrait, recasting their guest as an appearance for acquisition and exhibition. At that moment, they encounter the object of their speculation/specularity. As if refusing to sit for her portrait, Elizabeth quickly inverts the visual economy by assuming the position of artist who studies and composes them: "No, no; stay where you are.—You are charmingly group'd, and appear to uncommon advantage. The picturesque would be spoilt by admitting a fourth. Good bye." Running "gaily off," she still defies any attempt to capture and frame her. A volume and a half later, Elizabeth approaches Pemberley with a similarly assertive eye. She wants particularly to see the area without being seen by Darcy: "But surely I may enter his country with impunity, and rob it of a few petrified spars without his perceiving me." Driving through the park she gazes long and delightedly over the grounds. After "examining the nearer aspect of the house," she enters the building and surveys the dining-parlor with appreciation, admiring the good taste of the furniture. With increasing excitement, she stares out of every window, commands the

1. *Ways of Seeing* (London: Penguin, 1972).

view from each room. She does not merely look, but looks with a desire
to possess—from thinking to rob Darcy's county "of a few petrified
spars," she now imagines herself mistress of his estate. Challenging the
usual gender of the aggressive gaze, she positively leers.[2]

In the picture gallery, Elizabeth's desire to behold Mr. Darcy's portrait seems part of the visual assault she has mounted thus far. "At last
it arrested her—and she beheld a striking resemblance of Mr. Darcy,
with such a smile over the face, as she remembered to have sometimes
seen, when he looked at her." Like Darcy's letter, his picture is terribly
compelling. Though she sets out to track it down, it arrests her and,
before she can leave the gallery, draws her back to it again. Most
remarkably, it reorganizes the pattern and sexual politics of seeing—
for even as Elizabeth looks at the painting, it reminds her of Darcy
looking at her. She marvels at the vast proportions of his influence "as
a brother, a landlord, a master."

> And as she stood before the canvas, on which he was represented,
> and *fixed his eyes upon herself, she thought of his regard* with a
> deeper sentiment of gratitude than it had ever raised before. (my
> emphasis)

Elizabeth, visual libertine, is suddenly shy and conventionally vain.
Now her act of looking unexpectedly fixes his eyes on her; now her
gaze sees only how she looks to him. It is clear from this passage that
Elizabeth's deepening gratitude, the change of heart that propels her
into marriage, coincides with a novel concern for Darcy's "regard," a
heightened awareness of herself as the object of his gaze and estimation. But surely this bit of description, dramatically reversing what people usually do in front of a painting, is self-consciously strange; for the
woman positioned as spectator to fix the eyes of the image upon herself
cannot but strike us as perverse. As with Darcy's letter, which seizes
the female reader and turns her into the object of its force and her
own hatred, here is another striking inversion—one that by flipping

2. My remarks throughout this section are indebted to the body of work on looking and power
developed in the past fifteen years primarily by feminist film theorists. Much of this work,
following the lead of Laura Mulvey's "Visual Pleasure and Narrative Cinema" (*Screen* 16
[1975] 6–18; reprinted in *Visual and Other Pleasures* [Bloomington: Indiana University Press,
1989]), has emphasized the aggressive "maleness" of the gaze intrinsic to classical cinema's
way of seeing. More recently, however, critics like Judith Mayne, Mary Anne Doane, Linda
Williams, and Mulvey herself have raised questions about women as spectators—for example,
as the audience addressed by the "woman's film" of the 1940s (Doane); as classical and
avant-garde filmmakers (Mayne); and as female characters whose active looking and desiring
is often violently punished (Williams). These last may have something in common with the
investigative Elizabeth Bennet, well aware of her crime against propriety in gazing on Pemberley and an image of its master, without herself being seen. In the terms suggested by
Williams's "When the Woman Looks," Elizabeth's humiliation may be the punitive fate of
a woman who dares to look aggressively; I have been arguing, however, that Austen leads her
readers to question the naturalness and rightness of this fate. The essays by Mayne, Doane,
and Williams can be found in *Re-vision: Essays in Feminist Film Criticism* (Frederick, MD:
University Publications of America, 1984); see also *Feminism and Film Theory* (New York:
Methuen, 1988), edited by Constance Penley.

the idiom sets up the moment as a problem, making the reader pause and consider. The result, I would say, is once more to phrase Elizabeth's humiliating loss of pride as an awkward disordering, to defamiliarize the clichés of female development.

Of course, one continues to admire Elizabeth. She may care for Darcy's regard, but she is never so utterly enslaved by it as Miss Bingley. She may hesitate to laugh at Darcy, but she does show Georgiana that a wife may take (some) liberties. She is admirable because she is not Charlotte, because she is not Lydia. I want nevertheless to insist that Elizabeth is a better friend to Charlotte and closer sister to Lydia— that one version of her story runs more parallel to theirs—than previous readings have indicated. The three women live in the same town, share the same gossip, and attend the same balls. Why, as some critics have claimed, should Elizabeth alone be above the social decree?[3] There are, in Elizabeth's marriage, elements of both crass practicality and coercion. Elizabeth is appalled by Charlotte's pragmatism, yet in her own preference for Darcy over Wickham she shows herself beguiled by the entrepreneurial marriage plot.[4] And though clearly embarrassed by the family connection to Lydia, Elizabeth, too, is implicated by the formal intersection of their stories: in the course of the novel she loses not her virginity but her authority. For while the heroine marries a decent man and a large estate, Austen seems concerned to show that she pays a certain price. If Mr. Bennet embodies the post-Enlightenment, modified patriarch, Mr. Darcy harks back to an earlier type and time, before fathers were curbed by Lockean principles, before aristocrats began to feel the crunch. Recall how ambiguously his power looms before Elizabeth: "How much of pleasure or pain it was in his power to bestow!— How much of good or evil must be done by him!" Darcy disempowers Elizabeth if only because of their unequal positions in the social schema—because he is a Darcy and she is a Bennet, because he is a man and she is his wife. * * *

3. I have in mind D. W. Harding ("'Regulated Hatred': An Aspect in the Work of Jane Austen" *Scrutiny* 8 [1940]) [see pp. 296–99 in this volume—*Editor*] and Marvin Mudrick (*Jane Austen: Irony as Defense and Discovery* [Princeton: Princeton University Press, 1952]), old guard of the subversive school. While I am indebted to this tradition, I disagree with Harding's and Mudrick's view that Austen challenges her society by having Elizabeth transcend it. Mudrick contends, for instance, that "the central fact for Elizabeth remains the power of choice" (124); to his liberal imagination, Elizabeth represents the "free individual" (126). In my opinion, *Pride and Prejudice* is about the heroine's inextricability from the social context, not her independence of it.

4. It is interesting that Hollywood—of venal habits and puritanical tastes—should recognize and be uneasy with the suspiciousness of Elizabeth's position as Austen wrote it. In the 1940 film version of *Pride and Prejudice* (directed by Robert Z Leonard, with a screenplay by Aldous Huxley and Jane Murfin), Lady Catherine De Bourgh threatens to cut Darcy out of her will if he goes ahead and marries a Bennet. Elizabeth proves her romantic integrity by vowing to marry him anyway. Needless to say, Austen conspicuously chose *not* to test Elizabeth in such a manner. Agreeing that "Austen is at pains from early in the novel to show us Elizabeth's response to Darcy's wealth," Karen Newman ("Can This Marriage Be Saved Jane Austen Makes Sense of an Ending," *ELH* 50 [1983] 693–710) adds that critics as early as Sir Walter Scott remarked on the heroine's fascination with Pemberley (698)

* * * By the end of the book, Mr. Bennet's paternal role has been assumed by Elizabeth's uncle, Mr. Gardiner. Though "gentlemanlike," Mr. Gardiner lives by trade "within view of his own warehouses" and represents, more than Mr. Bennet, the rising middle class. No wonder Elizabeth fears that Darcy will rebuff him, given that nobleman's past intolerance for her vulgar relations. She is quite unprepared for Darcy's civility to Gardiner and for the apparent power of fishing to overcome class differences. Perhaps their shared fondness for Elizabeth, their lengthy haggle over Lydia, as well as their equal passion for trout serve to reinforce the shared social/economic advantages of Darcy's and Gardiner's alliance. They become, in any case, suggestively close; indeed, the very last paragraph of the novel informs us that

> with the Gardiners, they were always on the most intimate terms. Darcy, as well as Elizabeth, really loved them; and they were both ever sensible of the warmest gratitude towards the persons who, by bringing her into Derbyshire, had been the means of uniting them.

At first this seems an oddly insignificant note on which to end. On second glance it appears to confirm the suspicion I have had—that just as the Gardiners have been the means of uniting Darcy and Elizabeth, so Elizabeth has been useful as the means of uniting Mr. Darcy and Mr. Gardiner. *Pride and Prejudice* attains a satisfying unity not only between a man and a woman but also between two men, an intercourse not merely personal but social, a marriage of two classes no less than a marriage of true minds.

DEBORAH KAPLAN

Circles of Support†

Biographers and critics, in stressing the role of Austen's kin, have ignored the general impact of their community's culture while insisting that the influence of the novelist's family, after getting her started as a writer, continued unchanging. Throughout her life her family is said to have stimulated and supported her talent.[1] "Her novels remained to the last a kind of family entertainment," according to Mary Lascelles.[2]

---

† From *Jane Austen Among Women* (Baltimore: Johns Hopkins University Press, 1992) 96–97, 99–106, 108. The author's notes have been edited to provide references to the recent edition of Austen's letters. Reprinted by permission.
1. Park Honan provides the most elaborated version of this view in *Jane Austen: Her Life* (New York: St. Martin's Press, 1988) [see pp. 267–69 of this edition—*Editor*] and in his subsequent article, "The Austen Brothers and Sisters," *Persuasions*, no. 10 (1988): 59–64.
2. *Jane Austen and Her Art* (Oxford: Clarendon Press, 1939), 146, 32.

Mary Poovey concurs with Lascelles' representation of Austen's relatives: "Jane Austen wrote her first stories for the amusement of her family. . . . Austen's first longer works . . . were also apparently family entertainments, and, even after she became a published author, she continued to solicit and value the response of her family as she composed and revised her novels."[3] But just as the family's influence was permeated by the culture of Austen's community in her childhood, so that influence was reshaped by the community's values in Austen's adulthood. "Family" became a smaller circle in Austen's adult life, but that group, though private and exclusive, was still not disconnected from the community and patriarchal culture surrounding it.

The literary interests and pursuits of Jane Austen's family *and* community explain how, as a young girl, she came to be interested in literature and to try imaginative writing, but they cannot account for Austen's mature writing. In the second half of the 1790s Austen was becoming a serious, committed writer. We can follow the transformation by considering her productions. The majority of her juvenilia, like the works of her family and neighbors, are very brief; some mere fragments or, as she called one selection of them, "Scraps." Most of the longer pieces are unfinished. *Lady Susan*, the first composition written after the juvenilia in 1793–94, while not incomplete, is brought to a quick finish with a short, tacked-on conclusion. But beginning in 1795, Austen wrote and completed three extended manuscripts: "First Impressions" [*Pride and Prejudice*], "Elinor and Marianne" [*Sense and Sensibility*], and "Susan" [*Northanger Abbey*] and those efforts changed the nature of Austen's creative life, differentiating it both from her work on her earlier fictions and from the leisure-time composing of other members of the gentry. The manuscripts required sustained concentration. They took time.

We have only to remember the dictums of the widespread ideology of domesticity to appreciate the potential subversiveness of that writing. The ideal woman was to engage in activities that served her family, contributing either to the pleasures of her husband or to the education of her children. Certainly, a young girl or even an adult woman who whiled away an occasional solitary afternoon by composing a poem or by writing brief parodies could not be accused of putting herself first in an "unfeminine" way. But to write three books in four years? Although biographers and critics have routinely portrayed the charming family context for Austen's girlhood precociousness, they have not provided a persuasive rendering of that context for the novelist's dif-

---

3. Mary Poovey, *The Proper Lady and the Woman Writer: Ideology as Style in the Works of Mary Wollstonecraft, Mary Shelley, and Jane Austen* (Chicago: Univ. of Chicago Press, 1984) 202. See also Alison Sulloway. *Jane Austen and the Province of Womanhood* (Philadelphia: Univ. of Pennsylvania Press, 1989), 86, 87, 92. Sulloway stresses the lifelong role of the family, particularly Austen's father and her brother Henry. She also singles out Austen's mother and sister as decidedly unsupportive and unhelpful.

ficult transition from play to professionalism, a transition that began
in the second half of the 1790s and extended into the second decade
of the nineteenth century. They have not been able to do so because
they have ignored the increasing cultural pressures on females in Jane
Austen's community who were becoming adult women.

*   *   *

Austen's letters suggest that by the end of the 1790s she had a small
inner circle of enthusiastic female supporters. Only two references to
readers of her manuscripts appear in her letters from the period, but
we can conclude from them that her writing was a source of entertainment to which those to whom she was closest returned frequently. In
1799 Austen's mocking responses to Cassandra and Martha Lloyd's
requests to read one of her manuscripts suggest that both had already
done so several times.[4] * * *

Although Austen joked about Cassandra and Martha's requests, she
was also expressing self-confidence in her response to Martha. Such
expressions were not consistent with domestic femininity, though they
were typically encouraged by the women's culture. The audience for
some of Austen's responses to her own work, however playful, was shifting in the late 1790s. Austen's writing and her consciousness of that
effort were becoming part of the distinct culture of her female friend-
ships. To be sure, most of these ties, particularly in future years, were
to be to female kin, but "family" nonetheless was beginning to have a
meaning different from that evident during Austen's youth and early
adolescence.

* * * In 1809 Austen's father had been dead for four years. Her
brothers were preoccupied with careers and families of their own—all
except George, who had not, in any case, whether because of illness or
disability, lived among the family since he was a child.[5] Although Frank
and his new wife, Mary, lived with the Austen women in Southampton
from the fall of 1806 to 1808, Mary was the more longterm housemate,
for Frank was at sea from April 1807 to June 1808. Martha Lloyd had
also set up housekeeping with Mrs. Austen and her daughters beginning in 1805. The four people who moved to Chawton Cottage in the
spring of 1809, then, constituted a considerably altered, all-female version of the Austen "family." Austen's housemates had a more sustained
and immediate effect on her writing than her brother's gift of the
cottage.

In these later years Austen continued to try to restrict knowledge of
her writing. She signed the first edition of Sense and Sensibility "By a

4. Jane Austen's Letters, 3rd ed., ed. Deirde Le Faye (Oxford and New York: Oxford University,
   Press, 1995), 8–9 Jan. 1799, 11 June 1799, 35, 44.
5. For a comprehensive review of the information that has survived about Austen's older brother
   George, see George Holbert Tucker, A Goodly Heritage: (Manchester: Carcanet New Pross,
   1983), 115–17.

Lady" and her subsequent novels "By the Author of," listing some of her earlier works. Family and close friends knew; neighbors and acquaintances she tried to keep in the dark. The Middletons, who leased Chawton Manor from 1808 to 1813, were unaware of the writing going on in the cottage across the road.[6] And one of her letters from January 1813,[7] shows Austen and her mother trying to keep the authorship of the just-published *Pride and Prejudice* a secret from their houseguest, Miss Benn—even as they read the novel aloud to her. Jane or Cassandra also habitually enjoined family members to be discreet. The September 28, 1811, entry in the diary of their niece Fanny reads, "Another letter from Aunt Cassandra to beg we would not mention that Aunt Jane Austen wrote 'Sense & Sensibility.' "[8] As late as 1817, the year she died, the novelist wrote to Fanny, "I have a something ready for Publication, which may perhaps appear about a twelve-month hence." She followed this announcement with a warning to her niece *not* to pass the news on to her Kent acquaintances: "This is for yourself alone. Neither Mr. Salusbury nor Mr. Wildman are to know of it."[9]

The female *and* male members of her immediate family knew of her work, of course, but because over time her family had not only changed but grown, adding a new generation, Austen's reliance on the support of women is even more visible in this period. Her niece Fanny became part of the inner circle of confidantes, as did Fanny's sister Lizzy. James's daughter, Anna, also probably had intimate knowledge of her aunt's writing when they became quite close in the last four or five years of the novelist's life. The younger nieces and nephews were locked out of the secret, presumably until they were old enough to control their tongues.

Only Anna could report anything of her aunt's years at Steventon, but others of Austen's nieces and nephews were able to remember something of her years at Chawton. Their testimonies inadvertently help to reveal her choice of confidantes. What is striking about their descriptions of their aunt as a writer is how little some of them had to remember. They knew retrospectively that she was beginning a career as a novelist, but they saw very few signs of that career when they called up their memories.

Austen did no fiction writing while fulfilling her domestic duties, even when that meant no more than entertaining young relatives. We know that she did, however, write letters within gatherings, at least of family members, because part or all of her letters voiced their concerns

6. This information appears in a letter of reminiscence written by one of the Middleton children more than fifty years later, probably in the 1870s. Two of her letters were published in "Recollections of Chawton," *Times Literary Supplement*, 3 May 1985, 495.
7. *Letters*, 29 Jan. 1813, 201–202.
8. Quoted in Deirdre Le Faye, "Fanny Knight's Diaries: Jane Austen Through her Niece's Eyes," in *Persuasions: Occasional Papers*, no. 2 (1986), 15.
9. *Letters*, 13 March 1817, 333.

and interests. As Caroline Austen half recalls and half guesses, "My Aunt must have spent much time in writing—her desk lived in the drawing room. I often saw her writing letters on it, and I beleive she wrote much of her Novels in the same way—sitting with her family, when they were quite alone; but I never saw any manuscript of *that* sort, in progress"[1] James Edward Austen-Leigh, who had read Austen's first two novels before he learned that they were written by his aunt, can only assume in his *Memoir*[2] that Austen wrote in the company of just the women closest to her at Chawton: her sister, mother, and Martha Lloyd. But he *knows* that she put the duties enumerated by the domestic ideology before her writing and never revealed any hesitancy to do so. Or, rather, she never revealed any reluctance to him and other kin who were outside her circle of confidantes:

> In that well occupied female party there must have been many precious hours of silence during which the pen was busy at the little mahogany writing-desk, while Fanny Price, or Emma Woodhouse, or Anne Elliot was growing into beauty and interest. I have no doubt that I, and my sisters and cousins, in our visits to Chawton, frequently disturbed this mystic process, without having any idea of the mischief that we were doing; certainly we never should have guessed it by any signs of impatience or irritability in the writer. (102–3)

One of Austen's nieces, however, was able to recall Austen's writing with more certainty and specificity because older sisters of hers were allowed to hear works in progress. Marianne Knight advanced the "behind shut doors" imagery about her family's estate at Godmersham, which, along with the stories of the squeaky door and the blotting paper at Chawton, biographers have often evoked in order to describe Austen's working conditions. According to Marianne's reminiscence, when Austen stayed with the Knights in Kent, she shared her manuscripts with Fanny, Marianne's eldest sister, and probably with Lizzy, the next eldest sister, but only with them. As Marianne tells it, "I remember that when Aunt Jane came to us at Godmersham she used to bring the MS. of whatever novel she was writing with her, and would shut herself up with my elder sisters in one of the bedrooms to read them aloud. I and the younger ones used to hear peals of laughter through the door, and thought it very hard that we should be shut out from what was so delightful."[3]

In such restricted gatherings Austen received affirmation of her work as a writer. In accordance with feminine dutifulness and deference, she generally hid her work and kept silent about it. Even to show the pages

1. Caroline Austen, *My Aunt Jane Austen* (London: Jane Austen Society, 1952).
2. J. E. Austen-Leigh, *A Memoir of Jane Austen*, 2nd ed. (London: Bentley, 1871).
3. Constance Hill, *Jane Austen: Her Home & Her Friends* (1901; rpt. Folcroft: Folcroft Library Editions, 1977), 202.

of a manuscript, then, and to read from them was a striking, liberating change. Moreover, by sharing work in progress, she was not only acknowledging the fact of her products but the labor of creating them, and she was welcoming her female audience's participation in that labor. * * *

* * *

Austen volunteered less information to the male members of her family than she offered to her small female circle about works in progress, about what and when she was writing. Her allusion to a scene in *Mansfield Park* in a January 1813 letter that she wrote her sister indicates that Cassandra was very familiar with that still unfinished manuscript. By contrast, Austen mentioned it to Frank in July of 1813, when she had already completed the manuscript, telling him simply that a novel was "in hand."[4] And Henry embarked on his first reading of the completed novel in March, 1814, without any prior information on its plot or characters.[5] In a letter to Fanny Knight, written in 1817, we find more evidence that, despite his help with the business of publishing, Henry was—perhaps because he was not discreet enough to suit his sister—generally one of the last to learn of Austen's manuscripts. "Do not be surprised at finding Uncle Henry acquainted with my having another ready for publication," Austen wrote. "I could not say No when he asked me, but he knows nothing more of it."[6]

We can see an even more dramatic difference between what Austen said to contributors to her women's culture and what she said to her brothers and other members of her wider community in the way she represented herself as a writer and assessed her novels. Her biography-writing male relatives, beginning with Henry Austen, have insisted that she had little confidence in her work and was meekness itself in discussions of her writing.[7] More recently, literary critics Susan Gubar and Sandra Gilbert have radically altered this vision of the novelist by arguing that Austen consciously crafted modest, even self-abasing images of herself and her work: "With her self-deprecatory remarks about her inability to join 'strong manly, spirited sketches, full of Variety and Glow' with her 'little bit (two Inches wide) of Ivory,' Jane Austen perpetuated the belief among her friends that her art was just an accomplishment 'by a lady,' if anything 'rather too light and bright and sparkling.' "[8]

Austen's letters suggest that Gilbert and Gubar, though closer to the truth than biographers such as Henry Austen, are still only partially

4. *Letters*, 3–6 July 1813, 217.
5. See *Letters*, 2–3 March, 5–8 March, and 9 March 1814: 255, 258, 261.
6. *Letters*, 23–25 March 1817, 335.
7. See pp. 257–59 of this Norton Critical Edition [*Editor*].
8. Sandra Gilbert and Susan Gubar, *The Madwoman in the Attic. The Woman Writer and the Nineteenth Century Literary Imagination* (New Haven: Yale University Press, 1979), 108.

correct. Austen did indeed consciously construct self-deprecating images. She contributed them, however, only to the culture of the gentry. It was to her nephew James Edward that Austen represented her work as "the little bit (two Inches wide) of Ivory on which I work with so fine a Brush, as produces little effect after much labour."[9] To the Prince Regent's Librarian, J. S. Clarke, she offered a similarly self-deprecating pose: "I think I may boast myself to be, with all possible vanity, the most unlearned and uninformed female who ever dared to be an authoress."[1] Austen advanced such humble, albeit witty, self-representations with the intent, no doubt, of countering her society's general distrust of the femininity and gentility of women with public reputations as writers. She was always conscious of how she might appear to others if she were known as a writer. After the publication of *Pride and Prejudice*, a Miss Burdett expressed the desire to meet Austen. "I am rather frightened by hearing that she wishes to be introduced to *me*," Austen wrote her sister in dread of becoming a very unladylike public spectacle. "If I *am* a wild Beast, I cannot help it."[2]

In the discourse of her women's culture, Austen did not similarly depict herself as barely competent. Since her close friends generally promoted female assertiveness and pride in accomplishments, Austen could be sure of appreciative support when she announced to them the success of a dinner, a charitable act, some fine handiwork—or a piece of fiction. Thus, in her private discourse with female friends, Austen was able to develop a self-assured, even professionalized persona as a writer, a self-image that surely helped her to write. She was sometimes critical of or, to be more exact, sometimes a critic of her own writing but hardly in a self-demeaning way. When she told Cassandra that *Pride and Prejudice* was "too light, and bright, and sparkling," she was wondering if "the playfulness and epigrammatism of the general style" would be fully appreciated without "something unconnected with the story; an essay on writing, a critique on Walter Scott, or the history of Buonaparté, or anything that would form a contrast."[3]

She was also proud of her work. She spoke triumphantly to Cassandra, for example, about Elizabeth Bennet and the novel in which she figures, declaring her own superiority over those who either would not like or would not understand *Pride and Prejudice*: "I must confess that I think her as delightful a creature as ever appeared in print, and how I shall be able to tolerate those who do not like *her* at least I do not know. There are a few typical errors; and a 'said he,' or a 'said she,' would sometimes make the dialogue more immediately clear; but,"

9. *Letters*, 16–17 Dec. 1816, 323.
1. *Letters*, 11 Dec. 1815, 306.
2. *Letters*, 24 May 1813, 212.
3. *Letters*, 4 Feb. 1813, 203.

Austen continued, adapting a passage from Scott's *Marmion*, no less, " 'I do not write for such dull elves / As have not a great deal of ingenuity themselves.' "[4]

Only to women did she reveal the power she felt as an author. She may have pretended to a trivial "feminine" art before her nephew, but she was quite in earnest when she told her niece Anna about one of her manuscripts: "I *do* think you had better omit Lady Helena's postscript;—to those who are acquainted with P. & P. it will seem an Imitation."[5] Mine is the originating and original work, she was, in effect, declaring. * * *

Biographers have made the women so quiet and static that when chroniclers discuss Austen's writing, her companions sometimes seem to disappear. Life-writers, in fact, often invoke visions of Austen as a solitary genius or even of her double life at this point in their narratives. For James Edward Austen-Leigh, the quiet of Austen's female household enabled the "mystic process" of creation.[6] To David Cecil, whose vision of the female society at Chawton is a good deal less reverent than Elizabeth Jenkins's, Austen's life there "apparently so stagnant, served rather to provide the needed time and incentive for her genius to operate"[7] Because none of them supposes that Austen had a community at Chawton worthy of or necessary to her talents, many life-writers have insisted, as John Halperin does, on Austen's "loneliness" as a writer.[8] Even Jane Aiken Hodge, whose biography, *Only a Novel: The Double Life of Jane Austen* [1972], shows a good deal more interest in Austen's relationships with women, has maintained that "the artist is inevitably alone" when describing Austen during this period (116).

It was not her housemates' quiet or apparent capacity for invisibility that enabled Austen to write her novels. Before and after she moved to Chawton, her all-female "family" served as the crucial bridge between modest, self-effacing femininity and the self-assertion and self-expression of authoring. They formed a social circle among whom she could produce fiction and to whom she could talk—easily, confidently—about that work. We may never know the specific catalyst for the novels on which Austen embarked in 1809, but this much is clear: Had she only devoted herself to the interests of male and female neighbors and kin, had she always spoken a discourse filled up with their voices and concerns, she could not have become a novelist. Thus her alternative culture enabled her to do something for which the gentry's culture alone did not prepare her and to diverge considerably from the domestic ideal of womanhood without coming into conflict with it.

4. *Letters*, 29 Jan. 1813, 202.
5. *Letters*, 10–18 Aug. 1814, 268.
6. J. E. Austen-Leigh, *Memoir*, 102.
7. David Cecil, *A Portrait of Jane Austen* (London: Constable, 1978), 141.
8. John Halperin, *The Life of Jane Austen* (Baltimore and London: Johns Hopkins University Press, 1984), 190.

TARA GHOSHAL WALLACE

Getting the Whole Truth in *Pride and Prejudice*†

Of all Jane Austen's novels, *Pride and Prejudice* ends most serenely. The marriage that will perfectly balance Elizabeth Bennet's 'ease and liveliness' with Fitzwilliam Darcy's 'judgement, information, and knowledge of the world,' the stability of Pemberley and the capitulation of even Miss Bingley and Lady Catherine all point to a closure which eliminates ambiguities and achieves coherence. Impediments (the Bennet family's vulgarities, for example) become irrelevant, and mysteries (such as Mr Bingley's inconsiderate behaviour) are cleared up. Looking back at the narrative, however, I locate three puzzling moments not adequately explained or contained by the text's impulse towards clarity and closure. And in attempting to 'solve' the mysteries of these moments, I discover not only their resistance to my efforts to fix meaning but also a general epistemological uncertainty. *Pride and Prejudice* thematizes a narrative problem: it exposes the inadequacies alike of careful reticence, of ambiguity, and of absolute assurance, demonstrating how each of these strategies serves to block access to the 'whole truth' in narrative.

The first of the baffling but provocative moments describes a reaction to one of Mrs Bennet's many mindless assertions. To Elizabeth's generalization, 'people themselves alter so much, that there is something new to be observed in them for ever,' Mrs Bennet adds, 'Yes indeed . . . I assure you there is quite as much of *that* going on in the country as in town.' Then follows narrative commentary on the effect of her statement: 'Every body was surprised; and Darcy, after looking at her for a moment, turned silently away. Mrs. Bennet, who fancied she had gained a complete victory over him, continued her triumph.' There is no explanation as to why this innocuous inanity should give rise to so much surprise, silence and triumph.

The second instance is even more baffling. In March, on her way to Hunsford, Elizabeth visits the Gardiners in London. 'On the stairs were a troop of little boys and girls, whose eagerness for their cousin's appearance would not allow them to wait in the drawing-room, and whose shyness, as they had not seen her for a twelvemonth, prevented their coming lower.' We are to understand, then, that the Gardiners did not take their children to join the family Christmas celebration

† From *Jane Austen and Narrative Authority* (London: Macmillan; New York: St. Martin's Press, 1995) 45–46, 52–58. Copyright © Tara Ghoshal Wallace. Reprinted by permission of Macmillan Ltd. Some bibliographic citations have been added by the editor of this Norton Critical Edition.

at Longbourn. This seems very odd, given the Gardiners' roles as exemplary family members. Finally, in a sentence less puzzling than ambiguous, we hear the text's last statement about Lydia: 'in spite of her youth and her manners, she retained all the claims to reputation which her marriage had given her.' Here, there is a question of deciding the focus of irony. Is Austen mocking the social respectability that marriage inevitably confers? Or is she pointing out the fatuity of such claims by someone whose reputation is permanently tainted by her belated and purchased marriage?

These moments of indeterminacy are worth noticing, because the questions they raise are thematized in *Pride and Prejudice*. Mrs Bennet's victory over Darcy is part of the text's irresolute attitude toward silences, conversations and, ultimately, writing itself. The odd behaviour of the Gardiners illustrates a motif in *Pride and Prejudice*—how to reconcile apparent inconsistencies of character as well as narrative. And the ambiguous irony regarding Lydia points to an indeterminacy that subverts the textual closure asserted by the absolutes and superlatives of the ending: 'With the Gardiners, they were *always* on the *most* intimate terms. Darcy, as well as Elizabeth, *really* loved them; and they were both *ever* sensible of the *warmest* gratitude towards the persons who, by bringing her into Derbyshire, had been the means of uniting them' (my emphases).

*   *   *

Since it is largely plausible but untrustworthy talkers who inhabit the linguistic world of *Pride and Prejudice*, audiences have to be particularly alert and hard-working; again and again, characters and readers need to puzzle out the truth from a mass of inconsistent data and to examine their grounds for belief. And because there is no clear congruence of character and speech, those who attempt to evaluate the actions of others do so not by scrutinizing individual character but by appealing to general, immutable truths—to moral values and communal standards. When Jane and Elizabeth discuss Charlotte Lucas's willingness to marry Collins, neither attempts to psychoanalyse Charlotte; instead both press towards the abstract and the social. Jane urges Elizabeth to 'make allowance enough for difference of situation and temper', to 'consider Mr Collins's respectability, and Charlotte's prudent, steady character', to '[r]emember that she is one of a large family', and to 'be ready to believe . . . that she may feel something like regard and esteem' for Collins. The series of mild imperatives—make allowance, consider, remember, be ready to believe—all posit a stable, intelligible social framework within which Charlotte's behaviour can be understood. Jane presents Elizabeth with a coherent narrative, one which makes sense of Charlotte's choice.

To this, Elizabeth opposes a view which insists upon 'the inconsistency of all human characters,' but the binary oppositions she sets up present an equally coherent picture: 'You shall not, for the sake of one individual, change the meaning of principle and integrity, nor endeavour to persuade yourself or me, that selfishness is prudence, and insensibility of danger, security for happiness.' Neither account allows for real inconsistency—that Charlotte can be prudent as well as selfish, that an eligible match can also be a dangerous one. Nor do they posit a world in which moral absolutes and pragmatic choices coexist in permanent conflict; both insist upon ontological certainties which are always available as measures of judgement. Both explanations, therefore, proceed from partial and confining systems of belief, necessarily inadequate in the search for the whole truth.

In turning to a consideration of Bingley's desertion, Jane and Elizabeth again run into troubles generated by fixed values. Jane's generous reading of the Bingley sisters derives not from her knowledge of their characters but from her belief in deductive logic based on absolutes: 'They can only wish his happiness, and if he is attached to me, no other woman can secure it', and Elizabeth participates in this abstract level of discourse by challenging the formal argument—'Your first position is false', she claims. Elizabeth's cynical evaluation of the Bingley women owes less, I believe, to 'a judgement . . . unassailed by any attention to herself' than to a more generalized 'knowledge' about selfishness and hypocrisy, the same knowledge that impels her admiration for Jane: '[a]ffectation of candour is common enough;—one meets with it every where. But to be candid without ostentation or design . . . belongs to you alone.' While Jane protests that by reading the Bingleys cynically, 'you make every body acting unnaturally and wrong,' Elizabeth sees nothing unnatural in selfishness or weakness. Elizabeth's disappointment in Bingley comes from another treasured certainty: her belief in personal autonomy. Just as she rejects Colonel Fitzwilliam's contention that a 'younger son . . . must be inured to self-denial and dependence,' she cannot 'for a moment suppose that [Caroline Bingley's] wishes, however openly or artfully spoken, could influence a young man so totally independent of every one.'

Elizabeth's conviction that a wealthy man is beyond coercion or influence is closely connected to her certainty that even a poor woman like Charlotte (and herself) can claim autonomy and personal desire. Because Elizabeth's version of the world accommodates behaviour inconsistent with established norms, it seems to us less fixed than Jane's world of naturalness and rightness; but in its seeming inclusiveness, it asserts a kind of authoritative certainty that excludes the inexplicable. In Elizabeth's coherent world, baffling behaviour can be explained by '[t]houghtlessness, want of attention to other people's feelings, and want of resolution,' so that it is no longer baffling.[1] But where in this confident and judgemental world is there an explanation for the Gardiners? Without doing violence to the text, we cannot say they are bad because they abandon their children at Christmas; without doing violence to my own feelings as reader *and* parent, I cannot pretend that the lapse is understandable. With more real confusion that Elizabeth feels, I have to borrow the words she uses about Charlotte's behaviour: 'It is unaccountable! in every view it is unaccountable!'

Jane Austen is too meticulous a reviser to have overlooked unwittingly even so small a point as the unaccountable behaviour of the Gardiners. In showing us that even the Gardiners act in ways that defy comprehension, she shows us, I think, the futility of ontological certainties, the slipperiness of grounds for belief. Yet she is unwilling or unable to embrace fully the implications of her own problematized text. She therefore goes the route that Thomas Pavel urges on modern authors who, he says,

> have the option of building worlds that resist the radical workings of indeterminacy. In order to construct fictional systems accounting for the difficult ontological situations in which we find ourselves, we do not need to opt for maximizing incompleteness or indeterminacy. An important choice left to contemporary writers is to acknowledge gracefully the difficulty of making firm sense out of the world and still risk the invention of a completeness-determinacy myth.[2]

In *Pride and Prejudice*, Austen locates the determinacy myth in the competing narratives of Darcy and Wickham. *Pride and Prejudice* explicitly asserts that Darcy's and Wickham's stories not only compete with but exclude each other. When Jane casts about for some way to

---

1. Even at the end of the novel, Elizabeth retains a coherent world view. The lightness of her tone does not disguise her desire to edit the troublesome past; when Jane reminds her of her former dislike of Darcy, she responds, 'That is all to be forgot. Perhaps I did not always love him so well as I do now. But in such cases as these, a good memory is unpardonable. This is the last time I shall ever remember it myself.' She recasts indeterminacy as dynamism; like the Augustans, Elizabeth possesses 'a security that is always susceptible of revision and correction and which thus, finding its own stability in change and correction, mirrors the dynamic stability of the world to be known' (Frederick V. Bogel, *Literature and Insubstantiality in Later Eighteenth-Century England* [Princeton: Princeton University Press, 1984] 10).
2. Thomas Pavel, *Fictional Worlds* (Cambridge: Harvard University Press, 1986) 112. It must be acknowledged that Pavel's argument, though complex and attractive, has something of a rabbit-in-the-hat quality. Having shown the inadequacy of analytic philosophy or structuralism or speech-act theory to explain or reject fictional worlds, he moves to a kind of arbitrary model which relies disconcertingly on intuition. For example, discussing metaphysical problems confronting those who 'aim at comparing fictional entities and statements with their nonfictional counterparts', he finds that 'well-defined borders between these two kinds of statements are counterintuitive when dealing with specific fictional texts from an internal point of view' (16). Still, his notion of the self-conscious narrator/mythmaker strikes me as a useful approach to Austen's fiction.

exonerate both men, Elizabeth responds, 'You never will be able to make them both good for any thing. Take your choice, but you must be satisfied with only one. There is but such a quantity of merit between them; just enough to make one good sort of man . . . '. One man's credit must annihilate the other's, and one narrative must displace the opposing one. In order to maintain the binary opposition and to authorize its own discovery of the truth, the text turns to a sustained examination of grounds for belief. At first, partisans on both sides seem equally prejudiced. If Elizabeth's reasons for believing Wickham are unconvincing—she bases her belief on circumstantial detail ('names, facts, every thing mentioned without ceremony') and on his physical attractiveness ('there was truth in his looks')—the Bingleys' faith in Darcy is also dismissable, since Miss Bingley bases her opinion on class prejudice and Bingley has only vague recollections of the relationship. What is significant here is not that Elizabeth is wrong, but that Austen so carefully stacks the deck against her. It is hardly necessary here to rehearse the points about her superficial attraction to Wickham and her much deeper anger at Darcy's perceived indifference. I would merely point out what has not been so often noted, that Elizabeth is guilty of exactly the same credulity she ascribes to Bingley: 'Mr Bingley's defence of his friend was a very able one I dare say, but since he is unacquainted with several parts of the story, and has learnt the rest from that friend himself, I shall venture still to think of both gentlemen as I did before.'

By the time we read Darcy's letter, we are thoroughly prepared to find that Wickham is a scoundrel and Darcy a true gentleman. Wickham's superficial amiability does not stand a chance against Darcy's sincere and troubled affection for Elizabeth, and we, well ahead of Elizabeth in our evaluation of the two men, merely wait for character to catch up with reader. The problem is that if we were to apply to Darcy's account the same standards of proof that we do to Wickham's, we would find ourselves not far beyond Elizabeth's own initial perplexity—'On both sides it was only assertion.' Darcy's fluent pen has no more inherent credibility than Wickham's smooth tongue, and he, too, mentions 'names, facts, every thing'. The appeal 'to the testimony of Colonel Fitzwilliam' could be seen as a calculated risk, like Wickham's when he depends on Darcy's silence in Meryton. To a truly impartial and unengaged reader (and I freely admit the impossibility of locating one), 'truth' is still elusive.

Of course the text gives us more than Darcy's letter; it gives us Pemberley and the evidence of Mrs Reynolds. But even here, Austen has not forgotten that testimony can be tainted. Although Elizabeth is wholly converted to Mrs Reynolds's view—'What praise is more valuable than the praise of an intelligent servant?'—Mr Gardiner is 'highly amused by the kind of family prejudice, to which he attributed

her excessive commendation of her master' and Mrs Gardiner speculates that 'he is a liberal master . . . and *that* in the eye of a servant
comprehends every virtue.' We remember, too, that Wickham's
account accommodates a view of Darcy as praiseworthy landlord; his
pride, Wickham has said, 'has often led him to be liberal and generous—to give his money freely, to display hospitality, to assist his tenants, and relieve the poor.' If Darcy's acknowledged public virtues can
coexist with and arise from selfish pride, then we are again dangerously
close to moral uncertainties.

Because Austen needs to ensure that no uncertainty remains about
Wickham's duplicity, she provides the comic melodrama of Lydia's
elopement and piles on evidence of Wickham's perfidy. Not only is he
a seducer of maidens, he is also extravagant, dishonest and addicted
to gaming. In the post-elopement discussions about Wickham, we have
a reprise of earlier debates about grounds for belief. Mr and Mrs Gardiner, like Jane and Elizabeth earlier, appeal to large social and moral
certainties as grounds for their optimism. Mr Gardiner counts on
Wickham's self-interest and knowledge of the world—'Could he
expect that her friends would not step forward? Could he expect to be
noticed again by the regiment, after such an affront to Colonel Forster?
His temptation is not adequate to the risk'—while Mrs Gardiner
applies immutable moral values: 'It is really too great a violation of
decency . . . ' Elizabeth, who has learned that what is logical is not
necessarily true, counters with specific readings of Wickham and
Lydia—he 'will never marry a woman without some money' and she
lacks a 'sense of decency and virtue.' In other words, she turns to her
knowledge of their characters and history rather than to general truths.
Elizabeth and the reader have learned that a well-regulated society
includes the illogical and the anarchic, which can be contained only
by the energetic efforts of a reliable actor/narrator like Darcy. Darcy's
generous activity on behalf of Lydia finally validates his earlier narrative
and reassures us that we were right in crediting his words rather than
Wickham's.

The power and truth of Darcy's narrative are further demonstrated
in its ability to force concessions and revisions in Wickham's false
one. In their last dialogue, Elizabeth consistently makes Wickham
retreat from his former positions. He concedes that Georgiana, whom
he has described as 'very, very proud,' has 'uncommonly improved
within this year or two,' and he is driven to claim lamely that his original narrative had included information congruent with Darcy's version
of the story. His stammering repetitions—'Yes, there was something
in *that*; I told you so from the first, you remember' and 'it was not
wholly without foundation. You may remember what I told you on
that point, when first we talked of it'—attest to the fragility of false
narrative. Confronted by truth, Wickham loses fluency, and the reader,

together with Elizabeth, is 'pleased to find that she had said enough to keep him quiet.'

We see, then, the usefulness of the narrative conflict between Wickham and Darcy, the resolution of which powerfully denies uncertainty and indeterminacy. Wickham's discomfiture proves that Darcy has behaved consistently, that both Elizabeth and reader have learned to discover truth in narrative, and that true narratives will, in the end, silence false ones. The reader's absolute conviction of Darcy's truth and Wickham's falsehood spills over to the rest of the text, so that all anomalies seem to be erased. As Elizabeth confidently looks forward to a serene future at Pemberley, the reader comfortably looks back on a text that makes sense. But such comfort is partial and temporary; as recent readings have pointed out, there is something contrived and manipulative about the serene closure.[3] Austen knows the debate about Darcy's or Wickham's truthfulness cannot really be a model for a narrative as a whole and that slippage is inevitable. Miss Bingley and Lady Catherine may visit Pemberley, but the story they will tell others and themselves about Darcy's marriage won't be the one we have just read; their version will emphasize Elizabeth's 'arts and allurements' which 'have drawn him in.' And who can doubt that Wickham, though banished to the north, will resurrect the narrative that makes him out a victim of Darcy's pride and envy? Those who are ignorant of the 'true facts' of the case will believe these false narratives, just as those who have missed being educated by *Pride and Prejudice* may still judge badly—may still believe, for example, that true affection arises 'on a first interview with its object, and even before two words have been exchanged.' The triumph of true values as asserted in *Pride and Prejudice* can be available only to those who read it, and Austen knew her audience was limited. Even those who have experienced the text have no objective evidence to support its assertions, no *absolute* confidence

3. See, for example, Mary Poovey: 'in *Pride and Prejudice* Austen substitutes aesthetic gratification . . . for the practical solutions that neither her society nor her art could provide' (*The Proper Lady and the Woman Writer* [Chicago: University of Chicago Press, 1984] 207). D. A. Miller points out that in Austen novels there is always pressure towards unifying closure because 'Ignorance, incoherence, or ambiguity must never be enjoyed, but always submitted to as an enforced evil' (*Narrative and Its Discontents: Problems of Closure in the Traditional Novel* [Princeton: Princeton University Press, 1981] 52). Julia Prewitt Brown notes that a comic conclusion in Austen 'calls to mind the memory of some incident of absurdity or insensibility and in so doing, gently undermines the conspicuous gaiety of the marriage' but then herself presses toward coherence when she adds, 'It is as if the modes of resistance to the truth become part of the truth itself' (*Jane Austen's Novels: Social Change and Literary Form* [Cambridge: Harvard University Press, 1979] 69). Martha Satz sees the problem as one of authorial bad faith: 'the author herself, by foisting on her reader, in spite of all the evidence to the contrary, a metaphysically and morally certified view of knowledge, projects a supreme arrogance about what is true, thereby ultimately contradicting the fabric of the entire novel' ('An Epistemological Understanding of *Pride and Prejudice*: Humility and Objectivity', *Jane Austen: New Perspectives, Women and Literature 3*, ed. Janet Todd [1983] 183). Thomas R. Edwards sees in the novels Austen's recognition of 'a problem about fiction itself. ∴ . We are asked in some way to credit and care about untruth, to trust an illusion we have good reason not to trust' ('Embarrassed by Jane Austen', *Raritan* 7 [1987] 79).

that its narrative resolves all inconsistencies, includes all truth, and silences all falsehood. Unlike Darcy's letter, *Pride and Prejudice* will continue to compete with other texts and other values; it will always be susceptible to suspicious readings and reinterpretations; and it will always contain in it baffling moments that dismantle its coherence and provoke fresh inquiries. When Austen juxtaposes her indeterminate narrative to Darcy's closed one, she acknowledges authorial fantasizing. It would be pleasant to believe that the truth of her story could be wholly validated, that the reader could use it to construct a true vision of the world. But Austen the author knows what the meta-narrator of Darcy's story denies—that 'the apprehension of fictional texts can never be brought to an end'.[4] In leaving intact moments that elude comprehension, Austen consciously and conscientiously admits that her text, in spite of its seamless surface, is neither coherent nor comprehensive, that the indeterminacy that keeps it alive also kills its claims to be truth.

4. Karlheinz Stierle, 'The Reading of Fictional Texts' in *The Reader in the Text: Essays on Audience and Interpretation*, ed. Susan R. Suleiman and Inge Crosman (Princeton: Princeton University Press, 1980) 97. Richard Handler and Daniel Segal emphasize the epistemological openness of *Pride and Prejudice* when they argue that 'Austen's narrative techniques privilege multiplicity in and of itself. But her use of multiplicity does not require unquestioning acceptance of all opinions, nor a total relativism in which anything that anyone says is true. Rather, it conveys a profound conviction that among competing opinions, assessments, and ideas, all possess significance because each force a rereading of any other; (*Jane Austen and the Fiction of Culture: An Essay on the Narration of Social Realities* [Tucson: University of Arizona Press, 1990] 110).

Darcy on Film

SUE BIRTWHISTLE AND SUSIE CONKLIN

A Conversation with Colin Firth†

Colin Firth played Darcy in the 1995 BBC television production of *Pride and Prejudice*. Andrew Davies wrote the screenplay; Simon Langton was the director.

Andrew Davies says that he wanted to convey that there is more to Darcy than we at first think. How did you try to communicate this?
You really can't walk into a room and start acting your socks off, and doing all sorts of ambitious things, because Darcy wouldn't do that. But *not* doing anything is one of the most difficult things about acting. I remember thinking before I started that I was going to have to get together a very lively, dynamic, varied performance and then not act it. For example, in that first assembly-room scene I have to go in and be hurt, angry, intimidated, annoyed, irritated, amused, horrified, appalled, and keep all these reactions within this very narrow framework of being inscrutable because nobody ever knows quite what Darcy's thinking. I've played some far more physically energetic parts, but I don't think that I've ever been as physically exhausted at the end of a take as I have with Darcy.

I remember this particularly from the scene where Elizabeth and I have the argument at Netherfield: Darcy's emotional and doesn't want her to know it, he hates her because he fancies her, he hates her for being cleverer than he is during this particular conversation, and he's got the Bingleys as an audience. So there are a million things going on inside him, yet he has to keep himself together and not show that he is in the slightest bit ruffled; he mustn't reveal his turmoil. So he sits there, as still and calm as his emotions can possibly allow. Technically, you just try to assume all that and then play against it.

* * *

† From Sue Birtwhistle and Susie Conklin, *The Making of Pride and Prejudice* (London: Penguin, 1995) 99–105. Reprinted with the permission of the publisher.

What's interesting when you're doing a part like this is if you can find fluidity from moment to moment. When something is somehow not truthful, it jars because you've got to try to force your imagination to think up justifications for what you're doing. I never had to do that with Darcy—or very rarely—and it suddenly hit me that Jane Austen really did have an instinctive grasp of Darcy's inner self, even though she didn't have the arrogance to write it. But she writes the outer man so logically that the inside 'plays'.

Can you think of a specific example?
I remember thinking that it makes sense when Darcy slights Elizabeth at the Meryton assembly. I agree to go to a party with my friend Bingley. He encourages me: 'Come on, it'll be a great party with lots of women.' I arrive. I'm terribly shy—terribly uneasy in social situations anyway. This is not a place I'd normally go to, and I don't know how to talk to these people. So I protect myself behind a veneer of snobbishness and rejection. Bingley immediately engages with the most attractive woman in the room, and that makes me feel even less secure. He comes bounding over with a big, enthusiastic smile and tells me I should be dancing. I say, 'You've got the best-looking girl in the room,' and he replies, 'Well, never mind—what about the less attractive sister?' and this exacerbates the position I've put myself in. Then I say, 'She's okay, but not good enough for me,' but what I'm really saying is: 'Look, I'm supposed to be better than you, so don't give me the plain sister. I'm not even going to consider her.' By keeping this in mind when filming, I found that the scene actually played itself.

At the end of the story Darcy tells Lizzy that he doesn't know when he first fell in love with her. But you would have needed to plot his journey more specifically.
Yes, it's very interesting to watch out for the triggers that lead to Darcy's falling in love. Of course, love often starts with something trivial that attracts your attention. In Darcy's case, very little had ever attracted his attention. So I think the first trigger is the moment when Elizabeth rejects him so impertinently—when she overhears him saying, 'She's tolerable, I suppose, but not handsome enough to tempt *me*.' When she walks past and gives him a cheeky look, Andrew was very helpful here in writing: 'Darcy was used to looking at other people like that, but was not used to being looked at like that himself.' So at that moment, I think, he notices her simply out of bewilderment and curiosity; he becomes intrigued by her, which, I suspect, is the first time he has ever been intrigued by a woman, and he has to know a little bit more about her. It strikes me that you can be on a fatal course from a moment like that whether you know it or not.

Darcy starts to show his interest in Elizabeth during the Lucases' party, when he asks her to dance and she refuses. What did you feel was happening to him at this stage?

Up to this point I don't think Darcy has ever really looked at a woman—I mean looked with real eyes, with real interest—though he's admired women in a casual way. The truth is that he's very bored. He's one of the richest men in England, and until now that's always been enough to make him attractive to women. I remember reading a very helpful saying: 'A man who is eligible needs to entertain no one.' For me, that was a great key to understanding Darcy—I thought that if he were charming as well, life could be intolerable for him. So out of both shyness and a lack of necessity he remains aloof. Then Elizabeth comes along and actually gives him a chance to respond, and it's probably the first opportunity he's ever had in his life to be the pursuer rather than the pursued: it's irresistible. That's when he first notices her eyes. What starts off as intriguing becomes profoundly erotic for him.

And she finally does agree to dance with him at the Netherfield ball . . .

Yes. I think the sequence where they dance together is wonderful because it lays out the whole of their relationship at that point perfectly. We see an honesty and playfulness in Elizabeth, while there's something slightly comical about Darcy trying to maintain his formal manner while holding up his end of the repartee. She'll say something that stings him, and he has an entire eight-step circle to do before he is permitted to respond.

Jane Austen offers some clues here as to Darcy's resolution to hold back and cure himself of this 'madness' he's just contracted, but he's in over his head before he realizes what has happened. To begin with, it was a bit of sport. And then suddenly he's feeling vulnerable and resents it bitterly. Several times he decides that he is going to pull himself together, and this is when his behaviour becomes rather confusing and paradoxical—he's pursuing and rejecting Elizabeth at the same time. He's certain he won't dance with her, and then he asks her to dance; he waits in places where he knows he'll find her walking and then doesn't speak to her; he shows up at Hunsford Parsonage and then acts as if she had called on him.

You had to film Darcy's first proposal scene in the second week of filming. How did that affect you?

It seemed a catastrophe at first. Everybody knows how important the scene is. For scheduling reasons we had to film a lot of Darcy's later scenes first—where he appears a much nicer person—and then do this scene with him at breaking point. Because it's so inappropriate to do it early and it's so nerve-racking, we gave it a tremendous amount of attention and got a degree of adrenalin working up to it, so that perhaps it's invested with something that it would never have had if we had done it later, when everyone had settled in. It was a case of jumping in at the deep end, and Simon Langton handled it brilliantly.

How did you approach this scene?

I asked myself some extremely basic questions about what it was I wanted to do in the scene. I asked, 'What's my character trying to get?' and then, 'How will he overcome any obstacles that are in the way?' In this case, the main question was: 'How is Elizabeth going to make it difficult for me, and how am I going to make it difficult for myself?' If you address problems like these, you come up with ways and means that help to make the approach clear.

I felt, for instance, that when Darcy goes into that room and says those shocking things—'I'm too good for you, but will you marry me anyway?'—if I played it as if I knew I were being shocking and arrogant, it would never work. I realized that I had to make it the most reasonable thing in the world to say, but I wondered, 'How do I do that? How do I turn that extraordinary speech about her family connections being utterly disastrous into something reasonable?' And I thought, 'Okay, let's think ourselves into the time for a moment, into 1813,' and from Jane Austen's perspective this business about appropriate and inappropriate marriages made an awful lot of sense. It might be a disaster to cross class barriers; it could lead to all sorts of misery and unhappiness; the social fabric of the time was threatened by it, and so on.

He is also arrogant enough to think he has bestowed an enormous gift on her. Every woman he has ever met would say 'yes' to a proposal from him. It would be insane for Lizzy to say 'no', not because he assumes she finds him attractive—I don't think that's the reason—but because it's the most practical offer that even someone considerably her social superior could ever hope to receive. I think he assumes, as everybody would at that time, that it would be a Cinderella ending for her.

And so Darcy is coming in with a very imprudent proposal, as he sees it. He's saying to her, 'I'm going to put to you a proposal that may make me seem rash, irresponsible and even, possibly, juvenile, but I don't want you to believe I'm those things. I have thought through every detail of this; I know that my family will be angry, that people will frown on us and that our social positions are very different. So don't think that I haven't dealt with these issues—don't imagine that I'm just some reckless schoolboy. Nevertheless, having thought it all through, I find that my love for you is so overwhelming that these objections are rendered insignificant.' And, from that point of view, it's a terribly romantic proposal. I was a bit hurt when we filmed it, and everybody thought I was saying something terrible: I had got myself so far into the notion that he had come in with a really charming thing to say. Of course, when you watch it, you don't see it from his point of view. You see a self-important man entering and expressing these pompous sentiments as if they were the most natural reactions in the world and then having the gall to be astonished by Elizabeth's rejection—and I think that's right. But I couldn't have played that astonishment without approaching it the way I did.

*   *   *

Does Lizzy's rejection effect any real changes in Darcy, then?
Oh, yes. You cannot think that Darcy is simply going to return to the way he was. The fact that he writes her a letter explaining himself and disclosing some very personal information—which is ostensibly a tremendously out-of-character thing to do—suggests this. I think he suffers enormously as a result of her rejection because he loves her. I think he endures torment because a lifetime's behaviour, even his very character, has been thrown into relief by her words.

His real crime, I think, is silliness. I know that's a terribly undignified way to look at him, but I believe his failing is foolish, superficial, social snobbery, and that's the bitter lesson he has to learn. And I think in that sense he does change. He actually says in the book that his father instilled in him good values but also taught him to think meanly of the world outside his own social circle. He is rather afraid of anything outside his immediate experience and is quite convinced that he will encounter nothing but barbarianism. People do make assumptions about other areas of civilization, and that's precisely what Darcy does. It's ignorance.

He learns his lesson when he falls in love with one of those barbarians and realizes that she's at least his equal, if not his superior, in terms of wit, intellectual agility and sense of personal dignity. He is so profoundly challenged by her that his old prejudices cannot be upheld. I still think he'll always have something of the old view—he'll always be disgusted by ridiculous, boring people who talk too much. I don't think he'll ever learn to adore Mrs. Bennet or develop an enormous admiration for Sir William Lucas.

And, of course, he hasn't quite learned to laugh at himself. He's learned to criticize himself, which is probably the first step, but he doesn't yet know how to find himself ridiculous and enjoy it. With Lizzy as a partner, however, married life will be a matter of survival, and it's plain that he's going to learn *that* lesson before too long.

*   *   *

CHERYL L. NIXON

[Darcy in Action]†

* * *

In [Andrew] Davies's screenplay of *Pride and Prejudice,* Darcy is cast as an awkward hero tortured by an excess of emotions he cannot express. With his tousled dark hair, smoldering eyes that stare deeply into middle space, and a pained self-consciousness in social situations, he is convincingly reimagined as a vaguely Byronic hero. A brooding loner who can neither physically contain nor verbally express his inner emotional battles, Darcy engages in a roster of physical activities that do not appear in the novel but which convey these battles to the viewer. The film's additions envision Darcy playing billiards, bathing, fencing, and swimming. As Darcy's pursuit of Elizabeth becomes more certain, his physical activities are increasingly replaced by meditative stares which, in turn, become increasingly direct; this expression of longing peaks when he spends a tumultuous night pacing back and forth to his window while attempting to write a response to her rejection of his marriage proposal. Darcy's physical activities reveal the violence of his emotions while his longing stares restate his inability to express verbally those emotions. While Darcy displays emotional restraint, he physically displays that which he is restraining. Darcy's physical activities create a cinematic form of self-expression, a dialogue between his mind and body that runs throughout the entire film but is absent from the novel.

* * *

Darcy's physical reactions to Elizabeth quickly order themselves into an easily interpreted grammar of emotional signs. In [a] fabricated Netherfield scene, Darcy's physicality is emphasized as a complement to Elizabeth's, signaling an emotional connection between the two. The film intercuts images of Darcy taking a bath with images of Elizabeth frolicking with a large dog. Darcy's uninhibited physicality mirrors Elizabeth's. After seeing the naked Darcy being bathed by a servant while lounging and sighing in a large tub, we see Elizabeth walking outside and coming upon a large dog, which she laughs at and immediately starts to chase. This image is interrupted by that of the bathing Darcy, getting out of the tub and being helped into his robe. While still wet and tousled, Darcy peers out the window at Elizabeth, who is tugging at a stick in the dog's mouth. Darcy longingly gazes at Eliza-

† From "Balancing the Courtship Hero: Masculine Emotional Display in Film Adaptations of Austen's Novels," in *Jane Austen in Hollywood,* ed. Linda Troost and Sayre Greenfield (Lexington: University Press of Kentucky, 1998) 31–35. Copyright © 1998 by Linda Troost. Reprinted with permission of University Press of Kentucky.

beth for a lengthy space of time. Each character's natural self is revealed; each is removed from his or her constraining societal role, enjoying an unguarded moment and reveling—sighing and laughing—in bodily pleasure. At this early stage in the film, when the novel still has Darcy and Elizabeth bristling at one another, the viewer cannot help but feel that the two are connected both physically and emotionally.

* * *

These added scenes of masculine physicality are easily equated with their unspoken emotional content: Darcy's growing and continuing love. The film's interest in Darcy's bodily struggle with his emotions is best evidenced by the scene in which he writes a letter responding to Elizabeth's rejection of his first marriage proposal. In the novel, the letter's text is given to the reader after it has been received by Elizabeth; its content is, in effect, voiced by Elizabeth because the reader reads it as Elizabeth reads it. In contrast, the film gives the viewer the text of the letter as Darcy is writing it. The letter is read aloud by Darcy, not Elizabeth. The mental activity of reading is translated into the physical activity of writing. The letter is no longer a symbol of Elizabeth's misinterpretation and reevaluation of the past "text" of Darcy. Rather, the letter becomes a means of showing Darcy's emotional depth and conveying his struggle at self-expression. A quiet scene of silent reading in which the female reader is being persuaded becomes an emotionally charged scene of masculine writing in which the writer argues his case. The activity of letter-writing creates another opportunity for Darcy to express his internal self through external activity—and another opportunity to note that this is how the twentieth century, and not Austen, expresses masculinity.

* * *

The "extra Darcy" presented in these scenes is extra emotion. Darcy's added physical display of emotion provides a radical revision of the masculine balance Austen advocates between personal expression and social restraint. For example, in the film adaptation, Elizabeth's rejection of Darcy's first marriage proposal can be read as a rejection due to his inability to voice his full emotions. Compared with his doting stares, billiard playing, bathing, fencing, and swimming, Darcy's proposal seems restrained; although he expresses his love, he is unable to put his hidden emotions into a verbal vocabulary that matches the intensity of his physical vocabulary. His private desires are held back by public considerations of social inequality. Viewing the film, we feel Elizabeth is right to reject him; he has not given full expression to the depth of the emotions we, the audience, know him to have. In contrast, the novel can be read as constructing the scene according to completely opposite dictates. Darcy's proposal is rejected because he has displayed too much of his emotions rather than too little. Darcy does not show proper courtship restraint and propose according to proper social form; after Elizabeth rejects him, he himself says, "These bitter accusations might have been suppressed, had I with greater policy concealed my struggles, and flattered you into the belief of my being impelled by unqualified, unalloyed inclination. . . . But disguise of every sort is my abhorrence. Nor am I ashamed of the feelings I related." In contrast to the film, which places the same verbal expression within the context of emotionally charged physical expression, the text positions this verbal expression as an unexpected outburst from a character who has displayed almost no emotion in any form. Austen's Darcy has suddenly displayed too much emotional freedom: he expresses his love openly and then openly states the frustrating barriers his love has overcome. Is Darcy's proposal too expressive, as the novel might have it, or not expressive enough, as the film has it? The answer is both; he exists as both in two different *Pride and Prejudice* texts. Masculine emotional display has been envisioned differently by each; it provides a telling example of how Austen's "balance" has been reformulated and paradoxically maintained by today's audience, an audience that expects masculinity to evidence balance through emotional display.

*   *   *

Class and Money

DAVID SPRING

Interpreters of Jane Austen's Social World: Literary Critics and Historians†

* * *

It would be fair to say that the bulk of Jane Austen interpreters have had no trouble in agreeing that the world of her novels is real, a part of the real England. But they have had trouble in agreeing on what to call it, on how to characterize it. In the course of more than a century and a half, Jane Austen interpretation has boxed the compass of social respectability. It began by describing her as the annalist of the "middle classes," of "ordinary and middle life." Later she was said to be the aristocracy's annalist, or more commonly the gentry's. Most recently interpretation seems to have turned back to its beginnings and plumped for a bourgeois Jane Austen.[1]

High on the list of reasons for calling Jane Austen's society bourgeois, it would seem, is the ubiquity of money in her novels. Things and persons seem all to have their price. Even naval officers go to sea in a great war to make money. This pervasive monetarization of the novels was in itself perhaps enough to catch the eye of literary critics. But there were also historians, looking to other evidence than the novel, who reinforced this conclusion. So influential an historian as R. H. Tawney, in his famous essay on the gentry, characterized sixteenth- and seventeenth-century landowners as bourgeois because they were more intent on making money than their predecessors. For later centuries, something like this was also said by Marxist historians like the

---

† From *Jane Austen: New Perspectives*, ed. Janet Todd, *Women and Literature* 3 (New York and London: Holmes and Meier, 1983) 56–63. Copyright © 1983 by Holmes and Meier. Reproduced with permission of the publisher. Some bibliographic citations have been added.
1. The early critic was Sir Walter Scott, in B. C. Southam, ed *Jane Austen: The Critical Heritage*. For a modern critic who was assigned her to the aristocracy, see D. Daiches, "Jane Austen, Karl Marx and the Aristocratic Dance," *The American Scholar*, Summer, 1948: for one (among many) who assigned her to the gentry, see D. Monaghan, *Jane Austen: Structure and Social Vision* (New York: Harper & Row, 1980).

equally influential E. P. Thompson.[2] Not surprisingly, the bourgeois label found wide acceptance.

But some critics have had their doubts. Graham Hough, for example, observed in 1970 that the bourgeoisie was "too blunt an instrument to have much explanatory value."[3] And almost two decades earlier, in one of those revealing footnotes where professors choose to argue with themselves, Marvin Mudrick said almost as much. His admission is especially interesting, for in the text of the same book he came down heavily on the bourgeois nature of Jane Austen's novels. He wrote there, for example, of "the particularities of bourgeois courtship," meaning by this its monetary aspects. He also described Captain Wentworth in *Persuasion* as "possessed of all the new bourgeois virtues—confidence, aggressiveness, daring, an eye for money and the main chance." On the other hand, in his interesting footnote he observed that expressions like "middle class" and "bourgeois" did less than justice to a society which in his opinion was a hybrid society— one that combined "dying feudal tradition and progressively self-assertive bourgeois vigor."[4]

Mudrick's dilemma is well worth pondering. It touches on a number of confusions that have marked Austen interpretation—and, for that matter, the writing of eighteenth-century English history. It would be worthwhile to identify these confusions. Three suggest themselves. The first has to do with what Mudrick calls the hybrid nature of Jane Austen's society, of the world of neighborhood. What were its several elements? The second has to do with the group that Mudrick calls bourgeois. Who precisely made up this group, and in what ways was it related to the others? The third has to do with the group that Mudrick sums up as possessed of "a dying feudal tradition." Who were they, and were they dying, let alone feudal—at any rate, any more so than the group called bourgeois?

The world of neighborhood, the world of the rural elite, was indeed hybrid, hence the disagreement on what to call it. Strictly speaking, it contained three groups, two of which—the landed aristocracy and gentry —were less distinctive one from the other than both were from the third group. What brought them close together was the ownership of landed estates. They made their money in the same way—mainly by letting land to tenant farmers.[5] * * * Where the aristocracy and gentry chiefly differed was in what—to use one of her favorite phrases—Jane

2. R. H. Tawney, "The Rise of the Gentry, 1558–1640," *Economic History Review*, XI, No. 1, 1941; E. P. Thompson, "The Peculiarities of the English," *The Socialist Register* (London: Merlin Press, 1965).

3. Graham Hough, "Narrative and Dialogue in Jane Austen," *Critical Quarterly* 12 (1970): 201–29.

4. Marvin Mudrick, *Jane Austen: Irony as Defense and Discovery* (Princeton: Princeton University Press, 1952), 15, 235.

5. There is a very large literature on this subject. See especially G. E. Mingay, *English Landed Society in the Eighteenth Century* (London: Routledge & Kegan Paul, 1963); F. M. L. Thomp-

Austen called "style of living," that is, in their status, in how they spent their money.

Aristocratic landowners, having more money, had more to spend. A few had a great deal more to spend, as much as £100,000 of gross income annually. To appreciate what a very great deal this was, remember that in the first decade of the nineteenth century a skilled worker with a family to support would have been fortunate to enjoy an annual income of £100, an unskilled worker of £40.[6] Even the lowest annual income of an aristocratic landowner was something like £5,000 to £10,000, Mrs. Bennet's measurement of the lordly life. Aristocratic incomes, therefore, made for splendid status: great houses, great estates (perhaps several), great parks, a house in London, a seat or seats in the House of Commons for sons and relations, a hereditary seat in the House of Lords for titled fathers, perhaps a position at Court. Like the gentry, the aristocracy had local roots, but they also enjoyed a more metropolitan existence. They were less likely to marry locally: they traveled more, as Elizabeth Bennet once suggested to Darcy, up to London, and among "a range of great families."

The gentry had less money to spend—although relative to the income of a working man, even modest gentry incomes were still impressive, probably on a level with the income of a large town merchant and exceeding the incomes of most professional men. A modest gentry income was something like £1,000 to £2,000 a year. It was Mr. Bennet's income in *Pride and Prejudice*, Colonel Brandon's in *Sense and Sensibility*. * * * At the other end, at somewhat below £1,000 a year, at the income of John Willoughby's estate in *Sense and Sensibility*, the gentry landowner approached that uncomfortable region, so aptly summed up by Jane Austen as "comparative poverty," where status demands outran income, where the affliction of frustrated expectations became acute. To the unpleasant but aristocratic Lady Catherine de Bourgh, even Mr. Bennet's Longbourn with its £2,000 a year was scarcely adequate: deficient in park, servants, and whatever else was needed to impose on the imaginations of social inferiors. But these modest gentry estates, covering England in their thousands, managed to supply their owners with comfort and status sufficient to make them the natural leaders of their local communities. Assisted principally by the resident Anglican clergy, they ran their parishes and counties, acting as overseers of the poor, and as magistrates. They were more at home in the local county town than in London's West End.

Of the two, gentry and aristocracy, Jane Austen preferred the former.

son, *English Landed Society in the Nineteenth Century* (London: Routledge & Kegan Paul, 1963); D. Spring, *The English Landed Estate in the Nineteenth Century: Its Administration* (Baltimore: Johns Hopkins University Press, 1963).
6. See H. Perkin, *The Origins of Modern English Society 1780–1880* (London: Routledge & Kegan Paul, 1969), pp. 20–21, for a table of the several categories of income.

Not that she was uncritical of the gentry. She had her gallery of gentry fools like Sir John Middleton [in *Sense and Sensibility*] and Sir Walter Elliot [in *Persuasion*]. But socially she stood closer to the gentry than to the aristocracy, especially to the smaller-incomed gentry. Morally she approved of their more settled habits, of their less ostentatious patterns of consumption, of their limited capacity—compared with that of the Court aristocracy led by the Prince Regent—to perpetrate a national scandal. Her novels are thus not much populated with aristocratic figures. Moreover, when they appear, they are almost invariably silly, both men and women. * * *

Strictly speaking, then, Jane Austen belonged to neither of the first two groups in that hybrid world of the rural elite—neither to the aristocracy nor to the gentry—but to a third group, so far unnamed. This group comprised the nonlanded: the professional and rentier families, first and foremost the Anglican clergy; second, other professions like the law—preferably barristers rather than solicitors[7]—and the fighting services; and last, the rentiers recently or long retired from business. I have described them as nonlanded, by which I mean that if they owned land, and doubtless many of them owned some, they owned comparatively little, perhaps 100 acres and less. Sometimes they merely rented a house and its adjoining land, as did the Bingleys in *Pride and Prejudice*; and often, notably in the case of the Anglican parson, they held land (and sometimes farmed it) for life.[8] By and large, they were neither lords of manors nor collectors of rent from tenant farmers. But they lived in big houses, held or owned enough land to assure privacy, that most cherished of social delights, like the Woodhouses in *Emma*, who owned a corner of Mr. Knightley's Donwell Abbey estate. Some did with less land, less privacy, less floor space of an impressive sort. These were lower in the scale of the nonlanded, a sort of village patriciate, like the Coles in *Emma* or the Edwardses in *The Watsons*, and inferior to them, touching the very bottom of the rural elite, within a hair's breadth of falling out of it, the humble and garrulous Miss Bates [in *Emma*], the impecunious spinster daughter of a defunct parson, living with her mother and two servants behind a village shop.

This third group, the nonlanded, is the one most likely to be described by Jane Austen interpreters as bourgeois—although some (as we have seen) have also described the entire world of neighborhood as bourgeois. The word, however, ill suits both the smaller as well as the larger social unit. For bourgeois evokes an urban—or at least an actively trading—milieu. It also evokes a degree of social hostility—of class antagonism, to use the Marxist phrase—that was also inappropriate to

---

7. Both barristers and solicitors are lawyers, but barristers could plead in higher courts and therefore had a higher standing [*Editor*].

8. For a good account of the eighteenth-century Anglican clergy, see G. F. A. Best, *Temporal Pillars: Queen Anne's Bounty, the Ecclesiastical Commissioners and the Church of England* (London: Cambridge University Press, 1964).

the several groups within the world of neighborhood. There were tensions within that world, but these were something different from the deeply divided outlook of class antagonism. In sum, a word that breeds such misunderstanding might well be scrapped—at least in this particular context. Compared with sociologists and anthropologists, historians are timid inventors of language, a practice admittedly not always advantageous. But here, I suggest, it would be useful to find a new word.

As it happens, this has already been done. Some years ago, the Leicester historian Alan Everitt invented the word pseudo-gentry as a helpful substitute for the word bourgeois, having in mind the latter's misleading overtones. He used it first for seventeenth-century English society, later for a time more appropriate to Jane Austen's society.[9] There is some sign that it is being taken up, although as yet there is no great rush to do so. It strikes me, however, as a profitable addition to the social historian's language, as well as to the language of the historian of culture.

The pseudo-gentry were "pseudo" because they were not landowners in the same sense as the gentry and aristocracy were. They cannot be said to have owned landed estates. But they were gentry of a sort, primarily because they sought strenuously to be taken for gentry. They devoted their lives to acquiring the trappings of gentry status for themselves and especially their children: the schooling, the accent, the manners (from style of conversation to dressing for dinner), the sports, the religion, the habit of command, the large house in its own grounds, servants, carriages and horses, appropriate husbands and wives, and, last but not least, an appropriate income, which Jane Austen called "independence," that most desirable of all social states. In short they had a sharp eye for the social escalators, were skilled in getting on them, and (what was more important) no less skilled in staying on them. They were adept at acquiring what the economist Fred Hirsch has aptly called "positional goods"—those scarce services, jobs, and goods which announce social success.[1] In this they helped to inaugurate a "positional competition" inevitably more widespread than that indulged in by landowners, which has set the style for all modern societies, once those societies achieve a certain level of wealth and enterprise sufficient to feed the voracious appetite for positional goods. * * *

---

9. See A. Everitt, "Social Mobility in Early Modern England," *Past and Present*, April 1966; and A. Everitt, "Kentish Family Portrait: An Aspect of the Rise of the Pseudo-Gentry," in C. W. Chalklin and M. A. Havinden, eds., *Rural Change and Urban Growth 1500–1800: An Essays in English Regional History in Honour of W. G. Hoskins* (London: Longman, 1979).

1. F. Hirsch, *Social Limits to Growth* (Cambridge: Harvard University Press, 1974). See also Christopher Kent, " 'Real Solemn History' and Social History," who makes something of the same point, in David Monaghan, *Jane Austen in a Social Context* (Totowa, NJ: Barnes and Noble Books, 1981) 86–104.

Marriage, of course, had an important place in positional competition. As anthropologists have told us, marriage makes society and tends to confirm its arrangements. Jane Austen's was a rich, differentiated society, and marriage, being largely endogamous, tended to keep it that way. This is not to say that marriage among the pseudo-gentry and their superiors was exclusively a matter of status. That "trade of coming out," to use Jane Austen's bitter phrase, managed as it was reputed to be by marriage-making mothers, furnished increasing room in the eighteenth century for marriages of affection. But status accommodation was never lost sight of. * * *

In the business of positional competition, none among the pseudo-gentry equaled the strivings of the Anglican clergy, particularly its upper reaches, that is, the rectors and vicars who held prosperous livings. They derived their income mainly from tithes, thus being ultimately dependent, as landowners were for their rents, on the fortunes of agriculture.[2] Of clerical incomes, as might be supposed, Jane Austen had a precise and extensive knowledge. She knew the terrible depths to which an impoverished curate might fall—"a country curate without bread to eat." Colonel Brandon's living at Delaford [in *Sense and Sensibility*] was only £200 a year—a sum judged in all quarters as too small to permit Edward Ferrars' marrying; even £350 was found inadequate to supply "the comforts of life." Only when clerical incomes began to approach the lower levels of gentry income—somewhere above £500 a year—did they begin to give some assurance of gentlemanly status. * * *

This was the scale of clerical income which permitted the Anglican clergy to come closer to realizing the ideal of the English country gentleman than any other pseudo-gentry type. The rise of the clergy was an eighteenth-century rise, partly a product of the agricultural revolution, of the beneficial effect of enclosure [of land formerly opened to public use] on the receipt of tithe.[3] Not surprisingly, many of the clergy became enthusiastic farmers of their glebeland; some of them became agronomists, acting as enclosure commissioners and writing county agricultural reports. Some of them hunted; one of them wrote a treatise on fox-hunting. A good many of them became justices of the peace, in some counties virtually taking over the business of local government; and some of them became local political bosses. In their religious capacity, they were among other things the chief agents of social legitimacy and whatever measure of social control was attainable. In short, enjoying a superior education to that of most Englishmen, they were well fitted to becoming a kind of rural managerial

2. On tithes generally, see E. J. Evans, *The Contentious Tithe: The Tithe Problem and English Agriculture, 1750–1850* (London: Routledge & Kegan Paul, 1976).
3. See W. R. Ward, "The Tithe Question in the Early Nineteenth Century," *The Journal of Ecclesiastical History*, April 1965.

class for the landed gentry, forebears of a sort of the modern service class.

The rise of George Austen and his family paralleled the general rise of the clergy. The orphaned son of a country surgeon—and country surgeons came low in Jane Austen's social scale—he managed in the seventy years after his birth in 1730 to make a secure position for his large family in the world of the pseudo-gentry. Luck, family connections, the eighteenth-century patronage network, a superior marriage—all joined together to do the trick. His prosperous, kindly solicitor uncle, Francis Austen, started him off, steering him away from the apprentice-oriented but less gentlemanly callings. He went to Tonbridge School, which had its special road to Oxford and a St. Johns fellowship. From there the rest of the road into the church was easy: his uncle's help again, and a distant cousin's (Thomas Knight of Godmersham in Kent), made him a pluralist, the holder of two clerical livings, at Steventon and Deane in north Hampshire. He also married Cassandra Leigh, of the Leighs of Adlestrop, a family whose genealogy reached social heights unattained by the Austens. Six sons and two daughters came of this marriage. Five of the six sons did well; one was an incurable invalid. Luck would have it that one son was adopted by the childless Knights, to become in time the master of a great gentry estate [Godmersham] of the order of Mr. Rushworth's in *Mansfield Park*. Two other sons followed their father into the church. The remaining two, like Horatio Nelson, also a parson's son, entered the Navy, eventually to become admirals. The daughters fared less well, remaining spinsters and dependents, both luck and family doing less for them than for their brothers, although doing much for the world in supplying the raw material for some of the greatest novels in the English language.

The story of the Austens is but a single episode in the general rise of the pseudo-gentry. The historian Alan Everitt found the origins of the pseudo-gentry in the late seventeenth century; they were then an urban phenomenon. Sometime during the eighteenth century, presumably, they also became a rural phenomenon, settling on the outskirts of towns and villages. * * * Look into an early *Kelly's Post Office Directory* for any English county, and there you will find the pseudo-gentry in their hundreds and thousands, arranged alphabetically under the proud title of "Court," as opposed to the humdrum and inferior title of "Trade." Historians have long dwelt on the rise of the bourgeoisie and the rise of the gentry. They might now profitably turn their attention to the rise of the pseudo-gentry, which was well under way during the years Jane Austen composed her novels. In a sense, her novels celebrated that rise.

* * *

EDWARD AHEARN

[Radical Jane]†

*   *   *

The class dimensions of Elizabeth's marriage have attracted attention by critics who have come to see Austen's fiction as "the very evidence of social history."¹ Of punctual historical detail there is indeed
little. Rather, the indication at the end that Lydia and Wickham
remain unsettled "even when the restoration of peace dismissed them
to a home" has a deeper sociohistorical significance. Although shad-
owed by undesirable elements, the marriage of Elizabeth and Darcy is
seen (or wished) to coincide with the peaceful resolution of a period
of international turbulence that had shaken the social world of Austen's England.

That world includes aristocracy (Lady Catherine, Darcy), gentry
(Bennet), a "pseudogentry" of clergy, lawyers, and businessmen (Lucas,
the Philipses, Collins, and—unsuccessfully—Wickham), and an
urban-based commercial class (the Gardiners). Mobility within this
framework is remarkable and accounts for many of the work's strains
and satisfactions—Bennet's and Lydia's inferior marriages, the social
ascension capped by Bingley's purchase of an estate at the end, the
Gardiners' association with Darcy, the elder Bennet sisters' marriage
into vastly superior status. Satire of pseudogentry and rigid aristocracy
in the figures of Lucas, Mrs. Bennet, and Lady Catherine is clear. But
Darcy overcomes such limitations. That he is early on attracted to
Elizabeth, defending himself only through "the inferiority of her connections," indicates the extent to which the narrative *retard* derives
from the dynamics of class. Further, since Lady Catherine's project of
uniting two noble families fails, and since the daughters of these
families are presented as sickly or unnaturally shy, whereas Darcy
benefits from the lively Elizabeth, it is hard not to see their marriage
as a historical allegory with overtones of class stagnation, mobility, and
reconciliation. By her arrogance Lady Catherine precipitates Darcy's

---

† From "Radical Jane and the Other Emma," in *Marx and Modern Fiction* (New Haven: Yale
    University Press, 1989) 41–46, 49–50. Copyright © by Yale University. Reprinted by permis-
    sion of Yale University Press.
1. Christopher Kent, " 'Real Solemn History' and Social History," in *Jane Austen in a Social
    Context*, ed. David Monaghan (Totowa, NJ, 1981) 102. For what follows see Terry Lovell,
    "Jane Austen and the Gentry: A Study in Literature and Ideology," in *The Sociology of Lit-
    erature: Applied Studies*, ed. Diana Laureson (Hanley, England: Wood Mitchell, 1978), esp.
    20–21; David Monaghan, *Jane Austen: Structure and Social Vision* (Totowa, NJ, 1980); and
    David Spring, "Interpreters of Jane Austen's Social World," in *Jane Austen: New Perspectives*,
    ed. Jane Todd. *Women and Literature* 3 (1983): 56–63 [see pp. 392–99 of this volume—
    Editor].

second proposal, and her "infinite use" in that regard is noted. But even more "useful" are the Gardiners, who in the last lines of the book deserve Elizabeth's and Darcy's gratitude for bringing them together.

* * *

* * *[T]hough largely "about" the landed classes, the novel keeps calling our attention to London, where other forces—undescribed but evidently determining, even in the countryside—are at work.[2] This is a literary equivalent to Marx's arguments about country and city and to the concept of the historical opposition, persistence, and coexistence of competing modes of production. In Marx's terms, the urban capitalist mode of production, despite the persistence of earlier forms, is already achieving a position of dominance, but such characters as Lady Catherine and Mr. Bennet do not know that—although, in some profound way, their creator does. We can appreciate this further by examining the Gardiners, Lady Catherine, and Darcy in terms of the city-country dialectic and related social and economic elements.

Lady Catherine's adherence to aristocratic forms is flagrant, and most extreme in her argument with Elizabeth. Her assumption that the assertion of noble prerogatives will win the argument is countered by Elizabeth's self-assurance in being "a gentleman's daughter," which provides a readerly satisfaction based in class identity and antagonism and which reduces Lady Catherine to repeating the code words for noble values in an almost incantatory way: "You have no regard, then, for the honour and credit of my nephew!"; "You refuse to obey the claims of duty, honour, and gratitude." But the mere expression of such values is inefficacious, we might say, in changed historical circumstances.

Yet at Rosings Lady Catherine operates in a resolutely feudal way. Elizabeth observes that

> though this great lady was not in the commission of the peace for the county, she was a most active magistrate in her own parish, the minutest concerns of which were carried to her by Mr. Collins; and whenever any of the cottagers were disposed to be quarrelsome, discontented or too poor, she sallied forth into the village to settle their differences, silence their complaints, and scold them into harmony and plenty.

In addition to Elizabeth's insightfullness * * * we note the interactions among aristocracy, subordinate clergy, and cottagers and the unmask-

<hr>

2. This has not been much recognized, even by Raymond Williams, *The Country and the City* (New York: Oxford University Press, 1973) 18, 166. In addition to Gardiner's London business, Elizabeth's meeting with Darcy occurs because of his landed property affairs, "business with his steward." Different modes of production conflict and intersect around Elizabeth's marriage.

ing of the economic nature of the relations of superiority and inferiority in the discordant series "quarrelsome, discontented . . . poor" and "settle . . . differences, silence . . . complaints, . . . scold . . . into harmony and plenty."

In the context of our earlier discussion of the implications of certain names, we should consider Lady Catherine's, which like Darcy's, suggests ancient French lineage. To be named de Bourg(h) while asserting claims to aristocracy, however, is to be caught in a historical paradox, since the word in medieval French designated a fortified town, whose inhabitants, possessors of a special status, existed in contradistinction to the landed nobility. The adjective deriving from the word is of course *bourgeois*. Lady Catherine is not only an anachronism; her name, associated with the origins of the modern European city and of the bourgeoisie, belies the purity of class hierarchies to which she is devoted. Perhaps this fits with her house, described as a "handsome modern building," and with her ultimate reconciliation to Darcy's marriage despite the "pollution" of Pemberley by Elizabeth's city relatives.[3]

If Lady Catherine is a negative and contradictory figure, the Gardiners, unambiguously associated with the city, are presented in celebratory fashion. Their role is important and is developed with systematic care. We learn at first only that Mrs. Bennet has "a brother settled in London in a respectable line of trade"; Mrs. Hurst reveals that he lives in Cheapside (Miss Bingley appropriately exclaiming, "That is capital"; later Mrs. Bennet mentions his name. In volume 2, we meet him and his wife and learn of their estimable qualities and their influence on Elizabeth and Jane. In the final volume their role becomes major. They contribute much to the union of Darcy and Elizabeth, and in the Wickham-Lydia affair Gardiner shows himself to be generous and at ease in the city—as opposed to Mr. Bennet. Again in opposition to Bennet, the Gardiners' family life is highlighted, particularly through the happiness of their children. If Elizabeth's marriage to the family-oriented Darcy is meant to repair some of the damage done by the Bennets' deficiencies, the Gardiners contribute much to this rehabilitation.

* * *

Austen hints that Darcy's wealth may not be exclusively of the landed kind. Lucas immediately sniffs out that he has a house in town, where his sister lives; Elizabeth later meets her London companion.

---

3. On the rise of the bourgeoisie and the conflict of codes of values, see Karl Marx and Friedrich Engels, *The German Ideology, Part 1*, in *The Marx-Engels Reader*, ed. Robert C. Tucker (New York: W. W. Norton, 1978) 153, 173, 179. Austen also shows finesse concerning contradictions of money and class by having Miss Bingley, whose money comes from "trade" but who wanted to marry Darcy, submit to his marriage in feudal fashion, paying off "every arrear of civility" to Elizabeth. The possible double meaning of her use of *capital* cited below is unique; elsewhere the word means "of highest quality."

Darcy himself spends more time there than anyone else but his sister and the Gardiners, for example the ten days during which Bingley proposes to Jane. In handling the Wickham-Lydia matter he functions more effectively there even than Gardiner. Perhaps some of those business letters that Miss Bingley would find "odious" to write concern interests "in town"?

This conjecture may gather support from an important passage that to my knowledge has not drawn commentary, the late revelation by Lady Catherine about Darcy's (and her daughter's) lineage: "My daughter and my nephew are formed for each other. They are descended on the maternal side, from the same noble line; and, on the father's, from respectable, honourable, and ancient, though untitled families. Their fortune on both sides is splendid. They are destined for each other by the voice of every member of their respective houses." Lady Catherine's vocabulary of aristocracy is still in evidence. The verbiage cannot hide the fact that neither Darcy nor her daughter comes from absolutely noble lineage; aristocracy in the novel as in history turns out to be a pseudoconcept. There have been in her generation two marriages with "untitled families," with another kind of wealth, presumably commercial in origin. The lateness of the revelation, just before the union of Darcy and Elizabeth, is suggestive; it is as if, before a new fusion of social elements can occur, an earlier one must be admitted. Admitted—but not foregrounded, in contrast to the narrator's early detailing of Bingley's economic and social background. Bingley's father did not marry into nobility and did not purchase an estate, but we are not told if Pemberley has been in Lady Catherine's family for generations or if Darcy's father purchased it. Either way, the traditional mode of life that reigns there has been infused with wealth deriving from another economic mode. And Darcy himself may easily be thought of as the "protocapitalist," whose business in the city is not narrated but whose power exercises a discreetly sexual fascination, at a time when the countryside is only beginning to be marginalized and the new economic forces seem to contribute smoothly to the maintenance of the marvelous "aristocratic" world of Pemberley.

* * *

DONALD GRAY

A Note on Money

It is very difficult to compute contemporary equivalents of the sums of money named in Jane Austen's novels. One commentator uses a factor of 33 to estimate that Mr. Bennet's annual income of £2,000 is worth about $66,000 in 1988 US dollars. Darcy's income by the same calculation is over $330,000, and Bingley's is about $165,000.[1] Another commentator uses a multiplier of 70 to 80 to suggest that Mr. Bennet's income is $165,000 in 1989 US dollars, and Darcy's is $800,000—about the sum, Mr. Bennet guesses, Darcy spent to bribe Wickham to marry Lydia ("Wickham's a fool, if he takes her with a farthing less than ten thousand pounds").[2] Mary Mogford, figuring that Darcy's income is 300 times that of the per capita income of Britain in 1810, multiplies the per capita income of the US in 1989 by that number to give him an annual income of over six million US dollars.[3]

Even were these calculations consistent with one another, they cannot take into account the difference in purchasing power in a time when labor was cheap, income taxes low, and landowners like Darcy and Mr. Bennet could partially supply their households from their own farms. (Mr. Bennet's daughters sometimes cannot use the horses because they are required for farmwork.) A more accurate measure of the economic status of characters in *Pride and Prejudice* is a comparison of the incomes Austen ascribes to them and the actual incomes of some of her contemporaries. In 1810 the nominal annual income of agricultural workers was £42, of skilled laborers between £55 and £90, of clerks £178, of clergymen £283, and of lawyers £447.[4] David Spring in an essay reprinted in this volume suggests that the income of a large merchant (perhaps such as Mr. Gardiner) was about that of a member of the "modest gentry," or pseudo-gentry, such as Mr. Bennet (see pp. 396f).

The income of the Austen family, early and late, was less than that of merchants and holders, however temporary, of estates like Mr. Bennet's. Like most other clergymen, Jane Austen's father derived his income from tithes levied on his parishioners and from the profits of farming the "glebe," a section of land set aside for the benefit of the

1. James Heldman, "How Wealthy Is Mr. Darcy, Really." *Persuasions* 12 (1990): 38–49.
2. Edward Copeland, "The Economic Realities of Jane Austen's Day," in *Approaches to Teaching Jane Austen's "Pride and Prejudice,"* ed. Marcia McClintock Folsom (New York, 1993) 33–45. See also Copeland's essay, "Money," in *The Cambridge Companion to Jane Austen,* ed. Edward Copeland and Juliet McMaster (Cambridge and New York, 1997) 131–48.
3. "Darcy's Wealth: An Addendum," *Persuasions* 13 (1991): 49.
4. B. R. Mitchell, *British Historical Statistics* (New York: Cambridge University Press, 1988) 153.

church.[5] Mr. Austen's income from both sources at the beginning of his career was perhaps £200 a year from tithes and additional money from the lease on a nearby farm.[6] During her childhood he still needed to supplement his income by taking in pupils in the parsonage. But at the time of his retirement Jane Austen wrote in one of her letters, "I do not despair of [his] getting nearly six hundred a year" from his interest in his livings.[7]

Upon his death in 1805, however, this interest lapsed. His wife and two unmarried daughters were left with an annual income of a little over £200. Jane Austen's brothers agreed to contributions that doubled that sum.[8] After living for three years in Southampton—during one of which Austen recorded her personal expenses for the year as £50[9]— they were given the use of the cottage at Chawton. While she was resuming her work as a novelist and revising the novel in which Elizabeth Bennet becomes mistress of Pemberley, Jane Austen was settling in, with a maid, a manservant, a cook who was paid a little over £8 a year, and a new piano that cost about £30 (Tomalin 207; Nokes 346), to spend the rest of her life in a household managed on an annual income of about £460.[1]

Jane Austen's earnings from her writing have a place in these comparisons. During her lifetime Austen made less than £700 from her novels (Honan 393). She sold the copyright of *Pride and Prejudice* outright for £110 and made no more money from the sales of what even during her lifetime proved to be her most popular novel. All her other novels were published on commission, which meant that she was responsible for losses as well as eligible for profits after the publisher subtracted his costs and commission. She received £140 from the sales of the first edition of *Sense and Sensibility* (1811), the first of her novels to be published, and at least £60 from a second edition. The sales of the first edition of *Mansfield Park* earned her perhaps £320, and she wondered whether to risk a second edition: "People are more ready to borrow & praise, than to buy—which I cannot wonder at;—but tho' I like praise as well as anybody, I like what Edward calls *Pewter* too" (*Letters*, 30 Nov. 1814, 287). She did agree to a second edition, but in a memorandum on her earnings as a writer she notes that in 1816 the edition still posted a loss in her account at her publisher of nearly £200,

5. See Irene Collins, *Jane Austen and the Clergy* (London and Rio Grande, OH: Hambledon, 1993) 49–60.
6. Claire Tomalin, *Jane Austen: A Life* (London: Peters, Frances and Dunlop; New York: Alfred A. Knopf, 1997) 7.
7. *Jane Austen's Letters*, ed. Deirdre Le Faye (Oxford and New York: Oxford University Press, 1995) 3–5 Jan. 1801, 69.
8. David Nokes, *Jane Austen: A Life* (London: Fourth Estate; New York: Farrar, Straus, and Giroux, 1997) 274–75.
9. Nokes, 310; Park Honan, *Jane Austen: Her Life* (New York: St. Martin's Press, 1987) 244–45.
1. John Halperin, *The Life of Jane Austen* (Baltimore: John Hopkins University Press; Brighton: Harvester Press, 1984) 145.

which reduced her earnings on the sales of *Emma* (1816) to less than
£40 (Honan 393). (Eventually the second edition of *Mansfield Park*
made a profit, although not until after Austen's death.) The sales of
Persuasion and *Northanger Abbey*, published posthumously in 1818,
returned about £500 to her sister Cassandra (Tomalin 272). In 1832
Cassandra (who inherited Austen's copyrights) and one of her brothers
sold the copyrights of all the novels except *Pride and Prejudice* (which
they did not own) for £210 (Honan 320). In sum, in twenty years Jane
Austen's writing brought her and her family less than £1,500, undoubtedly a welcome supplement to the discretionary incomes of two women
who principally depended for support on their mother and brothers,
but less than the annual income Austen imagined for Mr. Bennet.

As I have in the preceding paragraph, Austen typically states the
wealth of women in lump sums, the wealth of men as annual income.
The meaning of a woman's money is not that its income will support
her, although at a 4 percent annual return Miss Darcy's £30,000 (Volume II, Chapter XII) and even Miss King's £10,000 (II, IV) would keep
a single woman comfortably. (As Mr. Collins makes clear, that is not
true of the £1,000 Elizabeth will inherit from her mother [I: XIX].)
Rather, its meaning is that on her marriage a woman's money will pass
as capital to her husband.[2] Having been one of the reasons for her
desirability, her money will become one of the sources of the income
by which his economic status is measured.

---

2. Judith Lowder Newton, *Women, Power, Subversion* (Athens: University of Georgia Press,
1981) 56; Mary Evans, *Jane Austen and the State* (London and New York: Tavistock, 1987)
20–21.

Jane Austen:
A Chronology

1775 Jane Austen born December 16 in Steventon, to Rev. George and Cassandra (Leigh) Austen, seventh of eight children, and the younger of two daughters.

1783–86 Attends boarding schools with sister Cassandra (1773–1845) in Oxford and Reading.

1787–93 Writes "Love and Freindship," "Catherine," and other short fiction for her own amusement and for that of family and friends.

1793 Britain at war with France.

1793–95 Writes manuscript novel "Lady Susan," the first of her fictions to graduate from the mostly parodic character of her juvenilia.

1795 Writes manuscript novel "Elinor and Marianne."

1796–97 Writes manuscript novel "First Impressions," which her father tries unsuccessfully to sell to a publisher. Begins to revise "Elinor and Marianne" into *Sense and Sensibility*.

1799 Writes manuscript novel "Susan."

1800 Brother Francis (1774–1865) attains rank of captain in navy (later rear-admiral).

1801 Rev. George Austen retires, moves with wife and two daughters from Steventon to Bath. Brother Henry (1771–1850) resigns commission in militia to become partner in a bank in London.

1802–03 Revises "Susan" and sells it for £10 to a publisher who holds the book without publishing it. Peace of Amiens (1802) broken and war with France resumes (1803).

1804 Writes manuscript novel "The Watsons." Brother Charles (1779–1852) promoted to first naval command (later rear-admiral).

1805 Rev. George Austen dies; son James (1765–1819) succeeds him as rector at Steventon.

1807 With mother and sister leaves Bath for house in Southampton.

1809 Asks publisher about plans to bring out "Susan"; he offers to sell the novel back for £10. Moves with sister and mother to cottage at Chawton owned by brother Edward (1767–1852).

1811 *Sense and Sensibility* published. Begins revising "First Impressions" into *Pride and Prejudice*.

1812 Britain at war with United States.

1813 *Pride and Prejudice* published. Completes *Mansfield Park*.

1814 *Mansfield Park* published. Begins *Emma*. War with United States ends.

1815 *Emma* published. Begins *Persuasion*. Battle of Waterloo ends war with France.

1816 Purchases "Susan" from publisher; revises it as *Northanger Abbey*. Upon failure of his bank, brother Henry takes orders and becomes curate at Chawton.

1817 Begins manuscript novel "Sanditon." Dies July 18. *Northanger Abbey* and *Persuasion* published posthumously, with biographical notice by Henry Austen.

Selected Bibliography

• Indicates works included or excerpted in this Norton Critical Edition

JANE AUSTEN: NOVELS AND OTHER WRITING

The Novels of Jane Austen. Ed. R. W. Chapman. 5 vols. 3rd ed. Oxford, 1932–34. A sixth volume, *Minor Works*, was added in 1965. Austen's juvenilia has been published in: *Volume the First*. Ed. R. W. Chapman. Oxford, 1933; reprinted London, 1984; *Volume the Second*. Ed. B. C. Southam. Oxford, 1963; *Volume the Third*. Ed. B. C. Southam. Oxford, 1951. Another edition of the novels, and of Jane Austen's letters to her sister Cassandra, is available online: http://www.pemberley.com.
• *Jane Austen's Letters*. Ed. Deirdre Le Faye. Oxford and New York, 1995.
Jane Austen's Manuscript Letters in Facsimile. Ed. Jo Modert. Carbondale and Edwardsville, IL, 1990.
Jane's Hand: The Jane Austen Songbooks. Sound recording. Produced by Mary Jane Newman. Englewood Cliffs, NJ, 1996.
The Poetry of Jane Austen and the Austen Family. Ed. David Selwyn. Iowa City, 1997.

BIOGRAPHY

Austen, Caroline. *My Aunt Jane Austen*. Alton, 1952.
———. *Reminiscences of Caroline Austen*. Guilford, 1986.
• Austen, Henry. "Preface." *Persuasion and Northanger Abbey*, by Jane Austen. London, 1818.
• Austen-Leigh, J. E. *A Memoir of Jane Austen*. 2nd ed. London, 1871.
Austen-Leigh, Mary. *Personal Aspects of Jane Austen*. London and New York, 1920.
• Austen-Leigh, William, Richard Arthur Austen-Leigh, and Deirdre Le Faye. *Jane Austen: Her Life and Letters*. London and Boston, 1989.
Cecil, David. *A Portrait of Jane Austen*. London and New York, 1978.
Chapman, R. W. *Jane Austen: Facts and Problems*. Oxford, 1948.
Collins, Irene. *Jane Austen: The Parson's Daughter*. London and Rio Grande, OH, 1998.
Cornish, Francis-Warre. *Jane Austen*. London, 1913. A volume in English Men of Letters series.
Fergus, Jan. *Jane Austen: A Literary Life*. London and New York, 1991.
Halperin, John. *The Life of Jane Austen*. Baltimore and London, 1984.
Hodge, Jane Aiken. *The Double Life of Jane Austen*. London and New York, 1972.
• Honan, Park. *Jane Austen: Her Life*. New York and London, 1987.
Jane Austen Family History. Ed. Louise Ross. 5 vols. London, 1995.
Jenkins, Elizabeth. *Jane Austen: A Biography; with a New Postscript by the Author*. London, 1938, 1986.
Lane, Maggie. *Jane Austen's Family Through Five Generations*. London, 1984.
Laski, Marghanita. *Jane Austen and Her World*. London and New York, 1969.
Le Faye, Deirdre. *Jane Austen*. London, 1998.
Myer, Valerie Grosvenor. *Jane Austen: Obstinate Heart*. New York, 1997.
Nicolson, Nigel. *The World of Jane Austen*. London, 1991.
• Nokes, David. *Jane Austen: A Life*. London and New York, 1997.
• Tomalin, Claire. *Jane Austen: A Life*. London and New York, 1997.
Tucker, George Holbert. *A Goodly Heritage: A History of Jane Austen's Family*. Manchester, 1983.
———. *Jane Austen the Woman: Some Biographical Insights*. New York, 1994.

BIBLIOGRAPHIES AND CONCORDANCES

De Rose, Peter L., and S. W. McGuire. *A Concordance to the Works of Jane Austen*. 3 vols. New York, 1982.
Gilson, David. *A Bibliography of Jane Austen: New Introduction and Corrections by the Author*. Includes bibliography of commentary to 1978. Winchester and New Castle, DL, 1997.
Roth, Barry. *An Annotated Bibliography of Jane Austen Studies, 1973–83*. Charlottesville, 1985.
———. *An Annotated Bibliography of Jane Austen Studies, 1984–94*. Athens, OH, 1996.
———, and Joel Weinsheimer, *An Annotated Bibliography of Jane Austen Studies, 1952–72*. Charlottesville, 1973.

HANDBOOKS

The Cambridge Companion to Jane Austen. Ed. Edward Copeland and Juliet McMaster. Cambridge and New York, 1997.
A Guide to Jane Austen. Ed. Michael Hardwick. New York and Reading, 1973.
A Jane Austen Companion. Ed. F. B. Pinion. London and New York, 1973.
A Jane Austen Encyclopedia. Ed. Paul Poplawski. Westport, CT, 1998.
The Jane Austen Handbook. Ed. J. David Grey, with A. Walton Litz and B. C. Southam. London, 1986. Published in New York as *The Jane Austen Companion*.

ESSAY COLLECTIONS

Approaches to Teaching Jane Austen's "Pride and Prejudice." Ed. Marcia McClintock Folsom. New York, 1993.
Critical Essays on Jane Austen. Ed. Laura Mooneyham White. New York and London, 1998.
Critics on Jane Austen. Ed. Judith O'Neill. Coral Gables FL, 1970.
Jane Austen: A Collection of Critical Essays. Ed. Ian Watt. Englewood Cliffs, NJ, 1963.
Jane Austen and Discourses of Feminism. Ed. Devoney Looser. New York, 1995.
Jane Austen: Bicentenary Essays. Ed. John Halperin. Cambridge and New York, 1975.
Jane Austen: Critical Assessments. 4 vols. Ed. Ian Littlewood. Mountfield, 1998.
Jane Austen in a Social Context. Ed. David Monaghan. Totowa, NJ, 1981.
Jane Austen: New Perspectives. Ed. Janet Todd. *Women and Literature* 3 (1983).
Jane Austen: The Critical Heritage. Ed. B. C. Southam. 2 vols. London and New York, 1968, 1987.
Jane Austen's Achievement. Ed. Juliet McMaster. London and New York, 1976.
Jane Austen's "Pride and Prejudice." Ed. Harold Bloom. New York, 1987.
Readings in Jane Austen. Ed. Clarice Swisher. San Diego, 1997.
Twentieth-Century Interpretations of "Pride and Prejudice." Ed. E. Rubenstein. Englewood Cliffs, NJ, 1969.

LITERARY CRITICISM 1820–1940

Farrar, Reginald. "Jane Austen." *Quarterly Review* 228 (1917): 1–30.
Forster, E. M. "Jane Austen." In *Abinger Harvest*. London, 1936. 145–59.
Garrod, H. W. "Jane Austen, a Depreciation." *Essays by Divers Hands* n.s. 8 (1928): 21–40. See also R. W. Chapman. "A Reply to Mr. Garrod." *Essays by Divers Hands* n.s. 10 (1931): 17–34.
• Harding, D. W. " 'Regulated Hatred': An Aspect in the Work of Jane Austen." *Scrutiny* 8 (1940): 346–62. Reprinted in D. W. Harding, *Regulated Hatred and Other Essays on Jane Austen*. Ed. Monica Lawlor. London and Atlantic Heights, NJ, 1998.
Hopkins, Annette Brown. "Jane Austen the Critic." *PMLA* 40 (1925): 398–425.
Hutton, Richard Holt. "From Miss Austen to Mr. Trollope." *Spectator* (16 Dec. 1882): 1609–11.
Lewes, George Henry. "The Novels of Jane Austen." *Blackwood's* 86 (1859): 99–113.
"Literary Women. No. II Jane Austen." *Athenaum* (27 Aug 1831): 553–54.
• Oliphant, Margaret. "Miss Austen and Miss Mitford." *Blackwood's* 107 (1870): 291–313.
Scott, Walter. "Emma." *Quarterly Review* 14 (1815): 188–201.
• Simpson, Richard. "Jane Austen." *North British Review* 52 (1870): 129–52.
• Whately, Richard. "Modern Novels." *Quarterly Review* 24 (1821): 252–76.
Woolf, Virginia. "Jane Austen." In *The Common Reader*. London and New York, 1925. 191–206.

LITERARY CRITICISM 1940–70

Babb, Howard. *Jane Austen's Novels: The Fabric of Dialogue*. Columbus, 1962.

Bradbrook, Frank W. *Jane Austen and Her Predecessors*. Cambridge, 1966.

Brower, Reuben A. " 'Light and Bright and Sparkling': Irony and Fiction in *Pride and Prejudice*." In *The Fields of Light*. New York, 1951. 164–81.

Cady, Joseph, and Ian Watt. "Jane Austen's Critics." *Critical Quarterly* 5 (1963): 49–63.

Craik, W. A. *Jane Austen in Her Time*. London, 1969.

Daiches, David. "Jane Austen, Karl Marx, and the Aristocratic Dance." *American Scholar* 17 (1947–48): 289–96.

Elsbree, Langdon. "Jane Austen and the Dance of Fidelity and Complaisance." *Nineteenth-Century Fiction* 15 (1960–61): 113–36.

Gooneratne, Yasmine. *Jane Austen*. Cambridge, 1970.

Gorer, Geoffrey. "Poor Honey: Some Notes on Jane Austen and Her Mother." *London Magazine* 4 (Aug. 1957): 35–48.

Greene, Donald J. "Jane Austen and the Peerage." *PMLA* 68 (1953): 1017–31.

Hogan, Charles Beecher. "Jane Austen and Her Early Public." *RES* n.s. 1 (1950): 39–54.

Kliger, Samuel. "Jane Austen's *Pride and Prejudice* in the Eighteenth-Century Mode." *University of Toronto Quarterly* 16 (1945–46): 357–70.

Lascelles, Mary. *Jane Austen and Her Art*. Oxford, 1939.

Leavis, F. R. *The Great Tradition*. London, 1948. 1–27.

Leavis, Q. D. "A Critical Theory of Jane Austen's Writings." *Scrutiny* 10 (1941–42): 61–87, 114–42, 272–94; 12 (1944–45): 104–19.

Liddel, Robert. *The Novels of Jane Austen*. London, 1963.

Litz, A. Walton. *Jane Austen: A Study of Her Artistic Development*. London and New York, 1965.

Moler, Kenneth L. *Jane Austen's Art of Allusion*. Lincoln, 1968.

Mudrick, Marvin. *Jane Austen: Irony as Defense and Discovery*. Princeton, 1952.

Phillipps, Kenneth. *Jane Austen's English*. London, 1970.

Ryle, Gilbert. "Jane Austen and the Moralists." *Oxford Review* 1 (1966): 5–18.

Schorer, Mark. "Pride Unprejudiced." *Kenyon Review* 18 (1956): 609–22.

Southam, B. C. *Jane Austen's Literary Manuscripts: A Study of the Novelist's Development through the Surviving Papers*. London, 1964.

• Van Ghent, Dorothy. "On *Pride and Prejudice*." In *The English Novel, Form and Function*. New York, 1953. 105–23.

Wiesenfarth, Joseph. *The Errand of Form: An Assay of Jane Austen's Art*. New York, 1967.

Wilson, Edmund. "A Long Talk about Jane Austen." *Classics and Commercials*. New York, 1950. 196–203.

Wright, Andrew. *Jane Austen's Novels*. London and New York, 1953. 72–91.

LITERARY CRITICISM 1970 TO THE PRESENT

• Ahearn, Edward. "Radical Jane and the Other Emma." In *Marx and Modern Fiction*. New Haven and London, 1989. 31–75.

Amis, Martin. "Jane Austen's World." *New Yorker* (8 Jan. 1996): 31–35.

• Auerbach, Nina. "Waiting Together: Two Families." In *Communities of Women*. Cambridge, 1978. 33–73.

Batey, Mavis. *Jane Austen and the English Landscape*. London and Chicago, 1996.

Beer, Patricia. *Reader, I Married Him*. London and New York, 1974. 45–83.

• Birtwhistle, Sue, and Susie Conklin. *The Making of "Pride and Prejudice."* London, 1995.

Brown, Julia Prewitt. "A Feminist Depreciation of Jane Austen: A Polemical Reading." *Novel* 23 (1990): 303–13.

———. *Jane Austen's Novels: Social Change and Literary Form*. Cambridge, 1979.

Brown, Lloyd W. *Bits of Ivory: Narrative Techniques in Jane Austen's Fiction*. Baton Rouge, 1973.

Brownstein, Rachel M. "Jane Austen: Irony and Authority." *Women's Studies* 15 (1988): 57–70.

Burgan, Mary. "Mr. Bennet and the Failures of Fatherhood in Jane Austen's Novels." *JEGP* 74 (1975): 536–62.

Burrows, J. A. *Computation in Criticism: A Study of Jane Austen's Novels and an Experiment in Method*. Oxford, 1987.

• Butler, Marilyn. *Jane Austen and the War of Ideas*. Oxford, 1975.

———. "Novels for the Gentry: Austen and Scott." In *Romantics, Rebels, and Reactionaries*. Oxford and New York, 1981. 94–109.

Carr, Jean Ferguson. "The Polemics of Incomprehension: Mothers and Daughters in *Pride and Prejudice*." *Tradition and the Talents of Women*. Ed. Florence Howe. Urbana, 1991. 68–86.

Copeland, Edward. "Fictions of Employment: Jane Austen and the Woman's Novel." *Studies in Philology* 85 (1988): 114–24.

Cottom, Daniel. *The Civilized Imagination: A Study of Ann Radcliffe, Jane Austen, and Sir Walter Scott.* Cambridge and New York, 1985. 106–23.

Deresiewicz, William. "Community and Cognition in *Pride and Prejudice.*" *ELH* 64 (1997): 503–35.

De Rose, Peter L. *Jane Austen and Samuel Johnson.* Washington, 1980.

• Duckworth, Alistair. *The Improvement of the Estate: A Study of Jane Austen's Novels.* Baltimore and London, 1971.

Erickson, Lee. "The Economy of Novel Reading: Jane Austen and the Circulating Library." *Nineteenth-Century Fiction* 30 (1980): 113–36.

Evans, Mary. *Jane Austen and the State.* London and New York, 1987.

• Fraiman, Susan. "The Humiliation of Elizabeth Bennet." In *Unbecoming Women: British Women Writers and the Novel of Development.* New York, 1993. 69–87.

Galperin, William. "The Picturesque, the Real, and the Consumption of Jane Austen." *Wordsworth Circle* 28:1 (1997): 19–27.

Gard, Roger. *Jane Austen's Novels: The Art of Clarity.* New Haven, 1992.

Gilbert, Sandra, and Susan Gubar. "Inside the House of Fiction: Jane Austen's Tenants of Possibility." In *The Madwoman in the Attic.* New Haven, 1979. 146–83.

Gordon, Jan B. "A-Filiative Families and Subversive Reproduction: Gossip in Jane Austen." *Genre* 21 (1988): 5–46.

Handler, Richard, and Daniel Segal. *Jane Austen and the Fiction of Culture.* Tucson, 1990.

Handley, Graham. *Critics in Focus: Jane Austen.* Bristol and New York, 1992.

Hardy, Barbara. *A Reading of Jane Austen.* London, 1975.

Harris, Jocelyn. *Jane Austen's Art of Memory.* Cambridge and New York, 1989.

Heldman, James. "How Wealthy Is Mr. Darcy, Really?" *Persuasions* 12 (1990): 38–49.

Hudson, Glenda. *Sibling Love and Incest in Jane Austen's Fiction.* New York, 1991.

Johnson, Claudia L. " 'A Sweet Face as White as Death': Jane Austen and the Politics of Female Sensibility." *Novel* 22 (1989): 159–74.

• ———. *Jane Austen: Women, Politics, and the Novel.* Chicago, 1988.

• Kaplan, Deborah. *Jane Austen Among Women.* Baltimore, 1992.

———. "The Disappearance of the Woman Writer: Jane Austen and Her Biographers." *Prose Studies* 7 (1984): 129–47.

Kirkham, Margaret. *Jane Austen: Feminism and Fiction.* Totowa, NJ, 1983.

Koppel, Gene. *The Religious Dimension of Jane Austen's Novels.* Ann Arbor, 1988.

Lane, Maggie. *Jane Austen and Food.* London and Rio Grande, OH, 1995.

Lauber, John. *Jane Austen.* New York, 1993.

Lawson-Peebles, Robert. "European Conflict and Hollywood's Reconstruction of English Fiction." *Yearbook of English Studies* 26 (1996): 1–13.

Litvack, Joseph. "Delicacy and Disgust, Mourning and Melancholia, Privilege and Perversity: Pride and Prejudice." *Qui Parle* 6:1 (1992): 35–51.

MacDonagh, Oliver. *Jane Austen: Real and Imagined Worlds.* New Haven, 1991.

McMaster, Juliet. *Jane Austen the Novelist: Essays Past and Present.* New York, 1995.

Magee, William H. *Convention and the Art of Jane Austen's Heroines.* San Francisco, 1995.

Mansell, Darrel. *The Novels of Jane Austen.* New York, 1973.

Marshall, Christine. " 'Dull Elves' and Feminists: A Summary of Feminist Criticism of Jane Austen." *Persuasions* 14 (1992): 39–45.

Mayne, Judith. *Private Novels, Public Films.* Athens, GA, 1988. 40–50.

Menand, Louis. "What Jane Austen Doesn't Tell Us." *New York Review of Books* (1 Feb. 1996): 13–15.

Michaelson, Patricia. "Reading *Pride and Prejudice.*" *Eighteenth-Century Fiction* 3 (1990): 65–76.

Miller, D. A. "Austen's Attitude." *Yale Journal of Criticism* 8 (1995): 1–5.

Moler, Kenneth L. *"Pride and Prejudice": A Study in Artistic Economy.* Boston, 1989.

Monaghan, David. *Jane Austen: Structure and Social Vision.* Totowa, NJ, 1980.

Mooneyham, Laura G. *Romance, Language, and Education in Jane Austen's Novels.* London, 1987.

• Morgan, Susan. *In the Meantime: Character and Perception in Jane Austen's Fiction.* Chicago, 1980.

———. "Why There's No Sex in Jane Austen's Fiction." *Studies in the Novel* 19 (1987): 346–56.

Morris, Ivor. *Mr. Collins Considered.* London and New York, 1987.

Nardin, Jane. *Those Elegant Decorums: The Concept of Propriety in Jane Austen's Novels.* Albany, 1973.

Newman, Karen. "Can This Marriage Be Saved: Jane Austen Makes Sense of an Ending." *ELH* 50 (1983): 693–710.

Newton, Judith Lowder. *Women, Power, and Subversion.* Athens, GA, 1981. 55–85.

• Nixon, Cheryl L. "Balancing the Courtship Hero: Masculine Emotional Display in Film Adaptations of Jane Austen's Novels." In *Jane Austen in Hollywood*. Ed. Linda Troost and Sayre Greenfield. Lexington, KY, 1998. 22–44.

O'Farrell, Mary Ann. "Austen's Blush." *Novel* 27 (1994): 125–39. Reprinted in *Telling Complexions: The Nineteenth-Century English Novel and the Blush*. Durham, NC, 1997. 13–27.

Page, Norman. *The Language of Jane Austen*. Oxford, 1972.

Parker, Jo Alyson. "*Pride and Prejudice*: Jane Austen's Double Inheritance Plot." *Yearbook of Research in English and American Literature* 7 (1990): 159–90. Reprinted in *The Author's Inheritance: Henry Fielding, Jane Austen, and the Establishment of the Novel*. DeKalb, IL, 1998.

Patteson, Richard F. "Truth, Certitude, and Stability in Jane Austen's Fiction." *Philological Quarterly* 60 (1981): 455–69.

Perry, Ruth. "Austen and Empire." *Persuasions* 16 (1994): 95–106.

Phelan, James. "Character, Progression, and the Mimetic-Didactic Distinction." *Modern Philology* 84 (1987): 282–99.

Piggott, Patrick. *The Innocent Diversion: A Study of Music in the Life and Writings of Jane Austen*. London, 1979.

Polhemus, Robert. "Austen's *Emma*: The Comedy of Union." In *Erotic Faith: Being in Love from Jane Austen to D. H. Lawrence*. Chicago, 1990. 24–59.

Poovey, Mary. "Ideological Contradictions and the Consolations of Form: The Case of Jane Austen." In *The Proper Lady and the Woman Writer*. Chicago, 1984. 172–207.

Roberts, Francis Warren. *Jane Austen and the French Revolution*. New York, 1979.

Ruderman, Anne Crippen. *The Pleasures of Virtue: Political Thought in the Novels of Jane Austen*. Lanham, MD, 1995.

Sales, Roger. *Jane Austen and Representations of Regency England*. London and New York, 1994.

Schaffer, Julie. "Not Subordinate: Empowering Women in the Marriage Plot." *Criticism* 34 (1992): 51–73.

Siebers, Tobin. "Jane Austen and Comic Virtue." In *Morals and Stories*. New York, 1992. 135–58.

Smith, LeRoy W. *Jane Austen and the Drama of Women*. New York, 1983.

Southward, Dennis. "Jane Austen and the Riches of Embarrassment." *SEL* 36 (1996): 763–84.

Spacks, Patricia Meyer. "Austen's Laughter." *Women's Studies* 15 (1988): 71–85.

———. *The Female Imagination*. New York, 1975. 111–21.

• Spring, David. "Interpreters of Jane Austen's Social World: Literary Critics and Historians." In *Jane Austen: New Perspectives*. Ed. Janet Todd. *Women and Literature* 3 (1983). 53–70.

Stewart, Maaja A. *Domestic Realities and Imperial Fictions: Jane Austen's Novels in Eighteenth-Century Contexts*. Athens, GA, 1993.

Stokes, Myra. *The Language of Jane Austen: Some Aspects of Her Vocabulary*. New York, 1991.

Sulloway, Alison G. *Jane Austen and the Province of Womanhood*. Philadelphia, 1989.

Tanner, Tony. *Jane Austen*. London and Cambridge, 1986.

• Tave, Stuart. *Some Words of Jane Austen*. Chicago, 1973.

Thompson, James. *Between Self and World: The Novels of Jane Austen*. University Park, PA, 1988.

Todd, Janet. "Jane Austen, Politics and Sensibility." *Feminist Criticism: Theory and Practice*. Ed. Susan Sellers. Toronto, 1991. 71–88.

Trilling, Lionel. "Why We Read Jane Austen." *Times Literary Supplement* (5 March 1976): 250–52.

Turner, Martha A. "The Aristotelian Logic of Settlement in Austen's *Pride and Prejudice*." In *Mechanism and the Novel: Science in the Narrative Process*. Cambridge and New York, 1993. 43–62.

Wallace, Robert K. *Jane Austen and Mozart: Classical Equilibrium in Fiction and Music*. Athens, GA, 1983.

• Wallace, Tara Ghoshal. *Jane Austen and Narrative Authority*. New York and London, 1995.

Weinsheimer, Joel. "Chance and the Hierarchy of Marriages in *Pride and Prejudice*." *ELH* 39 (1972): 404–19.

Weldon, Fay. *Letters to Alice on First Reading Jane Austen*. London, 1984.

Wilkie, Brian. "Jane Austen: Amor and Amoralism." *JEGP* 91 (1992): 529–44.

Williams, Michael. *Jane Austen: Six Novels and Their Methods*. New York, 1986.

Wiltshire, John. *Jane Austen and the Body*. Cambridge and New York, 1992.

Wright, Andrew. "Jane Austen Adapted." *Nineteenth-Century Literature* 30 (1975): 421–53.